A FALKLAND ISLANDER TILL I DIE

A FALKLAND ISLANDER TILL I DIE

Terence S. Betts

www.falklandislander.com

The Book Guild Ltd
Sussex, England

First published in Great Britain in 2004 by
The Book Guild Ltd
25 High Street
Lewes, East Sussex
BN7 2LU

Copyright © Terence S. Betts 2004

The right of Terence S. Betts to be identified as the author of
this work has been asserted by him in accordance with the
Copyright, Designs and Patents Act 1988.

All rights reserved. No part of this publication may be reproduced,
transmitted, or stored in a retrieval system, in any form or by any
means, without permission in writing from the publisher, nor be
otherwise circulated in any form of binding or cover other than that in
which it is published and without a similar condition being imposed on the
subsequent purchaser.

Typesetting in Times by
Acorn Bookwork Ltd, Salisbury, Wiltshire

Printed in Great Britain by
Antony Rowe Ltd, Chippenham, Wiltshire

A catalogue record for this book is available from
The British Library.

ISBN 1 85776 885 X

CONTENTS

1	A Brief Introduction	1
2	Betts and Goss, Native Falkland Islanders	8
3	Mysterious Deaths in the Goss Family	13
4	Father and His First Family	20
5	Mother and Father	26
6	Growing up in the Falklands	33
7	Packed off to Work at 14	66
8	I Join RRS *Shackleton*	79
9	Sports Champion at 18	101
10	Marriage – Fatherhood – Policeman – Contract Worker	108
11	A Sister-in-law Dies, A Daughter is born	124
12	Chile and Argentine Nearly go to War Whilst I'm in Chile	128
13	1980s and the Falkland Islands Company	134
14	Why War?	140
15	The Day Before, and Invasion Night	158
16	Under Argentine Military Rule	172
17	Should I Stay, or Should I Go?	184
18	Refugees	190
19	The Waiting is Over – It's War	206
20	The Pebble Island Story	215
21	Events in May, and My Brother Joins the Fray	219
22	Islanders Assisting 3 Para	228
23	Teal Inlet and Back	236

24	Green Patch, and Then Back to Estancia	241
25	Bombed by the Argentines	247
26	Civilians Die, and the Final Push	256
27	Surrender and the Aftermath	261
28	Brothers Meet	271
29	Were You an Argentine Spy?	276
30	I Tell my Parents About Alec	285
31	The Words of 'Two Fifty-Five'	291
32	Back to Work in Difficult Circumstances	294
33	Trade Unionism in the Falklands	302
34.	I Join Up	326
35.	Catapulted to Vice-Chairman	336
36.	Failed Industrial Action	342
37.	Elected to the Summit	350
38.	With the TUC in London	373
39.	From Member to President	382
40.	Sir Rex Invites Me on Board	386
41.	The Hospital is on Fire	389
42.	From the Boy to the Boss	393
43.	Controversy and Politics	399
44.	How Politics Worked in the Falklands	402
45.	Nominated for the United Nations	415
46.	New York, Brothers Clash	420
47.	The Falklands Within the United Nations Machinery	426
48.	Warming up for Centre Stage	428
49.	My Speech to the UN	431
50.	A Stroll, a Chat, and Back Home	438

51.	I Quit Employers and Start My Own Company	441
52.	The Workload, Plus Political Ideas for the Future	446
53.	Labour Party Conference and CPA in Bermuda	453
54.	Prayer Breakfast with the President of the USA	460
55.	A Tragic Death and the End of my Political Road	463
56.	Marriage, Cold Stores, Office Blocks, Fishing Companies	474
57.	Lunch and Dinner with Royalty	484
58.	Pleasure, Leisure and the Cruel Side of Business	490
59.	New York and Washington DC for a Drop of Politics	498
60.	Political Forum in Salta, Argentina	506
61.	I meet a Brother for the First Time in my Life	516
62.	When Father is Father, Son is Son, and Father Dies	522
63.	This and That	531
64.	President of the Chamber of Commerce	533
65.	I Take Mother to Argentina to See Her Son	542
66.	Another Royal, and a Few Other Things I've Seen and Done	545
67.	The End of the Marriage, then the Business	551
68.	I Have Been a Fortunate Man	561
Appendix 1 I'm a Falkland Islander Till I Die		570

1

A Brief Introduction

As I glanced out of the bedroom window, the red flashes of tracer bullets were shooting through the night air, others whizzed past the house and smacked into the concrete wall across the street. The house was shaking violently, as mortar bombs and other ordnance exploded with deafening thumps and bangs. The still night air had suddenly erupted into anger as small arms crackled with ferocity.

The children were crying, dad was in his bed, too frightened to move, my wife was shaken and pale, whilst I was frantic, confused and shitting myself.

Patrick was on the local radio, trying to keep the general public informed of what was going on in and around our tiny town, as the Argentines' invading forces carried out their will against the people of the Falkland Islands in a most aggressive and violent manner. The Governor, Rex Hunt, would come on the radio every now and again and conduct interviews that seemed so unreal they had to be fiction. If only they were. More gunfire and explosion would confuse or numb the senses still further. The one thing Falkland Islanders had always felt might happen was now unfolding in terrifying circumstances.

Wait a minute, I must be dreaming, this is the Falkland Islands, backwater islands in the middle of nowhere. The Argentines had been making noises about the Islands belonging to them, but surely they were not that pissed off about it, to land thousands of highly skilled troops, armed to the teeth, with the intent to kill. How the hell could all this be happening?

I was born a fourth-generation Falkland Islander, on 2 October 1950, in the King Edward VII Memorial Hospital (KEMH) in Stanley, the capital of the Falkland Islands. I was the second child of Cyril Severine Betts, who had also been born in the Falkland Islands on 16 November 1912. My mother, Malvina Ellen Betts, formerly Goss, was born in the Falkland Islands on 22 January

1928. Mother had two older brothers, Roderick Jacob Goss (known as Stan) and Darwin Jacob Goss (known as Darwie). She also has an elder sister, Lillian Beatrice Goss, who emigrated to the United Kingdom in May 1945. So what, you might be thinking.

Well, the reason for me opening with the details of my immediate family is to clearly demonstrate to you that I am indeed, a 100% born and bred Falkland Islander; it is an indisputable fact that I am a native Islander, as were several generations of my family before me, which I will further highlight for nothing else but political reason.

I am going to walk you through my family tree, both sides, Betts and Goss, to further demonstrate to all who might be in doubt that such a people as native Falkland Islanders do actually exist, and as such, we must have the right to self-determination and the basic right to choose our own government, just as any civilised and native race of mankind should be entitled to, as enshrined in the United Nations general charter.

The comment about the United Nations is deliberate and, I trust, a little provocative, because the Falkland Islands and its people are central to a complex and hotly disputed political issue between Argentina and Great Britain.

Furthermore, I do not want anyone discussing the future of the Falkland Islands without including its native population in such debate, or without a clear policy of planning the long-term peace, security and prosperity of Islanders as the key issues. Therefore I believe my family roots, and how it was that I would become a fourth generation Falkland Islander, are very relevant on the international political stage in this ongoing argument.

As I unfold the first 50 years of my life story, you will notice that I touch on many topics, including various aspects of Falklands politics. Whilst I may feel many of my comments and views are indisputable, others will argue that my opinions are, at the very least, certainly open for debate.

Some of my personal viewpoints on Falklands politics, past and present, will be considered highly controversial. But by expressing them, open and freely, as any member of a democratic society should be allowed to do, I trust it will enable you to understand why I, and other Falkland Islanders, feel so proud and passionate about our homeland. Also why it is, in my opinion, that any claim made by our neighbours in Argentina to the sovereignty of our homeland is groundless. It has only ever been based on extremely inconclusive evidence, drawn from a very blurred record of history indeed.

I will explain briefly where the Falkland Islands are geographically. I recognise this information is much more widely known today than, say, 20 years ago, but for those of you who might still be unaware, it should prove helpful to enable you to complete a better overall picture of the Falkland Islands and my story. I will, at the same time, give a brief factual resumé on the Islands' size, climate, history and suchlike. Spiked with personal attitude.

The Falkland Islands lie in the South Atlantic, in a latitude of 51º and 53º south and a longitude of 57º and 63º degrees west, approximately 250 miles to the northeast of Tierra del Fuego, and some 300 miles east of the Patagonian coastline. The Islands of South Georgia are a further 800 miles to the east and slightly south of the Falkland Islands. Just to finalise the geographical picture frame, the Falklands are approximately 1,000 miles southeast of the Uruguayan capital, Montevideo; from England, they are a mere 8,000 miles.

The capital since 1845 has been Stanley, but at the time of the resettlement by the British in 1833, the capital was Port Louis. Stanley is sometimes incorrectly referred to as 'Port Stanley'. Interestingly, the capital's latitude south is very similar to the latitude north of London, which means that the Falkland Islands are no closer to the South Pole than London is to the North Pole. This information often surprises people, but now that you know, it should help to dispel any misconceptions that you, or friends, might have about the Falklands sitting on the Antarctic ice shelf, covered in snow and ice, all year round.

They are also much larger then many people realise; their total land area is approximately 4,700 square miles, slightly larger than Jamaica. There are two main islands, East and West Falklands, with approximately 700 smaller islands scattered around the two main islands.

The Falkland Islands extend approximately 160 miles from east to west, and almost 80 miles north to south. The two main islands make up nearly 80% of the total land area, with the East Falklands, the larger of the two, some 2,500 square miles; the

West Falklands covers approximately 1,750 square miles. The two main islands are divided by a stretch of water called the Falkland Sound. Of the hundreds of other islands dotted around, the largest of these is Weddell Island, located on the west of West Falklands. It is approximately 100 square miles, five times the size of the beautiful island of Bermuda. For another example, Pebble Island, which is situated up to the north of West Falklands, the island where the Betts family would take root in the 1860s, is approximately 40 square miles, or twice the size of Bermuda.

Regarding the climate, I will not go into all the statistics, but rather an overview of it. Falklands weather unfortunately always seemed to appear as a bad news story in the United Kingdom's daily papers, especially after the Falklands War. It took a carefully planned campaign, by representatives of the Falkland Islands Government and others, to counteract these wild, often-inaccurate stories, so a more balanced and accurate picture of the Falklands weather is now transmitted.

I will not disagree that it can be very harsh at times, and yes, we do have horizontal rains, which can be bitterly cold. It is also true that we get sleet and snow, and it is equally a fact, just to add to the fun, that we sometimes have all the elements of weather known to mankind, in the same day. However, I do not accept that the Falklands weather is as bleak and miserable as some too often tend to portray it. We also have glorious long sunny days with temperatures peaking to near 30º C on East Falklands in the high summer, which is mid-January. On the West Falklands, recorded temperatures would be three or four degrees higher in the summer. Take your clothes off in the Falklands during sunny summer days, for just a short while, without protective creams, and you will become a serious burns victim, as many unsuspecting young servicemen and visitors have found out.

The prevailing winds from the west are constant in spring and summer, thus cooling the air temperatures on sunny days; in winter, the winds often die away to leave a crisp and clear air with temperatures on average at two or three degrees above freezing. The wind-chill factor can cause temperatures to plummet to 20 below, Celsius. In concluding this general overview of the Falklands weather, I will end by saying that it is a meteorological statistical fact that the Falkland Islands capital, Stanley, has more sunshine and less rain than London.

Turning to the history of the Islands once again, I will just generalise, even perhaps take a light-hearted approach to it, prior to 1833; to be honest, I really cannot take any other attitude, because I would not be so presumptuous as to be precise about the comings and goings up to that point. Such is the extent of the distorted recording of the historical picture of the Falkland Islands during that time that even truly great scholars are baffled as to who did what, when and where.

It seems that a few explorers, and others, from various nations, prior to 1833 stumbled across the Islands as they sailed on by. Some even had the misfortune to sail into, or upon them, quite literally. Which is why the coastline and seabeds around the Islands are littered with shipwrecks. Some – French, Dutch, Spanish, and Portuguese and of course British – on occasions, just popped in, stayed a short while and went off again, from the 16th century to 1833. This chain of events resulted in several nations being opinionated about ownership of the Islands. However, whilst most are fairly flippant about the matter, one, Argentina, remains deadly serious in her belief that the Falkland Islands belong to them, not to the British. A claim, in the writer's opinion, which is a terrible misjudgement, all based on some theory about Argentine inheritance from the Spanish Vice-Royalty in the early part of the 1800s, which presumed it owned the Falklands. A notion that I regard as as near to insanity as one dare go, without in fact being diagnosed as insane.

I conclude my peppered guide to Falklands history, this time from a British perspective, prior to the establishment of a permanent settlement in the Islands. Captain John Davis in 1592, in his ship *The Desire*, made the first British sighting of the Islands. John Hawkins followed a couple of years later. But it would be almost a hundred years after Davis, in 1690 in fact, before the British made their first landing on the Islands, when Captain John Strong moored his sloop *The Welfare* and stepped ashore at Bold Cove on the West Falklands. It was Strong who named the waterway between the two main Islands 'Falkland' in honour of Viscount Falkland.

John Byron established the first British settlement in the Falkland Islands when he arrived at Saunders Islands on 12 January 1765. The British left again in 1774. From then until 1883, you can gain any amount of repetitive chronological history about the Islands, none of which in my unqualified opinion is helpful to anyone in trying to conclude who might be the rightful owner of the Falkland Islands. It is also my opinion that it is irrelevant anyhow.

What I do consider to be extremely relevant to the case is this. It was not until the British resettled the Falkland Islands in January 1833 that once again they began to resume control over the Islands, which at the time *had no indigenous population*. From that date, the Falkland Islands have been in open, continuous, effective and peaceful possession, occupation and British administration. During this period, I believe the second, and most important factor of all, regarding the Falkland Islands sovereignty issue emerged. Although it always seems to be inexplicably and amazingly tossed away like a piece of wastepaper by such organisations as the United Nations.

What I refer to is the situation of my kin, the Betts and Goss families, and many others who became part of the first permanently established population of the Falkland Islands, and who indisputably created the first truly native Falkland Islanders, a people that never existed before in the entire history of the Falkland Islands. It is for this reason that I couldn't care less how many people, or nations, jump up and down making a claim on the Falkland Islands. In all of our time in the Falklands, for five generations at least the Islands have been under British administration, with the Union flag flying as the national symbol – with the notable exception of a brief period which was enforced upon us in 1982. Therefore, I am firmly of the opinion, that if the Falkland Islands are not indeed British, I can only conclude they must belong to the Falkland Islanders.

Incidentally, this is an opinion sure to infuriate my elder brother, Alec, who has left his birthplace, to live in Argentina, from where he champions the Argentine claim to sovereignty over the Falkland Islands, known in Argentina as 'Las Malvinas'. This has created a long-standing political feud between two brothers, quite unique to the history of the Islands.

In this story of life's experiences thus far, I will go on to highlight the divide of loyalty and passion between, not two, but three Betts brothers, which has carried on during the Falklands War, the occupation and liberation, and followed later in the corridors of politics, perhaps climaxing at the United Nations in 1987.

The Falklands War may have ended in 1982, but for the Betts brothers, the war of words uniquely goes on.

My remarks about ownership could appear a little simplistic and arrogant. But just imagine, if you and your family had owned and lived in the same family home for 160 years, then some stranger came up and told you that it was theirs, I am sure you would feel more than a little pissed off, wouldn't you? I am equally certain you would tell them to bugger off, or words to that effect.

Let's get back to the short history lesson. British control of the Islands as I am sure you are aware, was lost for a period of 74 days, from 2 April to 14 June 1982, due entirely to an unprovoked act of aggression by the Argentine military junta, led by their alcoholic General, Leopoldo Galtieri, who instructed his armed forces to invade my homeland. They then occupied it, and attempted to make us accept and adhere to their military edicts.

Fortunately, they only succeeded in getting themselves evicted from our islands as a result of a remarkable will by the population of Great Britain, and the bravery of her armed forces, who restored our democratic way of life – as I have mentioned, something the United Nations still fails to endorse.

What I do find rather interesting, and at times amusing, is that we call it war, whilst others refer to the whole traumatic experience as the 'South Atlantic Conflict'. Well, believe me, it looked pretty much like bloody war to me, from where I was standing. Anyway, war – or conflict – stories follow later.

2

Betts and Goss, Native Falkland Islanders

I am going to map out a little more of my family roots, so I can demonstrate to you once and for all, what I mean about Falklands families, and how it is simply preposterous to ignore us in the ongoing Falklands dispute. I would go as far as to say that I demand that we be recognised as the core issue to the problem, and it is us who should ultimately make the final and lasting decision on our future. I map out my Falklands heritage as the foundation to my claim, and I challenge any Argentine to match it.

All my immediate family, over five generations (that includes my two children, Severine and Amelia), have been born in the Falkland Islands. My elder brother, Alexander Jacob Betts (Alec), was born on 28 October 1947 and named after our grandfathers, Alexander John Betts and Jacob Napoleon Goss. Our younger brother, Peter James Betts (Popeye), was born on 21 January 1954, whilst my only sister, Vivien Delia Betts, was born on 26 April 1957. Another brother, Kevin, was born on 14 November 1951, but he died when he was four months old from meningitis.

My father married twice, therefore I have half-brothers and half-sisters, who were also born in the Falkland Islands. The original Betts, the first to arrive in the Falklands, was John Betts, my great-great-grandfather. He landed in the early hours of 9 August 1855, rather cold and wet; he had been shipwrecked when his ship, the *Carlton*, 60 days out of Swansea heading for the Panama with a cargo of coal, ran aground off Cape Carysfort which is on the north-east coast of the Falklands. I have not done any extensive research yet, but it is thought that he was born in Liverpool. What is certain is that he married Margaret Johnson in the Falklands on February 1858, and they would go on to have 18 children – that is not a typographical error, I do mean 18 children.

As we open the family book, as it were, and blow the dust off the fading pages to take a better look at my family heritage in the

Falklands, we see the original traces of Betts and Goss. I will start with the Goss family, because it was they who arrived in the Falkland Islands first.

The first Goss to arrive was my great-great-grandfather, Jacob Napoleon Goss, with his wife Ann Pedrick, apparently, on a ship called the *Alarm*. The year was 1841/42. Before immigrating to the Falkland Islands, Jacob Napoleon worked as a stonemason in the West Country, where he met and married Ann.

Jacob was born in England, on 17 June 1825, and was the eldest brother of William Henry Goss, whose family became famous Staffordshire pottery makers, operating a highly successful business in the United Kingdom from 1858 to 1933. This Goss family in fact, invented the heraldic porcelain theme. I suppose you have worked it out for yourself that William Henry Goss was therefore my great-great-uncle.

Once settled in the Islands, Jacob Napoleon recognised the potential of the land and the reasonable ease of acquiring it. Jacob was energetic and very keen to get going on developing land. But before he did so, even from afar, he was soon encouraging his father, Richard Victor, and his mother, Sophia, formerly Mann, to come to the Islands and join him. It's worth reminding ourselves that the first settlers had only arrived in 1833, therefore Jacob was a very early immigrant. It is also worthy of note that the population was a mere 200 souls at the time of his arrival.

Richard Victor was eventually convinced by his son's endless enthusiasm to come to the Falklands, and he duly arrived with his wife in 1850. Jacob then quickly got down to business, and after securing some crown land, started building properties for use as dwellings and for commercial activities.

As a stonemason, Jacob was able to put his skills to very good use during the construction of buildings. The stone had to be transported by horse and cart from where it lay to the building site, and naturally all building work was manual. Jacob and Victor would build what has now become the very famous Upland Goose Hotel. They built the structure as six terraced houses, with 20-inch thick stone walls. Even today there are still very few buildings in the Islands built from local stone, probably due to the lack of local skilled stonemasons over the years. Once finished, Jacob named the whole building block Marmont Row. He later opened the first tavern in the Islands, by utilising the east end unit as a public house, which he called the Eagle Inn. The family heraldic arms depict a goshawk, which family members often incorrectly referred to as an eagle.

Over the period of its history, the Eagle Inn has had only two name changes, firstly to the Ship Hotel, and finally the Upland Goose Hotel, which was a name given to the property by a very hard-working, astute and enthusiastic businessman. Well, at least in my opinion. He was an English immigrant called Desmond King. Des was fortunate enough, however, to have the support of his devoted and hard-working wife, and their equally hard-working young daughters during the operation of the hotel.

I am also delighted to record that he sold the very fine establishment, for considerable capital gains, some time after the Falklands War. A perfect example of his business prowess, and a fitting compliment to the craft and labours of my forefathers, for their landmark is held in such high esteem today as a rare and original building, and much prized and valued as a place to conduct business.

The Goss family prosperity grew rapidly, and it is believed they made acquisitions of some very large areas of open land, some of which have become important public landmarks in the capital of the Falklands today; I refer to Victory and Arch Greens in particular. Sadly, they never had time to develop these areas because of their untimely deaths, but one thing is for certain: Jacob Napoleon Goss achieved much in the Falklands, and when the definitive, full and true story of the Islands is told, he must go down in the history books as one of the great entrepreneurial pioneers.

With the Goss family already established, the other side of my family arrived and put down roots in the Falklands.

As I have mentioned, my great-great-grandfather John Betts came to the Islands due to misadventure. However, John Betts quickly found work and settled, not in Stanley, but on and around Keppel Island, which is located to the northwest of West Falklands and some 450 miles to the northeast of Tierra del Fuego.

The Patagonian Missionary Society (later called the South American Society) had leased Keppel Island just before my great-great-grandfather's arrival in 1855, where they established a station, called Cranmer, which had been set up as a base to service and support the organisation's aims, which were basically to indoctrinate the native Yahgan Indians in Tierra del Fuego and Patagonia of their religious ways, whilst using several of them as nothing more than slave labour, as they toiled away on the small island farm growing crops and caring for animals for food and to trade. One of the pioneers of the missionary Society, Allen Gardiner, from Berkshire in England, was a former Royal Naval Commander who apparently resigned his commission to establish the mission. He met his death, along with his shipmates, in Terra Del Fuego in September 1851 when the gifts they had come to offer the native Indians ran out, thus he and his companions either starved to death, or were murdered by the Yahgans in the winter of that year.

My great-great-grandfather, when not working on Keppel, worked on the ship named after Allen Gardiner. However, whilst on the Christian Missionary farm, my great-great-grandparents would create their own piece of unique Falklands history on the island, on at least two counts. Firstly, their first child, John Cranmer (no doubt named after the station) Betts, my great-grandfather, was born on Keppel Island on 29 December 1859, thus, he was the first boy, perhaps even the first child, ever born on Keppel Island. Secondly, John Cranmer Betts was the first Betts to be born in the Falkland Islands; he, and the 17 other children of his family become the first generation of native Falkland Islander Betts.

Apart from my great-great-grandfather's toils, it is clear he must have been a passionate man who found the time for pleasure with his wife, as she presented him with such a big family, most between 1863 and 1882. This meant, my dear great-great-grandmother was pregnant for virtually 19 straight years.

John Betts and his wife were almost certainly some of the very first British settlers in the West Falklands, which was populated some time after the settlement of the inhabitants on East Falklands. They moved to nearby Pebble Island in the middle of the 1860s. It is interesting to note that at that time, the Falklands population had doubled from the recorded figure of 287 in 1851, which was just after the arrival of my great-great-great-grandfather Richard Victor Goss, to 541 inhabitants in 1861.

Once John moved to Pebble Island, the Dean family soon appointed him as farm manager. John Henry Dean had leased

Pebble Island and three smaller islands in the vicinity – Golding, East and Middle – in 1846 which he later purchased apparently for the sum of £400. He had been the first person ever to be granted freehold of land in the West Falklands.

John Betts' arrival on Pebble Island would also start an amazing, possibly even a unique, family record in the Falkland Islands. For at least 140 years, one member of the Betts family would be living and/or working on Pebble Island. Some would go on to follow in his footsteps and become the manager of the tiny island farm for the United Kingdom-based Dean family. I had better come clean now, and put the record straight once and for all, thereby removing any hint of guilt on my behalf. I was the only one of dad's children who reached working age and did not work or live on Pebble Island. It is also true to say that because of this, large chunks of my life developed away from the larger family fold and I can tell little of life on a small island farm, first hand, with the exception of a brief period spent on Lively Island during 1964/65. I should also say, to my knowledge, none of the family has held it against me (I think).

Okay, that rather neatly brings both sides of my family forebears in parallel up to the mid-1860s. Now what happens next to the Goss family, in 1868 to be precise, was to change the future and fortune of this family in the Islands for ever. Whether the stories I am going to relate to you are true or false, I have no idea, and one thing is for sure, we will probably never know. But I find the allegations fascinating and riveting stuff. Not, however, if you were, or are, a Goss I suspect.

3

Mysterious Deaths in the Goss Family
(And tragic death in the Betts family)

On 11 September 1868, Jacob Napoleon Goss died very suddenly and mysteriously, without any previous complaints or signs of illness and many local residents and family members became deeply suspicious. Suspicion turned to despair and panic when just three days later, on 14 September, his father, Richard, also died. Allegations and gossip soon started flying around the town of a double murder.

The story also goes on to portray an unbelievable alleged act of betrayal by a representative of the Anglican Church. This has never been proven. The Goss family were certainly very staunch members of the Anglican Church. However, I should also add that it was being rumoured by the locals, at the time, that traces of poison were found on the dead men's bodies. Rather intriguing stuff, don't you think? Well, double murder or not, poisoned or not, one thing that was definite, both men were dead within three days of each other.

It is alleged that Richard and Jacob had entrusted the church official with the administration of their affairs, which included the deeds to their considerable lands, many buildings, a schooner, and a large amount of cash, for that time anyway. I must repeat, none of these allegations have ever been proven beyond reasonable doubt.

One thing that is beyond any reasonable doubt, Jacob's widow, Ann, ended up with nothing, and by some odd coincidence, the Anglican priest disappeared from the Falkland Islands, apparently on the family schooner, which he claimed to have purchased. Jacob's widow, or other dependants, never saw the deeds to properties and other elements of the accumulated family fortune again.

It is also alleged that the cleric met a most violent death in

Chile, and upon further investigation after his death, it is believed the family schooner was still registered with Lloyd's in the Goss family name. Well, well, there you go.

I suppose you will hardly find it surprising if I tell you that the direct descendants of the Jacob Napoleon Goss family quickly changed their Christian allegiance and adopted the Catholic Church for their holy place of worship. Several generations on, and to this very day, they remain hardcore members of the Catholic congregation. Whilst I accept this murder story is full of conjecture, I do suggest that something quite dramatic and mysterious must have happened in the remote and isolated Falkland Islands during those few dark days in September 1868.

But there would certainly not have been any Sherlock Holmes type of character in the community, to carry out any sophisticated investigation, and I suppose law, and the administration of it, was probably pretty ad hoc. The Church would also have been very influential with authority and administration in the tiny community of the Falklands in 1868. Whatever, one thing is certain, something of a very serious nature must have taken place between the Goss family and the Anglican Church, for them to slap their bibles down on the back of a pew and strut up the road and throw themselves into the arms of the Roman Catholics. This kind of action, you must agree, is not an every day occurrence.

In his passing, Jacob left behind his devoted widow, Ann, and their nine children: six daughters – Lousia Ann, Sophia Jane, Georgian Ellen, Ann Elizabeth, Emily Jane and Margaret Fanny – and three sons – Richard William Napoleon, Abner Cosmopolite and my great-grandfather, William Henry Goss.

When Louisa Ann Goss, was born on 31 October 1852, she became the first Goss to be born in the Falklands Islands. However, all her brothers and sisters were born in the Islands also, thus making them the first generation of Goss Falkland Islanders. Just like the Betts's at the time, they were being indisputably marked down in Falkland Islands history, as some of the new, and native, populace.

There could be no doubt, had the children of Jacob Napoleon Goss reaped the full rewards and benefits of their father's exploits, they would have inherited the basis for a very secure life and to build and expand the family empire. Whatever actually happened back in 1868, it condemned many of the Goss family in the future to being nothing more than someone's employee. Just like every other Falkland Islander. Sadly, it would take a war before that situation changed to any great extent.

The second generation of the Goss family directly connected to me were the 12 children, 9 daughters and 3 sons, of my great grand-parents, William Henry and Ann Goss, formerly Aitken. Their fourth child was my grandfather, Jacob Napoleon Goss, no doubt named after his pioneering and commercially minded grandfather. My grandfather was born on 2 January 1900. He lived a short, hard and eventful life, mainly working on sheep farms and small boats, until his death on 19 August 1954 on New Island. From some of the stories my mother tells me about him, I think he might have been something akin to pirate and poacher. One thing that is for sure, he certainly did not follow in the footsteps of his productive and far-sighted grandfather.

However, granddad did once leave the Islands. This was during World War II, when he responded immediately to a call to join a British fuel supply vessel which was anchored in the outer harbour of Stanley (Port William) and was in desperate need of additional crew to carry out her contribution to the war effort. Granddad Jacob eventually found himself stationed on the Rock of Gibraltar until the war had ended, after which he returned to the Falklands to rejoin his wife, my grandmother, Rebecca McCallum, but the marriage was never stable, so he would leave home and go back to working on small islands and boats.

I only ever recall seeing him on one occasion. He was about 5 foot 7 inches in his socks, with dark hair and a big bushy brown beard which seemed to highlight his sunken deep blue eyes. I remember him as being a gentle and quiet man, but mum tells me he had a terrible temper.

As I have indicated before, my grandparents had four children, my mother being the youngest. Although I never really knew my grandfather, I got to know my grandmother very well, because I would live with her, on and off, until her death on 22 January 1974, oddly and sadly enough, on my mother's 46th birthday.

Switching back to the Betts side of the family, I have told you that the original Betts, John Betts, moved quickly to the West Falklands upon his arrival in 1855, which meant the early Betts families were not very well known in the Islands capital, Stanley, because once established at Pebble Island, they stayed put. Due to the sheer number of John and Margaret's children, I could not, and will not, make any attempt to describe all their movements and destinies. But I can say that not all lived, worked or died in the Falklands. Three at least, William Henry, Amy Margaret and Sarah Anne, emigrated.

However, the Betts family are synonymous with Pebble Island and its history. Diana, who is a fifth-generation Betts, still lives and works on the island today. Another, her sister Susan, was a prisoner on the island during the Falklands War, when British Special Forces carried out a night raid on Argentine positions and destroyed several aircraft. The event would shoot this little island into worldwide news headlines.

John was a fortunate survivor of a shipwreck. He lived to be 65, he had been struck down with paralysis 6 years prior to his death on 13 July 1889. However, the seas would not be so forgiving towards his family as they had been to him 46 years earlier.

On one fateful day in August 1901 his twin sons, George Robert and Edwin John, my great-great-uncles, were taking passage back to Pebble Island, after a rare visit to Stanley, on the *Thetis*, She was a 305-ton barquentine built for the Falkland Islands Company in Dumbarton, Scotland in 1893 to operate as a shipping service between the United Kingdom and the Falkland Islands, and to provide an inter-island service within the Falklands.

The ship departed Stanley carrying 21 passengers and crew and some large deck cargo, a huge sheep dip, actually. As the vessel was heading for an East Falklands port called Salvador, tragedy would strike, and hard.

The vessel never reached her destination and was never seen again, all 21 crew and passengers were lost. Wreckage was found washed ashore on Pebble Island off the north-west of West Falklands believed to be that of the *Thetis*, miles away from her intended destination. If that were not bad enough, the bodies were never recovered. Losing a family member is always sad, but to lose twin sons, in their mid twenties, must have been a devastating blow for my great-great-grandmother.

Moving on, I will now deal strictly with my direct branch of the Betts tree. As I have said, the one interesting statistic about my great-grandfather, John Cranmer, the eldest son of John and Margaret, if you recall, was that he was the first boy to be born on Keppel Island. It might be that he was the first *child* ever to be born there. Who knows? But what is certain, he is one of only a handful of children ever to be born on this remotest of islands.

John Cranmer Betts married Elizabeth Ann Kiddle in 1883. Ann was born in London in 1865 and had come to the Falklands with her parents in 1873 on a ship called *The Sea Witch*. She was just seven years old and went to live with her parents at Port Stephens. Then, at the young age of 17, she married my great-grandfather in Stanley. They did not make their home in the capital; instead, they moved to the West Falklands to live, not at Pebble, in the first instance, but to a place called Roy Cove, where they stayed for two years, before eventually, and almost inevitably, moving on to Pebble Island, where they remained for a further fifty years. Like his father before him, my great-grandfather became the manager of the island sheep farm.

My great-grandparents were married for 52 years, until my great-grandmother's death, at her daughter's home in Stanley, in 1935. The couple had celebrated their golden wedding anniversary in Stanley during the Islands' centenary year celebrations of 1933; apparently, it was the first visit they had made to the Falklands capital for 20 years.

A special and unique silver coin was struck to commemorate the Islands' first 100 years of unbroken administration and British rule, and my half-brother Arnold (same father), who was born on 27 January of that year, would be the youngest inhabitant to receive one. Which, I am happy to say, he still has among his possessions in New Zealand.

My great granddad died three years after the death of my great-grandmother in 1938. During their long and presumably happy marriage they had six children; three sons and three daughters. Their eldest son was my grandfather, Alexander John Betts. He was born in 1884, and married Vivien Gladys Carey (his 1st cousin) in 1909. They lived on Pebble Island all their lives, naturally.

Granddad Alexander was the farm's carpenter and built several of the farmhouses and other structures in the island's compact settlement. My grandparents had just the one child, my father, Cyril Severine Betts, who was born on 16 November 1912.

Tragically, my grandmother died a month before her 27th birthday, apparently from some form of tuberculosis in 1917, when my father was just 4 years old. Her body rests in the tiny cemetery on Pebble Island.

Although very young at the time of his mother's death, my father had obviously held extremely fond memories of her. I can vividly recall that he often carried a photograph of her in the inside pocket of his jacket. Even in the latter part of his own life, he would still tell me with great pride that she was a very accomplished pianist, singer and poet.

His most cherished memento of my grandmother was a love poem called 'To my Baby' which she wrote for him a short while before her death. Some of the lyrics indicate she was aware that her illness was not going to be cured, and death was imminent.

Because my father adored the poem so much, we, as a family, decided it was only fitting that it be recited at his own funeral. This Canon Stephen Palmer did very eloquently on 13 March 1996, which I trust pleased both him and my grandmother. I now have the original poem in my home.

Dad once told me a lovely story about granddad Alec and my grandmother. After returning from a very rare visit to the United Kingdom, granddad was asked by several people on the farm, 'What did you think of England, Mr Betts?' In reply, my grandfather said, 'Oh, it was all right, but it isn't as pretty as Pebble.'

After my grandmother Vivien's untimely death, granddad married Hyacinth Emily Peck in 1921, and they had two sons. Arthur John, who was born in 1922 and always known simply as John, who lived and worked all his life on Pebble Island.

He actually died in the house he had shared with his mother for nearly 70 years on Pebble, in 1996, just six months after my father's death. I vividly recall uncle John saying to me in the lounge of my house, after dad's funeral, 'I'll be next, Terry'. He was right. Like his mother before him, my uncle was buried at Pebble Island.

His brother, Henry William Betts was born in 1929. He emigrated to New Zealand in the 1960s, where he still lives today. I can recall Uncle Henry being a very keen and accomplished accordion player.

Following my grandmother's death, my father spent much of his time in the care of my great-grandparents. As granddad had to spend his day out and about working on the farm, it was simply not practical for him to stay at home and look after my father. That said, my father told me he had a very strong and loving relationship with his father.

4

Father and His First Family

Dad began his working life at Pebble in the mid-1920s. He met and married my great granddad's housemaid in 1931, oddly enough, not on Pebble, but in Stanley. Her name was Daisy May Rowlands. Both were just 19 years old, teenagers marrying in the Falklands in those times was a very common occurrence.

My father and his first wife had a short marriage – just nine years, they divorced in 1940 – but there was time enough for four children; two girls and two boys, my half-brothers and sisters. Arnold Cyril was born on 27 January 1933, almost 100 years to the day of the arrival of the first permanent settlers in the Falklands; Bernard Keith, born on 19 January 1939, and Olive Joan, born on 28 January 1937. Yes, I know that only makes three. The first child, Olga May, was born on 28 August 1931, but she died on Christmas Day of the same year, just four months old, a cruel twist of fate that would repeat itself with my father's second family 21 years later.

Following a family trend, and a father and son discussion in Stanley, Arnold began work at the tender age of 12 years as a houseboy on Pebble Island, earning a mere three pounds a month. Arnold's immediate boss was our uncle, William David Noah Betts. Uncle Willie would be the third, and last, Betts to be manager of the farm. But before mentioning anything else, I must recite a tale Arnold often tells me about those days and the daily chores he had to perform whilst there.

'It was like this, Terry. Everything, everyday, was a monotonous routine. Uncle Willie would wake me up in the early hours of the morning, in his long johns. I would get up and go down to the kitchen, to make sure the fire was still smouldering away. If so, I would rake and stoke it up, to enable a cooked breakfast to be prepared. After breakfast, I would then have to go and fill all the peat buckets. Then it would be time to feed the hens and check to see if there were any eggs. I would collect them up and take them back to the house.

'After that, I would then have to go to the lavatory, and if the bucket was full, I would be required to carry the bloody thing down to the beach, and empty it. It was quite heavy for a 12-year-old boy, and its contents stank to the heavens. The floors of the outhouses around Uncle Willie's house had to be scrubbed from time to time, and you had to get down on your hands and knees, using a scrubbing brush to carry out the task.

'Once I had finished my jobs for the morning, I would go down to the carpenter's shop to work with our grandfather. It was my favourite place to go, because granddad would teach me a lot about carpentry. There were no electrical power tools in those days, and all the wood had to be cut by hand. He would teach me how to saw a piece of pine timber, and how to keep on the thick black pencil line. In the afternoon I would go back to the big house (local terminology for the manager's dwelling) and fill more peat buckets.'

After four years on Pebble Island, Arnold left the Falklands in 1949. He had taken a job on board the Royal Mail Ship *Lafonia* as a pantry boy, a job secured for him by our father. Anyway, the owners, the Falkland Islands Company Limited, had sold the vessel, and Arnold sailed back to the United Kingdom on her. He settled in Southend on Sea, taking a job in a timber yard. He eventually moved to New Zealand in 1978.

My other half-brother, Bernard, has lived his entire life in the Falkland Islands, working on sheep farms, firstly on Pebble Island, as you would expect, where he met and married his most incredible hard working, loyal and loving wife Marion. Both were horse riders and racing jockeys of considerable renown.

At one time Bernard was the 'cowboy' who tamed the wild horses on the farm at Pebble. Marion is the quiet-spoken member of the family, but behind that smiling face with the gentle and polite gestures is a rock, a character so strong, which bonds the whole of their family together.

Bernard and Marion purchased their own farm, the Boundary, a sub-division of Hill Cove Farm, on the West Falklands in 1982. They had only been able to achieve their dream because of a new Falkland Islands Government initiative, prompted by Lord Shackleton in his economic reports on the Falkland Islands in 1976 and '82, in which he recommended the buying-up of the large farmland from absentee and other landowners, to sell back to Falkland Islands residents by providing repayable and affordable mortgages – based entirely on a willing seller, willing buyer policy.

The first of these transactions had taken place a year or so earlier when the Falkland Islands Company sold land on East Falklands. The FIC is a UK-based and owned company, who at the time owned at least 30% of the Falklands entire land area.

Regrettably, in the mad scramble that followed, the Islands Government policy was not very well planned, possibly due to the intense pressure from many members of the public to distribute land quickly. The distribution system made no allowance for error or market forces, which has resulted in a long, hard battle for economic survival for many who entered into the scheme. Most were saved from collapse by regular and varying types of Government Grants, which were equally not very well thought out.

My brother's planned timing of ownership and no doubt, popping of champagne corks, received a very unexpected delay. Having just settled into his new home and surroundings, he, and the other new owners of the sub-divided sections of Hill Cove, were expecting a visit from the Governor, Rex Hunt (later Sir Rex) on 2 April 1982 to receive the deeds of title for their newly owned properties.

However, Rex was to be otherwise engaged on that day, because the Argentine Armed Forces had decided to pay us all in the Falkland Islands an unexpected visit, and a most hostile one at that.

If there was any sort of consolation to Bernard and Marion, then it was that they were not directly caught up in the nastiness of invasion, occupation and liberation, to the same extent of some others.

Olive Joan, my only surviving half-sister, married Gordon Peck and they had one child, a daughter, Darlene. I never saw very much of her because they rarely came to Stanley, where I spent most of my life in the Islands. I do recall staying in their house when I went to Pebble for a holiday around 1963, and they did come and stay with us on one occasion whilst we lived at the Victory Bar, prior to their emigration to New Zealand in the 1960s, but since her departure from the Islands, we have never been in contact (my fault, I'm sure). However, I do know that she and Darlene still live in New Zealand.

My father was to break a long family tradition by moving away from Pebble to Stanley. When he married his first wife Daisy, they moved to a farm called Fitzroy on the East Falklands, owned by the FIC. But an injury of a personal nature would not allow him to sit in the saddle. His injury became progressively worse and required more regular medical treatment, not readily available on the farm, thus forcing him to move to Stanley.

The switch from camp to the Islands capital would be the beginning of dad's travelling, but not the end of his personal links with Pebble Island. He joined the Falkland Island Company's vessel the *Fitzroy*, which was formerly the *Lafonia*. These *Lafonias* will get bloody confusing, I promise you. This one was built in 1931, and lengthened in 1936, remaining in service until being replaced by the Royal Mail Ship *Darwin* in 1957.

Father would also venture down to South Georgia during the industrial whaling period. He worked there in 1937/38 for the South Georgia Company Limited which was established in 1909 at Leith Harbour. The attraction for my father, and many other Falkland Islanders at that time, was the exceptional earning capacity, in comparison to local salaries. The temptation was just too great, also a factor was that not many people in those days had too much sympathy or regard for the poor old whale.

After his whaling exploits, he came back to the Falklands, and promptly went back to the sea, sailing the South Atlantic Ocean between the Falklands and Uruguay, which included a period during World War II.

Dad was actually in Stanley when HMS *Exeter* arrived in the port after the battle with the pride of the German naval fleet, the pocket battleship the *Graf Spee*, which had been severely damaged by HMS *Exeter*, *Ajax* and *Achilles* during the 'Battle of the River Plate'. He was among many Falkland Islanders who went on board the *Exeter* to assist in cleaning the ship up, after the horrors of battle. Sometimes he would tell me about some of the terrible scenes he witnessed, pretty gory details, of body parts and blood all over the place. I do remember seeing a black and white photograph, as a child, of a sailor standing in a gaping hole in the ship's hull, which had been pierced by a German shell. Other damaged areas had been filled in, or covered up, with mattresses and pieces of timber.

Whilst dad was working on one *Lafonia*, another, formerly the

Southern Coast, built in 1911, had in fact been designated as a hospital ship in the South Atlantic during World War II, but was never called upon. The ship was in service for the Falkland Islands Company from 1937 to 1942.

Father actually received a couple of medals, I believe they were the Southern and Atlantic Stars, for his services in the South Atlantic during World War II.

At this point, I would just like to throw in a little comment or two, before moving on. Interesting, don't you think, that the Argentines are all mouth now about the Falkland Islands being theirs, yet they were nowhere to be seen during World Wars I and II. However, Falkland Islanders were laying down their lives, and volunteering to join the war effort for Great Britain, in both of the wars. We had not opted to operate sheep farms in Patagonia.

In World Wars I and II, the Falkland Islands themselves were also a strategic base in the South Atlantic, from which Great Britain was able to protect the whole of the south-west Atlantic area from German occupation and worldwide dominance.

In World War II, 10% of the Islands' adult population sailed away to join His Majesty's forces and support services, of which 20 per cent lost their lives. The Falkland Islands contribution was not limited to human resources. In 1940, the Islands' Legislative Council approved the funding for the purchase of ten Spitfires. Funds were also raised by a local charity to purchase an additional fighter plane, Sadly all were lost in combat with the enemy.

The Argentines on the other hand, were preoccupied with sitting at home, on neutral territory, making a quick buck, whilst the rest of the world was tearing itself apart in armed combat. They did not have the slightest interest in the Falkland Islands then. Isn't it obvious why? Because it was not something they owned or occupied, they had no native people on the Islands, no connection, no history. Therefore, it was not something they concerned themselves about. Oh I'm so sorry, I can be so naughty at times, with my personal viewpoints.

Back to dad and his medals. I remember getting more than one telling-off and cuff around the ear from him, for marching around the passageways of the Victory Bar, with the bar and four medals pinned to the front of my pyjamas, which hung loose from my skinny chest, complete with a British Army tin helmet, which sat very insecurely on top of my head, broom handle in hand, and singing out at the top of my voice, 'Quick march, left, right, left, right,' pretending to be a British soldier. I also recall, after his death, gathering up some of his personal items with Arnold. Only one of the medals ever appeared, whatever happened to the others only God knows.

After the departure of the *Lafonia* in 1942, my father came ashore for a short time. It was during this period, that he contracted, and almost died, from quinsy, whilst living with friends. Arnold recalls that he was so ill he decided to make a last will and testament. But he made a dramatic and speedy recovery, and was soon back to work, with renewed vigour. In addition to his regular job as a stevedore with the FIC, he started to operate a small shoe repair business in an ex-Army nissen hut, which he and a friend, Les Halliday, had purchased. I wonder about that, because Islanders rarely purchased anything from the Army – they acquired it.

Dad had the sea bug, and it would not be long before he rejoined the *Fitzroy*. In 1946 he travelled to the United Kingdom to collect the Falkland Islands Company's new vessel. You've guessed it, the *Lafonia*. This one was formerly called the *Perth*. Built in 1915, she was much larger than all before her, being some 2,259 tons. My father remained on this ship until she completed her service for the FIC in 1949, when she was sold, taking my brother Arnold back to England with her.

5

Mother and Father

My mother and my father married in the register office in Stanley at 6 p.m. on 27 October 1947. The wedding party was very small, consisting of just my mother, father, grandmother and my uncle Darwin. The group had all walked down to the register office from the family home in Callaghan Road. The reason for this, apparently, was that my grandmother did not want anyone in the community to know my parents were actually getting married. All very bizarre. After the wedding ceremony, the bridal party all walked back home again, and shared a few drinks with a small number of guests.

In the early hours of the following morning, mother and father, with suitcase in hand, were walking as fast as they dare, down to the hospital. Once there, the first addition of the newly married couple arrived: my oldest brother, Alec. This was the reason why my grandmother had been so coy about the marriage the previous day. In those days it was deeply frowned upon by the tiny community for anything to happen outside the perceived normal way of life. Anything which did was soon seized upon, and rapidly became hot gossip for the energetic and often highly hypocritical, all too eager to wag their tongues.

At the time of my brother's birth, my father was working as a barman/captain's steward on the *Lafonia*, and just days after mother returned home from hospital with Alec, the ship was bound for the UK for a refit. Dad would not come back home again for a further six months. Most of this time, which he often told me was a very enjoyable, he spent in a place called South Shields.

Mum was convinced he had a girlfriend there. Who knows? One thing is certain, my father was not about the house for the first six months of Alec's life, therefore he was of no support to my mother in very difficult times. Regardless of that, even when dad did return to the Falklands, the frequent movements of the vessel in and out of Stanley meant he would only visit mum and my brother fleetingly.

It is now the middle of 1948, mother is still living at home with grandmother, and she continues to be an unpaid housekeeper. However, she tells me, that the highlight of the year was a free trip with dad, for her and Alec, on the *Lafonia*. This was a working cruise for dad around the West Falklands for ten days, a busman's holiday, but the voyage did include a short stopover at Pebble Island. Time enough for my parents to have a meal with granddad Alec and step-grandmother Hyacinth, and show off the new grandson. Mother recalls that my brother actually took his first steps in life on the settlement green that day.

With the sale of the *Lafonia* in 1949, my father was paid off in Stanley, but remained in the employ of the Falkland Islands Company by joining the 'Jetty Gang', as it was locally referred to – a group of stevedores/labourers.

During this time a serious incident took place. Someone, or some persons, had broken into the Royal Navy warehouses, situated at the naval depot, locally called 'The Camber'. The storage buildings were full of all sorts of bounty, such as liquor, cigarettes and clothing, and some of the goodies disappeared. The local constabulary soon became involved, and as the FIC stevedores were working over at the site at the time, they soon became the prime suspects.

One night, my mother and father were visiting friends, when the police came to the door and invited my father to accompany them to the police station, where he was promptly interviewed and held for several hours, before being released.

The police followed up their questioning by searching gardens and outbuildings at the family home. Nothing was found. I understand, the local police force would never solve the case. However, father had been sufficiently rattled by their close attention and he decided to seek employment elsewhere. He was successful, and the family moved to Carcass Island, a tiny island in West Falklands.

My parents, with brothers Alec and Bernard, took passage to this remote island on the *Fitzroy*. My mother was six months pregnant again, this time with me. Within a few months mum was winging her way back into Stanley with Alec in the tiny, and only, float aeroplane, which was operated by the Falkland Islands Government to provide the community with a somewhat limited inter-island passenger and mail service.

This time, mother had a normal labour and returned to Carcass with Alec and the new addition to the family, one Terence Severine Betts. However, before taking us back to the Island home, I was christened in the Christ Church Cathedral by the Bishop of the Falkland Islands, Bishop Evans, who by pure chance just happened to be in the Falklands on a very rare visit from the United Kingdom to his South Atlantic diocese.

My parents' stay on Carcass Island was a short one. Unfortunately, mother needed to accompany me back into Stanley when I was just six months old, to allow me to receive urgent and sustained medical treatment.

Whilst we were in Stanley, Bernard had an unfortunate accident out on the farm. He badly injured his sensitive parts whilst climbing on the house water supply barrel to get his football, which had got stuck in the roof guttering. One of his feet slipped on the wet edge of the drum, and he fell, straddling the rim of the steel container and causing himself considerable pain and discomfort. Father had to accompany Bernard into Stanley, so his injured son could receive medical attention.

Once medically examined, it was decided Bernard should remain in hospital for a week or so. Father, therefore, decided to remain in Stanley until Bernard was fit and well enough to take back home. But, one day, as he was walking down the street, he came across the manager of Carcass Island, who was rather surprised to meet my father in the town. He asked dad, 'What are you doing in Stanley, Cyril?' Not satisfied with my father's reply, he fired him on the spot. All because my father had not made contact with him, thus he had not given him permission to leave the farm. That's how it was those days in the Falklands.

By the winter of 1951 my father, who had gone back to Carcass Island to pack up the family belongings, as a result of his unceremonious dismissal, returned to Stanley to join my mother, brothers and me to live with grandmother, at 1 Callaghan Road.

This family abode had been built by my uncle Darwin towards the end of World War II, mostly from ex-Army material. Oddly enough, some items had actually been purchased; but most had been borrowed on a long-term basis. I think it is possible many homes had been similarly built in those times, because it was the only way affordable to many Islanders. (The materials derived from the stationing of the British Army in the Falklands – the West Yorkshire Regiment, I understand.)

Bernard, by now, had fully recovered from his accident, and was no longer singing soprano, Alec was four years old, and living a normal life for a child that age. I, however, had still not recovered from my abscess problems. In fact, they had worsened. Father had rejoined the FIC jetty gang and become a very keen darts player. He became a member of the Stanley Arms team, which would go on to win the inaugural league championship.

The third member of this Betts family was born in the Falklands summer of 1951, a third son to my parents. They called him Kevin Charles. Charles, because he was born on the third birthday of HRH Prince Charles. If you recall, I mentioned before that my father's first child, Olga, from his previous marriage, died at the age of four months. For those of you who strongly believe that lightning doesn't strike in the same place twice, then you had better think again, because Kevin also died at the same age from meningitis. What a weird and cruel coincidence of fate for my father, and very heartbreaking for my mother.

Tragic as it was, however, my brother's death would eventually relieve my mother of some of the terrible stress and strain she had been suffering during his short and ill-fated life. At that time, she had been walking me in a pram to and from the hospital daily for medical attention. Then, when she got me back home, she would have to repeat the journey with Kevin. For the whole of Kevin's short life, my mother would not know what a proper night's sleep was. Kevin was in constant pain and needed almost continuous attention.

I asked my mother once, why my brother was not admitted to hospital to get the medical attention he so obviously required. She said, 'They would not take him in until I went down one day, completely mentally and physically exhausted, and demanded that he be taken in.' But it had always been an uphill struggle to save his life, from the day of his birth. Even with all the best medical care, he lost his battle to survive, just one week after being taken into hospital.

Should you be wondering why my mother had not been more demanding about having her son cared for in hospital, it should be remembered that in 1951 the ordinary people of the Falkland Islands lived not only an isolated, but also a parochial life, with basically no opinions, and very few civil rights. Defending and speaking up for oneself was certainly not considered appropriate for the working class – a situation that would not change greatly for quite some time.

At the time of my birth into the world, or more accurately, the Falklands Islands, the Islands' economy was entirely based on the production of wool for export to the United Kingdom woollen mills, as it had been for nearly a century.

Land was almost entirely owned by absentee landlords, and the farmers were flush with cash. It was the time of the Korean War, and the market price for wool was sky high, perhaps even at its peak. The landowners were very wealthy people because they were operating low-cost and very high turnover businesses, I suspect that they were also highly influential in the Government.

However, before I get too critical, and at times cynical, I would agree that the Falklands Government kept a balanced budget and did not need, and nor did it receive, any financial support from the United Kingdom Government at this time, and neither does it require so now. A point well worth highlighting, because there are many who believe that we have always been a burden to the British taxpayer and the United Kingdom Treasury. Not so. In fact, in 1950 the Falkland Islands, as it had been for a very long time, were actually contributing to the United Kingdom economy by way of import tax from the wool shipments. Surprised you, haven't I?

I was born into a colonial society. The sheep farmers not only controlled the land and the assets on them, but directly or indirectly they affected the lives of every citizen living and working in the Islands. They had money, property and power, therefore they expected to be, and were, treated as god-like figures. An ordinary Islander, and there would not be too many who did not fall into this category, addressed these affluent members of society as 'Mr Bob', or 'Mr John', at the very least, often it was 'Sir'. If these jokers were your employer, they generally controlled all aspects of your and your family's lives. I explain this in some detail in the union experience part of my book. The tied cottage system was believe me, very tied. If a married man lost his job, he and his family would lose their home, the manager would evict them, usually on a month's notice, but it was not unheard of to be a shorter period.

The worker never received his salary in cash, weekly or monthly. Instead, he would receive an account statement from his employer every three to six months. The regularity of this depended upon whether the farm had its own bookkeeper. The purpose of the statement was nothing more than to advise the individual if his financial position was in credit or otherwise with the farm owner.

Even more galling when I think of it now, but not surprising at the time, the worker's cash was almost certainly tucked away in the bank accounts of the farm owner, or the owner's agent, which was probably the Falkland Islands Company, and the worker would only get his money if he wanted to purchase some goods, and only then, after much pleading with the farm manager, or if he was fired or left his place of employment.

The owners of the larger farms also owned, operated and stocked the farm store, a very neat arrangement, which meant that they recovered a large part of the salary paid to their employee. It was just another cog in the wheel of total domination of the working class.

However, even if you did not live in this environment of near oppression in the camp (the countryside), working for the farm owner/manager, this in itself did not mean you would escape their influence, power and arrogance by living in the Falklands capital.

The reason for this is very simple. In general the landowners were also the appointed or elected members of Government. Those members not elected to Legislative Council, would be appointed by the Governor of the Islands, and those appointed would invariably be a farm manager/owner, or the head of the FIC.

There was no such thing as a truly, fully elected government by the people. This would not happen until as recently as the General Election of 1985, following the enactment of the first Falkland Islands Constitution in October of the same year, just three years after the Falklands War – a point worthy of noting, don't you think?

The farmers' powers were as good as total because, as members of the Legislative and Executive Councils, they would make and pass laws which often never affected their day-to-day living on their farms in the camp, which, in terms of facilities and administration, was isolated and separated from Stanley.

There were no roads, therefore few, if any, daily visitors, in fact, there were never any visitors without the manager's knowledge because you always had to seek his permission to enter upon his land. Anyway, my point is this: if the Council were to increase tariffs for the utilities, such as electricity, water supply and refuse collection, or raised the tariff for a driving licence or vehicle road tax, the effect was felt by the residents of Stanley only. Hence, no escaping their power and influence.

6

Growing up in the Falklands

Getting back to family matters, my mother was starting to recover from the loss of her son. She spent the remainder of 1952 at home, looking after my elder brother Alec and me. I made a slow but full recovery this year from my health problems; this seemed to coincide with the arrival of a new doctor in the Islands who began to take care of my treatment.

At this time, my father was for the first time living at home on a permanent basis after many years at sea, but I understand he was of little support and comfort to my mother once again, because as well as his working hours, he would go out in the evenings, working as a barman in a local pub called the Stanley Arms. This resulted in many drunken nights, with him coming home in the early hours of the morning, and eventually led to arguments and mistrust. It's a familiar life story.

Mother tells me it was also very difficult sharing a house with my grandmother and her lodger. Actually he was also her lover, a huge man, Herbert Summers, nicknamed 'The Bear'. With so many different personalities all living under the same roof it was not surprising that we kids were subjected to many moments of high tension, which would often result in the adults screeching and yelling verbal abuse at each other, and us. Mum continued to spend her days in this environment as the skivvy. She was not alone, of course. So were many housewives in the Falklands, and the world, for that matter.

The house was of a medium size, but all the rooms were small. My brother and I shared one bedroom. There were no luxuries in this Falklands house, as was the case in just about every home in the 1950s and 60s. Facilities and aids such as insulation, central heating, double-glazing, plumbed hot water, bathrooms or indoor water closet, were no part of this home. There was a limited supply of electricity, but not enough for the use of electrical appliances which are taken for granted today, such as fires, carpet cleaners, steam irons, kettles, toasters, freezers or fridges. There were also no fitted kitchen units or bathroom suites.

I can remember mother ironing clothes with flat irons which were heated on top of the peat fire, which at that time was usually a Modern Mistress or a Stanley Range, always situated in the kitchen. Also, on top of the fire would be a cast-iron boiler, called a fountain, which would contain the total hot water supply for the house, but there would only be hot water if you kept the home fires burning.

The kitchen was the main living room in a Falklands home, because it was the warmest part of the house. It was always furnished with a dining table which held the household cutlery, and chairs (meals were eaten in the kitchen). There would also be a settee, with the family cat asleep upon it, and a unit which held the crockery and cooking utensils. A peat bucket or two would be placed at the side of the fire.

Lounges, in most homes, had an open peat fire, locally called, 'an open grate', but they would only be flashed up for a special occasion, or during the winter. Both kitchen and lounge would have a goose wing placed somewhere by the fire-side. Their normal use was for sweeping up dust, and getting bits and pieces out of corners, but they had many purposes – one of which was whacking children's backsides if we had been up to mischief.

Unfortunately, as a result of another calamity, I ended up in hospital again in 1953. This time, I had been playing with a toy truck in the house, and somehow I managed to jam my thumb between the cab and tip-up back. Impatiently pulling it free, I partially pulled off the thumbnail. My mother marched me down to the hospital, and the doctor opted to remove the nail with a good old Wilkinson Sword razor blade. Although not a serious injury, I was kept in the hospital so that my thumb, which was now in a splint, could be treated and attended to until the new nail grew.

Life for the nursing staff was never simple, trying to attend to the medical needs of an active three-year-old who found it quite amusing to play games on them, like hiding under the bed or running away to another ward.

My six-week stay in hospital also meant an additional workload for my mother, who was also caring for my elder brother's daily needs, plus all the other domestic chores expected of her. Once again, she had the added burden of walking up and down from the house to the hospital twice a day, in all weathers, to visit me, fetching and carrying clothes and attending to other things I might require.

On this occasion in hospital, however, the medical care was not restricted to my injured thumb. I had also developed asthma and eczema, which I would have to live with for a while, but I would be cured of eczema at a very early age and free from asthma by the time I was fifteen.

After returning home to convalesce, unbelievably, disaster struck again, towards the end of the winter of 1953. Despite having my thumb in a splint, wheezing with asthma and covered in a rash from my skin disease, nothing affected my high spirits. For convenience and health reasons, my parents had made up a bed in the sitting room. This meant my mother could just pop in and out from the kitchen to make regular checks on me, and because it was one of only two rooms in the house that had a fire.

Winters in the Falklands can be very harsh, and bedrooms, due to the lack of insulation, double-glazing and central heating, were exceedingly cold. Walls were usually covered with wallpaper, which would become damp and mouldy from the moisture. The nights of heavy frost and/or snow often resulted in one waking up in the morning and being able to scrape the ice off the inside of the windowpane. I remember admiring the wonderful frost patterns that formed on the windows.

It was during one of these winter mornings that Alec and I were larking about, neither playing nor fighting, on my bed. I was in my pyjamas and dressing gown and Alec was teasing me for having such a luxurious robe – he was probably jealous because he did not have one. Whatever, he was taunting me about being a bit of sissy.

We started pulling one another about, then he pulled off the waist cord and ran off towards the kitchen, with me in hot pursuit. As I have mentioned before, we had a cast-iron hot water fountain on top of the peat-fired stove, which held approximately 15 gallons of water. Unfortunately for me, it was full, and the water was boiling. As Alec continued to run through the house with the dressing gown cord streaming out from his hand, somehow it managed to hook itself over the protruding brass spout, and my brother's speed was sufficient to bring the heavy container crashing to the floor. I was perfectly placed as it spewed its entire contents of boiling hot water all over me, scalding me from head to lower chest.

I do not recall any immediate pain or burning sensation, I seemed to be more aware of the total pandemonium that immediately broke out; people began running here, there and everywhere. I vividly remember my mother screaming at Alec as she chased him out of the house, smacking her head on the telephone as she was in pursuit of her fleeing son. So hard was the impact that she was stopped in her tracks and bent down, rubbing her aching head vigorously. Simultaneously my uncle Darwin leapt from the settee and grabbed my wet and steaming clothes and stripped me naked as fast as he possibly could in an attempt to avoid any further burning. I still carry some scars from this accident, but the doctors later told my mother, had it not been for my uncle's quick thinking and actions, I would have suffered much more serious burns which would have left me badly scarred, as it was, I lost the skin off my forehead, nose, around my eyes and ears, cheeks, neck, shoulders and upper part of my body.

My brother tells me that, unfortunately, the telephone which my mother had hit her head on had only recently been installed and was not yet connected. A friend of my uncle's who was visiting at the time jumped up and ran to his father's house just around the corner and alerted him to the problem. This neighbour had both telephone and motor car, so he alerted the hospital and then came to the house in his car to transport me there.

The next thing I recall was being wrapped up in something, probably a sheet, then being carried out to the waiting car. I was in the back seat, with my head on my mother's lap. Much later in the day, I woke up on the bed in the doctor's consulting room, with my mother sitting at my bedside. I think I said to her, 'What time is it, mummy?'

I was only hospitalised for a fortnight. The hospital was not fully equipped to deal with a case such as mine, so once the staff were satisfied that there was little else they could do, I was allowed home and mother once again became my nurse. I can remember her picking out the dressing bandages from a tin with tweezers. The dressings were yellow in colour and wonderfully cool as she placed them on the raw parts of my body. Thanks to her loving care, by Christmas I had made a full recovery, with just a few scars on my right shoulder and the right side of my chest to carry for the rest of my life. Taking all things into consideration, I had been a very fortunate boy in the end.

Another calamitous moment was not far away. In the January of 1954, my younger brother, Peter James (Popeye), was born a day before my mother's 26th birthday. Shortly after returning home she began to feel unwell, suffering from continuous headaches and tiredness. After examining her at the hospital, doctors were horrified at the condition of one of her lungs, and it was decided that she should be admitted for care and treatment immediately.

This dramatic and unfortunate situation meant that we children were farmed out, so to speak. Alec and Popeye would be taken care of by our adopted aunt Mildred (Auntie Middy to us kids) and Uncle Bertie (Bert), whilst I would spend my time between grandmothers and Harry and Betty Ford.

Six months later, mother was still in hospital, still recovering from a major operation for a collapsed lung. Then there was more bad family news. This time my uncle Darwie was admitted to hospital with TB, which many Islanders contracted during the early fifties. Fortunately the Falklands by then had a TB specialist, and he eventually ensured my uncle's return to good health.

If mother had not suffered enough over the last couple of years, even more tragedy would fall upon her. My granddad, Jacob Napoleon Goss, died in August, days after Uncle Darwin was struck down. My mother received the news of her father's death after being summoned to the office of the senior medical officer. She thought he was going to give her good news about her pending return home. Instead, the doctor said, 'I am sorry, I have bad news for you.' He paused for a second, then continued. 'Your father passed away on New Island. We are not actually sure when, because his body was found in bed, in a small isolated hut, probably several days after his death.'

The news was a devastating blow for my mother; she was extremely close to her father, even though she did not see a lot of him after her parents unofficially separated (they were never divorced), but whenever he was in Stanley, they always spent time with each other. My mother was aware that granddad had become very attached to New Island, he had even told her, that when he died, he wished to be laid to rest there. The manager's reaction to granddad's death was all rather weird. Allegedly, he would not even allow anyone to lay his body out, or have it put into a temporary coffin. The corpse was eventually flown to Stanley.

The year 1954 had started with a happy occasion of the birth of my brother, but for my mother, the remainder of the year was nothing short of miserable. The misery climaxed when I was taken ill with suspected TB. However, after a short period of dedicated treatment, the year ended on a brighter note, with my mother, brothers and me returning home to my grandmother's house in time for Christmas.

The next couple of years would bring some sort of normality and happiness into life, I started school in February 1956, and struck up my first real best-mate relationship, with my cousin Roy Hansen. We became almost inseparable, but we had a flair for the most unusual and varied forms of entertainment. On one occasion, when my mother was out shopping, I suggested we should climb onto the roof of grandmother's house and go down the chimney, just like Father Christmas.

I had discovered an easy way to climb up onto the roof of our house, by means of a steel water barrel at the edge of the back porch, and a wooden fence.

Once we made it to the chimney, we were disappointed to discover that it was too high, and thus, impossible to get on top of. So we walked over to the other side of the house and sat chatting on the edge of the roof, with our feet resting in the fragile guttering. We were completely unaware of the fact that if the guttering, which we were resting our feet in, was to give way, we would fall some 20 feet, which would surely have resulted in serious injury at least.

Once mother returned from her shopping trip, grandmother immediately told her that we were on the roof. In a fit of panic, mother called the neighbour, Jim Watson, for assistance. After an hour or so, he succeeded in getting the two of us off the roof by offering Roy and me sweets and sparkling orange drinks. However, once we were safe on the ground, the remainder of the day was spent in bed, without the gifts that had been on offer.

Roy and I remained very close friends until he emigrated, with his parents, to New Zealand in 1965. We would spend hours and days together, playing in the paddocks around my grandmother's house. Other favourite play areas were the white sandy beach at Surf Bay, the common, and the peat banks in that area, the small forest to the south of Government House, or just out and about on our bicycles.

One of my favourite pastimes as a very young boy was to go the local dairy. This meant getting up at 5.30 a.m. to help the dairymen with milking the cows. The dairy was only 100 yards or so from our house, and my parents would be woken up by me running down the stairs at the most ridiculous hour.

The dairy was tiny. It could only hold four cows at one time, and once finished milking, they were let out into a paddock, and the next four cows would be let in from a holding corral across the road, which, in the winter, would be knee-deep in mud and cow dung.

I remember filling their feeding bins with pollard and cow cake. I would eat the cake myself. I found it quite nice.

What I really enjoyed most was the milk delivery rounds, which were twice a day. Few people had a vehicle of any type in 1956, so it was very exciting to drive around the town, hopping on and off the van, putting milk bottles into people's boxes and placing the empties into the crates on the back of the truck. It was also a wonderful way to get to meet, and know, a large part of the community.

I also helped the dairymen cut and bag up grass. I would get six old pennies a bag (2.5 pence), but you had to jump the grass into the bag until it was solidly packed. I would watch the dairymen in total admiration as they swung and sliced the long grass with a large scythe in a fluid and graceful manner, Chuck and Gug were past masters, it was so elegant to watch.

Equally as gripping was the way they sharpened the long curved blade with a sand stone. I would lie on the ground thinking: One slip, and a finger would be severed from a hand, like a knife cutting butter. I will always remember the Christmas present Gug gave me one year, it was a fishing rod and a 10 shilling note (50 pence). My father was only earning £5 a week those days, so it was a considerable amount of money for a young boy. Christ, it was five cinema tickets, a box of Mars Bars, or enough money for two good nights at one of the local church bazaars.

When I was growing up in the Falklands, there was no such thing as televisions, only a few motor cars, and no public transport, such as buses and trains. We had 78 rpm records, which were played on a wind-up gramophone. I was always getting into trouble for scratching the records. By the end of the 1950s record players and vinyl records appeared. Our house, like everyone else's had a loudspeaker, rented from the Falkland Islands Government, for listening to the local radio station. It was a horn-shaped thing which had two knobs on it, for volume control: one for high, the other for low. But it didn't matter much where the controls were set, because there was very little difference between high and low volume.

Anyway, the local station was only on air for a couple of hours each evening. Sports programmes were very popular, football and boxing in particular. We children enjoyed the Saturday early evening programme *Children's Corner*, which was a music request show with a story midway through. Once the programme was over, it was Saturday night bath time.

We kids would share the old tin tub, which mother would drag into the kitchen and place in front of the peat stove, to gain the maximum warmth. We would be scrubbed down from head to foot, with Lifebuoy soap. We never wanted to get out, and there were always lots of protests and a struggle, to get us dried and dressed for bed.

The year 1957 would also bring a change to our family life which did not please me greatly at the time. My sister Vivien Delia was born. It did not fill this six-year-old boy with the greatest of pleasure when she arrived home one afternoon with my mother. I announced to my mum, and everyone else who was in the house, that I was leaving. There was no way I was going to live at home with a girl. I was going to pack my bag and go and live with Auntie Middy.

Alec started teasing me and tried to make me kiss my sister to welcome her home. As we had a pair of boxing gloves in the house, I decided I would challenge him to a fight, and if I won, I could leave.

We made our way to the back porch of the house, and duly set about punching each other. I guess we were ignored, and left to get on with it. After a while, my brother had beaten me to a standstill. I was finally reduced to tears, and ran up to my bedroom to escape everyone present, to try and console myself that a girl was now going to share our lives.

In the winter of 1958, my father got a job as barman at the Victory Bar. At this time the pub was only one of four in town, but it was an exciting prospect, because this would be our first independent home, free from living with other members of the family. The deal for my dad was £25 per month, with potential for additional earnings through a profit-sharing system, plus the rent-free house.

The house was small, but it had three bedrooms – one was only used as a storage room in the beginning. There was a kitchen, a large lounge, a cloakroom and a most wondrous contraption called an inside toilet. We had only known the outside water closet until the last year of our stay up at Callaghan Road, which was bloody cold in the winter and stank like hell all year round, wiping your backside on the sheet of the *Daily Mail* was far from a comfortable experience.

I can remember the guys on the old horse-drawn night cart coming around and collecting the buckets and slopping most of the contents into the cart. I understand that once it was full, they took it to a small jetty and emptied the load into the Stanley harbour. My uncle Bert use to swim in that harbour. What a terrible thought!

Alec and I shared one bedroom, whilst Peter and Vivien stayed in the same room as our parents. Moving in was a fantastic time of exploring and running around the interior and exterior of the Victory Bar. I wasted no time in busily opening and closing doors and windows, running around the gardens, climbing trees and searching outbuildings, until I had exhausted my parents' patience. I got myself sent to bed with a thick ear when I accidentally knocked out the stick that was propping one of the windows up and open, which brought it crashing down, trapping my sister's fingers. She screamed out in agony and I screamed all the way to my room, all on the first night.

Getting up the next morning was so exciting. We were in the middle of the town, the bakery and shops were just around the corner. Although it was a tiny little town, we had lived up on the hill, right on the back road, all our lives, out in the sticks, with open fields and the common to the back of us, so if the weather was particularly shitty, we were that much more exposed to it. I remember the winters always seemed much worse up there, downtown was considerably more sheltered, being lower down the hill and surrounded by other houses and the odd tree.

In Callaghan Road, snow would drift higher than the garden fence, five or six feet high, and build up to the back door and the lower part of the roof. When it was really bad we would have to dig ourselves out from the doorway to the gate.

The cold water pipes would freeze up, and sometimes burst, especially at the lead joints, which would split under the pressure of the water freezing to ice. The first one down to use the toilet in the morning would often be greeted by freezing cold water spewing out of the broken joint and splashing against the wall, with and an inch or two of water lying on the floor.

During any freeze-up, it also meant the toilet was inoperable, there would be no water to replenish the cast iron water fountain to provide hot water, which of course was required for washing dishes, clothes and making tea, etc. If the water supply became really desperate, we would go outside and fill galvanised buckets with snow, which we then melted down. Let me tell you, it takes an awful lot of buckets of snow to make one bucket of water.

A big fall of snow was also a time for potential conflict with freezing parents huddled around the kitchen fire, trying to keep warm, whilst we kids would be outside building snowmen, and throwing snowballs at each other, which often missed the intended target, and would thump against the side of the galvanised clad house, or smack against a windowpane. This resulted in a screeching parent yelling, Stop throwing those bloody snowballs at the house, or words to that effect. It was not unusual for the odd windowpane to come to grief during the winter.

Another thing that got up adults' noses was that we would keep running in and out to get a quick warm in front of the fire, traipsing a path of snow indoors, which would quickly melt to water and make a mess on the floors. Then, as we went out again, we would invariably forget to shut the back door, which would allow wind and snow to blow in. The gales and winter storms would often cause electrical power cuts, which meant that candles would be lit to provide light; on some nights dad looked more like Wee Willie Winkie in his nightshirt and hat, carrying a lighted candle around the house.

Winter nights were especially long. In mid-winter it would be dark indoors from 3.30 p.m., until 8.00 a.m. the following morning.

An alternative source of light to candles was the wondrous paraffin lamp, which I found quite hypnotic, romantic and soothing as it gave off a wonderful glow as it purred away. The whole apparatus was a simple and effective work of art. The bowl-shaped bottom was filled with paraffin and fitted with a small pump, which you pushed and pulled several times to build up pressure. Before lighting the contraption, you took a pair of tweezer-like objects out of a small jar, where they had been soaking in methylated spirits. Its simple function was in fact as a torch, which you clamped around the vertical fuel supply tube, at the appropriate distance below the mantle. Once you lit the torch, it would heat the mantle, turning it to a reddish colour, then you opened up a tiny valve, which released the pressurised fuel up the tube, and the mantle would bust into a bright clear light and give off that soothing humming sound as it burst into life.

Another delight in those dark cold nights was the brick. As I have said, we did not have the luxury of central heating, nor did we have hot water bottles for some years. I can still picture grandmother putting a building brick in the oven of the peat-fired cooker. When it was hot, she would take it out and wrap it in a woollen sock and put it in our beds. It was so lovely on the feet at night, but bloody hard on the toes in the morning, when you had forgotten it was in the bed and accidentally kicked it.

We were not in the Victory Bar for long, before I started to become very ill again. The house was very cold and damp, especially in the winter, much worse than in Callaghan Road. Unfortunately, the damp was not restricted to the walls of the bedroom, it also affected my feather mattress, which soon had my asthma raging again. I can remember being so bad, on many occasions, that I would be gasping and struggling for my next breath. I would sip water, which I found gave me some little relief, but the main remedy was inhaling the smoke of Hickman's asthma powder.

A portion of this dark green powder was taken out of the tin, tipped into the oval shaped lid and then set alight. It did not burst in to flames. Rather it would smoulder away. The smell from the bloody stuff was quite awful, but I would spend many hours lying over the edge of my bed, breathing it in, and it would help me to catch my next breath, which at times I would think was never coming.

However, as the house got damper, I became weaker. A common cold would turn into a severe attack of asthma, and I would be in bed for a week or so at a time, and because of my aliments, I was starting to miss school on a regular basis. Soon I contracted bronchitis, and I was heading for hospital and a lengthy stay in bed. I will come back to that in a moment.

I will always remember the musical evenings which my parents organised in the house at the Victory. We had a piano in the lounge, which Ken Mills would come in and play. Other friends of mum and dad would bring their musical instruments along, such as accordions, devil's fiddles', violins, banjos and guitars, which would result in Scottish and country music being played during the evening, and it was never too long before dancing and singing would break out also. They were joyous occasions. There would always be plenty of refreshments, not limited to tea and coffee. Often a traditional supper of mutton bangers and mash, with green peas and mutton gravy, or tripe and onions, with mashed potatoes and peas, would be served. Mum would be working all day, with one or two of her mates, preparing the food for these festivities.

The noise of the merry making was always too tempting for Alec and me, and we would sneak down the stairs and see what was going on. Unable to keep my nose out of things, I would go down first, but my father would usually spot me and tell me to get to bed. Then Alec would go down and, often as not, he would be shown off to the gathering and invited to do his rendition of 'Davy Crockett'. Whilst Alec was performing his song, my father would think I had gone off to my bedroom, but I hadn't, I would be peeping round the corner of the door at the foot of the stairway, enjoying the entertainment.

I can also remember going over to Fitzroy Road to watch the German road gang laying tarmac roads. We kids were fascinated at the thought of Germans being in town, because we had been educated to believe they were a little evil and dangerous. It was just ten years or so after World War II. The Germans were housed in a camp to the back of the town. Presumably, it was thought by the authorities that they should not be in the main community. Their accommodation was very basic, World War II Nissen huts, to be exact. I do not recall many speaking English, and I would be captivated as I stood and listened to small groups of them speaking in German.

It was also very exciting to witness new and smooth roads being laid in the town, and for the more curious of us, it was just too tempting not to walk about in the hot steamy tar. The problem was, it would stick to our wellington boots, so once we got home we would walk it through the house.

Just before my eighth birthday, I was on my way to hospital again. This time, the combination of asthma and bronchitis had become pretty serious, I needed full-time medical care. I was taken to the hospital in the doctor's motor car, which was a Rolls Royce, the first and only one in the Islands at that time. The owner was a Scottish doctor, a kind and gentle man who had a very quiet and reassuring voice, which made me feel secure rather than apprehensive about leaving home for the hospital, with my little suitcase in my hand.

Once we were in his car, he turned to me and said, 'Let's take a little spin, shall we, Terry.' Then with a wink of an eye he drove off. I think he knew I was going to be in confinement for some time, so he was going to give me a little pleasure before it all began. I was so excited and proud to be driven around the little town in the front of the most prestigious car in the capital. For the ten minutes or so that we drove about, I felt like a prince, perched in the passenger's front seat, with a broad grin on my face, waving at people as we passed by.

As it turned out, I would spend the next six months in hospital; it was a period of X-rays, umpteen pills, injections and loads of toys. A routine of waking up early in the mornings, taking tablets, having breakfast, using the bedpan, followed by a bed bath, more pills, lunch, a visit from mum every afternoon, which I always looked forward to, when we would share tea and cakes. More medicine, supper, another bed bath and a further visit from my concerned and caring mother would follow this, before I went to sleep.

There was also the weekly visit from the various priests, inquisitive members of the public and, on odd occasions, a snappy visit from the Governor of the Islands, whilst he was doing his rounds.

I would lie in my bed for hours, looking at the wallpaper, which had a multitude of characters from nursery rhymes. Humpty Dumpy always got a low rating in my mind, but I adored Snow White, angels and fairies. For me, there was something magical about the notion of creatures flying about the place, and often I would fantasise that I was winging my way down the corridors of the hospital, swooping on some unsuspecting nurse or doctor.

I also developed an interest in the weather. I would sit up in my bed and watch the sun through the large ward window as the light sparkled and danced on the clear blue seas. The colours and movements were hypnotic. It was often deceptive, I would imagine that it was quite warm outside, because the view was one of wondrous colour. However, my mother would often tell me that it was chilly and a little bitter with the sharp wind, which would make me feel a little less envious of people walking by as I lay in my bed.

Some days I would be struggling for breath and doing nothing more than sleeping and taking medicines – I was taking sixteen pills a day – and often had staff and parents on full alert, but eventually, I was allowed home. However, it would not be long before I got very ill again, and once again the root problem was the damp.

After a few months of continuous suffering, I recall one morning lying in my bed, all alone in the largest bedroom of the house. My body was fatigued from the constant coughing and choking, wheezing and puffing. The fighter was down, and this time I felt I could not take any more, I was giving up the war. I remember lying on my side looking out of the tiny window, it was a moment of peace and calm. The sky was blue, with a few big puffy white clouds. Then I noticed on the left hand edge of the nearest cloud an image of a man's face. Then a very strange thing happened.

There was a feeling of physical presence, a kind of eye contact was made between me and the image, which appeared to be staring directly at me, if that makes any sense. Then I started speaking to the image, in my mind. I told it I was tired and I wished I could float into the sky and go to heaven. The expression of the face changed, a smile appeared, then I heard a voice saying to me, 'Not yet, not yet, you are not ready; you have much to do before you come to heaven.'

As I listened intently to the words and stared at the face in the sky, I imagined an eye winked, then it started to fade away, slowly, until it finally disappeared. Suddenly I could feel strength seeping back into my frail body, and I started to sit up and look around the room. Whatever it was that was happening to me that morning, I was uplifted and inspired to battle on. Okay, I know you are thinking I was hallucinating. God knows.

Eventually I got strong enough for my parents to move me down stairs, to continue on my road to recovery. But it was to be a long struggle, and it would be a further 18 months before I climbed out of bed and stood up, unaided, on very shaky legs, to make a full recovery and finally make my way to school for the first time in two and half years.

My parents had got Harry and Pud, two family friends, to come in and put up a partition wall in the lounge. One end had a peat stove, so the idea was to make a small and snug bedroom for me. Apart from going to the toilet, this room would be my solitary confinement for one and a half years.

My tutor, companion and source of entertainment during this time was a Telefunken valve radio. I would have it tuned into the BBC World Service all my waking hours, my mother tells me. Often I would drop off to sleep and she would come up to my bedside and switch it off. The signal was frequently poor, but at a young age, your ears are sharp and finely tuned. Listening would start in the mornings, in the 13-metre band, by the evening, I would have moved up to the 49-metre band. The reception was always much better at night. The news, sports round up, current affairs, drama, comedy, music and adventure programmes were favourites. It was a wonderful source of comfort to me whilst in bed all that time.

I was in my own classroom, getting one-to-one tuition on history, finance (such as worldwide currencies), geography (I got to know the names of the capital cities and places of the world). I knew who the political leaders were, and their political parties, the world dictators, wars, who was fighting whom. The only problem with this private teaching system was, I was not required to read and write, just listen. Which meant that by the time I returned to school, I knew plenty about people and places, sport and industry but I could only talk about it. I could not write an essay, I was not able to spell at all, and my reading was poor.

It was during this period of convalescence that I started to take an interest in music, listening to the latest hit songs of the 1950s. Buddy Holly's 'Oh Boy' became my first favourite record. When I had the puff, I would sing away in bed at the top of my voice. Unfortunately I did not follow my brother's footsteps and learn to read and write music, Alec had a private teacher, Jim Peck-Betts; there was little to no music taught at school. Several years later I grabbed a microphone and leapt out on stage as the lead vocalist for several bands

If I was not listening to the BBC, I would have the radio tuned into the local radio telephone system (the RT). This was quite entertaining. Many people listened in to it to get the local gossip. I would pretend to be the man in the Stanley radio shack (Sid Summers). My parents had got hold of an old and inoperable microphone, which I would sit up in bed with, holding it to my mouth like a football commentator. I would go, 'Fox Bay, Fox Bay, this is Stanley calling Fox Bay. Can you hear me? Over.' Then I would read out imaginary telegrams, copying the way Sid would relay them to the farm manager.

Managers would take messages and pass them on to the intended recipient – even one's messages were not private. In fact, most of the Falklands would listen in as dear old Sid read them out. Interestingly, if there was a personal message for the manager, then Sid would be instructed to relay them via another, more private frequency.

The most popular listening period, by far, was the doctor's session each morning at 9.00 a.m. Everybody's aches and pains, and illnesses of a more serious and personal nature, would be relayed by the farm manager, or his deputy, over the radio telephone to the doctor, who would be sitting in the radio shack beside Sid, listening intently. Then the doctor would reply with a series of questions, to be sure he could analyse the individual's problem, as best he could anyway. He would then issue instructions to the manager, by issuing a series of codes which related to pills and other medicines contained in a medicine chest which the manager held in his office, within his house. Sometimes an individual would have broken a limb. Then, the doctor would describe how to make the suffering victim as comfortable as possible until the local floatplane could be diverted, or made ready in Stanley, to fly out and collect the person concerned, and fetch them to hospital in Stanley. This could take many hours. I know this from personal experience, which I will detail later.

Whilst in bed at home, I would get regular visits from the minister of the United Free Church, locally called 'the tabernacle'. Dr Forrest Mcwan became, and deservedly so, a legendary figure in the tiny Islands community. The perfect example of Christianity, he was a quiet and upstanding figure who devoted his entire life, not just to the teachings of the Bible, but to caring for all members of the population. He also provided entertainment by showing black and white silent movies in the church hall, and organised outings for children and families – communal picnics at a local beach were very popular. It is said that Dr Mcwan leapt into the freezing cold water of Stanley harbour (you remember, the one those nice gentlemen would tip the effluent into) each morning to freshen up, before he took his breakfast.

One day, he was visiting me at the Victory, and the conversation got around to the subject of birthdays. For some reason, I told him it would be my birthday the next day. After he left, I forgot about my little white lie, therefore I got quite a surprise the following afternoon.

When he entered my bedroom, and loudly announced, 'Happy Birthday, Terence'. I was a little shocked, and mother was hugely embarrassed. My birthday was actually months away. As I was regaining my composure, mum rushed off to make a pot of tea and, no doubt, to collect her thoughts. As she scurried away, Dr Mcwan pulled up a chair and sat beside my bed, then he passed me a birthday card.

Mother soon returned with a tray of tea, and joined us as we all tucked into the most wonderful chocolate cake you could imagine, and a little rendition of Happy Birthday was sung to me.

After half an hour or so, Dr Mcwan got up, patted me on the head, wished me luck and went on his away. My mum told me, as she was letting him out of the house, she was being deeply apologetic to him for my prank and his fool's errand. He calmly replied to my mother, 'Don't worry, Mrs Betts, we knew it was not the boy's birthday, but Nelly was happy to do it for him.' That was so typical of the man and his good lady wife.

Eventually the day came when it was time for me to get out of bed and take my first steps about the house. Because of the long period off my legs, I was initially unstable, but, driven on by the determination and a growing desire to get out and about to join other kids who were leading a normal life, it was not long before I was able to walk about the house unaided.

I was both excited, and nervous on the first morning I was getting dressed to go off to school, I was excited, because at last I was going to be like all other kids and go out into the fresh air and mingle in the playground. But I was nervous because I knew so few of the children at the school; I had not been in their company for so long, nor did I know the teachers.

Getting to school that day was just like starting all over again, which in reality it was. The major problem now was, I was 11 years old, not 5, and way behind my age group in all the lessons. But I was always that fighter, and rarely short of confidence, so I found methods to deal with my shortcomings and obvious disadvantages. I soon fitted in with the class, and it wasn't long before I became a bit of a ringleader. I don't know why, but I was never content with just being part of a team, I always wanted to lead it.

I still had the odd attack of asthma, up until I went to sea when I was 15, but never a bout serious enough to confine me to bed again for any long period of time – even if I did have to flash up the old Hickman's asthma powder and take in a few deep breaths to my lungs before going off to school. Fortunately, I had a natural love for sport, which meant that I was taking regular exercise, just the thing to speed up my rehabilitation.

When I joined the Life Boys and later the Boys' Brigade, I got very excited about dressing up in the uniforms and going off to the drill sessions, in the aptly named drill hall. I remember the bloody awful woollen socks and jersey of the Life Boys uniform, which made my legs and neck itch something terrible. We also had physical training nights, which consisted of exercises on the wooden horse, and the mini football league, naturally, was a favourite.

The Life Boys and the Boys' Brigade always formed part of the national parades, held to commemorate the Battle of the Falklands (8 December) and the 11 November Remembrance Day. These were very serious occasions for everyone and practically nerve-racking for a young boy. Shoes had to be shining, the hat properly placed on one's head, and the rest of the uniform immaculate.

All those hours of drill practice were now going to be put to the test, in front of the watching general public, who would be observing proceedings with a very keen eye, whilst lined around the main streets of Stanley. You always hoped you would be the boy the Governor would stop to talk to, when inspecting the parade.

If the weather was inclement, it could be most uncomfortable standing in file in a pair of short pants, vest and woolly jumper. Once the parade was over, we would all group together at the drill hall and tuck in to liquorice allsorts and Madge Biggs's milkshakes. The thought of a glass or two of this wonderful concoction, which was thick, sweet and purple in colour – a mixture of blackcurrant syrup and Nestlé's Ideal Milk, encouraged many boys out on parade who would normally have stayed at home with the excuse of a cold or whatever.

Once I had settled in to school, I became a central figure in a group of friends, Roy, Derek, Les, Clem, Brian, Robin, Owen, the Ross brothers and others. My younger brother, Popeye, was always hanging around as well.

In our age, boys had to be creative and imaginative, parents could not afford to hand out pocket money willy-nilly, so if you wished to go to the cinema on a Sunday evening, or have money for a church bazaar, you needed to earn it.

There were a few options available: filling someone's peat buckets (the 'peat boy' could earn £2 a month), be an errand boy, cut and bag grass, or build yourself a cart. The latter was my preferred choice, because I found it an enjoyable activity. You made contact with the community as you earned your money to buy chocolates and fizzy drinks.

But let me explain the technicalities of building the cart. Firstly, you got yourself a wooden box 24" x 18" x 18" deep, then you made a pair of wooden handles – we called them shafts – which you nailed on either side of the box. A steel rod was fixed to a substantial piece of timber on the base of the box, and wheels, usually from a baby's pram, placed at each end of the steel rod completed the splendid vehicle. You were now set-up to do your rounds and earn yourself some money.

There was one unwritten rule; you never went on another boy's territory, no tapping someone else's established clients, each had his established households where he would collect from.

There were three rates of pay for empty bottles, half an old penny, a penny, and two old pennies for the lucrative Patricia beer bottles – this was an imported beer from Uruguay. I remember one day, father had forgotten to lock the outside shed, which contained a huge pile of these much sought-after bottles. It was all too tempting for me, and I loaded my cart up in a flash, then nipped round the corner to the Globe Store, delivered my prize cargo and pocketed the money, which was at least three times the normal Saturday earnings.

Flushed with my success, I put my cart away and went off to find my mates, who were all extremely jealous of me, as I continuously bragged about it.

Saturday was also English football day. Well, at least during the season, my mates and I would meet at someone's home, usually mine, and listen to the radio commentary, if transmitting conditions permitted. If we couldn't pick up a signal, we would impatiently wait for *Sports Review*, which would come on later in the day, to get all the Saturday results. In those days of course, it was a full football programme on Saturdays, no Sunday matches.

Kick-off time for us was midday, so it was very important to get the bottle run finished before then, and any messages mother wanted done.

In the Falklands summers, we would spend most of the day outside playing. Children in the Islands have always been able to play freely, safe from the worries and concerns parents might have in so-called civilised communities. No murders, muggings, rapes or any of those sorts of nastiness.

We would often play up on the common. The British soldiers had built gun emplacements there during World War II; all that remained now were the concrete wall structures. We converted a section of the building into a small hut, constructed from some light timbers and a few sheets of corrugated iron, with peat turf placed over the iron for the roof. Before covering the iron with turf, we cut a hole to let the pipe through from the stove, which was made from an oil drum picked up from the common.

Once the fire had been set up, it was time to turn our attention to some home comforts such as seats – empty wooden Johnnie Walker whisky boxes, or such like. It was very convenient living in a pub, because it was easy to get your hands on furniture material for the hut.

After its completion, six young boys could use the hut comfortably, any more, and it would be a bit crowded. We would sit around the warm and glowing peat fire whilst excitingly chatting away about the day's events, sipping away at a steaming hot cup of tea from a thermos flask, if you were fortunate enough to own one. If not, then it was a tin, brewed on the stove. If we were really adventurous, we would heat up baked beans and fry eggs and sausages, providing we could get our parents to let us have some. Failing that, we would try and nick them. It was all wonderful harmless and healthy fun, because we were exercising our minds and bodies at the same time.

There were only two things that could spoil our fun on these days out. One was the rain, because if it rained too hard, then water would start running down the unsealed roof, causing the hot chimney pipe and stove to let off clouds of steam, and after a while, it would eventually put the fire out. This, combined with the water which would now be running freely under the door, would soon drive us out and home, or to make a mad dash to my grandmother's place, which was very conveniently situated only a couple of hundred yards away. There was also the likelihood of my grandmother serving up some goodies in sympathy for a few half-drowned kids.

The other thing that would sometimes curtail our amusement was the older boys, the group of my elder brother Alec's age, because if they felt like doing the same thing, at the same place, at the same time, they would march up and boot us out.

We might put up a mild protest whilst explaining that we had put the hut together and all that stuff, but they did not care about that, and if we didn't get the hell out of it fast, they would chase us away, or sometimes give us a beating if we got too rebellious – usually my problem. Then it would be running home to grandmother's in tears, to tell her of the terrible deeds the older boys had done to us, which usually got the response of 'Don't worry about it, son', as she would pat each of us on the head and give out sweets to console us. But you should not feel any pity for us, because a couple of years later as the older lot went off to work, we replaced them as the bullies, and it was us who were kicking my young brother and his crowd out of the place, and it would be them running off to grandmother's.

I have mentioned before that *Children's Corner* was a must-listen-to music, request and story programme for us kids on Saturday nights. It came on about 5.30 p.m. and started off with birthday requests. The exciting part about having a birthday request played for you was having your name mentioned on the radio, then being told where to find your birthday present.

The record itself rarely got listened to, because as soon as the announcer mentioned the whereabouts of your present, you were off running through the house to find it, then unwrap it and look whatever it was over, usually in great excitement. By the time all this was done, the record would have finished.

I must tell you about one remarkable statistic regarding *Children's Corner*, which is that Jim Reeves singing 'Bimbo', was played every week for over 40 years. Now the other thing about *Children's Corner* was story time. This was always in the middle of the programme; I remember one series called *Journey into Space*, a story about outer space, rockets and all that stuff. At the end of each episode, and after *Children's Corner* had finished, Robin Luxton would come down from his house in John Street to the Victory Bar. He and I would go out and climb the small tree in the front of the house, and play out our imaginary space journey. It was one of those rare occasions when I was happy for someone else to be the leader. Robin was more aware about the subject of space, so he was always the leading astronaut as we, in our mind's eye, transformed the tree into our rocket.

Whilst in our very serious roles of astronauts, we eagerly waited to be counted down from 10 to zero, then blasted off by our pretend ground control. Then we would frantically fiddle around with various parts of the tree's branches, which were the imaginary rocket's controls, as we whizzed off on our fantasy journey to space and back again.

On a clear night in the Falklands, the sky could be full of stars, which gave us the perfect backdrop to our space scene. An hour later, we would safely return to both earth and reality, because Robin would have to dash home for his bath, food and bed. Yes, growing up without television was so wonderful for the creative mind.

Although I was now part of a normal school life, and very much involved with a group of schoolmates, life at home was starting to take a turn for the worse. Dad was starting to drink too much and he would have fights with mum, which was pretty upsetting. As he became more and more violent, he often turned towards me; for some unknown reason, he started to dislike me, and often needed no excuse to give me a beating. Perhaps it was because I would always try to defend my mother when he was drunk and saying or doing something nasty to her. Perhaps it was just because I was the eldest child at home (Alec had left for work at Douglas Station in 1961). Whatever it was, it was a very unpleasant time. Anyway, by 1962 my mother and father had separated.

In the beginning it was a bit of a relief for me, I had got tired and at times very frightened of dad's actions, and it was ever so nice not to have the arguments and fighting going on in the house. For mother it would begin another period of turmoil in her life. It meant we were a bit like gypsies as we moved around the town from one place to another, carrying the barest essentials with us.

Finally, mum managed to secure the job of running the pub, which meant we could all go back to the Victory and resettle in the house. I was very happy about that, because I was now back to base and pretty much allowed to do my own thing. But I did have to take on a lot of responsibilities. I had to help mum out as best I could. I would fill all the peat buckets, do the shopping, wash up the dishes and make sure that my younger brother Peter and sister Vivien were okay. I was only 12 at the time, and in the beginning it was very hard for me, but I adjusted and coped.

It had not been all bad when dad was home. He was a champion darts player, and as soon as I was able to throw darts into a board, he would let me go into the bar for half an hour after lunch to practise with him. It was he who taught me to always think about working out a finish on double 16. The logic was simple: if you missed and hit a single sixteen, you then had double 8 to finish, if you missed that, and got a single 8, you then required double 4 and so on, all the way down to double 1.

Eventually, one day, I began to beat him more often than not, then lessons stopped, but he was one of the great players in the Falklands in his time. His teams always seemed to win the league, or the knockout cup, often both in the same season. Darts was the most popular and organised sport in Stanley during the long Falklands winter nights.

By the time dad left home in 1962 he had a large collection of trophies, gained from playing with the Stanley Arms and the Victory Bar. In 1961, he was the individual league champion, I often showed off his cups to my schoolmates. I should also say, at 11 years old, darts was tremendous for one's mental arithmetic.

I often drove my dad up the wall with my non-stop football. I would be kicking the ball around the lounge, using the lower part of the piano as a goal, be doing some fancy dribbling whilst also commentating on Spurs beating their opposition 3–1. Then the climax; as I kicked the ball against the piano, shouting G—O—A—L and turning away with my hands aloft like all elated strikers, dad would appear. Flushed in the face, having stormed from the bar, he would begin shouting at me.

'Stop the bloody noise' usually waving a fist, and saying, 'how many times have I told you not to play football in the house? I have told you time and time again, but you never bloody listen.' I would drop my head, pick up my ball, sheepishly say, 'Sorry, Dad,' and go off into the garden to continue my football romances there. In these fantasy games, Spurs always seemed to win after going a goal down.

Dad's frustration and annoyance with my football was not limited to the house. A group of my mates would come around and start a game of goal to goal. There was no problem whilst the ball was in play, but once someone took a shot at the goal, which was one end of the house, it would make a bang as it crashed against the building.

However, every now and then, we would get a telling off or punishment for something we did not actually commit. 'Sod's Law' I suppose. Uncle Bertie worked at the Globe Store, which was just below us at the Victory. He was a great sportsman and loved football, so he would often pop into the garden when we were playing and join in the kick-about, until he whacked the ball against a window, on occasions breaking it. He would run off the scene as fast as possible to work and I would get collared and punished for the damage.

By the time I was 13, I was still hopelessly behind my classmates in English and spelling, but I was overtaking most in subjects like mathematics, history and geography. My old tutor, the BBC, had done a good job in these areas. But I knew that I had no hope of catching up in English. I remember adopting the attitude of why should I care anyway, because school would all be over in a year's time. At 14, it was the end of a child's legal educational term in the Falklands, unless you were one of two fortunate enough to win a scholarship to the United Kingdom. But the odds of that were so extremely long, because your chance only came once in your school lifetime, I believe at the age of 12.

The general attitude was one of, 'not to worry, a Falkland Islander only needs a very basic education anyway'. He or she was not going to run their own business, be a political leader, or have any say or influence in the day-to-day affairs of a colony and its inhabitants. Therefore, we only needed to be fit and obedient, to carry out work on a sheep farm, or to be a stevedore/labourer, office worker for the FIC or FIG.

A Falkland Islander had reached a pinnacle if they qualified as a carpenter, electrician or plumber in Stanley; and foreman or head shepherd was the summit for an Island worker living in the camp.

However, despite these moments of apathy, even at the age of 13, in the middle of this social narrow-mindedness, I always believed I was destined for something different – even though I had no idea at all what that might be. Like all children, I had my dreams, such as being the next Jimmy Greaves, but that was what it was, just a dream.

Also, by the time I was 13, my out of school activities were starting to get me into trouble. I think I always begged attention, and if I could not get it in a conventional way I would improvise. This would lead me to organising a small group of boys who would go out and do naughty things, just to test adults' wit and minds against ours – naughty and annoying things, rather than criminal and nasty.

But our luck eventually ran out. Dear old Sergeant Williams, of the local constabulary, came and collected me from my house one Saturday afternoon, and took me and three others off to the police station, where we received a serious lecture from the chief of police. He then decided we should serve punishment for our mischievous and devious deeds, by cleaning out the station henhouse and cutting the grass around the police station in some of our free time.

It all seemed a little over the top, I thought. After all, we had only been helping ourselves to people's milk, collecting eggs from the odd henhouse, pulling up vegetables out of people's gardens and taking the stuff home to consume. Sure, we did not have their permission, but I thought that was a minor detail, and yes, okay, there was, I suppose, the odd home with a broken windowpane as a result of a misdirected stone which had been intended for a nearby street lamp, but had missed its target and flown on until it came to rest against a window.

The trouble was, by the time Sergeant Williams had got to my house, he had already collected the rest of our compact gang, who, in the process, had all needlessly admitted to the felonies. Because of this development, I had been given little scope for creative alibis and even less for denial. I quickly realised the game was up, when I saw one of my mates standing beside the police officer, with tears rolling down his cheeks and sobbing. 'Sorry, Terry, I had to tell him.' Don't worry, I said, with a slight sigh, it's not your fault. As a leader I was always prepared to take the blame. After all, that was what leadership was all about, wasn't it? Stand up and be counted, and all that jazz.

I will move on to a couple more of my childhood memories. Everything in the Falklands was about making do with what you had, spending money was never an option or a solution, even our bicycles were second-hand, or built by ourselves. Okay, we would get a new football for a birthday or Christmas, maybe a new *Beano* or *Dandy* hardback. But the football was one of those plastic things that stung like hell on your bare leg when it and you were wet and cold. Many times, I was left with the imprint of the ball markings on my leg after someone, usually Les Biggs, had smashed the thing against me, as I blocked one of his powerful shots.

There was always a galvanised nail sticking out from some fence or wall that would pierce the ball upon contact, which would mean that it would rapidly lose pressure and lie like a balloon devoid of air. Because of necessity, Les and I became past masters in the repair of these things. One boy would squeeze the ball with all his might to expose the point of penetration, whilst the other welded the plastic over the hole with a glowing red-hot poker. This would leave the kitchen full of the smell of burning plastic and black smoke, as we ran off to find the nearest bicycle pump, to pump the ball up again. One could make a ball last for along time using this method of repair, the option of no football until someone had a birthday, or waiting for next Christmas, was inconceivable. After all, football was a huge part of our lives.

As I was saying, our bicycles were never new. Often we would build them ourselves, usually by going down to the refuse tip to the east of Stanley. I recall there was one of the local dairies down that way them days, operated by the Goodwin family. Anyway, we would spend all day rummaging through the broken glass, ashes and rusted iron objects, frightening wild cats and rats in the process of trying to find enough bits and pieces to put on a frame to make up a bike.

Interestingly, despite our means, other lads must have been more fortunate, because we could often source spindles and brake cables from the tip, but other parts, such as gear cogs, would be much harder to find this way. At times we would have to go out and beg, steal or borrow these items; if we were really unlucky, then we would need to spend some of our bottle money on buying a new part, which in turn, could mean missing a Sunday night cinema once in a while.

We would spend hours in a shed building our bikes. Sometimes it took us weeks. We would always give the frame and mudguards a new coat of paint, which, like the spare parts themselves, had to be found by one means or another. Once completed, it would be a really proud moment as you took your self-built machine out onto the streets to show off to other boys.

I do remember one boy who rode his bicycle around the town like a king. He was a bit older than me, and always seemed a bit on the cocky side, just a bit too sure of himself, always teasing me about the second hand rubbish that I was riding.

One afternoon, just after lunch, the moment of opportunity presented itself to me. I was walking across Philomel Hill from the Victory Bar to my aunt Sibby's to collect Owen May for a game of football.

I do not know why, but for some reason I was carrying a long pole. Anyway, this boy, who was also a bit of bully, was coming along Fitzroy Road at full speed. Then, as he was opposite me, with the full width of the road between us, I simply could not resist the temptation, so I swung around and in one movement poked the end of my pole in the front wheel of the boy's bike between the spokes and the front forks.

As all three objects locked together, bringing his front wheel to a grinding and immediate halt, the back part of his bike reared up like a bucking horse. Then it jack-knifed, and he began to depart from the saddle and free his grip involuntarily from the handlebars, all in one wonderful graceful movement. As he started to begin his journey of flight, I dropped my end of the pole, and took off hot foot to my auntie's. I never once stopped to look behind me, to see how my unsuspecting victim returned to earth, but once inside the safety of my auntie's house, I started to laugh uncontrollably. Fortunately, that boy did not get too badly hurt, and rather interestingly, he and I became good friends after that little incident and he never teased me again about the type of bikes I rode.

Another wondrous source of entertainment was sleighing in the winter days and nights, Once again the majority of the sledges would be home-made. One or two people might have a flex, a local name given to a very flexible model, but mine was always built in the back shed, made up with bits of timber and some steel rods for the runners, which I had acquired from somewhere. However, it was always among the fastest.

Philomel Hill was the town's favourite slope for this activity, very fortunately for me, because it was right outside our front gate. The peak hours of sleighing nights would involve a good cross-section of the community, it was one of those rare times and events where the class barrier disappeared into the snow around you.

There was no admission fee, no front seats, no special or reserved runs. People mingled, chatted and laughed as they enjoyed the winter sport being played out on a piece of public highway, which by now was unofficially out of bounds for any foolhardy motorist who dared to try and cross one of the three road junctions during the sleighing sessions.

I have no idea of speeds reached on this slope, but I can tell you I could go down from the top of Philomel Hill to the end of the public jetty in 14 seconds. Mickey Clarke, on his flex, would do it in 12 seconds.

You actually spent most of your time pulling your sledge back up the hill. Once at the summit, you would push off again, laying yourself flat out on your stomach, using only the toes of your footwear as steerage. Sometimes we would build small snow mounds, to give a little lift-off, but usually people just preferred a straight and fast run.

As the snow became more compact, speeds would build up, and a hard rope would be laid over the wooden decking of the jetty to act as a pull-up area, to prevent people and equipment going straight over the end into a very cold sea.

I never saw anyone going over the jetty, although many boasted they actually had. It made a good story. I do, however, know someone who did go over the seawall once, whilst going down Hebe Street. One day I went over to the next hill eastwards from Philomel, to look at some of the novices. My cousin Denise Hansen was there, so I invited her to come down the hill on my back. As I have said, my sledge was fast. Before I knew it, we were flashing past everyone as I approached the road at the bottom of the hill. I called out to Denise to jump off, She did, but in the second or so that followed, I whizzed across the small grass verge and over the seawall.

The next thing I remember was lying flat out on the stony beach. My sledge had hit the sewerage pipe, upon impact, it went one way, and I the other. As I came to rest on the rocky surface, I knocked the wind out of myself and hit my chin on a rusty old piece of fire grating, splitting it open in the process.

Abby Alazia quickly come to my rescue, as I lay pole-axed from my fall from grace. Fortunately, the tide was low, so I had not got a very cold bath. I was hurt more from having the wind knocked out of me than the injury I had to my chin. But as Abby was pulling me up to my feet, I could feel a warm liquid running down my neck It was, of course, blood.

Abby was the publican of the Globe Hotel, just a few hundred yards away, once there, the caring Alazia family were satisfied that I needed further medical attention, so I was off to hospital to be patched up.

I mentioned sleighing was a community activity, equally so were the church bazaars which were run by the three mainstream religious sects. the United Free Church, at their headquarters at the Tabernacle, the Roman Catholics, at St Mary's and the Anglicans, of Christ Church Cathedral. Each had a variation on the theme, which was to raise money from the general public to support administration and other specific costs.

A bazaar was a good opportunity to meet your friends over the two nights, as you strolled around the hall, going from stall to stall, playing games and seeking out that special bargain with the few coins you had in your pocket. You might even seek out a potential girlfriend. It was one of those rare occasions when parents would let you stay up until the end of proceedings, which was always pretty close to midnight – although the church organisers would make sure that such jollification never spilt over into the Sabbath.

The Church had a powerful influence over many aspects of life, which included entertainment, as I was growing up. Events such as dancing and sports would not continue after midnight on a Saturday, and football was played on a Sunday afternoon to avoid clashing with mass or church services.

By the time I reached my teens, life at home was starting to get a bit disorganised. I think mum was wilting under the pressure of running a pub and not having a husband around to support the family, especially financially. During this period a young women living with us became very ill and eventually died in the bedroom opposite to mine. I never saw her body. I was ill in bed, and I remember mother coming up the stairs calling out, 'Dorothy, I've got a nice hot cup of tea for you,' then she went into Dorothy's bedroom. Next I heard mum say, 'Oh my God,' then I saw her galloping down the stairs.

Shortly afterwards, a group of people arrived, which I noticed included a doctor and a priest. Even at my young age, I was aware what had happened. But I did not make any attempt to be inquisitive, like children can be in these situations. Instead, I remember lying in my bed, wondering if she was feeling any more pain as she was floating off to heaven. I always seemed to have a bit of a different kind of mind. Sometimes, I would even scare myself with my sense of imagination.

After a year or so, mum decided she could not carry on with running the pub any more. It was time for us to move on once again. I was terribly upset about having to leave, although I expect the neighbourhood was probably quite relieved. After leaving the Victory, until I went to work, it was to be a period of considerable uncertainty and instability as we skipped around the houses of Stanley, like gypsies once again, a month here, two months somewhere else.

Money had obviously become an even more acute problem, as

meals were fewer and smaller, clothes would be hand-downs, my shoes often had holes in them. We were poor, and trouble and pain just seemed to follow us around.

Mum would take in the odd lodger for a bit of extra cash, and I remember going to a house in Fitzroy Road east, which we called Kirk's House. It was large, compared to what we were familiar with. But bugger me if another lodger didn't go and die on us. I only ever knew of him as Otto Rip, he was a Scandinavian sail maker who, I guess, died of old age. He took his last breath on the kitchen settee.

Mum got herself a job as a shop assistant in the FIC West Store once, and I would go in and watch her serving customers. No such thing as self-service in 1963 in the Falklands. Mum would stand opposite the client with duplicate invoice book lying in front of her on the store counter, pen poised, ready to write down each article into the book as the customer called out the item. The drill was something like this: the client would ask for one tin of syrup, mum would then write down '1- tin of syrup @ 2/6d', and go and fetch the product. This would be the procedure, item after item, until the customer had completed their shopping list. Then mother had to do a numbers check of items with the customer, and a little piece of mental arithmetic as she would tally up each item's price to reach a gross total. No calculators or cash tills for the shop assistant to use. There could be hiccups to this method, however, if mum wrote down an item and then discovered it was not in stock. Then it was a matter of crossing out the item penned in and starting over again. After completing the exercise, the goods were put into shopping bags and the customer would be handed the top copy of the invoice. They were then required to go to a central cashier, where they would pay for the goods.

I was very proud of my mum, because I knew she could not spell, but she developed a technique to overcome that minor problem, and I thought she was the best shop assistant in town.

My last year at school was my best in terms of learning and progress. I had developed a desire to learn, term results and class positions started to rise, I was studiedly progressing and by the time I left, I had managed to hoist myself into the top five of the class of about 20 children. Not a bad effort, on reflection, for one who had missed so much classroom time.

It was one of the happiest times for me as a child, although I had maintained my mischievous and original mind all the way through my short school life. It rewarded me with a lot of amusement and enabled me to establish many lifelong friendships, some educational development, and of course, a whole series of canings for being too outrageous with some of my pranks.

I also experienced one of my first successes in life, on the football field, winning a school trophy which had not been played for in years. At 13, I had also managed to play in the final of the adults six-a-side tournament.

But now it was the last day at school. I remember being very sad about leaving; perhaps it was because I was about to walk out into the unknown, or maybe it was because I thought I would be leaving friends behind. Perhaps it was none of these things, but because I had started to build up trust and believe in some of my schoolteachers.

I had a special liking for two, Jim and Mike. Jim was an Islander, an old hand who was even older than the school itself. He had a certain kind of wit and an unorthodox way of teaching, more like a buddy than a teacher.

Mike was just different altogether than any other teacher I had come across, he was upfront, straight to the point, no pissing around type of teacher. I liked that sort of approach. If you performed, he would get behind you and support you in your times of need, whatever that might be. But if you didn't toe the line with him, you could be the target of a flying blackboard rubber, or threatened with a beating from a blackboard ruler. He was aware of my educational shortcomings, but never showed any signs of contempt. He worked on it with me, whereas I felt other teachers were far less understanding. That said, I did try their bloody patience.

During the whole of my last day at school I had been clock-watching, and for some strange reason I did not want this final school period to end. But the final teaching session slipped by all too fast, and right on the stroke of 4 p.m., as usual, the school bell rang. It was ringing for the final time for me. It was Friday afternoon 9 October 1964, one week after my 14th birthday.

As all the other children got up and ran out of the class as fast as possible to go off and enjoy the weekend, I got up from my desk rather slowly. I felt empty, lost, I was close to tears. It was all over. What was wrong with me? All the other kids couldn't wait for this moment in their lives, they were so excited about their last day at school, going off to work to make money.

I remember slowly putting together and picking up my few possessions, then I began walking out of the classroom, looking around at the girls' and boys' various works of art hanging on the wall. When I got to the outside door, I paused and stood at the top of the steps, staring into the empty playground which had been a place of so much activity, filled with fun and a fair amount of sporting success. I somewhat melancholically walked down the steps and slowly ambled my way out of the grounds for the last time.

7

Packed off to Work at 14
(On Lively Island. Where the hell is that? I asked)

If leaving school had been a moment of remorse for me, I would have little time for reflection and sadness about my departure. As soon as I got home, mother, Aunt Middy and my grandmother were all patiently waiting in the kitchen for my arrival, so they could announce one unexpected and hugely shocking piece of news.

As I entered the house I knew something was up because I was greeted by all of them sitting around together with big smiles on their faces. I asked mum, 'What's up?'

'Nothing's up', she said, 'but we have a big surprise for you'.

'Oh what's that?' I asked, thinking it was some school farewell gift, or a party had been organised.

'We've got a job for you', my mum said, as Aunt Middy and grandmother excitedly joined in and said 'yes', the ideal job for you, son'. 'You're going to Lively Island and you leave on Monday's Beaver flight.

'Lively Island, where the hell is that?' I said, rather alarmed by the announcement and prospect.

They all sang out the reply together, 'Oh, it's a lovely little place and you will like it there. Besides, there is nothing here in town for you to do.'

I was totally flabbergasted, but I quickly realised there was little point in arguing, My fate had been decided and I would be on my way to God knows where, first thing Monday morning. Suddenly, I felt leaving school was even worse than I had first thought.

My mum could tell I was not happy with the situation, but she tried to console me by saying, 'It's £19 a month, son, you will be able to save your money there'. I felt sorry for her really, she was struggling to clothe, feed and house us all, so I suppose, in a way, she was doing her best for me. One less mouth to feed and one less person to clothe, would be a welcome lifting of a bit of financial pressure from her very shallow purse. I think my aunt, who I knew liked me a lot, and my grandmother had different thoughts, but they were no less caring. They had decided it would be best to get me well out of harm's way from any potential trouble, due to my readiness for devilish exploits.

So that was it, the die had been well and truly cast. Jesus Christ, I was going to camp and I did not know a soul where I was going to work and live, nor did I have a clue about camp life and working with animals. The sudden realisation quite horrified me.

I had been for one holiday to Douglas Station, and on one other occasion with my father on Pebble Island. Each had been an enjoyable experience, but going to a remote little island such as Lively Island was a bit extreme. I was terrified of dogs and I had limited experience of horse riding – my uncle Stan had put me on the back of one within minutes of arriving at Douglas, and I had a couple more rides during my stay at Douglas Station. He taught me that you should get off the beast the same side as you got on, that was my total horseback riding knowledge.

Actually, I will always remember the occasion when a group of us went across the creek between Douglas and a part of the neighbouring farm, called Teal Inlet, at a place called Hope Cottage. A Chilean family were living there and one of the boys went to school at Douglas. Anyway, the water was too high for the horses to walk across, so they began to swim. It was an incredible sensation sitting on the back of a horse as it was going through its swimming motions underneath your straddled legs.

During my holiday at Pebble Island I gained my only experience of working with sheep. This came about when the main gang went off to a small island called Golding Island. I had been allowed to go along with my father, who was going to do the cooking for the boys as they toiled away shearing the flock.

The journey was made on the farm boat *The Malvinas*. Apparently, this vessel had been purchased in England, and sailed out of Greenhithe, with my uncle Henry as one of the crew. Once we reached the island, we all went ashore and quickly settled into the only house. The building had two large rooms upstairs, which would be used as the sleeping quarters for all the gang. I think there were about a dozen or so men in all, although the house had been empty all year, I was surprised to find it remarkably dry.

The manager of Pebble Island was a man called Adrian Monk. I did not know him, but instantly I liked him. He gave off a sense of authority, but at the same time was warm and open. He enjoyed a game of poker dice or cards, and was not uncomfortable sitting around a table and chatting with his workforce.

The first day of our arrival, Adrian came into the kitchen of the house, as dad was preparing to flash up the fire. He bid dad a greeting and then asked me if I had enjoyed the trip. I told him I had, he then went on to say, 'I think you'll get bored pretty quickly, don't you? Would you like to earn some money for yourself? What about you filling the pens in the shed? Work starts at six in the morning and it's a ten-hour day, I'll pay you a shilling an hour.'

This was 1963. Ten shillings (50 pence) a day! I had never known of money like that in my entire life before.

The next morning I was at the shearing shed bright-eyed and ready to go. However, I was soon to find out that the work was hard, and very heavy going. The sheep on Golding Island were like I had never seen before, they were huge, and like all bloody sheep, extremely stubborn bastards. By the end of each day, I did not need any rocking to sleep, I was always ready for my bed.

Each morning seemed to arrive too quickly, but I never missed a second of my work. But I made up my mind that I did not like sheep, after this experience. I found them incredibly stupid animals, and after pushing and shoving them around for ten hours each day and getting my clothes covered in their grease and oil, I had no desire to have to work with them any more in the future. Now I was heading to Lively Island to do just that. I could not believe my ill fate.

I must admit, I have never been a great lover of any animals, other than the family cat, and they would play up hell with my asthma. So how was I going to cope on Lively Island? After the weekend I was going to find out. I had been thrown into the deep end big time, and make no mistake about that.

I spent most of the weekend with some of my mates, Les, Roy, Owen and Clem. I told them about my imminent future and they reacted with total disbelief, which did nothing at all for my self-confidence and tore my ego to shreds Then I started to reflect on what I was going to miss.

This bloody job at Lively Island would bring about an abrupt end to football sessions, playing in the gun pits and the cinema. The cinema was not just about going to the movie, it was a social occasion. And what about the boy gang warfare with Peter Biggs's lot? I recall we had bombarded them with rotten gull eggs, launched from the safety of the Victory Bar roof the last time they had come around our area looking for a fight. It had been great fun watching them scamper for cover and safety as the stinking eggs broke upon them.

Monday morning 7 a.m., I was having a bite to eat as mother was putting together my bag. Once ready, we walked off to the Government jetty together. That was the point where I would board the Beaver floatplane. As I stepped onto one of the floats and began to climb inside the plane, I heard mother wishing me well. I could not look back at her, I was too heartbroken and I did not want to upset her, and soon enough I was winging my way to the unknown.

Lively Island is situated to the southwest of Stanley, slightly south of east to the entrance of Choiseul Sound, which is the waterway leading to the now very well known settlement of Goose Green.

After 35 minutes or so, the Beaver plane, a De Havilland, Canadian-built DHC-2, which struggled to reach a speed of 120 knots with its single 450 hp engine, touched down at Lively. As the pilot taxied the plane up towards the small jetty, I noticed a man sitting inside a dingy and every now and then dipping the end of an oar in the water to maintain his position. Finally, when the single engine had been shut down, the pilot unbuckled himself, opened his door and jumped down onto the float below, bidding a boisterous good morning to the man in the boat.

The person in the dingy then motioned the boat towards the plane, and once the pilot made fast the small craft's line to a cleat affixed to the plane's float, he walked along the float decking and opened the door of the plane where I was sitting, then announced, 'Lively Island, Master Betts. Would you like to step down this way and climb into the taxi that awaits you.' Then he laughed and said, 'Be careful as you go, Mr McMullen will get you to the shore.' Oh my God, what am I in for, I thought.

Okay, I said to the pilot, rather timidly. As I was getting down and into the boat, a strong firm hand grabbed my skinny and fragile arm, and for the first time I clapped eyes on my new boss. He was a very stockily built man with a deep gruff voice. Once my bag was in the dingy, the pilot released the line and pushed us away.

As boat and plane drifted apart, Mr McMullen started pulling on the oars and the pilot cranked up the plane's engine. My new boss said, 'Ever rowed a boat before, son'?

'No, I haven't,' I nervously replied.

'Well, you'll soon learn, because this will be one of your jobs from time to time.'

'What's that?' I said.

'Coming to meet the plane,' he said. 'I haven't got time to do this every bloody time the plane comes here.'

'How often is that?' I asked.

'Two or three times a month.'

'What! I shrieked.

As we were approaching the jetty, I noticed that there were only a couple of houses and very few people about. I had been a townie kid, and from that very moment, I thought to myself that I was in for a whole new experience.

Once everything was out of the boat, it was made secure and we began to walk up the jetty. 'Now then, I am Dave, just call me Dave,' said my boss. He put out his hand and I shook it.

Then I said, 'Oh, just call me Terry.'

He laughed and said, 'Cheeky little bugger. Well, this will be where you will stay,' as he pointed to a small bungalow on the rise straight up from the jetty, 'We'll drop your stuff off, then I'll show you around the settlement if you like.'

I replied, 'Okay, that's fine.' I had perked up considerably as a result of his friendly attitude.

Upon entering the bungalow, I was happy with what I saw. I had lived in many worse in Stanley, in fact, I had lived in few better. My bedroom had nothing in it other than the bed itself and I would have to wait until the next boat arrived before mother could send any of my stuff out to me.

The worst thing about this period was not having my dear old companion, the radio. What an earth was I going to do without the BBC World Service to listen to in my spare time? As it turned out, I had to wait a month before I was accompanied by my trusty old Telefunken radio once again.

I had learned another hard lesson about life in the camp long before my dear old radio arrived. This unexpected surprise actually hit me on the first night of my arrival, when, at 10 p.m. the electric lights went out and I was left in total darkness. I discovered the next day that the lights only came on for a few hours each day in total.

My conducted tour of the settlement did not take long and my fading memory does not allow me to accurately describe the whole layout of the island or everyone who worked there during my time. I do recall Dave taking me to meet Olga and Charlie Coutts, I learnt Olga would be providing me with my daily meals, and that Charlie's brother, Fred, was also working on the island.

I remember a small stone house, which was operated as the farm store, standing outside the structure. Dave said, 'We open this once a week. It's got most things you need inside.' Actually, I think there were four other houses on the farm, but I do not clearly remember.

After a little while, Dave said, 'Let's go to my place and have a cuppa.' We headed off to the far end of the settlement, to the 'Big House'. Even in this tiniest of communities the big house syndrome existed. Fortunately, I would find out that Dave had no care or desires for such a culture.

After tea he showed me the garage and the farm machinery, something that did not take long. In a shed to the back of the house was an old World War II Willis jeep. As he presented the rather tired-looking vehicle to me, he said, 'She's a bit difficult to start in the mornings, and she's got no brakes, but it beats walking.' Also in the garage was an old Ford tractor. Pointing to it he said, 'that's it, every thing else is done by horse, dog, walking or by hand.'

By the time he had finished showing me around the vital infrastructure, stables, woolshed and suchlike, I was deeply depressed. Not with Dave – he appeared to be a nice man – but with the life I was now going to be forced to live. It was like being sent to some remote prison island for a crime I had not committed, and I knew from that very moment I had to find a way to leave.

As it turned out, my stay at Lively Island would be short, and also split in two parts.

To my surprise, I would have a reasonably enjoyable time on Lively Island. I certainly have some happy memories of my only time working in camp. Working is a word I need to use very loosely, because I soon discovered that living in a remote island did have some very distinct advantages over working on a mainstream farm.

Dave was certainly not a lord-and-master type boss. The worst thing about him was his appalling temper – not a side to get on. Work times were pretty flexible, perhaps even very flexible; when there was something to do, we got on with it.

On many occasions, the most difficult task of the day for Tony McMullen, Tony Jaffray and me was to try and bowl each other out, or be the first to reach 100 runs in a very competitive game of cricket. The batsman had to reach his target against a bowler and a fielder, in the endless series of our three-man version of the sport.

The award for the first man to reach the milestone of 100 runs not out, was a tin of Tate and Lyle golden syrup or a large bottle of Lea and Perrins sauce. I have to say, I was the first one to reach the coveted prize, as I lofted the tennis ball over a paddock fence off the bowling of Tony McMullen, which indicated a six, and I had clocked up my 100 runs. As I jumped for joy, the two Tonys stood with hands on hips, bemoaning the fact that they now had to share the cost of purchasing my winnings.

Because of the relaxed atmosphere, I found myself quickly settling down and getting involved in things on the farm, and I began to learn. I discovered that riding a horse was not that difficult, at least not on the 19-year-old nag I had been given to ride. Fortunately I didn't need to work with dogs, but interestingly enough, it would be a dog that would contribute to bringing my camp life and employment to an abrupt end. I will get back to that.

I never got to liking bloody sheep, but again, this was not a big deal on Lively Island. The flock was not that large and even though sheep work, as on all farms, was a major part of the daily chores, it was not on the same level as the big farms.

Shearing was all done by hand, and there were four shearers, so in my job as a wool boy, I was never really pushed to keep the board clean. Tony McMullen and Charlie Coutts were the top shearers, but I do not recall them ever shearing any more then 170 sheep a day; 200 a day was considered exceptional for any shearer by the hand method.

Spring in the Falklands is a wonderful time of the year, and perhaps even more so in the camp than in Stanley. It is the time when the lambs are born. Many of the birds' chicks appear. Wildlife becomes highly active.

One bird I could never stand, which always put the fear of Christ up me, was locally called 'the sea hen'. I had been frightened of this bird because of an experience whilst on Golding Island. I was taking a walk about a mile from the house when suddenly I looked up and noticed a dark brown bird soaring up in the air. Then it turned and made an approach flight directly at me. Firstly, I stood still and watched it coming closer and closer, until I thought it was going to hit me. At the very last moment I ducked. Like a fighter-bomber aircraft that had just swooped in and dropped its bomb load, it flew away and soared up in the air, and then it circled and repeated the same action. Only this time, it came in lower, and after three or four incoming flights, I was reduced to lying flat out on the ground; then, as it winged away to come in at me again, I got to my feet and ran as fast as I could. Eventually it gave up on me. I got back to the house totally exhausted, and told my father what had happened. He laughed and said I must have been close to its nest or young, it was nothing personal, it was just their way of protecting their patch. These birds had hit many people, some were even knocked out with the force of impact.

It was a terrible experience, and I was going to keep a bloody good look out for sea hens whilst I was on Lively Island.

The worst thing about Lively Island at times was sheer boredom. I would eagerly await a mail drop to receive my football magazines, but often they would come in a bundle of two or three, and be three or four months old by the time I received them.

I had two holiday breaks during my time on the island. The first was Christmas week, which I spent in Stanley. I had a great time there with all my old mates and my family. Christmas time in the Falklands is traditionally horseracing time. There was a two-day race meeting, mixed with athletics and traditional sporting activities, all held at the Stanley racecourse.

It seemed the entire community would venture up to the course, gathering around the racetrack and patronising the food stalls and the very popular bar. I would find it quite amusing watching the drunks stagger out, sometimes even falling out, of the bar door as they misjudged a step and went crashing to the ground. During this particular sports meeting I was amazed and delighted to see one of my schoolmates, Tony Andersen, win the top horse prize, the Governor's Cup, on Mr King's horse Pegasus. The race is the Falklands equivalent of the Epsom Derby.

Having been marooned on Lively Island, I had money in my pocket, and I was able to have a bit of a flutter on the Tote. By the end of the two-day meeting I was actually well up on my wages. I had managed this purely by watching a man a couple times. He would go and stand in front of the blackboard, study the list of riders and runners, then go up to a Tote window and ask for his chosen number. I soon noticed, he was always in the winners' queue. So I thought the best thing I could do was wait until he had selected his horse, listen to the instruction he gave out to the Tote assistant, and then go up and request the same number. I never lost a bet that year, my mates never knew how I did it.

When it was time for me to return to Lively, straight after the New Year celebrations, I was much less apprehensive about going back to the island, on two counts. I was no longer a stranger to the people or the environment, and I knew in two months there would be another week's break. This time it would be the traditional camp sports week, which was going to be held at Goose Green. With this in mind, my farewells to friends and family were much less painful.

Upon my return to the farm, the main occupation, other than cricket, was getting the shearing completed before the summer ended. The boss also let me have a few goes at putting the jeep and the tractor into the garage. You might think that this task was pretty much a routine matter. Well, I agree it should have been, but not on Lively and not with this particular tractor and jeep: neither had brakes. It required a great deal of skill to get the right speed up to ride the small wooden ramp at the entrance of the garage, then let the vehicle freewheel to the end of the building, so that when the front of the vehicle gently nudged the timber 4" by 2" framing of the garage, it would stop and you could switch the engine off.

Any misjudgement of speed could have a pretty devastating effect on the overall shape of the garage, which would then require the additional work of putting the building back to something like its original design, or as near as one could. On one occasion, Dave made a bit of a hash of manoeuvring the tractor into the garage and he only managed to get the vehicle to stop inches from the garden fence, having gone right through the end of the garage, which was now in a pretty sorry state and took several days to put right again. Oh yes, putting those two vehicles away was a very complex task and required extreme and delicate skills.

The week long sports holiday at Goose Green arrived soon enough, I will always remember my first night's sleep there, which was between a couple of mattresses in the lounge area of the new bunkhouse. We had arrived late one night on the small company boat, the *Penelope*. When we moored alongside the jetty, our arrival had not exactly caused much excitement with the folk at the settlement. There was not a soul there to greet us.

I had been warned that the people of Goose Green were not very open and friendly to strangers, so I arrived there rather guarded and a little nervous. I need not have been. One chap did approach me to say that he had been keeping an eye on me and if I approached any of his daughters, I would know all about it. I found out later it was all a joke and he and I became very good friends, we would spend many a successful darts night together when he retired from the farm and came to Stanley to live.

The week turned out to be great fun and I was a little disappointed when it was time to leave. All too soon I was back on Lively Island, which I was now finding too quiet, especially after the jollifications at Goose Green. I was not looking forward to the coming winter. However, my life as shepherd and farm hand came to an unscheduled and abrupt end.

I had just got back to the settlement from a ride out in the camp area known as Spring Point, and was climbing out of the saddle of my old horse, when I noticed one of Charlie's young dogs coming full pelt towards the horse and me. The dog had a bit of a reputation for being a little out of control. I was far less complimentary I thought the bastard thing was quite mad.

I do not have a clue what happened next, but without warning, the horse was bucking and jumping all over the place. I had no hope of staying aboard. I was in midair, then crashed to the ground in an unceremonious heap. I landed on my right side with a mighty thump; the wind had been knocked out of me, I then began to feel a tingling sensation in my left wrist, a similar sort of feeling to when you hit your elbow on the funny bone.

I did not know whether to laugh or cry, but in a very short period of time Charlie Coutts was at my side, asking me if I was okay. He helped me to my feet, but I soon realised I could not use my left wrist and it looked as though it was beginning to swell. Charlie looked at it and said, 'I think we had better get you home, and I'll get Dave to give Stanley a call. If it's broken, you will need to go into town to see the doctor.'

That's how it was in the Falklands those days; communication on a very remote island was by radio telephone, transport to Stanley in case of emergency was by the Beaver floatplane.

In my case, I was fairly lucky, I had only broken my left wrist, which was not considered a big deal, by that I mean not life-threatening, therefore all I had to do was to sit and wait to be picked up. But this was a pretty uncomfortable period as my wrist continued to swell and the pain was growing. From the time I had actually broken my wrist, to when I finally got to hospital in Stanley, to have it confirmed by the doctor that it was indeed fractured, then put in plaster for support and protection, almost six hours had elapsed.

Once I had been attended to, it was then time to walk to my grandmother's house; there were no taxi services, nor a member of the family with a vehicle to transport me home. She was shocked to see me, she had no idea I had been injured, let alone was in Stanley. Obviously she had not been listening to the radio telephone.

The silver lining to this particular cloud was that the doctor had informed me I would have to keep my arm in plaster for six weeks, then providing everything seemed okay, I would only need a light bandage on it for a couple more weeks. However, I would not be ready to go back to Lively Island for about two months. It was difficult to refrain from breaking out into a broad grin as I said to the doctor, 'Flipping nuisance that, doctor.'

I spent much of the two months with my mates; in particular, Clem Harrison and Les Biggs. Les and I were football crazy, we would spend hour upon hour and day after day on the football field, in all sorts of weather. It wasn't long before I would forget I had my lower left arm in plaster, as I flung myself to my left and made a spectacular midair save from one of Les's thunderbolts. I would flop to the ground clutching the ball to my chest, then pick myself up, and do a quick check for any damage to my arm. Once satisfied everything was in order, we would play on.

All my other mates liked football, but Clem always needed to devote a little time for girlfriends. Girls were species that I had not thought much about at this stage of my life; in fact, I had given them no time at all. Reading, talking, playing and thinking about football was just about all I did do, other than a bit of singing.

Two months on, it was time to go back to Lively Island. The system employed to inform someone if they could expect to be flying the next day was by the reading of a flight schedule over the local radio station in the early evening. It would go something like this: 'First Beaver from Stanley to Darwin, Lively Island, North Arm, Fox Bay East and Pebble Island, passengers are: Messrs Hardcastle, Middleton, Betts, Morrison, Porter, Evans, Watson and Ford.' From this, I knew I was on the flight, and so did the rest of the Falklands.

However, the next morning there could be a long period of waiting as the flights office collected weather data from around the islands. It was not unusual to have to wait until the middle of the day before it was confirmed that the aircraft would indeed fly, and even if it did, it was possible that due to the time delay, or a narrow favourable weather window pattern, or the short period of daylight hours left in the day, the original schedule would be revamped, and as a consequence, your destination could have been deleted all together.

At the time I was due to go back to Lively Island, the Falklands was in the grip of a typical weather pattern in the middle of winter: wind in the east and dense fog. We have a saying in the Falklands, 'Wind in the east, three days at least'.

Well, I had been preparing myself each day for the last three mornings to set off back to camp, and each day the weather prevented any flying. Each day my prayers had been answered. Then at about 11 a.m. on the fourth morning the fog suddenly lifted, and it was time to go, but I decided I wouldn't. I was in the kitchen of my mother's house and I announced to her I did not want to go.

She did not persuade me otherwise and made a hurried call to FIGAS and told them I would not be taking the plane that day. I never returned to Lively Island and that was the end of my sheep-farming experience, which in total barely extended beyond six months. As a result, my life would take a completely different direction.

I would say that although Lively Island and its lifestyle were not my cup of tea, the people, with one exception, were very good to me there, especially Dave McMullen. I was greatly saddened when I heard sometime later of the way in which he ended his own life. He had been one of the first men in my life that I respected. I had acquired more than a touch of admiration for him because he gave me a little bit of responsibility and demonstrated elements of trust in me. No man had done that before.

8

I Join RRS Shackleton
(Whaling, volcanic eruptions, fire, sinking, you name it)

My decision not to go back to Lively Island meant it was time to look for new employers. The opportunities in our one-horse town were very limited, even more so because I had just snubbed one of the two major employers, the Falkland Islands Company, by not returning to Lively Island.

So it seemed to me the only option was the Falkland Islands Government, who, as it happened, were seeking persons interested in taking up a five-year apprenticeship as a carpenter. I thought this was something I should go for; here was an opportunity to hit the heights of all expectations for a local boy who didn't want to be just another camp employee.

The civil service did offer work, but promotion in it was structured in such away that it only ever offered dead man's shoes possibilities. I am not entirely convinced that much has changed today. Anyway, with my educational background and perceived capabilities, I could forget about a career in that department, which would have only offered the post of messenger boy as the first step in a pretty closed shop environment.

No, this apprenticeship thing was it, I thought, a chance to gain a trade, a skill that would perhaps open a few doors of opportunity, once I had qualified. I knew of several Falkland Islanders who were able to emigrate and get good jobs because they had a skill. This was one of those narrow channels of opportunity not normally available to an Islander, so without further ado I tendered an application.

However, my destiny was not to be a carpenter. Before the Government could respond to all the applications they had received, which I am sure would have been quite a lot, the British Antarctic Survey office, based in Stanley, advertised that they required a galley boy to join one of their Antarctic re-supply and scientific research vessels, the RRS *Shackleton*. Bloody hell, it was just like waiting for a bus to come, there's nothing for ages then two come at the same time.

Uncertain when I could expect to find out anything from the Government, and as the odds of me being accepted could not be high, I decided to apply for the job with BAS also. I had nothing to lose, especially as I would know within a very short period of time if I had secured the job with them or not, without affecting my interest in the apprenticeship.

After a week or so, the vessel arrived into Stanley harbour following her 33-day journey from the United Kingdom, which included a two or three day stopover at Montevideo, the Uruguayan capital. She moored at her usual spot alongside the public jetty. Mother was in the kitchen of the house and I was upstairs in my bedroom when she called me to say that I had to make my way to the ship for an interview. 'Interview? What the hell is that?'

They want to speak to you, stupid,' she snapped back.

'Oh, okay, I'll waddle down later.'

'Bloody get going now, don't keep them waiting or you might miss out.'

It was one of those rare moments when I actually listened to what a parent had said. Without further hesitation I made my way to the ship.

I walked up the gangway, then along the deck and up a couple of flights of steps towards the boat deck, where I was greeted by two very upright gentlemen looking immaculate in their officers' uniforms. They were the Captain and the Chief Steward. One asked, 'How old are you?'

I replied very nervously and accurately, 'Fifteen years and one month, sir.'

The Chief Steward responded immediately, frowning as he did so. 'You are very young. We were looking for someone a little older than that.' Then he asked, 'Why do you want to join the ship?'

I hesitated for a moment because I was not sure how to reply. Then I said something which I was sure blew my chances completely: 'I'm looking for some security and stability,' and then preceded to dribble on about how troublesome life was at home.

When I finished my explanation, there was total silence and the two men just stood and stared at me. Upon reflection, I suppose they were a little surprised by my openness, but I was certain I had not given them the type of answer they were expecting or wanting to hear. The silence was only lifted when the Chief Steward said, 'The Captain and I will have a chat and we will let you know. By the way, do you have any travel documents?'

Looking somewhat puzzled at him, I replied, 'No.'

'Well then, you will need something if you intend to join this ship. Passport, seaman's card, something like that. If I were you, I would go and get something sorted out, and fast. That's all for now, and as I have told you, we will be in touch.'

I thanked them for their time and I left the ship as fast as I could.

Once I was inside the house, I started crying and proceeded to tell my mother how awful I had been at my first job interview in life and equally, how sure I was that I would not get the job.

A day passed. Just as I had given up all hope, mother received another telephone call. They wanted to see me on the ship again. I trudged off again, totally convinced that I was only going to be told that I was unsuccessful.

When I got to the boat deck once again, I was met this time by the Chief Steward only, who once again asked me how old I was. I repeated I was 15 years and 1 month.

'Yes, well, that is bloody young for this ship, but we think you have the right attitude for us, so you can start tomorrow morning at six o'clock sharp.'

I could not believe it, I wanted to dance a jig right there and then, but the Chief Steward made me focus in on things when, he said, 'Now go and get your seaman's book from the Customs department. Without it, no job, do you understand?'

The reason I did not have a passport was because I was not expecting to be going anywhere; there was no prospect of leaving the Islands so why would I be travelling? My situation epitomised the level of expectation for many Islanders. There was one thing which was a bonus about life in the Falklands those days: bureaucratic things such as the issuing of passports or seaman's books could be dealt with the same day.

The deal with the British Antarctic Survey was this: after the Antarctic season had been completed, you would sail back with the ship and stay in the United Kingdom, usually from early May to early October. The *John Biscoe*, the other British Antarctic vessel operating in the area, left and arrived back a little earlier.

Whilst in the UK, the Falkland Islander crew were paid off, but remained on a rather acceptable retainer of half salary. Many would take up part-time employment during the UK summer. Butlin's holiday camps were a big favourite for many of them. But, before I could think about fulfilling a lifetime dream of going to the UK, I had another experience immediately ahead of me. I had to endure several months at sea in the wild and windy South Atlantic Ocean. I was even going to be going so far south that I would travel inside the Antarctic Circle.

There was no gentle introduction to the deep sea for me on my maiden voyage. We were actually at sea for ten straight weeks. I would be fortunate in one aspect, however. I did not have to deal with one common problem for many first-timers and others, the dreaded seasickness. But it was to be a little while before I actually got my sea legs. It takes some time to get used to the ship pitching and rolling, before being able to walk about without knocking into things, I suppose it was a week before I got the hang of it.

The work itself was definitely not for the tired and lazy. I had to be out of my bunk by 5.45 a.m. every morning, every day of the week, to prepare myself for work at 6 a.m., scrubbing passageways. The only tools required for my trade were very basic: a scrubbing brush, bar of soap, a tube of Vim, floor cloth, a bucket and very hot water. Once I had finished the floors and cleaned out the shower units, I was required to go to the galley and wash the pots and pans and anything else that had been utilised in the preparation and serving of breakfast and lunch. This would keep me occupied until approximately 1.30 p.m. each day. I could then relax until 5 p.m., unless it was my turn to serve afternoon tea to the officers, which was every third day at precisely 3 p.m. Preparing and serving tea and biscuits could be a very tricky exercise at sea, especially when conditions were rough. The final work session was from 5 to 7.30 p.m., once again scrubbing pots and pans and cleaning dishes, peeling vegetables and so on.

There are all sorts of tricks you need to be aware of, even when carrying out the most mundane task at sea. Never put too much water in your scrubbing bucket or the galley sinks. If you did, as soon as the ship rolled or pitched, it would displace the water everywhere but where you had intended it to be. You would then spend the next 15 minutes or so cleaning up the bloody mess.

Pots and pans can never be stacked to one side of a drainer as you clean them, like you do at home. You soon learn this lesson very quickly, once you have stuck the shits up yourself, and everyone else in the galley, as they all go crashing to the floor, creating a terrifying noise. Once the chief cook has recovered, he then comes up to you waving his finger and telling you, 'Do that again and I'll break your fucking neck.'

I guess I was pretty much like all the boys who had gone off to sea before me and at my age, in that I developed a process of rapid learning, gained from immediate mistakes and threats. There was always someone around willing to take advantage of your inexperience, or to threaten to give you a beating, or order and push you around.

Even though I was on my guard for some of these dubious characters, I was not prepared for other situations which I was about to encounter for the first time, which seriously shocked my innocent mind about the sometimes dark and dangerous roads of sexual predators and their methods of advancement towards the unsuspecting prey.

My family had not taught me anything about this subject, it was never something discussed at home – we children all came from the vegetable garden, according to my parents. Nor was it a subject in the classrooms. It was a taboo topic altogether; therefore, I knew nothing about sex other than masturbation.

I may as well get this story out of the way, then it is done with. One day when I was working away in the galley, the chief cook kept winking at me each time I looked his way. I thought he was satisfied with my work, or in a good mood, and the winking was all a sign of praise or happiness. After a while he came up to me and said. 'Why don't you come to my cabin after work? I'll show you some of my photographs.' As I have said, I was completely innocent and naïve. I somewhat excitedly said okay, and the cook was a very happy bunny for the rest of the day.

After dinner had been served and everything cleaned up and put away, I went off to the cook's cabin with him. I was really looking forward to seeing the photographs of his worldly travels. However, I was only in his cabin for a matter of minutes, before he was displaying his huge erection. I dropped the photo album and began screaming at the top of my voice, 'Let me out, I want out.' Fortunately for me, my screams scared him and he did let me go. Equally fortunately, he never tried anything on me again for the rest of our very long season at sea. But I will always remember my first brush with homosexuality and it was one hell of a rude awakening.

In all, I would spend four consecutive southern hemisphere summer/autumns on the RRS *Shackleton*, covering the period 1965 to 1969. Thirty-five years on, I have only one major disappointment from the whole wonderful experience. I never took a single photograph.

All I have from those long days of journey in to some of the wildest, most rugged, peaceful and beautiful scenic parts on God's earth are the memories, which I find are fading each passing day. But I do remember going ashore for the first time at South Georgia and stepping onto the jetty at King Edward Point, because I nearly fell over as I did so.

I had become so used to walking around a moving object for the last 70 days, that once I stepped onto something that wasn't shifting about, neither my legs nor mind were prepared for it. It was quite a shock to the system. I felt a bit of a fool for a while as I was staggering about the jetty decking. Anyone watching would have naturally assumed I was drunk.

My first landing at South Georgia was in January 1966. The Japanese were still whaling commercially and it was quite an eye opener to see the operation firsthand as it was winding down. I did not see any whales being slaughtered, but I did see one being carved up on a slipway with the long flensing knives. It was not a sight that shocked me, because I had been educated by my father and others, that whaling was just a job, it was a very normal thing to slaughter whales, because it was a way to earn very good money. Therefore I did not take onboard the scale of the brutality, or the dangers to the existence of the whales, or the environmental impact. The majority of the world's population, for that matter, were not yet sensitive to such major issues as the extinction of whales and the damage to the ecosystem and environment.

The sight of the Japanese did startle me. They were operating the whaling station at Grytviken, in Cumberland East Bay, one of six stations that were, or had been, in operation. But I was very surprised to see a dozen or so Japanese running to catch one of our mooring lines as we moored alongside the jetty.

As soon as I was able to get ashore, I felt I was walking into another age, even another world. The stench from the rotten whale carcasses, and the sight of mounds of clean white whalebones, were beyond belief. There were many buildings and pieces of infrastructure for the whaling industry, all of which appeared to be littered with tools and equipment.

Groups of Japanese would stop their conversations and turn and look at me as I appeared at a building entrance. I recall a large factory ship (large compared to the *Shackleton*) moored at one of the jetties. My curiosity was so great, I just had to go and take a look at. It stank more than anyone could imagine, especially in the area around its cargo of whale oil.

There was a diminutive figure guarding the ship's gangway, in a brown uniform. He looked at me very sternly as I walked directly past him and made my way onboard to take a closer look at the vessel. I did not stay long, I could not stay long, the whole atmosphere very nearly made me throw up, and I was more than a little bit concerned about the Japanese gentleman, who had not kept his gaze off me since I went onboard the ship.

Despite my nervousness, I was somewhat fascinated by the sight of the Japanese about the place. You should remember I was only 15 years old, and up until then, I had spent my entire life on the very remote Falkland Islands. We Islanders rarely saw visitors from anywhere, certainly not from Japan, therefore I had never seen a Japanese person in the flesh before.

Naturally, I was a bit apprehensive of them at first, because I had been told many horrible war stories and seen the movies, which had only portrayed a very bad image of them. I remember being really puzzled that they seemed to be running the place pretty much as though it was their own. I thought everything in South Georgia was British, nobody had told me the Japanese were in South Georgia. It came as one hell of a shock and I thought it most odd.

Looking around the place, there was also the most amazing sight of dozens of whale catchers; some were moored up, some floating, others grounded, and some partially submerged, but all abandoned and slowly rusting and decaying year by year. This place, and others, had clearly been a hive of activity over the years, as thousands upon thousands of whales had been slaughtered from 1904 to 1966.

Before leaving South Georgia, I received a telegram from the Falkland Islands Government, informing me that my application for the post of apprentice carpenter had been accepted and they would be grateful if I would advise them of my intentions.

Bloody typical, I thought. Now I had two jobs. But I did not hesitate with my reply. I was enjoying myself, I was having my eyes opened as I was travelling and gaining experience of life first hand. There was also the matter of salary. I was receiving £80 a month with BAS. As an apprentice, my first year wage would be £3 2s 6d a week. Oh, sorry, that is £3 12½p a week. There was no contest. I politely replied to FIG, thank you, but no thank you. It was a decision which resulted in Terence (Nobby) Clarke, one of my old schoolmates becoming a qualified carpenter in 1971, and a bloody good one at that. I have never regretted my decision, and I quickly forgot about it.

Once we left King Edward Point, we went to other whaling stations nearby, Leith, Stromness and Husvik, each in their respectively named harbours. Each in turn was different in size and layout, but they were all designed for an activity that would become a scene of endless blood-letting and butchering of whales.

Different things at each one caught my attention. When I first landed at Husvik and saw the houses, which were all abandoned, I was amazed by their condition. They were bone dry and full of excellent furniture. But over time, they would be seriously looted, as were many of the stations.

I remember the floating dock facility at Stromness, where they carried out ship repairs during the height of the whaling season. But going a shore at Leith Harbour was a little emotional for me, something unique for family reasons. You will recall my father had worked here at the whaling station in the 1937/38 season. Twenty-eight years later I had followed in my father's footsteps. I can assure you not many fathers and sons in this world have been to Leith Harbour.

I know not why, but as Captain Turnbull took the *Shackleton* around what seemed like every bay and harbour for a few days, as if we were on a package tour, every now and then my mind would go back to our stay at King Edward Point.

Apart from the surprise of meeting the Japanese, I had met a few people I actually knew whilst we were there. One of them was Peter Biggs, who had not been over the moon to see me, probably because he remembered the last time we had seen each other, when I had covered him with the contents of several rotten gull eggs outside the Victory Bar.

His mood when seeing me walking past his parents' house at South Georgia was one of extreme displeasure. I quickly assumed he felt like a little bit of old-fashioned revenge on his home patch, as he hastily started to gather up missiles which I was certain he intended to hurl at me. I did not need to be told that it was time for evasive action, and fast.

RRS *Shackleton*'s main tasks were to re-supply the British bases with provisions and equipment, deliver, collect and transport scientists and other personnel and carry out scientific operations in support of collating scientific data. The latter could be a very bloody boring exercise for the crew as we often went up and down the same stretch of water for weeks on end. It would only be livened up by the scientists or some over-enthusiastic bomb disposal expert letting off block after black block of TNT from the ship's stern, shooting seawater tens of feet high, sometimes interspersed with mud from the seabed, and probably killing the odd unsuspecting bird and God knows how many fish in the process.

It was very dangerous work; two crew members of the Royal Naval ship HMS *Protector* had lost their lives when someone mistakenly fired one of these things off whilst still inboard, in the belief that it was outboard, a safe distance off the stern of the ship. Many others of her crew were only saved from injury by a mound of potatoes stacked on the ship's helicopter deck which took the main force of the blast.

The first season on the ship was wonderfully exciting. I must single out the first season because each year after, it all becomes a bit repetitive and then you start to take everything for granted. We humans tend to do that a lot in life.

Fortunately, I settled into my surroundings quickly. I was a pretty adaptable sort of lad and the ship's crew were a good bunch of guys, therefore making friends was easy. I also got to grips with my daily work routines very quickly, thus everything was becoming a bit of an adventure. I would be fascinated by each base and island, because all had their own specific features. I would see the various island groups, South Sandwich, South Shetlands and South Orkney Islands, I would visit bases such as Signy and Deception Island, then as we moved down the Bransfield Strait we would fall upon the Antarctic Peninsula, where we would call at all the British bases, some of which have now changed nationality, others have changed their names; The odd one has done both.

The *Shackleton* operated mainly outside the Antarctic Circle, but on one occasion we went deep inside, to Stonington Island (base E) which was below 68 degrees south. This base was usually supplied by the *John Biscoe*, but she had problems one season and was unable to service the base, so we took over and got the job done as usual. I am especially grateful that I had that opportunity to visit Stonington Island, because 30 years later I would enter the Arctic Circle. It is still a rare achievement for men to enter both polar regions.

The sights that greet you in the Antarctic are truly amazing. Much has now been written about them, so I will tell only of the ones I thought were the most breathtaking and eye-boggling.

One has to be travelling through the Lemaire Channel, which is situated between the Antarctic Peninsula and Booth Island. I have been fortunate enough to travel this wondrous sea passageway on several occasions en route to the British base, oddly enough named Argentine Island, later renamed Faraday and now called Vernadshy and owned by the Ukraine.

Each time I travelled these seas I would be gripped by their stunning beauty. I would also have the luck for the waters to be still, deep and dark, with just the ship's bow wave disturbing the sea surface. The high and spectacular peaks, two of which were referred to by the old hands on the ship as 'Una's Tits', because they proudly pointed to the heavens side by side, presumably much like a women's cleavage, when she is lying on her back, were of a green tarnished colour from their heavy copper content.

Add in the scene of snow, ice, blue skies with heavy white clouds all providing a multitude of colours and movement. It's a scene that will last in one's memory for a very long time, and certain to get you repeatedly pressing the button of your camera shutter.

The Antarctic season of 1965/66 would turn out to be slightly more dramatic than expected for the RRS *Shackleton* and for those of us on board her. We were sailing along, or should I say punching our way in heavy seas, from South Georgia to the South Orkney Islands, to the base at Signy Island (base H), which was normally a two or two and a half day trip for the *Shackleton*, at her best cruising speed of 10/11 knots.

We had hit really rough weather; the sea conditions were appalling at times, at least force 10. One day the seas were so bad, it was too dangerous for the cooks to prepare anything to eat as it was simply impossible to keep pots and pans battened down on top of the cooker, so it was sandwiches for the day.

Anyway the two-day voyage had turned into three, then four, and finally five. I remember going out on deck one day, at considerable risk, to sling the trash from the galley overboard, much to the delight of the seabirds who always seemed to be flying about the ship no matter how far out to sea we were. I was only out on deck a very short time, but it did appear to me that the ship was down at the bow. It was impossible to be certain, given the sea conditions.

I thought no more about it until one morning, after the weather and seas had abated, when the boatswain came into the crew's mess room and announced, 'I don't want anyone to panic, but we're sinking.' There was some nervous laughter, then he repeated his words, and it soon became evident that he was not joking.

Apparently he had gone to sound the ship's tanks, and was somewhat amazed when he dipped the forward ones, to find the watermark at the top of his measuring chain. Soon it was obvious that the number one forward hold, between lower and between decks was full of water. Fortunately, the *Shackleton* had been built with watertight bulkheads, and once the hatches were battened down, each hold became a separate compartment; therefore, the water was contained in a single hold of the ship.

The problem was, no one had a clue why the vessel had taken in so much water. There were other serious unanswered questions. Had we been holed? If so, what was the extent of the damage? The only thing for sure, it was time to get into action, and everyone then had his station and role to play. Pumps were set in motion, but it soon became clear that they were not reducing the water level in the hold.

Once the Captain had satisfied himself that the ship was not going to sink, he ordered that we change course for Deception Island, which was in the South Shetland Group and had a nice soft black volcanic ash beach, upon which he intended to run the ship's bow, so the water could be pumped out and the damage assessed. Then makeshift repairs would be carried out, if possible.

We reached our destination in two days, then as we squeezed our way through the narrow entrance, we turned into Whalers Bay, before pushing the bow of the ship carefully onto the soft beach bed. Safety now seemed assured.

My descriptions of these events have been very simplistic, but everyone was greatly relieved. I am sure, for Captain David (Frosty) Turnbull and his officers, it had been a much more complicated matter to get the ship to safety. Our arrival would permit them a great deal more comfort, and a little more sleep, than had been possible over the past week. I should say, once we had changed course for Deception Island, the journey passed without further incident.

But life on board was far from normal as you could imagine. We all went to our bunks at night with lifejackets hanging at the ready. We three boys, who were sharing the one cabin, went to our beds fully dressed and ready to go as soon as the alarm bells might ring.

Once the ship was safely and firmly aground, the hatches were opened. I remember looking down, with many others, from the upper deck at the scene below. The hold was still full of water, with some of the ship's cargo floating about on top, like a duck in the bath. The scene was one of total devastation. Everything inside the ship's hold had been smashed to pulp, nothing had been saved, stores, provisions, clothing and scientific equipment had been completely destroyed.

Large seismic buoys the size of a 45-gallon drum had been crushed to the size of a can of cooking oil. So extensive was the damage that *Shackleton*'s seismic programme was lost for the rest of the season.

The pumps were again started and this time they reduced the water level rapidly. When the debris was removed, the reason for the chaos become apparent. Somehow we had sheared a rivet from the ship's starboard bow, which made a hole about the size of the drain in a kitchen sink. The pressure of water from the sea against it must have produced a pretty impressive waterspout, and consequently filled the ship's hold very quickly.

I do not recall any state of panic during our moments of potential danger on the high seas, in the middle of nowhere, with part of the ship full of water. But I do recall a mood of relief and relaxation once the ship was in Deception Island.

With the problem now identified and the clean-up completed, a cement patch was placed over the offending hole. Then we could all start to stand easy and enjoy some of the rewards for successfully manoeuvring our way out of a rather tricky situation.

Our cabin was full of bounty. Damaged bars of Cadbury's chocolate and other confectionery adorned the place, until we had finally managed to consume it all, with considerable help from other crew members.

The other bonus which lifted spirits dramatically, was the news that we were going to the Chilean port of Punta Arenas, in the Straits of Magellan, to carry out proper repairs. The main attraction at Punta Arenas was not the windswept city itself, but the bustling nightlife, which lightened many of the crew's hearts and pockets as they fell in, and out of, renowned places of entertainment. This would be just another experience that I was going to gain, my mind was to be opened just a little bit further, as I travelled a new road on the journey of life. But let me deal with those stories another time.

I have mentioned the wonders of the Lemaire Channel; well, let me tell you, Deception Island is no less remarkable. It is another one of my favourite places, because of its spooky atmosphere, with all its mystical features and its dangerous and most violent temper. You had to treat Deception Island with the greatest of respect, or it would boot you severely up the ass.

The experience of going through the island's only entrance, and exit, is an event in itself. Once seen, never to be forgotten. The name given to this narrow passageway, about 220 metres wide, with its unseen jagged rocks not more than 2.5 metres below the sea's surface, ready to punch a hole in any ship's bum that dares to touch them, is Neptune's Bellows.

Actually, it is a gap in the top of a surface ring of a sunken volcano wall. Once inside, you are greeted with a mass of black volcanic ash making up the shoreline. The hills rise skywards, towards the clouds, covered in snow.

I was to see my first whale in Whalers Bay at Deception Island. Once you have fixed your gaze on the shore, you will wonder if you are hallucinating, because you will see a wall of steaming water coming from the sea at the shore's edge. This is due to the warming of the waters by subterranean volcanic vents. Many people who go to Deception cannot leave until they have paddled about in the lovely warm water. Although in total contrast, it often reminds me of the Blue Lagoon in Iceland.

During my times on the *Shackleton*, (the *Shack*, as everyone called her), Deception Island decided it would flex its muscles on a couple of occasions. Once we just happened to be in the area at the right time to witness the volcano get in one of its foul moods. I told you it had a terrible temper. As we lay about a mile off shore, it spewed out enormous clouds of steam and black ash, high, very high, into the air. Some of the fine grains of ash fell upon the decks of the *Shackleton*. Much, much more, however, was descending upon the neighbouring Chilean base, which had forced the personnel to evacuate hurriedly, some barefoot, to the British base before they were completely engulfed. At the same time, the volcano was shaking the ground so violently that all the bases in the area had buildings, and other structures like huge oil tanks, vibrating and moving, some even collapsing.

At some point, we were instructed that our role of spectator should switch to one of rescuer; we should go in and lift the personnel off the British base to safety at once. It was not a pleasant prospect, but when you've got to go, you've got to go. The command was crystal clear and the task very simple. Get in, pick everyone up, and get out as fast as possible.

It is at moments like this that you become acutely aware that Deception Island has only one way to get in and one way to get out, and if the moody volcano decided to close the door whilst we were in, we would have to concede that we were fucked. Happily, we got everyone off without any major problems.

We did get one little surprise as we carried out the operation. From past experiences of taking cargo ashore in the ship's motor-boat, we would run the bows of the small boat on the tapered soft volcanic ash beach. Then carry items ashore in waders. Following the eruption, we could put the boat alongside the beach face without touching the bottom of the beach. The whole structure had changed, just as if something had sucked the bottom out of the bay. I often wonder if that is exactly what had happened.

I found lifting the people off to safety very exhilarating and rewarding. It had also been an extremely wise decision, because going back sometime later, it was noticeable that a chunk of ice had broken away from the rise behind the base hut and had come tumbling down and gone straight through the middle of the building, leaving a gaping hole in the structure. There had also been several mudslides and surface movements.

Deception Island can be a little nerve-racking, but it is not to be missed. One other odd thing that took place during one of my visits to this island during the 1965/66 season. I was in the base hut lounge with my cabin mates, Bill Giles and Bryn Hopper listening to the Beatles album 'A Hard Day's Night', and we decided it would be appropriate to sign the visitors' book. Bryn had just finished writing in his autograph and was leafing back through the pages, when he suddenly found that his brother had signed the book two or three years previously, to the very day. What an odd coincidence, don't you think?

Naturally, I have many memories of the Antarctic, aside from the sheer beauty of the place, one of which is when I had just gone to the wheel at 6 a.m. The *Shackleton* did not have automatic pilot. Deckhands would manually steer the ship in typical four-hour watches, of two men, who would take the helm alternately hour about. I had just taken the wheel from my cabin mate, who disappeared in a flash. This was normal routine, because the officer of the watch did not permit anyone on the bridge who was surplus to requirement.

Once I had familiarised myself with the ship's heading, I immediately noticed we were approaching an iceberg on our starboard bow. Suddenly it started to rock 'n roll. At first, the motion was slow, but it picked up speed. Then it began to turn over, throwing out water and spray as it flipped, it created quite a wave in what had been a calm sea. It rocked to and fro for a little while, before finally settling down and showing off its new features, displaying an ugly black mud mark, in complete contrast to its former pristine white and blue colours before capsizing. It was quite a show thoroughly enjoyed by the officer of the watch and myself.

I will tell you about another moment of extreme excitement and danger for us all on the ship. We were sailing along quite happily, somewhere in the Antarctic. It was mid-afternoon, and I was at the wheel, when suddenly, the alarm bells started ringing. They had been set off by one of the officer engineers, who had smelt smoke whilst relaxing on his bunk. He went off to investigate, and discovered that a fire had started in the engineer's workshop, which was at the end of the passageway to his cabin.

Let me tell you right now, one of the worst incidents that can happen on a ship at any time is fire, when at sea. Everyone on board is in grave danger; I cannot overstate that fact.

In a flash, the intercom system was highly active as messages and orders were being sent to and from the Captain, who had hurried to the bridge immediately the clattering of the bells had begun.

Captain 'Frosty' was a portly and often grumpy man, ice-cool and in control of any situation. But not this time. If I had not known better, I would suggest he was white with fear, but one thing was for sure, he was visibly shaking. I was relieved from the wheel and I went off to my fire station, which was the starboard aft fire hydrant. What a stroke of luck, more or less, above the seat of the fire. As I grabbed the end of a fire hose and started making my way down below, I thought, oh well, if she blows, I'd be in heaven before the rest of them.

The fire was starting to take hold, fire extinguishers in the immediate area had been exhausted, or were now inaccessible. Word was spreading that the fire had been started when a spark from a grinding wheel ignited a rag, and other bits and pieces of material as one of the lads had been working with some metal object on a stone. He had gone off oblivious to what he had started.

The major concern right now was two bottles of acetylene gas that were starting to hiss and pop with the ever-growing heat. If they were to explode, or take off like unguided missiles, there was no telling the damage they could cause. Then, as I suppose is often the case in a situation like this, someone reacted a little faster than the rest, without hesitation, in a way that was quite exceptional. (After everything is over, we often refer to such people as heroes.) Well, our hero was the second navigating officer, Peter, who dropped all fire-fighting appliances and ran into the workshop, and wrestled the two cylinders out. But before he could, he had to unclip them from the bulkhead. As each one was pulled out, they were passed along a human chain, until up on the top deck, they cooled off and became safe again.

Once the potential vessel-damaging, life-threatening objects had been taken out of the fray, the fire was quickly under control. The only damage was blackened deck and bulkheads and flooding to the cabins of engineer officers as a result of a severely flooded passageway. By the look on some of the fire-fighters' faces, it did appear that one or two of them might have needed to change their underwear. It had been a close call. The lesson should have been learnt, always to keep a clean and tidy work area. After a week of scrubbing, cleaning and drying, everything was pretty much back to normal, all thanks to the quick-thinking of one man.

Christmas time on board ship was a great occasion. Everybody mucked in, and for one of the Christmas Day meals, the officers and junior staff reversed roles. We wore their officers' uniform jackets, and they would be decked out in the stewards' attire, with cloth draped over a forearm and paper hats strapped to their head as they served our meal, which was accompanied by a very palatable red wine and rounded off with a brandy or whatever might tickle the fancy. It was all light-hearted stuff, and for the duration of that one meal, everyone was on first name terms.

I remember that we spent one Christmas anchored at a place called Potters Cove. The *Shack* was not the only vessel in the area, we were accompanied by the Royal Naval vessel HMS *Endurance* and our friendly rivals the RRS *John Biscoe*, whose captains had decided to join us.

Not surprisingly, pranks were being conjured up by the crews of all the ships to carry out on one another. We had decided that we would sneak upon the HMS *Endurance* and embarrass Her Majesty's ship's company by painting the number ½ along side her bold A171.

I have to admit, we were much more successful then the Argentines would be 24 years later, simply because we actually achieved our objective. We were all very amused as we watched some of the sailors busily painting out the huge white ½ with red paint in the early morning of Boxing Day. For a few hours at least, HMS *Endurance* was unofficially registered and marked on her port side, as A171½. Our fun was to be short-lived, however.

As we were all busting our sides with laughter, the officer of the watch appeared and enquired who had been the night watchman. All fingers pointed in my direction, 'Some bloody watchman you,' he said very disgruntled, 'Have you seen what they've done?' Not giving anyone a chance to react, he went on, 'The bastards have boarded us during the night and painted a fucking big black footprint on the funnel.'

I went as red as the hull of HMS *Endurance* with embarrassment, and now it was my turn to break out paint roller and paint, and restore the ship's funnel to its original design. I had to endure stick from the crew for a week or more.

Sometimes we would go and collect food for the husky dogs that were still very much a part of base life in the Antarctic those days. I vividly remember some of the ship's crew climbing over the rail with rifles in hand, dropping down on an ice flow which the vessel had sidled up to, and shooting some crab-eater seals, who in fact do not eat crabs at all, they feed on the abundant krill. The crab-eaters did not think much of our hunting expeditions, but the dogs were very grateful and enjoyed the fresh supply of food.

I can still see the eager faces of base personnel as we arrived at the bases in a new spring, after they had spent a winter in the remotest places on earth. We arrived like Father Christmas, with mail and gifts from family and friends, fresh supplies of food and other materials. Some just enjoyed seeing new faces to hold different conversations. Several of these hardy devils would actually stay back-to-back winters. Now that is achievement.

I often think too of the wonderful social nights spent in Shackleton House games room at South Georgia, with snacks provided by the caring hosts, Ada and Andy Smith. There were also the highly competitive football matches played out between the ship and the lads in King Edward Point – mostly enthusiastic Chileans – on what had to be the world's worst football pitch. Well, at least one half of it, because it comprised small stones that would penetrate the leg like a shot, if you fell to the surface.

Other memories of my Antarctic experience still remain: the amazing and abundant scenery of the Antarctic, and the variety of wildlife, all claiming their piece of Antarctica, as they would swim, fly, walk and feed whilst living in one of the world's least polluted environments. The camaraderie and friendship of the people who worked and lived in Antarctica will stay with me for as long as my memory permits me in my lifetime. Travelling the Antarctic when I did, and as I did, was a bit like travelling to the moon today: few of us were doing it, and many of those who were would be pioneers.

I recall lying out in the sun one day, thinking how lucky I was to be travelling to the United Kingdom. Going 'home' was every young Islander's dream, no, it was every Islander's dream. My mother still calls England home, and she did not realise her wish until she reached the age of 70.

I arrived off the south coast of England, for the first time in my life, just before the FA Cup Final between Everton and Sheffield Wednesday in May 1966. Southampton and the English Channel at the time, were both covered in a thick blanket of fog and mist. I had been given the thankless task of standing at the ship's bell, ringing it at regular intervals, to warn other shipping of our presence. Finally we made our way to a berth and officials cleared the ship, then the vessel was swarming with family and other well-wishing members of the public.

Travelling to the Antarctic in the 1960's was still a journey into the unknown, in the eyes of the great British public, so the ship's return after seven months away was quite an event, particularly for families who would not have seen a father, son, brother, husband or boyfriend for anything between seven months and two years.

I stayed with my cabin mate, Bill Giles' parents in the first instance. His father, also called Bill, was a Southampton taxi driver. There was quite a homecoming party for Bill on the night we arrived, and with seven sisters present, there was plenty of female company about.

I had a wonderful time in England during the summers of 1966 and 1968, but especially in '66, football World Cup Year. England were the hosts, and eventual champions. I watched as many games as I possibly could on television in the lounge of the sea boys' home, Toc H, where I was now staying, for 17s 6d a day, (87½p) with three meals and a room included.

On the day Geoff Hurst scored three and Martin Peters one goal, to make England champions of the world, the whole of Southampton, like the rest of England, became a place of parties and serious drinking. Publicans were in such party mood, that they were offering the first drink, free on the house. My friends and I soon rumbled this, so we went on a pub-crawl of the area, taking our free drink, then moving on to the next pub. We got stoned without spending a penny. I was only 15 at the time, but no one cared.

I also did something else which you could never do today. I went to a football match between Manchester City and Southampton. It was the last game of the season, and as it happened, ended in a nil-nil draw, so both sets of fans were happy because their team was promoted. Anyway, I was invited by a Southampton fan to grab one end of his huge banner, and join him to run around the perimeter of the Main Road football pitch, waving the thing at the fans as we circled the ground. I jumped over the rail and duly obliged. The stadium was full, and as we waved the sign at City fans, they would boo, hiss and shake a distant fist. It was exhilarating stuff, and when I got back to my seat I was jumping with excitement. It was a special moment because, as I have said, you could never do that today. You would be arrested and slung out of the ground for life.

The United Kingdom in 1966, was really alive and kicking, the pipe-smoking Harold Wilson was the Labour Party leader of the country, the Beatles were top of the musical world, it was the age of the Mods and Rockers. I was shocked by the daily newspapers' coverage of the violence on the Brighton beach, as members of the two groups had clashed and fought battles.

It was a wondrous merry-go-round, a mystical tour, as I saw for the first time in my life live sporting events and their hyped-up personalities. Lester Piggott at Newbury, the great footballers Best, Charlton, Law, Greaves, Mackay, Moore, Peters and Hurst. My first live pop concert had the Equals top of the bill, performing their number one hit 'Baby Come Back' in the Royal Pier in Southampton.

I would also see and experience other things for the first time which people took for granted in their everyday lives in the UK: television (black and white then), big red double decker buses, trains, stations and miles of railway track, motorways, coaches, zebra crossings, traffic lights, taxis, street lamps lit all night, daily newspapers, tramps, pimps, lesbians and homosexuals (I have not forgotten the *Shack* cook).

I recall there was a pub in Southampton called the Horse and Groom, with three bars, which were unofficially segregated: one for the lesbians, one for the homosexuals and the other for the assumed straights, which, as it happens, was the one I frequented.

I suppose you could say the old Horse and Groom was years ahead of its time. Someone who was working for the *Southampton Evening Echo* told the newspaper editor about my lack of knowledge and experience, and they duly ran a story on me. (I wish I could find a copy.)

Whilst in England on this first occasion, I broadened my sexual knowledge considerably by living with a lady twice my age. She taught me many things about a physical relationship. As a matter of fact, I do remember her name, and I am very grateful to her.

Also during my first visit to good old Blighty, I experienced running out of money and having nowhere to live, so I had to sleep rough, admittedly only for one night. I remember the Beatles being number one with 'Paperback Writer' at the time, so as I crawled under a piece of old carpet, underneath some trees in a park in Southampton, I forgot my problems by singing myself to sleep to the words of the song. Ah yes, such memories.

My final voyage on the *Shackleton*, in March 1969, was yet another wonderful adventure, as it took me through the Straits of Magellan. This is the waterway between the tip of South America and Tierra del Fuego, which has an enormous tidal current that could reduce the *Shackleton* to 2 knots pushing against it, and have her running at 16 or 17 knots with it.

After stopping over in Punta Arenas for a couple more of those nights of wild entertainment in the dimly lit 884, we set sail and continued our journey, this time going out of the straits on the Pacific side, weaving an endless course of compass heading changes through the Cockburn Channel heading back for the

Falklands via the notorious Cape Horn. My one experience of 'rounding the Horn' was one of near calm seas, as we passed between Tierra Del Fuego and the islands of Lennox and Nuevo, and finally between Tierra Del Fuego and Staten Island, before ending the trip by mooring at the public jetty in Stanley harbour.

My adventures with **RRS** *Shackleton* were over. The ship had been sold to new owners, and was now going back to the United Kingdom. Therefore, it was time for me to pay-off where I had signed on. I could not sail to the UK and sign off because I did not have the right of abode in England. Never mind, my love affair with this ship still lives on.

9

Sports Champion at 18
(I didn't want to be champion. I expected to be champion)

In May 1969 I could only think about what I might be doing back in England, if I had been allowed to travel back on the *Shackleton*. I admit, for a while, I missed the whole lifestyle very acutely. However, I had money, I had been paid off with £250 – not a fortune, but if you consider that an hourly paid worker in Stanley was earning something like £115 per year, then I was not exactly living in poverty – and I was in no hurry to find a job. Much to my mother's husband's frustration, I think.

I did not get on too well with Eric in the early years of their marriage. He was the caretaker of the town's cemetery, and I was living with them in the cemetery cottage. Later on in life, I got to understand him much better, and we got on okay. Sadly, actually tragically, he died too young, just 58 years old. Although he and my mother had separated and divorced, I think they still loved each other to the day of his death.

The winter of 1969 was my first winter in five years. It was very harsh, with lots of snow and freezing cold temperatures. Which was just another reason why I did not rush out for a job. Who in their right minds, if they did not have to, would volunteer to expose themselves for a pittance to those antisocial elements? So I stayed in the warmth of the cottage kitchen, practising my darts, listening to the Beatles top the charts, and man land on the moon. The only time I ventured out was to play my darts matches with the Victory Bar team. I wanted to emulate my father's achievements, and win the Kendall Cup (the team league title) and the Knock-out Cup (the major team knock-out tournament). But most of all, I wanted to win the Governors Cup (the major singles title). Dad had only made the semi-finals of this tournament back in 1961.

As it happened, I completed two thirds of my darts ambitions in that very first season. We had a good league team, and I am convinced we would have won the league title that year, had we not lost one of the league's most talented players, Stanley McAskill. Stan was an outstanding player, but he fell ill and was hospitalised. Our stand-in, Eric, was a good player, when he could see the board, but Johnnie Walker often blurred his vision and also had a strange effect on his legs when he attempted to stand up.

Dear old Eric was also banned from one of the pubs, which was a further handicap to us, because that's where some of the league matches were played. So from the moment we lost Stan, we were playing at a great disadvantage, and we had to eventually settle for third place, behind the Ship Hotel and the eventual champions, the Rose Hotel.

I would only lose twice in all the league games, but on each occasion, I got hammered. League matches were three games of 301, double to start and double to finish. The two guys who beat me so comprehensively were William (Jumbo) Whitney, who was the best player in the Falklands, at that time, and for a few years after. The other fellow was Tony Pettersson. He was a team member of the league champions and was a very good player indeed. Each of these chaps didn't give me a sniff of a chance in our one-off league encounters: 3–0 to both of them. But I would get even with each of them. I was only 18, and I was the youngest player in the league. You had to be 18 to join a team, because of the Falklands licensing laws, which did not permit anyone under that age in the pubs, which was where most of the competition was played out.

The biggest indoor sporting event in the Falklands and arguably the biggest sporting event in the Falklands calendar, right up there with the football shield matches against **HMS** *Endurance*, from 1955 to 1967 with **HMS** *Protector*, the rifle competition, known as the local Bisley and the Governors Cup horseracing events in Stanley and camp, is the Darts Governors Cup. As a darts player, to win the Governors Cup is the pinnacle of achievement in the sport. Your name goes down in Falklands sporting history. Equally so, if you win or participate in winning any of the aforementioned sporting competitions.

To win the Darts Governors Cup tournament in July 1969, which was to be played out over two evenings, in the Drill Hall, of the local defence force, I would need to win seven rounds of individual combat. The rules were slightly different to the league: the first player to win two games out of three of 301 double in double out would triumph and progress into the next round. In addition to the 150 players, several hundred of the local community would turn out, thus making the event one of those very special social occasions as they chatted away to friends, had a tot or two of their favourite tipple, and placed a wager off the record. There are no bookies in the Falklands, and betting was illegal – not that anyone cared too much. We had a magistrate and seven policemen to administer and uphold the law. They themselves were probably all in the hall having a bet anyway.

The first night is a bit of a drag for a player; there is too much waiting around – with only four dartboards being played on you would be lucky to get two matches. I won my first match very easily, and then I had to play my namesake and cousin, Ron Betts.

It was very late in the night but I was fired up; so were the crowd of several hundred people. I do not know what triggered off my behaviour, perhaps it was the large crowd that had gathered behind the chairs which separated the spectators from the players, maybe it had been Clemmy, who had now taken a coach and mentor role. God knows. But by the time I reached the mat, I was jumping with the adrenaline flowing through my body.

I knew nothing of Ron's darts-playing capabilities, but I did know he was one of the Islands' most disciplined and accomplished sportsmen in a whole variety of sports. Perhaps it was this knowledge and my mental state at the time, or the buzz of the crowd, heaven knows, but I started playing the showman, acting out my antics to the crowd, who I soon whipped up into a total frenzy. Some were jumping about with their arms in the air, others were screaming, 'Come, on, Terry,' and the remainder were in a state of rage yelling, 'Get the bastard, Ron.'

I started calling the numbers I was going to get, and each time I hit them. I had won the first game finishing on double four. But before getting the double I required, I turned to Ron and waved the dart in front of him, and said, in a voice loud enough for the crowd to hear, 'Shall I finish it? Shall I finish it?'

Ron tapped me gently on the shoulder and said softly, 'Get on with it.'

I turned and fired the dart right into the heart of double four. I threw my hands aloft, and swaggered up to the dartboard to retrieve my darts. When I turned around I was stunned to see the behaviour of the crowd, they were going berserk.

When I was down to double one in the second game, first dart straight in, contest over 2–0, the din from the crowd was deafening. Just to complete the night's entertainment I said to Ron, 'Shall I show you it was no fluke?' and promptly put another dart alongside the first one that had clinched the victory. There was another huge roar from the spectators. The show for the evening was over, and people started drifting out of the building to head home. Comments ranged from 'I love him' to 'I hate him'. The scene had been set for a spectacular second and final night.

It has to be said that Ron's behaviour during my period of virtuosity had been impeccable. He never once lost control. At times he was even polite, and at the end of the night, he and his wife Pam took me back to their house for a nightcap. Ron had many critics in the community for being a bad sport. This night, I learnt that it was not true.

Before the second night got under way, I had a little practice and a get-together with Clem and Les. Les was not 18, so he could not come into the hall to watch the proceedings. He would spend the whole of the night peering through a window from the outside, or standing at the main door to wait for Clem to get the latest news.

My form, and the crowd's mood, carried on from where we had left off the night before. Each time I won, so the crowd would react one way or the other. I was getting ever closer to my goal. I had reached the quarterfinals, but such was the draw that I had to play William 'Jumbo' Whitney. In the game of darts, he was the king.

Whilst I was sitting with Clem talking tactics, people would come up and wish me luck. Others would be brutally honest and say, 'I hope to fuck he gives you a good hammering.' William was the 1967 champion, and the clear favourite for this tournament. He did not want to lose his crown. I was the cocky little teenager wanting to be crowned. The announcer called us out to the mat, inviting us to have a quick warm-up before battle commenced.

What he and the general public did not know, was that Jumbo and I had already had a bit of a go at each other before we even got out in front of them.

I knew the crowd were up for the match also, because I had noticed and heard many saying, 'I bet you a fiver he wins' or 'I bet you a tenner he doesn't'. Anyway, Jumbo had said to me, 'I'll have a vodka and orange when I'm finished with you, Terry.'

I snapped back, 'Take it easy, will you, old chap. You can get me a vodka lime and water in five minutes' time. It will only take that long.'

He laughed hysterically. You see, it was customary for the loser to buy a drink for the winner, a gesture of good sportsmanship, something like that. Don't let anyone fool themselves, there was no love lost between Jumbo and me leading up to this game. In normal life, I thought he was a bloody fine chap, but right now, he was the boss, and I was the pretender wanting his crown.

Clemmy was panicking. He kept saying, 'Be careful, he's dangerous.' Les was outside as nervous as hell, but I was calm. So it was game on, the crowd were even more boisterous than previously. I got off to a flyer of a start and Jumbo was always chasing me, one–nil, I had gone straight out.

I followed with another quick start. I looked at Jumbo. I could tell in his eyes he knew his number was up. I was as high as a kite on adrenaline, I knew I had him, but I also knew this was not Ron, this was a completely different type of character. With Ron I could be the showman, play around a bit, William was lethal, and I knew once I had him down, I had to make bloody sure he was not going to get up again. So I did the only sensible thing I could do, showed him no mercy, and I polished him off, just like the four other opponents before him, 2–0. The only thing I had got wrong, was that I had asked Jumbo to give me five minutes, it actually took four and a half.

My opponent was naturally dejected, Clemmy was jumping for joy and people were pushing and shoving me, trying to slap my back or shake my hand, or yelling at me all rather excitedly how much money they had won. Eventually I had my very sweet vodka lime and water with Jumbo. He was sore, and I was pleased. I was pleased because he showed the signs of a great champion, truly great champions hate losing; winning is great, but if you beat someone of real class, it is so much better.

I was now in the semi-finals, and the Whitney family were not finished with me yet: I had to play Jumbo's father, Fred. It was all a bit of an anti-climax, I put Fred away also 2–0, with complete ease. So now it was the big one, I had reached the major individual darts final without losing a single game. But my opponent was Tony Pettersson, the only guy, aside from Jumbo, who had beaten me in the league. It was the final act. Win, I'm in the record books as a champion. Lose and I'm soon forgotten, a nothing, a might-have-been, if only I had done this or that.

Again I got off to a fast start in the first game, I was always in front, and was thinking about how to finish on my double. Then bang. Tony still needed 116, but the bugger went out with a fantastic three-dart finish. The noise of the crowd almost lifted the roof off the building. I had lost my first game of the tournament; lose one more, and I would be chump not champ.

Officials called for the spectators to calm down. No one listened, or if they did, then they took not the slightest bit of notice. There was too much money riding on this game, I guess. Before starting the second game I glanced towards Clemmy. I noticed he was fidgeting about in his seat, a complete bag of nerves. I said to him, 'Don't worry, it is just a minor hiccup.'

'I bloody hope so,' he said.

The next game went according to plan, and scores were level at 1–1. It was now bull up, and the winner of this game takes all. I was again off quickly, and soon I was left with double one, and I had three darts to do it. I knew if I didn't, I could kiss the championship goodbye, because Tony was waiting to have a go at his finishing double.

First dart, bang, right in the centre of double one. I shook Tony's hand, but before I could do anything else I was surrounded by a huge crowd of people. One chap was so excited he started kissing me, and yelled, 'I have just won 200 quid on you.' That shocked me. That was a bloody lot of money in those days. What was one man doing trusting me with so much money? But my own thoughts and feelings were soon overcome with the elation of having just won the Govenors Silver Cup, and the prize money of £2.

I enjoyed my moment of triumph, and I still have the memory to cling to. I would never reach the same level of success in that sport again, although the Governors Cup was not my only victory that year, I also went on to win the individual knock-out tournament.

I have told you this sporting story only because I believe it is so relevant to life itself. I won the Governors Cup because I trained and practised hard, because I wanted to win it. In life, it is the same story: if you want something badly enough, and you are prepared to make sacrifices, you will achieve your aims, I promise you that. The euphoria of victory is but a brief period, it is the memory of success that lives on and on and on.

The decade ended with me having my first steady girlfriend and being capped for the Falkland Islands national football team. The 1960s were over and I had much to look forward to in the coming decade, but the sixties will always have a special place in my heart. The Beatles, man landing on the moon, Mods and Rockers, the assassinations of John F. and Robert Kennedy and Martin Luther King, and the rebellious youth movement across Europe. I can only imagine that not to have experienced growing up in the 1960s must be like living in a world without the moon and sun.

10

Marriage – Fatherhood – Policeman – Contract Worker (And that attempted murder case)

For the next 12 years of my life I would spend nearly all of my time living and working in the Falkland Islands. Life in the seventies was to be completely different from the decade before. I did not travel outside the Islands much at all during this period. The main reason for this is because I had found my first real love, and I would eventually get married and become a father.

I now had new challenges and responsibilities. I carried on playing sports, but I lost the enthusiasm for darts and got much more involved in football and my new hobby, music. I started work again with a local contractor, John Rowlands.

John was one of those local rarities in the Falklands: he had entrepreneurial spirit and was well educated. He had also been a former member of the legislative council.

I had worked for John previously in 1967, building concrete roads in the town. He always said I mixed the best concrete he had ever seen. In those times almost everything had to be done manually; the only machine we had was a cement mixer, but even that had to be loaded by hand. We did not even have a dump truck to carry the wet and heavy cement from the mixer to the gang waiting to lay the material, sometimes 200 metres away from the site of the mixer. It was all moved by two-wheeled wheelbarrows over very rough terrain. Pickaxes, spades and shovels were the only tools we had.

It had changed now. John was getting more adventurous. He was still building roads, but he was also carrying out works such as extensions to the local power station. This included pretty technical matters, such as laying out firm and reliable foundations for diesel generators. We also prepared and laid foundations for buildings, even constructing car ports and suchlike.

I remember one day when I was working on the power station

with a lovely guy, nicknamed 'the Pope' (Fred Biggs was his real name). We were breaking rock with 28lb sledgehammers, then Fred suddenly stopped, threw his hammer down, bent down and picked up a piece of rock. After looking at it for a moment, he turned to me and said, 'That rock is ten million years old.'

I stopped myself from laughing, then I said, 'How do you know that, Fred?'

'It's that bloody rotten it fell apart with the slightest touch,' he replied.

Fred Biggs was one of the Islands' characters; many thought he was a little bit off the wall. I never thought that. He was certainly different, though.

Many years later, I would travel on the same flight as Fred from the Falklands to RAF Brize Norton. As we were waiting at a baggage carousel in the arrivals lounge, he came up to me and said, with a deadpan face, 'You know, I could live up there, up in the sky. It's very comfortable and really good food.'

I ignored the comment, and asked where he was going. He said he was heading to Swindon. I asked if he had anyone meeting him or did he have transport. No, was the answer to the first question, yes to the second. Tragically, within a week, the Falkland Islands Government representative in London was having to organise his safe return back to the Falklands because he was in some sort of accommodation for the homeless, apparently devoid of any finances.

I must tell you another amusing story about an event that took place whilst I was working with John. We were doing ground works, laying foundations and putting in services such as foul water systems for the British Antarctic Survey, on Race Course Road. The pipes we were using were made of a new material to the Islands, called pitch fibre. Well, one morning, just before breakfast, we had these things lying about the place ready to lay in trenchers, and suddenly we noticed this black smoke and flames filling the air just 200 yards up the road.

Some of us stopped whatever we were doing and immediately ran off to where the smoke and fire was coming from. It was in the area where the government had its stable and some other buildings, just below the racecourse.

As we entered the compound, we were greeted by a somewhat shocked Bikey, Steve and Hector, who were all outside their hut looking up at the spectacular fire display.

'What's up?' I asked.

'Oh the chimney's on fire, Che,' Steve replied. Then I realised what had happened.

Some boys must have helped themselves to a length of the pipe as they were walking by, deciding it would make a nice new chimney for the stove in the hut which they used for shelter and to cook up breakfast. No doubt unaware of the materials the pipe was made from, and delighted with their new fixture, they flashed up the fire with great anticipation of a smoke-free breakfast, only to receive the shock of their lives as the chimney burst into flames, and ejected the most dense black smoke, which filled their little accommodation, forcing them outside, whilst exposing their act of theft. We all had a good laugh at their expense. Nothing more was said and we went back to our job.

John (Ski) Rowlands will always be a man that holds a special place in my heart. He taught me self-belief and never to accept second best. He not only encouraged me to take on responsibility, he actually gave it to me. He taught me many things about local issues such as politics and the trade unions. John was a big union activist himself. He also explained to me the various functions of many FIG administrative departments, and their personnel.

But what I liked about John most of all was that he was bloody interesting. He was also very critical of Government and the system. Another thing he would say was, 'Never be a yes man, Terry. The Falklands are full of yes men.' Over the years, John became one of my closest friends, and I am proud to say one of my mentors. We spent many late nights together, firstly in the Working Men's reading room, chewing the fat over one thing or another, and later on in life, in the Falkland Club, locally called the 'Glue Pot', always discussing the latest topics, local or worldwide.

He was especially critical of the system of employing overseas contractors brought into the Islands to take up senior positions in administration on short-term contracts. His displeasure was mainly because he felt that such a policy meant that Islanders would often be denied the opportunity to take up middle and senior posts.

'Well, Terence, I think these buggers are just down for a good time. They can't believe their luck. We educate their children for free, accommodate them for free, then give them all the administrative power, and just to top it off, they are all on grossly exaggerated salaries.' He would suck away on his cigarette and then continue.

'The blighters can afford to go out and buy up a house for an inflated price, on the pretence that they have been converted and have fallen in love with the Falklands. Suddenly they want to stay here for the rest of their lives. Then bugger me, as soon as the kids have finished their education, they sell the house for a huge profit and push off, leaving us with the bloody mess they have probably made whilst they were here.' I must say, I found it very difficult to disagree with his sentiments.

I found John's assessment of the Government structure and how it operated such a refreshing point of view, it was this kind of spirit in a man that I liked, and I got to like and respect John Rowlands very much. I felt he genuinely cared for his fellow Falkland Islander. He certainly was a straight talker.

When John died a few years ago, it was a very sad day for me, although his death had not come as a great surprise – he had been suffering from terrible respiratory problems for some time. John was more than a close friend; in many ways, he had become a father figure to me. The reassuring bus driver, guiding me through some of the complicated roads of my life.

As I have said, I would go to the Falkland Club late at nights, just to talk to, and listen to him. This man had given me employment when I needed it, he gave me self belief when I needed it, he always showed interest in what I did, when I needed it, he gave me a lot of encouragement and advice, as I ventured out into business myself when I needed it.

John was always in touch with things; he had been a doer in his own life up until ill health curtailed his activities. Anyone who had the time or the opportunity to be in John's company, and have the privilege to sit and listen to his wealth of knowledge, would have been much better educated for the experience. If there is a heaven, which I am sure there is, John will be there, a just reward after his wonderful contribution to his fellow man, as a trade unionist, local politician and civil engineering contractor, all in an attempt to provide a better Falkland Islands for Falkland Islanders. I know I owe him much. I also know I am not alone.

The 1970s did not get off to a great start. I was more than a little sad when one of my best mates, Clem, left the Islands to pursue a career in the Royal Marines, but I was happy that he was going off to do something he really wanted to do. Then just before Christmas in 1971, my girlfriend and future wife Melody Lee, gave birth to our first child. She had a long period of labour, and sadly, things would end in a tragic way. Our son died just six hours after his birth with some intestine difficulties. I was not present at the birth, and when I was told of the terrible events I was totally gutted. I was invited to go and see the body, but I declined. Perhaps I took the easy option, perhaps I will never know, but I remember thinking to myself, what was to be gained from subjecting myself to further pain. It was supposed to have been a moment of great joy. Instead, it had turned out to be so painful. You must also remember I was living in a society which did not have much understanding or caring for single parents. I was just a young man (20) who had got a young girl (16) pregnant, so my feelings were of no importance.

For Melody, it must have been many times worse to go through nine months of pregnancy, then give birth to a child, and then to be confronted by such a devastating outcome. Only she can know the extent of grief. Officially, our first child was buried at a very simple ceremony, as James Lee, named after his uncle. Thinking back, I doubt if I gave Melody much useful support; I was too immature. But she did have a very strong family, who were all firm and active believers, and that certainly did help her and them. Melody had lost a sister who was just 16 years old, a few years previously.

However, on 18 August 1973, happy times. I got married after three years and three days of going out with Melody Christine Lee. We tied the knot and settled down together. I remember we had £80 between us, £50 of it belonged to Melody. We had a wedding reception in the Parish Hall of the Christ Church Cathedral for 250 guests. It was one and a half hours of feasting and drinking, customary for such occasions in the Falklands. The bill for the hiring of the hall and the catering was £30. I will tell you this, I might have been in love, but I was certainly not prepared for the struggles of maintaining a home and, before too long, bringing up children. I do not think any man at 22 years is prepared or equipped for marriage and its varying responsibilities.

One of the most unsettling things in the first year or so of our marriage was that we seemed to be packing our bags and moving house every other month. The reason for this was because we could only secure very short-term lets within our budget. But we were also struggling to cope with the bills and within five months we had the additional responsibility of parenthood.

This was the first major event of our marriage, although we did have some great times. Following all the pain and hurt of James's death in 1971, which will always linger in my mind, the events of 7 January 1973 helped to greatly relieve that awful experience. This was the day we had our second child, this time fit and well to cherish, a beautiful carrot-top boy we named Severine.

It had been planned that I would be at the birth (a novelty in those days). I had been with Melody, at her bedside, until midday. The doctor, Derek Cox, had a little chat with me and said, 'If you want to nip home for a bite of lunch, it will be okay, Terry. You won't miss anything. I expect it will be a few hours yet before we have any action.' I was feeling a bit hungry, so after discussing things with my wife, it was agreed that I should pop up to my in-laws and join them for lunch, and collect a few things Melody needed.

After lunch finished, I relaxed for a short while. Then I casually strolled back to the hospital with a small bag of goodies for my wife. When I opened the door to the hospital ward, I got one hell of a surprise. I will not go into graphic details, but it was all over, Severine had been born minutes before I arrived. So quick was the event that there had been no time to move my wife to the maternity ward, but who cared, we had a very healthy baby boy, and we were both over the moon.

We had moved home once again, and this time, we were living in a small house at No. 1 Davis Street. It got so damp in the winter, the mattress was almost wringing wet. We had a small electric heater, and we would sit it on the mattress during the day to try and dry it out. Oh yes, times in the early part of our marriage were very hard, but we struggled through.

I also recall that we had a difficult period with Severine when he first came home. I guess we were overfeeding him or something. He would wake every hour, day and night, but once we had fed him and put him down, he would throw it all up again and an hour later, he would be screaming to be fed again.

Melody was working as a nurse, which sometimes meant she had to work nights or go to work very early in the morning. I also had to get up early to go to work. The lack of sleep got us very fraught at times. But eventually, we got the hang of things and Severine became more enjoyable as he became more satisfied. I would get the hang of helping out in all aspects of fatherhood. Yes, including changing nappies.

Then in 1974 life changed again. I became a police constable. I felt there was a need to inject further stability into the partnership of marriage by having a more secure job. The police force did that. When I first went out on the beat, one very kind member of the public who was very surprised to see me in the Queen's uniform said, 'What's this, Terry? If you can't beat 'em join 'em.' I thought the comment was very funny, even though I knew it was meant to be sarcastic.

I enjoyed most of my time in the Falkland Islands Police Force, as it was then called. The entire force totalled seven officers: four constables, a corporal, sergeant and the inspector. The force infrastructure consisted of a police station, jail and exercise yard and short wheelbase Land Rover.

The Land Rover was used for special needs only, foot patrols of Stanley were the norm. I soon learnt that it was also the most effective way to police Stanley, and as you walked about, you had regular contact with the town's population, who would stop and chat with you in the street. Many would even invite you into their homes for an afternoon cup of tea. Foot patrolling meant that you built up a kind of trust with the community. Some would be a bit shy and stand-offish, but most people were open.

One of the pleasures of being a policeman was on the nightshift (from midnight to 8 a.m.) at about 3.00 a.m., after checking the grounds at Government House, it was customary to stroll down to the King Edward Memorial Hospital and pop in for half an hour, to sit, chat and often as not, have a very early breakfast with the night staff. On more sombre occasions, you would be called out to help the staff to move the body of someone from the hospital ward to the mortuary. That was one task I did not like.

Although the Land Rover was supposed to be used for special occasions or emergencies, whenever a fellow constable and I were on the late-night shift (from 7 p.m. to midnight) – considered the busy time of the capital, so two policemen were deployed – we would do the pub closing round at 10 p.m., and often transported members of the general public home or off to a house party. We became very popular for this friendly gesture.

One night when most people were off the streets, I remember driving along St Mary's Walk at a speed much less than the legal limit of 20 miles per hour. Just as well, because I had time to notice something lying in the middle of the street. As I got closer, I realised it was a man, so I pulled up just short. I was not sure at this point if the person was dead or alive, because he appeared very still.

I climbed out of the vehicle, more than a little concerned. When I reached the figure I bent down to check who it was, then the individual began to move. I quickly realised it was my old bass guitarist mate from the band 'Since'. I tried for about ten minutes to help him to his feet so I could get him off the street and into the vehicle. By the time I had achieved my objective, I was quite exhausted.

His home was just a short journey away, so I decided to take him there. When I got alongside his garden gate, I stopped the vehicle and helped him to the front door of his home. Believe me, taking him home was to be a far greater punishment than putting him into a prison cell for the night to sleep it off. Anyhow, how could you put your mate in a cell for the night? By the time I had let myself out of the garden gate to get back into the Land Rover, I wondered if I had done the right thing, because, as I looked back, I noticed that he was in the arms of his highly agitated wife, who was now wide-awake and threatening to give him a good lesson in the art of boxing.

He might not have been enjoying the welcome, but I was to be free of any unnecessary paperwork which I would have had to deal with if I had put him in a cell. But, as I have said, he was the band's bass guitarist, so how the hell could I put him in jail. Only two of us knew anything about the incident – his wife and me – he sure as hell didn't.

The main offences in our pretty well-behaved population were drunk and disorderly, speeding and domestic unrest. We all hated dealing with the latter. There was one lady who was well known for beating up her husband as a private drinking session would turn into a fight, then she would call the station and demand that we go up to the house and arrest the man. Once you got there, things would have calmed down. Then just as you were ready to walk off, both of them would start verbally abusing you. Sometimes, the sensible thing to do was to take the husband away for a while, for his own safety, and to let the wife get some much needed sleep – which was all a bit of a drag because now you had to file a report.

We had a thing in the Falklands, locally called 'The Black List'. It was an official and legal document which was posted in all liquor outlets, listing the names of persons prohibited from entering public houses, or being allowed to purchase or consume alcohol, also prohibiting any member of the public from purchasing alcohol for consumption by the named person/s. It also specified the period of prohibition, which would be either three, six or nine months, or one year. It was done in the sincere belief that it would protect the individuals' lives, or save others from suffering in one form or another from alcoholic abuse. Wife-beating was a favourite Saturday night sport at one time.

The Falklands has had a few murders in its history since the resettlement of the Islands in 1833, but one day, a husband cold-bloodedly murdered his wife in front of their young son. Because that boy and his family have rebuilt their lives and are still very much part of the Falklands community today, I will spare them the pain by not giving you graphic details.

In 1974 the Falklands still had its inner circle, the untouchables. There was much pretence that no such thing existed, but I would find out that indeed it did. My former window-breaking schoolmate was on a nightshift with me, and we were sitting in our stationary Land Rover, registration mark 333, opposite the old Beaver aircraft hangar, when I noticed the headlights of a vehicle coming towards us. We both assumed the driver was heading for Stanley. We were also aware that there had been a party for distinguished guests at the barracks of the Royal Marines at Moody Brook, no doubt hosted by the commanding officer of Naval Party 8901.

Anyway, as the car drove by, I was a little surprised that the driver had not noticed us, so I said to Rossi, 'Do you think we should follow for a little while?'

'May as well,' he said. 'It beats sitting here.'

I let the car get about 20 metres down the road, then I drove out and followed the vehicle all the way to the owner's home. Whilst in pursuit we could clearly gauge his speed at 28 miles an hour by reaching that speed ourselves and maintaining the same distance from him. The driver was also driving very erratically, going virtually from one side of Ross Road west to the other. There were no other vehicles on the street at the time, or I would have attempted to stop him long before he got home. By the time he had passed Government House, we were pretty certain who the driver and passenger were.

For the rest of the journey, the debate between Rossi and me was should we or should we not make a charge against the driver. Rossi was certain we should not. Then I said to him, we must. If it were an ordinary Islander, we would not hesitate. As we were passing the Town Hall, the driver had become aware that he was being followed, and who it was that was following him. I observed him repeatedly looking in his rear-view mirror. When opposite the man's house he drove straight into the garage. As he did so, I parked up, and jumped out of the police vehicle and ran into the shelter. I was just in time to witness the man getting out of his car; he was unable to rush because it was a very tight squeeze between the car, and the wall of the garage.

'You all right, sir?' I asked.

'Oh, yes officer,' came a slurry reply.

'Driving a little bit fast weren't we sir?' I questioned.

'Me?' said the man, who was also visibly unstable on his feet. 'I don't think so.'

'I would estimate that you were doing 28 miles per, sir. The speed limit, as I am sure you will know only too well, considering you were one of the persons who passed the law, is 20 miles per hour, sir.'

'Hum, I didn't realise the old girl would do that much.'

I sarcastically replied, 'Would you be referring to the car or the wife, sir?'

Rossi burst into laughter.

I was, of course, well out of order with such a comment, but the elected member of legislative council said, 'Damned funny that, officer. Bloody funny indeed. I think I will bid you goodnight.'

Then I said, 'I am sorry, sir, but I will be filing a report, which might lead to you being charged for driving a vehicle whilst under the influence of drink or drugs, and also for exceeding the lawful speed limit.'

Oh, I should point out that the police force in the Falklands did not have fancy toys such as breathalysers. Nor laws which stated the limit of alcohol permissible in one's blood. If you really wanted a drink-drive case to stick, without the person charged, having a cat's chance in hell of avoiding conviction in the courts, you only had to get a doctor's report, or for a doctor to testify in court, that in his opinion, and as the result of a simple urine test, the person charged had sufficient alcohol in his body to deem him under influence of alcohol. Naturally we opted for the urine test in this case. Once completed, the gentleman went off to bed, and Rossi and I went back to the station and filed our reports.

A few days had passed, then the inspector came up to me one morning and said, 'Do you really want to press charges?'

'Of course I bloody do,' I angrily replied. 'If he can get away with things like this, then how can I pull someone else in?'

'Okay,' he said, 'you're right, I am just checking.'

Another week or so passed. Again I was in the office on a day duty, when the sergeant answered a call, and promptly announced to the inspector that the call was for him, and who the caller was. Once the inspector had finished his telephone conversation, he hung up, then turning to me, he said, 'Do you know who that was?'

'Yes I do,' I replied.

'Well,' he said, giving a big sigh, 'your report will not go any further. I've been instructed that any charges are to be dropped, there will be no charges, and that is the end of it, do you understand?'

I could tell he was slightly shocked. The caller had disturbed him, and I was livid. I proceeded to tell the inspector what a bunch of hypocrites they all were, and from now on, I would not be able to carry out my duties properly. He tried to calm me down, but I got up and walked out of the office and went home. The inspector did not reprimand me for my actions, but I had learnt a very hard lesson about colonial life, and who held all the power within it. I and my fellow Islanders were second-class citizens in our own home. Come to think of it, what home?

I have one more story which I must tell of my police force experience. One afternoon, between 5 and 6 p.m., a group of us were holding a football committee meeting in the police station. The fact that we were doing this in the station once again typified life in the Falklands. The boss was a keen footballer, and had no objections. Few people were prepared to take up responsibility in anything, and those that did were soon on more committees than they could count. Therefore, there was a tendency to hold meetings wherever, and whenever, possible.

Well, back to the story. We were just starting to get into the agenda when we were all distracted by some kind of commotion outside. None of us took much notice at first – it was not unusual for the general public to be walking or running through the police station yard. It was pretty much used by the general public as a thoroughfare; even though there were signs posted that this was not permitted, no bugger took the slightest bit of notice.

However, our meeting was brought to an abrupt end when, without any further warning, a windowpane was broken in the office west wall. I also heard a clicking sound, two, three, four times. I can still recall seeing Ron Betts taking cover behind the end of a filing cabinet. Then my attention was drawn in the direction of a voice. 'Bang, bang, you should all be fucking dead by now. You had better get outside quickly and save the bastard who's dying out here. If he's not fucking dying, he should be.'

Looking towards the window, I saw the familiar face of an ex-Royal Marine, and the tiny barrel of a pistol. I immediately recognised it was a German Luger, which, unfortunately, was now aimed right at me. I only knew of the whereabouts of one of these guns in the entire Islands. It belonged to a very close friend of mine.

I saw little point in shitting myself. There was nowhere to hide, nowhere to run, so I walked towards the crouched and partially hiding figure of the man staring through the broken window and asked, 'What do you mean?'

He did not answer my question, but shouted back, 'Don't stand there, you cunt. Get outside and look for yourself.'

Seconds passed which seemed like minutes, but I went outside. I heard a voice call out to me. It was my old schoolmate, who was bent over holding his stomach. 'He stabbed me, TSB. The bastard tried to kill me.' My friend had been stabbed in the lower abdomen with a short-bladed penknife. Once satisfied he was not in a life-threatening condition, I helped him to his feet and we walked together to the police chief's house, where he was checked over and comforted until a doctor arrived.

Unfortunately, the inspector was not available for advice and guidance. He had gone off to camp somewhere, but within a few hours of getting the news of the attack, he pulled the throttle back on his motorcycle and was back in town in record time.

It was not long before the victim of the knifing was able to go back home and rest up; equally, it was not that long before the attacker was in a prison cell, being held in custody until a court hearing could be convened.

Allegedly both men had a desire for the same attractive female, which is always a complicated and messy situation, especially when one is the husband and does not approve of the other male's attention to his wife. Apparently, the two men agreed to meet each other to try and sort things out. But whatever was being discussed, things quickly got out of control, and threats were being exchanged. My dear friend knew he would get a serious beating, at least, in a fistfight from the well-trained ex-Royal Marine who had seen active services in places like Aden. But he made a grave error of judgement by pulling out his pistol, aiming it straight at the ex-Marine and pulling the trigger several times.

Terrified that his only meaningful form of defence had failed – in hindsight, thank God, or the ex-Marine would have been very dead, and my friend would have had to serve a very long prison sentence for murder – he turned and ran for his life. The ex-soldier was soon in hot pursuit...

I can remember the former soldier being in custody for 49 days, because on one occasion when I went to the prisoners' dayroom to see him, he was at a table, with a ring of salt lying on top of it, and holding a pack of playing cards. I asked him what he was doing. Magic, he replied, and then he went on to tell me that he knew on the 49th day of confinement, he would be released. I thought no more about that encounter until the day of the trial verdict.

When I went back to the station, he showed me the calendar he had in his cell. Pointing to a date, he said, 'That was the day when I came in,' then turning a page, he started to tap a date. 'And this is the day I am going out. Count the days, you'll find it's 49.'

After he had gone, I did, and it was. Bloody odd coincidence, don't you think? I was deeply saddened that my friend had to serve a custodial sentence. I felt he had been more the victim, rather than the criminal, in the whole sordid affair.

I am sure that the incident with the councillor and the imprisonment of my schoolmate dampened my enthusiasm for a career in the police force, and certainly made me very cynical of what is perceived to be justice. It is strange how everything finally turned out. The ex-soldier left the Islands, allegedly just short of deportation. The councillor who thought he was untouchable lost his seat. My harshly imprisoned friend became one of the Falkland Islands Government's most senior administrative officials. Poetic justice indeed.

On New Year's eve 1975 I resigned as a police constable. I used the excuse of a lack of contract as my reason, but in honesty, I had lost faith in the system. My only regret is that I never told the inspector that, or he might have been more understanding when I handed him my uniform and told him that I would not wear it again, and that I could not recommend to anyone that they join the force.

At the time, a new thing was exciting the community. There were a lot of new faces in the town, and it was all down to the building of the new airfield which was being constructed towards the east end of the Stanley harbour. It was one of the few positive outcomes from the communications agreement signed by the United Kingdom and Argentina back in July 1971.

The arrival of the United Kingdom contractors, and the commencement of the construction project itself, provided a bonanza in earning capabilities for Islanders. They were able to move from their previous employers, who were paying 30p an hour, to the airfield contractors, for a minimum of 70p per hour. I guess it was a bit like the 'Gold Rush' in the USA.

There were negatives to the huge leap in salaries and the spending power of the construction consortium, who it seemed had money to burn. The price of retail goods and homegrown produce soared just as dramatically. Before their arrival, you could buy a beef carcass from a farmer for £8, now it was costing £40, much to the alarm of those not able to directly benefit from increased earnings.

I soon contacted my old mate John Rowlands, who was subcontracting labour to the project, and I was off to dig a little piece of gold as well. I have to say that I never really enjoyed my work at the airfield site. I was working a wagon drill, drilling four-inch holes in very hard rock, getting covered in sand and rock dust day in and day out. Conditions on the site in the winter were dreadful. Everywhere was knee-deep in mud and you were also totally exposed to whatever foul weather the South Atlantic decided to throw at you.

There were some funny moments. I remember an Irish foreman called Tommy Costello. Tommy was full of energy, and was a tremendous motivator. He had a long wheelbase Land Rover, which was in immaculate condition when it had been purchased from its previous owners. I think its maximum recommended carrying capacity was nine persons. Well, be that as it may, this particular evening, Tommy was driving the vehicle back up to the town with reportedly seventeen passengers on board, mostly Chilean labourers.

Tommy took a bend just a shade too quickly, and the machine rolled over onto its side. Once most of the people were on their feet, Tommy instructed the terrified Chileans to lift the vehicle upright and climb back on board to head home. As soon as the Land Rover was back on four wheels, Tommy roared off with his overcrowded vehicle as though nothing had happened. That night Tommy became a kind of legendary figure, and the Chileans remained wary of Tommy for the duration of the contract.

Another incident that epitomised Tommy's character was when he and a Scotsman, the same one that would later murder his wife, met in the pub one night. The Scotsman had been off work for a week or so, on the booze. The man had been prodding Tommy all night about going back to work the following Monday, and demanding that he give him his truck-driving job back when he went back to work. After a while, Tommy said to the Scot, 'Sure, sure, I'll give you a driving job when you come back.' With that comment, the Scotsman seemed very happy.

On the following Monday morning, the Scotsman duly turned up to the site at 6 a.m., but by 9 a.m. he was still standing in the site mess room, waiting for Tommy to appear and advise him which truck he would be driving.

At this time of the day, the mess room was always full because it was breakfast time. Suddenly, Tommy burst through the doorway with a shovel in his hand, he walked directly up to the Scotsman, thrust his arm out full length, and held the shovel in front of the Scotsman's face and said to him, 'There you are, you drunken piss head, drive that until your heart's contented, you bastard.' Everyone in the mess room burst into laughter, seeing the funny side of the situation. The Scotsman was not so amused, however, and he brushed past the Irishman, storming out of the building and slamming the door behind him, never to be seen on the site again.

It would be possible to go on with Tommy the Irishman stories for ever, but alas I shall not. The airfield project was a success, and once finished, several Islanders had made enough money to buy a house, the price of which had also risen threefold since the contractors' arrival. However, when the contractors packed up and left, work was once again difficult to come by. John did not have enough work around the town to keep us going, so he paid me, and others, off.

In the Falklands winter of 1977 it was not a good time for me to be out of work, because my wife and I were expecting another child. Fortunately, I was only out of a job for a week before I secured employment with another local man who had taken the plunge into the private sector, Willie Bowles. Willie's core business was operating a carpenter's shop, but he had acquired some maintenance work at Navy Point. This kept me, and about ten other men, employed for the whole of the 1977 winter, which would be quite severe.

11

A Sister-in-law Dies, A Daughter is Born
(The mysterious Johnny Green, and bloody peat)

On the family front, the winter of '77 brought great tragedy and extreme happiness. The tragic event which brought such sadness was the unexpected death of my sister-in-law Candy. Unexpected because she had gone into hospital for what was supposed to be a routine operation, and was only 25.

Alec was full of beans when he popped into our house on his way down to collect Candy from the hospital. He stopped by for about half an hour, chatting about their plans and how they were looking forward to fresh challenges as they mapped out a new life of hope and ambition together.

My brother was not long gone when he returned alone. 'Where's Candy?' I asked, rather concerned.

'Oh, she's still in hospital. When I got down there, I met her in the passageway and she collapsed in my arms. They've taken her back into the ward and they'll give me a call later.'

After a period of time, he went back to the hospital because he had not received a call. When he got there, he was to be completely stunned with the news that Candy was now in the emergency ward, with doctors making every effort to save her life.

Unknown to us, Alec waited for several hours, until a doctor finally appeared, only to inform him that the fight was over, and it had been lost. Candy had died of massive blood clotting, just 25 years old, with what was supposed to be a bright future ahead of her. Doctors told my brother had she survived, she would have been cabbage for the rest of her life. Scant comfort to him, and the two young children, Dawn and Paul, who were just eight and nine years old respectively.

In total contrast, Melody, Severine and I were to have a moment of great joy in the early morning of 19 July 1977. This was when our third child, Amelia, was born, a sister for

Severine, who was now three and a half years old. Severine was pleased as punch. When his little baby sister arrived home, he was eagerly waiting to show her off to his best friend. This friend would take up much of Severine's free time for about a year or so and was rather interesting. He was a little different to most young boys' mates. Why? Well, you see, his best mate did not exist. Severine's best friend was imaginary, invisible to his mother and me. But as two very understanding parents, we did not make any attempt to interfere with his imagination; instead, we went along with it.

Every once in a while, when either his mother or I set the table for lunch, Severine would ask if Johnny Green could stay and have lunch with him. Oh yeah, this invisible boy also had a name, Johnny Green. We would say sure, and set an extra place alongside Severine, so he and Johnny could sit, in his mind, to eat lunch and chat together.

The other thing Severine would do, he would be happily playing away with a truck or some other toy on the kitchen carpet floor, then he would suddenly jump up and ask for his coat, so he could go out and play with Johnny Green, who was apparently waiting at the door for him.

We would get his coat and help him to put it on, then walk to the door with him, open it, and say hello to Johnny Green, who was supposed to be waiting on the doorstep, then he would go out of the house into the garden, beaming from ear to ear, wave, and say, 'I'll see you later, okay?' This phenomenon went on for about a year, and then I guess Johnny Green moved away from the Falklands.

The seventies were happy times for our small family. I was a contented father and husband. I enjoyed gardening, and spent many hours tending to it as I listened to the BBC World Service on my radio for company. Despite the difficult elements, gardening was very rewarding, and you could grow enough vegetables to supply the family needs for most of the year.

Being parents was delightful. We were always taking the two children out for walks. Bedtime was fun, too. Melody would read stories to them, or I would go and sit on the bed and play my guitar and sing to them, often with original tunes and/or stories.

We were just one nice and neat little family in the seventies. But there was always one dark cloud about. Bloody peat.

I hated the dreaded peat-cutting. I said I would get to this subject once again. Peat, as I have told you, was a fuel in abundance, and providing you put considerable effort into it, you could supply your family with all the fuel required for domestic purposes, such as providing hot water, central heating and cooking. Most homes required approximately 120 cubic metres of peat for a year's supply, but your labours were never finished with bloody peat or its by-products. Every day of the year, you had to do something with it. I had better explain why.

The first task is to cut the peat, originally and traditionally, in 64 blocks, which we called sods, of 9" × 9" × 9" in a cubic yard. Once the glorious sight of machines were introduced to cut the peat, these precise measurements went out the window, along with the peat spade, which was the hand tool required to cut your peat, and which also blistered the palms of your hands in the process. The spade had to have a hole bored through the centre of the blade. This was to avoid suction against the blade with a wet sod of peat.

Peat was cut in the spring and/or early summer, and always in your own time, after work, in the evenings, through the week or at the weekends, or during your holidays. Once cut, it was left to dry in the fresh and plentiful prevailing westerly Falklands winds, and after a few weeks, the sods were picked up off the ground and placed into small heaps, locally called rickles. Once totally dry, it was then loaded by hand into the back of a lorry or trailer. Then it was transported home, and dumped at the main door of your peat shed, which was one of the main outside buildings of any property in the Falklands. The method in camp was slightly different. Peat would be stored in large stacks, in bins, rather than in a shed.

Once the peat had been delivered to your peat shed door, then another backbreaking phase had to be entered, which was throwing and stacking the goddamned stuff into the shed. This was always a dusty job, and small bits of peat fragments would get in your eyes and ears, or up your nose, as the wind swirled the dust around your working area. By the end of a day throwing peat into your shed, the first thing to do was have a bath (few homes were fitted with showers). When you finished, and let all the water out of the bath, the bottom of the tub would be covered with a fine layer of peat dust, which you would then have to wash away, so the wife didn't scream at you for leaving a mess behind.

Some guys would cut enough peat to be a year ahead. If you did this, you would be required to put the peat into big stacks on the top of the peat bank to stand out through the winter, before fetching it home the following spring. Peat that stood this way was invariably better to burn.

Even with your yearly supply now stacked in your shed, the trials, tribulations and horrors of peat continued. You were never free from working with the bloody stuff, each day you would have to fill your peat buckets (cans) and carry them from the shed to the back door of the house, along with two sods. The sods were called 'bankers', and were used to put in the firebox, then you closed all dampers for the night. Then each morning after you got up, the same boring routine began again: open dampers, rake out the ashes, take the ashes out to your ash drum.

From the moment you opened your eyes to the time you closed them, bloody peat had played a part in your daily life, and not in labour alone. Peat caused many a domestic situation in the Falklands, especially if it was a cold winter's morning and there was no peat in the shed because the husband had not summoned up enough energy during the spring/summer to provide enough peat to keep the home fires burning all year round.

I do not know if anyone still cuts their peat, but if they do, I cannot think for one moment of a reason why. I always hated it, or was there some truth in the legendary stories? It was said that a man always had a much more active sex life if he ensured that the peat shed was always full, and, I believe, not necessarily with his own wife.

My only lasting memory of a specific occasion at the peat bank was on 8 December 1980, the anniversary of the Battle of the Falklands (1914), so I was spending my national holiday cutting fuel. Then I heard the news on my radio that John Lennon had been shot dead in New York. I stopped what I was doing and trudged home. My hero had been killed. I was devastated.

12

Chile and Argentina Nearly go to War,
Whilst I'm in Chile
(And a few rock band stories)

I have mentioned that I did not travel off the Islands very much in the 1970s, but on one occasion in 1978, my wife and I went to my brother's wedding in Punta Arenas, Chile. He married a Chilean lady, Rosita, who he had met in the Falkland Islands, and he had asked me to be a witness for the wedding. How could I say no? Our journey, on a Fokker-28, took us from Stanley to the Argentine coastal port of Comodoro Rivadavia, where we stayed the night.

Argentina was under military rule at the time, and armed soldiers appeared to be everywhere. There seemed to be many more military personnel than civilian passengers at airports. I was travelling with a bit of discomfort because I had seriously damaged ligaments in my left knee playing football. It was still very swollen, and I was unable to walk on the leg very freely.

Well, after a night's stay in Comodoro Rivadavia, we took a domestic flight to an even more hellish place in Argentina called Rio Gallegos. I must say that after seeing these two cities of the Republic of Argentina, I knew the Argentines had nothing better to offer us than we Falkland Islanders already had. We stayed a night in Gallegos, where, by chance, we happened to bump into a Falkland Islander in a local supermarket.

Our trip from hell on earth to Punta Arenas was by bus, which took us some ten hours or so on what seemed like an endless long and winding gravel road, with nothing to see but the flat pampas. The only thing that caught my attention during the whole trip was the ostriches. These huge birds seemed to be running around freely in the abundant wide-open countryside, and they also appeared to be moving faster than the bus we were travelling on.

If the boredom was not bad enough, what was making matters worse, I had got myself into a bad frame of mind as I felt sure that at the Argentine border post we were certain to get some trouble or bullshit from the Argentine border guards because of our Falkland Island passports. Sure enough, I was not disappointed. But the first thing I had to do, when we arrived at the border was to find the nearest toilet. When I did find it, I wished I hadn't. It was a tin shelter with a hole in the ground. Many who had used the site previously had missed the hole, and there was filth all over the place. The stench was appalling. I was in and out of that place as fast as possible.

When it was our turn to hand over our documents, a tall man looked at me and said, 'Malvinas.'

I replied, 'Falkland Islands.'

He angrily shouted 'NO, NO. Las Malvinas, Las Malvinas es Argentina's' or something like that.

'No, Falkland Islands,' I said.

Melody touched me on the arm, and said, 'Don't antagonise him Terry. We have a wedding to go to.'

'Okay.' I then turned to the border guard and said, 'I don't speak Spanish.'

After a bit more of his blabbering, he finally said it was all right to go back on board the bus.

We got to Punta Arenas late in the evening, very tired. But all our troubles were soon forgotten when we were introduced to the couple who were going to be our host and hostess during our ten-day stay. They didn't speak a word of English, we didn't speak a word of useful Spanish, but we got along just fine, even if meal times and other occasions were a little bit comical as we tried to communicate with each other, one word at a time, as we flicked through the pages of a pocket Spanish/English dictionary.

The wedding went off well, and there were plenty of parties and feastings. However, our host came running home one morning in a state of anxiety, and tried to explain something to us. We did not have a clue at first what the hell he was on about, but after half an hour of hand signals and frantic and sometimes hilarious body language, plus searching for words in the Spanish/English dictionary, it became clear that he was trying to tell us the Argentines might attack the city with fighter planes and bombers. Therefore, if we heard the air raid alarms, we were to go to a certain place to shelter. Bloody wonderful, I thought to myself, my brother asked me to be a witness for his wedding, not to witness a goddamn war between Argentina and Chile. Our plans had been to stay for a short break, but the news of potential conflict meant we had only one decision to make, and that was to get out of this troubled area as fast as possible, and go home.

Having discussed the matter with Alec, Melody and I packed our bags and took the Penguin bus service, in reverse order, from Rio Gallegos. It was very noticeable as we approached the border on the Chilean side that they had moved their ground troops right up to it.

Once we had travelled across an area of about 400 metres of open land, I suppose a 'no-man's-land' between the two countries, we reached the Argentine border. The Argentines had also positioned hundreds, perhaps thousands, of ground forces up to their boundary, supported with some artillery and tanks. The opposing forces were as good as eyeball-to-eyeball, with weapons no doubt cocked and ready to fire, as soon as the order was given.

We got home safely, two days later, to learn that the tension between the two countries had intensified and that they had closed the borders. We were out just in time. For what it is worth, the two sides later cooled down and backed their troops off, and combat was averted. It had been a close call, the two South American neighbours had got very hot-tempered with each other. It also made me aware how much Argentina was spoiling for a fight with someone.

I had no idea at the time that just four years later it would be with us, and they would be launching their fighter and bomber aircraft from that bloody miserable hell-hole of a place, Rio Gallegos, to cause so much death and destruction on British troops and Falkland Islanders, in the seas and on the land, in and around the Falkland Islands.

No doubt that tall bugger who had given me so much grief about the Falklands being the 'Las Malvinas', on the Argentine border, took some part in the war. He needed to be taught a serious lesson about the fact of ownership of the Falklands, because he wouldn't listen to me. I wonder what he thinks now? Perhaps it even took his life.

I had started to get seriously interested in music; I had had no music lessons, music was not taught in school in my time, but I was full of enthusiasm, and I enjoyed exercising my lungs as I sang away. I quickly learnt the words and timing of all the big hits of the day.

I had my first go as lead singer in a local band, called The Hallucinations. Clemmy was on rhythm guitar and Terence 'Nobby' Clarke, the guy who had taken my place as an apprentice chippy, was on the drums. We managed to get a few gigs, playing as second string to the only other group in the Islands, Preamble Spectrum. They were in great demand, and had even developed a fan base. We were just a few kids having a go, but even then I wanted to be part of the best band in town.

I would get a little envious when I heard the girls talking about what a lovely singer Barry or Bob was, and how they turned them on. I wanted to be the man up on the stage that the girls got excited about. I really fancied myself as a bit of a showman. It is the front man in any band who always gets the attention of fans and gets the crowd going.

Late in 1969, my chance came. Barry Lowe had left the Islands, and Bob Gilson was going. Preamble Spectrum needed a lead vocalist. At first, I was doubtful about being selected, but Clemmy was sure that I was the man to take up the microphone, and after some kind of audition, I was accepted. I have to admit, I loved every moment I was onstage. I know this might appear terribly egoistic, but it was just made for me. I was in a world of my own, as I sang out the words of songs that people enjoyed and danced away to.

The band became so busy, we would be playing at several functions a week, and when we weren't playing, we would be practising and learning new songs to build up a very large repertoire. I should point out that we were not professional, although an old friend told me once that the only difference between professional and non-professional is that one declares some of their earnings, the other doesn't declare any. Nevertheless, we were not doing it for a living, it was a hobby, a pastime. Alas, as is always the case in music, after a while you get a little tired of doing the same old thing over and over, which results in the whole thing becoming boring, and arguments start to creep into practice sessions, etc.

Preamble Spectrum eventually split, and five of us formed a new band, which we called Since. Peter King, Ray Robson, James Lee,

Gerard McKay and me. Even though there were no session musicians, no wind section and no orchestra, nor musical director or arranger down the road, and very limited recording facilities, with no professional recording engineer to help build the sound you imagined, I still wanted to have a go at writing lyrics, trying out my own tunes and making my own sounds.

It was extremely frustrating, trying to explain to someone what type of melody you had in mind for the lyrics of a song you had just written, when you lacked the ability to play a musical instrument or write a single note of music. One guy, however, Ray Robson, was wonderful at this period; he would listen to me ever so patiently, for hours upon hours, as I tried to explain my lyrics whilst humming the melody. Eventually, I would write, and he would slap something out on his six-string electric guitar which provided the musical interpretation of my inspirations. The rest of the boys in Since warmed to the idea of making our own music. Many people in the community did not like what they heard at first, when we played out our new songs to live audiences at various public gatherings – not so much because it was poor material, probably because it was new, previously unheard music, and it would take the public a bit of time to get used to it.

This was Stanley, not London, so the only time they would hear our music was when we were playing it live. You could not cut a disc in the Falklands, or get much radio coverage. So our works would rarely be played, if ever played at all, over local radio. Over a two-year period, I suppose we wrote many songs, but the band only really had moderate success with one or two of our own numbers. One song in particular stuck with the public. It was called 'Women' – not the John Lennon one, that came years later – but I did not write the lyrics.

After a while I split with the band, and it was then I decided to teach myself how to play guitar. I did, over many years, and I am so sorry for, and extremely grateful to, those people, who had to endure the awful noise, as I started out strumming E and F, or C and G, hour after hour, and day after day – especially two wonderfully understanding landladies, May Binnie and Hazel Bonner, who not only put up with the din, but also made sure I ate.

During the 1970s and in the beginning of the '80s I sang with all the bands, the last being Agatha Christie, which I founded during a one-off show. Patrick Watts stuck his head around the curtain and said, 'You're on next, Terry. How shall I introduce you? What is the band's name?' Without thinking I said, Agatha Christie. Later, another formation of the band changed the spelling of the name to Khristie.

But I have to admit that although I have had great times with these bands, I have never fulfilled all my dreams with my own music. I continued to write lyrics and sing and played guitar well enough to lay out a basic melody.

In 1983 I wrote the song called 255 – the lyrics are in this book, and they are self-explanatory. In 1992, I recorded a version of it at East Coast studios in London, to commemorate the tenth anniversary of the battle for the Falklands and to raise money from the sales of the record to contribute towards a fund for the British victims of the war. Although I had some genuine help, still no one completely understood the music, nor what it was I was trying to do with the commercial plan. So the project failed then.

However, I am not deterred. If anything, I am more determined to achieve my aims to record my music. Remember the 18-year-old boy who wanted so badly to win the major darts prize in darts 35 years ago? Well, he still has the same fighting spirit and one day finally hopes to succeed in realising this particular dream.

13

1980s and the Falkland Islands Company

So the sixties, and suddenly, the seventies have now expired, and it is the years of the eighties that start to unfold. I have been working for the Falkland Islands Company for three years, mainly as a stevedore. I am enjoying my employment and, for an unskilled employee, I am now earning the best money I could in the Islands.

The Falkland Islands Company has had many critics in the Islands over its history of commercial activity, not because it dominated the private sector, but because it monopolised it. This monopoly had not been fought for by the company itself, they had in fact gained it by purchasing the Falkland Island landmass, which was owned by the English businessman Samuel Fisher Lafone.

Mr Lafone had bought some land in the Islands in 1844, with the objective of establishing a farm, presumably to raise cattle. For reasons best known only to the British Crown, Mr Lafone was also granted 200 leagues of camp land (a league is 3 miles), also presumably signed and sealed by the Crown's representative on the Islands, at the time, Governor Moody.

One might assume that it was the acquisition of all this land which attracted the Falkland Islands Company to the Islands in the first place. But in all probability, it was part and parcel of the Company receiving a Royal Charter from Queen Victoria in 1852 to develop the Falklands. Whatever the reasoning, it meant that the Falkland Islands Company owned a huge part of the Islands land area, which included everything south of the Choiseul Sound on East Falkland, and contained most of the best grazing country.

What an incredible stroke of luck for the Company then, when Governor Moody's successor, Governor Thomas Moore, decided somewhere around 1855 that sheep farming, for the production of wool, was the way forward, as opposed to cattle ranching.

Thus as wool became the Islands' only raw material production, and wool prices soared due to world demand, the Falkland Islands

Company became very powerful within the Islands – not just commercially, but also politically. Because they held so much land, they were unrivalled in sheep breeding and wool production. This power base enabled them to monopolise everything. They took control of the only commercial shipping link to and from the Islands, which meant more profits and more power. Anyone who wanted anything to be shipped in, and out, of the Islands, had to do it via the FIC.

They also controlled the Islands' internal shipping links and owned and operated the largest retail outlet. So not only did FIC control the transport that fetched goods to the Islands, they set the freight tariffs, and by owning the largest and best-stocked retail outlet, they were the biggest consumer provider, setting consumer prices. I am not just talking about foodstuffs when I talk about consumables, I mean everything one needed to live and maintain life on the Islands. This also generated still further profits, and just to cap it off, because they controlled so many things, they were one of the largest employers, which they fully exploited. I think you understand by now what I meant when I said they monopolised the private sector. They *were* the private sector, for Christ sake.

Nevertheless, I was to have 11 very enjoyable and rewarding years with the FIC. Perhaps that was all down to attitude. I respected them, but in return, I expected them to respect me. Even when I started work for them in 1977, painting their warehouse roof in the company colour of Buckingham green, I would look towards the office block, and say to myself, 'I will work in there one day, I will have a manager's job one day.'

Now that was attitude. To get a manager's job in the FIC would be a major achievement. Very few Islanders had achieved that. No one had any capital of his or her own to branch out, and if he or she wanted to, what the hell would you do anyway – the FIC had everything stitched up. Okay, there were a few extraordinary exceptions to the rules, people I held in the greatest respect, who inspired me and who I wanted to emulate, but in the meantime I needed to learn, and the FIC management network would be a great place to start learning. There were no facilities in the Falklands for commercial studies in those days.

When we Falkland Islanders are ready to really start believing in ourselves, we should formulate a list and boldly display it, with the names of the greatest Falkland Island entrepreneurs. People who built a successful business from nothing, or from sheer inspiration, and as a consequence, contributed so much to improving the standard of living and way of life for fellow Islanders. A hall of fame, if you like.

The Chamber of Commerce building in Stanley would surely be the appropriate place to honour such people, and when we get around to it, the list in my opinion, would have to include: Les Hardy (arguably the greatest of them all), Des Peck, Des King, Don Ross, Jimmy and Freda Alazia, Peter and Emily Short, Joan and Horace (Nap) Bound, Terry Binnie, John Rowlands and Ernest Barnes.

These names are obvious, but there are others who must be strong candidates as people who have changed the face of our only industry at the time, wool. I refer to Peter Goss, Keith Heathmann and Trevor Browning, the pioneers of the Contract Shearing Gangs at the beginning of the 1970s. Their imagination changed labour relations and introduced a much more efficient method for conducting the labour practices of the industry. However, what strikes me, after 170 years of commerce in the Falkland Islands, is that the names of native Islanders on the list will be alarmingly few, all because of those years of monopolisation. Thankfully there is a new generation of business people in the Islands today, who I am sure will make a justifiable claim into the private sector hall of fame in the future. I sincerely hope so, and as each name is added to the list, I will proudly toast them.

I drifted off again, didn't I? After three years with the jetty gang, I made my move from stevedore to office worker in 1980. I was well short of the manager's job and management material, but I was on my way. At this stage in my life, I was on top of the world. I was secure and happy at work, happily married, with two wonderful and healthy children, and we now lived in our own home for the first time – our first real tangible asset. Things were indeed looking up.

Melody and I knew we would never have owned 6a Pioneer Row, if it had not been for Harry Milne, the Stanley manager, who pushed the directors in the London office to break with in-house rules and provide me with the £9,000 I needed to purchase the property. As a result of Harry's actions, I made up my mind that there was only one way to repay him for his amazing support.

That was to become someone he could be proud of, not simply a forever grateful and grovelling employee.

By now I was also very involved in the trade union. Being a blue-collar daytime worker, whilst negotiating working and pay conditions for the employees of my own employers and of the Falkland Islands Government, as well as the agricultural workers, was a tremendous learning curve, and a very exciting challenge. But I never once found it too daunting because I made a simple promise to myself, a golden rule if you like, never to allow myself to be bought, and never to sell my soul for anyone or anything, and to be honest, unselfish, open-minded but firm.

During this time in my life, I was always aware that some, perhaps even many, in the tiny community, found the concept of me being able to do all these jobs at the same time, as incomprehensible and not possible. I knew I was treading where no man had gone before, and it was an exhilarating feeling.

Just prior to the Falklands War in 1982, I spent time as a member of the company's shipping agency team. It was a strange period in the Falklands; the Islands were basically bankrupt, the only industry, wool, was no longer paying its way, wool prices were plummeting, and each year they got progressively worse.

The economic stagnation and lack of opportunity because of it, along with the very unstable political situation in the Islands, had driven the Falklands population into decline, and in the census of 1980 it showed very alarmingly that the Islands' population was a mere 1,813 inhabitants, the lowest since 1891. We had, regrettably, become for the first time in our history, a 'Grant and Aid' far-flung Colony. Therefore, working for the FIC was as good as it got, and the Company was actually making very healthy profits from its Stanley operations. The shipping agency was very busy working for the Eastern-bloc fishing fleets.

Actually, the plight of the economy was totally unnecessary, because although the Falkland Islands had huge fish reserves, the fishery remained uncontrolled for several years. Therefore, the Government was not deriving any meaningful revenue from the hundreds of fishing vessels from Poland, Russia and East Germany. These fleets were gleefully hoovering up our fish stocks without paying any licence fee to the Falkland Islands Government, all because the Conservative Government of the United Kingdom, led by a certain Margaret Thatcher, had ignored the expert advice of the Labour Party peer, Lord Shackleton, who had informed both the UK and Falklands Governments that fishing could be a very useful source of revenue in his economic report of 1976, and in a following report in 1982.

Well, if the Falklands Government were happy just to collect revenue from harbour dues out of this uncontrolled fishery, it was proving to be a very good source of revenue for the Falkland Island Company, which charged a flat agency fee for the first four days of a port call, plus an additional sum for each day thereafter. The company also provided launch services for the fishing fleets and the Falkland Islands Customs Department. Cash advances, repatriations, mailbox and postal services were all provided for, at the appropriate fee, plus 5% commission.

On a personal front, it was a very rewarding job. At times, you were like a district nurse, postman and errand boy. You also needed to be very patient, a good listener and more than prepared to work all hours of the day and night. On many occasions, I would receive a call from Customs at two or three in the morning, requesting me to arrange a launch so a doctor could be transported out to a ship, or to bring an injured seaman into the hospital for urgent medical treatment.

By the beginning of 1982 I knew I was on top of my game. I would be made warmly welcome the minute I had climbed up the pilot's ladder and put foot on the ship's deck. All the ships' captains called me by first name, Mr Terry. There was one problem; I was always struggling to get away from a meal or a bottle or two of Polish or Russian vodka as the guest of a very friendly captain. Because there were so many ships to attend to, I was starting to find that I was spending more time on board the fishing fleets in port than in the office or at home.

The small launch crew would enjoy themselves doing a little bit of trading with the crews, buying good working gear for greenback dollars as they waited for me and a Customs officer to reappear from a captain's cabin, sometimes with a little gift, to head back to the city.

Then on 2 April 1982, everything dramatically changed in the Falklands. It was never going to be the same again. In some ways that was a good thing. As we now all know, the leader of the

Argentine military junta, Leopoldo Galtieri, ordered his forces to invade the Falkland Islands, for what he called 'the recovery of Las Malvinas'.

Oddly enough, and certainly without overdoing it, Falkland Islanders might take some time out every now and then, and thank Leopoldo Galtieri for his woeful folly.

Have I gone off my rocker? Certainly not. Remember, if he had not been so bloody stupid, we would have all been fucked. The Islands were financially hamstrung, the begging bowl was out, and the British Government was, or already had, lost interest in us. The combination of these, and other factors, meant it would only be a matter of time before we were finally abandoned by the United Kingdom Government anyway, and then we would all have been citizens of the Republic of Argentina and, no doubt, abandoned by them also.

Well come on, they do not live in the southern part of their own country, it is too inclement for them, also, the Argentines can never seem to get their own finances sorted out, and as a consequence, they never have enough money to support themselves on the South American mainland, let alone a new small island colony.

I choose the word 'colony' very carefully, because that's what we would surely have been. So with that very sobering thought, that is why I would like to offer my sincere thanks to the former leader of the Argentine Republic; and whilst his passing from planet earth brought no tears from Falkland Islanders, they should never forget that his mistake was part of our saviour.

14

Why War?
(A Falkland Islander's viewpoint)

The Government of the United Kingdom never officially declared war on Argentina in 1982, therefore on a technicality the British Government refer to the armed struggle in the Falkland Islands as 'The Falklands Conflict'. Believe me, from where I was in the Falkland Islands at any time from 2 April to 14 June 1982, along with the lasting impressions of being bombed and shot at, diving into holes in the ground for cover, swooped on by hostile fighter aircraft, the bomb craters, destroyed and shrapnel-peppered houses and other buildings, gun emplacements and the streets of Stanley and its surrounding areas littered with military hardware and other materials, the incarceration of civilians in some of the camp settlements, which are now littered with mine fields from the aftermath of those events, it seemed very much like war to me and my fellow Islanders.

I will admit, what was to unfold in the early hours of 2 April 1982, as the military activities of invasion were played out around the streets of Stanley, all seemed to be a comfortable near miss away. A fortnight earlier, all the attention was focussed on South Georgia. But as the first automatic rifle fire rang out and the mortar bombs and hand grenades started to explode, the belief, and fear, that one day the Argentines would take the Falklands by military force, had become a terrifying reality.

To be fair, Islanders thought it would happen simply by the British Government continuing to lose interest in these far-flung islands, and eventually through negotiation stitch up a deal with the Argentine Government whereby it was all theirs, just allowing them time to take out their handful of Royal Marines and pull down the Union Flag in a dignified manner.

Why? Well although we Falkland Islanders had always been extremely loyal to the British Crown and the people of the British

Isles, over a period of time, especially from 1966 to the date of the invasion, most of us had developed a great mistrust for successive United Kingdom Governments regarding their position on the sovereignty dispute with Argentina over our homeland. Islanders seemed to accept as a matter of fact that one day the British would pull out.

Naturally, my tale of the Falklands War must be read as a very personal story; other Islanders may have experienced a very different situation to mine during the invasion, occupation and liberation of the Falklands.

By the time Britain had decided to evict the Argentines and be in a position to land their own forces on the Falklands, to complete a truly remarkable victory, few native Islanders were left – not more than 400 perhaps. We were also scattered far and wide, therefore there were very few people alive who can even tell of their own experience of the whole affair. Although many people remained in the Falklands capital, Stanley, tiny communities would experience war and its fall-out in varying degrees at such places as Goose Green, Fox Bay, Port Howard, Pebble Island, San Carlos, Teal Inlet, Fitzroy, Estencia or Green Patch. As a result all have their unique stories to tell. Others, remarkably and fortunately, witnessed little or nothing of the horrors of the war at all because of their extremely isolated locations.

I must also say that my overall views on the politics of this whole subject are likely to differ from the majority of islanders' opinions. I am comfortable with that. However, I believe this war story cannot be told without first giving you some background to the build-up of the war and perhaps as to why it might actually have happened. An Islander view, probably not very well known, mainly because we have not fallen over ourselves to write about the encounter. Therefore I grasp this opportunity with a sense of eagerness.

Few people in the United Kingdom, let alone other parts of the globe, knew where the Falkland Islands were before 1982. Even fewer knew anything about the Islands, and still fewer cared anyway. However, that was not the case with the people of Argentina. Nearly the entire population of the Argentine Republic has had it drummed into them from the earliest possible age, not only as to where the Falklands ('Las Malvinas' to them) were but that they also belonged to them; they had been stolen from them by the British, and one day they would take them back.

We Islanders, on the other hand, had only known British rule. English was our native tongue, very few people spoke Spanish, and those that did had gone to the British School in Uruguay, or Argentina, after the 1971 communications agreement, or had met a Spanish-speaking partner somewhere. We were taught English history in our schools and, until 1971, we had never had any direct contact with Argentina. As the most obedient of colonials, we sang 'God save the King/Queen' and therefore never considered any other rightful owner than Her Majesty's Government.

Argentina and the United Kingdom have disputed sovereignty, with varying degrees of vigour, on and off for the last 175 years or so, and unfortunately, despite the war, nothing has been conclusively resolved. By this I mean Argentina still asserts its claim to our Islands, a situation that bothers me greatly for the long-term peace and stability of future Islander generations.

In my opinion Argentina has always based its claim on a very chequered and shaky piece of historical activity up to 1833. Thus, many experts on the subject of the Falkland Islands pre-1833 have become frustrated and confused whilst grappling over the barest threads of evidence in an attempt to make sense of it all. Whatever the Argentine arguments, I shall repeat: it is the British who have administered the Islands uninterrupted from 1833 until today, obviously with the exception of the 74 days during 1982 (indisputable).

There is, however, one issue which I must highlight again: at the time of resettling the Falkland Islands in 1833, they had no indigenous population, not one Argentine or Spaniard. Furthermore, since then, and until today, several Falkland Island families have known no other home, they have worked and lived on the Islands for many generations, and our forefathers produced the first truly native Islander. Because of these simple facts, I am inclined to think that it is time to seriously consider the possibility that perhaps the Falklands belongs to none other than the Falkland Islanders themselves, and all three parties, Britain, Argentina and the Falkland Islanders, should be spending much more time, thought and effort on realising this goal, which might just be a win, win, win situation for all.

However, irrespective of Argentina's continuous screams of foul play and the Falkland Islanders' unequivocal loyalty to the United

Kingdom, up to the events of 1982, it was always the British Government who held all the cards. It would be they who would decide if the Falklands would remain theirs, or if they would hand them over to Argentina, a fact that troubled Falkland Islanders greatly, mainly because until after the 1982 war, we had no safety net, we had no right of abode in the United Kingdom, and if the British made any decision to offload us, we would almost certainly be forced to accept Argentina's administration and nationality, all very much against our will. There was also the distinct possibility that once the Argentines had gained control of the Islands they would punish us for our undivided devotion to the British.

As a 31-year-old at the time, it seemed to me that for a 16-year period prior to the Argentine invasion, we Falkland Islanders, with considerable help and support from the Falkland Islands lobby group inside the United Kingdom, had fought a gallant but uphill battle against successive British Governments not to cede sovereignty of the Falkland Islands to the Argentines. Britain's continued wavering on the sovereignty issue had the effect of indicating to the Argentines that the British had an increasing lack of commitment to retaining the Falklands. Which, in turn, eventually led to a desperate Argentine military junta believing that if the Falklands could not be taken at the negotiating table, they would take the Islands by force.

This, the Argentines believed, would result in nothing more than several sessions of vigorous finger-wagging, along with written and verbal protests from the British Government at the United Nations. The Argentine Government also knew that by taking the Falklands when they did, it would have the enormous benefit of distracting their riotous populace at home from the mounting economic difficulties and their regular demonstrations in the streets against the Government's indiscriminate killings of civilians in the country – a campaign that was to be called 'The Dirty War'. Just two more reasons why we Falkland Islanders had no desire to be any part of Argentina.

We had had good and reliable transport links with Uruguay and Chile for many years, which made us independent of Argentina, to their annoyance and frustration. The British, and I suppose, the Argentines, knew that forging these lifelines with Argentina would introduce a self-imposed dependence on Argentina for vital daily needs, advanced education, emergency medical services, and cultural, sporting and social activities. Both were also aware that important infrastructure to augment these services would need to be built on the Islands, which would require Argentine nationals being allowed to move freely in and out of the Falklands to live and work (not the case before). This freedom would produce a deadly double-edged sword for us Islanders.

One was the creation of total dependence on Argentina, the other was the neat little trick to create a process of integration and seduction, which would result in amorous relationships leading to marriages and children. Add in the spice of many new cultural activities, and the cocktail is complete for breaking down Islanders' resistance and mistrust of the Argentines. Also whilst this courtship was going on, the United Kingdom Government would be able to make its planned withdrawal with the minimum of fuss, perhaps even without anyone noticing.

The first time I had taken any notice of the Argentine claim was back in 1964, when an Anglo-Argentine called Fitzgerald landed his single-engine light aircraft on the Stanley racecourse, where he promptly planted his Argentine flag and delivered a statement to the Governor of the Islands (Arrow-Smith) and then buggered off again.

The most exciting part of the whole fiasco for me at the time was watching the plane fly over our house on a couple of occasions, a rare and enjoyable spectacle indeed. Aircraft were few and far between in the Islands.

The next Argentine political activist stunt to take place in the Islands would be a far more dramatic event. In fact, it was in itself an act of terrorism. I would learn about it from reading a UK daily newspaper sitting in the mess room of the British Antarctic research ship the RRS *Shackleton*, which was in port in Southampton. It was 28 September 1966. I was amazed to read that an armed group of extremists, headed by a Mr Dardo Cabo and his 17 young members of the Condor group, had hijacked a scheduled DC-4 domestic flight from Buenos Aires to Rio Gallegos and forced the pilot to alter course for the Falkland Islands and land the plane on the Stanley racecourse, a considerable feat of pilot skill, given the confined space (even if he did bog the plane down in the process).

The 18 militants, which included a female blonde beauty, quickly took some inquisitive Islanders and others (including the police chief) as hostages. They raised several Argentine flags in the vicinity of the plane and, like Fitzgerald before them, handed the Falklands Governor (this time a chap called Haskard) a statement, which apparently contained a wish list. The aircraft was quickly surrounded by members of the Royal Marines and the local Defence Force (Territorial Army), which resulted in a 36-hour stand-off. However, after a few cold nights and a total lack of response from the Islands' authorities to any of the Argentines' demands, plus some gentle and influential persuasion from a representative of the Catholic faith, who also managed to smuggle the somewhat embarrassed police chief out of captivity by hiding him under his robes as he walked away from the plane after one period of negotiations, the Argentines voluntarily surrendered.

Following a short period of confinement in a section of the property belonging to the Roman Catholic Church, St Mary's, they were duly evicted from the Islands and shipped off on the Argentine vessel the *Bahia Buen Suceso*. Surprisingly, they did not return home to a warm welcome. Instead, they were tried and sentenced by a federal judge in Ushuaia. However, their exploits had brought them considerable success in terms of media coverage both at home and back in England.

It is understood that neither the Fitzgerald nor the Condor group's adventures had any Argentine Government support, at least not on the surface. But in parallel to these events the Argentine Government had started to flex its political muscle once again on the sovereignty issue, which had been dormant for many years. This time, the activity was taking place at the United Nations, where Argentina had decided to latch onto a resolution that had been passed four years before Fitzgerald's flight of fantasy. This was resolution 1514 (15) of 1960, which simply put stated 'that all colonisation should be put to an end in all its forms'.

The Argentines claimed that this resolution was applicable to the Falklands. The C24 Committee noted the existence of a sovereignty dispute between the Argentine and the Government of Great Britain and Northern Ireland and recommended peaceful negotiations between both parties to resolve the problem, with the caveat that whilst reaching a solution, the *interests* of the Islands population had to be 'taken into account'. The resolution was basically a halfway-house stance to the positions held by the British, who had been pushing for our *desires* to be taken into account, whilst the Argentines had been claiming that we had artificially been implanted by a colonial power, Great Britain, in the Falkland Islands, therefore we Islanders were not a people and our aspirations should not be considered at all.

The political sands started to shift for Falkland Islanders in the United Nations in 1965 when the C24 report was ratified by the full committee and presented to the General Assembly, where it was approved by a vote of 87–0. Amazingly, Great Britain abstained. They had settled for our interests to be taken into account only, not our wishes. The local view on this was that it was the thin edge of the wedge and Britain was starting to prepare itself to cede sovereignty to the Argentines. Further meetings between the representatives of the British and Argentine Governments in the sixties only increased Islanders' fears.

By 1968 we Falkland Islanders were on tenterhooks. Trust in the UK Government was evaporating rapidly, and an Argentine takeover was starting to look like a very worrying possibility. In November, bloody Fitzgerald poked his nose into matters once more by flying another aeroplane into the Islands, this time not alone, but with the editor of a respected Argentine newspaper and another journalist. However, he failed to land his plane on the racecourse and had to settle for a narrow strip of rocky road, called Eliza Cove, which he did not navigate very well and he ended up in a ditch on the side. This time there was no quick getaway, no planting of flags. He and his buddies were unceremoniously shipped out on the Royal Navy vessel HMS *Endurance*, which was also carrying Lord Chalfont, the British Foreign Secretary, who was also leaving the Falklands after receiving a political battering from Falkland Islanders. Ironically the purpose of Fitzgerald's uninvited visit was to disrupt Chalfont's. He needn't have bothered. Falkland Islanders saw to that. His plane was dismantled and shipped away, but many interior fittings would end up in Islanders' homes as spoils of a failed bloodless coup. (I'm joking.)

Lord Chalfont had turned up in the Islands to push the Wilson Government's 'memorandum of understanding' with Argentina, which basically accepted Argentine sovereignty of the Falkland Islands providing our interests could be safeguarded. However, Chalfont's motives had been rumbled by the newly formed and effective Falkland Islands Committee. This lobby group, which was based in the UK, was established by Bill Hunter-Christie, a Falklands-caring English barrister and formerly of the Foreign Office. The group advised their Falklands counterparts of Chalfont's intentions, and a mass rally was organised on Arch Green. Placards with the likes of 'Keep the Falklands British' and 'No Sovereignty sell out' were brandished. There were also plenty of anti-Argentine slogans, and a very firm 'Get stuffed' message was rammed down the throat of the Foreign Secretary.

Simultaneously, back in the UK the Falkland Islands Committee lobbied very successfully and the Wilson Government beat a retreat. But the stage had been set for a political battle of wits and various games of cat and mouse between Islanders, the UK and Argentine Governments, until the Argentines' patience snapped and they invaded.

If we Islanders had been successful in 1968, which I suppose we had, it is generally agreed that in 1971 we suffered a most telling blow. Actually, I think we had been more mugged. This might just have been the single most important issue that would lead to the Argentine Government's misinterpretation, or perhaps, clear understanding, of the British Government's medium-term intentions on the sovereignty issue of the Falklands.

It was in July of 1971 that the British and Argentine Governments released a joint declaration, called 'the communications agreement', which recognised each side's sovereignty claim. The hammer blow for us was that Argentina would be allowed to introduce and operate air links with the Islands, which would provide for other essential services. We were told we had nothing to worry about, Britain would maintain a sea link with the Islands, and because of the new agreement we would be able to visit Argentina free of any possibility of being called up for military service. We would also have the benefits of a better standard of education by attending British schools in Argentina, there would be improved medical services, easier access in and out of the Islands etc., etc. Whilst all this might have been true, we were neither convinced nor fooled, and it wasn't long before the British Government reneged on the shipping link, which then meant we became further dependent on the Argentines, who only too gladly filled that vital service also.

Another thing that really pissed Falkland Islanders off was that we would be issued with, and required by the Argentine and British Governments to carry, 'the white card', a miniature identity document, which would effectively replace our own Falkland Island passports, whilst travelling in and around Argentina.

Another result of the political instability, which would continue during the 'black years' from 1966 to 1982, was that many of the most naturally talented and skilful inhabitants left the Islands to escape the prospect of becoming Argentines. Few have ever returned to the Islands to resettle. Most emigrated to the United Kingdom and New Zealand, but, like the Scots, a Falkland Islander can be found in every nook and cranny of the globe.

This migration period was the reason for the decline in population figures from the 1960s to 1982. In fact, by the time of the Argentine invasion, the Falkland Islands population had dropped to the lowest figure since 1891, just 1,813 people. Furthermore, just as we anticipated, the Argentines took full advantage of the communication agreement and established footholds in Stanley very quickly. We noted that every piece of infrastructure to support their services to the Islands had an appearance of permanency.

The Argentines also flooded the Islands with their nationals as tourists on ships and by the weekly airline connection, which was pretty soon increased to two flights a week. Oddly enough, many Argentines came to the Falklands in those early days of free access to buy British goods; many more came to catch a glimpse, and put foot on what was previously considered to be 'the forbidden fruit'.

However, once seen, few, if any, were interested in living in the Falkland Islands – it was too cold for them.

The year 1973 epitomised the confusing signals we received about our political future. Firstly, in April the British Government refused to negotiate with Argentina on the question of sovereignty, arguing that it could not give up the Islands without our consent, and as a result talks practically stopped. Then in December the General Assembly of the United Nations passed another Revolution, 3160, which was once again more helpful to the Argentines, than the British or, of course, ourselves. This time they expressed grave concern at the lack of progress on the sovereignty issue and urged the two governments to renew negotiations.

In between these significant political events and at a time when we had been pushed into dependence on Argentina via the communications agreement, Britain took another decision that would leave us once again feeling betrayed and abandoned, pushed still further into the arms of the 'big bad wolf'.

As I have mentioned, under the communications agreement Britain had agreed to maintain a shipping link with the Falklands, but when the old trusted and popular regular shipping link with Uruguay was terminated, when the Falkland Islands Company withdrew the loss-making Royal Mail Ship *Darwin*, the British Government typically failed to honour their pledge on the basis of costs. The Argentines gleefully offered to fill the void, leaving us with no option but to accept.

The loss of the link with Uruguay was a double blow. It had stripped away our last thread of independence from Argentina, and many Islanders had made good friends with the Uruguayans through trade, and especially in the bars and clubs of Montevideo, where the ship's crew of the RMS *Darwin* and many before her had become very welcome guests on many a joyous evening. But just as importantly, there was the loss of employment factor; upwards of 20 Islanders worked on the *Darwin*. This represented a high percentage of the Islands' labour force.

In the following year, 1974, we had a remarkably lucky escape, I suppose as a result of UN Resolution 3160. Edward Heath, still leading the Government of the United Kingdom, suggested to the Argentines the possibility of shared sovereignty or condominium. We as usual had not been consulted, and when we first heard the news via our trusted friends the Falkland Islands Committee back in London, we were naturally gutted. But amazingly, the Argentines rejected the idea. Why on earth they did, we will never know. Perhaps they had become overconfident, believing it was now just a matter of time before the British would cave in altogether on the sovereignty matter.

Even more unexpectedly, the actions of the Argentines actually hardened the British Government's attitude for a short while, and as a result we felt, for the first time for some time, that the British were back on our side. They sent a group headed by the well-respected Lord Shackleton to the Falklands in October 1975 to analyse and report on the possibility of exploiting the natural resources of the Islands to provide economic development and security.

This was all wonderful music to our ears, but it displeased Argentina's President, Isabel Peron, immensely. She got really shitty knickers, and in the January of 1976, she withdrew her ambassador from London in protest at the Shackleton mission and the British attitude on the question of sovereignty. Edward Heath, in turn, pulled the British Ambassador out of Buenos Aires. Argentina eventually lost its patience, and showed its true colours later in the year when the Argentine Navy firstly harassed and then fired several shots across the bows of my old ship, the RRS *Shackleton*. This action took place just 70 miles off the Falklands, with the Argentines claiming the vessel was in Argentine waters. The captain of the *Shackleton* chose to ignore repeated demands to stop his ship and receive a boarding party. Instead, he took a calculated risk and made a course for Stanley. The Argentine vessel followed, until just six miles out of the Falklands capital, it then changed course and headed back to where it came from.

The following year, 1977, the Argentine military were once again back in power in Buenos Aires, further hardening our reasoning for not wishing to become any part of the Argentine, as we surely would have been at any time the British ceded sovereignty to them. Furthermore the matter of an awful economic situation was crippling the nation. This all too common factor with Argentina naturally deters any Falkland Islander from voluntarily becoming a part of it. For a couple of years the dice seemed to be rolling in our favour, but quite amazingly, the imposition of a military government in Argentina did not secure our position with the United Kingdom Government, as we had all hoped and expected. Instead, and quite unbelievably, the Conservative Government of Great Britain, now led by Margaret Thatcher, reinstated diplomatic relations at ambassadorial level, and the Government reopened dialogue and once again began to explore solutions to put an end to the sovereignty dispute. One of these would be 'leaseback'. The thinking behind this theory was that Britain would recognise Argentine sovereignty of our homeland, and simultaneously they would lease it back for a period of time.

The British Government decided to take no action on the Shackleton findings in 1976, followed by Thatcher's Government patching things up with the Argentines in '77. It is my belief that the UK did not want to develop the Islands into economic self-sufficiency. Why do I say this? Surely it would have had the effect of buggering up any intentions they might have had of eventually getting rid of us.

In view of what happened in the Falklands War of 1982, I suppose it is all too easy for one not to care to remember that quite unbelievably, the leader of the British Conservative Government at the time of reopening talks with an Argentina military government on the question of sovereignty over the Falkland Islands was none other than the triumphant Falkland Islands War Prime Minister, Margaret Thatcher. I also find it interesting that it was also during Thatcher's Government that our loyalty to Great Britain would receive a further and most terrible body blow; in a vote to decide if Falkland Islanders should be granted British citizenship, it was denied. The result of the vote was actually a tie.

By now, a mood of despair had started to filter through the Islands community, because the result of the citizenship vote which had gone against us had come too closely on the heels of a visit to the Falklands of the Minister of State at the Foreign Office, Nicholas Ridley, who made his journey down to the Islands just over a year before the Argentine invasion (as it happens) with three little rabbits in his bag: condominium, sovereignty freeze or leaseback. All we Islanders had to do was simply choose which one we wanted. After many meetings with a wide and varied section of the community all over the Islands, Ridley himself appeared to be selling the concept of leaseback the hardest to us. We, as you can imagine, were pretty sore with anyone who represented the British Government at that time, especially as he seemed to be like too many before him, on a mission of further punishment.

Most Islanders obviously wanted a sovereignty freeze, and this message was officially confirmed by our councillors in January 1981, with the caveat that there be no further talks with Argentina on the subject of sovereignty. The majority of the people also made it clear that they wanted nothing to do with the other two options. Some, however, did show minor interest in the leaseback system, and fewer still wanted to know how long the leaseback period would be installed for. For what it is worth, I personally think if Ridley had clearly stated a time period of something like 99 years, he might have just about got away with the leaseback concept. Why? Because one thing that we Islanders had become was tired and weary of the constant pressure to talk and cede something to the Argies. That something, we knew, could only be sovereignty as far as the Argentines were concerned. (I must admit, at the time, I would have gone for that.) I am sure it would have been a close call, but we will never know.

However, Ridley appeared to many Islanders to be getting too pushy, intimating a much shorter period of leaseback – 25 years was a figure being bandied around. To be absolutely honest, I do not recall him ever stating such a figure, but the Falklands inhabitants never have any problem in starting a rumour, especially if it might have the effect of scuppering something they didn't want anyway. As he was getting towards the end of his visit he did appear to be getting irritated with the lack of positive response to his offerings.

I remember first meeting Ridley in my capacity as the vice-chairman of the Falkland Islands Trade Union. A meeting had been scheduled in the Trade Union headquarters with members of the union's committee and others. I recall that he was being constantly questioned by a well-informed and intelligent union stalwart named Fred Cheek. Ridley became tired of Fred's persistence and direct questioning and in the end appeared to lose his composure. Over time your memory can play tricks with you and I cannot recall exactly what was said, so I will not claim 100% accuracy of his words, but looking directly at Fred, he bellowed something to the effect, 'If you don't accept things, I will sell you down the river'. I was stunned by this remark, and thought to myself it was extremely fortunate for Mr Ridley that the media were not present at the meeting. Had they been, Ridley's comments would have made the headlines in both the British and Argentine press, thus he might have been put under extreme pressure to consider resignation.

Anyway, as it turned out he got himself crucified in the public meeting that followed in the Town Hall in Stanley. I vividly remember him replying to a speaker from the floor which might have been my cousin Eric Goss, who said to him something like,

'No deal, no talks', to which Ridley replied, once again showing signs of agitation, 'So on your head be it then'. I will never forget those words, they would ring in my ears several times when the Argentine armed forces were running around our Islands. Ridley would also get a hostile send-off as a large crowd gathered at the airport to demonstrate our considerable displeasure with the proposals he had to offer and the manner in which he had offered them. He most certainly left the islands with a flea in his ear.

If Mr Ridley had thought his troubles were over after his departure from the Falklands and that the Islanders' protests were a mere hiccup, he was in for an unexpected surprise when he returned to the UK, because his report to Parliament was received no better there. We in the Islands felt some degree of satisfaction as we heard via the trusty old BBC World Service that he had got another terrible slating. Some even questioned who gave him the authority to promote the leaseback concept in the first place. Interestingly, whoever this person or persons might have been, they kept their heads down and didn't volunteer to step forward.

We Islanders became even more annoyed when it became blatantly obvious that whatever Ridley had been offering to us on the leaseback concept must have been discussed with the Argentines previously and been generally acceptable to them before he came to the Falklands. When they got news of the failed effort their Foreign Minister, Camilion, conveyed the huge disappointment of the Argentine Government to his counterpart in England, Lord Carrington. I think it is fair to say, from that point on, the Argentines had decided that further dialogue with Britain on the sovereignty issue would be slow, even endless, and they then started to seriously consider the military option.

The Argentines were becoming very aggressive on the sovereignty issue, with jingoistic and highly charged statements in their principal newspapers, all part of their propaganda programme as they tried to deflect attention away from the real domestic issues: economic austerity measures and the murdering of many innocent people by the authorities. Anyone who protested against the three-man junta headed by General Galtieri did so with considerable risk to their own lives. Given these facts, it is even more incredible that the Thatcher Government might want us to accept this brutal regime, which held no regard for its people or civil rights, as our possible new government. Sometimes the British attitude was beyond all sensible comprehension.

But once again, and true to form, Britain would send out another message of encouragement to the Argentines, to the horror of the Falkland Islanders, by announcing the withdrawal of the Royal Navy ice patrol vessel HMS *Endurance* – dear old 171½ – from the South Atlantic. We in the Falklands felt this action was a clear signal that the British intended to cut back, and eventually, remove any meaningful British presence and military defence from the Islands. HMS *Endurance* and the 40 or so Royal Marines who were stationed in the Falklands, were the total sum of that presence and defence. In fact, defence was a loose term; the words used in the corridors of Whitehall were, 'a trip wire', which basically meant any attack on either *Endurance* or the Royal Marines by Argentina would be seen by Britain as an attack on the United Kingdom herself. Scant comfort for us, because we were well aware that we would be caught up in the middle of any war games played out between the two powers, as the events of 2 April 1982 would only too clearly demonstrate.

No matter how you look at it, as the year 1982 began, events started to turn nasty pretty quickly between the Argentines and Great Britain. Following the 16 years or so of political pushing and shoving, we Falkland Islanders, without doubt, had fallen between a rock and a hard place. Let's face it, we had little to no power, nor for that matter, any influence over our destiny. Then we got ourselves into financial difficulties – not I hasten to add, as a result of my Government's mismanagement of funds, but simply because of the worldwide collapse of wool prices, the result of which forced us to seek a subsidy from the United Kingdom. But it is worth remembering all this could have been resolved if the British Government had taken any notice at all of the astute Lord Shackleton's economic report of 1976, in which he appeared to put together clear directions on the potential to exploit natural resources and covered other areas such as land reform, all focussed on the purpose of making the Falkland Islands economically self-sufficient. Instead, the British Government's response to this crucial report was to ignore the advice. Can anyone explain to me and my fellow Falkland Islanders why the bloody hell that was?

The British can never use the excuse that they did not know our thinking; they knew all right because of the incredible work carried out by the Falkland Islands Committee in London, and the local branch in the Falklands. I remember four people especially, involved in the Falklands committee. Neil Watson, Joe King, Velma Malcolm and Gerald Cheek. Via them and other members, we had become politically active, making it abundantly clear to the United Kingdom Government that we had *no desire whatsoever* to become Argentines. Unbelievably, the Margaret Thatcher Government ignored us and reopened negotiations on the sovereignty issue, surely only for the purpose to eventually transfer the Islands to the Argentines. What other point was there?

Despite the fact that we had made it crystal clear to the British Government that we did not want any links with Argentina, the British Government reacted by forcing us into a communications agreement, which stripped away our independence from the Argentines, whilst making two honest, and honourable, Falkland Islands Legislative Council members appear like clowns in the process. We had been very happy with the existing sea links to Uruguay and Chile, for the very reason that it gave us independence from the Argentines. The Communications Agreement of 1971 promptly dumped us right into the palms of the Argentines and, like putty, they could play with us and shape our way of lives as they desired. One perfect example of that was when they decided to decrease the weekly flights from two to one because we had pissed them off on our stance on the sovereignty matter.

I, along with most Islanders, was pretty much unaware of the extent of the diplomatic and political shit that was flying around between Argentina and Britain during the first three months of 1982. Unless the Falkland Islands Committee got wind of things, we were kept very much in the dark. Because of this, we would all get a serious jolt on 20 March 1982, when we learnt that there was a lot of Argentine naval activity down at South Georgia. The dear old *Bahia Buen Suceso*, that's right, the same ship that took the rebel Condor group back to Argentina, after hijacking the DC-4 to the Falklands, was delivering and discharging workmen and equipment at Leith Harbour and they had hoisted the Argentine flag, all illegally, under the pretence that they were simply ashore to assist a scrap metal dealer who was working under contract for the company Salvesen's. (Salvesen's had been a principal company in the whaling industry; they were the people dad worked for during the 1937/38 whaling seasons on a staggering £16 per month, triple his potential earnings in the Falklands.)

The story we were getting in the Falklands was that the Argies had invaded, which seemed a realistic possibility to us, and although they had not apparently landed a military force, we did not know that. But we did know they had raised the Argentine flag, which in itself, to us, constituted an invasion of Falklands and British territory, because South Georgia at the time was a Falkland Islands dependency administrated by the Falkland Islands Government. I remember being at a friend's house with others the next day, and we all agreed what a lucky escape it had been for us that it was South Georgia and not the Falklands that had been invaded.

At the time we never really understood, or knew, the real goings on down south between 20 March and 2 April. South Georgia is over 800 miles away from the Falklands, a good three days' sea journey, but one thing we had noticed was that HMS *Endurance* had departed Stanley harbour on the morning of 21 March, therefore we surmised she was heading down to South Georgia to give the Argies a good 'boot up the arse', or at least we hoped so.

Another thing that we could not understand was the total lack of any hard and factual information on the South Georgia crisis. Nothing was coming out of Government House or from the Islands representatives. Given the potential gravity of the situation it was extremely worrying and annoying. We felt that we were once again being kept in the dark and not worthy of trust by the British Government. We had no idea that the British intelligence service and political leaders were in a boxing match with the Argies and they didn't know whether to punch, or put up their guard, so to speak.

A couple of days before the invasion of the Falkland Islands, the RRS *John Biscoe* arrived in Stanley from the Uruguayan capital Montevideo, carrying the new detachment of 40 Royal Marines, who were coming for what they expected to be a one-year tour. She had transported the soldiers to the Falklands because of the *Endurance*'s deployment to South Georgia. The arrival of both the ship's crew and the Royal Marines, we thought, was bound to bring us fresh and up-to-date news on the South Georgia situation; alas, we would be disappointed. They knew little, or nothing, of any substance.

15

The Day Before, and Invasion Night

In the afternoon of 1 April I got a call from my mate Pete, suggesting I meet him, with our wives, in the Globe Hotel bar for a before-supper drink. I needed no encouragement. As soon as I finished work I took a drive up the front road and past the Secretariat. As I did so, I noticed there were an unusual number of government civil servants heading towards the east driveway of Government House, but I had no idea that heads of departments had been directed by the Governor, Rex Hunt, to attend a meeting at which he would deliver notice of the harsh realities that were expected to unfold upon us in the early hours of the following morning.

I met my friend, and as we got to the corner of the Globe Hotel, one of the Royal Marines' four-ton lorries pulled up alongside us and we immediately chatted to a couple of Marines we knew. They were hanging out of the back of the truck with blackened faces and rifles in hand. I do not recall them saying anything about the Argentines coming, nor do I believe we asked them that question.

After they pulled away, we went off into the pub, which had its usual gathering of loyal locals. We had a few drinks but the girls had not arrived, so we decided to go back to Pete's house, on Racecourse Road. We were all sitting at the kitchen table chatting away and sipping our drinks, when suddenly there was a lot of activity on the racecourse nearby. One of the local aircraft landed and was parked up; fire tenders, fuel trucks, and other such items were placed round about – we assumed to stop someone using the racecourse as a landing strip. I recall thinking the whole thing was a Falkland Islands Defence Force exercise against the Royal Marines.

Suddenly, my attention was drawn to the local radio station, which had broken off rather abruptly from its regular programme to inform listeners that the Governor, Rex Hunt, would be making a very important announcement, to which we should listen.

Melody and I looked at each other. We now knew something serious was up, therefore it was decided that we should get back home and listen to what Hunt had to say in the company of my dad, who was staying with us, and Severine, who was eight years old, and Amelia, who was only four.

At approximately 8.15 p.m., Rex Hunt addressed the Islands population via the local radio station. The Falkland Islands Broadcasting Station, to give it its full title. I was alone on the settee in our kitchen. Dad was perched on a chair underneath the telephone, which was hanging on the wall directly above his head, at one end of our Rayburn peat stove, whilst Melody was sitting at the end of the dining table. We were all a little tense and extremely silent as Hunt started to deliver his speech, which started with a very bright 'good evening'. Then he appeared to ramble on about a whole lot of diplomatic activity which was taking place at the United Nations, in New York, London and Buenos Aires, which, quite frankly went over our heads. It did not mean a hell of a lot to us gathered in our tiny room. Why should it? Such matters had never been discussed with Islanders before.

I remember dad looking up at me with a worried expression on his face, then he said in a rather annoyed manner, 'For Christ's sake, Rex, get on with it.' Governor Rex Hunt did just that, finally. He advised us that the Argentine Armed Forces were heading our way and invasion was imminent; also, if Argentina did not heed the Security Council's request, which was not to resort to armed force on the Falklands dispute, he would need to declare a state of emergency.

I thought to myself, what an incredible remark for him to make, the bloody Argentines were just hours away from landing on the shores of the Falkland, yet Rex Hunt was still not yet in a position to declare a state of emergency. The Argies were going to *invade* us. What the hell was he waiting for? Instead, Rex requested that we all keep calm, stay off the streets, remain in doors and keep away from windows, he also recommended that we continue to listen to the local radio station because he would be back later in the evening to give us all a further update on the situation.

At the end of his announcement we all got up. Dad shook his head in disbelief, I suggested to Melody that we should put the kids to bed – we had put them to play in the lounge whilst the speech was on the radio; they were unaware of what was going on and we both felt we should keep it that way. Once we had got them off to sleep we all gathered together again in the kitchen and discussed the content of Rex Hunt's address. Still not 100% certain that the Argentines were going to invade, we did not make any plans for that eventuality, and even if they were going to attack the Falklands, what the hell could we do about it anyway? What did strike me, right there and then, was that despite the potential for Argentine military aggression against the Falkland Islands and its people for many years, no one in authority had made plans for a system of civil defence with useful things such as air raid shelters. I must admit I did wonder if that was now going to be a costly error of judgement, which could have terrible consequences.

I had noted Hunt's advice to stay off the streets, but I decided, to hell with it, so I popped over to the Rose Hotel bar for a quick drink, just before closing time. As I started out along the road, I remember thinking to myself, the house was the first piece of property that we had ever owned. Would it still be standing in the morning, I wondered. Even if it was, I was certain I wouldn't be owning it once the Argies took over.

When I reached the pub, there was not a single customer inside. The only person there was George Malcolm, the husband of one of the owners. I walked up to the bar counter and said, 'Good evening, George.'

'Hello Terry,' he politely replied. 'What would you like?'

'Give me a whisky, George, will you. Come to think of it, make it a double, it might be my last.' We chatted away rather glumly about the current state of affairs, then suddenly, right on the stroke of 10 p.m., George turned and looked up at the clock on the wall. Lifting the trap hatch, he walked towards the bar door and opened it widely, then at the top of his voice shouted, 'Time, ladies and gentlemen, please.' I had great difficult in keeping a straight face, but I finished my drink and walked towards the door. Before I walked out into the street, I stopped in front of George and shook his hand and said, 'Goodnight and God bless, George.'

'The same to you, Terry,' he calmly replied, patting me gently on the shoulder as I began to walk away.

I was still smiling to myself as I made my way back home along the deserted street. Here we were in the middle of a major crisis, about to have our peaceful little island environment brutally abused by the fucking Argentines, and dear old George Malcolm was sticking rigidly to the letter of Falklands law. Yes, even in our most desperate hour, we Falkland Islanders remained law-abiding citizens. I felt extremely proud of him, and it gave me a warm and satisfying feeling to be British. No matter what was in store for me in the coming hours, no one, especially the Argentines could take away my pride in being British. Once home I closed and locked the door (God knows why – it was a simple wooden door and it was not going to keep any invading forces out).

I spent most of the night glued to the radio, with my wife. We decided we would take the radio upstairs to our bedroom. That way we would be close at hand to the children and dad. We knew that sleep was not in the equation, but at least we would be able to stretch out on the bed and let the radio guide us through the night's events as they developed. Sometime after midnight, Rex Hunt came back on the radio and indicated that little had changed, therefore we must assume that the Argentine task force had not changed course – thus, they would be off Cape Pembroke by dawn. He repeated that we should remain indoors and he would continue to keep us informed by radio.

It was all very agonising. It felt a bit like standing before an execution squad waiting to be shot down. The radio station continued to play music and relay BBC World Service news. The music was quite relaxing, strangely enough, and at times very apt: 'How Deep is the Ocean?' and 'Strangers in the Night' were very fitting songs. The news, however, was never good.

Looking back, I remember we were just a few hours away from attack and I was still being totally naïve. I never dreamt of gun battles, people shooting at one another with the intent to kill, the Argentines taking power, house arrest, edicts, deportation of friends and allies, curfews etc. – all these things might have been quite normal for the ordinary Argentine back in Argentina, but they were completely alien to the culturally British way of a democratic-thinking Falkland Islander, even if democracy had been handed out very sparingly to us. I also remember thinking to myself that all of this was not a great surprise to many of us – we had been anticipating something of this kind for some time.

I was more upset, hurt and disappointed, because I felt the British Government had finally let us down, and big time. We Falkland Islanders had shown tremendous loyalty to the Crown for over a century and a half. Islanders of all ages were quick to stand up and be counted and offer their services, and several would lose their lives to defend Britain in its hour of need in the world wars of 1914–18 and 1939–45. During the Second World War we made a financial contribution to the war effort of £50,000, an amazing amount of money from just two thousand people. The money was used to purchase a squadron of ten Spitfires.

Apart from the human factor, the Falkland Islands themselves had been strategically very important to the United Kingdom in both World War I and II. During this time they provided an ideal base and platform for Britain to defeat the powerful German Pacific fleet of Admiral Graf von Spee in the battle of the Falklands Islands on 8 December 1914, when a Royal Navy squadron sank the *Scharnhorst, Gneisnau, Nurnberg* and *Leipzig*, along with all the support vessels. It is estimated that more than 2,000 German sailors perished in the deep, dark and cold waters off the Falkland Islands during the battle, but this victory secured naval superiority for Britain in the area for the remainder of the war.

The Falkland Islands would once again become vitally important to Great Britain during World War II. This time they were used as a badly needed friendly home port to rest up and repair a severely battered Royal Navy squadron after the victory of the Battle of the River Plate. This British naval victory would once again allow Britain to control the seas of the South Atlantic.

But this time it was not just ships that needed a friendly home port; crew needed medical attention, some urgently, whilst for others it would become their final resting place. Many more simply needed some rest and recuperation after the horrors of the battle. They would stay and be cared for by Islanders in their homes, suffering from extreme shell shock. My grandmother told me that the men who stayed with her were that nervous they would almost jump out of their skins if a door or window rattled or slammed. The British also utilised the Falklands during the Second World War as a military base where they stationed several thousand troops of the West Yorkshire Regiment.

The Falklands remains today ideally located for any activities relating to the south west Atlantic and Antarctica. Nothing lasts for ever: the Antarctic Treaty will expire and is bound to change in content in the not too distant future. Any potential commercial development, such as tourism in the Antarctic, might be well served from the Falklands. Equally in these unsettled and uncertain days there is no telling when the Atlantic Seas passageways might be of significant importance once again. So with all this British history, tradition and loyalty in the Falkland Islands, plus the other factors I have highlighted, how was it that the British Governments of Wilson, Heath and Thatcher would lead us into this very sorry state of affairs? It felt to me that in our hour of need they had abandoned us. Or was it our own fault? Had we been too stubborn and unrealistic about the sovereignty issue and now we were reaping our just deserts? Surely not? Whatever, there was one thing that was absolutely certain, we were in deep shit.

Lying on the bed fully clothed, I was talking away to Melody. When I realised I was not getting any response, I lifted my head up off the pillow and noticed she had dropped off to sleep. Amelia was sound asleep also as she lay between us, completely unaware of our trials and tribulations (thank God for that). I ran my hand across her tiny and warm soft-skinned brow and bent down and kissed her tenderly on the cheek. This prompted me to get up off the bed and check on Severine, who was in his own room. I tiptoed along the short passageway, and poking my head in the open doorway I could see that he too was in another blissful world. I wondered if I should pick him up and bring him into our room so we would all be together, but then I thought if I did I was surely going to wake him up, so I decided to leave him where he was. He was no more or less safe where he lay. Then I carried out the same tender loving actions with him as I had just done with his sister a few moments ago.

I knew dad was in his room, so I went along the corridor and as silently as possible I opened his bedroom door. He was lying in his bed but was not asleep, he was listening to the radio with the volume very low. I asked if he was okay. 'Yes, I am fine, son,' he said in a quiet voice.

'Good,' I whispered back. 'If you need anything give me a shout.'

'Don't worry,' he said, 'I'll be fine.'

He was 70, but in good shape mentally and physically for his age. He had always held a strong and deep anti-Argentine feeling; I suddenly remembered that he had received three or four medals during the Second World War and was British to the core. God knows what he must have been thinking and feeling right now.

The night outside was incredibly quiet and still, no movement of any kind, no wind, nothing. Then suddenly I could hear a vehicle approaching our way and being pulled up. Then I heard voices and doors opening and closing. We guessed that Carlos was being rounded up by the civil guard. He was an Argentine living in a house opposite with a Falkland Island lady. I remembered pulling his leg about two weeks previously regarding an Argentine C130 Hercules, which had landed on our airstrip. 'I suppose that was a dummy run, just to see if a Hercules could land there.'

He sheepishly and very defensively replied, 'No, no, it had a fuel leak.'

'Come on Carlos, pull the other one,' I said, laughing. But I later found out that Carlos had in fact been telling the truth; the plane had developed a fuel problem.

Anyway, shortly afterwards the vehicle pulled away and all fell still again.

We had been waiting for what seemed an age before we heard anything more from the Governor. I think it was about four in the morning when he did come back on the radio. The news was not good. Pretty much as expected, the Argies were still coming, and going to take the Falklands by force. He told us that last-ditch efforts by the United States President, Ronald Reagan, had failed to get Galtieri to call off the invasion. Rex Hunt went on to inform us that our handful of gallant and extremely professional Royal Marines, along with members of the local Defence Force, had been deployed and were in good spirits. From the moment he mentioned the Defence Force, I immediately hoped and prayed that none of them would be harmed and that he, as the Governor, who was also Commander in Chief of all our armed forces (about 100 in total, I suppose), would not expect the ridiculous or impossible from these brave souls.

We all knew the Royal Marines were well trained and prepared for this type of situation. After all, they were professional soldiers and this was the purpose of their posting here. On the other hand, members of the Defence Force were made up of good honest-to-God citizens who earned their living by being carpenters, butchers, lorry drivers – whatever it took to support themselves and their families. They were the most loyal and obedient of employees, and they were now out there waiting for the might of the Argentine task force; it was natural to them, and all other Falkland Islanders, to be prepared to do whatever was asked of us in the name of the Queen of the United Kingdom and Northern Ireland. It had been said many times previously that we Falkland Islanders were 'more British than the British'. It was an undeniable fact.

With a state of emergency now declared and no hope of turning the Argentine task force back home, it was just a question of sitting and waiting for the inevitable to happen. I really believed that they would land en masse on the beaches to the east of Stanley. Then it happened, the waiting and guessing was all over. Suddenly the still and silent night was shattered by loud explosions and the popping of gunfire, and not from the east, but the west. I guessed it was the Royal Marines barracks at Moody Brook which had been attacked. I turned to Melody and said, 'Jesus Christ, they're shooting at each other.'

Sure I know it sounds a dumb bloody thing to have said, but I did not expect a battle, a war. Briefly I panicked, but Severine had been woken up by the thunderous sounds and came running into our bedroom, rubbing his eyes and saying, 'What is that noise, daddy?'

Without hesitation I said, 'I think it is an exercise, son.' I bent down and picked him up. My brief moment of lost control was over, I had to take care of my family as best, and in whatever way, I could. I put my son on the bed with his mother and sister, Amelia, who amazingly was still fast asleep. I was going to check on dad again, but I stopped, because the Governor came back on the radio. He told us that Argentine ships had been sighted and a landing craft was approaching the harbour narrows. He also said things were under control (I doubted that). He confirmed the loud bangs had come from the Moody Brook area, and Government House was under attack also. I suppose the Argies had anticipated that the Marines might still be there. I too thought that some of them would be, and I supposed they were engaged in battle with the enemy and that was what all the noise was about. I found out afterwards that they had in fact pulled out of the barracks. How extremely sensible of their commanding officer.

For a fleeting moment I wondered where dear old A171 was – that was the Royal Navy Antarctic guard vessel HMS *Endurance*, remember. The last I knew of her was that she had left Stanley on 21 March to sort out the Argies down in South Georgia. We had heard nothing concrete about her since, but there had been some stories about her being chased by Argentine warships. I thought to myself, if she had been here with the extra manpower, helicopters and weaponry, our boys on the ground would not feel so exposed and hopelessly outnumbered tonight. But I quickly realised that whilst she and the ship's company would have been a welcomed added boost, and would most likely have contributed to giving the Argentines a far more serious bloody nose, their involvement would have certainly escalated the whole level of combat at the cost of British lives and perhaps even the loss of *Endurance* herself. With that sober thought, I was glad that floundering British intelligence and dilly-dallying diplomats had ensured that most likely she was neither in South Georgia nor the Falklands.

The Governor had been on the radio very briefly and almost immediately after he went off the air, the bangs and small arms fire intensified to deafening levels. I ran around to dad's bedroom and asked if he wanted to come into our room, he was still lying in his bed. 'No,' he said. 'If the bastards are going to kill me, it may as well be in my bed. I'm happy to die here, rather than anywhere else.'

I ran back to my bedroom. As I got to the doorway, Amelia suddenly woke up and, getting to her knees, started rubbing her eyes. Then when she saw me, she put out her arms and in a very frightened and whimpering voice said, 'Daddy, daddy, the Germanies are coming.'

I picked her up, and as she flung her arms around my neck, I whispered into her ear, 'Not to worry. Everything will be okay.' I passed her down to her mother and grinned to myself. Then I thought, why the hell would a little four-year-old girl in the middle of the Argentines invading the Falklands suddenly wake up and associate the whole fracas with the Germans? I don't ever recall talking about the First or Second World War, or the Germans, to any extent in her company. I was amused and amazed by her innocent comment.

Patrick Watts had been manning the local radio station all

night; he had been, and would continue to be, a great source of comfort to me, and I am sure to all those who were listening. The music was subtle and appropriate, often poignant, sometimes even humorous. I will always remember his amazing interviews with the Governor as fighting around Government House was taking place, and the most incredible live debates and interviews with members of the public, who described all that they could hear or see as the Argentines advanced towards Stanley whilst the Royal Marines employed a hit-and-run tactic from the east of the town, through the tiny capital and back to Government House.

In one such interview the Governor had reported that there had been a lull in fighting around Government House, but he expected it would only be a matter of time before the Argentines would be back and almost certainly overrun them. Then came the dramatic moment when Patrick asked the Governor if he was going to surrender. I stood stiff and absolutely still to the spot where I was standing as I waited for the Governor's reply, which was a clear and determined 'I'm not going to surrender to any bloody Argie.' Even though we knew he would have to, his statement was extremely uplifting.

We also received the news that the Royal Marines had knocked out an armoured personnel carrier. The adrenaline was starting to pump and once again I felt so bloody proud to be British, even if I was shitting myself from time to time over being in a completely hopeless situation which was well out of my control.

Two interviews that I found quite unbelievable, and captivating, were held between Patrick and Alistair Grieves and a neighbour of Alistair's, Tom Davies. They were both expatriates, living in a small housing unit of bungalows to the east of Davis Street, locally called 'White City'. Patrick was asking them to describe events following a shoot-out between the Argies and the Royal Marines. The Argentines had got very pissed off after the loss of the armoured personnel carrier and anyone who might have been inside. They had started firing back at the retreating Royal Marines, and Alistair reported that all hell had suddenly broken out around his house, with loud bangs from mortar bombs, the crackling of machine and small arms fire, and there was lots of smoke. Then he went on to say that he and his family were now lying on the floor and that he was not going to get up and pop his head out of the window for Patrick or any bugger else to see what anyone or anything was doing. I thought he was being incredibly brave, given the circumstances he and his small family were in. As he was describing events, you could hear the noise of battle in the background over the radio.

Patrick's interview switched to his neighbours, who had just had the most remarkable escape. Tom Davies and his wife Gwen told us that they were soaking wet and up to their ankles in water. They, like Alistair and his family, had been flat out on the floor, when suddenly, their attic had taken a direct hit and the water supply tank had disintegrated into thousands of metal fragments and dropped its entire content of water down on Tom and Gwen below. Had that mortar bomb hit the ground floor of the house, they surely would not have been able to tell us this most dramatic tale in such graphic detail.

Other members of the public called Patrick with news of Argentine flags flying at the airport and helicopters landing. Staff at the school hostel reported the well being of the camp school children living in the capital. Their mothers and fathers must have been in a terrible state of mind, now completely cut off from their loved ones and unable to do anything about it. News of their children's safety must have been a tremendous relief for them, even though they would anguish for many hours and days ahead.

Hearing that most of the interviewees were lying on the floor, I thought perhaps it would be the best place for me and my family too. The trouble was, our bedroom was on the first floor, which was quite high. I felt we needed to get lower down, to the tiny cellar we had below the floor of the scullery. (A cellar was a very unusual thing to have in a basic Falklands home.) I knew if we could squeeze inside, it would be the most secure place we could be, at least from automatic and small arms fire. Most homes in the Falklands did not keep the cold out, let alone bullets, bombs and suchlike. I was just about to suggest to my wife that we make the move, when I heard a commotion in our back garden. At first I thought it was the Argies and my mind started thinking all sorts of things, but as I pricked my ears to listen to the heavy and fast approaching footsteps, I heard a loud crack, then someone fell to the ground with a thud. Then I heard someone say in beautiful crystal clear English, 'Oh fuck it.' Another person asked what the matter was. 'It's okay, I'm okay. The bastard fence broke. Come on, let's get the fuck out of here.' I was slightly amused by the brief entertainment and also mighty relieved that it was friend, and not foe, that was galloping through my property.

Moments later gunfire rattled out again, interspersed with bangs and pops of varying levels of noise, but the combination of all together seemed much louder and more deafening than at any time before. I thought I could hear bullets whizzing past the house, others smacking into a small concrete wall in front of the house. God knows, the mind can play all sorts of tricks in this situation, I suppose. 'Bugger it,' I said to my wife, 'let's just stay here.' She readily agreed, and so we flattened out on the floor where we were.

News came through that there were some casualties, Argentine, up at Government House, and arrangements were being planned to get them collected and delivered down to our hospital, where doctors and staff were at the ready. I hoped and prayed they would not be harmed or overrun that night.

Then a most terrible thing happened. Patrick, a long and close friend of mine, was playing music on the radio station and I was thinking to myself, by now he must be out on his feet with fatigue from hours of unbroken toil, coupled with a total lack of sleep and high emotion. He had two young daughters and I supposed he must be terribly concerned about their safety. Then we heard in the background loud voices shouting in Spanish. It had to be the Argentines and they were obviously inside the studio and approaching him, because their voices were getting louder. Patrick said something like, 'Well, I expected this.' Pausing momentarily, he went on, 'We're being taken over, the radio station is being taken over.'

I immediately thought to myself, please don't hurt him, please don't hurt him. As I have said, he had been a great friend of mine and he had only been doing his job. No, in fact, he had done far more than his job that night. He later received the MBE. Patrick's only problem in life was that he was a Preston North End fan. There was some scuffling, then Patrick could be heard to say something to the effect of, 'Just a minute, take that gun out of my back.' Then obviously speaking to the listener, said, 'I've got a gun in my back. We've been taken over. They want me to play some tapes. Now they're arguing with themselves. Three Argentine soldiers are here in the radio station and they are arguing with each other. Now they have gone.' Patrick, understandably, was now very emotional and my heart went out to him.

Then the Governor came back on to say he was sorry about how things had panned out. He told us that he had warned the Argentine Admiral that he had landed unlawfully in the Falkland Islands and should leave, but the Admiral replied he had taken back what belonged to Argentina. Then Hunt repeated, he was sorry it had happened this way, and that it would most likely be the last message he would be able to give to us. He wished us good luck and then finished by saying, 'Rest assured, the British will be back.' I must say at that time I held out little hope of that. For what it was worth, I had not been taken in by Hunt's much more open approach with Islanders than any previous Governor I had known. It was nothing personal. True, his willingness to mingle and chat with us locals had been very refreshing. But I believed he, like all before him, had a line to follow, that of the Foreign and Commonwealth Office, which I felt was not in our long-term interest. That said, I think we, and the Islands, had got inside his heart and on this night he was most definitely with us. For that, I will always be grateful to him. He is now justifiably regarded as a national hero by many Falkland Islanders. It would be very unyielding of any Islander to begrudge him that.

But that was not it from the Governor. Patrick went straight back to him, mainly because the Argentines in the studio had not sorted themselves out, I do not know the topic of the discussion, because I suddenly realised I had not checked on my dad for a while and I had not heard any sound coming from him. When I reached his bedroom and went in I found he was underneath the blankets. I asked, 'Are you okay, dad?' I moved quickly across the bedroom floor and lightly touched the bundle that lay undercover.

He pulled the blankets down to his shoulders and gazed up to me. 'It's getting pretty rough out there, isn't it?'

I realised that he was very edgy but I did not have a clue what to say or do to comfort him. 'Do you want me to stay with you a little while?'

'No,' he said, 'you go and take care of Melody and the children.'

As I reached my own bedroom I heard the Governor uttering some final words as he went off the air. I had always had a lot of respect for Patrick Watts, but on this night he had become a real hero in my eyes. He had been relaying historic events all night long, in an extremely professional manner, and completed a magnificent and unselfish radio marathon in tears – all very understandable. But before he was finished, he suffered the indignity of having to put on those bloody Argentine propaganda tapes. The only thing I remember about them was the sickening sound of their mournful national anthem – a bloody awful thing it is, no rhythm. Clearly it was all over, Stanley the capital of the Falkland Islands, my homeland, had fallen into the hands of the enemy and we were now under Argentine military rule. That, I can assure you, was a very worrying prospect indeed. They were butchering their own people back in Argentina. What the hell lay in store for us?

16

Under Argentine Military Rule

Suddenly it was quiet and still again, so I looked out of the bedroom window. The morning sun was shining brightly and the harbour sea was like glass, reflecting mirror images of the camber coastline and hills. I felt drained. Amelia and Severine had gone back to sleep and Melody was sitting on the side of the bed. 'I think I'll go down and make a cuppa. Do you fancy one?' I asked her. This might sound as though I was being pretty cool, but believe me, inside I was jumping.

We were not down in the kitchen very long before dad joined us. Soon enough we started to get the Argentine edicts, numbers 1, 2, 26 and so on. They began by telling us that they had liberated us from the terrible British oppressors and we should rejoice in the knowledge that we were now all free Argentines. They also told us we had nothing to fear and that we should continue life as normal, but for the moment we were not allowed out of our homes and we should stay off the streets until further notice.

They went on to tell us we could continue to speak English, but Spanish would be mandatory in school. It was also pointed out that there would be religious and employment freedom and that we had the right to enter and leave the Islands as we wished. That statement did not make a hell of a lot of sense, after being told we had to stay in our homes. We were informed that public services would resume as normal but from now on we must drive on the right hand side of the road, the opposite to our normal system.

Sometime later in the morning, I suppose about an hour or so after the surrender, an Argentine APC drove past our house. The driver was having great difficulty keeping it on the narrow street of Pioneer Row, but once he had managed to squeeze past, we got our first look at some of the Argy troops who had invaded our country. These were special forces, 20 or 30 very well equipped and fit men, extremely mean-looking bastards, I thought to myself as they marched past us in double file. One or two looked towards us and waved or smiled at us as we were looking out of the kitchen window. They really did believe they had come to free us. Dad responded to their friendly waves with a back-to-front Winston Churchill two-finger sign. Then a split second of high tension: I was resting against the front rail of the peat stove, a favourite position for many Islanders, but when I moved quickly to get closer to the window, one of the Argies stopped immediately from his stride and swung around with his automatic weapon pointing straight at us. I froze on the spot for a split second, fully expecting him to empty his gun on me and my family. He was clearly very jumpy, but fortunately not trigger-happy. Something must have stopped him pulling that trigger, God knows what, but he lowered his gun, spun around again and marched off.

I relaxed from my frozen stance and said something stupid to dad like, 'He was bloody nervous, wasn't he?' Dad said nothing, but I could see he was shaken. As I looked out over the roof tops in the direction of the Secretariat building, which was just a short distance from our house, my gaze fixed on an enormous Argentine flag. The sight of this massive symbol of Argentine authority broke my heart, and my resolve. I cried unashamedly and uncontrollably for a while.

The rest of the day was mostly spent indoors, as dictated to us by the Argentines. I would only venture out to fill the peat buckets and collect vegetables from the garden, or for other essential needs. We had taken the Argentines' instruction seriously, but some Islanders, in the area of the radio station in particular, had chosen to ignore the Argentines' edicts and went out to bid farewell to Rex Hunt as he went in and out of the radio station to yet another broadcast. This would be his final, final speech. Which was, as you can imagine, extremely sombre, but he finished his address with a clear and determined promise: 'We will be back. Until then, goodbye.' His words signalled the beginning of the eviction by the Argentine military of anyone who represented British authority, which I knew would include the very brave Royal Marines who had put up such a bloody good show against overwhelming odds in our defence. I got this feeling that whilst the Governor and others wished us luck as they departed, either by force or by choice, most would all be over the hill as fast as possible, breathing a huge sigh of relief and leaving us behind to face the music. No one, of course, could be blamed for that.

Whilst sitting indoors on invasion day, we would have to endure the Argentine radio broadcast of the swearing in of their Military Governor of their Las Malvinas. Some fellow called Garcia was the first, followed a few days later by General Mario Menendez. On this and other days there were also those bloody edicts, endless they seemed. I had two radios in the house, one tuned in to the local station, the other to the BBC World Service, who confirmed some four hours after the Argentines had taken over that the Falklands had in fact been invaded. There we also heard that in the streets of Buenos Aires back in Argentina the general public were out dancing and singing, celebrating a famous Argentine victory, Oh yes, General Galtieri had achieved his aims of turning street protests into a massive wave of joy and happiness, with vitriolic cries of '*Viva Argentina, viva Las Malvinas*'. In one stroke he had diverted their attention away from the problems at home and for the next ten weeks he would operate a programme of misleading propaganda to the Argentine population that would eventually lead to his downfall, just days after the Argentine surrender on 14 June.

The invasion had not damaged Stanley's very basic telephone system, so we were able to speak to fathers, mothers, brothers sisters etc. From the conversations we had with them, it dawned on us that it had been a miracle that during the attack on our small compact little capital, not a single one of the Islands' community or defence forces had been injured or killed. Truly remarkable, someone had surely been looking down upon us that night.

Having two young children at this time was a blessing; they required time and attention for their needs and desires, and this ensured you took your mind off the bloody Argies for a while, even if only momentarily. The kids had been fantastic throughout the invasion and the embryonic stages of occupation, but they could not understand why they were not allowed out on such a beautiful sunny day to play in the back garden or to go and see their friends. This meant we were forced into making some indoor entertainment for them, taking turns at telling stories, singing songs etc. There were no televisions or computers in the Falklands in those days. Anyway, they had become far less enthusiastic about going out after Argentine fighter jets flew over the house at about midday, causing the most deafening of noises as they did so. It really frightened the pair of them.

By night time things had quietened down considerably and tiredness started to creep in, so we went off to bed fairly early, all of us in the one bed. There was not much else to do, the radio news bulletins had become repetitious and somehow when a war story is being told about a war zone that you are sitting right in the middle of, it is far less interesting and gripping, especially as it is not necessarily 100% accurate – and a little dated.

After a reasonable night's sleep – it was certainly a night less dramatic than the one before – I spent the next day listening to the news broadcasts, analysing them and speculating upon our lot. One thing was sure, we were most definitely under Argentine military rule. There was no more British leadership for us to follow, or to protect us. One major plus was that the Argentines did not appear to be hostile towards us. They were clearly organising themselves in the business of administrating their newly gained territory, and I suppose for them too there must have been a great deal of uncertainty. They would be aware, like ourselves, that international politics had taken a firm stance against Argentina, because the result at an emergency meeting of the United Nations Security Council had voted overwhelmingly in favour of the Argentines making an immediate withdrawal of their armed forces from the Falklands, and for Britain and Argentina to commence negotiations to reach a peaceful settlement on the dispute. Well, that was the nuts and bolts of Resolution 502.

I must say, at the time this act of diplomacy gave me some hope that the Argentines just might see sense and agree to the request. Why? Because I felt if they would agree to it, it would allow us to get back to some sort of normality after they pulled out their troops, even if it were only for a short while. I suggest a short while, because I felt that even if the Argentines did agree to sit down with Britain at the negotiating table, they held all the trump cards, therefore they would be able to exert extreme pressure on Great Britain to cede sovereignty, and if the British did not agree to these demands, then surely they would immediately reoccupy the Islands, and Britain would be unable to do anything about it.

Furthermore, in view of the fact that they had failed to negotiate with Argentina on the sovereignty issue, the UN Security Council would most likely be far less sympathetic and supportive to the

British cause, and the general populace of Great Britain might have been far less willing to support a military response. In hindsight, it is extremely fortunate that the Argentines were not that intelligent.

With constant listening to BBC World Service Radio, which included our very own programme called *Calling the Falklands* and reports from the BBC Latin American correspondent Harold Briley, I started to get a general picture, but most importantly perhaps the British Government's reaction to the events. I formed this image of all the Members of Parliament and the House of Lords choking on their early morning breakfasts from hearing the news of the invasion, then scooping up their briefcases and hurrying off to an emergency meeting of the House of Commons called by Prime Minister Thatcher the following day, to admit how embarrassed they all were and that they should send the strongest note of protest to the United Nations condemning the Argentines' action and agreeing that the two sides should get together to resolve their differences. After all, I thought to myself, what the hell else could they do?

I was astonished at the reaction of the Members of Parliament, which seemed to be a combination of anger at the Argentines, and a united belief that positive action should be taken to force them out of the Islands by whatever means necessary. I wondered if all I was hearing was just a load of hot air, mainly because in reality we were far too far away and under occupation. I was made to think again later in the day when it became obvious that it was not just the Members of Parliament and the House of Lords that were fired up and pissed off, so were the general public, and if they, the British Government were not going to do something about it they would make bloody sure they did.

I had reached this conclusion by listening to my beloved Tottenham Hotspur play Leicester City in the semi-final of the FA Cup. Spurs had two Argentines playing for them in the match, Ossie Ardiles and Ricky Villa, and every time they touched the ball there was a tremendous noise of hissing and booing. I vividly recall saying to my father, 'Listen to that, dad. The British public are well and truly annoyed, they might be going to do something after all.'

He looked at me somewhat quizzically and said, 'It will have to be war, because these bastards won't pull out.'

I did not reply to his very pronounced statement, because my heart sank knowing he was probably right. But there was one bright note on this pretty grave day, my beloved Spurs won their match and were into the Cup Final to play Queens Park Rangers in May.

In the afternoon we decided we badly needed some fresh air, so we all gathered up some things and went down the road to stretch our legs and do a bit of essential shopping at the largest supermarket in town, the West Store, which is owned and operated by the Falkland Islands Company. Our journey and the shopping under normal circumstances would have taken us an hour; however, today was far from normal circumstances and we took some time as we stopped and talked to friends and other members of the community to discuss the Argentines' attack, our individual experiences of invasion night, the edicts, the volume of Argentine forces and military hardware in the streets and the prospects for the future, which for most of us seemed pretty hopeless.

There were also the tales of defiance in response to the Argentine dictatorial demands. One especially gave us a great deal of satisfaction and amusement. Islanders completely ignored the order to drive on the right, therefore as they went along the street in the usual manner in their Land Rovers, they would come face-to-face with an Argentine military vehicle approaching them head on from the other direction. Finally at bumper to bumper, the Argentines would blow horns or make various types of hand signals, demanding that we Islanders move our vehicles out of the way. It was more a petulant form of defiance than anything else, but it was one of those little things that allowed us to demonstrate our unwillingness to cooperate with the Argentine dictatorship and express our refusal to relinquish our British-ness.

The Argies eventually painted big white arrows on the streets, pointing the direction in which the traffic should flow. Even then, no one took any notice, and Argentine drivers would eventually give up, shaking their heads in disbelief or waving a fist in anger, as they backed off and went around a Falkland Islander's vehicles, shouting obscenities in Spanish as they passed by, which would get a two fingered response from a satisfied and grinning Islander.

Sunday, 4 April was a gathering of families, Sunday lunch and all that sort of stuff. It might surprise you to read that we appeared to slip back into a normal lifestyle so quickly after being invaded. Well, it was far removed from normal but we were completely isolated, living on an occupied island hundreds of miles away from any friendly populated continent. The nearest country was Argentina, the home of our occupiers, and our nearest friends were 8,000 miles away. So it made sense to try as best as one could to live a normal life, especially as our plight could take a decided turn for the worse at any time.

I seem to recall that this was the day that I first heard that South Georgia had also been taken over by the Argies, but we were pleased to learn that they did not have it all their own way; the Royal Marines, led by Keith Mills, had downed a helicopter and everyone inside it before having to give up the fight against ridiculous odds. Much more sobering was the report that a British soldier had been injured in the fighting. I then started thinking more of the next day and a return to work. How were we going to carry out our daily work routines? I had made my mind up about one thing, I would not accept Argentine pesos as payment for my labours. I believed that if I did, it would be a symbol of accepting Argentine rule, and I was not going to do that without it being rammed down my throat. But I will be honest with you and say, given the choice to live, or die for this belief, I am not certain I would have chosen death.

I had mixed emotions about the UK's decision to send a task force to evict the Argentines. In one sense I was happy, but it would be a long time yet before the British would be in any position to implement a strike-back, and there was plenty of time for diplomats to work out a peaceful solution, which I was sure would not go in our favour. I was also aware that if a negotiated settlement could not be reached, the Argentines would get more and more aggressive towards us, with potentially dire consequences. If that were not serious enough, I realised for the British to retake the Falklands by force they had to take the capital Stanley. This would require a war, and we would be in the middle of it. So, although not easy, it made an awful lot of sense to try and live our lives as normally as possible.

Monday morning, 5 April, and it was time to go to work and see how things might work out in this area. I walked down to the Falkland Islands Company shipping agency office. Our main clients were 80 or so Polish fishing trawlers. One of their 'mother ships', *Zulawy*, the name given to a large factory vessel, was lying at anchor in the outer harbour called Port William. The ship acted as a floating cold store and also as a resupply vessel providing the trawlers with fuel and provisions whilst they discharged their cargoes. This enabled the trawlers to make a speedy return to the fishing grounds. Crew sometimes came ashore in Stanley to take a drink in one of the local pubs or do a little bit of shopping, but this practice had been discouraged following the imposition of martial rule back in Poland, which had inspired nine crew members from various trawlers to jump ship and seek political asylum on our peaceful and tranquil islands. What a bloody awful stroke of bad luck to have jumped out of the frying pan and into the fire.

Once at the office, I joined other members of staff at a meeting. My brother Alec was there, to my surprise. It was the first time I had seen him since the invasion and I asked him how he was. He had been working part-time with the FIC doing accountancy work, but in February had switched to the Argentine airline company LADE and their fuel and gas supply people Gas Del Estados, both of which had established themselves in the Falklands since the signing of the 'communications agreement' which had been thrust upon us.

Alec spoke excellent Spanish and was anti-British, therefore I supposed he was at least one Islander who was not so disturbed by the present situation. But I will say, he was not showing any signs of pleasure either. Oddly enough, he had been waiting to receive news from the LADE head office in Buenos Aires to confirm his appointment to their office in Ushuaia when the war broke out. Perhaps that's why he never received the news of the appointment.

Once we were assembled in the general manager's office, Harry Milne very quickly outlined the position of the company. He also recognised the difficulty of trying to maintain a normal way of life and then in a highly commendable piece of heart-and-soul management, he went on to tell us that we were free to make our own decisions for ourselves and our families. If that meant we wished to stay at home with them and not attend work, that was perfectly understandable, and we could return to work whenever we wished with no fear of any negative consequences. Unfortunately, I would need to remind him of this after the liberation.

Harry warned that it was highly likely the Argentines would be extremely prominent in the area of the jetty and the office, therefore we had to expect to be subjected to their harassment when entering and leaving the premises. He also indicated that it would be wise from now on to carry some form of identification. The idea of having to carry a passport around in the Falklands to identify yourself was completely alien to us. Before these bloody Argentines had turned up, everyone knew everyone else and there was never any need for such authoritarian measures. Harry did not prolong the meeting. He finished by thanking us for our loyalty to him and especially to the Falkland Islands Company and then wished us well in whatever we chose to do and prayed that we would be safe and well.

As we all filed out of his office to head back to our various posts, I stopped to talk with Alec. We exchanged greetings and then he made it apparent that anyone wishing to leave the Islands could do so by hopping on the Fokker 28 jets that LADE were still operating to the Argentine mainland – providing you could beat the rush. He went on to say he would be able to arrange seats for my family and me. I had no reason to disbelieve he could, he was now working for the Argentine airline in their Stanley office and they knew he was supportive of the Argentine claim of the Islands, so I assumed that would carry some weight in terms of priority in getting his family members off the Falklands.

I was still a little confused at the time and to be absolutely honest, I had no clear idea about what to do for the best that morning, so I said to him that I had no particular interest in leaving the Islands but thanked him for his offer. Then I asked him what he was going to do.

'Oh, I'm staying put, I'll carry on living here with the Argentines. There's nothing to worry about,' he said.

'I would not be so sure about that, Alec,' I told him. 'Well, I'd better be going. I need to go and see how the Poles are doing.'

The Polish ship anchored out in Port William had also had quite an eventful time on invasion night. Some of the Royal Marines had taken shelter behind her in a high-speed rubber dingy during a daring getaway from Argentine forces. The Marines were still hiding away somewhere in the hills and it was annoying the Argentines immensely, so much so that they had been requesting via the local radio station that anyone who had information on the Marines' whereabouts should come forward. They also took time out to warn us that if we were helping to hide the British soldiers or were withholding any information from the authorities, then we could expect to be punished.

Although many Islanders had a good idea where the Royal Marines might be, and some in fact knew exactly where they were, there was no mad rush from Islanders to aid the Argies in finding the Royal Marines. A Falkland Islander giving up a Royal Marine to the Argentines would have been an unthinkable act of treachery, like giving up a member of the family – which is exactly how we viewed the Royal Marines.

When I reached my office, it was not long before I heard on the VHF radio the call of 'Fleetwing, fleetwing, fleetwing (this was our radio call sign), this is Port control calling fleetwing (Port control was the radio call sign for FIG Customs department). Fleetwing, fleetwing, Port control calling fleetwing, do you copy? Over.'

I picked up the mouthpiece to acknowledge the call and replied, 'Port control, Port control, fleetwing calling Port control. Copy you loud and clear, over.'

'Good morning, Terry,' came the reply. 'It's Les here. I would be most grateful if you could arrange a boat for us to go up to the *Zulawy*. Over.' As the Customs department did not have a work boat of their own, the routine was for Customs and the ship's agents (FIC) to go out together on our little wooden tug *The Lively* to complete the formalities and to attend to any other needs the ship's captains might require of us.

I put the hand piece to my mouth and paused for a second, then pushed the button on the side and said, 'Good morning, Les, if you can call it a good morning. Just wait a moment and I will get back to you about a boat, over.' I put the mike in its cradle on the wall and walked back towards my desk and looked out of the window down towards the jetty where the *Lively* usually berthed.

I will always remember the sight before my eyes. Neil Jennings, one of the stevedores, was coiling a rope on the stern of the vessel and there were a few Argentine soldiers milling around with what appeared to be no real purpose in life. Then I noticed the Argentine flag flapping away in the gentle breeze on the short flagstaff on top of the *Lively's* wheelhouse. That was it; Instantly I knew I could not go on board her, not with that fucking Argy flag flying so proudly on our little vessel. The Argentine flag seemed to hurt me most; it symbolised their total control of the situation. Right there and then I decided once again that not only would I not accept Argentine pesos for my salary – this had not been suggested, by the way – but that I would, for as long as it was possible anyway, not work anywhere where the Argentine flag was flying. The idea of punting down Stanley harbour on the *Lively* at seven knots maximum, whilst standing on the tiny deck presumably with some Argentine soldiers on board to observe our every move and with their flag stuffed in my face, was simply not an option.

I lowered my gaze from the window, turned around and walked swiftly towards the radio. When I told Les I was not going on the boat, he asked why not. 'We've been told to carry on as normal, so I think we should.'

I responded angrily by saying, 'It might be fucking normal for you, but it is not for me and I will not go on the *Lively* with that bloody Argentine flag flying on it and that is it.'

I rammed the microphone into its wall clip and then, looking down at Bob Peart, who was trying desperately hard to concentrate on his work, I said, 'Fuck it, there is no point me being here. I'm off, Bob,' and disappeared out of the room.

On reflection I suppose I was being a bit awkward and difficult. The situation was certainly not Les's fault, he was simply doing what he thought was right, though I was upset by his comments, which seemed so matter of fact. But I knew I could not bring myself to work in that environment that day and I was going to need some time to think things out, therefore the only sensible thing to do was go home. Before leaving the office, I decided I should go and tell Harry Milne of my intentions. Once I had entered his office I wasted no time explaining to him my problem and that I had reached my conclusion. He was very understanding and instantly said, 'Not to worry, go home, be with your family, do whatever you think is best for them and yourself. Everyone must make their own decisions now, Terry.'

He looked up at me with glazed eyes and I took his hand and

shook it firmly thanking him for his comforting words and then I turned away and walked towards the exit door, but before going out, I turned around to look at him once more. He was sitting in his chair looking rather forlorn. Before exiting the office I said to him, 'I will be back, Harry, and I will see you sometime soon. In the meantime, please take care of yourself.'

Strangely enough, walking home that morning I felt good. I had made a clear-cut decision and it was a wonderfully uplifting sensation.

Once home, I could tell instantly that Melody was pleased to have me around. Apart from being husband and wife, Melody and I were also good friends. I pottered about the house trying to make myself as useful as possible. I was also never very far away from the radio, which was constantly tuned to the BBC World Service rather than local radio.

That day they relayed the news of Lord Carrington's resignation as the British Foreign Secretary. He had taken the rap on behalf of the British Government for their enormous cock-up. Rightly or wrongly, a head or two was bound to roll, and it came as no great surprise to me that it was his. I also thought to myself, however, that a senior official resigning over the invasion of the Falkland Islands was in itself only an acceptance of blame, not much use or comfort to me and other Islanders at the time. The British Government's negligence meant we were living under Argentine occupation and authority.

We were also told that day that ships of the task force had started to set sail from ports in the United Kingdom, and other vessels were being assembled and prepared to be despatched to the South Atlantic at incredible speed, due to the fantastic efforts of dockyard workers who were working unselfishly day and night to pull out all the stops to complete work in record time. I had often doubted the British Government's motives regarding the Falkland Islands and the Falkland Islanders, but I had no such doubts about the British people, and knowing they were right behind us was a great source of comfort and gave me some degree of hope.

17

Should I Stay, or Should I Go?

The remainder of April was a strange period of time for us in the Islands. Although we were most definitely under occupation, there was no war as such, no visible conflicting armies in combat. Argentina continued to build up its military defences on the Falklands and Britain sailed its massive task force towards the Islands, but guns were generally silent. Furthermore, with the exception of the first couple of days after the invasion, from 5 April to the last LADE flight, which left at 14.02 local time on 29 April 1982, local inhabitants and others continued to fly out of the Falklands. It is estimated that nearly 400 civilians left over this period of time. Interestingly, the Argentines had at least complied with their edict that we were free to enter and leave the Islands as we wished. I should point out that no-one flew in.

Okay, it was an option for Falkland Islanders, providing you had the means to pay for your journey and that you had contacts and somewhere to live once you reached your journey's end. But where was journey's end? The UK was not a choice for me and many other Islanders as a long term option because of the British Government's refusal to grant Falkland Islanders the right of British citizenship. It appeared the only other choice was Argentina, so, no, thank you very much. For those of us who did choose to stay in the Falklands, we basically had two options: one was to remain in Stanley, the other was to move out to or around various camp settlements, to be with friends and family or simply because we felt a little more comfortable and safer there.

I suppose for the British Government, April was a very busy time. They were being active on several fronts, diplomatically and militarily, at home and abroad. Domestically, politicians were grappling with the politics concerning war, or how to avoid it, both in the House of Commons, and at the general public's level, whilst fully utilising friendly envoys and embassies overseas. Meanwhile the military were pulling together every possible piece of the war machine jigsaw to fight a potential war. The logistics involved to carry out such an action 8,000 miles away must have been daunting, perhaps even unprecedented, I use the words 'potential war' very carefully, because all peace options had NOT been exhausted and war might still be averted. Well, officially anyway.

For the invading Argentines the month of April must have been a strange and difficult period also. They had thought that they had liberated Islanders from the British, they wished to be our brothers and friends, but instead, for their efforts we locals were unhelpful, cold and resentful. They were trying to introduce a normal way of life, there had been no raping and pillaging of the local community, no one had been shot. But we only wanted them out and off our Islands and for the British to come back before we would consider anything remotely like normal.

I also suppose, for them, they did not really feel at war either, because they were spending most of their time ensuring public services were operating, and digging in and strengthening military positions around the capital Stanley, Goose Green on the East Falklands, and places like Port Howard, Fox Bay and Pebble Island on the West Falklands, whilst at the same time building up equipment and supplies. This was all being carried out unimpeded by direct contact with their homeland on the South American continent. With no apparent opposing forces to fight, they might even have been thinking that even if the British were coming, there was plenty of hope they could beat them off, with their ever-growing military presence and equipment and the more than adequate support from their navy and air force based around the Islands or just 400 miles away on the Argentine mainland. Or perhaps they thought that there would be no war at all, because some form of peaceful settlement would be reached as the result of the efforts of people such as Alexander Haig, the US Secretary of State, who was on an intensified shuttle diplomacy mission, trying to get all the sides to see sense and negotiate a deal before the British were in any sort of position to begin to fight.

In the absence of any British Government leadership, Islanders constantly listened to the radio to get as much up-to-date information as possible. People would often make decisions about where it might be best to locate themselves and their families based on the information gained from the radio. The LADE flights out of the

Islands twice a week allowed 60 passengers to depart each time, and this was an opportunity readily taken up by a lot of expatriate contract workers and their families, all eager to leave the Islands and escape the troubles and return to the safety of their homes in the United Kingdom. I am not attempting to be cynical with this statement, because you could certainly not blame them for leaving. After all, their homes and families were in another part of the world.

But I will tell you this: many who departed had made good friends with Islanders and as each one departed it seemed a part of us was leaving with them. It also seemed to make our situation so much more hopeless and harder to bear, because it was someone we knew, a friendly and familiar face, and their ability to just freely get up and leave also made us feel very much more like second-class and abandoned citizens as we were left in the middle of total chaos to take whatever was coming our way. It is true that some Islanders also left the Islands, but they must have been the lucky ones with a fortunate birthright and thus not affected by the British Government's decision that Falkland Islanders should not have the right of abode in the United Kingdom.

I had no knowledge of military tactics – remember, I was the one who turned round to his wife on invasion night and said, 'Christ, they're shooting at one another' – so I had no real idea if I should stay in Stanley, go to camp or try and get off the Islands. If I was going to do the latter, I needed to do something about my passport, therefore it was in this area I decided I should act first, to broaden the options for me and my family before making a final decision.

I had a good friend in the Government Secretariat who dealt with passport issues – well, at least before the invasion. I knew that all senior members of the service who were expatriates had been invited to leave the Islands by the Argentine authorities, which meant that the most senior official left was Harold Rowlands, the head of the Islands Treasury. But shoving my passport firmly into the back pocket of my trousers, I took a walk down to the Secretariat to see if my friend was at his desk.

Although it was only a short distance from my house, I passed many Argentine military personnel along the way, and when I got to the Secretariat building itself, I was greeted by a mixture of military and civilians as I stepped inside the building. There appeared to be people all over the place, queuing and fidgeting in corridors, up the stairs and in doorways, and clusters of confused and bemused civilian staff. There were calm, impatient or outraged residents, and just to complete the scene, there were Argentine military people rushing in and out of the building, others standing at various positions almost motionless, whilst some were being shouted at or having their chests prodded by a superior officer or an irate civilian. Amid all this chaos and pandemonium, I went straight up the stairs, pushing past people in the process, and found the place I was looking for. I had even better luck, I found the person I was looking for, my old rock band drummer mate.

Now I hoped he would be the right guy in the right place who could rearrange some discreet, but highly significant details to my passport, if he dared. He was pleased to see me and we greeted each other with a joke about where the band was going to play tonight. But there was no time for small talk, so I told him of my problem and desired requirements. He winked, then said, 'Give it here, TSB' as he thrust out his hand and snatched the passport from mine in a flash. 'Keep an eye open, just in case any of those Argy bastards come this way, and if they do, just act dumb.'

I watched nervously as he turned the pages of the document then when he got to the relevant page he started folding the passport back and forth, then flattened it out a little more and laid it down on a desktop. Then with a few quickly written words, a rapid initialling and dating to make it all effective from 31/03/82, in an instant my wife, children and I were legally allowed to enter and stay in the United Kingdom. My friend had completed something for me in seconds that had proved impossible in the past 31 years of my life for the Government of the United Kingdom. What's more, here was a Falkland Islander taking care of a fellow Falkland Islander and his family in the most positive way possible, all with the stroke of a pen, not a gun.

He looked up at me and then he pushed out his right arm with the document in his finger tips. Giving me a big broad smile, he said, 'Good luck, TSB. That should take care of things for you.'

I grabbed the passport and said to him, 'As always, you are a star. Take care as well, my friend. If the Argies catch you doing this, you could be in deep shit. I'll see you soon.'

I turned and left, quickly pushing my passport in the back pocket of my pants once again. As I made my way out of the

Secretariat building, some lady was giving an Argentine officer a serious verbal attack. He was upright and pale as she laid into him. God knows what it was about. Once I was outside and a comfortable distance away from the building and any Argies, I pulled out my passport to check on my friend's piece of handiwork. I could see he had done all that was required. No one could have any idea how liberating it felt, nor what it meant that I now had the wider option to take my family out of this troublesome situation. In fact I now had three options at least: to stay put in the capital, leave for the UK, or go to camp.

I must say that the first choice was now becoming the least attractive. Some friends had already gone to camp and felt much safer there. They suggested we should go and join them and it had been agreed we could stay in a house that had been used as a school.

Once I got home and showed off the rearranged passport to Melody, she was delighted with my friend's efforts. But after a little while, we agreed that for the moment she and the children should go to camp and I would follow on if they felt safe and settled in their new environment, and if we chose not to get a flight out of the Islands.

Within a day or two of my wife and children leaving for camp, Long Island in the first instance, I started thinking about getting someone to stay in our house. I knew if I left the house empty the Argentines would move in pretty damned fast. I was also aware that before making any final plans about destinations I had to discuss things with my father and uncle Johnnie Blyth (Melody's uncle). They had to be considered and cared for as well. After daily conversations with my wife, who was obviously much more relaxed at Long Island, plus the knowledge that the Argentines were increasing troop and equipment levels in Stanley at a steady rate, it was obvious it was now decision time. The question was, Should we stay or should we go? Camp or the United Kingdom?

Before making a final decision I spoke with my brother once more about getting a flight out of the Islands, and he once again assured me that it would not be a problem. I was not bothered in any way about possessions, they were the least important thing on my mind, so leaving them behind was not an issue. But I had to get my decision right, because if I chose to go to camp, that was probably it. Okay, there would be time to come back into Stanley and take the UK option, but not for long. However, after discussing things with my father, mother and wife, camp it was. Why? Very simple really. Although I had sorted out my own passport, I had overlooked the fact that dad only had a Falkland Islands passport, therefore if we had left the Islands that would have meant leaving him behind, and that was unthinkable.

Furthermore, if we did go to the UK, where would we have gone? I had a few family members in England – my sister Vivien and my brother Popeye (I was not aware at the time that he was making plans to join the task force). Anyway, neither had the facilities to put five extra people up at short notice. Even if we did go to England, what the hell would we have done? How would we have supported ourselves? We had no money. Few Falkland Islanders had money. We also had to think about Uncle Johnnie, who was very handicapped with arthritis. So in the end, it was a simple decision, camp, and in the beginning Long Island.

Naturally I was concerned about my mother, but she did have her Scottish husband, Eric. for support and company. He was a member of the crew of the small coaster the *Forrest*, which had acted as a floating mobile radar station on the night of the invasion. Even though they could have left the Falklands they had decided to stay put in Stanley, so I offered them my house to stay in and happily they readily agreed.

18

Refugees

On the morning of my departure for camp I put the barest essentials into the back of Pat Whitney's Land Rover, the last thing being the family cat, and like refugees, off we went, heading for Long Island. There was no road network between Stanley and the camp in 1982, the terrain is white grass, diddle-dee bogs, peat, ditches, rivers, stones and mud, which required bags of skilful driving, a knowledge Pat had gained from hundreds of hours of driving in such conditions. Once at Long Island, I was pleased to be reunited with my family, and also to be with our old friends from the capital who had also made the decision to leave Stanley, Neil and Glenda were good friends and hosts at the best of times, but given the circumstances we were all in, they were now exceptional.

The first thing that struck me about moving out of Stanley and arriving at our destination was the total lack of Argentine soldiers about the place. That alone had made the decision to move out of Stanley a sensible one. Without realising it, my nerves must have been a bit on edge, because when I went to bed on my first night at Long Island I did not really sleep much. The night was still and because of that I was aware of the slightest sound and imagined I could hear approaching helicopters or something else that could only be sinister. I was expecting to hear Argentine soldiers knocking on the door and ordering us out of the house and taking us all off somewhere. So when I got out of bed, I was more tired in the morning than when I had gone to bed the night before.

Neil was the type of guy who would not have needed much encouragement to start some sort of guerrilla group against the Argies if it had been in any way possible; he was one of the strongest anti-Argentines in the community, possibly because he was one of its better-informed members via his involvement in the local branch of the Falkland Islands Committee. Neil was proud and passionate about being a Falkland Islander and British. There was no doubt we all were, but Neil was definitely at the top end of the scale. You will recall that a small group of Royal Marines had managed to evade the Argentine invading force on 2 April, firstly taking shelter behind the Polish mother ship and then speeding off in their rubber boat to the shore, where they then ran hot foot and disappeared into the hills. Anyway, from something he said one day when he and a few other guys were chatting, I thought Neil at least knew where the Marines were hiding, and if he knew, it seemed logical it had to be somewhere pretty close, which made Long Island mountain a distinct possibility. The small group that was huddled together seemed to be discussing a rendezvous, which I assumed was most likely the Royal Marines. When the group finally broke up they began climbing into vehicles and moving off. I had not been invited to join them so I assumed I was not required.

It would not be long before my presumptions were confirmed. Neil returned to the house later in the day. I was in the kitchen when he entered with a grim-looking expression on his face. Greetings were exchanged but he clearly had something on his mind and he proceeded to tell Glenda, with disappointment and a touch of fretfulness, of his meeting with the Marines. He was disappointed because his plan of keeping the Marines in hiding whilst providing them with food and whatever for as long as possible had been reluctantly and respectfully turned down by the Royal Marines. And he was fretful because they had informed him that they had no option but to call it a day and offer themselves up to the Argentines. This disturbed Neil because he was sure it would lead to their mistreatment.

The Marines had decided not to remain in hiding – and perhaps eventually get involved in a gun battle in and around the Long Island area – not because they were heavily outnumbered by the Argentines, but probably because it would be too high a risk to the civilian population. They also felt that the Argentines would be likely to carry out reprisals against Islanders for assisting them in hiding. The decision must have been an extremely difficult one for these highly professional soldiers who were more than eager to fight the Argentines. Neil could not be consoled, not even by the fact that it had been agreed they would hide their automatic weapons and suchlike around the Long Island area before walking in to the enemy. It was a terribly bitter pill for Neil to swallow, given he was so passionate and loyal to the British, and the Royal Marines in particular.

After a few days, my family and I moved on to Green Patch, and a small convoy of us drove off in Land Rovers to our destination just five or six miles away. Upon our arrival we met up with some more old friends – and during the course of this bloody war we made many more new ones.

The day had been a long one for some of us because we had been in to Stanley, travelled back to Long Island, delivered stores and collected my family and others, before driving off to Green Patch. However, once settled in, we quickly became members of one big family group. The community had rapidly grown from approximately 15 to 50 people. The regular residents were some of the new farm owners living in a settlement which was now owned by the Falkland Island Government, but was still acting as a hub for the individual farmers to live and carry out their sheep farming businesses cooperatively, by utilising infrastructure and facilities on hire from the Government.

Green Patch turned out to be a perfect choice of location during the Falklands War. It was only 20 miles or so from Stanley, but the war, as luck would have it, most of the time just happened to go around, rather than through or in, the settlement. Upon reflection, it does make me wonder why the Argentines did not pay more attention to the place, because it had been a base for the Royal Navy's HMS *Endurance* helicopters. This did get the Argies a little excited later into the war, but I will get back to that tale later on.

My mate Pete told me that before I had arrived he and others had moved a lot of useful provisions and equipment which had been placed in the community hall by the local FIG representative. The gear had been left behind by the members of Royal Naval Parties 8901 (the Royal Marines) and 8902 (the Royal Navy) in the tractor shed when they had to make their rapid exit to join the *Endurance*, which had been instructed to leave Stanley immediately and head for South Georgia after the incident down there with scrap metal workers. Those who did not join *Endurance* regrouped with the HQ of the Royal Marine detachment at Moody Brook in Stanley. Just to remind you, the South Georgia incident was just short of two weeks before the Falklands invasion.

The decision to remove the gear had been an extremely intelligent one, for the interior of the community hall had apparently looked more akin to a British military museum with all the equipment and ration packs neatly laid out, and anything slightly resembling a British military base was not the cleverest thing to show off to the Argentines, should they decide to make an unscheduled visit to Green Patch, as they surely would do. They would be deeply suspicious and perhaps believe that some British military personnel were still about the place.

Remember, they had been searching for missing Royal Marines and their discovery of all this gear would have certainly led to a considerable amount of questioning and mistrust of the local community, thus harassment for us all. This in turn would have surely resulted in a permanent Argentine presence, which just might have meant that our war story would have been more akin to the residents at Goose Green or Pebble Island. The people at Goose Green would find themselves shut up in one small building for 30 days under appalling conditions, whilst on Pebble Island the community were held in the manager's house – all much different to the war we would experience.

There was also an extremely good logical reason for moving the stores. Over time, we might be in real need of the additional food supply contained in the many boxes of ration packs. Still in their original packaging, the rations were in perfect condition. (As it turned out, we would be very glad of them.) The guys had been very clever when they decided where to hide the boxes away. They dug out holes in peat banks and placed the packs, wrapped in plastic, inside, then covered them up again. With the natural terrain, it would have taken an extremely intelligent, or very lucky, Argentine to have found them there and fortunately we did not run into too many of them during our piece of the war.

Also stored in the hall were flat beds (sorry, I do not know the military term), which were extremely useful given the additional amount of people now in the settlement. The arrival of my family and Pete's had increased the population by 11.

After unloading vehicles and having one or two excellent cups of tea and a good old chat about the present situation, it was time to think about moving into our new home. It was clear from the moment of our arrival that my family and I were more than welcome to stay in the settlement, for which we were exceedingly grateful. We were informed that the small house at the far west end of the settlement would be at our disposal. It had been used as the school prior to the war and I think the children in the settlement were quite happy it was now closed, and even more pleased that someone was going to live in it, because that would surely mean it was not going to reopen for a while. We were also told to help ourselves to the peat supply which was stacked near the house, and that the vegetable garden, which was fully cultivated and situated in close proximity to the house, belonged to Peter Goss (my first cousin); if we needed a feed of potatoes or other vegetables, we should help ourselves as they were sure he wouldn't mind. I never knew if he did or didn't. If he did, we were truly thankful to him and Margaret anyway, because by the end of the war I do not think there was an awful lot of anything left in their garden, but I did make a good job of tidying it up, ready for him to cultivate the next year.

Once we moved into our new abode we were all in a good frame of mind. Our home, as it would turn out to be for the rest of the war, was compact, but it provided enough space for a family of six to live in. My wife, the children and I took one bedroom, whilst dad and Uncle Johnnie shared the other. We had a reasonable-sized kitchen, the scullery and bathroom were large, but most important of all, there were no bloody Argies, which, given we were under occupation, was totally blissful.

The kids settled in right away and they were delighted that they had plenty of young friends to play about with. After a day or two it was soon routine for them go down to Carol and Terance's house, especially after nightfall, to watch a video. Although we had no television network in the Falklands, there were a few television sets knocking around, and even fewer video recorders, but as good luck would have it, Chuck from the Globe Hotel had both, and fortunately he had the presence of mind to bring them out to Green Patch. Now they took centre stage of the lounge at Terance and Carol's house, which provided entertainment for adults and children alike. The limited supply of video tapes had become pretty badly worn by the end of the war.

Many of the days in April were spent visiting people in their homes to exchange news or just plain old gossip, and in doing the domestic chores, taking walks and so on. Every once in a while I would go into Stanley with a few other people to buy stores and/or collect a few more essentials for our families and other members of our tiny community who did not have the means to go in themselves. However, by the end of the month this practice was not possible as the Argentines had closed Stanley off, and once the *General Belgrano* had been sunk on 2 May, war was most definitely on and it would have been totally disregarding one's health to try it.

It was always amusing and pleasurable to go and visit Jock and June McPhee at their house on the Farm. Jock had a quick wit. No sooner were you in his house than he would say, 'Let's go in the office and see what we can find.' The room he called the office had a wonderful piece of furniture full of pigeonholes and drawers. It didn't seem to matter which drawer he selected, because they all seemed to contain a bottle of Johnnie Walker Red Label whisky, which he would pluck out with a very contented smile on his face and immediately proceed to screw off the cap. Announcing, 'I don't think we will need that any more,' he would crush the cap between fingers and thumb and throw it into the waste bin, then vessels of all shapes and sizes would be seized and used for drinking the whisky, to the enjoyment of the appreciative gathering. Eventually June would politely break up the party by calmly informing Jock that his meal was ready and waiting on the table for him.

As luck would have it, my best mate at the time Pete, a small group of children and I were enjoying the fine weather and the stroll to Brookfield Farm one morning. We were slightly over half the distance to our objective when we heard the unmistakeable sound of a helicopter. There was no need to guess who would be flying and occupying the craft. Pete and I stopped as one and turned to each other. Despite a brief moment of panic, we decided there was no way we could get back to Green Patch in time to do anything which might be helpful in supporting our families. We also concluded there was certainly nothing we could do to assist the Argentines. Therefore we decided we should pick up the pace and get our backsides to the house at Brookfield, but in a fashion that would not alarm the children.

The people at Brookfield were great, but I was on edge, I could not relax. I was concerned for the remainder of my family still at Green Patch. Anyway, after a while we heard the helicopter again. This time we assumed it was on its way and we were breaking our necks to find out what had been going on, so we made our way back to the settlement as fast as we could. I was delighted and mighty relieved as we reached the farm gate and got our first clear glimpse of the settlement, because at once I noticed some children playing around and a couple of adults going about their tasks in what appeared to be a relaxed fashion. I headed directly home, whilst my friend broke off and went towards his house at the other end of the settlement, no doubt every bit as concerned about his family as I was about mine.

Once home, I could see that Melody was fairly calm. She told me that the Argentines had come into the house and done a thorough search, then carried out a head count and took everyone's name. They also asked dad about his gun licence and the whereabouts of his weapons. Apparently they did not ask any particularly difficult questions. Melody also told me that the Argentine officer spoke exceptionally good English and he proudly told her that he had been educated in England. One thing this incident did drum home to me and my family was that although we might have been out of sight of the Argentines, we were now certainly no longer out of their minds. From now on they could, and probably would, drop in unannounced any time they liked. Quite a worrying prospect! But my thoughts were suddenly distracted when completely out of the blue, four-year-old Amelia touched me on the hand and said, 'He was a nice man, he gave me a bar of chocolate, daddy.' I smiled at her, touched her on the top of the head and thought how blissful the innocent mind can be – and hoped she and Severine would not come to any harm during this godforsaken war.

I will always vividly recall my first encounter with a piece of Argentine military weaponry. It was one of those unforeseen and unique moments. I was walking along the coast on one bright and sunny but chilly morning with Severine. He had been enjoying himself watching the various animals and birds feeding, swimming or flying about the place, and we were about half a mile from our house, making our way back towards the farm in a leisurely manner and chatting away about this and that, whilst we threw stones in to the mirror-like water. Then we were suddenly somewhat startled by a plane which appeared from nowhere and was now heading straight at us as it hugged the coastline. I remember getting the words 'what the bloody hell' out of my mouth, then stopping in mid-sentence as we both froze to the spot and looked up towards it. It was coming up the shoreline like one of our giant petrels in flight as it glided along with wing tip just off the ground.

I remember having a firm grip of Severine's hand as we ran inland a few yards then stopped to turn and look at it again. I had no idea what type of plane it was, but as it got closer and closer then flew past us just above our heads, I could clearly see the pilot sitting strapped in his seat. He turned his head and looked towards us and gave a wave and smile, but I did not respond, for I was totally dumbfounded. I did recognise that the aircraft had Argentine markings, and once it had flown by I got Severine home as quickly as possible.

The plane, as it turned out, was an Argentine-built Pucara. A couple of members of the 3rd Parachute Regiment who I was talking with at the Estancia later on during the war told me it was a nasty piece of work which enjoyed itself most shooting up ground troops. With this new-found knowledge I was rather pleased that it, and the pilot, were in a good mood that day, or it might just have spoiled our stroll in the sunshine.

During April we made a couple of trips to Stanley to stock up on food and other essential supplies and also to take the opportunity to see a few friends and members of the family. During the later visit it was noticeable that the Argentines were much more jumpy and irritated. Curfews were now in place, with civilians ordered off the streets and windows blackened out between dusk and dawn. There were also many more Argentine military about the place, there had been an obvious build-up of forces since the first two weeks of the invasion.

One of their checkpoints in and out of Stanley was at the cattle gate at the old Royal Marines barracks, which was now being utilised as a barracks for Argentine ground forces. The whole area was bristling with troops. They were also in the surrounding hills to the back of the Moody Brook barracks and up around Wireless Ridge and Moody Valley. Field kitchens were in place, vehicles, men and equipment were on the move or being set up, the place was a hive of activity. Once in town, we heard a rumour that Galtieri was making a short daytrip to Stanley to visit his military governor, General Menendez, to boost his forces' morale, and because of that there were extra precautions and more stringent inspections of civilian vehicles and personnel. I have no idea if he did visit the Falklands that day. None the less, on our way out of Stanley that wet and cold day the Argentines were very uncooperative and they held six of us, Terance, Carol, Peter, Jackie, Neil and myself, at gunpoint for nearly an hour before allowing us to move on from the checkpoint at Moody Brook.

During our short stop in Stanley, Peter and I called into the Falkland Club – we were both members of this strictly male-only establishment – to have a quick drink and to collect some supplies of beer and whisky for the farm. For some reason, before I went behind the bar to get my requirements I thought I would take a look inside the lounge, which was adjacent and separated only by two sliding doors. I pulled back one of the doors rather vigorously, and as it rapidly slid open, to my astonishment I saw an even more surprised figure down on the floor and huddled in one corner with a steel billiard cue in one hand and fiddling knobs on a radio with the other. He looked up at me with an expression of horror, because he expected to see a very irate Argentine military person who had finally discovered where the radio signals were coming from and who was transmitting them. I realised instantly what was going on, patted the man on the head and said, 'Don't worry, Reg, it's only me. I've just popped in to get a few things and I'll be off. Carry on with whatever it is you're doing, my friend.' His face relaxed and without another word I took a step or two backwards and closed the door again.

Reg was a fellow club member and a man with considerable radio skills. He had been using the club as a radio shack and, coupled with his improvised equipment, was transmitting messages back to the UK. The Argentines knew someone was doing it because they had been picking up the signals with their mobile tracking station, but they kept raiding the Rose Hotel Bar, which was just across the road, mistaking it for the source of the signals.

Happily, the Argentines never did find Reg during the whole period of the occupation, and I told very few people of my discovery that day. He would go back to England shortly after the war, having done his little piece of Argentine resistance. Reg was like many civilians left in the Falklands during the war, doing their own little thing to assist British forces where and whenever possible, and being as unhelpful as they dared be to the occupying Argentine forces, sometimes at considerable risk to themselves and other members of the civilian community who knew of their colleagues' actions and gave them full and unselfish support, in the hope that one day we would all be free again.

It wasn't all about underground and resistance movements, as one might associate with France. The Falklands War was something completely different, but wherever possible the Falkland Islanders and other civilians pulled together to achieve the same goal, which was to stuff the Argie one, good and proper. Whilst in Stanley on this occasion – our last as it would happen, until after the war – I was told a wonderful tale which epitomised the type of compassion and camaraderie within the town's community at the time of the occupation. My old football mate Les Biggs and a cousin, Chris McCallum, had a Land Rover; I am not sure if it was theirs, because more and more people were going away and leaving their vehicles behind, and it made very good sense to acquire and use them or they would have been taken and used by the Argentines. Anyway, I learnt that Les and Chris had been going around the town to many people's homes, usually the elderly, infirmed, or those who were just too frightened to go out of their houses, and helping them with domestic chores such as getting in the peat, collecting and delivering stores, or just sitting down with them and have a chat over a cup of tea and a cookie. I was really moved and very proud of their unselfish and tireless work for the good of others.

Just before leaving Stanley I ran into to my long-standing friend Patrick Watts. We started to talk about the night I went down to the radio station with a belly full of whisky to see him the last time I had been in the town.

I had decided that I would go and see what he was up to. Upon entering the studio I found him in the transmitting room, which had a small L-shaped desk with a single suspended microphone and two record turntables. Around the walls were shelving for storing the radio station's record collection, tapes and other bits and pieces. Behind the control desk was a large solid glass window which allowed you a complete view of the adjacent recording studio. I recalled having been in there on many occasions as quizmaster of the children's sports quizzes on their *Children's Corner* programme, also as a member of a winter quiz team, or with various bands recording half-hour programmes for shows like *Music Unlimited*, with Patrick on the other side of the glass as the responsible production and recording engineer. Now, that all seemed to be days long gone.

I think Patrick must have been going on air. Whatever, I decided to leave him in the main transmission room and I was about to step inside the adjacent workshop room when I was immediately addressed by an Argentine officer in the doorway, who looked me straight in the eye and said in very good English, 'What do you want?'

'Oh, nothing,' I said. 'I've just come down to see Patrick and he's busy at the moment so I thought I would come and see what you guys are up to.'

He was more than a little surprised and amused by my attitude. As I looked around I noticed there must have been about another six or seven Argentines in the shop, fixing, fetching and carrying this and that. 'Really,' he said. 'Well, come in, but don't touch anything, and don't get in the way, or I'll throw you out, and as soon as he' – pointing in the direction of Patrick – 'has finished you must leave.'

I nodded and went up to the workbench and rested my backside against it, and I started to talk with the officer about football. He opened up, saying how Argentina was going to win the World Cup – they were the World Champions at the time. I remember saying to him I didn't think they would and I hoped they wouldn't. He took my bullish comments fairly well.

Slowly, I started to get more and more confident as the conversation went on. Finally I got on to the subject of the invasion and told him that in my opinion Argentina had made a big mistake and that he and the rest of the Argentines should get back home before it was all too late.

'What do you mean?' he snapped.

'Well, the British are coming and if you're still here when they arrive, they will kick your ass,' I said.

He glared at me but did not get angry at my statement; rather, he appeared to become more intrigued. 'What do you mean?' he repeated.

Without hesitation I said, 'Well, the British troops are the best in the world and if it comes to fighting you lot have no chance.'

'Don't be so bloody cocky. Don't be so bloody sure of yourself,' he went on.

By now I was beginning to get a little bit carried away. 'You wait and see.' I was now upright and pointing my finger at him, just as Patrick entered the workshop. 'For every one British soldier that dies, ten of you guys will.'

He coolly looked towards Patrick and said, 'I think you should take your friend away.'

I quickly realised I had pushed my luck a very long way indeed, and I left, never to see him or his Argentine colleagues again. God knows if he survived or not. I hope he did, because I think he was probably a decent sort of chap who was just doing his job. Otherwise I doubt if he would have put up with my bullshit that night.

Jumping on a bit, the last rendezvous that we made for stores was on D-Day 21 May, when a small group of us went to a place called Corner Pass. This is a small waterway between Long Island Mountain and the Two Sisters. Ron Buckett had come out from Stanley to meet us. Once the exchange of goods and messages had been completed we went our separate ways. On our return towards Green Patch the Argentines stopped us on the top of Long Island Mountain, where they were now dug in. They were not a very sporting bunch of chaps at all and were very aggressive as they started to jostle us about a bit. One fellow was particularly pissed off and kept prodding his rifle into my side. They searched our vehicles thoroughly and at one point it seemed they might take everything we had on board. Eventually they settled for our offer of all the luxury items such as Cadbury's chocolates, cigarettes and liquor, which, considering they held all the bargaining chips, was not an unreasonable compromise. When we arrived back home there were a few disappointed children and adults, and dad thought we were rather childish to have given up the whisky. But that was soon forgotten as we sat down for dinner, which was served with a few extra delights on the plate to celebrate the British landings at San Carlos.

One other thing that happen to us during April which I should mention was that the Argentines started to cut normal communications between the communities. Those farms that had a telephone link with Stanley were cut off. I should point out that there was no telephone communication between West Falklands and Stanley before the war other than the radio telephone (RT). They also began jamming the BBC World Service programme *Calling the Falklands*, until the BBC got wind of it and moved to a frequency which remained unimpeded for the remainder of the war. They also put a total ban on the use of two-metre radio sets and all aerial masts had to be taken down. The idea was psychological warfare. Depriving us of information, it was hoped, would add to our insecurity. But let me tell you, it worked. The few days without the radio programmes had a numbing sensation on one's mind; psychological warfare is a lethal weapon.

The two-metre radio and telephone network between Stanley would remain inoperable for the remainder of the war. However, we in the north camp were able to keep in touch with neighbouring farms with the old antiquated telephone system, which was worked by cranking the handle and dialling a farm. It had a quite unique numbering system, one long ring, one short ring and then one long ring, would be someone's number. When communications with the BBC and *Calling the Falklands* were restored, they became compulsive listening, as we received news and messages from friends and family in the UK and other parts of the world. I remember one day dad was over the moon to receive a message of good wishes from Arnold, Mary and family. That was just what the programme was about, to inform and lift spirits. Peter King was magnificent in his role as presenter. He became a household personality and everyone took note of his signing off words 'Keep your chins up and your heads down'.

I met him a couple months later, when he came down for the occasion of the 150th anniversary celebration, and later at the BBC in London, where he interviewed me, after which he was then kind enough to offer me a lift back to my hotel. Peter was as he sounded on the radio, a huge loveable character, light-hearted, quick-witted and extremely intelligent and a genuine friend of Falkland Islanders. When he came to the Islands in 1983 and again in 1992, I know he had a deservedly enjoyable time. Another man to lift the spirits through the media in no less a manner was the BBC's Latin-American correspondent Harold Briley, who reported from inside Argentina. When Harold arrived in the Falklands I remember taking him back to my house on one occasion and giving him a very large whisky and a supercharged rendition of my song '255', all at 4 a.m.

One of the most amusing announcements I remember coming from the Argentine authorities during April informed us that we were free to celebrate Queen Elizabeth II's 56th birthday on 21 April – they wished Falkland Islanders to enjoy the day. We didn't need telling that, we had every intention of doing so. I just found the whole thing funny. Did they really think they would be able to stop us? What the hell were they going to do to us, round us all up and lock us away for the day? Upon reflection, I suppose it was meant as a gesture of goodwill. At Green Patch we had a good gathering and enjoyed a few tots of spirits or cans of beer, according to fancy.

One thing that we always tried to do during the occupation was to try and keep up traditions as much as possible, including 'glory hour'. This was traditionally a Sunday drinking hour between midday and 1 p.m. We would get together at someone's house and pool our supplies of refreshments and sit around and chat about the week's events or whatever. Towards the end of the war, bar stocks were getting alarmingly low and we were finally left with various types of Bols liqueurs, which in my opinion is terrible stuff, and it was exceedingly difficult to try and stretch one's imagination to the point where you could pretend you were enjoying an excellent blend of malt whisky, Jamaican rum or Gordon's gin, because once you had swallowed the stuff it left you gasping for breath.

The highlight of the month was undoubtedly the news that the British had retaken South Georgia. Its effect on morale was extremely uplifting, especially as HMS *Endurance* had been involved, which in turn meant that so had a Falkland Islander. John Ferguson was one of the ship's company, and we were proud of his participation. The knowledge that the British forces were now much closer to us and that they had given the Argentines a serious warning that they meant business and that they had the capabilities to cause serious damage and pain – demonstrated by the demobilisation of the Argentine submarine the *Sante Fe* – gave us at Green Patch suddenly real hope of the possibility of giving the Argentines more to think about than issuing bloody edicts to us.

The Argentine surrender at South Georgia on 26 April was a great way for me and dad to celebrate my sister's 25th birthday. What I did not know, however, was that on the same day my younger brother Peter (Popeye) had arrived at Ascension Island to play his individual role in the British task force as a crew member of the Royal Fleet Auxiliary ship the *Tidepool*, which he had joined up with off Curacoa. Interestingly, the *Tidepool* had been sold by the British to Chile, but now they had borrowed her back again.

It was the beginning of the Betts brothers' triangular involvement in the Falklands War. Peter was in the task force, Alec was working alongside the Argentines in their LADE airline office in Stanley, and I was soon going to be involved in moving British ground forces and equipment around the Estancia area.

Following yet another edict, this one towards the end of April, we were informed that all communities within the Islands had to comply with blackouts at night. Previously it had applied to Stanley only. It was yet another signal that real war was ever closer. Therefore, we decided it might be a good idea to make use of the bales of wool in the woolshed and build ourselves a kind of air raid shelter.

It was also a good exercise for another reason, because it got all the able-bodied men together as a unit with a common goal. The structure, once finished, was quite impressive, built like Lego bricks on top of each other with tunnels weaving this way and that. There is no doubt that the 385 kilo bales of solidly compressed wool would have given us reasonable protection from bullets and shrapnel. Well, at least we believed so.

As I have mentioned, the lack of any sort of civilian shelters was one of the things that frequently came to my mind during the invasion night. This type of civil defence system had never been planned, and even today there are no installations for the civilians' protection against hostile attack. Quite amazing really when you consider that a military threat from Argentina might still exist.

19

The Waiting is Over – It's War

The month of May opened with a bang, or should I say with a series of them, and quite literally. I was outside the house when suddenly there were huge bangs and thumps and the ground beneath my feet began to shake. I could not comprehend what the hell was going on at first, there had been no sound of incoming shells or mortar fire – hey, I am becoming an expert now – so what the hell could it be? I began to run as fast as I could towards the top of the hill at the back of the settlement. Terance Phillips was already up there. It was 8 a.m. and another fine, clear and still morning, not unlike invasion day a month earlier. As I got closer to Terance I shouted out, 'What the hell is it?'

'Christ knows,' he replied, 'but they are bloody big bangs.'

He was right about that. With each thud the ground would shudder. The only thing I knew for sure was that the Falklands doesn't have earthquakes to contend with, so it had to be explosions of some sort created by the military.

After a little while the commotion stopped, so I decided to go home. Curiosity was killing this particular cat, but I would not find out for about an hour or so after all the activity had calmed down what had actually happened. Once again it would be our dear old friend the BBC World Service who would inform us. As dad, Uncle Johnnie, Melody and I were huddled in a group around the radio, the latest news bulletin informed us that the British had bombed Stanley airfield with a Vulcan bomber, dropping 1,000lb bombs, and that attacks had also been made on installations at Goose Green with Sea Harriers. All of us in our little household broke away from our hunched positions and did a jump and jig for joy after hearing the news. I know this comment might seem a little jingoistic to some of you readers, but before you pour scorn on me and my family, just remember it was not us who created this bloody mess, but it was us who were right in the middle of it, and anything that gave us hope that one day soon we would get our freedom back and return to some sort of normality was very welcome news indeed.

Like waiting for Christmas, suddenly the waiting was over, and the war had begun in all earnest. It was all a little unreal and very scary, but we would adapt to the new situation in pretty quick time. The bombing of the airport at the beginning of May, had brought the combat right into our back yard and up to our front door.

Despite the fact that this action raised the level of the hostilities, and with it, the risks and dangers to us all, very frightening as it was to me and my family, and I am sure for many other Islanders, we knew that we had to accept this phase of the conflict as inevitable.

There was a positive side about this next stage of operations: there was no more need for guessing games about what was going to happen next, no more wondering if someone would come up with a peaceful solution. Alexander Haig, the United Nations and others had been trying, but from this day on Haig admitted failure. The United States decided it was time to get down off the fence and fully support the British effort to remove the Argentines from the Falklands, and offered military supplies, as well as imposing trade sanctions against Argentina.

Keeping abreast of the latest news was now of paramount importance, therefore dad, Uncle Johnnie and I decided that one of us would listen to the radio all day and night, taking it in turns to get sleep, just in case something really dramatic happened which might require us to make a speedy departure from the house or take some kind of evasive action.

We all went to bed that night pretty much satisfied with the day's events, but I did spare a thought for my mother in our house in Stanley. I knew she was frightened but she wanted to be with her husband. I noticed on our final trip to Stanley the Argentines were starting to get a bit jumpy. Stanley was becoming with each passing day a more and more dangerous place to be, and it would become increasingly so as the tension and military activities built up.

My mother did tell me a funny story the last time I had been in Stanley. Eric, who came from Scotland, had been working on the little coastal vessel the *Forrest*, the one that had been the floating radar on the night of the invasion, if you recall. Well, one day Eric was at the Government jetty and apparently strolled up to a small group of young Argentine soldiers who were milling around, and said to them, in his most colourful Scottish, 'Ye better watch oot when the Black Watch coom after ye.'

I must say, not a lot of English people understood what Eric was talking about, so God knows how the Argentines understood him.

The next few days were action-packed, full of high drama which resulted in huge emotional swings as the events between 1 and 5 May unfolded – not before our very eyes, but you lived and reacted to each piece of news being relayed by radio, which described every episode of tragedy and the terrible repercussions of war. Why is man so stupid?

The first of these incidents was the sinking of the Argentine cruiser the *General Belgrano*. I was in my bedroom when there was a knock on the door. It was dad. As he looked at me his eyes appeared as though they were on fire, and he had the look on his face as if he had found a pot of gold. He just said, 'They've got the *Belgrano*.' Throwing his arms in the air, he shouted, 'They've sunk her!' He was all very excited, then he went on to say, 'I have just heard it on the radio.' I was clueless, I didn't know who the *Belgrano* was, nor did I appreciate the significance of her demise. Dad was a little shocked that I had not heard of the ship and disappointed because I did not immediately join him in rejoicing at her fate. But he wasted no time in putting me straight on the potential strike power and threat to British forces which had now been extinguished.

The thing that struck me from dad's lesson was that it was totally amazing that an ex-United States of America warship which had survived Pearl Harbor was involved in the Falkland Islands War 40 years on.

Prior to the war, I had no interest in such matters. My trouble was, I was a bit of an idealist. I would not join the local Territorial Army because I believed man should put away all his weapons; having them only gave him the tools to self-destruct. I never accepted that weapons were for defence alone, I believed they started wars not stopped them. And I never accepted the idea of teaching men and women to kill their fellow man under the pretext of self-defence. Surely it made much more sense not to go into conflict in the first place.

My mates often laughed at me for my opinions on this subject. They also wondered why I couldn't swallow my opinionated pride and join up. That way I could be with them for the late-night drinking sessions in the Defence Force Club. Dad didn't think much of my, as he put it, 'way-off ideas', and I had to admit that right now, I was bloody pleased that the British forces were equipped with the weapons of destruction, so they could hopefully return our much treasured freedom.

I will also admit that once I understood the importance of the *General Belgrano*'s removal from this war game, it was not too long before I was joining in the celebrations with father and Uncle Johnnie. I am aware that the sinking of the *General Belgrano* has been controversial, but all I can say is this: on that day she represented the Argentine Navy, the enemy, and she constituted a serious threat, therefore I firmly believe the British Armed Forces were absolutely correct to take her out of action once and for all.

Since the war, there have been some who believe that the action was unnecessary, others would even go as far as to say that Margaret Thatcher committed a war crime. In my humble opinion, both views are totally preposterous.

I have never wavered in my belief that had the British not sunk the *General Belgrano*, many more, perhaps hundreds more, British service personnel and civilians would have lost their lives during the Falklands War. It is even possible the war itself might have been lost.

Some may argue that is not the point, the issue is that the ship was sunk outside the military exclusion zone and heading away from any potential battle scene. I would only ask these people now who is being really naïve? Do you really think that she could not have entered the fray at any given time, utilising all her military might against the British Forces and creating death and destruction as she did so? Whilst you are all mouth and condemning, would you have also had the balls to accept the responsibility of the additional loss of life? I rather think not.

What I do find most bizarre about this whole subject is that it is the British who seem to have the biggest problem of guilt about the issue. Everyone else, including the Argentines, readily accept it was a very sensible action by the British forces and the tragic loss of Argentine lives came about purely as a necessity of self-defence in time of war.

Several Argentine naval officers are on record as saying that, had they been in the same position, they would have done the same thing and taken British lives to save those of Argentines.

The sinking did do one thing to me. I became too elated, too confident, which in turn gave me the false belief that the war would be over in a matter of days. I was so sure the British were so powerful, so well equipped and organised, they would wipe the floor with the Argentines. It would only take two more days for me, and perhaps others who were thinking like me, to get a shocking rude awakening.

I think the shock was so pronounced because the day after the sinking of the *General Belgrano* we received news that another Argentine ship had been attacked and taken out of active service. This time it was the *Alferez Sobral*, a patrol vessel found to the north of the Falklands.

Then came the unthinkable, like someone punching you firmly in the stomach quite unexpectedly as you are standing with your hands in your pockets, knocking the wind out of you. I remember being totally overcome by the shocking news, completely numbed by the dreadful information, a tragedy that I had simply not prepared myself for.

Again, it was dad who broke the story to me. This time, however, I knew something had gone horribly wrong, or was about to. His face was pale and his hands were shaking as he approached me. I wondered if the Argies were about to descend upon us imminently and with serious intent.

He looked at me with glazed eyes, and with a quivering voice said, 'They've got one of ours, 'they've hit the *Sheffield*.'

I stood upright, took a deep breath and stood still, staring at the ceiling. It felt like the blood was draining from my entire body. Then I said, 'Oh my God, oh my God, what happened? How the bloody hell did that happen?'

'She's been hit by a missile.'

I could not understand how a ship could be hit by a missile. A bomb, shells, torpedos – yes, I could understand that. But a missile?

'I don't know,' he said, 'but that's what they have just said on the radio.'

'Has anyone been hurt? Has anyone been killed?' I questioned. I don't know why it is but you always ask that useless dumb ass question, don't you; it has no relevance to the situation whether it is one, or one thousand, but you always ask it. It generally makes no difference to your feelings, no difference to the gravity of the situation.

I was completely gutted and for a moment I could not speak. My grand illusion of an easy victory and a quick return to Stanley, getting back to work and living under a government of my choosing, had been shattered. Many other tragic events followed during this war, but they did not have quite the same impact upon me as the strike on HMS *Sheffield*.

The *Sheffield* would eventually sink whilst under tow to South Georgia. I was somewhat pleased about that. I felt, like someone's body, better to put it to rest and hold on to fond memories, rather than display her with all her ugly and horrifying scars.

There would be other days when I was down, but never as low as I was this day. My thoughts were not of self-pity and concern for me because the British might now have a real struggle, perhaps even lose the war. No, I was thinking of the families who were all those thousands of miles away, who had probably never heard of the Falklands until the Argentines had invaded, and how distraught they must all be. I was also concerned about the injured and the other survivors. Sickening as it was, I spent the day glued to the radio to try and get every piece of detail as to what had happened.

Within a few hours of going to bed, I was up again and, still upset from yesterday's events, I started doing the domestic chores to try and divert my train of thought from the horrors of the day before. But all of yesterday's events were being repeated by the BBC. I was truly floored, completely overcome. To add to the woes we were informed that a Harrier jump-jet had been lost whilst attacking Goose Green. Oh yes, 4 May 1982 was a very sorry day indeed.

For the rest of the war, life for me and my family would be different. Everyone's attitude changed, everyone would be much more alert and much more aware of the level of danger that might lie ahead. We all understood we were living in a life threatening environment, and we needed to be calculated in everything we did. We simply lived life on an hour-by-hour, day-by-day basis.

There was still talk and hope, by a few, that despite the fact that Britain and Argentina were shooting each other up, there would be a peaceful outcome. But in truth, in my opinion, once the task force was in a position to carry out a military campaign the diplomats never really had a positive role. They had had their chance and quite frankly had made little impact on the two opposing forces.

It might shock you somewhat, but now that we were in this predicament, I don't think that we wanted a peaceful solution any more anyway, because we were pretty certain that this situation could only mean something that would be highly satisfactory to the Argentines, which could only mean that we Falkland Islanders would suffer one way or another.

It was also pretty clear to me at this stage, perhaps even before, that Britain needed a military success as much as we did. The United Kingdom had not been having the best of times in the international political world – nor, for that matter, domestically. Many old friends had joined her enemies in regarding her as the poor relations, the 'has-beens'. After all, no one could reasonably deny that Russia and the United States of America were now the superpowers who held all the political and military clout.

On 6 May, the Argentines turned up again at Green Patch, and once again by helicopter. This time we were all in the settlement. It was on this occasion they found the helicopter landing lights and other bits and pieces, which got them terribly upset.

We were all ordered out of the houses. I was down at Terance and Carol's house at the time, so I was with them as we all grouped on the settlement green. Their senior officer, as it always seemed, could speak excellent English. He warned us that we had better not be clever, that we should tell him all we knew about the British and why it was that the helicopter equipment and other military gear was stowed away in the tractor shed. I must say, Carol was pretty impressive in dealing with inquisitive Argentines and she answered his questions in a direct and effective manner, even if her style was a little unorthodox and sometimes a little short on the complimentary side.

It was pretty easy for me when I was questioned, I genuinely did not know a thing about how they had come to be there. After all,

I was only a visitor, a townie.

Just as some of his men began carrying out the equipment from the building the officer got very aggressive and started shouting, 'If you lot don't tell me something soon, I will gather you all up and take you to Stanley.'

Carol then blasted back at him, 'Don't be so bloody stupid. How do we know where the British might be? The people who brought this stuff here are probably long gone.' It was obvious he was quite unused to having a woman talk to him in such a direct manner and he was struggling to deal with it.

Anyway, it mattered not, because just at that moment one of the flight crew of the helicopter began shouting and waving at the officer, signalling that he had received some kind of radio communication.

Whatever it was, God knows, but once the crew member had finished passing the message on, the officer turned to his men and reeled off a whole string of instructions in very rapid Spanish indeed. The men responded by hurrying towards the helicopter and piling in as quickly as possible. As the last of the men were still scrambling aboard, the helicopter was already off the ground. It gained height, circled and flew off.

The war had escalated considerably now. In addition to the naval bombardments the fighting started to take to the skies in a meaningful way. There were daily reports of Argentine ships, aircraft and land bases being attacked.

One of the Argentine ships that would go to a watery grave in the Falkland Sound was the *Isla De Los Estados*. I had some fond memories of her coming to Stanley and berthing at the Falkland Islands Company east jetty with supplies of gas, kerosene and petrol. I had worked on her many times as a stevedore, unloading and loading her cargo. They were lucrative contracts for us.

From the BBC report, I got the impression that HMS *Alacrity* had stormed through the Falkland Sound in a cavalier sort of fashion, with all guns blazing, and upon sighting the Argentine ship, *Alacrity* had literally blown poor old *Isla De Los Estados* out of the water. I assumed from my experiences of working on board her in the past, and the BBC report that she blew up in one great fireball, that the explosion gave the crew little or no chance whatsoever.

It was a strange kind of sensation listening to the news about the destruction of ships and places you knew first hand. But I could be a callous bugger at times, and especially upon the news of any Argentine adversity. I turned to my father and said, 'Well, I guess I won't be unloading the *Isla De Los Estados* any more dad.'

Five days later came news of another of the old Argentine supply vessels which had become a familiar sight to the stevedore gang in Stanley, the *Bahia Buen Suceso*. That's right, the same old bugger who had taken the Condor group away from the Islands after their antics in 1966, and also transported Davidoff and his scrap metal workers to South Georgia just before the war. She had finally come to grief when she got herself strafed whilst moored near the farm settlement of Fox Bay on West Falklands, where she lay for the rest of the war.

One night in the middle of May, members of the SAS landed by helicopter on Pebble Island and proceeded to destroy 11 Argentine aircraft on a grass landing strip and an ammunitions dump. This news was particularly uplifting because it signalled British soldiers were at last on the ground. It was comforting to think that it was likely we had a few other welcome friends about the place, too.

On this occasion, however, the good news was tempered somewhat, although dad and I were thrilled that Pebble Island (the Betts's original base) would go down in the history books as the first place that British forces put foot on in the Falklands after the invasion of 2 April. However, the mood was somewhat subdued by the news that the civilian population had been locked up in 'the big house' by the Argentines, including dad's granddaughter Susie Hansen and her husband Ian, and also his halfbrother John and stepmother Cinty. That is, my niece, uncle and step-grandmother. This news was especially worrying as there was no word about their safety or treatment by the Argentines. It would be sometime later that we learnt all the civilians on Pebble were alive and unharmed.

20

The Pebble Island Story

It is only in recent months that I have contacted my niece and asked her about their experiences. I was very curious to learn about what it was like for other members of my family who lived through a different kind of war. Theirs was to be on a tiny and isolated island, where they were eventually imprisoned by the enemy.

My niece Susie has told me how the Argentines arrived at Pebble the day after the invasion, did a head count, took away radios and any other form of communications equipment, firearms etc., then announced that they were off and would not be back. However, to her surprise and shock, the next day the Argentines were back and, it appeared, back to stay. Several aircraft landed at the tiny grass airstrip and dozens of armed soldiers piled into the settlement and began settling in.

For six weeks the small civilian population tried to carry on with daily farming chores as best as possible but it was difficult to ignore the fact that the place was now crawling with Argentine soldiers.

However, as Susie explains, on 15 May things took a dramatic turn for the worse:

> That night, members of the SAS came through the settlement and blew up aircraft and an ammunitions dump on the airstrip, which isn't very far away from the settlement.
>
> Our house was in the valley of the settlement and it was very dark, so we couldn't see very much. However, we could see large flashes and hear the deafening explosions which appeared to come from the hill behind the manager's house, which, next day, became our prison for a month. There was also a lot of small arms fire, I think mainly from panicking young Argentine soldiers, who I presumed were shooting at anything that moved.

Following the attack on the airstrip, we were all rounded up by somewhat annoyed and nervous Argentinians, then taken to the manager's house and incarcerated. I suppose we were taken there because it was the largest house on the farm. There were 23 of us, with grandmother Cinty, now 82, the eldest, locked in a house with half a dozen bedrooms and two bathrooms.

Every night we would queue outside the bathroom doors after lights out with torches in hand. One night I recall one of the children was in the bathroom when delayed-action bombs started exploding, causing tremendous noise, and the house began shaking. Then as the young boy tried to let himself out of the bathroom the doorknob came off in his hand. His father spent the next few minutes telling his son what to do, so between them they could put the knob back on again and the boy could let himself out and the others could use the bathroom.

Susie also told me that when the British dropped their bombs on or around the airfield, it would shake the house so badly that windows would break. In fact it was discovered afterwards that the end of the house had moved and was very close to collapsing. The safety of the house was not helped by the fact that the Argentines had set up an anti-aircraft gun alongside the house, which shook the structure as much as any bomb landing. I think the Argentines had developed the idea of civilian human shields long before Saddam Hussein.

To provide a shelter the men had cut a hole in the floor of the lounge so the women and children could climb in under the floor for a little bit of added protection when the night-time bombardments and shelling from the British started. Susie explains that she was too claustrophobic so she would often stay above ground.

She recalls that one night, whilst lying on a sofa, one of the Argentine guards, called George, who spoke good English, was lying on the floor in front of the fire, when he suddenly began crying.

> We were being bombarded at the time and I felt sorry for him because I thought he was frightened. It transpired, however, that he was crying for our safety, because earlier in the evening

a particularly nasty officer, whom we nicknamed 'Bad Man' had made a search of the house, including looking up chimneys of fireplaces, even those that had a fire burning. He was totally convinced that we were collaborating with the British and were responsible for the bombardments. Apparently 'Bad Man' had informed George the guard that if there were any more bombardments we were all to be shot.

Susie highlights another common factor throughout the Falklands War:

I recall there were many frightened and hungry Argentine conscripts. The officers had taken over grandmother's house, and after the surrender it was discovered that the officers had lived in relative comfort with any amount of stores and food, whilst the conscripts had spent six weeks on the island in trenches, cold and starving. They were so hungry, they would beg us for scraps of food.

We were lucky, we had plenty of stores, we also had fresh meat and vegetables, and the women took turns at baking cakes and bread. We had a routine after we were locked up. A couple of us, escorted by an armed guard, would go and milk the cows. The conscripts would queue up outside the cowshed door in the hope of a mug of milk, straight from the cow to warm themselves up. Sadly this routine was curtailed, and so was our milk supply, when the Argentines eventually shot all the cows for fresh meat.

Afternoons were spent looking out of windows and watching the activity outside – Harriers dropping bombs and Argentine aircraft being chased by missiles. When things were much less playful, time was spent reading and playing cards. After blackout times it was a routine of supper and clean up, and whatever surprises were in store courtesy of the military from both sides.

Fortunately one of the guys had hidden his radio when all the others were confiscated. We had it rigged up in the house and tuned in to BBC World Service. Our Argentine guards knew we had it, but they did not mind because they would join us to listen in and get updated on news because they were not informed otherwise.

An example of this was the day HMS *Coventry* was hit, and lost, off Pebble Island. We had seen lots of helicopters flying up the Pebble coastline, and a few hours later we learned via the BBC that the *Coventry* had in fact been hit and we had been witnessing a rescue mission.

We had good views from the windows of the house we were locked up in. People would rush from one room to another to watch incoming Argentine aircraft, especially prior to the SAS attack. As I have indicated, we even witnessed Argentine aircraft being pursued by missiles and shot down. The only Argentine deaths on Pebble were the pilots. We saw several aircraft shot down and only on two occasions did I witness a pilot eject.

After the surrender we all went back to our homes. The Argentines had turned our house into a makeshift hospital and they had managed to burn a hole in the kitchen floor. For a hospital the place was filthy, but we did have some luck, most of our personal effects were still in the house. A neighbour lost all his personal items when the house the Argentines were occupying was burnt to the ground.

Many other people lost things or had them damaged. The Argentines spread excrement everywhere, they soiled everywhere with their inconsiderate and unnecessary behaviour.

In many ways, I am sure it was worse for our families as they knew the Argentines occupied Pebble, and that the island was constantly being bombed, shelled or suchlike. They would also be aware that we were imprisoned for 30 days in pretty difficult circumstances, and they did not know if we were dead or alive. Or, perhaps, even taken to Argentina.

I find it quite amazing that although Susie was in very grave danger for more than a month, her final comments about the war were her concerns about the fears and traumas of other members of her family. But then, she is a Betts, that's what really counts.

21

Events in May, and My Brother Joins the Fray

May was a topsy-turvy month for morale. No sooner did your spirits get lifted by word of a British success in one form or another, than it would be quickly followed by a tragedy of varying magnitude, because it was not, and of course it was never going to be, all British successes; British ships and aircraft were being hit, some damaged, others lost, with loss of life and serious injury, either in combat or by accident. One of the most dreadful accidents resulted in the loss of 21 lives as a helicopter ditched in the sea between two ships just a couple of days before the Falklands D-Day, 21 May 1982.

Strangely enough, even in times of war, I still found time to reflect and analyse things other than the war itself, but in relation to the consequences of it, I had become sure about one very important issue – hardly surprising, I suppose, considering I was having these thoughts whilst living this war out in reality.

My thinking was this. If the Argentines were successful in keeping the Falkland Islands as a result of their unprovoked military takeover, it would almost certainly be the spark for many more such acts worldwide, areas that were all little powder kegs just waiting to explode.

For example, our other neighbours just across the water, Chile, certainly did not want an Argentine military success in the Falklands, because it would surely encourage the Argentinians to attack Chile at some time, because they had been disputing territory with each other for many years.

A British victory was not only desirables just for me, and other Islanders, but it was essential for Britain and other countries, because it would demonstrate to the whole world that the principle of taking someone's land against the wishes of its inhabitants was totally unacceptable, and as we all know now, this was the same basic principle that the United States of America, Great Britain and others would uphold against Iraq when it invaded Kuwait just nine years later.

Had Britain not won the war, I guess it is fair to assume that Britain would also not have recovered domestically to rebuild her economy and regain a credible place in international politics to the levels it enjoys today, and equally as certain, the map of the world would be much different today.

You will note through this book I have very personal political opinions and I am not worried about sharing them.

A remarkable thing about our war at Green Patch is that we all got on with each other in our small and now even more isolated community. We were all living in an atmosphere of extreme tension and there was plenty of scope for personality clashes and bickering, but people generally put them to one side in the interest of all.

From what you have read so far, you might be thinking that life for us was all a bit of a doddle. It was never that. True we were fortunate beyond all expectations not to ever be up to our ears in Argentines and eventually have ourselves interned in the community hall, but we like everyone in the Islands, irrespective of where you were located, were right in the heart of a full scale war with nowhere to run and very few places to hide, a war which by now was escalating daily. Once the bridgehead was established on 21 May, anywhere from Darwin to the north on the ground, in East Falklands in particular, was a potential battleground. Of course until our D-Day, no one actually knew where the landings might take place, but there was plenty of speculation amongst ourselves. We reckoned a farm in Berkeley Sound could be one such place.

During the daily broadcasts of *Calling the Falklands*, it was also clear to me that the British Government and the British forces had continued overwhelming support from the people of Great Britain, who were doing everything possible to ensure that the huge fleet of ships of all shapes and sizes were refitted, replenished and prepared by working around the clock to ensure that the military machine had all the resources available to liberate us 8,000 miles away.

Although the highly professional British forces would pull off an incredible victory in the South Atlantic, I was also well aware that without the massive public support in Great Britain and the involvement of civilians in the task force it would surely not have been possible. As a Falkland Islander I must record my sincere gratitude to each and every one of you, and may God bless you all.

My younger brother Peter (Popeye) had left the Falklands in 1977 and joined the British merchant navy, because he did not have the right of abode in the United Kingdom. The merchant navy gave him the opportunity to earn a reasonable living and the ability to move in and out of the UK, so as not to become an illegal immigrant.

In April 1982, he would find himself in quite a dilemma. He and his wife Shirley were expecting their first child and he had been granted extended leave to be with her at the birth, which was expected sometime in April. When the news of the invasion broke, Peter desperately wanted to be with Shirley and to hold their first child after the great event, but he equally wished to do what he could to support the British cause to recover the Falkland Islands, which after all was his birthplace, and where a majority of his family were still living.

At first Peter decided he would stay put and would offer his collection of photographs, slides (he was a keen amateur photographer) and movie film of the Islands to Royal Marines Intelligence. He also volunteered to have a debrief about the Islands at Seaton Barracks in Plymouth.

Despite Shirley telling him that he should do whatever he felt he needed to do, his decision to volunteer with the Merchant Federation to join the first ship available, was a heart-wrenching one. But there was little time to dwell, because he would soon be boarding an aircraft to fly out of Heathrow airport to join, as I have mentioned before, the RFA *Tidepool*. He signed on just ten days after the invasion.

The *Tidepool* was a 27,400-ton tanker, which as I have mentioned had been sold to the Chileans and lent back to the British. My brother was not the only Falkland Islander on the ship. To his surprise and delight, he was accompanied by an old schoolmate, Kelvin Summers. They sailed from Curacao, destined for Ascension Island, which they reached on 26 April, coincidently our sister's 25th birthday and the day the Argentines surrendered at South Georgia.

The *Tidepool* would enter the war zone on 15 May 1982, once again, rather fittingly; if you recall, it was the day members of SAS raided Pebble Island.

His son, Scott, was born on 22 April but he would be two weeks old before Popeye got news of the birth, although Shirley had attempted to send a telegram to him. Communications were very restricted, and even when he did receive the joyous news, he was not permitted for security reasons to send a radio reply, which resulted in him and his skipper having serious words.

Falklands D-Day, 21 May, was one of those typically mixed days of ups and downs emotionally and physically. I have told you the story of collecting the stores from Corner Pass that day. Upon reflection, I suppose the Argentines' reaction towards us was hardly surprising, considering the British had just landed at San Carlos and a bridgehead was being established.

San Carlos quickly became a hot spot. The Argentines' reaction to the British landing was swift, with vicious air attacks, as they swooped down on the supporting ships in San Carlos waters. Although the Argentines took heavy losses, our hearts would be heavy also because we learnt that HMS *Ardent* had to be abandoned with many losing their lives. HMS *Argonaut* had also been hit, with casualties.

The bridgehead at San Carlos meant that the land war was now under way on the Falklands mainland. It had progressed from individual Special Forces raids on designated targets, to gaining a foothold.

The BBC's descriptions of the troops landing and digging in, ship movements in San Carlos and firing off anti-aircraft fire at the Argentine fighter aircraft as they flew in at ridiculously low altitudes, conjured up movie scenes of World War II. Ships were being hit left, right and centre, fighter aircraft being shot out of the skies, soldiers attacked and killed on the ground – no wonder the waters at San Carlos would be called 'Bomb Alley'. And in the middle of all this scene of active warfare was the unlikely sight of the huge P & O liner *Canberra*, which appeared like a stranded iceberg and would be nicknamed the 'Great White Whale'.

Oh my God, the week 21 to 27 May was a time of terror, destruction and, worst of all, death and injury. In this one week five British ships would be lost, along with Sea Harriers and helicopters. One of the ships lost was the merchant vessel *Atlantic Conveyor*. Popeye had sailed on her in 1978 and he actually knew two of the men who lost their lives on her.

Popeye was himself in Bomb Alley on several occasions with the *Tidepool*. One such occasion was on 25 May, Argentine national day, the day *Atlantic Conveyor* and HMS *Coventry* were sunk. He told me that his emergency station was in a fire crew. Air raids were so frequent that no sooner had they received orders to stand down and get their fire suits stowed, than they would be ordered to fire stations and kitting up again. Eventually he and his fellow fire-fighting crew members decided to remain in their fire-fighting gear.

My brother said, on some of the raids the bombers would be in, drop their bomb load and be out the other end before the warning alarm had even sounded. So frequent and rapid were the attacks that the atmosphere was surreal. In the beginning they would look up to see which direction the aircraft were coming from, then they would whoosh past below their line of sight. But you soon got used to the idea, he would say.

'With the loss of the *Atlantic Conveyor*, *Tidepool* had to release her two helicopters to support the land forces, thus taking with them *Tidepool*'s only anti-aircraft weaponry. We didn't even have any chaff rockets,' he told me. I always knew Popeye was a cool character, but I never knew he had such a sense of humour. Listening to his stories about sitting on an oil tanker in the middle of a war, I realised he had both.

One day Peter Gilding and I took a trip from Green Patch over to a neighbouring farm called the Estancia, which is situated about ten miles to the southwest. As we approached a paddock, a helicopter suddenly appeared and was heading straight in our direction. Neither of us knew whose it was, nor what it was. We stopped the vehicle and got out. It was then very evident that it was going to land in the field nearby. We watched it, then as it landed a side door opened and a figure appeared. To our delight, he was British, the helicopter was British. Bloody hell, we were in the company of members of Her Majesty's Armed Forces.

We quickly climbed over the wire fence and began to assist the crew with the unloading of its cargo, which from memory were cans of fuel and boxes. God, it was so good to see the British troops and it was just wonderful to be doing something to help, no matter how small that was.

Soon enough the cargo was stacked a short distance away from the helicopter in cargo nets, and the helicopter lifted off and was on its way. Peter and I stayed around for a little while longer just in case any more appeared, but alas after half an hour none did, so we somewhat excitedly jumped into Pete's Land Rover and headed back to Green Patch. Once home, we made a little tour of the houses in the settlement to tell our story, with great enthusiasm, over a beer or two.

One afternoon I was on top of the ridge behind the Green Patch settlement, to get a tripe from a beef that had been slaughtered, when suddenly, an Argentine helicopter appeared, coming in very low. At first I thought it was going to land nearby me. I wasn't sure what the hell to do, but I did know that if they were going to act rough, I was completely at their mercy.

I knew they would be on high alert and looking out for British troops, which also made me realise that they themselves were taking a big risk flying about in this area. As it got ever closer I saw it was not going to land, and that they had no interest in me, thankfully, because it maintained its height and then veered slightly away in another direction. Just as it did, dad appeared, shouting, 'It's okay, son, they're heading for Brookfield.' With those comforting words I quickly relaxed again.

Once dad had got his breath back he said that the Argies had come out to collect young Allan Steen. The Steens were another family from Stanley who decided to move to camp and were staying at the McPhees at Brookfield Farm.

Apparently their young son, who I guess was about six or seven years old, had fallen seriously ill with acute appendicitis and they had called for assistance to get him to Stanley for urgent medical attention. I remember thinking that the decision to call for help must have been a very difficult and brave one for them, given the increased level of hostilities and the likelihood of a full-scale battle at Stanley itself. But, I suppose, being aware that their young son's life was already in danger, they were left with no option. Nevertheless, I was full of admiration for their courage.

I stayed and watched the helicopter disappear, then soon afterwards reappear again and fly on towards Stanley – a weird situation really, the enemy was carrying a desperately ill young Falkland Islands boy and a very concerned mother to hospital in Stanley, which was under the enemy's control, and as such, was potentially the most dangerous place in the Falklands for them to be going to.

Another thing that caught my attention a couple of days after the San Carlos landing, was that the Argentines were very active, flying helicopters non-stop during daylight hours, which we assumed was to carry troops and equipment to Goose Green and/or Darwin for the expected British attack.

I say expected, because the one odd thing about the battle of Goose Green was that it was not a surprise to anyone because the BBC was telling the whole wide world of the imminent attack. The Argentines only had to listen in to the news bulletins and they would be left in no doubt that the British were going to attack them.

Sure enough, the news soon broke that the battle of Goose Green was under way and that the 2nd Parachute Regiment had met heavy resistance from the Argentines at Darwin and Goose Green and come up against a larger than expected number of enemy soldiers. I think the BBC might well have contributed to that statistical fact, and it came as no surprise to me that after this battle the BBC were much more subtle about the information they released.

The battle of Goose Green was particularly vicious. The Argentines apparently out-numbered 2 Para by five to one. The British were extremely courageous and brave, achieving a vitally important victory in the first major land battle of the war. The landing at San Carlos had been responded to mainly by Argentine air attack, with little resistance from the ground.

Following the victory and the subsequent Argentine surrender on 29 May, the news broke about the plight of the hundred or so civilians. Goose Green and Darwin combined made up the largest civilian population in the rural area of the Falklands, and there had been many additions as a result of the invasion.

For many who had made the decision to move somewhere they believed would be much safer, it was sometimes to be a luckless choice. I know of one family that went from Port San Carlos to Goose Green to be with parents. It was a natural decision, but it resulted in them being imprisoned in the community hall for a month, with very sparse facilities. Being inside this building during the ferocious 12-hour battle of Goose Green must have seemed like an eternity and a nightmare of an experience. The prison, because surely that's what it was, offered no protection and they were totally exposed to whatever was to come their way. It can only be described as a miracle that no civilians lost their lives, because so intense was the fighting at Goose Green, the British victory on 28/29 May reportedly took the lives of 250 Argentines and 17 members of the 2nd platoon of the Parachute Regiment.

I, like everyone else who was not there, can never have any real understanding of the hell the local people must have gone through, and for those people who were there, 28/29 May 1982 will always be their liberation day, and quite rightly so.

I have been told that one poor Falkland Islander was often taken out on to the village green and forced to lie down, then the Argentines would put a pistol to his head threatening to shoot him, because they believed he had been using a radio to communicate with the British.

It's a story that often makes me think, whilst I continue my life pretty much free of any mental scars, a fellow Falkland Islander will surely be haunted by his experiences at Goose Green for the rest of his life.

After the British landings I would meet up with my old boss and friend from my police force days, Terry Peck, from time to time as he breezed in and out of Green Patch on a Suzuki motorbike – not his, that I was sure of, but neither of us cared much about who it belonged to originally, that was a minor detail.

Anyway, before Terry had departed Stanley, he had rather wisely removed and buried a pile of what might be regarded as sensitive documents from the filing cabinets at the police station in Stanley, then just as wisely, took leave of absence shortly after the Argentines invaded. Terry quite rightly felt that anything that could be done to hinder information-gathering from civilians by the Argentine intelligence branch was an agreeable exercise. The Argentines' intelligence strongman in Stanley was a particularly nasty chap and he would dearly have loved to have got his hands on Terry Peck.

Terry was much like my good friend Neil at Long Island, a fireball, full of energy, fit, and up for a fight, especially now, with the British on dry land. He was giving that little Suzuki hell as he tripped about the north camp of East Falklands.

Somehow he had acquired the name of Rubber Duck, as he and others, like Carol Phillips at Green Patch, used a system of code names to inform each other about Argentine whereabouts.

Even though the Argentines had ordered that radio masts be taken down and telephone links with the capital and other areas cut, and declared all other forms of communication off limits, with the warning that anyone disobeying this order did so at serious risk to their health, if caught, neither the order, nor the warning, deterred people in the Green Patch area. They had small two-metre radios and gathered and exchanged information to pass on to the British forces. Terry seemed to be full of beans and enjoying his new role in life, fully kitted out in his camouflage gear.

22

Islanders Assisting 3 Para

On 31 May, seven of us from the Green Patch area, Terance Phillips, Pete Gilding, Vernon Steen, Pat and Keith Whitney, Angus Robertson and Ray Newman, set about fuelling up our vehicles ready for a move to the Estancia Farm early the following morning.

As 3 Para had arrived at the farm, we were now going to commence our little effort to support the British troops. The sitting around was over at last, and we were all very excited about the prospect of helping out, doing what we could and whatever would be asked of us.

We were only seven, but we had seven vehicles. The loss of the *Atlantic Conveyor* meant that many forms of transport had been lost, which resulted in the Paras tabbing miles across the Falklands, from San Carlos to the Estancia. So our Land Rovers and those of others who would join us from Brookfield, Port Louis, Douglas Station, Long Island and Teal Inlet could be put to good use, plus of course utilising our local knowledge and driving skills over the camp.

Well, the latter might have been applicable to the other six chaps, but I knew bugger all of the camp and had done little driving over it. I had been presented with a short wheelbase Land Rover to use at my pleasure because the owner had climbed on one of those LADE flights and was now back in the UK, but I was a bloody townie, I didn't know anywhere beyond Moody Brook, situated at the far west end of Stanley; I knew nothing of the camp, or the skills required to drive a Land Rover around and upon it. But we all agreed that was a minor detail and we didn't see any good reason why it should stop me from getting involved and doing my little bit to help.

The night before our intended departure from Green Patch, I was sitting at home with the family, when we were interrupted by a knock at the door. Before I was able to go and see who it was, the door opened and Carol appeared in the front porch.

She was quite excited, and without hesitation she announced, 'We have some visitors at Jock's place. Would you like to come over and see them?' Before any of us were able to make a response, she added, 'But you can't bring the children.' Finally taking a breath, she then went on, 'They have said they can't be seen by the children because it's a security risk.'

Naturally, full of curiosity, we got ourselves dressed for the cold night air and took the short trip from our house across the green to June and Jock's house.

Reaching the small front garden, we saw a group of people gathered at the flight of concrete steps. As I got closer, I noticed four soldiers who were not dressed in any kit I was familiar with. They had blackened faces and some mean-looking firearms and equipment strapped upon themselves. As you know by now, I would not have the slightest clue what type of goodies they were carrying, I only knew they were for the protection of themselves, and to make life for the enemy pretty damned miserable.

The men were, in fact, members of the Special Boat Service. I was soon being introduced to them all and they gave me their first names as we shook hands firmly, and warmly. I remember one gentleman being called Terry. I excitedly replied to him, 'I am Terry too.' Christ, I thought to myself, this little settlement is full of Terrys.

Then I remember saying to each of them how bloody good it was to see them all. They told us that they had been around the settlement for some days lying low. One of them had even been run over by someone on their motorbike. We all agreed it had to be Derek, because he was always roaring about the place between Port Louis and Green Patch.

The reason, apparently, that the SBS had not come into the settlement sooner, was because they could not work out what the engine noise was at nightfall. They thought it must have been the motor of an approaching enemy boat, but after a day or two they realised it was not. The noise they were hearing was in fact the farm's diesel generator, used for domestic power supply.

They also mentioned that they had been to the farm across the sound, at the historically famous Port Louis, the capital of the Falklands before Stanley. We all had quite a laugh when we heard how they introduced themselves to a local man named Mike

Carey, at his house in the Port Louis settlement.

Mike had heard a knock at the door. Assuming it was someone local, he expected them to let themselves in. After a moment, no one had appeared and then there was another knock. This time Mike thought he had better go and see who was at the door. When he reached the door and opened it, there was no one to be seen. As he was gazing up to the starry night sky somewhat confused, he then heard a whispering voice say in plain English, 'Put the light out, mate.'

Somewhat surprised he looked down to the general direction of where he thought the words had came from and got an even bigger surprise as he fixed his gaze on the barrel end of a rifle, which was aimed right at him. As his gaze followed the length of the weapon his vision fell upon a blackened figure, lying on the ground.

Slowly getting a grip of his senses, he responded by telling the gentleman, who was in a rather unique posture for one who had just been knocking at someone's front door, that he was an Islander. Then he hurriedly rushed to put the lights out, at the second request of the visitor, which instantly threw everything into total darkness. 'That's much more comfortable,' said the stranger, as he then got up and offered his hand, and introduced himself to a much-relieved Mike.

The four SBS men stayed in Green Patch chatting to us for as long as they felt sensible and then they moved on. Before they left, we gave them as much useful information as we could about the Argentines: that they were up in the hills at a place called the French Wreck (the correct name, I believe, is the Salvador Hills). One of the guys said, 'Perhaps we can give them an early morning call tomorrow.'

Someone did ask why they did not want to be seen by the children. The explanation was simple and logical: children in their innocence can talk freely to anyone, and if the Argentines got the news that the SBS were around, it would be unhelpful to them and to us.

The whole experience of meeting them gave me a great deal of comfort and satisfaction. To know they had been looking over the settlement gave one less of a hopelessness feeling. Now, I suppose, they were off to create a little bit of devilment.

I knew I was not alone with my thoughts. Their visit, as you can imagine, caused quite a stir and lots of excitement as everyone drifted off to their various homes.

Incidentally, if the SBS had been confused by the engine noise, we in our little home had been equally dumbfounded by a droning-like sound every night. None of us could work out what the hell it was all about, but it sounded much like a plane or a helicopter engine in the distance. It was dad who finally worked out what it was. As the temperature dropped to freezing and the frost fell on the steel telephone wire, a section of which passed in the front of our house, it created a loud humming sound. It was quite a relief to know what was making the noise and sleep was a little easier afterwards.

There was plenty of frost on the ground at 5.30 a.m. on 1 June as we drove out of the settlement to head off to the Estancia. We formed our little convoy of vehicles at the settlement gate and made our departure under the cover of darkness. We had agreed to meet a few more vehicles from Brookfield Farm, which included Jock and June's daughter Trudi, who was just as determined as the boys to do her bit to help the British forces.

Once all together, we made our way the ten miles to our final destination. It was daylight by the time we arrived. I have no idea how long the journey had taken us, but by the time we reached the top of the ridge overlooking the farm, instantly it was noticeable that the farm had been transformed from my last visit just a few days earlier.

Then it had been peaceful until the sudden appearance of the Sea King helicopter. Now the scene down in the flats below was of soldiers all around the place, figures moving this way and that.

We drove down the hill across the creek and up to the house. Everywhere you looked there were British soldiers in their camouflage clothing. They were dug in around the fence line, along the banks of the creek, in the open fields, around the large peat stack, everywhere. The Paras had arrived the day before, after a very long walk of more than 20 miles from San Carlos.

As I got out of my Land Rover, I walked into the garden. The first thing I noticed was that the small outside sheds, so typical of farmhouses in the Falklands, had been occupied and was now transformed and fully operational as a radio communications centre.

Looking around I noticed that a makeshift flagpole had been erected near to the front of the garden fence, which had the Union Flag at the top and the regiment's flag just underneath. They fluttered together gently in the light breeze, It became a popular site for the soldiers to have their photographs taken, usually with a colleague or two, during their short stay.

I was thrilled to be at the Estancia. Just seeing all these wonderful British soldiers about the place gave me a sense of belonging and a feeling of enormous protection, and I was equally delighted that I was going to be doing something positive. Our main task during the first few days was to assist the troops in moving them and their equipment from the settlement area up the Estancia Mountain.

The weather during these two daytime tasks was generally shitty, grey and wet, and by the middle of the second day these conditions made moving our heavily laden vehicles up the shoulder of the mountain very difficult.

The first day had gone pretty well and I was very satisfied with my efforts. I had also astounded myself with my driving skills, even if it had not impressed one or two of the Paras But the second day was a different story. The ground had been badly cut up due to the constant drizzle and rain and the continuous running up and down of vehicles, and the Land Rovers started to slip and slide all over the place.

I remember on one occasion getting about halfway up the slope. My Land Rover was full to overflowing with Paras and their gear. Then the vehicle started to slide sideways, ever so slowly, down the hill. I was struggling to keep control, and I could not get the wheels to gain traction to move the vehicle forward.

Then almost in slow motion the Land Rover stopped sliding and I could feel my side dip; simultaneously, the passenger side started to rise. I knew our fate if I did not act quickly. I looked around to the men squashed into the back of the vehicle and coolly but clearly said, 'I think it might be a good idea if some of you move to the passenger side and damned quick.'

The response was instantaneous. A couple of the men immediately moved from my side to the other; the passenger side of the vehicle dropped back down to the ground. I then shouted out instructions to others to jump out and push.

With their assistance I was soon able to get the Land Rover

heading in the right direction again. But when I suggested to the lads that they could climb aboard again, with pleasant smiles and very polite gestures, they all declined, and said, 'I think we will walk the rest of the way thank you very much, Terry.'

I could tell that I was not going to restore their confidence in me getting them to their destination in one piece, and as they had a war to fight they wanted to start fighting it in the best possible shape – a reasonable point of view.

Before moving off with the remainder of my passengers I put my hand out of the open window and shook each one of their hands and wished them all good luck and God's protection. They thanked me for my help and I simply nodded, saying nothing more, but as I pulled away from them, giving a final farewell wave, a lump came to my throat. I could not get over how young many of these soldiers were and what enormous danger lay before them.

As I progressed up the hill I kept wondering about the chaps I had left to walk on and then about all the guys I had taken, or was to take, up Mount Estancia over the two days. How many of these brave men would not return home to their loved ones? It was a dreadful moment of thought and I have remembered the occasion many times since.

There were lighter moments; times when you just had to laugh, even in the midst of war. It was one of those periods of time when groups of men were doing things for themselves, rather than preparing for war – taking a crap in the field loo, cooking up food from ration packs on tiny hexamine stoves, drying bits of clothing, repairing footwear, cleaning a rifle, enjoying a cigarette, chatting, all that sort of stuff. Anyway one of the Paras came up to me and said, 'Do you think it would be all right if I cut off a slice of that beef?' He was pointing with a knife in his hand at a full beef carcass hanging from the palinkey. (Before carrying on with this tale I had better explain what a palinkey is. It is from the Spanish *palenque*; the word is used in the Falklands to describe a wooden frame, like a gallows, used for hanging newly slaughtered beef or mutton. Okay, back to the tale.) The palinkey was some 30 yards away. I had not noticed the carcass before and I guessed it had been killed recently because the meat looked fresh.

I looked at the soldier, shrugged my shoulders, and said, 'It's not mine, mate, but if you feel like a piece of it, I would think it would be no problem.'

He gave me a broad smile and a slap on the shoulder and said, 'That's bloody great, a piece of fresh meat for a change.'

As he hurried off, I turned away and got on with my chores, then about an hour or so later I noticed Jack McCallum very purposely making his way towards the palinkey, presumably to get a joint of beef for the family. Then suddenly as my eyes turned to the palinkey, I was astounded at what I saw. Jack must have got the same picture as me simultaneously, because he had suddenly stopped in his stride.

The scene was quite unbelievable. Just an hour ago there had been a full carcass of beef hanging there, now there was nothing left but a clean and complete skeleton. Jack was transfixed, with one arm hanging straight down by his side with knife in hand, looking up at the huge rack of clean bones, whilst scratching his head with his other hand. Instantly I realised I had been involuntarily responsible for a mass dinner of Falkland Islands beef for the 3rd Parachute Regiment in the middle of the Falklands War.

Obviously when the guy had gone over to cut his piece of beef off, others must have done the same, and like flies they must have attacked the carcass to get their little bit of unexpected and very welcome diet change.

I was feeling extremely guilty, but then, as Jack walked away in a completely puzzled frame of mind, I had to laugh, and I felt the Heathmans would also see the funny side of things once they realised what had happened. I looked around and could see that dozens of little plumes of smoke coming from tiny fires, camouflaged figures in various positions appearing thoroughly satisfied with their latest supper, and this scene quickly transformed my feeling of guilt, to one of considerable pleasure and satisfaction.

Whilst at the Estancia, I also remember on a couple of occasions during the early evening, some of the senior officers, including Hew Pike and dear old Rubber Duck (Terry Peck) gathering around the kitchen table at Tony and Ailsa Heathman's house, looking over maps that had been laid out on the table top as they discussed tactics for probing night patrols near to or into Argentine positions – extremely dangerous work.

I was full of admiration for the soldiers, but seeing Terry full of enthusiasm and taking a very active part in the patrols made me ever so proud of him. In a way, for me he was flying the Falklands flag for us, but he was not alone. Vernon Steen (the father of Allan) was a very brave man also, he too would be involved in forward skirmishes.

I also had a great deal of respect for Tony and Ailsa Heathman as well, because they just took everything in their stride. They had willingly allowed their house to be completely taken over. Not only had they accepted it, but I think they actively encouraged it. You might think that was an obvious course to take, believe me that is not so; even in times of war you try to keep a little bit of privacy and dignity.

23

Teal Inlet and Back
(The terrain is inhospitable, it's dark and it's wartime)

When we set out on our mission to drive to Teal Inlet, it was a grey, misty sort of afternoon and the time was about 3.30. Trudi had been talking with a sergeant, who had asked her if some of the civilians would be prepared to go to Teal Inlet to collect some men and gear, and no sooner had he asked the question than we were getting into our vehicles and making our way out of the Estancia settlement.

Now Teal Inlet was 17 miles or so away, and to get there you had to cross some of the most inhospitable terrain you could imagine. Added to that fact, it was now getting dark and it was wartime. This was going to be some challenge for a novice like me.

As we headed for the coast, about 12 vehicles in all, we were driving with full headlights on – quite crazy, given the situation. Surely we had to be seen, and if we were seen by the Argies, then it was pretty obvious we would soon know about it.

As it turned out, we were spotted, but not by the Argentines. Instead the commanding officer and men of the 'Blues and Royals' had their Scorpion and Scimitar tanks and their guns aimed right at us. The CO told us later of his quandary as he and his men were all sitting with twitchy trigger fingers in their tanks, deciding whether they had a target to hit or not.

Fortunately, the CO thought to himself, it could not be the Argentines, surely they would not be so bloody stupid to be driving in the early night, in convoy, lit up like a Christmas tree. But if it were not the Argentines, then who the hell could it be? There was only one thing he was sure of: that it certainly could not be any of the British forces.

As he unfolded his story to us it became abundantly clear what had happened. You see, the trouble with the Para sergeant's request, and our rapid response in travelling to Teal Inlet, was that nothing had been relayed to the nearby tank regiment of our movements.

But we were lucky on two counts. One, we were completely ignorant of being potentially blitzed by the tanks, and secondly, the commanding officer had decided that although he did not have a bloody clue who these idiots were driving around the countryside, they were not Argentines, and therefore refrained from giving the order to open fire. Had he done so, it would surely have taken us on a trip to heaven, (or would it have been hell?) rather than to Teal Inlet.

None the less, we made remarkably good time to Teal Inlet. There had been a couple of times when vehicles got bogged down, but we were there in just over three hours. As we were approaching the settlement itself, I remember seeing the small tracked BVs for the first time. I was mighty impressed with their speed and mobility over the soft peaty ground. There were also many soldiers marching out from the settlement with huge kitbags on their backs.

Once at the farm, I parked my vehicle outside Mrs Newman's house. There were soldiers all over the place, mostly Royal Marines, I seem to recall. I would meet some old friends from old Naval Party 8901 in Mrs Newman's house that night, as we stopped for a cuppa and a chat.

Whilst in the house chatting away to some of my old Royal Marine mates, the most unexpected thing happened to me in the entire war. Mrs Newman re-appeared and said, 'There is someone at the door asking for you, Terry.'

Well, as you can imagine, I had had the wind completely knocked out of my sails. Who on earth would even know I was here? When I got to the door I was stunned to find my sister Vivien's boyfriend, Glenn Hills, standing in the doorway.

He was a Royal Marine, and with the Commandos who had travelled down on the *Canberra*, but he had been pulled out of active duty because he was recovering from an operation en route on a growth that had formed in his neck.

I was pleased to see him and to get the latest news about my sister. I asked him how the hell did he know where to find me? It transpired that he had done so purely by chance. He had come ashore and decided he would knock on the first door that he came to and ask for me, fully aware that I lived in Stanley normally and believing that's where I would be. He got the shock of his life when Mrs Newman announced that she would go and fetch me.

We went on to exchange stories and news about my family in and around the Falklands. It was during this conversation that I learnt my brother Popeye was on board RFA *Tidepool*. That pleased and worried me in equal amounts.

Unfortunately we did not have a lot of time because soon enough it was time to go and prepare our loads and vehicles for the return journey to Estancia. Glenn came with me to my Land Rover and chatted away as I carried on loading fuel, ammunition, weapons and men into the vehicle.

I knew from our conversation that he was somewhat dejected by the fact that his incapacity would not allow him to have a go at the Argentines, which was precisely what he had come down to do. He had served for a year in the Falklands with Naval Party 8901 and I know he was wishing he could have made a personal contribution now that he was in the Islands, but it was not to be.

As we drove off out of the settlement we soon started to pass troops still making their way out on foot. Before long we started to leave them behind, and our problems began. As our convoy of about 12 approached the first tricky ditch crossing, a couple of vehicles manoeuvred the obstacle successfully, passing over it one at time, but then as expected someone would fail, and get stuck in the middle of a bloody muddy ditch. This meant that everyone would climb out of their transport and start to mill around the bogged vehicle. A tow rope would be secured to the front of the Land Rover, and one or two vehicles now situated on firmer ground would pull, whilst as many people as possible would push from behind and eventually the vehicle would be out and free to move on to the other side of the ditch.

Whilst the driver would be relieved, those left behind were often up to their ankles in mud and/or water, and if you had got in line of the mud being fired out by the spinning wheels of the Land Rover as it struggled to safety, you would also be pebble-dashed with mud.

This was to be the procedure for the entire night as we came to each soft stop on the 17-mile return trip. We were making a miserly one and a half miles an hour. It would be a laborious nine over the ditch, three down. Six through, six down. Three safe and nine bogged.

It had been easy coming up but now we were fully laden it was a much different situation. We did have one stop, at the Top Malo house. We all parked our vehicles outside the house and climbed out of our machines. It was not long before someone organised a little time-out session, which resulted in passing around one or two bottles of Lamb's Navy Rum. As we stood behind the Land Rovers, each one of us would take a sizeable swig out of the bottle then pass it on to the nearest person.

The night was cold, but clear, and the sky was full of stars, as I gazed up to the heavens and started to think about events that had taken place at this very spot. Just a few days earlier it had been the site of a swift and intense gun battle between British troops and some Argentine special forces. After the British landing at San Carlos the Argies had dropped in some of their special forces to create as much trouble and havoc as possible, but before they could get into action they were confronted by the Royal Marines and deactivated.

Normally Top Malo was a quiet little place, which was home to a single shepherd and his dogs. Then it had become a battlefield and now it was surrounded by a group of soldiers and civilians downing rum in the middle of night in the middle of a war. I began thinking to myself, what was my little Falklands in for next?

Party time was called to a halt; it was time to move on and complete our journey. On our approach to Estancia, whoever was leading us must have had a mighty helping of rum and got confused. We found ourselves on some flat open land, and to our left was the high rise of Mount Kent. As we turned in towards the peak to do our U-turn, we saw the red flashes of tracer bullets stringing out in their arched lines in the night sky. I did wonder if the shooting was aimed at us, but then I thought, well, even they are, their bullets are not reaching their intended target – and I was rather pleased about that.

If the trip up to Teal Inlet had been pretty uneventful, thanks to the Blues and Royals holding their gunfire, then the return journey had been a bit of a nightmare. By the time we got to Estancia, it had been 12 hours and it was now broad daylight. I was completely knackered. But once parked up and unloaded I had time to reflect and I soon began to feel extremely satisfied. Sure, it had been a bloody hard night's work but it had also been very rewarding, and if I had been asked to do the same again the following night I would have done it without hesitation.

After a couple of hours back at Estancia, it was felt that it would make sense if we went back to Green Patch to get some rest and a proper sleep. I had been curled up in the back of my Land Rover lying very uncomfortably on top of the spare wheel and trying to get forty winks, when someone told me. The ten-mile journey home was a light-hearted affair, everyone was on a bit of a high.

When I arrived home I soon learnt that information was now being fed into the communications system at Estancia House by various people in the surrounding areas. They were reporting Argentine sightings or known positions. It was during this period Islanders used the code name system for each place, 'Cardiff' for Long Island, 'Leeds' for Johnson's Harbour and so on.

24

Green Patch, and Then Back to Estancia

Carol told me a lovely story about how she transmitted her messages. You will recall that the Argentines had declared that all radio masts and aerials had to be taken down and made inactive, therefore Carol, or perhaps it was Terance, had made a DIY aerial by simply tying the halo of her two-metre set to a broom handle and poking it out of the kitchen window to improve her transmitting and receiving signal. Then when she was finished, she would pull it in again and stow it away in a cupboard. Because of the Argentine edict, people like Carol were taking a great risk.

I was horrified to learn, as it happened, that the Argentines had actually turned up at Green Patch whilst we were at Estancia. They had apparently flown into the settlement searching for a couple of their Argentine comrades who were in trouble. They had been at the 'French Wreck' (Salvador Hills) and the people in Green Patch knew they had appeared hotfoot and barefoot at Port Louis as a result of being shelled by the Royal Navy. I guess the information we had passed to the SBS during their brief visit at Green Patch had been subsequently passed on to the appropriate people, who in turn had decided to give the unsuspecting Argentines an 'early morning call'. Which must have been a little too exuberant for their liking.

I found that piece of the story about the Argentine visit very amusing, but I felt awful, and completely incompetent, when my wife told me that the Argentines were very hostile later on after they had gone up to our house to ask a few questions and had found my military sleeping bag, which I had inadvertently left lying in the bedroom. Whilst I was making my quick getaway in the early hours of the morning to head for the Estancia, I had rather stupidly forgotten to pick up the bag and take it with me or hide it away. The Argentines were enraged when they found it and consequently ordered all of the family out of the house whilst they then searched the house high and low, throwing things about and pushing and shoving Melody, dad and Uncle Johnnie about as they asked questions. They were now fully convinced that British troops had been staying in the house and might still be in the vicinity. They became especially aggressive towards Melody, asking her to admit where the British soldiers were, and if she did not cooperate they would take her and the other adults to Stanley to be interrogated by the infamous Mr Dowling, their head of intelligence, who had gained a reputation of being a right bastard and was considered quite capable of carrying out torture to gain any information he required, even though there had been no reported cases that he had.

As Melody continued to recite her tale, I felt responsible for her dilemma and realised she must have been terribly frightened, but she finally convinced the Argentines that it was dad's sleeping bag, which had been given to him before the war by a Royal Marine who was leaving.

At last, the Argentines were satisfied that the British were not about the place and they made their way off again, much to the relief of the Betts family. From that day on, I would make sure that I did not leave anything about that could expose my family to such actions again.

After telling my stories of the activities with 3 Para and the trip to Teal Inlet, I decided I would go and have a bath. It was a wonderful feeling as I disrobed and slipped into the nice hot water. I lay there with my head resting on one end of the bath, feeling the aches and pains seeping from my body as I allowed my thoughts to take me on a voyage of memories. Slowly, but surely, I completely relaxed and drifted off to sleep, until I was suddenly woken up in a somewhat startled manner by Melody shouting out, 'Are you all right, Terry?'

Slowly gathering my senses, I stated the obvious and said, 'I must have gone off to sleep.'

'I reckon you did,' she replied. 'You had better get yourself ready and have a bite to eat because the boys are heading off for Estancia soon.' With that announcement, I was up out of the bath and drying myself down as fast as possible, then getting dressed and hurrying into the kitchen to share lunch with my family before heading off again.

It was nice to be sitting down at the table with everyone, and especially nice to see the children. Severine and Amelia were unaware of what I was up to, and it was better it remained that way. I was delighted that they were also not showing any obvious signs of stress as a result of the war, and I would pray daily that no harm would come to these two very innocent souls who I loved so much. But I was a realist, therefore I knew there was no guarantee.

I then realised that everyone was holding up pretty well considering we were all in extreme danger. Dad and Uncle Johnnie were pleased that I was getting involved in things, but dad was frustrated that he could not take part. Although very fit for his 70 years, there was nothing he could do except help around the home here at Green Patch, which in itself was very important. Uncle Johnnie was crippled with his arthritis, and there was nothing he could do but try and make the best out of a pretty shitty situation.

Immediately after lunch I prepared for my departure, I asked the family if they had any mail they wanted me to take with me. There had been a fortunate and welcome change of circumstance since the arrival of the troops at Estancia: the communications now built up with the British military were not limited to passing and receiving messages by radio, we were now enabled to send out letters also.

I had written a couple to Popeye and I remember Melody writing one to Margaret Thatcher, which I took to the Estancia with me and passed on to guys who were travelling back to Teal Inlet, who in turn would pass them on to someone who was going back to a ship. Eventually, the mail would reach its intended destination.

The letter Melody had written to the British Prime Minister had obviously been received, because Melody would receive a reply after the war. I remember her so proudly showing it off to family and friends.

Once back at Estancia, I started to dig myself in. It had been decided we should try and take some defensive measures because there was a real threat of Argentine air attacks at any time. It was funny really, because I had no idea how deep to dig my foxhole. A friend, Mike Luxton, was giving me a hand at the time, but we would be frequently interrupted to go and help someone with moving one thing or another.

It was also one of those moments when the original group of civilians had been split into two. Some of us remained in the settlement, whilst others were going as far out as Mount Kent, which was two or three miles out from Estancia, and just a dozen miles or so from Stanley. It was a very forward position and, as such, that much more dangerous I suppose. But then every fucking where was dangerous. But Mount Kent was certainly in range of regular Argentine mortar attack, Estancia was not, or at least we didn't think so.

I had just finished moving some stuff about for the Paras and I was going back to dig a little more of my foxhole, which by now was getting more the shape of a grave, when Pat Whitney came roaring into the settlement with a broad grin on his face. He was pleased as Punch because he had stumbled across a Suzuki motorbike whilst up Mount Kent, which he decided should be his Falklands War trophy.

Stopping alongside, he then started to tell me how he had captured his prize. He had found the bike lying in a piece of open ground, so he decided if he could get it going he would take it away. He began vigorously jumping away on the kick starter lever just as the Argentines started to sling in mortar rounds. Pat realised things were getting a little too hairy, so he decided to have one final go. If it didn't start, then he would abandon it and take cover. Much as he wanted the bike, losing his life for it was not a sensible act.

The motorbike roared into life and Pat jumped aboard, opening the throttle fully, to speed off down the mountain and away from a trail of mortar bombs which were now landing on the mountain and exploding behind him. I was pleased for him, but I thought to myself if it had been me, I know I would have left the bloody thing where it was, and I walked off to carry on digging my hidey hole.

Whilst I was digging away and chatting to Mike, a Para came up to me and said, 'How deep you going to go, mate?'

I looked up at him from my hole and said, 'I don't know really, maybe when I get to Australia.'

He grinned and said, 'Well, there's no point going too deep. If a bomb explodes and you're in range of the down blast, it will kill you anyway. It's not just a direct hit that takes your lights out.'

I was surprised, and now a little more concerned about my

general welfare. The Para must have noticed my change of mood and said, 'Don't worry, dig for as long as you like,' and then he walked off.

Suddenly it seemed that everyone would stop as they were walking by and chat for a moment or so. I eventually finished my shelter, but not that day. It had grown to such a size that it could accommodate several people, which was very fortunate the day *Sir Galahad* and *Sir Tristram* were attacked.

Later in the day, Pete Gilding arrived back from Mount Kent. This time I was fiddling around with the Land Rover as he approached me, bellowing out, 'How is it going, TSB?'

I replied, 'It's good to see you in one piece. You haven't got a motorbike, I see.' Then I went on to say, 'I'm okay.'

'Hey,' he said, 'I've got something to tell you.' We sat down and he proceeded to tell me a story in his usual jovial manner, but as the tale unfolded, it was apparent that it must have been quite a scary experience.

Pete and Neil Watson had been on Mount Kent helping the military. In the middle of a short break, Pete noticed a couple of onions lying on the ground and he thought to himself, they would be a welcome addition to a homely cooked stew, so he walked towards the onions, stooped down, picked them up and shoved them in his pocket.

Unknown to him, he had been spotted by the Argentines, who proceeded to fire in mortar bombs, which although dropping well short of Pete, prompted him to pull the onions out of his pocket and hold them aloft, shouting towards the direction the mortars had come, 'Look, I've only got three. If you're that upset about your bloody onions you can have them back,' and he proceeded to throw them in the air and headed off for reasonable cover. We laughed together, but clearly Mount Kent was a very dangerous place to be. He went on to tell me that because of intensive artillery fire the night before he could not get back down off the mountain.

Some of the nights at Estancia were spent bedding down in a huge 20-man tent. I would climb into my sleeping bag and lie out flat on the solid ground, which was as hard as concrete from the heavy frost, and lie there talking to some of the guys whilst we listened to outgoing artillery fire and incoming mortar bombs, all two or three comfortable miles away.

Just after bedding down one particular night, my thoughts drifted back to the enlightening conversation we had had with the commander of the Blues and Royals following our trip to Teal Inlet. I wondered to myself if I would have held my fire if I had been in his position. I concluded I would not have, which would have meant that I would probably have killed a bunch of civilians who were only trying to help out a little.

I would eventually fall off to sleep having exhausted myself from laughing at Robin Jaffray's jokes, which made a welcome change from the Ministry of Defence spokesman Ian McDonald's crisp and solemn voice giving out hard facts on the course of the war.

25

Bombed by the Argentines

From the beginning of June to the surrender on 14 June, we made many trips to and from Green Patch and Estancia. A group of us had returned to Green Patch on 4 June and many of the families had been having a lunchtime drink at a friend's house. I remember it being one of those wet, cold and grey days, with very low cloud. The party had broken up and we had made our way back to our house, and were sitting around chatting about various things, when suddenly I heard a high-pitched whistling noise.

I stood up, and could hear the noise starting to peter off. In a flash I realised what the sound signalled – I had heard it many times whilst watching war movies. 'It's fucking bombs, we're being bombed, hit the bloody floor,' I said. In a split second we were all flat out on the kitchen floor lying side by side. Then there was one hell of a commotion, thuds followed by deafening bangs, and then the house began shaking so violently that I was certain it was going to collapse.

As I lay on the floor I was looking at the window, expecting it to blow out any second and throw glass splinters all over the place. When these events are happening to you, even the shortest period of time can seem a lifetime, but on reflection I suppose it lasted less than a minute. Equally, when you're being attacked blindly you never quite know when it is over and at what time it is safe to poke your head out again.

But within seconds of everything going quiet we were up on our feet. The first thing I noticed was that Uncle Johnnie was in a squatting position. 'Are you okay?' I asked him.

He looked at me and said rather angrily, 'It's all right for you bastards, you can just get up and down as you like, but I can't.'

It then dawned on me that when I had shouted out for everyone to hit the ground, everyone did just that and no one thought about helping Uncle Johnnie. He was still on his way down as we were all leaping to our feet with the bombing over. I put my arm around him and helped him into the chair that he had been trying to get out of.

Melody was hugging the children and I said to her, 'Just wait here a minute. I'll take a look outside and see what's going on.'

I got to the door and as I opened it to go outside, I saw Terence Newman running towards the house shouting, 'Terry, Terry, did you see the sparks flying? There was lots of flames too,' he said, all rather excitedly.

I was horrified by the thought of what he had witnessed: he had in fact seen the shrapnel from the exploding bombs. 'Come into the house,' I said to him. I went back inside with him and suggested that we all go down to Terance and Carol's place to see if we could find out what the hell had happened. Everyone got ready and off we went.

When we got to their place, there was quite a gathering. Some people were actually coming from the woolshed – they had obviously gone to take shelter in our wool bale shelter – others were appearing from other homes. Many had been shaken by the experience, and I would not pretend not to be one of them.

But some people who were normally pretty cool were now indicating we should leave Green Patch as fast as possible and move over to Port Louis because they believed we had been shelled and therefore were extremely vulnerable to further attack, and moving the short distance to Port Louis would be just that much further away and put us out of reach of any artillery fire.

The idea that we had been shelled made no sense to me. No, it had to be bombs. That said, it also made no sense to me that we should be bombed, unless the Argies had found out that we were helping the British forces and decided to put us out of action. That made little sense either. They could have flown out a few Argentine troops by helicopter and taken us away or pretty much whatever they liked, just as they had demonstrated two days earlier.

After further debate it was agreed that it could not have been artillery that had rocked the settlement, but it was suggested that everyone should go and take shelter in the woolshed for a while just in case there was a follow-up attack. So 26 of us responded to the suggestion without hesitation. Once there, we started to calm down again, and after a period we all began to come out of our hideout. Once we had all gathered back at her house, Carol received a frantic telephone call from Neil and Glenda at Long Island. Naturally, they heard the bangs and knew exactly what had caused them, and were worried that some of the houses in the settlement might have been hit and people hurt, or worse.

Once again Carol assured them that everything was okay, although even she was now starting to wondered if the Argies had picked up her radio signal whilst transmitting messages to Estancia and had decided to bomb us for her efforts. She later admitted before making a dash for the woolshed, she had picked up the makeshift radio aerial and thrown it into the upright freezer, just in case some snooping Argentines did turn up rather irate.

In fact, what had happened to us was that an Argentine Canberra bomber (British-made, I believe) which was looking to dump its load on the troops at Mount Kent could not locate its target because of the appalling weather conditions, so thinking they were near enough in the vicinity, and not wishing to take their bomb load back home again, they dropped their bombs anyway.

The intended target was nearly ten miles away from where the bombs eventually landed, which was in the dip paddock (so called because a large sheep dip had been erected there) at Green Patch, about 500 metres from our house, which was the closest house to the paddock. Other bombs had landed in the harbour between Green Patch and Port Louis settlement, throwing up huge plumes of water and mud.

Okay, the Argentines hadn't meant to bomb us on that grey and murky afternoon, but dropping their bombs indiscriminately could have killed a lot of innocent civilians. Once again, it had been a very near miss; once again, God must have been looking down on us. He had really been batting overtime on our side of late.

We remained at Green Patch for a couple more days, and I can remember on a clear sunny day watching the Harriers circling in the clear blue sky above an Argentine plane, just like an eagle waiting to pounce on its prey. It was an incredible sight. I never actually saw any dog fight, but just being in a position to watch the spectacle was quite a remarkable privilege. It was also a little surreal.

During some of the nights Green Patch would rock and roll to the music of the guns of the Royal Navy, as they let off salvo after rapid salvo of shells on the Argentine defensive positions. I could imagine some of them landing in our impressive stone runs and spewing out millions of splinters of shrapnel, just like confetti being thrown about at a wedding.

I found it quite amazing how humans could adapt to things so quickly. After a night or two of the Navy bombardment, once they began to open up in the evening, you would just carry on with whatever you were doing – sipping a drink, playing cards or listening to the radio – and make a comment like, 'Sounds like the Navy's giving the Argentines a roasting again.'

On 8 June we were on our way to Estancia again, this time seven of us. As we were crossing through a valley, a plane suddenly appeared and was making its approach rapidly towards us. At first I thought we were going to get ourselves seriously shot up, we were in a totally hopeless position right out in the open with nowhere to hide ourselves, let alone vehicles.

I assumed everyone else felt the same as me because, like me, they just drove on. Soon the plane roared overhead and banked away to the left. It was an Argentine Pucara. I was sure that it would now come back with all guns blazing and let us have it. The suspense was awful, but we never saw it again. Why the hell the pilot didn't rattle our cage I will never know, perhaps he had other things on his mind.

Once we arrived at Estancia House we got straight to work moving things around for the Paras. I noticed that the soldiers were getting more and more edgy as the days went by. They did not like being held up in one place too long, they much preferred to be on the move. Perhaps they felt too exposed. There was also evidence that several men were suffering from trench foot, which was taking soldiers out of the action, to allow their soft and very sore feet to recover from having been constantly wet.

I also learnt that Terry Peck (Rubber Duck) and Vernon Steen, had continued to go out on night patrols with the Paras. Terry being there in the thick of things was completely predictable and when I saw him he appeared to be enjoying himself, equally predictably.

But I was somewhat surprised that Vernon was going out on

reconnaissance missions. None the less I held him in great esteem. I would also say one other thing about Vernon: if you under estimated him, you did so at your peril.

It was mid-afternoon when the loveable little sergeant started blowing his whistle like an infuriated football referee. It was the signal for an air raid. I started climbing into the hole in the ground and, peering out of the open end, I could see Ailsa running along towards us with her small child in her arms. As she climbed into the shelter, she was a little bit out of breath. I anticipated that all hell was about to break loose. I could see the sergeant standing his ground, poised for action.

We waited and waited and waited, but nothing happened. I was expecting the sergeant to blow his whistle any time to indicate the threat was over, but no whistle came and then I noticed he had disappeared. I decided I would go out for a look.

When I got up on the ground, soldiers were dotted all over the place and I heard one of the Paras, who was carrying a radio pack, say in a shocked voice, 'Fucking hell, they've got a couple of our LSLs at Fitzroy.' Fitzroy was just about 15 miles away as the crow flies. After a brief pause he shouted out again, this time very glumly, 'Fifty casualties.'

I did not have a clue what an LSL was, so I decided I would ask the nearest Para. 'Landing support ships,' he said impatiently. If the abbreviation LSL did not register, then the statement of 50 causalities certainly did penetrate, and just as I was thinking about the tragic human loss and the terror and horror going on nearby, my mind and attention was suddenly diverted, just like a stranger walking unannounced into your house.

I heard someone shout, 'Incoming enemy aircraft.' I immediately looked up and to my disbelief, approaching us was an Argentine fighter plane, which I assumed was one of the Skyhawks or Mirages (I could not tell one from the other) that had been involved in the attack at Fitzroy. It was low, very low. Then I thought perhaps I had climbed out of my shelter just a little too soon, and now it was our turn to be shot up and there was absolutely nothing I could do about it, so I just stood where I was and fixed my eyes on the plane, waiting for the pilot to throw everything he had at us.

I do not remember anyone shooting at it as it appeared from around a bend, then I noticed black smoke coming out from the left hand engine as it flew past, barely 30 or 40 feet above the ground. It sounded as though the engines were popping and spluttering. Hearing the noises the engines were making, I felt a little bit easier, because I guessed the pilot would be more preoccupied with keeping his plane in the air than with us on the ground below him.

I was sure he had no chance of reaching his home base, and I fully expected the plane to fall out of the sky at any moment and burst into flames as it hit the ground. It didn't, and I have no idea whatever happened to the plane, or its pilot.

Once out of sight, it was soon out of my mind, because I turned expecting to see one of his companions fly in behind him, but thankfully it was not to be.

Soon, everyone else who had sensibly got themselves in holes in the ground started to climb out. The news of events at Fitzroy had changed the mood, which, as you can imagine, was very sombre for the rest of the day. Everyone was now on high alert, with one ear cocked for the sergeant's whistle.

Even though I had heard the shocking news shouted out from the Para earlier in the day, almost within seconds, many of us still got ourselves to the nearest radio to listen to the next BBC account of the war. But when the news bulletin was released, the BBC were much more guarded about the things they had to say this time, unlike the events leading up to the battle of Goose Green and its aftermath.

This time, they only reported that the ships had been attacked and damaged, also the approximate location, which was incorrectly reported as Bluff Cove. Perhaps that was deliberate. They also did not give details of the numbers of casualties. I thought this was intelligent, because I felt it would surely have only served to lift the Argentine forces' morale, which, equally, would have surely encouraged them to carry out further attacks the next day. I was pleased from a personal viewpoint, because I felt we could be a target for their aircraft, especially if that pilot had made it home, or had reported our position.

That night, we remained with the Paras in Estancia, but early the following day, we were making our way back to Green Patch. Terance Phillips and I would return to Estancia on 14 June, but until then, we remained home with our families, glued to the radio and waiting for the word from someone to tell us to go back to the Estancia to help out again, if we were required.

I remember once listening to my transistor radios – I say radios, because I had been told that if you got two radios and tuned one of them to a scrambled signal, then placed the other radio face into the other one and turned the tuning knob, you could descramble the signal. The information was correct, you could, and on this one occasion I did, but I could only receive one side of the conversation. I was amazed to hear a voice in very clear and concerned English snapping out to someone, 'I wish your coloured berets would stop shooting at our coloured berets.' I quickly assumed separate ground troops had mistakenly been firing upon each other.

Although much was obviously happening in many areas of the Falklands, Green Patch was relatively quiet during the next couple of days. The Navy would have their standard gun practice at night, which would sound like being inside a vibrating drum, and after that the rest of the night would be relatively peaceful. However, since the bombing at Green Patch and the Fitzroy incident, I was always on edge, ready to jump into action at the slightest noise. Or at least I thought I was, but when the next hair-raising moment came, I was no more prepared then, as I was the night of the invasion.

I was casually strolling back from a friend's house with Severine. We were between two houses, the night was pitch-black and the small light from my torch gave us just about enough visual assistance to avoid walking into clothes lines, peat stacks etc. Then, without the slightest warning, an almighty eruption of cracking and banging thunderously echoed in the still night, accompanied by a multitude of illuminations as rockets fizzed and lit up the sky. It was if I had activated a tripwire and set a whole array of apparatus into spontaneous action.

We both nearly jumped out of our skins. Then in one movement I scooped Severine up into my arms and ran off to hide behind the first building I came to, which was one of Jock and June's outside sheds. I squatted down and held Severine close into my chest. At first I thought the Paras at Estancia were being attacked, and I expected Argentines to come running over the hill screeching and yelling into Green Patch settlement.

It took a little time before I realised they were not, and once other people started to appear, I began to relax a little more and I let Severine go. Then I stood up and joined a group as we all looked to the heavens together, watching the spectacular lights, but so loud was the noise that some people had their hands over their ears. Not even on the night of the invasion, or on the day the airfield was bombed, was the noise so intense.

Once I was satisfied we were not under threat ourselves, I began making my way up to the ridge to get a better look from the vantage point. I looked to the east, in the direction of Stanley, and was horrified at what I saw. The skyline appeared to be just one massive ball of fire – flashing lights, flares, tracer bullets and suchlike. My first thoughts were that Stanley was being blitzed and was now ablaze, and if it was, no one in the small town could surely survive such an onslaught.

I then started to think all sorts of terrible things that could be happening to my mother and other members of the family. For the first time since the war had started I was sure this was the end for Stanley and all its civilian inhabitants, which by now were barely 400 people.

I stood on the hill feeling so helpless, feeling sick to near throwing up. Then I realised I should get Severine home, so I took him by the hand and said, 'Let's go and see mummy and granddad.'

He looked up at me and said, 'They are big fireworks, daddy. What's happening?'

The innocent comment made me smile briefly, then I said, 'I don't know, son, but it is nothing to worry about.' Then we hightailed it home.

Once again the reaction was guessing games, we could only wait for news from the BBC. My worst fears for the people of Stanley did not, and could not, ease until I heard that the entire fracas was due to attacks which had been launched on Mount Longdon, Two Sisters and Mount Harriet. It took a second for the penny to drop that Mount Longdon was being attacked by the Paras. Now I started to think about the chaps I had been with at Estancia. I was numbed by the fact that they were in the middle of this assault.

Dad tried to console me by saying this was what they were trained for, they were some of the world's most professional and finest soldiers and they had to do this so they could go back home. He was of course so right, but it was little comfort to me.

Mount Longdon was taken that night, but at a terrible price: 21

Paras and 2 supporting engineers lost their lives, and nearly 70 were injured.

When hearing about the success of the battle at Mount Longdon and the other battle sites that night, and the awful human cost in achieving it, I turned to dad, looked at him and said rather angrily, 'Fuck this bloody war.' Then I rambled on, 'When this is all over we Falkland Islanders had better pull our fucking finger out and make fucking sure we win the peace and make bloody certain that we secure a long-term and stable future for generations, not just for today or the next week, but for centuries. That's why those soldiers were out there last night risking life and limb.'

I stopped abruptly. I was on my political high horse again and once more dad was getting the brunt of it.

26

Civilians Die, and the Final Push

One truly remarkable thing about the war so far was that there had been no civilian casualties – quite extraordinary, given the environment. But surely this could not continue as the war progressed. No, was the simple answer to that.

Whilst I was coming to terms with the loss of life from the battles of the night before, more bad news came. The news I had always been expecting, but was always dreading, so I tried and tried to put it at the back of my mind: two ladies, Doreen Bonner and Sue Whitley, had been killed in the house of close friends of ours, to the west of the town. A third, Mary Goodwin, died later from the same incident.

Although it had been amazing that it had taken so long, and even though it was expected, the news of the first civilian casualties hit me like a ton of bricks. What's more, I always knew that when it did happen, it would inevitably be someone I knew; our community was too small for it not to be the case.

What surprised me was the location because I had understood that the civilian population had all been moved to 'safe houses' (a rather misleading term this, because I didn't think such a thing existed in the Falklands). Anyway, it was reported that they were all in stone or brick built buildings in the centre of Stanley, like the local supermarket and the nearby Christ Church Cathedral. Therefore to learn that people lost their lives in a house in an area locally known as 'Little Italy', located west of the war memorial which commemorates the battle for the Falklands during the First World War, was quite a shocking piece of news.

An even more bitter twist of fate was the fact that the ladies had died due to British shelling. Once again, it demonstrated no matter how much you prepare there will always be accidents. Needless to say, we were all very low that day, and once again I thought about my mum.

I did not worry about my brother Alec in the same way, as he was working for the Argentines in a civilian capacity, and I did not consider he would be in any trouble with them. It was a silly notion really, because in reality everyone in Stanley was now in a potential blood-bath zone.

I had become even more acutely aware of this following my many conversations with members of 3 Para at Estancia. In their considered opinion, to take Stanley might require street-to-street and hand-to-hand fighting. No British soldier that I knew, at Estancia or anywhere else, expected the Argentines to collapse in the manner they would eventually do. Thus, it was assumed that as the British entered Stanley, with all guns blazing from both sides, to secure the final victory would mean certain civilian casualties and, it was assumed, many of them.

I felt sure that the the first civilian casualties were only the beginning of one terrible human catastrophe in Stanley. Although there had been major British successes, the Argentines were showing no signs of giving up the fight. In fact, they immediately demonstrated their intentions of quite the reverse, by hitting HMS *Glamorgan* with an Exocet missile fired from the outskirts of Stanley, whilst she was withdrawing out to sea after providing support to the British attacks on mountaintops. The news of this action served to amplify their determination to fight to the very end.

The outskirts of Stanley were getting squeezed more and more by advancing British troops, and cramped with defending Argentine soldiers as they were falling back from lost positions.

I was now certain that if I were to survive this war, it would be because others had encouraged me to leave Stanley and come to Green Patch. I shall never forget these people, nor their very sound advice and the genuine concern they displayed to my family and me. We were so few, who shared so many memorable, unique and, at times, extremely nerve-racking moments together.

By 13 June the Argentine forces had been pressed back even further towards Stanley. Royal Marine 42 and 45 Commandos had secured Mount Harriet and the Two Sisters respectively, whilst 3 Para had been victorious at Mount Longdon. This was followed by the Scots Guards conquering Tumbledown Mountain, after a most bitter and furious fight, and 2 Para had taking Wireless

Ridge. It seemed that all was set for the final push on Stanley; I just hoped to hell that as many Islanders would survive the anticipated onslaught as possible.

With the Argentines now boxed off in Stanley and the very immediate outskirts of the town, it seemed to us that victory was fingertips away. Even though it was not difficult to form an overall picture, we could not know the exact situation – we were, after all, in isolation. I, like everyone else, was on the outside trying to look in through steamy glass.

I knew thinking negatively was not a good thing to be doing, but who could not have a troubled mind, knowing that although the liberation of the Falklands might just be a day or two away, the price for this could be the the lives of your mother and brother.

The next morning, 14 June, Terance Phillips and I went over to the Estancia once more. This time our load was purely food, baskets of freshly baked bread and buns, and steaming hot pastries, such as the famous Falkland Islands sausage rolls, along with other goodies, like free range hen eggs. All had been prepared and arranged by the industrious and caring Carol for the Para boys.

Reaching the Estancia, I immediately noticed that there were very few troops about. We approached a small group of two or three men who had a radio set with them, and announced we had a nice hot breakfast for them.

They flashed smiles, but seemed to preoccupied with some information being received on the radio. After a moment, the radio was put on the ground, and the troops stood up and replied with a somewhat belated 'good morning', and proceeded to munch away on the food.

The early morning air was chilly, and the ground was quite hard from the night's frost and patchy white with a sprinkling of light snow. Then one of them said something about Harrier jump jets going to strike Stanley. My heart missed a beat and I asked him what he meant, as I still had family there and I was concerned for them.

'Well, mate,' he started, 'I am not 100% certain, but as I understand it, everything to the south of Davis Street, west of the war memorial and east of the town's cemetery is going to get a peppering from the Harriers as a prelude to an attack on Stanley by ground forces.'

Although the information was all a bit vague, I was really fearful for my family in Stanley now. I could only hope they had somewhere to shelter, and would survive the fighting ahead.

Then came a piece of quite unbelievable news. One of the Paras, who now had the radio set strapped to him, was standing in front of me, with his grubby-looking camouflage clothing, slightly dirty and unshaven face, and glazed red eyes, obviously from the lack of a good night's sleep, peering out from underneath his hat, said, 'I think they have called off the Harriers' attack.' Then he went on, 'There's word that the Argies are running back. They're retreating and there's white flags.'

It was so sudden and totally confusing, it was difficult to contain one's emotions. Was he right? If he was, fantastic – or was it all a case of false alarm?

Then he said, 'I think the boys have been held back, they are not going into Stanley. I don't know anything else.' It was just like listening to Spurs on the radio, they have been awarded a penalty, Hoddle is about to take the penalty kick and the radio goes dead, leaving you not knowing if he scored or missed.

I fell silent and bowed my head. One of the guys must have realised that I was worried, and broke the silence by telling me that there was an Argentine prisoner in the woolshed. 'Why don't you go over and see him?' he said. I asked the soldier if it was safe He laughed and said, 'Sure it is.' I needed no second invitation.

There was no one guarding the building, or if there was, I did not see them. Once inside, I could see a lone figure hunched in one of the sheep pens. I went directly up to where the man was and leaned over the sheep pen rails and said good morning to him. He did not reply, and I could see he was very nervous. I assumed he could not speak English, and as I could not speak enough Spanish to get into deep conversation, I decided not to try and talk with him.

I noticed that he was about five foot eight, very leanly built, with sunken dark brown eyes and dark greasy brown hair. Then taking a closer look, I observed he had problems with his hands, which he was holding in front of him about hip level in a kind of U shape, and they appeared to be very stiff.

He was extremely frightened and jumped backwards to maintain his distance from me each time I took a step forward. Given his state of mind, I thought I should walk away and leave him to whatever he was thinking, because I knew if it had been me in his position, I would be crapping my pants.

As I hurried out of the building and back towards the Paras, it crossed my mind that I did not hold any animosity towards the Argentine soldier, who, I guessed, was in his early twenties. In fact, I felt some pity for him, and I hoped that he would get back home to Argentina and his family, where he belonged, safely. I also hoped he had learnt a lesson and would never harbour any more notions about the Falkland Islands belonging to Argentina.

As soon as I reached the small group of Paras again, I asked if they had any more news, but there was only a shake of the head and a 'sorry mate, nothing new'. We asked if there was anything we could do. Once again the response was brief, 'Don't think so, mate. Thanks anyway. If things go okay we will soon be out of here.' It was clear that there was nothing useful we could do for the few soldiers left at Estancia, so Terance and I decided we should head back to Green Patch and be with our families and wait for the latest word on Stanley at home. Before driving off we wished the guys well and thanked them for everything.

As Terance and I made our way back home, I was thinking that it was just a few days earlier that nearly a hundred of their colleagues had been lost or injured in the battle of Mount Longdon. I also now knew, and was very proud that Rubber Duck, Falkland Islander Terry Peck, had fought that battle with them and come through the whole episode unscathed. For me, it symbolised that we Falkland Islanders were with the British forces every step of the way.

There was not just Terry Peck involved, of course. Other Falkland Islanders, such as my brother Popeye and Kelvin Summers on the *Tidepool*, Ian Cantlie on another merchant vessel and Mike Smith in HMS *Glasgow*, John Ferguson in HMS *Endurance*.

I shook myself out of my inner thoughts and looked at Terance. 'If the bloody Argies have surrendered, it's magnificent news. Perhaps everyone in Stanley has been spared after all. If so, we can have a tot or two.' Poking him in the ribs, I added, 'What do you think?'

He looked at me with a grin and replied, 'You can say that again, TSB.'

27

Surrender and the Aftermath
(Shock, shame, happiness and sorry)

As soon as we arrived back at Green Patch I went into Terance's house with him, just long enough to find out if there had been any further news on developments in Stanley. But the only thing that was clear, was that a ceasefire was in place. I left to head for home as quickly as I could. Just like me, everyone was hoping it was the end, but we needed solid confirmation before we could really start to relax and celebrate.

The day seemed to drag on and on. We had been informed that a small British negotiating team, which apparently included a Lieutenant Colonel Rose and a Captain Bell, had been dropped into Stanley by helicopter to try and thrash out a permanent ceasefire and surrender settlement.

We would later learn that one of the Islands' doctors, Alison Bleaney, had been instrumental in getting a senior Argentine officer to convince the Argentine Governor, Menendez, of the folly of fighting on, which was only bound to cause tremendous human suffering both for the civilian population and the Argentine military.

I understand that the British and Argentines had communicated via the local radio telephone system, which had been allowed to remain in operation during the war, apart for a brief period, to maintain a link between Stanley and the camp for urgent medical needs for the civilian population, such as the Allan Steen case. The radio shack had been manned during the occupation by the loveable and extremely brave Everton fan, Eileen Vidal, who is the mother of my former police colleague and window-breaking friend of my youth, Lacky Ross.

Eventually, the word came through that there would be a meeting between Major General Jeremy Moore and the Argentine Governor, General Menendez, to discuss surrender terms, and later in the night the announcement came, the statement that we could only have dreamed about 74 days ago on the night the Argentines invaded our remote and peaceful homeland. But now, at 21.00 hours on 14 June 1982, Falkland Islands time, the Argentines had surrendered.

It was an extraordinarily emotional moment. People hugged and kissed each other, danced a jig, shook hands with each other, or simply yelled out with joy. Everyone was eventually reduced to tears. It was one of those unique moments, one of those occasions you know only comes once in a lifetime. A lifetime which now appeared to have some possibility of continuing in peaceful surroundings, and there were many people for us to thank for that.

Oddly enough, after the initial outburst of euphoria, I suddenly began to feel drained. I noticed that dad and Uncle Johnnie had found a bottle of Johnnie Walker Red Label from somewhere, and both were half submerged by clouds of thick blue cigarette smoke as they clutched glasses full of their favourite alcohol.

Melody also appeared tired, but she was busy entertaining the children, turning them around in circles and singing, 'If you're happy and you know it, clap your hands.' The two children had big smiles on their faces and their eyes were sparkling. They portrayed complete happiness.

I thought, Jesus Christ, we should all be happy, we had just survived a war fought in one of the remotest places in the world. But this was not just any place in the world, this was our home, as it had been for five generations for my family. True, there had been much talk of celebration when this moment arrived, but when it did, it somehow did not seem right to go over the top. Sure, we slapped each other on the back, and yes we did have a drink or two, but it was not a time for dancing and drinking yourself to a stupor, it was a time for reflection. The price for victory had been very high. As well as the loss of life, many very brave men had sustained permanent injuries, not just physical, but as it is now much more widely recognised, mentally also.

We might not have survived this ordeal, yet we had. It could have all been so different. The British might have lost the war, yet against all odds they had won. There was a surrender now, but there was still the question of 10,500 enemy troops in Stanley. Stanley in particular was still a very dangerous place to be.

I am sure that everyone wanted to be reunited with their

families, but that was not possible yet. It would take time before it was sensible and practicable to go back to Stanley and other places in the Falklands, due in the main to the lack of communication and transport, and, of course, for one's own safety.

I should point out that although the Argentine Military Governor, General Menendez, had taken a very courageous and humane decision to surrender his forces, he had done so against the orders of his superior, General Galtieri, and furthermore even though the terms of the surrender had included the laying down of arms by all the Argentine forces in the Islands, the Argentines at Fox Bay and Port Howard could have easily carried out reprisals against civilians in those two settlements before the victorious British troops had the time or the means to go and disarm their opposition and remove them from the farms.

So there I was, standing in this little house, which had been the old school room of Green Patch, the classroom for six or seven children, and the war was suddenly and dramatically at an end. But I felt like someone who had missed his supper, deprived of something I had been waiting so long for.

If I could not feel overly excited, I did feel mighty relieved. After all, my family was safe thus far. I also felt very grateful to many people, not least the wonderful people of Green Patch, who took us in, in our hour of need, and looked after us as though we were one of their family.

I was very grateful to the members of 3 Para, many of whom I had the privilege to meet and help in a small way, and to all the other British servicemen and women, also the incredible British public and the United Kingdom Government for taking the enormous gamble to fight and free the Falkland Islands from a heavily fortified, entrenched and much larger enemy.

Of course I realised that I would be a fool to believe the Falklands War was fought for me, and, you know, I didn't mind that at all, what was important to me was that the Falkland Islands were once again British. It was also important to me that I would now be able to feel mighty proud to be British once again.

Oh yes sir, I felt unbelievably honoured to be part of a people that champion and lead the world in democracy. By their actions in my homeland, they had signalled to the world that it is simply not right for anyone to invade someone else's land and that it is certainly not proper, or acceptable, for another government to try and impose its powers and will upon other people against their wishes and beliefs.

The population of the Falkland Islands might only have been 1,800 people, but it is not the size of the Falkland Islands population that is, or can ever be, the issue. The point must always be that we Falkland Islanders, like all other populations, must have the right to self-determination, as enshrined in the charter of the United Nations. It is this principle more than anything else that made the Falklands War a just war.

The following day, on the radio, I learned the reaction of the Argentine people in their homeland. They were now in the streets of Buenos Aires crying and yelling in hysterical disbelief that the war had been lost, in total contrast to their screams of joy as they danced in delirious delight in the same streets on 2 April.

Once again the population of the Argentine had been hoodwinked into believing something that was not real. Now, instead of two catastrophes, the military junta of Galtieri had three: the missing ones, a decimated economy and the humiliation of a defeated invasion of the Falkland Islands – a hopelessly lost cause, at the cost of still further suffering for the ordinary Argentine citizens, who were now in a total state of shock because they had believed their military government and its propaganda machine that the war was being won and the British forces were getting a terrible beating.

Surely, if the most patriotic of Argentines had paid proper attention to detail, they would have realised that it was highly improbable that a very large aircraft carrier could be sunk on more than one occasion as claimed by the junta.

Had they done so, they would have twigged something was not quite right about the distribution of information about the war, and the news of defeat might have been a little less surprising, and much less shocking.

I also remember feeling sorry for their plight, but I will admit not for long. I had to put reality into the equation, which was this: their stupid junta had attacked us because they believed they could bury appalling domestic problems by fooling a blind and patronising public, who were brainwashed from birth into believing the Falkland Islands was theirs; the truth is, it was not; it is not, and what's more, never will be.

My eagerly awaited return to Stanley would be put on hold for a while, mainly because on the day after the surrender an appeal was made for people not to rush back into the town, because it was in a pretty chaotic state. There were enemy soldiers to disarm and collect into a central point so they could be properly guarded and controlled.

Stanley was also a filthy mess. Infrastructure and vital services, such as electricity and water supply, had been severely damaged and disrupted. There was also the distinct possibility that booby traps had been set in and around the town. This was in fact the case. There was also an enormous amount of unexploded ordnance lying about the place, which not only made Stanley bloody dangerous, but also the approaches from overland, which the Argentines had heavily mined. These areas were unmarked and would have trapped many unsuspecting Islanders as they drove back into Stanley.

Later in the day I heard that the Argentines in West Falkland had also formally surrendered. To our relief, we learned that my brother-in-law James and his family were safe and well. When we eventually got together, he said he and his family had had a very hairy time, especially when the British were shelling the area at Port Howard. They had decided to take shelter underneath the floor of their house and were all huddled by the base of the brick chimney as shrapnel whizzed and popped over their heads, peppering the house as it did so.

One of my old workmates, Paul Bonner, also told me a story about the Argentines having a British prisoner bound and gagged under the floorboards. I had no reason to disbelieve him. I knew from reports that the SAS had been at Port Howard and that Captain Hamilton had lost his life there on 10 June.

It was wonderful to learn that all our Betts family, and the other civilians on Pebble, although shaken, were also well and safe. Dad broke into tears of joy and relief when he got this news, and bugger me, suddenly, another bottle of Johnnie Walker Red Label whisky appeared and seemed to evaporate in no time at all, with dad and Uncle Johnnie slumped in armchairs, looking rather satisfied with themselves.

Two days after the surrender we had a bit of a celebration. I had been asked to help Terance and a couple of other guys to re-erect the radio aerial which had been down since the Argie edict. It was a simple, but wonderful occasion, as we laughed and joked whilst we all huffed and puffed – well, at least some of us. There seemed to be more standing watching than doing the work.

Having radio communications once again symbolised our new-found freedom perhaps more than anything else. It allowed many of us to make radio contact around the Islands to speak with family members we had been cut off from for six weeks or more, not knowing if they were safe or otherwise.

With the radio up and running, and buzzing away with frantic communication, we began to settle down and enjoy a few drinks in Terance and Carol's home, in the company of a wonderful group of friends, new and old, who had shared with us almost everything they had to give. In a way, it was our first tentative step towards normality, even if things would never be quite the same for us in the Falklands again.

Shortly after the surrender, an appeal went out for accommodation for the British troops. Local people were asked to billet the soldiers, and those who had left homes in Stanley to consider letting them be used.

Within seconds of hearing the request, Melody and I readily agreed it was a good opportunity for us to assist out liberators in their hour of need. We hurried down to Terance and Carol's house to use the radio to call my mother and ask her to let the authorities know that we would be happy for six men to move into our place in Pioneer Row. I have no idea why we said six. Anyway, it didn't matter much, because I would get a little surprise when I arrived at the house a few days later.

Before that, however, a British helicopter landed in Green Patch and some Royal Marines appeared. They had come to collect names and normal residences so that families could be informed and the authorities could start to get a handle on where all the civilians were. If they thought their task would be a simple one and take little time to perform, then they had clearly misjudged the feeling of the local people towards them. Which was one of lengthy expression of gratitude. They would be treated as national heroes, as indeed they were, as they approached each house.

Everyone wanted to chat and spend time with them. Dad

hugged and kissed one of the chaps that came to our house, so did Melody. I was a little more reserved and I remember sticking to more formally shaking their hands.

Two of them came to our house, and I said to them, 'It is bloody good to see a Royal Marine again.' Then jokingly, I added, 'I have to admit that in your absence I've been a little unfaithful. I've been fraternising with 3 Para.' (There is a lot of good old-fashioned rivalry between the Parachute Regiment and the Royal Marines.) Both the Royal Marines laughed heartily and said, 'Don't worry, we will forgive you for this time.'

Once they had completed jotting down names and addresses, they took a little time out to play about with the kids. Before leaving they asked if there was anything we needed. We mentioned a few items of domestic importance, but finished by saying, 'We are all safe and well, and I think that is not a bad situation to be in at this stage of the proceedings.'

Somewhat surprisingly, a day or two later, another helicopter arrived. This time it was the Royal Navy. A chap in a Navy uniform started coming around the houses delivering parcels like a postman, dropping off bags of flour and sugar, tea bags and coffee. It was a bit like Christmas. The Royal Marines had obviously taken our requests for various items rather seriously, and we were being showered with all sorts of essentials.

Uncle Johnnie was especially grateful for a packet of what he called, 'real cigarettes' – English, not the goose shit that Terance and Carol had given him a few days ago in his moment of need. And Melody and I were mighty pleased that we would not have to endure that god-awful smell any more.

That night we sat down to a non-ration pack meal. Although extremely grateful for the rations when food supplies were getting low, one can overdo eating the same thing day in and day out. Part of the ration pack was a tube of Rolo chocolates. I don't believe I have ever eaten a Rolo chocolate since the Falklands War, and I probably never will again.

After a lengthy discussion with Melody, my father and Uncle Johnnie, it was decided that I should think about making a move back to Stanley. We all agreed that it made sense that I went alone in the first instance, that way I could check things out, and then decide whether, or when, the rest of the family should go in. We had been made exceedingly welcome by the good people of Green Patch, but it was a week since the fighting had stopped and sooner or later we would need to get ourselves back to home base and leave the people here on the farm to get on with their own lives and start running their businesses again.

The opportunity came for me to take a helicopter ride from Green Patch into Stanley on 21 June. The trip itself was a wonderful experience. I think the helicopter was a Gazelle, but don't trust me on these sorts of military detail. As the pilot flew it grass-top high during our 20-mile journey, we passed over some of the battle-grounds and I got excellent views of the aftermath of war. Abandoned and destroyed vehicles, gun emplacements, foxholes and a whole array of equipment lay on the ground, which had been peppered with bombs and shells, as the craters, many now half-full of water, highlighted so dramatically as we whizzed over them.

As we approached the racecourse to make our landing, I found the whole scene – of military personnel hurrying and scurrying about the place, with a backdrop of grey skies, a little rain, chaos and destruction – all too much to take in.

Soon we were touching down on the racecourse, which was now a mud heap. I quickly hopped out of the helicopter, which had been provided with the compliments of Her Majesty's Forces, and made my way towards home.

I could see now why we had been requested not to rush back to Stanley. The place was indeed in a state of disrepair. It was also the middle of winter, which contributed accumulating mud and filth to the problems.

The streets were broken and filled with litter and materials of all shapes and sizes. I passed a house that had been destroyed on the corner of Allardyce Street and Reservoir Road. As I continued along Allardyce Street, which ran on, taking a dogleg at the junction, into Pioneer Row, I began to pick up the pace.

As I reached the junction, I looked down King Street into St Mary's Walk, where I noticed a couple of 20-foot containers, which blocked the street off. Later, I discovered they were full of food and stores, which obviously the Argentines had failed to distribute to their forces. There had been many, and consistent, stories of Argentine conscripts starving during the later stages of the occupation and war.

When I finally reached my house, I was expecting to be welcomed by an overjoyed mother and perhaps five or six British military guests, with feet up, sipping a Carlsberg (mother's favourite beer) whilst listening to mother's continuous chatter. Not to be. It was quite a different welcome. I got one hell of a shock as I opened the door to let myself into the kitchen. My first sight was a scene similar to a Chinese laundry. I was greeted with clothes hanging everywhere. The washing machine was standing idle in the middle of the floor, full of filthy water. I went in a little further, ducking under some clothes hanging from very fragile galvanised water pipes.

I announced to the nearest chap I could see that I was the owner, and I questioned in a very loud voice, 'What the hell is going on?' I told him I had given instructions that we would take six men, not the whole army. He looked at me with a pained expression on his face and quickly moved to one side as I headed towards the lounge. Once again, all I could see was chaos – a sea of soldiers, mostly stripped to the waist, weapons and gear lying wherever you looked.

I was a bit pissed off, and I asked the guy I had spoken to before, where the hell was my mother. 'Don't know, mate. She said we could stay here.' Bang! Realisation hit me. My mum was a softy when it came to looking after the troops.

'How many more of you are there?' I enquired.

'A few more guys upstairs,' he said.

I climbed the stairs and began to rage when I saw a couple of guys lying on my bed with their boots on and a couple of other chaps lying on the floor.

'Come on, chaps,' I yelled. 'I don't mind you being here, but I wish you would have a bit more respect for the furniture and personal things.' Then I went on with a needless comment, probably. I said, 'It must have been hard enough for my mother to stop the Argies wrecking things, so surely you don't want to.'

As I have said, I was now raging, and for a while I lost control as I went into the other bedrooms and was greeted by the same sight. I know you might think I was being totally unreasonable, and inconsiderate, considering what these men had just gone through. Bloody extraordinarily ungrateful, you might say. Of course I was neither.

I soon cooled down, when the soldiers began to put their things in a little more order. It transpired that I had 17 Welsh Guards in my house, and I was mighty glad to have them, even if our introduction had not got off to the best of starts.

28

Brothers Meet
(Peter pops in and out, whilst Alec departs)

The next surprise of the day was the arrival of my younger brother Peter (Popeye). It was pure chance that I came into Stanley the same day as he was allowed ashore.

I was speaking with some of the guys in the house, when the door opened and a figure covered in camouflage clothing from head to foot and supporting a full beard appeared. I quickly thought someone else was coming to stay. Then mother came in, shouting excitedly to the soldiers, 'Look who I found in the street lads. What a wonderful surprise.' She hadn't noticed me in the kitchen yet.

Popeye, I could tell, was just as surprised as me to see so many soldiers about the place. Then he focussed his eyes on the odd one out, the strange guy in the civilian clothes sitting in the corner of the kitchen. He smiled and coolly said, 'TSB, how the devil are you?'

Getting to my feet, I said, 'Pretty good, Popeye. Bloody good to see you.'

As we started to shake hands, mother realised that she had not one, but two sons in the house and she immediately became emotional and started sobbing and saying, 'Oh my God, two of my babies are here.' Then turning to a group of Welsh Guards, shaking, crying and holding her arms out wide, she said, 'Look, boys, I have two of my sons here.' They were genuinely pleased for her but then decided it was a family moment and politely made their way out of the room.

It took mother a little while to get over the shock. It had only been a few minutes since she ran into Popeye in the street whilst walking home, so to get a double whammy in less than two or three minutes would take a bit of digesting, I suppose. Obviously we were all delighted to see each other. I was pleased to see that mother did not look any the worse for wear as a result of her war experience.

After a short while, Peter and I decided that we would go up to mother's house on Callaghan Road, where Alec, our eldest brother, had been staying. Mother was uncertain if he was still there, but Popeye was naturally keen to see him if possible, before he had to rejoin his ship. So I said to my mother that we would go up for a little while and then we would return before Popeye had to go back. As we were about to leave she touched Popeye on the arm and she said, 'For God's sake be careful up there.'

As we weaved our way through the littered and potholed streets of Stanley, we chatted about each other's war experiences. I told Popeye I thought being at Green Patch had been a much better option than sitting on the Royal Fleet Auxiliary oil tanker *Tidepool*, especially in places such as 'Bomb Alley' in San Carlos waters. Peter laughed, and said, 'Oh sure, we had our moments.'

As we reached the house that our grandmother had once lived in, it was very plain to see that the Argentines had been around. There were foxholes in the garden, fences were broken down, and some of the Argentines had even been hiding in the peat shed. Pieces of their military clothing were flapping about in the strong wind. There were abandoned vehicles, anti-aircraft guns, and small arms rounds lying in the dozens around the garden, the neighbouring paddocks and gardens, and all along the street.

We went inside the house, calling out Alec's name, but there was no answer. As I looked around, I thought to myself that, considering there had been a war, things appeared pretty orderly within the house. In the kitchen, my attention was drawn to the vacant armchair that our grandmother always sat in. For a brief moment I could envisage her hunched figure sitting there. She had passed on eight years ago and I thought to myself how glad I was that she had missed all this bloody carry-on.

There were candles and a paraffin lamp in the kitchen, and by flicking a light switch I found out why: there was no electricity. We also discovered that there was no running water either.

We were both feeling a bit disappointed that we did not find Alec. Although neither of us mentioned it, we both knew that Alec was surely not going to hang around in the Falklands. He had made his position on the Argentine claim well known, therefore he would not be the most popular guy around town for some considerable time. That said, I knew Alec still had many friends in the Falklands. But he had also made many enemies too. As for us, we just wanted the opportunity to say a quick hello, and most likely goodbye.

Just as we were going out of the door to leave, Alec appeared at the back garden gate. He was pretty startled to see two people standing in the doorway. He recognised me straight away. 'Fucking hell,' were his exact words. He continued to look past me and kept his focus on the figure alongside me.

Then I realised he was not sure who the guy in the British military uniform was. 'Oh it is okay, it's Popeye in fancy dress.'

We all shook hands and went back inside. Alec was very much on edge. He was clearly nervous, but then I considered so would I have been if I had been living in Stanley during the last few months. It was the first time we had been together for nearly two years, when Popeye had come down to the Islands with his wife Shirley for a visit, and it had taken a war to pull us together this time.

There we were in the kitchen of what had been the family home for almost 40 years, three brothers meeting together under incredible circumstances: one from the British Task Force, another reasonably fresh from being in the camp, whilst the other one looked a little strained from being in the eye of the storm and, perhaps, a little too close to the Argentines. But I was not going to be either judge or jury on that matter. For this brief moment, I was a brother sharing a little time with his other brothers. The fact that we had been apart was no big deal, we had been going our separate ways all our lives, and even now, Popeye would be heading back to England to see his wife and, for the first time, his first child, Alec would be going to make his new home in Argentina, whilst I would be staying put in the Falklands.

As we were gathered together in the house where we had spent some time growing up together, I thought to myself, this was going to be some war to remember for our parents. What the hell must be going through their minds? Ah, but there was no time to dwell on that. Popeye had to catch a helicopter back to his ship, so, after little more than five minutes together we had to leave Alec.

Before departing I said to Alec I would like to catch up with him later on, but Alec replied he had no idea where he would be.

Before I could say anything more, Popeye said to Alec, 'I suppose we will meet up again one day.'

Alec said, 'You never know, but I hope so.' Then Peter and I shook Alec's hand one more time and we left him standing in the doorway as daylight was beginning to fade.

It was only on the way home that I realised Alec's comment to Popeye was probably aimed at both of us. As we walked back towards my house we started talking about the times when we were children as we passed things and places where we used to play, which were now either broken or had their appearance dramatically changed. About ten houses had been lost and everything was in a godalmighty mess, but it could so easily have been a situation where the whole town was virtually erased. The Argentine General Menendez had spared everyone that awful fate, just in the nick of time.

When Peter and I got home, mother immediately asked if we had seen Alec. We duly told her we had. She said nothing, but the expression on her face was troubled. After a cup of tea, Peter said he should make his way to the football field, to catch his helicopter back to the ship.

We agreed to say our goodbyes at the front garden gate of the house. Mother, as she always does on such occasions, got very emotional, and through the tears wished her youngest son a safe journey, and thanked God that He had taken care of him thus far. When we finally parted, I shook hands with my brother and said, 'It has been great to see you, and the next time we should get the guitars out and do a few songs.'

'Good idea,' he said. 'Take care, and I'll see you soon.' I did not realise just how soon. My mother and I watched him walk along Pioneer Row and disappear out of sight. He never once looked back, and I knew exactly why.

I needed to console my mother for a little while, then I suggested she went into the house and joined the Welsh Guards in the lounge for a beer. The Guards were very understanding, and pretty soon they had her settled down again as they sipped a beer with her. It had been some day. By eight or nine at night I was quite exhausted, physically and mentally, and needed to get my head down. I decided to get into my sleeping bag and share the lounge floor with about ten other Welsh Guards, as two others had my comfy bed and I felt they were more in need of it than me.

The next morning I was awake pretty early, and no sooner had I finished a cuppa than there was a knock on the door. I found a military officer standing on the doorstep, asking if he could come in and organise his men to move out.

As he stood in the kitchen he appeared somewhat amazed as men popped out from every corner of the house, 'Christ sake, how many are here?' he questioned.

'Just a few,' I replied rather dryly. I was most satisfied that he had been every bit as surprised as me to see so many soldiers.

Soon he was slinging out orders left, right and centre, and men started hurrying about gathering up their kit, stuffing things into bags, picking up weapons, tying bootlaces. It was time for them to board their ship and begin their journey back home, presumably to eagerly awaiting families.

Before departing, every one of them took the time to shake my hand and say thank you for the hospitality as they left. Mother was again in tears and received a big kiss and a quick hug from each as they filed past her.

I was delighted for them; their war was now over, and they were going home. What was sad was the thought I would probably never see any of them again, and to this day I have not. I would love to be able to put that right one day, but I have no idea how.

When my mother and I were suddenly on our own in the house, it was strange. It seemed very empty – it *was* very empty, we could see walls and floors again, there were no clothes obstructing sight. It was still and peaceful, but it didn't feel right. One moment the house was packed to the rafters, the next nothing. Very odd.

I spent the rest of the day clearing and cleaning up. As I was busying away I noticed that one of them had doctored up the toy soldier that we had sitting on the mantelpiece in the lounge into the colours of the Welsh Guards. Sadly, I no longer know where that toy might be. It was the only memento we had of the Welsh Guards' stay in our house. The Guards did, however, leave a couple of other surprises, but I had not come across them yet. I will tell you this story a little further on in this book.

Soon I was satisfied that it was time to go back to Green Patch and help Melody to organise the rest of the family for the move back to Stanley, but before going I had a mission to complete, one only I could deal with.

29

Were You an Argentine Spy?
(I asked my brother Alec)

I would try and track Alec down one more time, just in case he departed before I could see him again.

I had not heard from Popeye, nor had I expected to, because I naturally assumed that he had caught his helicopter and was now back on his ship preparing to head back to the UK. I was very wrong. However, I would find Alec, once again up at the house at Callaghan Road, and also once again I was just in the right place at the right time, because I found him hurrying around collecting things to take with him. He had been given notice by the International Red Cross that he had one and half hours to get ready and leave on the Argentine hospital ship the *Bahia Paraiso*, which I had noticed was moored in Stanley harbour.

As he was scurrying around, I said to him I would wait and walk along Davis Street with him, I made no attempt to help him, because I had no idea what he wanted to pack to take with him, but I had every intention of making use of my time with him.

I began by asking him what it had been like living in Stanley during the two and half months the Argentines had been here. He told me that things had been a little strained between him and the Argentines but he continued to work for them in their LADE office. I was a little surprised to hear the news of friction between him and the Argentines. He went on to say that the Argentines had changed their booking office manager in February, and he didn't have a clue about flight arrangements, connections, weather forecasts, airplane pay-load sheets, flight manifests and plotting sheets. The list of this chap's 'don't knows' seemed endless, but Alec was in flow now, and he had a very keen listener.

During April he had his work cut out to help and train the twat (his words) whilst also trying to deal with the clamouring of expatriates, and Islanders, who were desperately wanting to get confirmed bookings on the next flight out.

At this point I did interrupt, and I asked, 'So a lot of people wanted to leave then?'

'Oh, for sure,' he replied, as he picked up a few pieces of clothes and pushed them into a suitcase.

'I suppose that was natural,' I said. By the look on his face, I felt he was not quite in agreement.

Then he went on, 'As you can imagine, tempers were extremely short, and when I tried to explain to some of them that all the flights were heavily overbooked and they would have to go on a waiting list, which was now stretching out to about a fortnight in advance, the comments made to me, were often far from complimentary.'

'What did you do?' I asked.

'What the hell could I do? It was not in my control. Anyway, virtually everyone got out before the first of May, but there were some unlucky ones who were stranded in town. Once the RAF started bombing and the Royal Navy began its nightly shelling of the Cape Pembroke, Tumbledown and Eliza Cove area, there were no more commercial flights to the mainland.'

'Yeah, I suppose it would have been a bit suicidal to try and operate a passenger airline service during a war,' I interjected.

'Why the hell you didn't take the chance to leave, Terry, I will never know. I thought you were pretty stupid, with small children and a wife to think about.'

I was a bit offended by his comment, but then perhaps he had a point. I tried to defend myself by saying, 'I think it was a bit like "heads I lose, tails I lose" sort of situation. Anyway, it doesn't matter any more. So with LADE closed, what did you do then, Alec? It must have been hairy in here with the bombing and all that stuff. Perhaps I wasn't the stupid one?'

He did not respond to my inspirational sarcasm, but went on to tell me more about his experiences.

'I was down at the airport during daytime, until the sixth or seventh of May. I was sent to the heliport which had been established at the racecourse, but I was only there for two or three days, and then I was instructed to stand down until they called me.' (Stand down from what? I thought inwardly.) 'Obviously my presence at strategic points around town caused a lot of suspicion among Argentine officials and military authorities.' (That comment surprised me somewhat also, because I thought he was on their side.)

'Finally I was left to attend to the Gas Del Estados business.' (I assumed he meant the fuel depot facilities, and fuel distribution.) 'This job was much quieter and less conspicuous than being mixed up with olive green uniforms. Obviously, it didn't require a great deal of time, and I made a daily practice of going around to Emma's Guesthouse, to the TELAM Correspondents Agency, and in the afternoon to an Argentine friend's house in Brandon Road – he had been a working colleague in the LADE office.'

At this point, I had to know the answer to two questions, and so I asked them. 'What the hell did you do when all the bombing and shelling was going on? And where was Santina?' Santina was his Argentine girlfriend.

To the first question he replied, 'Like everyone else, I suppose, I took cover wherever possible.' To the second, he said, 'We were together here at the house for a while, but things got a bit wild up here, so we went down to Jubilee Villas.' The Jubilee Villas are a unique block of four terrace houses built in the late 19th century.

Alec had now finished packing and was ready to get moving, but before leaving we sat down on the kitchen sofa and I asked more questions. I was aware that I was now behaving more like a media reporter than a brother, but let me tell you why.

I had become well aware of the comments being made about him by some people who regarded him as nothing more than an Argie spy. Some thought he should be shot for treason, others even promised to shoot him, if they got the chance.

I decided not to get my mind fucked up by the opinions of other people, or their emotions. I just wanted to hear from my brother, in his own words, his version of things. I had also made up my mind that it was up to him to tell me the truth or otherwise. If he chose to lie to me about it, it would be his own conscience that would be pricking him for the rest of his life. Whatever he said, I would have to accept as the truth and not doubt it, ever. That was the rule I made to myself before I began this very personal family inquest.

But before I got to the mother of all questions, in an answer to another question he said, 'As you know, I was looking after this place once mum went down to your house. The young conscripts and non-commissioned officers would come knocking at the door at all the imaginable hours of the day, asking me to go shopping for them at the West Store (the FIC supermarket which remained trading during the war). There was a military edict which forbade the Argentines from purchasing goods from local stores, therefore they began to beg. They would ask for chocolate, biscuits, soups, canned meats, whisky and cigarettes, anything to try and keep the body calories up, to beat off the cold.

'Because I would often get their requirements, purely as a humanitarian act, I received many insults from the other Islanders, who said I was a collaborator.' He ran his fingers through his hair and said, 'But I would just shrug off their hurtful comments, believing I had a heart in my chest not a stone.'

I felt a bit sorry for him at this point, and said, 'But I know several other people who gave the Argentines food when they went knocking on doors. In fact, I also heard stories that some Argentines actually forced their way into some folks' homes and threatened them, if they did not provide them with what they wanted.' I could tell my comment seemed to fire him up a little bit because I don't think he was aware of this.

Then Alec went on, 'I think the town's civilian population was two hundred and fifty at best throughout May, to the end of the war, and the general opinion of those who stayed on, was that the British forces would need little time to come and retake the Islands, with no British loss of life, or any damage to their properties.' With a slight grin, he added, 'This naïve option quickly changed to stupor, and shock, when the news of the *Sheffield* hit them.' I could sense anger and cynicism in his voice now, because I think his comment was aimed at all Islanders, including me. I wouldn't accept being in a stupor, but I would accept I was pretty much naïve up to the *Sheffield* incident.

Raising his voice a little, he carried on. 'When they suddenly realised there was a real war on, not something they had been watching in a town hall cinema on a Sunday night, people who had completely shunned me up to then suddenly began to stop me on the streets and ask how long this whole thing might last and if it were possible that anyone in Stanley might get hurt, or even killed. Without beating about the bush, I usually replied that there were even odds on casualties and deaths, and only God knew what the final outcome would be. Before the attack on HMS *Sheffield*, nobody even dreamt of this possibility, and if I made any comment about the likelihood of British troops overrunning the town to retake Stanley and the airfield and a few Islanders were injured or killed in the process, from a British military point of view, this was perfectly feasible and within the calculated losses in this type of military action, I was blankly looked at as though I was a maniac or just talking nonsense.' (I thought to myself he was absolutely correct.) Little did I imagine that these words would turn out to be so prophetic.

Giving me a slight stare, he said, 'I don't know if you knew, but the three ladies who died were killed during a British helicopter missile attack on the heliport at the racecourse.'

This version of events did make some sense, because the Fowlers' house was in the vicinity of the racecourse. I did not know it had been a missile attack, I was only aware that something had gone terribly wrong, and tragically the end result had been the loss of civilian lives.

Taking a deep breath, my brother continued to tell his stories. 'You might like to know that a few days after the landing at San Carlos and the British establishing a bridgehead there, the Argentine military authorities in town issued an edict.'

Putting my spoke in, I said, 'There were plenty of those bloody things.'

'Yes, well okay,' he said. 'The edict required all families still occupying houses considered to be in a dangerous position to move to other safer and more resistant properties towards the middle of the town. Quite a few families moved into the West Store and the few other stone houses around.'

I am not sure if he was inviting comment, but I made my thoughts known anyway. 'Oh, is that right? So that's why the Argentines actually placed some of their defences in between people's homes right in the middle of the town. Now that is a mighty strange way to show your concern for someone's safety, don't you think?' There was a moment of silence, broken when a plane flew over the house.

'I don't know about that, but I decided I didn't want to compromise anyone in the family or close friends with my presence, so I went to live with twelve Argentine civilian employees living in Tim and Eve Halliday's Jubilee Villa on Ross Road.'

His comments made me a little respectful of him. However, I was not convinced that the motives were entirely for the reasons

Great-grandfather and grandmother Goss, William Henry and Ann (née Aitken).
Photo courtesy of Gennie and John Luxton

Great-grandfather and grandmother Betts, John Cranmer and Elizabeth Ann (née Kiddle).

Photo courtesy of Susan Hansen

Grandfather and grandmother Betts, Alexander John and Vivien Gladys (née Carey).
Photo courtesy of Arnold Betts

Father and Mother.
Photo courtesy of Arnold Betts

The *Thetis*, Falkland Islands Company vessel, lost with all hands August 1901, including the author's twin great, great uncles George and Edwin Betts.
Use of photograph granted by director of Falkland Island Holdings

Grandfather Jacob Napoleon Goss, holding hand-shorn sheep on New Island.
Photo from author's mother's collection

Civil Engineer, John Rowlands, far left, a major influence on and inspiration to the author. The three employees in the picture are Eric Spinks, Bob Stewart and Clive Allen.
Photo courtesy of Robert Rowlands

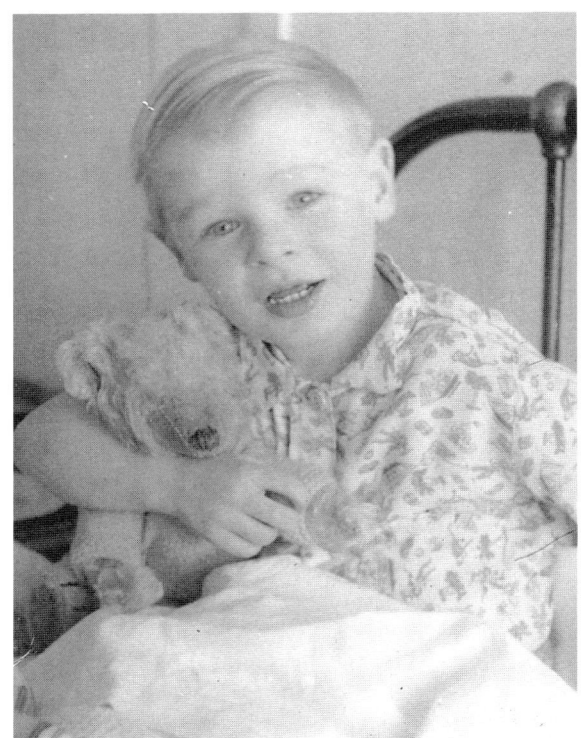

The author in a hospital bed (aged 4).
Photo from author's mother's collection

A Betts family snap, Father holding brother Peter, half-sister Olive cradling author's niece Darlene, with Mother holding author's shoulders, elder brother Alex, also in front, completes the picture.
Photo from author's mother's collection

Victory Bar, one of my first family homes, Christ Church Cathedral beyond.
Photo courtesy of the author

In uniform, and serious mode, for the Battle of the Falklands (1914) Parade, Brother Alec left of the author.

A proud mother with author, holding the Governors Cup for darts. The author won this most prestigious of tournaments at the first attempt in 1969.

Photo from author's mother's collection

Author taking a tea break during the construction of Fitzroy Road, Stanley.

Photo courtesy of the author

RRS *Shackleton*, which took the author to Antarctica as a fifteen year old crew member in 1965.
Photo courtesy of Gennie and John Luxton

Brothers Alec left, and Peter right, flanking sister Vivien, at Mother's wedding to Eric Spinks in 1967.
Photo from author's mother's collection

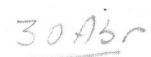

Nº. I 610	30 Abr
	BETTS
	Apellido (Surname)
	PETER
	Nombres (Fornames)
	Masculino
	Sexo (Sex)
	Soltero
	Estado civil (Marital status)
	Puerto Stanley
	Lugar de nacimiento (Town or settlement)
Firma del agente autorizado (Signature authorized agent)	**21 Enero 1954**
Otorgado **10 Abr.** de 197 **3**	Fecha de Nacimiento (Date of birth)
(Issued **10 Abr.** of 197 **3**	Firma del titular (Signature of bearer)

The 'White Card' depicts brother Peter. Following the communication agreement signed by Britain and Argentina in 1971 all Falkland Islanders were required to carry this document whilst travelling in and out of Argentina. Things changed after 1982.

Document courtesy of Peter Betts

The DC4 coming into land with the Argentine hi-jackers aboard Photo courtesy of Peter Betts

105mm gun emplacement (Argentine), Stanley Common, Sunday 17 June 1982. The concrete walls in the picture were built during WWII, where the author and friends played pretend war games as children.

Photo courtesy of Peter Betts

Argentine anti-aircraft weapon in a paddock off Callaghan Road, Sunday 27 June 1982.

Photo courtesy of Peter Betts

Police station, Stanley, hit by British missile fired from helicopter trying to target high-ranking Argentine Officers thought to be in the nearby Town Hall.
Photo courtesy of the author

Exocets - surface to surface miles (Argentine) - on trailer east of Davis Street, Stanley, Sunday 27 June 1982. (One such missile hit HMS *Glasgow*). Photo courtesy of Peter Betts

The 1982 War memorial in reflection   Photo courtesy of the author

Terry Betts (left) presents a Falklands silver coin to Glenn Hoddle, who accepts on behalf of Tottenham Hotspur FC   Photo courtesy of Holsten Distributor Ltd

The author's late father, Cyril Severine Betts 1912-1996.
Photo courtesy of Derek M. Slattery

The long white building made up the original six cottages forming Marmont Row, built by the author's great, great, great grandfather, Richard Victor and great, great grandfather, Jacob Napoleon Goss, sometime in the 1850s. The property is now owned by the Falkland Islands Company, and is operated as the famous Upland Goose Hotel.
Photo courtesy of the author

Terry Betts with daughter, Amelia, in East Coast Studios, in London (1992), during a recording session of *Two Fifty Five*, written by the author. Photo courtesy of the author

Severine (author's son) with author's companion, Sara Maria Fernandes.
Photo courtesy of the author

Author (far right) with Falklands Governor Tathum (2nd left) and first Chinese business delegation ever to visit the Islands, invited by the author's company JBG Falklands Ltd.

Photo courtesy of JBG Falklands Limited

Atlantic House, one of many pioneering projects involving the author, and his various joint venture exploits. This one included the building of an office block and retail unit, for let, whilst operating a stationery supply service.

Photo courtesy of the author

Roy Hattersley, chatting to the author at the Labour Party Conference of 1988 in Blackpool. Also in attendance is Falkland Islands Government UK representative Lewis Clifton O.B.E.
Photo courtesy of Falkland Islands Government

HRH Prince Philip, the author's ex-wife Arlette, the author and Falklands former financial secretary Harold Rowlands.
Photo by permission of Falkland Printz

Jordan Phillips, the author's grandson.
Photo courtesy of Paul and Shula Phillips

The author's daughter, Amelia, with son-in-law Craig Appleby.
Photo courtesy of Craig and Amelia Appleby

he said. But I was going to give him the benefit of the doubt anyway (I was not judge and jury, remember).

Alec carried on. 'By the middle of May, the nightly bombardments by the Royal Navy had caused serious damage to water pipelines, and virtually the whole of the town was out of fresh water.' (The British would, in fact, blow a bloody great big hole in the filtration plant unit.) 'Fresh meat and vegetable supplies had also been exhausted. Toilets were being flushed with seawater collected in buckets. It was impossible to take a bath and dishes were scraped and then cleaned with damp grass.'

'No luxuries then,' I quipped.

'You can say that again,' he replied. 'A cup of tea or coffee could only be made by melting down snow which we collected from outside. We had to get by with canned conserves that we might have in the larder and just simply make do the best way we could with whatever was at hand.

'This situation was only alleviated about a week after the capitulation.' (I must admit, I got a feeling of great satisfaction when he used the word 'capitulation'. But I needed to concentrate on his stories, because very few people had experienced what he had.) 'When the British military authorities replaced the Argentines they began to ration out the huge amounts of food supplies they found in various depots in and around the town.' (I was thinking to myself, why didn't he say, 'When the defeated Argentine Army were replaced by the victorious British Army'? This amplified the fundamental differences we had in our political viewpoints – not a question on this day, but tested to the full in the future.)

I jumped up from the settee and said, 'Interesting stuff, but let's go, or you'll miss your ship.' I must say, that was one thing I did not want to happen. I felt it was not in the long-term interest of Alec's health.

At this point I had not asked the question that I had sought him out to ask. I decided I would wait until we were walking along Davis Street. Before leaving the house, Alec did one more thing, something I will always remember. He picked up an unused envelope and began to scribble a message on it to our mother. I don't know why, but I stood back from him, so he could write his words in relative privacy. Once he had finished writing his note he put it on the kitchen table and we left.

These were Alec's last moments in the Falkland Islands, to this day. I felt the tension mounting and there suddenly seemed to be an uncomfortable atmosphere developing between the two of us. Maybe we were both thinking the same thing at the same time.

As we made our way along Davis Street, we found ourselves abreast of Pill House. Now I felt was the time to ask my question, the most difficult question any brother could ask of the other. We had been walking side-by-side, but I broke stride and said, 'I have one more thing to ask you, Alec, before you go. I have to know the answer to this question, Alec, because I would like to be able to tell our parents the truth.' I paused ever so briefly. 'Were you an Argentine spy, Alec?' Then I said, 'But before you answer me, remember, if you lie, you lie to yourself, but much more important than that, you will be lying to the two people on this planet who love you more than anyone else, and that is your mother and father, and I am their messenger.'

The last remark made him stand still and he drew himself upright. But without hesitation, he said, in a rather raised voice, 'Don't be so bloody stupid. What could I tell, or do, for the Argentines that could be considered espionage, that they didn't already know? Christ, before the war, they would have been invited to cocktail parties, and other functions, up at the Royal Marine barracks at Moody Brook, and also Government House, as the guests of the Commanding Officer and the Governor. They had all the information they needed long before they invaded. They had got it for themselves, probably via very friendly hosts, and other methods, at these social gatherings and suchlike.'

I was now all ears. This was not a time to interject. That would have been disrespectful and extremely distracting. Then he fired out the answer.

'No,' he said. 'I am not a bloody Argentine spy now, and I have never been any fucking Argentine spy. But what people can't get into their heads, including you, perhaps, is that I cannot support the British position over the Falklands. They have done fuck all for the place in 150 years, and now look at the bloody mess they have got you in. I say you, because you're stuck with it. I'm leaving, and furthermore, I'm leaving because I want to live in Argentina with the woman I love, simple as that.'

We began to walk on. I had asked a very direct question, and I was pleased that I had got a very direct answer. I did not follow up with any ifs and buts, that was the rule – in and out with the question and accept the answer. I have never had any problem with Alec's response. Others may judge as they think fit. That is up to them.

When we reached the junction of Davis Street and Philomel Hill, I decided this was as good a place as anywhere for us to say our goodbyes. From where I was standing I could see the ship he was to leave on, at anchor off the town's cemetery. There was a slight sea running in the harbour, with the waves showing white tops. The stiff breeze coming from the southwest was making the *Bahia Paraiso* lie back slightly on her anchor chains. Interestingly, this ship, in times of peace, was an icebreaker/supply vessel which operated in the Antarctic. She would come to grief there several years later, sinking off Graham Land in the Weddell Sea.

There were no emotional farewells. I thanked him for his understanding and for responding to all the questions. Also, for his honesty (I hoped that was right). I wished him all the best for whatever the future had in store for him. I must say, he looked very relaxed, and then he said, 'Thanks and good luck to you also.' He gazed around the town for a moment, then stopped and looked straight at me and finally said, 'Looks to me as though you might need it more than me.' He immediately spun around and walked off down Philomel Hill.

I felt quite relaxed, considering I had just carried out one of the most shitty jobs in my entire life, but I was totally content with the result. Of course I had no idea that the next time I would see my brother would be five and a half years later, alongside a security guard's sentry box outside the gates of the United Nations building in New York.

When I got back home, my mother immediately asked if I had met up with Alec.

'No,' I said, 'there was no one at the house. I'll try and catch him tomorrow, before I go.'

'That's if he's not already gone,' she said.

Her reply made me look towards her and I noticed that her diminutive figure was hunched in a chair as she hung her head gazing at the floor. I knew she was in painful thought about Alec, so I opted to go to my bedroom and leave her alone with her thoughts.

Should you be wondering why I lied to her, the honest answer is, I don't really know. I just felt the time was not right to come straight out with it and tell her that he was about to leave the Falklands or had in fact, already left. I hope I made the right decision. My mother has never told me either way.

30

I Tell My Parents About Alec
(The challenges of the war's aftermath begin)

I spent the next couple of days toing and froing between Stanley and Green Patch. One day I went on a walkabout of Stanley, before hitching a helicopter ride to Green Patch. I wanted to see what I was going to bring my family back to.

Homes had been erased by fire, and one of the town's most central stores, The Globe Store, had been burnt out and its stone-wall structure looked an even deeper grey, with large black smoke scars above the vacant window spaces. The remains of the roof and interior walls lay in a heap of ash and charcoal. It was believed the fire had been a case of arson by the Argentine POWs.

As I walked about, I was careful not to touch anything that looked the remotest bit suspicious. There was a high risk of booby traps, and many were later found. I was also aware that the Argentines had deliberately soiled many public buildings, such as the post office, with human excrement, and one morning as I was walking by, I remember passing Lewis Clifton, who was hosing down the post office to remove the filth.

I passed the police station, my old work site. A large piece of the centre upper wall and one end of the roof had been blown away by a rocket fired from a British helicopter. The pilot had missed his intended target, which was the Town Hall, on the opposite side of the road. Apparently, British intelligence sources had informed the British military that several very senior Argentine officers would meet in a room on the upper floor of the town centre's largest public building at a precise time, on a certain day of the week. Naturally, it was decided it would be most helpful if these gentlemen were eliminated from any further involvement in the war.

The British pilot popped his helicopter over the ridge opposite Stanley harbour, took aim and fired his wire-guided missile, which fizzed between the Town Hall and the gymnasium, hitting the police station and exploding upon impact – leaving the building obviously no longer watertight.

Realising he had missed his intended target, the pilot fired a second missile, which by all accounts went completely haywire and ditched itself into Stanley harbour, then like a torpedo headed straight towards an Argentine hospital ship, missing it by the narrowest of margins. This resulted in the Argentines screaming 'foul play' and claiming that the British had made a deliberate attack on the Red Cross vessel whilst it lay at anchor.

I was surprised to pass so many houses which had been damaged to varying degrees, with windows out, or covered up with plywood or corrugated iron. Many had also been peppered with shrapnel, as the many tiny holes in the walls displayed. There was Argentine military hardware abandoned and littering the town, both inside and on the perimeter in places such as the common. Missiles and launchers sat on trailers; light tanks, machine guns, 105mm weapons, spare parts and equipment, and various forms of transport sat in streets and in people's properties.

On the corner of Pete Gilding's house on Racecourse Road lay a light grey plastic egg-shaped thing, resting in a wooden cradle, which was leaking some sort of white powder or liquid. I found out later that it was in fact a napalm bomb. Fortunately, the Argentines had not got around to using it, but the fact that it was there at all showed their intent.

The public area known as the common, at the back of the town, was unrecognisable, except for the concrete gun emplacements built in the Second World War where we children used to play out imaginary war games 20 years earlier. Now the whole area had been transformed to a scene of total chaos as a real war game had been played out. With all the abandoned bunkers, gun emplacements and military hardware strewn all over the place, much of the area I was walking around was also an unmarked minefield.

All this was just a few hundred yards from the back door of the house on Callaghan Road. Hundreds upon thousands of live small arms rounds lay just about everywhere you could imagine. Oh yes, Stanley was indeed still a very dangerous place. So any decision to bring my family back into Stanley had to be very carefully thought out. But life had to move on, so there was no alternative, really. We had to bite the bullet.

As I bring some of my experience of the Falklands War to a close, I am going to tell you a story that I think is quite unique and brings out one of the lighter moments during a period of great stress and uncertainty. It is a tale of a father and his son meeting in the most peculiar and difficult of circumstances, at the end of a terrible event. As you read this story you will need to remember that, although my father knew his youngest son had joined the British task force flotilla, he naturally assumed he was somewhere on the high seas.

Popeye had not gone back to his ship. Despite waiting where he had been instructed to and spending a couple of days going to this place and that, his helicopter never turned up. In the end, he and fellow Falkland Islander Kelly Summers were told they could go to their families, providing they left contact details. So like a bad penny Popeye turned up at Pioneer Row again, much to our surprise and delight, and this time we did get the guitars out, and we played and sang a few old songs that we used to play with Alec in the garage at the house in Allardyce Street. But that is not what I want to tell you.

Dad and the rest of the family were coming in from Green Patch the very day Popeye showed up again. Dad, of course, had no idea that Popeye was in Stanley, so I suggested to Peter that he come up to the racecourse with me and meet him and the family when they arrived. The Sports Association Committee Hut was being utilised as some sort of meeting point, communications and control centre. Popeye and I waited rather excitedly in the building as the helicopter landed and the family climbed out one by one.

Melody and the children entered the building first and we greeted each other warmly. She eventually recognised Popeye alongside me and was about to scream out his name, but stopped when I put my finger to my lips and signalled to her to say nothing as we waited for dad. He took his time because I think he stopped and spoke to every British serviceman in the area. Eventually he walked into the building. I greeted him with a handshake and asked him if he had a good flight.

Then Popeye went up to him in his full military attire and bushy beard and proceeded to shake dad's hand. Dad turned to me and with a puzzled expression on his face and asked, 'Do I know this chap?'

'I would think you probably do – it's your son,' I said.

Popeye began to laugh and then took his hat off. 'Don't you recognise me, you old bugger?'

Dad looked up into Peter's face and suddenly the penny dropped. He yelled out, 'Popeye, what the bloody hell are you doing here?'

'I've come down to check on you,' he said.

As I stood back and watched the scene, I thought to myself, yes indeed, he had come thousands of miles to check on his old man. Then everyone broke into laughter and we made our way home a pretty happy family unit (almost).

We had only been home an hour or so when Popeye got a call to get on his bike and catch his helicopter back to his ship. This time, I decided I would go with him. Before leaving the house, Popeye went through the goodbye rituals with mum and dad.

We left the house with mother in floods of tears and made our way to the football field. A Sea King helicopter was sitting there with its rotor blades spinning rapidly. I watched him jump up on to his transport. He turned and gave a final wave. The helicopter lifted off; my brother was on his way home. It would be 16 August before he eventually made it home to his waiting wife and to see and hold his son, who was now four months old, for the first time.

When I got back to the house I could sense a bit of an atmosphere. I had put it down to mum and dad being a bit glum about Popeye going off, but I found out it was not that, they had been talking about Alec and were concerned about his well-being.

'I know where he is,' I said, in a rather schoolboy sort of fashion. 'He's gone. He left on the Argentine hospital ship. He's gone to Argentina.'

I had been rehearsing over and over again in my head how I was going to tell my parents in the most subtle way possible that their eldest son had left the Falklands. In the end, I spat it out like a tortured captive unable to take the pain any more.

In respect for my mother, who is still alive, I will refrain from describing her reactions and words. Dad was calm, in fact he appeared somewhat relieved, and he looked at me and said, 'It's probably just as well, son.' I knew exactly what he meant, but I had no idea what he must have been really feeling. Dad died almost 14 years after the Falklands War without seeing Alec again, but he never told me what he thought about his decision to go to Argentina, nor what he felt about his two sons battling it out in opposing camps a few years after the war in the very public eye of the local and international media and political forums. My mother has sometimes talked about the pain it gives her, but father never said a word on the subject. Which I will admit was one thing I thought about as I looked down on his coffin as it lay in the uncovered grave on his funeral on 13 March 1996.

The Falklands War was over and now the rebuilding of our homeland and lives was to begin. It was not going be an easy task and there were to be lots of heartaches along the way, to be sure. On 1 April 1982, the people living in the Falkland Islands were a nothing, nobodies, unknowns, living in one of the remotest parts of the world. Strangely enough, as a result of the Argentines' invasion of our Islands and their defeat, some very positive things came about.

Firstly, it would rid Argentina of military dictatorship and give the people a democracy. Secondly, Britain's victory reinstalled pride and passion in the nation and it was once again able to command respect on the international political stage. Thirdly, the people of the Falkland Islands had had a very narrow escape from a certain future of austerity, had the Argentines won the war.

Perhaps there is a case, after all due consideration, to build a statue of Galtieri in the Falkland Islands and for the Argentines to erect one of Margaret Thatcher in the main square of Buenos Aires. A fantasy maybe, but stranger bloody things have happened in this weird, wonderful and sometimes extremely cruel world of ours.

Shortly after the war, I felt compelled to write a song as a tribute to those who had fallen to restore freedom, peace and democracy to all the people of the Falkland Islands. The song is a very personal message, it is a simple thank-you from my family to the families of those loved ones who paid the ultimate price for my freedom with their lives. But of course my song does not exclude the people who suffered horrifying injuries that they will carry for the rest of their lives.

I do not exclude all the brave people who formed part of the task force. I do not exclude all the people back in the United

Kingdom who gave unflinching support in one way or another. Nor do I exclude the United Kingdom Government, Her Majesty the Queen and members of the royal family. Nor do I forget the other nations, and their peoples, who stood by us in our hour of need, and I shall never forget the three civilians, two of them Falkland Islanders, who perished whilst we were being freed.

I am sure all Falkland Islanders are grateful for their freedom, but each and every one will choose their own way, and moment, of showing their gratitude. But I do hope they are satisfied with the sentiments I have tried to express in my song, and that they can sing along with it at times, feeling a sense of pride, whilst believing that as Falkland Islanders, we are a people, in our own right, who do, and must have, the right to self-determination.

But please think about this: pride and determination are not enough. In the end, my only hope and concern is that we Falkland Islanders can justify all the aforementioned incredible unselfish deeds, and that we find the time, and make the effort, to build bridges with our Argentine neighbours to secure a lasting peace. If we fail to achieve this, we might just fail those who gave so few people, so very much.

Future generations of Falkland Islanders are looking for guidance, security and prosperity, but above all else they seek lasting peace. It's a huge responsibility but let's not fail them either. Rise and be counted, 'Two Fifty-Five'.

31

The Words of 'Two Fifty-Five'

Longdon, Tumbledown, two of the places, laid your life down
But your memory will linger on
You perished at sea, Sheffield and Coventry
Just two of the ships that went down

Rise and be counted, two fifty-five,
You lost your lives, so we may survive

Oh the pilots, hero's everyone, saved many a mother's son
But far too many lives were lost
Galahad, so tragic, liberation, fantastic.
God bless you all, two fifty-five

Rise and be counted, two fifty-five
You lost your lives, so we may survive

Soldiers, sailors, airmen too, freed you, back in eighty-two
Thank you so much, every one of you
Fourteenth of June is liberation day
And with pride we wipe a tear away.
God bless you all, two fifty-five

Rise and be counted, two fifty-five
You lost your lives, so we may survive

Music and Lyrics by Terry Betts
Arranged by Trevor Holman

293

32

Back to Work in Difficult Circumstances
(And Margaret Thatcher arrives in the Islands)

Returning to work after the war was not easy. There was a lot of tension between those who had stayed in Stanley and those who hadn't. The aggravation came from those who had remained in the capital. They would come up to me and say things like, 'Did you enjoy your holiday?' or 'I am surprised you can remember where Stanley was, seeing you've been away so long.'

I cannot deny that I would be hurt by the snide remarks, and at times I felt like exploding and telling them where I had been, and what I had done. But I always pulled up short because I realised the anguish, considerable pain and stress people in Stanley must have suffered during the occupation.

I could, and did, forgive friends, and others, for feeling the way they did towards me and the other people who chose not to stay in Stanley. But I was extremely upset and unforgiving towards my boss, Harry.

When I returned to the office to say hello and inform him that I was ready to come back to work, Harry, who was accompanied by the company's accountant, said, 'Well, I don't know about that.'

I sensed trouble brewing straight away. I could see by the expressions on their faces, and the look in their eyes, that they were both seriously thinking about telling me I didn't have a job any longer. Instinct told me, the 'well, I don't know about that' was big trouble, and I had better defend my position instantly, and the only way to do that was to kick ass, and big time.

Without further ado I went on the attack. I am a great believer that the best form of defence is attack; I was not going to give my boss a moment to regain his composure. I walked up closer to his desk, stared at Harry and said, 'Look here, I think I had better remind you of a few things. On the first morning back to work, after the invasion, you said that everyone had the liberty to decide what was best for them and their families, and if anyone wanted to leave Stanley, that was understandable, and it was okay by you, and the company. Furthermore, you went on to say, that no one need worry about their jobs. Right or wrong?' I snapped.

He was rocked, and looked at me rather sheepishly, then said, 'Right.'

'Okay, that's it then. I will be back to work in the morning.'

He made a slight move, then made an attempt to say something, but then decided enough had been said. It was the only time Harry and I ever crossed swords and, like John Rowlands, he became a kind of mentor in my life – but in a very different sort of way to John. Harry took a great interest in me, and gave me every chance to succeed in life, which I appreciated and duly accepted.

Immediately after the war the fishing vessels had disappeared and there was little work in the agency office. I was sent to waste away at the automotive spares section for a month or two, and I hated every minute. I knew nothing at all about vehicle spare parts, and spent most of my time sitting down writing out invoices in duplicate. It was a living nightmare, until I returned back to the main office block in Crozier Place and eventually became head of the company's shipping agency.

In just under six years, I had progressed from total obscurity, as one of the company's most junior employees, painting a warehouse roof, to head of a department in the largest commercial company in the Falkland Islands. I was responsible for the day-to-day administration, which included the proper invoicing and accounting of clients, flights and travel, launch services and their crews, ships' bunkering, liaison with Customs, Immigration and Medical departments of the Falkland Islands Government, and for the provision of other services to a fishing fleet of several hundred ships, ensuring efficiency and the highest standard of quality and service. I was very particular about the latter. I was now one of the management team, albeit not a senior manager. Not yet.

At the same time, I was fronting the Islands Trade Union as its chairman. One of my most important roles in the trade union movement was to lead the negotiating team in debating working and pay conditions with the major employers, of which the

Falkland Islands Company, my employers, were one. I refer to this period of life in much more detail later.

Obviously, leading the union to victory in the dispute over the future of further cost-of-living awards had done no apparent damage to my development and progress in the ranks of the administration team, and I continued to enjoy my time with FIC. I eagerly absorbed all the knowledge I was gaining on a daily basis. I was hungry for it, and would often go into the office on days when I was supposed to be off.

One thing that had annoyed me immensely after the war was receiving an invoice in the post from the Falkland Islands Government for rent. It was a charge made for the house we had occupied at Green Patch during the war. It was not the amount they proposed to charge that pissed me off, it was the bloody principle. The Government agent on the farm had been meticulous in his calculation of days we occupied the unit, something else that pissed me off. I would have thought he would have had better things to do than count the damn days we were in the house. There was a war on for fuck sake, and I had been out helping British forces during it.

With haste, and a very short fuse, I presented the offending bill to Sir Rex Hunt, and I wasted no time in pointing out that I was extremely miffed, and I also indicated that I had no intentions of paying the demand, and would he be kind enough to sort the matter out. I guess Sir Rex did just that, because I was not troubled with the levy any more.

I mentioned that I would get back and tell you about a couple of surprises the Welsh Guards had left behind, after being in our house in Pioneer Row. To be honest, the person who came across the surprise packages was my wife. She was meticulously cleaning the house, and as she poked the head of the Hoover underneath the piano a metal object appeared. Being well drilled not to pick any ordnance up, she dashed into the kitchen, just as luck would have it, as two military men were walking past the house. She rushed out and called them in to investigate. Not being bomb disposal experts, they were not over-eager to prod around with unexploded bombs, but they gingerly obliged Melody and pulled out a mortar bomb and a belt full of ammunition for something like a machine gun. We can only presume they were left behind by the Guards as they hurriedly left the house to catch their waiting ship.

For many months after the war, the population of Stanley became used to the bangs, thumps and shudders of the daily rituals of the military explosives experts detonating tons upon tons of explosive devices and mines left behind by the defeated Argentines. Mines, obviously, were destroyed on the spot, so were other items too dangerous to move, like cluster bombs, but other munitions would be gathered up, placed in a heap and then blown to smithereens.

I must thank those magnificent military men who showed tremendous courage and professionalism as they went about their daily tasks of clearing away and making safe so much unexploded material which lay all over the place in the Falklands. Some were obvious, but others were not so, which resulted in a very high personal price being paid by soldiers losing limbs. After a short while it was decided that to try and remove all the mines was too high-risk and, very sensibly, this operation was abandoned and a much more prudent policy of ring-fencing the danger areas was adopted.

I don't think anyone should be shy to admit that morale was not very high for some time after the war. It is even possible that some of the community, especially some of those in Stanley and perhaps one or two who endured the Goose Green, Port Howard, Fox Bay and Pebble experience, never really got over their misfortune to the day of their departure from this sometimes troublesome world. For some it is even suggested that it might even have speeded up their progress to eternal life.

But an exceptional event that would lift the community's flagging spirits was the arrival in the Islands of Great Britain's Prime Minister, Margaret Thatcher, the 'Iron Lady' herself.

It was January 1983. There had been whispers about an impending visit, but in the afternoon on a sunny 8 January, one day after my son's ninth birthday, local radio interrupted its programmes to hail the news that the Prime Minister had arrived. The whole family put coats on and walked down to the east driveway entrance of Government House. By the time we got there, it seemed the whole of the town's population had turned out. People were buzzing with excitement, some barely able to contain themselves. Even I got caught up in the electrifying atmosphere and although I was not a Thatcher fan, I would have to be very grudging not to understand the people's gratitude towards her, and it would have been extremely selfish of me to attempt to spoil Melody and the kids' enjoyment of seeing their heroine in the flesh.

I will never forget the most amazing atmosphere in the Town Hall on Monday 10 January. The hall was jam-packed with people, shoulder-to-shoulder stuff. A normal function would encourage 250 people along. Special events like the May Ball or the prize-giving dance of the Stanley Sports Association would swell the crowd by a further 150. On this occasion, there must have been more like 600 people. Everyone was on a high as the adrenaline was pouring through the body. Broad smiles were back on people's faces, everyone was totally exuberant, as Mrs Thatcher was presented with the freedom of the Falkland Islands, a unique honour, and one most would agree was thoroughly deserved.

Falkland Islander Harold Rowlands, the brother of John, the Financial Secretary, who was the Falkland Islands Government's most senior Islander official, had been given the honour of presenting the scroll to the Prime Minister. Everyone hushed as first Harold, then the Governor, and finally the Prime Minister herself, gave a speech. Each time a speaker said something to the public's liking, a deafening noise of approval would break out.

Thatcher's speech went on for some time, but it was masterful in its delivery, and each time she hit the right spot, a thunderous response would roar out, accompanied by rapturous applause that would rock the building and raise the electrified atmosphere to an even higher level.

As I stood among the people in the middle of the hall, not more than 20 metres away from the Prime Minister, who was standing in the middle of the stage, flanked by Harold and Sir Rex, a thought came to my mind. There was no need for security guards for Thatcher in the Falkland Islands.

I was captivated, as I watched her, and stood in absolute amazement as the people reacted to virtually every word she uttered. For the first time in my entire life, I was witnessing a professional politician at work, a world leader, who had been caught up by the atmosphere, and as a result, was pumped up herself.

The timing of her visit to the Falklands was bang on cue, a much needed shot in the arm. I am very grateful to the British Prime Minister, because she knew what needed to be done, and she did it in magnificent style.

(I am slightly confused about when it was that I was actually introduced to the Prime Minister in the Town Hall, but it might have been during her second visit, to commemorate the tenth anniversary of the war. The Falklands Governor, William Fullerton, introduced me to her when they stopped directly in front of me. He mentioned to Mrs Thatcher who I was, and what I did. As we shook hands, I was surprised to notice she was wearing so much powder on her face, and she was slightly shorter than I had expected. I also remember from seeing US President Ronald Reagan in the flesh in 1988 that television seems to give a deceptive image of world leaders' physical size. Anyway, after shaking Mrs Thatcher's hand, I said to her something like, 'You were a long way away on the second of April 1982.' She held a stare very briefly, and did not say a word. I thought to myself, perhaps I had been the one who had got things right on cue this time.)

Whatever anyone might think of Mrs Thatcher, for or against her, I was not going to walk around with a chip on my shoulder over the 'Iron Lady' for the rest of my life. I am glad that she took the stance she did in 1982, but I am also not fooled, that on 1 April 1982 she, like previous British Prime Ministers, was probably intent on, or in the process of, giving the Falkland Islands away to Argentina. So I am just trying to put things into perspective a little bit.

Although I would like to think the Falklands War was fought for me, and fellow Islanders, I am not that naïve. But there is one thing for sure, had Britain not reacted in the way it did, what would Britain be herself today? I think an awful lot of people in the United Kingdom, are intelligent enough to know the answer to my question. That is why they quite rightly demanded action, so God bless you all.

Following the PM's visit to the Islands, the Governor and others were determined to keep spirits high, and no better way than to celebrate the 150 years of British rule (excluding 74 days). Things kicked off with one very large carnival, which included a vast number of floats parading through the streets of the town.

The weather was a bit naughty, but it could not stop the community and the many special guests to the Islands from enjoying themselves. Two of the superstars from the Falklands War who joined us in our celebrations were Peter King and Harold Briley of the BBC. Peter and Harold had become hero figures to many of the Islands community and were made warmly welcome wherever they went. Other important Falklands friends, from the Lords and the Commons, shared a dram or two with us, Baroness Vickers, Lords Shackleton and Buxton, Eric Ogden and Michael Shersby, being just some of them.

After the carnival had ended, we elected our first, and I believe only, Falklands Carnival Queen, and thanks to the Island of Barbados, we could warm the body with a mighty swig of Barbados rum. Several military bands entertained us with a variety of music, fireworks displays lit up the night sky, and there were two days of horse racing. At the time, I was the secretary of the Stanley Sports Association, which meant I was very much involved in the arrangements for this event.

The racecourse was not really in a fit state for racing. The track was boggy soft, and I remember on one occasion looking out of the windows of the crow's nest of the committee hut as Stewart Morrison was riding his horse, Bonito, to certain victory. Suddenly, and quite horrifyingly, within the last few strides, his horse's right foreleg dropped into one of the many peat-filled holes, right up to its shoulder, and it came to a frightening halt, catapulting Stewart out of his saddle. As Stewart hit the sodden wet ground on his belly, he slid along the slippery surface across the winning line. A few racecourse officials quickly ran to the aid of horse and jockey, and for a brief moment I was certain the horse must have broken its leg. Amazingly, neither was injured. To be completely honest, I was truly amazed, that no horse or jockey was hurt during the meeting, but so determined was everyone that the races should go on, so go on they did.

We would get another huge morale booster towards the end of the festival week. This was the announcement that the House of Commons had passed an amendment to the Nationality Bill giving Falkland Islanders the right of abode in the United Kingdom.

Very fitting for a proud and loyal community to the British Crown who had just finished a week of celebrations to commemorate 150 years of British rule. What an awful shame it took a war and the loss of so many lives before we were finally awarded what we always should have been entitled to.

Life in the Falklands was never the same after the war, but I could never have envisaged the many changes my life would go through over the next 20 years.

During this period in life, I would travel the world, meeting representatives from governments, and other organisations, of many countries. I would meet members of the Royal Family, Presidents, Prime Ministers, Lords and Ladies, sports personalities, and many celebrities in the entertainment business. Some were very nice ordinary and honest people. I have also come across cheats, liars, pimps, bums, gigolos, prostitutes and plain old bullshitters.

The next twenty years (1982–2002) would be a roller-coaster life, two decades which contained more happy times than sad, a life full of responsibilities, in the public and private domain, which would be very demanding, and carry a huge amount of trust and accountability. New challenges which required my time and attention seemed to be on the horizon every day. But before I go into more detail, I would like to tell you about the Falkland Islands' only recognised trade union movement, and the small part I played in its history.

33

Trade Unionism in the Falklands
(Life in the camp)

Trade unionism in the Falkland Islands was almost a hundred years in coming from the time of resettlement of the Falkland Islands in 1833. The movement, the Reform League, was stirred into action at the peak of the worldwide depression, which did not exclude the remote and isolated Falkland Islands from a chronic economic decline and acute unemployment.

However, even a sympathetic Governor O'Grady, who himself had been a union activist back in the United Kingdom, and had also been a Labour Member of Parliament, could achieve little other than to create a kind of false employment haven.

Although workers now had a voice, and some organised meetings about labour relations were being staged, the movement did not become officially recognised and registered until 28 October 1943. It was known then as the Labour Federation. (I find the timing of the registration in the middle of the Second World War rather intriguing, but I have not been able to establish why this was the case.)

In early 1943 a small group of pioneers had realised the need for a recognised and organised body to represent employees, who were generally being used and abused, with no agreed contract or terms of conditions regarding their employment in either Stanley or the camp.

However, before getting into the nitty gritty of the trade union, I think it would help to fill in the overall picture of the living and working environment of employees in the camp around the time of the union's formation. In so doing I am aware some of the story-telling might offend. Be assured, I am not attempting to be deliberately offensive to anyone; I am just describing how things were, and why the union saw the need to change things. Also why it was oppressive as people adhered to such a system. The story of these times not only should be told, it simply must be told, because it is such an important part of Falkland Islands history.

My early experiences of the nature of farm managers would be gained at the negotiating table, and in general I found them in the beginning to be extremely stubborn and abrasive characters. But once they got to realise that you had a bit more than fresh air between your ears they became moderately cordial.

So let me attempt to set the scene. The only meaningful industry and export in the Falkland Islands in 1943 was sheep farming. Prior to sheep farming, the early settlers had derived an income from sealing, whaling and the slaughtering of wild cattle. But for nearly a century leading up to the trade union formation, and for a further 40 years, sheep farming would be the engine room of the Islands economy. Thus, with the exception of the Islands capital, most of the 3 million acres of land had been utilised for the breeding of sheep purely for the production of wool.

This operation was carried out on a small number of large farms on the two main islands, and on many of the other smaller islands, making up approximately three dozen sizeable settlements and communities. Farm numbers, and sizes, would begin to change in 1979, as land sub-division took place.

Breeding and raising sheep in the Falklands has always been a difficult and laborious task. Mainly, sheep have had to be raised on extremely poor quality white grassland, which is still very much the case today, even though efforts are being made by some to improve pasture. Farmers have wisely calculated that, on average, it requires three acres of this land to raise and graze one sheep.

The industrious landowners operated the farms very much in the style of sheep ranching, with a sheep population of approximately 700,000, which, in turn, produced more or less 2.5 million kilos of wool. This was all exported, as a raw material, to the woollen mills in the United Kingdom.

In general terms, the farm settlement infrastructure did not change greatly until the concept of land sub-division got into full swing in the 1980s. So let me guide you around a typical farm settlement, and as I hop from one piece of infrastructure to another, whilst describing its functions, you should be able to get a general picture of life in the camp.

Perhaps we should start with the woolshed, which, as you could imagine, was the hub of any sheep farm. This was where all the work force, either collectively or in smaller groups, would carry out the activities of sheep-shearing, wool-carrying, keeping the main floor (the board) clear of fleeces, rolling and classing the fleece at the wool table, storing the wool in separate bins, keeping the shed and the pens within full of sheep to ensure the shearers had a steady flow of sheep to shear. This was carried out with hand shears until the 1960s.

Then there was pressing the wool into bales of sacking. The bales would be marked with the initials of the farm owner and/or the farm's name in heavy black marking ink.

A bale of wool could weigh in excess of 400 kilos before the middle of the 1960s. Once pressed, bales of wool were stored either in the woolshed or transferred to another building closer to the jetty or shore, awaiting collection by ship.

From the woolshed we move across the green (local terminology for the land area in the centre of the farm settlement). As we stroll along this hallowed turf, we reach the sometimes infamous cookhouse – the main accommodation and eating quarters of the single employees on the farm.

Like all the dwellings on a sheep farm it was built in a very simple manner. It was usually constructed of light 2×4 inch timber framing, with very simple interior and exterior cladding of rough boarding. All rooms usually had a window. There would be brick chimneys, wherever fires and cookers were set.

In 1943, there were no luxuries, no central heating, insulated walls, floors of attics, no double glazing, vacuum cleaners, washing machines, toilets, bathrooms. Not even running hot water or electricity. These things would come, but very gradually, and often many years later.

Instead, candles flickered and paraffin lamps glowed for lighting. Brooms, scrubbing brushes, the irreplaceable goose wings, mops and buckets were the tools for keeping things clean. Copper boilers using wood and/or peat heated water for washing clothes and taking baths.

Clothes would be washed by hand, in wooden washtubs and rubbed on washboards of wood or glass, and if really dirty from sheep work, scrubbed clean with a scrubbing brush before being hung out to dry in the fresh Falklands breeze on clothes lines.

A bath would be taken in big tin tubs on Saturday nights. This was also the time when the men would have a change of clothes, which they would not change again until the following Saturday, unless absolutely necessary.

Going to the latrine was an invigorating experience, which would require going outside and taking a walk to the purpose-built water closet, often in the dark and getting bloody cold, wet, or both, from the wind and rain on the way. Once you had entered the timber facilities, it was time to pull down your trousers and underwear and perch yourself on the wooden bench-like seat, if that was the task before you.

Often the aroma inside these cubicles were a very poor substitute for Chanel No. 5. Such was the atmosphere, you were encouraged to get on with your business and get out again in the quickest possible time frame.

On the ground floor of the cookhouse was the one large communal room, which was a type of leisure-cum-mess room. It would have very sparse furnishings, usually a large wooden table, with long wooden benches down each side, and a grubby settee. The main feature would often be the large open peat fire, which was the only facility to keep the occupants warm.

In the spring/summertime, the men would often work from sunrise to sunset, all day on horseback, carrying out sheep work. Therefore, when they arrived back home they were totally exhausted, ready only for a meal and bed, with the knowledge that the next sunrise was not many hours away, and another long hard day's work lay ahead of them.

For the boys – and they were just that, often only 12 years old, certainly in the 1940s – life in the cookhouse was hard, and sometimes quite brutal, a situation which never really improved until the 1960s. They would be constantly bullied and harassed, always expected to keep their mouths shut, and to do the menial tasks in the cookhouse in their own free time – chores such as carrying in the daily peat supply from the peat stacks and taking out the ashes daily etc. The boys were the constant target of verbal abuse from the men. Many pranks were carried out, and frequently a boy would be the target of a joke, usually in extremely bad taste. I have been told that it was not unusual for boys to be victims of some form of physical and/or sexual abuse.

In the 1960s, men started to share the tasks of keeping the communal areas in order, and the person who would carry out this job during the week was referred to as 'The Peggy'. He would sign off his week's 'Peggy' by scrubbing and cleaning all the shared areas on a Saturday morning, whilst the remainder of the gang would be out doing farm work, in what was then a five and a half day working week at least.

Before the days of a recognised workers agreement between the GEU and the Sheep Owners Association (the SOA), men worked as and when the manager instructed them to do so, all for their basic monthly pay. The 40-hour working week was not introduced until the late 1970s in both Stanley and the camp.

Bedrooms were usually on the first floor of the standard farm cookhouse. They were small and had paper-thin walls; privacy was not something anyone could expect in a cookhouse, with perhaps one notable exception, that was the cook.

The farm cook usually lived in the cookhouse. The kitchen/galley, which was adjacent to the mess room/lounge, was his kingdom, and any man who entered the galley without an invitation from the cook did so at considerable risk. Cook was a term used very loosely for some of these prima donna-type characters (I need to be careful, my father was one for many years). They came from all walks of life, and all corners of the globe. But if nothing else, they all had one thing in common: they were temperamental buggers. Few had any training, and those that did tended to be worse than those who made up their menus as they went along.

The chef was not required to be particularly inventive, there were no gourmet dinners served in the cookhouse. It was generally good old '365', the local terminology for mutton. Mutton was served just about any way you could think of – roast joints, fried chops (a breakfast special), pickled, boiled, undercooked, and sometimes burnt to cinders, especially if the cook was having a bad day.

It would often be served cold for the evening meal, and would also be a prime ingredient in local favourites such as fritters and sandwiches, usually smothered in tomato sauce or mustard, as well as stews, meatballs (locally called rissoles), curry, sausages and sausage rolls.

Whatever the meal, no cookhouse dining table was ever complete without vital condiments to add a little extra spice to the meal being served. These items would typically be Lea and Perrin's sauce, tomato ketchup and a tin of Tate and Lyle Golden Syrup. The latter would be plastered over butter on a slice or two of white bread, perhaps even a fritter. Salt and pepper would be provided, but the other items would have to be purchased by the individual from the farm store. Which meant that each man guarded and cared for his personal items as treasures. Trouble was never far away if someone tried to, or accidentally, used someone else's sauce.

The vegetables were cultivated in the cookhouse gardens. The responsibility of planting and tending to them rested with the occupants of the cookhouse, just another 'in your own time' occupations for the employees.

The eating of offal would be seriously curtailed from the middle sixties, and as a result a whole generation of Islanders have become unaccustomed to eating it. This was because of a life-threatening disease which could be transmitted by dogs who had eaten offal to humans. Cysts would form in the human body and would require surgical removal, or death could be the final result for the poor victim.

At certain times of the year the old 365 would be accompanied or replaced by other seasonal delights. Lamb was everyone's favourite (three or four months old), which was traditionally served up at Christmas lunch, accompanied with new potatoes and mint sauce. Roasted upland goose packed with a sage and onion stuffing was another favourite. Autumn would see the roasted teal duck on the mess room table. Goslings were also a choice offering at the right time of year.

Spring/summer would produce a variety of eggs, which were prepared in the frying pan or in a pot of boiling water: penguin eggs, goose eggs, mollymawk eggs (local name for the black-browed albatross), steamer duck eggs (locally called logger duck), gull eggs, duck eggs and, of course, the trusty old hen eggs were all served up in one form or another. On odd occasions a wager might inspire someone to take any of them raw, sometimes including a bird in its embryonic stage.

I should point out that on the farms there were no facilities or services such as a greengrocers, bakery, fishmongers or butcher's shop. Therefore all the ingredients had to be collected up by the men or the cook. The cook would also be required to bake cakes and bread.

Local fish, such as mullet and smelt, would be a further diversification from 365, but chicken and pork were a rarity. Fresh milk was provided daily in a big bucket. Butter and cream were commonly produced, but I have never heard of anyone making cheese.

Now it is time to leave the cookhouse, and its many more dark secrets, and give you a description of other buildings on the farm.

Dwellings were provided by the employer, unfurnished, for the married employees, and considered part and parcel of the salary package. 'The tied cottage' syndrome, in general. These houses were built of the same very basic materials as the cookhouse. There were only a very few stone houses.

Each home had a sizeable garden, but the main garden for the cultivation of vegetables was usually appointed somewhere else. Like the men in the cookhouse, the occupier of each home had to plant and look after the garden in his spare time.

Despite the Falklands short growing season, which produced variable and often inclement weather, potatoes, carrots, turnips, cabbage, cauliflower, broccoli, sprouts, peas, radish and lettuce all grew well. So did many other things. Herbs and soft fruits were also grown.

The farm employer also provided milking cows to each family, and mutton was also supplied. Both of these items were provided free of charge, therefore they were also considered as part of the overall employment package. Mutton was butchered as required and usually delivered once a week.

The milking of the cows was yet another labour-intensive responsibility of the occupants, thus adding still more daily chores to an already heavy workload in a very long working day.

The housewife had all the familiar laborious tasks as the cook in the cookhouse, plus many more. Few women worked outside the home, but one or two might have been a domestic servant in some capacity at the manager's house. In those days in the Falklands, as in many other parts of the globe, it was firmly considered that a woman's place was in the home, nowhere else. This attitude did not really change much until the 1970s, and only very moderately then. Things are, quite rightly, very different now.

Leisure was a rare thing, for both wife and husband. However, even the most oppressed people find time to socialise, and when the small settlement community did relax, indoor social occasions took place in 'the hall'. If there was no main community centre, then the cookhouse often became the venue for jollification, usually on a Saturday night. Often it was a dance, with local entertainers providing the music, because until the 1960s record players with 78, 45 and 33 rpm records were not readily available.

The Betts's on Pebble, and the Lees at Port Howard, were just two families well known on the West Falklands for their musical talents. They would get many a dance into full swing by playing fiddles (both the devil and the standard type), accordions, guitars, banjos, drums, washboard and spoons – and blowing into fag papers on combs – to the timing of quicksteps, foxtrots, waltzes or the hell-raising circassian circle.

Not surprisingly, serious drinking was an accepted part of life at these social gatherings, and a laugh and a joke turning into a challenge to a bare-knuckled fist fight on the village green was not unusual. Often, the assumed winner of the unofficial boxing match on the night would be nursing a black eye the next day, whilst the rest of the men, who would not have missed a single blow of the entertainment, would be excitedly reliving the events and discussing the finer points of detail about the contestants' skills, or lack of them. Such as when Williams should have ducked, or 'what a right uppercut he got caught with'.

Horseracing was a very popular outdoor sport, and the sports week was a huge social occasion, bringing together communities from many other farms.

The community hall was the gathering point for a multitude of events: films, weddings, card and darts competitions, even funeral services – not necessarily in that order. When the Falkland Islands Government became a little more serious about education, some of the community halls were utilised as temporary schools for visiting teachers. One or two of the larger farms would have their own purpose-built school. At Darwin the school building was destroyed during the battle for Goose Green.

It must be said that the educating of Falkland Islanders was not considered very important in the 1940s and for many years after. In fact, many farmers, even some dignitaries, considered it as an extremely dangerous practice to educate the native Falkland Islander. The perception being, that if the lower classes were educated, they would become too adventurous and expectant about employment opportunities and quality of life. It is for this reason that so many of the children, male and female, went off to work at the tender age of 12. A truly disgraceful situation, which resulted in several generations of Falkland Islanders being unequipped and unprepared to take on responsibility and seek a more independent way of life.

Now, the farm store. The community purchased their supplies from the farm owner's general store. This system meant that the employer was in the enviable position of effectively paying a man his salary and recovering a large proportion of it by selling to him, and his family, their basic needs. (I should point out that this method was not exclusive to the camp; it was just as prominent for the employees of the Falkland Islands Company in Stanley.)

Opening times for these tiny outlets were very restrictive, and at the whim of the farm manager or his representative, the storekeeper. But usually, it would be on Wednesdays and Saturdays. It was a rare opportunity for the housewife and the dear old cookhouse cook to replenish their larders with essentials such as flour and sugar, which were purchased in 50-kilo sacks and stored in specially made bins in the house. These containers often played hosts to the weevil, and the odd mouse or two.

The shop would be open for about an hour or two, and it was also an occasion which enabled people to get together and catch up on the gossip. For the single men on the farm, it was one of the highlights of the week. It was an opportunity to purchase a bottle of whisky, rum, gin or vodka. For the beer drinkers, then a case of beer. The quantities of these items for purchase were rationed by order of the farm manager, so the men would discuss shopping tactics on opening day, to ensure maximum purchasing power and the widest possible selection of liquid refreshment.

The cookhouse would be a hive of activity after such a successful shopping venture, as it became the venue for the unofficial bar, which would be stocked, and very much opened, for a session of yarns and drinking.

The bachelor would round off his shopping experience by filling up his shopping bag with a bottle of Lea and Perrin's or tomato sauce, a tin of syrup, some soap, 200 cigarettes, or a tin of Capstan tobacco and fag papers, a box of candles, matches, a few chocolates, and finally, a new pair of rubber boots once in a while.

The store would also have a notice board, which would be adorned with company, or the manager's, edicts.

The alternative to purchasing from the farm store was to send your requirements to the retail outlets in Stanley and await the arrival of the ship that would carry them to the farms. A very small amount of goods could be transported by the local air service, but this was not introduced until the 1950s.

A visit from a ship was not a regular thing, and only once every six weeks or so. In fact, the arrival of the vessel was always a moment for great excitement. Not only was this a time when a much more serious supply of alcohol would arrive for those in need, it was also an occasion when members of the tiny hamlet community could receive packages from friends and families, or even receive family or friends themselves for a stay (subject to the manager's permission).

The ship would supply a whole range of goodies not normally available from the farm store: items of furniture for the house to make it a bit more comfortable, the local newspaper, UK dailies bound in monthly editions, usually three months old at best, new clothing, or some other luxury.

The visit of a new, or familiar, face would make an evening or two more interesting. One could sit down and listen to the news from town whilst tucking into some unusual treats.

Moving on to other facilities, you naturally had all the usual ancillary buildings dotted around the settlement: cow sheds for milking the cows, dog kennels, which from my memory were horrible rat-infested things full of mutton carcasses rotting away, horse stables, workshops for carrying out carpentry and other repair and maintenance works, hay barns and, as things progressed over the years, a diesel generator shed for limited electricity supply, garage and mechanic's workshop for repair, maintenance and shelter of the farm tractor/s and other automated agricultural equipment, plus the towering windmill which was used to pump spring water in to a storage system for domestic use.

Last, but by no means least, we come to the manager's house (locally called 'the big house' because it was by far the largest dwelling on the farm), which was always sited in a position of prominence, and usually stood well apart from the rest of the buildings in the settlement, thus allowing its occupants distance from the farm community. Which, I suppose, epitomised the social structure and divide even in those tiniest of communities.

The big house was the lion's den, the laird's castle. The

manager's house was strictly out of bounds for staff, with few exceptions – perhaps the foreman and the head shepherd. Lesser staff members would require a very serious need indeed to enter these most private of private premises.

The manager and his wife were so terribly aloof, each would have support staff to attend to their every need, and on many occasions, to those of their guests, such as other farm managers, or dignitaries from government.

The cowman/gardener was the manager's flunkey. He would attend to gardens, milk the cows, feed the animals, cats, dogs, hens etc., bring in the peat, take out the ashes, set and light fires. When the manager said, do this or that, the cowman/gardener jumped.

The female staff cooked and waited table, washed and cleaned around the house, changed bedding, washed and ironed clothes, by hand, and with flat irons.

The relationship between staff and their superiors was rarely one of friendship, but behind closed doors, and in private moments, there are many tales of pleasure between management and staff.

I remember my old friend Williams telling me once, 'One day when I was working with the boss, he said to me, "You know what, Williams, I have had it off with every woman on this farm."' (The manager knew that Williams had just got married and his remark was typical of their arrogance.)

I said to Williams, 'Christ sake, what did you do?'

Williams replied with a grin on his face, 'I think he expected me to get really angry, but I just told him, "Well, that's two of us, boss."' Then with a broad grin on his face, he added, 'He stopped what he was doing, threw down his tools and rushed off.' As I stood staring at Williams, rather quizzically, I noticed he had a very content expression on his face.

This neatly brings me on to the subject of working relations between managers and their employees. Farm managers, in the main, were arrogant, miserly and disregarding of their employees, who they viewed as nothing more than peasants. They did have some respect, however, for two key figures within their employ, the head shepherd and the general foreman. But the friendship was usually never more than at arm's length and was only forged by the awareness that they would be very dependent on them. These two men, completely loyal and competent individuals, would ensure that the day-to-day operational needs of the farm would be effectively and efficiently carried out, leaving the manager free to attend to a whole host of other administrative work.

The manager's all-encompassing authority meant he would be filling the role of postman, judge, telecommunications operator, marriage counsellor, diplomat and, on rare occasions, even reverend or spiritual advisor. The foreman and head shepherd also took care of many of these responsibilities in the manager's absence, such as long vacations in the United Kingdom, or visits to Stanley for council work or a winter holiday.

Sadly, the attitude towards mainstream employees never really changed to any great extent until the 1980s. I believe there were a few principal factors for this. A different type of manager appeared on the scene by the late seventies/early eighties, the first crop with a working-class background, Falkland Islanders who had slogged their way through the ranks, ex-union men mostly – ordinary people from exceptional families or, perhaps, exceptional people from ordinary families, perhaps even exceptional people from exceptional families. Such as Ron Binnie, Eric Goss and Tony McMullen. I am sure I do not offend the aforementioned. Rather, I hope they feel very proud of their achievements.

Another issue which shook the old regime manager's nest very severely was the dramatic collapse, worldwide, of wool prices, resulting in the woollen industry, in the Falkland Islands at least, becoming financially crippled. This sudden cold financial climate blowing down the corridors of the big house forced managers to seek new company and supporters, who in turn whispered different ideas and concepts to them.

Finally, the wind of change was also in the air from another direction – Government. This came about as a result of the findings of Lord Shackleton and his team in their two economic reports, which basically encouraged Government to buy out absentee and other landowners, thus bringing these very independent and affluent members of society down to earth with a thump as they sought new friends.

That said, many quickly got over their attack of frostbite as they quickly gathered their thoughts and worked out a very lucrative way to get their greedy little fists one more time on a large chunk of public funds. They only too willingly sold off all, or part, of a 'dead duck' of a business to a government too eager to pay too much, so as to get rid of them.

Probably, they were contemplating political Brownie points, as they handed the land over to too many ordinary people who followed their hearts and not their heads. Then reality would hit the new owners, as they peered out of their farm kitchen windows thinking, all that land out there is mine. Unfortunately, so were all the heartaches and the debt.

However, what I might think about the land sale is one thing, but what I do not believe anyone could argue is this: for many years before the formation of the trade union, and after, managers ruled with an iron fist, and true to ALL colonial systems ALL over the world, called for patriarchal authority. Anyone who stood out of line was fired in double quick time, often without compensation, if the manager could manipulate the situation, which was never very difficult.

Some would say that not a lot changed for many years even after the union's formation, but one thing is for sure, the union was a solid and secure buffer between the manager and his employee for 50 years, or more, whilst there was such a need.

It must also be said that managers could be incredibly deceitful to their loyal workers. I vividly remember a story my grandmother told me about Williams, who had decided to leave the farm he was working on simply because he fancied a change, and get work at a neighbouring settlement. As Williams was saddling up his horse to ride off to his next employer, the manager walked up to him and asked if he would take a letter with him to pass to his new boss when he arrived. Dear old Williams replied obediently, 'Certainly, sir, no problem.'

When Williams got to his journey's end, he reported to his new boss, and duly passed him the letter, and started to walk away towards the cookhouse to find his new accommodation. Hardly had he gone a few steps when he heard the manager roar, 'Williams, what the hell is this?' The man was waving the letter in the right hand of his raised arm. 'It says here that you are a troublemaker, a lazy bugger and very unreliable and I would be a fool to take you on.'

Williams was gobsmacked, but fortunately for him, on this rare occasion the manager was graceful enough to listen to his pleas of innocence and assurance that he was a good stockman. It was finally agreed that Williams would have one chance to prove himself, but one chance only. 'Any sign of trouble, and you're off the farm at a minute's notice,' growled the manager.

I think that pretty much sums up labour relations between employer and employee at that time.

Finally, I will try and give you a description of the daily chores on the sheep farm that made up the working day of a man's life in the camp. Female workers (land girls) would be introduced to the farm labour force in the 1970s, and they were a very welcome transformation to the working environment.

I should also enlighten you of the bizarre method of payment in those dark and laborious days, and even more bizarrely, how a man got his accumulated cash (if he had any).

Most of the work took place during 'the season', the spring and summertime, as you might expect. It revolved entirely around sheep, and it was at this particular time that the shepherd, especially, with the assistance from just about everyone else on the farm from time-to-time, became a key figure.

The season began with lambing. Survival percentages of lambs would vary; much depended on the elements. A combination of long periods of foggy damp weather, snow storms, or heavy rain in early spring (September/October) could wipe out newly born lambs in the thousands across the whole of the Falklands, due mainly to the almost total lack of shelter.

A shepherd was often subjected to these harsh climatic conditions himself, getting frozen and soaked to the bone as he toiled away trying to save as many animals as he could from near certain death, with only his horse and dogs. These creatures were a shepherd's working tools, transport and companions. Today this type of work is usually carried out on motorbikes.

In parallel to the lambing season, other important work had to be carried out by other members of the labour force, in particular peat cutting. This task was done by the navvy. Today, even in camp, fewer and fewer individuals rely on peat as a source of heating the home and as a cooking fuel. Gas oil, kerosene and even propane gas have replaced this fuel.

With lambing and peat cutting complete, all hands would muster at the lamb-marking pens, which would have been set up at strategic positions in the fields.

Lamb-marking was a very gruesome affair. My brother has told me the gory details of how the male lambs were castrated. I think I should tell you, even though it makes me squirm and fidget in my chair as I am writing it down, but here goes.

A man, armed only with a very sharp knife, would make a quick cut of the scrotum, then he would force a testicle out with one hand, giving it a quick tug with the other to expose the genital cord as he severed it with his knife. This practice, needless to say, could cause haemorrhaging and other internal injuries, which could perhaps lead to an agonising death. A much more civilised New Zealand system was introduced in the 1960s.

The poor male lamb would also be subject, along with all the other lambs, to having their tails cut off at the third joint, and just for good measure, a chunk or two would be cut out of their ear to indicate the sex and age of the animal. See, I told you it was a gruesome tale.

Then it was time to turn the labour efforts towards sheep shearing and pressing the wool into bales, so the annual clip could be shipped off to Stanley and then the overseas wool markets.

For many years there was also another task to perform with sheep, dipping. This was carried out usually after all the shearing had been completed. The reason for this exercise was simply to get rid of ticks (*Melophagus ovinus*) – another local name of these beetle-type things was keds. They would suck the blood from the sheep and could cause anaemia and also stain the wool.

The sheep would be made to swim through a long, deep and narrow trough, which would be filled with a disinfectant liquid – the dip. The animal would be pushed under the surface of the water so that the head of the sheep could also be treated to kill off all the keds that were living on the animal.

The process of sheep dipping ended during the late sixties, when *Melophagus ovinus* was finally and thankfully eradicated.

Work on sheep farms was not all about sheep, there was always new fencing to erect, or repair, gates to swing, buildings to scrape and paint, fields to plant, hay and other animal feed to gather and store.

Port Howard, on the West Falklands, was an example that few farms unfortunately cared to follow. They proved that farmers could grow acres upon acres of wheat, oats and suchlike, which they wisely stored and fed to the animals, especially during the winter months.

Life in the camp in late autumn, the winter, and very early spring, was very different to the rest of the year. It was a gentle period of repair and maintenance; as much work as possible would be carried out indoors to try and escape the bitter cold outside. Cleaning the woolshed floor gratings, digging out and carrying the sheep droppings to the community gardens and painting the sheep pens were standard winter tasks. Some of the chaps would make horse gear from cattle hide.

Daylight in the winter was pretty short. The sun would rise just before 8 a.m. and would be dipping away and setting by 3.30 p.m. in the heart of the winter. The long winter nights were conducive to many hours of darts and card games. One or two would play chess, but draughts was a much more popular game.

This was also a time when many of the farm managers would leave the farm for a long vacation either in the United Kingdom, or in Stanley. The assistant manager or foreman was often left in temporary charge, which usually meant there was a much more relaxed atmosphere about the place. However, things were never allowed to get out of control, or the stand-in, whose powers were very limited anyway, would have his nuts in a vice the moment the manager returned.

The farm employee was poorly paid for his labours, a mere £5 a month in 1943 for a navvy (general hand). He was *never* paid in cash. Each worker had a personal farm account. This was not a bank account as such, merely a bookkeeping tool, a financial statement, which recorded all the debit and credit transactions against the individual in question.

The account was controlled by the manager, or his representative or agent – the farm bookkeeper, or perhaps the FIC. They would be responsible for cataloguing all purchases from the farm store and other items of expenditure, such as postage stamps, procurements from shops in Stanley, electricity bills, money transfers to a third person, and so on. All of these business transactions would probably have been settled by a farm company cheque.

Once every three or six months the employee would receive a copy of his financial statement. It was usually the only time he had any idea of his overall financial position. This was the procedure until the man retired, resigned or had his employment terminated.

Even though the employee had earned his money through very hard work, and the money was his and due to him, the manager would still try and make him consider that it was much safer and wiser not to withdraw the money from the farm account. The employee rarely put up much of a fight for his cash. After all, his lord and master had advised not to do so, so it must be right. If one did become a little too persistent he would, likely as not, be discriminated against, as a 'meddling outsider'.

Oh yes, the farm manager was a TYRANT. The system was most certainly OPPRESSIVE, change simply had to come about.

In the 1940s, labour relations were little better in Stanley. There was no competitive private sector in the Islands capital, job opportunities were very limited and working conditions little less domineering. The Falkland Islands Company and the Falkland Islands Government were the main employers of the working man. Therefore, it was hardly a surprise, I suppose, that in 1943 someone, somewhere, came to the conclusion that enough was enough and began to think about putting a stop to the unabated employment abuse.

In the beginning, two of the trade union innovators, Jack Barnes and Maurice Evans, were given the responsibility of promoting the trade union organisation and recruiting potential members in Stanley and the camp. Recruitment in Stanley was relatively easy in terms of logistics, but the task of coordinating travel and meetings in the camp was a completely different proposition.

Travelling around the East Falklands would require the delegation to spend long hours going overland. Even reaching the nearest farm settlement, which might just be 20-odd miles away, could take up to five or six hours because there were no roads outside Stanley and the terrain was mainly made up of peat and boggy marsh land. Getting bogged would be a frequent occurrence, and average speeds of seven to eight miles an hour would be considered very good.

The mode of motor transportation in the Falklands in 1943 was very limited, probably a lorry, but horseback was probably a quicker and more efficient alternative.

If overland was not an option on the East Falklands, due to distance and time, the steamship *The Fitzroy*, at this time, steamed around the East and West Falklands periodically, delivering stores and provisions. It also carried passengers to and fro, whilst picking up the wool for export. A small amount of salted sheep and cattle skins were also exported, but this could hardly be described as an industry. The cargo would be fetched to Stanley for storage, then onward shipment to the United Kingdom by a specially chartered vessel.

The journey by sea was fine in terms of carrying promotional material and other union propaganda. It was also excellent for preparing speeches and setting out agendas. But there was one huge disadvantage. Once at the port of call there was very little time to organise meetings and promote the cause as the vessel would often depart within a few hours of arrival; in most cases, immediately after the ship's crew and farm hands had completed the discharge and loading of the vessel and farm's cargoes.

The only opportunity to call and hold a properly organised meeting would be if the ship stayed overnight. On these very rare opportunities the meetings would often be convened in the cookhouse.

During the shorter stops, the farm hands (the potential recruits) were also engaged in the unloading and loading of the vessels, so meetings (if you could call the gatherings that) would have to be hurriedly arranged during a meal or refreshment break. I have even heard tales of Jack and Maurice talking about the benefits of forming a labour organisation as they walked alongside a man carrying out his labours.

It should also be understood that the farm managers or owners, in some cases both, were not welcoming Barnes and Evans with open arms. I have been told, at times, their reception was even hostile as they stepped off the ship and began to try and hold meetings in a house or shed.

This was hardly surprising; the employers in the Falkland Islands had had a free rein regarding employees' working and pay conditions for over a century. They had hired and fired as they liked, totally free of any outside interference, so why the hell would they want to assist the employee in getting organised to fight for change?

Probably the worst thing of all for the farmers to tolerate was the unthinkable, perhaps even degrading prospect, of having to discuss such issues as regulated working hours, introducing a form of minimum wage, provision of sick leave (with pay, God forbid), offering leave entitlements and other revolutionary ideas, with people whom they regarded, in the main, as nothing more than peasants.

Even more terrible was having Barnes and Evans putting these ideas into their employees' heads under their very noses, so it was hardly surprising to hear stories of harassment and vindictive behaviour towards the men as soon as Jack Barnes and Maurice Evans were 'over the hill'.

I have been told, many times, of employers using all sorts of uncivilised behaviour towards their employees in an attempt to stop them joining the Labour Federation.

One man informed me, he was taken to a corner of the shearing shed, where he was told, 'If you have any ideas in your head about joining that fucking Federation, I'll fire you on the spot, at a minute's notice.'

Another man told the story of when he was riding his horse, gathering a flock of sheep. The boss rode up alongside him and said, 'How did the meeting go, Smith?' (referring to the visit of Barnes and Evans the day before). 'I hear you are going to be a father again soon. Is that right?'

'Yes sir,' said Smith, thinking the employer was showing some humanity towards him.

This idea was soon dashed, when the manager snapped in a loud and uncontrolled voice, 'Join that bloody Labour Federation and you and your miserable fucking family can find a new home and job.'

It has also been alleged that if the manager felt he was not succeeding in his game of mental warfare with verbal threats and other abuse, he would resort to trying to break the man's spirit by imposing additional labour on him, longer hours of intensive work in the worst possible conditions. If all his efforts failed to deter the man from joining the trade union, it was then extremely likely that he would seek the slightest excuse to fire him.

I should point out that while these actions were allegedly carried out by the majority of the managers, there were some who behaved quite differently, who actually understood what it was that Barnes and Evans were trying to achieve.

One of my brothers, Arnold, is able to tell a far different, and unusual, story. At the time the union was trying to recruit membership, he was working on Pebble Island, where our great-uncle, William Donald Betts, was the farm manager. Arnold and his colleagues were free of any such horrors and many were among the original members of the trade union movement. Our great-uncle was described as very sympathetic and understanding towards the working man and showed no resistance to the idea of a trade union movement.

One thing that is for sure, Barnes, Evans and the other pioneering colleagues of the trade union movement were causing a major revolution in the work place, on a scale never seen before in the Falklands, and despite the hostility and frequent threats towards the founders and the would-be new members in Stanley and the camp, the first employees' representative body The Labour Federation, was officially launched and registered on 28 October 1943.

But the inception of the trade union movement, hardly surprisingly, would not bring about dramatic changes in working and pay conditions straight away. This was not something that employers, both in Stanley and camp, were going to take lightly.

It also hardly came as any great surprise that the union and farm managers would lock horns shortly after the union's formation. The moment of dispute arrived in December of 1945.

At this time the membership of the union wanted its representatives to confront the managers about the task of shearing wet sheep. The men had grown tired and fed-up with having to grab hold of a big woolly sheep which was wet from the rain, then position the animal against themselves to clip its wool with hand shears.

Four or five sheep later, the shearers would be drenched themselves, but they would be expected to carry on working soaked to the bone until such time as they could get home to have a change of clothes, only to repeat the process a few sheep later into the next working session.

The employees also claimed that these working conditions were directly responsible for lost man hours and wages due to being off work, without pay, from illnesses such as colds and flu. No work, no pay, prior to the formation of the trade union. Thus, the union leaders, quite rightly, took up the challenge with employers.

The Labour Federation wanted a complete review of the

practice. They requested that sheep should be inspected before a shearing session, then, if agreed that the sheep were too wet to shear, shearing would not be carried out until such time as the shearing shed could be filled with dry sheep.

The employers' response was a united one of, 'The men had always done the job in the past without complaint, why the hell should they not carry on doing it now?' There would, no doubt, also be mutterings from the employers, in varying degrees of decibels, 'We knew that bloody union would be nothing but trouble.'

Following several attempts to resolve the issue in a manner of open debate, it became clear to the union that the employers would not yield. Hence, a complete breakdown of communications between the parties resulted, and the Falkland Islands would find itself in the grip of its first labour dispute. The 'historical test case', let's face it, if it had not been wet sheep, it would have been something else that would test the mental and physical strength of the union and its membership against the authorities.

As it turned out, history was to be made just before Christmas in 1945, when the men at Fitzroy Farm (owned by the FIC) refused to shear a woolshed full of wet sheep. Management, unused to having its authority contested, perhaps not surprisingly (in the writer's opinion) handled the situation tactlessly. Their 'will not listen' response was, effectively, the pulling of the trigger for industrial action in a dispute that did not limit itself to Fitzroy.

The Labour Federation was also in a bit of a spot, because it knew it had to be up for the struggle, otherwise its credibility as an organisation capable of representing and protecting its membership's interests would surely be seriously damaged. Therefore, they deployed a 'no holds barred' tactic, a strike. In doing so, they called all members out of their work place, in Stanley and camp, in support of the men at Fitzroy, thus implementing the first labour industrial action in the Islands' history. Over the years, there would be very few to follow.

The strike was short and, for the union membership, pretty sweet. Not only did the Federation get the employers to concede on the matter of wet sheep, but during the debate on settling the dispute, the union threw in a wild card on wages, as part of the deal to call off the strike.

My brother Arnold told me that Uncle Henry, who was just 16 at the time, saw his monthly salary rise from £4 plus the £1 cost of living allowance to £5 10s a month (£5.50), a pretty impressive percentage wage increase.

The worker had tasted his first moment of success over his miserly employer, thanks entirely to the trade union.

However, the new working practices had a distinct positive side for the employers and farm owners, by limiting the serious possibility of farm owners losing much, or all, of their wool clip as a consequence of compacting wet wool into very tight bales or storage areas.

I should explain. Wet wool, when it is very tightly compressed, becomes very hot and can cause spontaneous combustion. The process takes time to activate, but it can occur at any time, in a woolshed, or in a ship's hold. As well as property, people were being put at unreasonable risk. Should a fire have broken out on board ship, especially whilst at sea, the tragedy could have resulted in the loss of the ship and its crew. I wonder why no one ever had the sense to think of, and put into place, a safer working practice that would limit these potentially high-risk dangers before the Falkland Islands Labour Federation was formed?

Let's move on to other matters. After a period, the Labour Federation and the employers' representative body, the Sheep Owners Association, managed to forge agreements on the working and pay conditions through annual negotiations. But there would be periods of breakdown in communications which would lead to further strike action. Often the dispute revolved around the cost of living bonus.

The first industrial action on this very sensitive and extremely complicated issue took place in 1966/67, again in camp. On this occasion the argument between the two parties reached deadlock on a discrepancy about the way the camp cost of living bonus (COLB) was calculated.

The COLB was a system whereby a list of 100 shopping basket items, previously agreed between the two organisations, were monitored over a period of three months. Should there have been any alteration to the prices to the workers (an increase was usually the case), the cost would be averaged out and a wage increase awarded to the employee, and added to his/her monthly pay.

The items covered in the shopping basket for camp varied somewhat from those of the hourly paid workers in Stanley. Inter-island shipping freight rates was a cost to the workers living in camp, not to the workers in Stanley. House rents, utility charges and the cost of purchasing mutton and milk applied to workers in Stanley, not the camp.

Okay, back in the late 1960s, the trade union organisation and the body representing the sheep farmers could not agree on the method of calculation for the previous quarterly inflation figures. Farmers, in fact, were adamant that there was no upward adjustment due, whilst the Labour Federation insisted there was. Deadlock followed, the union called a strike, which duly lasted one and a half working days, a Friday and Saturday morning to be exact.

Unlike the strike of the 1940s, on this occasion the Stanley workers did not come out in support of their fellow workers, because of the speed in which the issue was resolved. The sheep owners quickly agreed to an error of judgement, and duly accepted the union's position was correct. Therefore, an increase in employees' salary was due, and paid.

However, a rather bizarre situation followed. Farmers insisted (quite rightly, in my opinion) that they would deduct the wages for the one and a half days they were out on strike from the men's monthly salary. Jubilation quickly turned to despair within the trade union membership, rapidly followed by anger, when realisation hit them that the industrial action had come at an individual cost, which would result in them receiving less money in their pockets at the end of that particular month.

The union's Executive Committee suddenly found itself on the wrong end of its own membership's fury. The men were now demanding reimbursement for the loss of wages from the union itself. Suddenly, the whole thing had turned the union on its head, and in the midst of the commotion the union membership would, for the first time, get the stark truth about the union's financial position; it did not have the means to entertain any such claims.

Red-faced, the Executive Committee had to explain to members that all revenues received from membership fees, the odd donations and the running of a weekly sweepstake, barely covered the operational and administrative costs of the organisation.

Therefore, there were no funds in reserve to entertain the idea of subsidising loss of salaries from any industrial dispute.

In this desperate situation, the negotiators came up with a quite unbelievable idea. They decided to go back to The Sheep Owners Association and suggest that they, the employers, reimburse the deducted salaries. God knows why, but just as unbelievably, the association agreed. Thus not only did the Labour Federation manage to get the employers to concede defeat on the matter of dispute, they then got them to fund the union members for the strike action against them. Surely, even Mr Scargill would have been very proud of that achievement.

34

I Join Up
(Not that there was any choice in the matter)

By the time I became involved in the trade union, some 30 years after its formation, much had changed. The union was now a fact of life even though elements of management, especially in the camp, had still not got used to the idea and some, in fact, really despised it.

To be honest with you, if I had not needed to take up employment in the Falkland Islands Government Public Works Department (PWD) in the early 1970s, I would never have got interested in its activities, let alone become its Chairman and head of negotiations team later on in life.

When I joined the General Employees Union, as it was now called, there were NO women members. This I am sure was more to do with the union's overall outlook, rather than anything to do with female apathy towards the trade union.

The union had concentrated its efforts on two main areas of employment; the hourly paid workers in Stanley, who were generally employed by the Falkland Islands Government and the Falkland Islands Company, and the monthly paid sheep farm workers.

Perhaps I should point out that there was also a type of blue-collar worker's organisation, the Civil Servants Association. This was not a trade union as such, but it did negotiate terms and conditions with the Falkland Islands Government for their members.

Unfortunately, the General Employees Union and the Civil Servants Association kept their distance from each other. Which, in my opinion, was a great shame and in neither party's interest. Whenever any attempt, or suggestion, was made to merge the two groups, it was quickly extinguished.

By the early 1970s, not only had the trade union gained its place in the day-to-day life of the working man of the Falklands, but, via its only paid officer, the General Secretary and Treasurer, Richard Goss (Dick), who was the great-grandson of Jacob Napoleon Goss, it had for the first time a friend and supporter who was in the upper circle, as he rose through the ranks of the local Territorial Army to eventually become Lt. Col. Richard Victor Goss, OBE, TD. He also became a member of both the Falkland Islands Government's Executive and Legislative Councils, something like the upper and lower houses of parliament. Dick often used the knowledge gained from his many roles in Government and from mixing with the social elite at various gatherings in a finely tuned and balanced manner. But it can surely be no coincidence that whilst he was involved, the union always seemed to be one step ahead of the game. He carried a heavy bag of responsibilities, ranging from part-time politician, military commanding officer, Governor's aide de camp and, of course, General Secretary and Treasurer of the General Employees Union.

Until 1973, I had spent my working life outside the Islands, or outside the trade union sphere. But from the moment I started my first day of work at the 'dockyard', all that was about to change, and in a manner I had not bargained for.

I had been working away at my new job and just getting used to my new work surroundings, when I felt a tap on my shoulder. I turned around and immediately recognised that the man was the union delegate (the equivalent to shop steward in the UK). He kicked a stone away as if he was Bobby Charlton and said, 'You a union member?' I somewhat nervously replied I was not.

He stared at me, and then said in a very polite but firm fashion, 'You had better be by the end of the week, son, or there will be trouble.' Then he added, 'I don't like trouble, do you understand what I mean?'

'How can I join, and how much is it?' I replied, without thinking much about the consequences of not joining.

'More or less a week's wages.' Then, with a grin, he added, 'You get protection then, see.'

'But I can't afford a week's wages,' I replied hurriedly and nervously. I had no savings to draw on and I had a wife and newly born son to support, and I suddenly realised I was not going to receive my first wage packet from my new employers for a further two weeks. Hourly paid workers were paid a week in arrears from the commencement of their employment.

Noting my obvious anxiety, the man said in a very gruff voice, 'Don't worry, lad, you can pay by the week until you're paid up in full.'

I should add that it was not compulsory to be a member of the trade union to gain employment in the hourly paid departments of FIG and FIC, but once employed, if you were not a member, you would soon be under intolerable pressure from the members. So I concluded that it simply was not worth the hassle, and I might as well join and be done with it.

As it turned out, I did not stay around long enough in the job at PWD to learn too much about the union's activities. That would come next time round. But I did take time out to read a copy of the four-page hourly paid workers' agreement, which was affixed to the wall of the restroom in a very ungraceful manner by a dart. This slimmest of documents did give me a feel for the basic and vital components which made up the workers' agreement with employers. However, it did not give the slightest hint about how much work had been put in by so few people to conclude the simplest of understandings between employee and employer.

One afternoon, about three or four months after I had been working at the Public Works Department, I was mowing the grass on Victory Green with a Flymo. Victory Green is a popular open green area of land of an acre or so, on the foreshore of the centre of Stanley. It is also used for ceremonial occasions and by the general public as the mood takes them.

Anyway, I was putting some fuel into the machine near the telephone exchange when the Chief of Police, Terry Peck, came up to me and said, 'I hear you are interested in joining up.'

'Yeah, that's right.' I was puzzled as to how the hell he knew.

To my total surprise, I became a police officer almost overnight, for what turned out to be a 14-month experience, some of which I related in Chapter 10.

The move meant that I would become a civil servant and out of the union and into the civil servants association net. It also meant a considerable pay increase and other long-term security benefits that were not part of the trade union member's agreement, such as: considerably better pension rights, overseas leave, free medical care for much longer periods than hourly paid workers.

I would not come back into the General Employees Union fold until November 1977. I had been working the winter of that year at Navy Point (locally called the camber). The area, on the north side of Stanley harbour, was the property of the Ministry of Defence, and comprised a fuel depot with the capacity to hold 18,000 cubic metres of fuel in two large tanks, ancillary services to distribute the fuel, some large warehouses and a very impressive stone house, which was occupied by the unit's caretaker.

I had been working for a local contractor, Willie Bowles, who had secured some work there. However, once the job had been completed, Willie politely terminated my employment. It had nothing to do with my labour contributions, it was simply a matter of not having any other work to offer me, and others.

As Willie handed over my last pay packet he advised me to talk with the Works Manager of the Falkland Islands Company. He had heard that there might be a job opportunity there.

I thanked Willie for the information and wasted no time in heading off to see the man at the FIC. In response to my question, he looked at me and smiled, then in a very jovial sort of fashion said, 'Sure. Go down to the jetty and tell the Jetty Foreman I've sent you and inform him I have taken you on. Oh, and you can start Monday.'

It was now Friday. I was thrilled. Work was not easy to find in the Falklands at this time, so a weekend break and into a new job was wonderful. In my excitement, I virtually ran down to the Jetty Foreman's hut, sometimes loosely termed an office.

I was full of the joys of spring as I announced the news to Billy Morrison. He dropped his pen, lifted his head rather rapidly from the timesheet that he had been diligently working on, then jumped up out of his office chair and thumped his desk top heavily before shouting out in a rage, '*I* decide who the fuck we take on here, not that jumped-up prick in the office.'

As you can imagine, my joy evaporated pretty quickly, to be replaced by shock and puzzlement all in seconds flat, just like someone flicking a switch.

Eventually I muttered something silly, like, 'Well, that's what he said.'

Still in a rage, and, I presume, not hearing my hopeless response, Billy shouted, 'How the hell can I run this place if I don't know who fucking well works here, and who bloody doesn't.'

I stood still in the doorway, beginning to wonder if the works manager had set me up, and was now in his office laughing his socks off.

Then just as quickly as the man had launched himself into his rage, he went calm and said, 'Well, this warehouse needs painting.' He was pointing to a long building sheathed in corrugated iron on the opposite side of the jetty. 'I suppose you can paint, can you? Okay, you can start Monday, but don't think I'm giving you a full-time job. I don't need any more stevedores at the moment. If someone leaves I might consider taking you on.'

Colour came back to my face and I began to feel normal again. As I turned around to walk back up the jetty, I was stopped in my tracks when I heard the Jetty Foreman shouting out to me, 'Oh, and by the way you'd better be a union member, or you can forget it.'

'Oh yes,' I said, waving my arm as I wheeled away and got off the premises as fast as I could.

Now I was in a state of panic. I had been untruthful to him, the port, locally known as the FIC jetty, was a rigid union stronghold and I knew it. Everyone in Stanley knew it. No, everyone in the bloody Falklands knew it, and I had just told the Jetty Foreman I was a member, and I wasn't.

I knew what to do, and quickly. I needed to get my ass up to the union office as fast as possible and rejoin. What troubled me now was that I could be pretty certain the Jetty Foreman would telephone the union office to check out if I was indeed a member.

The union office was only a five-minute run from where I was, but the question now was: could I make it before Billy called? I began to run as fast as I could, and by the time I got to the union office I was sucking air heavily. I was also terrified that it might all have been in vain.

I hesitated for a brief moment to catch my breath, then I knocked on the General Secretary's office door and went in.

A somewhat surprised General Secretary looked up from his

desk and said, 'Hello, Terry, welcome. To what do I owe this surprise visit? How can I help you?'

'I would like to rejoin the union,' I told him, staring at the telephone, expecting it to ring at that very moment.

'Certainly,' he said, 'my pleasure. Would you like to take a seat and have a coffee?'

'No thanks,' I said, 'I'm in a hurry.' Then I asked, 'How much do I need to pay?'

'I'll need to look at the register to check when your membership lapsed. That will take me a few minutes.'

Shit, I muttered under my breath, I am not going to make it. The Jetty Foreman is bound to call before the deed is done. I was inwardly tearing myself apart with anxiety. Every move Dick made seemed to take an age, from getting up out of his chair to dropping his pen on the office floor as he walked from his desk across the room to where a huge ledger lay on top of a table. Then when he got there, he was not able to find his glasses, then he could not find the page he was looking for, and when he did, he couldn't find my name.

I was desperate, but finally, and with great relief, the transaction was completed and after shaking hands, I left the office in great haste.

Just as I was getting to the outside door, I heard the telephone ring in Dick's office. I do not know to this day if it was the FIC Jetty Foreman who was making the call or not, but I remember thinking, too late, I am a member.

When I rejoined the union that day, in November 1977, I thought it was for employment needs only. I had no idea what was in store for me, nor did I have any idea to the extent I would become involved in the union's efforts and activities for the ordinary man over the next eight or nine years.

The FIC Jetty guys were the hardcore of the trade union, I suppose because the union chairman, Ken Summers, was the stevedore gang's intermediate boss.

Ken Summers was an exceptional man. Like most of his generation, he had had a limited education, but he worked very hard and always led his men from the front. He had a huge heart and was motivated by raw passion, but he could also be a very hard and stubborn man. However, the union was everything to him, and he expected it to mean everything to the men he led and to all the other union members.

In addition to the Chairman, the union also had a union delegate (shop steward) at the jetty. The union, in fact, had delegates at all its strongholds and depots in Stanley and at all the settlements in the camp. The jetty delegate at the time was Trevor Browning, a quiet man who basically jumped when the Chairman said jump. His main task usually amounted to checking everyone's fees had not lapsed and calling the very occasional delegates' meetings.

In our case, this would mean all the members from the various FIC departments in the vicinity: the garage, carpenter's shop, warehouses, etc., who would all have to cram into the small 'jetty hut' after working hours.

Before the meeting started, the men would get straight into small groups and start boisterous debates on the weather, sex, food, someone's cat, or how the peat cutting was going, if it was that time of the year.

Generally, there would be uncontrolled raucous laughter, men shouting at one another or the odd thumping of the table, which would only be called to a halt when the Chairman began unceremoniously banging a wall or kicking the door and bellowing, 'Okay, you buggers, shut up and listen. Let's get this thing over with so we can get to the Globe and get on with the more serious business of getting pissed.'

The Globe Hotel was an ideally located pub just a couple of hundred yards from the jetty, and a favourite watering hole.

My first union delegates' meeting was one of life's culture shocks. I had only ever attended local sports club meetings and a singular Civil Servants Association meeting, which were all tame and reasonably orderly affairs. This was quite different: no fixed agenda, and three or four conversations going on at once in response to the topics the Chairman would raise. No one was taking any minutes, or attempting to make any kind of record of the meeting.

Then, just as it appeared that chaos was in full swing, the meeting ended just as abruptly as it had begun, with the Chairman declaring that there had been enough bullshit tossed around for one night, and the meeting was closed and it was time to turn out the lights, lock the door and make a stampede for the pub.

I would also discover that it was the custom for the last person to arrive at the pub to pay for the first round of drinks. Something I only became aware of as I entered the pub last and in a rather casual manner, with everyone lined up along the bar counter and in one voice shouting, 'Your round, TSB.'

The evening did not end until 10 p.m., when the publican, the legendary Chuck Clifton, the old dairyman I used to do the milk round with, called time. Four hours of serious drinking had elapsed since the union meeting, of which no one any longer recalled or cared anything about.

All the important issues of the trade union were conducted and planned from the head office in Ross Road, under the eagle eye and cool head of the wary General Secretary and Treasurer, Richard Victor Goss.

Dick ensured that all union matters were discussed in a prudent and seriously democratic fashion, within its constitution. An Executive Committee was elected every year, at an annual general meeting. In addition to the permanent General Secretary and Treasurer, it consisted of Chairman, Vice-Chairman and seven other committee members, who were elected by show of hands. Camp members voted by postal ballot. The Falkland Islands, even by 1982, still had no road network, therefore it was impractical for employees to leave their employment on many parts of East and West Falklands, for a minimum of two working days in many cases, to go to Stanley and back.

Quite unexpectedly, one day as I was painting away on the transit warehouse, the Jetty Foreman, dear old Billy Morrison, came up to me and announced that a vacancy had become available on the jetty. Trevor Browning had left, and would I be interested in taking his place. I didn't need to think twice about the offer, and quickly responded with a rather excited 'You bet.'

Within a week of my becoming the new jetty stevedore, the union Chairman called a meeting to elect a new union delegate to replace Trevor. Once again a gathering of members took place in the jetty hut.

This time, the business of the day was clearly determined, thus the men seemed less inclined to indulge in the usual cross talk and other distractions such as the centrefold of *Playboy* magazine. In fact, when the Chairman opened the meeting in the usual boisterous manner, he simply asked for nominations for union delegate. An eerie silence immediately fell about the place, which was only broken when men started moving around uncomfortably in their chairs or flicking a pack of cards.

Then suddenly, Neil Jennings sat up straight and said, 'I propose TSB.'

Within a split second someone else snapped, 'Second that.' Then silence fell again.

It was blatantly obvious that no one else was going to be nominated, or volunteer, so I decided to bring an end to the farce by saying, 'If no one else is interested, I will give it a go.'

Hardly had the words left my lips, when the Chairman replied, 'That's that then. TSB is the new delegate and I declare the meeting closed.'

Once again, everyone made a mad rush for the exit door and headed in the direction of the Globe.

I didn't have a clue what I had let myself in for, but from that moment on I promised myself that I would do my very best to represent the union membership to the very best of my ability. But I quickly realised that to do this, I would need to go on a very steep learning curve.

I had planned to spend as much time as possible with the Guru, Dick Goss, the heart and soul of the whole movement. Alas, Dick had been suffering periods of illness and he fell ill once again, shortly after my election as a delegate, and all rather tragically, he never fully recovered and died at his home within months.

Dick, quite rightly, was granted the nearest thing to a state funeral. All sections of the community turned out to pay their last respects to a man who had given so much to the inhabitants of the Falkland Islands via his various roles. He was one of those very rare men on planet earth who really cared about and worked unselfishly for his fellow man.

However, despite the man's incredible efforts to build understanding and trust between the worker and his employer, even as

Dick's body was being laid to rest, there were some people hoping, even believing, that Dick's passing would be the end of the General Employees Union. They gleefully forecast a short period of turmoil, followed by eventual collapse.

Well, they were to be hugely disappointed, for they had underestimated the working man's ability to regroup and reorganise in the face of adversity. Of course Dick was a huge loss to the trade union, but there were motivating factors for the union to pick itself up and move on.

The workers quickly realised that it was only the union that stood between them and the potential return to exploitation at the work place from their employers.

They also knew that if they did not carry on with the trade union movement, all the many improvements the working man (and their dependants) had gained, would have been eroded away. That was much too high a price for the working man to pay.

35

Catapulted to Vice-Chairman

I, along with a massive turnout of union members, crammed into the trade union headquarters in Ross Road, a building that had been donated to the GEU by the Falkland Islands Government.

We had all gathered to attend an extraordinary general meeting to elect, not only a new permanent General Secretary and Treasurer, but also a new Executive Committee in the light of Dick's untimely death.

Many members appeared anxious and very uneasy that night, and some visibly showed signs of stress. They were not used to being at a meeting without Dick skilfully and democratically guiding it through its paces.

Following a minute's silence, the Chairman, Ken Summers, called for the meeting to proceed, but he was like a fish out of water. He had been thrust into the lead role involuntarily, and was clearly struggling to hold back his personal emotions. His eyes were glazed and he was visibly shaking. The combination of Dick's death – they were very close friends – and the load of new responsibility was weighing heavily on him.

Everyone with a heart felt for Ken that night. Somehow he managed, ever so bravely, to stumble and stutter his way through a very difficult meeting, for him and everyone else present. The atmosphere in the headquarters was charged with emotion and, as always, thick with cigarette smoke.

That night there was also a matter of personal consequence. To my total amazement, I was elected to the position of Vice-Chairman, the organisation's number two man. I had gone from non-union member, to member, to delegate, and now Vice-Chairman, all in a matter of a year. As a result, I was now directly in the line of the sniper's gun. Should the Chairman be incapacitated or unavailable for whatever reason, the buck would stop with me.

My sudden elevation through the ranks meant that I was to be thrust into the annual negotiations with the Sheep Owners Association, without the foggiest idea of the subject matter or the procedures. What was even more concerning, I would soon discover I was not alone.

It seemed to me that planning for such an important occasion was a term that had to be used very loosely. There was an obvious lack of solid leadership. Someone to coolly and intelligently structure and plan things within, and on behalf of, the trade union did not exist. I am not being disrespectful to the Chairman at the time, but no matter how passionate and dedicated Ken might have been about the trade union, Dick's sudden and tragic death had left a huge void in its leadership.

I remember being convinced that good leadership and teamwork was going to be the single most difficult issue for the union to achieve in time for the forthcoming meetings with the Sheep Owners Association, or there was a very good possibility that they would take full advantage of the situation. What made matters even worse for me, was that I knew I was completely unable to do anything about it. As Vice-Chairman, I was too inexperienced and totally lacking any knowledge about the camp employees' agreement to be of any use to the Chairman or the trade union's negotiation team.

The annual meetings also signalled the commencement of an event unique to the Falkland Islands, traditionally known as Farmers' Week. This was a midwinter break, when nearly everyone in the camp took a week off. Among other things, it was an ideal opportunity for the union organisation to bring in a couple of delegates to form part of the negotiating team.

Many members of the Sheep Owners Association would gather in Stanley for a week of meetings at their headquarters, Barton House, to discuss farming matters among themselves and meet with senior members of the Falkland Islands Government administration. Which, at the time, some people would argue they basically controlled, or at least heavily influenced.

The week would also result in a very heavy social programme, especially for the members of SOA. This would include lunches, dinners and other evening functions at top venues such as Government House and Stanley House, the mansion residence of the manager of the Falkland Islands Company. Therefore some members of the SOA delegation who had to meet the GEU might have considered themselves a trifle unlucky because they would be missing out on some of the jollifications to engage in discussions with the lower classes on such drab matters as employment issues.

The consumption of huge amounts of alcohol was not restricted to socialising. What I remember most about my second SOA meeting, held at Barton House, were the frequent calls for a 'gin and tonic' break, even in the morning sessions.

On a more serious point, one very important factor about holding the preliminary negotiations in July was that should the GEU and SOA run into negotiating difficulties which resulted in a breakdown of talks, there was a six-week safety time zone. So both parties could go back to their respective members and then reconvene to settle any unresolved issues. The agreement was effective for one year, from 1 September.

The campers' employment agreement took into consideration the varying types of work, and the periods of working hours reasonably required, to properly carry out the vastly differing employment tasks needed to operate a sheep farm.

My first experience of face-to-face dialogue with sheep farmers was to be gained in the smoke-filled conference room of the union headquarters. I remember being fairly calm, but feeling completely raw and totally exposed. This was hardly surprising as I was a townie who had no real understanding of camp life, apart from a brief period spent on Lively Island. It was not in my heart and soul. Things that got the blood pumping through the veins of a camp delegate did not pump through mine. Issues that would usually get them annoyed, excited or disappointed generally went straight over my head.

Thankfully, and most surprisingly, even to the experienced members of the GEU Executive Committee, the meeting of 1979 flowed swiftly and fluidly, with few moments of the anticipated hot air and tabletop thumping which had become an ugly and all too familiar trademark since Dick's departure from the union's side of the negotiating table.

There were moments of high tension, most keenly felt when the debate centred around the question of a rise in the basic level of pay. However, even this thorny issue was resolved to the mutual satisfaction of everyone pretty quickly.

For some unexplainable reason, I felt the farmers had agreed to come to battle with loaded guns, but on this occasion, with safety catches firmly on, metaphorically speaking. Also, rightly or wrongly, I sensed it had all to do with Dick's passing. It must have been the first time in many years that Dick had not been present, and his death was still very fresh in the minds of all, on both sides of the negotiating table. Therefore, I think, a kind of mellowness prevailed over these particular meetings as a mark of respect for the great man.

Once the meetings had been concluded, the SOA members left pretty quickly. There was some small talk between employer and employee from the same farm who had spent the week sitting on opposite sides during the negotiations. But once the opposition had finally all left the premises, most of the union participants broke into a serious session of hand-shaking and backslapping. I should tell you, when you got your hand shaken, or your back slapped, by a muscular farm worker, it took some time for both parts of your body to fully recover from the experience.

Committee members whose faces had shown signs of tension and stress now had expressions of relief, even joy. Then from nowhere, as if a magician had waved his magic wand, crates of beer and bottles of liquor suddenly appeared.

Like party parcels, beer can rings were pulled and liquor bottle tops were enthusiastically screwed from the necks of bottles and thrown into the nearest bin or ashtray, or if neither was readily available, then on to the floor. Once a bottle of liquor had been opened, there was no question of the entire contents not being consumed.

To be honest, I think many of the camp delegates found it quite a daunting experience to have to sit opposite their immediate boss, and other farm managers, to discuss improvements to their working and pay conditions. There was always the sense of class distinction in the air between the two. Some, I know, even worried about reprisals from their employer upon their return, especially if they felt they had been a little over-enthusiastic or vocal during the course of the meetings.

As for me, I was disappointed and confused. Disappointed because I had played no meaningful part in the deliberations. Confused, because following the SOA meetings there was no real serious debrief.

I was clear about one thing, however: if I was going to be involved in the SOA/GEU meetings next year, I was going to be much better prepared, and certainly much more educated, about camp labour relations matters. I was not going to be sitting around like a dummy, ever again.

Within a few months, I was part of the union's Executive Committee responsible for negotiating the hourly paid workers' agreement, between the GEU and the Falkland Islands Company and the Falkland Islands Government.

The Stanley meetings were a very different matter to the camp negotiations; the membership of each negotiating team was much smaller, usually, Chairman, Vice-Chairman and General Secretary representing the trade union. The head of administration and the Financial Secretary of the Falkland Islands Government would represent the employers, along with the General Manager for the Falkland Islands Company.

In comparison to the meetings with farmers, the atmosphere was much more relaxed. Everyone was addressed by first names, not Mr Jack or Mr Ben. I was also much more comfortable. I was a member of this working environment, therefore I understood everything that was being discussed, thus, I was much more involved, and found the whole experience rather exhilarating.

Unlike the camp negotiations, agenda items were debated, rather than argued, and as a result resolved much more quickly. Everything was concluded in two working sessions.

The hourly paid workers' agreement applied to union members only, but neither of the employers ever varied from the agreement for any non-union members who worked alongside union members. It was the same situation for monthly paid workers in camp.

The Stanley agreement was, in fact, a minimum wages agreement, but employers rarely paid more than the agreed minimum hourly rates of pay to any of their employees, skilled or otherwise, union member or non-union member.

Apart from salaries, the wages agreement covered issues such as paid leave entitlements, normal working hours, overtime payments, sick leave entitlements, termination of employment.

Outside these two main agreements, the GEU were also involved in two other labour relations issues which were discussed and negotiated annually. Their role was pretty much one of umpire.

One agreement defined the terms and conditions of an exclusive contract agreement between the FIC and their jetty stevedores, locally called 'the jetty contract'.

The FIC Jetty was the place that every ordinary hourly paid worker in Stanley wanted to work. Employment on the jetty offered many hours' work on lucrative contract rates whilst working the ships that fetched and carried freight from the FIC Jetty, or on odd occasions at other berths.

The small inter-island coastal vessel would also be worked under contract conditions as it brought in wool from the farms almost weekly.

Some of the most lucrative contracts for the stevedores were the Argentine vessels (up to 1982), which carried 45-gallon drums of petrol to replenish the fuel depot, kerosene and gas cylinders for domestic heating use and JPI fuel for the Government inter-island air service, along with general provisions on a regular basis.

The other prized contracts involved the quarterly freighter service, operated by Darwin Shipping Limited from the United Kingdom to the Islands. This vessel would bring in vehicles and spare parts, household fixtures and fittings, clothing, toys, games, books, food, drinks – everything one could imagine – in an effort to provide the community with all it needed to live on a very remote islands.

To give you a feel for the value of these contracts to the working man, the normal hourly rate of pay in 1980 was approximately £1 an hour. On these contracts, a man could earn anything ranging from £3 to £20 an hour, according to the number of tons discharged or loaded per hour.

Now you can see why I was delighted, when Billy Morrison offered me a job on the jetty.

The other important contract agreement involved the GEU and the SOA, and covered the terms and conditions for contract shearing, which had only been introduced into the industry around 1969/70 and had revolutionised the working practice of this aspect of the woollen industry.

36

Failed Industrial Action

My next union experience was to be a heartbreaking affair. Matters had been pretty much routine for three years, but then the ordinary was replaced by the extraordinary. It would prove to be a traumatic event for the hourly paid workers and their families in the Falkland Islands.

The issue at the heart of the troubles was the cost of living bonus. Employers had attempted to have the system abolished during the 1981 SOA/GEU meetings, and eventually a deal was struck with the union to reduce the benefits of the award by 50%. But the union executive had strongly indicated they would not accept such a deal with employers for the hourly paid workers in Stanley, when these negotiations came around.

However, the union must have been in no doubt that the employers would be back to make another attack on it during the Stanley negotiations, and so it was to be.

Why? Well, the cost of living bonus was one, if not the, most important component of the working man's agreements that the union had ever managed to negotiate. It was a near perfect shield for hourly and monthly paid workers against inflation created by consumer and other retail price increases, which, largely, were in monopolistic control of the FIC, who operated the main supermarket and the external shipping services. Only a few items within the cost of living index could be affected by Government fiscal decision-making. Issues such as the cost of utilities, postage and inter-island airfares.

One way or another, directly or indirectly, almost everybody in the Islands received some kind of protection and reward from the method, be it employees or their dependants.

It would be pointless in continuing this story if I did not try to explain the basic mechanics of the system. At the hub of the method was a list of 100 or so standard commodities and consumer items for a typical family of four, such as petrol, alcohol, beer, flour, sugar, soap, mutton, the price of electricity per kilowatt, entrance fee to a dance or cinema, local inter-island airfares, price of a pair of shoes or a pair of jeans, packet of cigarettes, cost of postage, local house rents etc.

To ensure the efficiency and effectiveness of the system, a type of watchdog group was set up. This body consisted of a representative from the trade union and the Falkland Islands Government, for the Stanley system, with a member from the trade union and the Sheep Owners Association overseeing the camp module. At the end of each calendar quarter, the monitoring bodies would analyse the fluctuations in all the index prices, and a bonus wage award would be made in proportion to the cost of living increase.

Even before the dispute, I always felt in my own mind that the union would be attacked on this front at some time or other, and I also knew who would lead it. That, however, was not my concern.

No, my worry was the union organisation itself, and how it would deal with the situation when the inevitable happened.

Before going on with this subject, I should mention that in 1980 I moved from the FIC Jetty to take up a job as a junior clerk in the shipping agency of the FIC. The move meant I was to switch from being an hourly paid worker to a monthly paid 'blue-collar worker'. The usual thing to happen in this circumstance would have been for me to give up my union activities, just as I had done previously when I joined the local police force. Not this time, however.

When I was invited to join the office staff of FIC, I did so with the proviso that I would continue my union work, and be able to remain as part of the union executive committee for as long as I was an elected member. I also requested that I could supplement my monthly salary by continuing to work the jetty contracts. This request surprised the General Manager, Harry Milne, but he eventually agreed to both conditions.

My move to the FIC office, however, did have the effect of moving me sideways in the trade union movement. Although I remained as Vice-Chairman, I was replaced as the union delegate on the jetty, and was not invited to participate in the negotiations with the SOA and the GEU in the winter of 1981. Thus, I missed out on the action and debate over the camp COLB reduction. I will not make any attempt to go into a blow-by-blow account of the meetings of that winter, but I do recall at the time that there was a new face about the place who had the ability to lead the attack for the SOA on the cost of living bonus, and had every intention of doing so.

This man had been creating quite a stir in the camp with his straight talking, which had put more than a few cats among the pigeons. He was a very intelligent man, full of energy, with a very devilish and pronounced moustache; the combination was to gain him the title of 'Electric Whiskers'.

Here was a man who could, and would, whip up the SOA troops into believing that a reduction in the COLB was not only just, but much worse than that, he believed the system should be abolished all together. It was clear the union would need to be sharp and at their very best to beat off this determined and very aggressive attack.

There was another issue that troubled me greatly on this matter. I knew that some of the senior members of the trade union negotiating team had believed, quite wrongly, that if the union had to concede on the question of the COLB for the camp, it was not necessarily a big deal; they would make their big stand if the employers of Stanley were to attempt such an action during the Stanley hourly paid workers meeting later in the year. It was a terrible misconception, which I also knew was likely to have catastrophic consequences.

Why? Firstly, it would surely mean that the union would not focus seriously enough on the matter in hand during the SOA meetings, and as a consequence, they would probably not do their homework, nor have enough fire in their bellies if the going got tough during the negotiations.

Secondly, and far more troublesome, to lose ground on this vital topic in the SOA meetings was bound to be a watershed for the forthcoming meetings on the hourly paid workers of Stanley.

Finally, I also knew that the intention was not reduction, but abolition. The union, amazingly, never took this crucial point on board until it was too late.

As I have said before, I am not aware of the full details, but during the winter meetings of 1981, the SOA won round one, and 50% of the cost of living bonus for the camp employees had been lost by the GEU.

I still believe, to this day, that was entirely due to the appalling way the union conducted itself prior to, and during the negotiations. They were a disgrace to their membership.

I vividly recall at the committee meeting following the SOA meetings that there was very little discussion about the torrid affair. The mood was just matter of fact, and any attempt to bring the subject into open debate was ignored or brushed aside by the various members of that negotiating team.

This behaviour was not entirely unusual. Falkland Islanders have never been very good at looking one another straight in the eye and thrashing things out. It was much more usual to talk about issues in a pub, or condemn some person/s behind their backs. Something that I appreciate is not exclusive to the Falklands, but it does seem to be much more pronounced within small communities.

Getting down off my high horse, the most obvious effect of the union's defeat, and the way it had come about, was that it completely undermined confidence and trust between the membership and the Executive Committee of the organisation. It also created an immediate and clear divide between camp and Stanley members. The principal aim of the employers, surely – divide and rule.

So, as the Stanley negotiations commenced in November 1981 over terms and conditions for 1982, I was once again sidelined and not invited to participate. Naturally, I was hugely disappointed, even if I was not greatly surprised by the move.

Not surprised? Sure, I had become aware that some in the union hierarchy felt I had become too close to management for the union's own good. This judgement was made on the basis that I now worked in the FIC office, therefore I must have become influenced by my employers and would be sympathetic towards them.

Anyone who really knew me would know that was quite a crazy notion, but, alas, I was to be out of the fray, and fray there was sure to be.

Sure enough, once negotiations began, dialogue became difficult, eventually bogging down and reaching deadlock, then subsequently collapsing.

The union had not only rejected any moves to reduce the award, but also refused to consider independent arbitration, the introduction of a minimum wages board and an agreed independent regulator.

It is true that at the eleventh hour the union did put forward a proposal to the employers which suggested the 100% award remain in place, but that it only apply to the straight 40-hour week, not to overtime and contract payments.

Employers agreed to consider the new initiative, but indicated they would need time because they would need to refer the matter to the Executive Council and the board of FIC.

The two sides separated, with some degree of optimism for a settlement. However, the following day, the union called an extraordinary meeting of its membership, and sought a vote in favour of strike action, effective from midnight that day.

This farcical motion was unanimously agreed, even with the knowledge that measures had been put in place by the Governor to convene an emergency meeting of the Executive Council the following week to discuss the union's proposal.

Why? Probably the union thought the employers were playing for time, firmly believing that employers wanted to string them along until the charter vessel (as the freighter from the UK was called locally) had been discharged, loaded, and sent off back to the UK, depriving the union of its negotiating trump card.

In my opinion, this argument did not hold up. The vessel was still several days away, and employers would be meeting and have time to respond to the union's proposal before her arrival.

In truth, the strike was an ill-timed and futile exercise, with potentially very serious consequences for the union. Futile, because the union had split itself in two. The members in camp were not going to come out in support, because they had already lost 50%, thus there would be no unity within the union.

The dangers of an ill-conceived and badly handled strike were that it could cripple the union in every aspect, in the short term, and failure to force the management's hand would certainly mean its membership going back to work very disillusioned with the union movement.

Failure would also mean the union would have an uphill struggle to maintain membership levels in the future, whilst the victorious management, fresh and buoyant from victory, would organise itself for the coup de grâce of the union in the meetings of 1983. There would, however, be other more dramatic events that would take place in the Falklands in 1982 which would interrupt these planned proceedings.

As things turned out, management were well prepared for the strike action. They knew where and when it was going to happen (no one needed to be a rocket scientist to work that out), therefore they had a plan of counter-action in place well beforehand.

The location would be the FIC Jetty; the timing would be the arrival of the charter vessel. The union always believed this to be the employers' soft spot in such circumstances, the theory being that this strategy would inflict upon the charterers (the FIC indirectly) the most serious financial pain.

It was understood that the vessel was on a daily charter fee, therefore each day the ship sat idle at the dockside, it would increase the overall charter costs, forcing the charterers to seek a quick solution with their FIG employer colleagues to settle the dispute and get the men back to work.

The union were totally confident the vessel could not move once moored alongside the jetty, because they were convinced the management would not be able to source the required skilled and unskilled manpower to discharge and load the vessel.

They also hoped pressure would be put on the employers to reach a speedy conclusion to the strike action by other sections of the community, such as small businesses, who relied heavily on the arrival of the vessel to replenish their stocks.

Once the charter vessel arrived and docked, in January 1982, battle lines were quickly drawn, but the union must have realised quickly that all their best-laid plans and ideals were going to go up in one big puff of smoke, all before their very eyes.

From the moment the gangway was down, to the vessel being cleared by Customs, slowly but surely management unfolded their counterplan. In no time, the vessel, warehousing, heavy plant and other machinery were crawling with FIC staff from the main office block and the supermarket, supported by Civil Servants from FIG, who took leave to earn some extra, and welcome, money. Even a few farm managers, friends and others were out in numbers to support the employers, and bust the strike.

Stunned by the employers' reaction, the union doggedly held out whilst the vessel was being discharged, still believing that victory was possible, because they thought that many of the office staff would not be able to cope with the physical demands of moving

375-kilo bales of wool from storage sheds into the ship's holds.

But that was to be another error of judgement. Soon the wool began to appear, and be lifted up and over the ship's rail, disappearing four bales at a time inside the ship, and as each one did, so the union's hopes of maintaining the COLB disappeared with them.

After ten days of futile strike action, the union had been resoundingly defeated once again. Round two of the COLB had been sadly, and very badly lost.

Now the General Employees Union was being set up for the knockout punch in round three, and there seemed to be little fight left from the defeated Executive Committee, or its dwindling followers, to stop it.

In contrast, Electric Whiskers and his team of employers were basking in the glory of their success, drinking until the early hours of the morning, behind the solid walls and interior comforts of the Colony Club. Ironically, the building had been constructed some 130 or so years ago by the pioneering Jacob Napoleon Goss, who was the great-grandfather of the trade union's legendary former General Secretary and Treasurer, Richard Victor Goss.

God knows what that pair were thinking, as they looked down from heaven to witness the employers celebrating in the premises gained from the Goss family in a dark and mysterious period of Falklands history, at the expense of the workers. Especially Dick, who had worked so hard to protect COLB in his lifetime. Needless to say, I did not work against the strike, but my action was nothing more than a token gesture in support of the union. It was gut-wrenching stuff for me, watching my present working colleagues toiling against my former workmates and fellow union members. But I inwardly smiled as I observed them gritting their teeth as their blistered and raw hands were racked with pain from carrying out the labourers' tasks. My pleasure was always short lived, however, as I glanced this way or that, and saw a distraught union member realising the fight was being lost.

I also knew I was not alone, for many who had worked against the strike did so with heavy hearts. They took no pleasure from doing what they were doing, but they had little option, they were not going to risk their jobs, or their families' well-being, by not cooperating with their employers, and that was surely understandable.

It was a truly sorry state of affairs, which, once again, demonstrated the need to always exhaust every channel of communication open to you before taking any offensive action that could just destroy the one thing you are trying so hard to protect.

This was January 1982, and little did we know it, but the Falklands and its entire population were just three months away from a disaster that would make the strike pale into insignificance.

37

Elected to the Summit
(The COLB buck stopped with me)

Once the Falklands had been liberated from the Argentines, we were eventually able to get back to the work of the trade union.

Following the union's defeat in January '82, a massive shake-up was required within the trade union movement. Like a defeated party in a general election (or the Argentine Army), heads were bound to roll. Sure enough, at the AGM a virtually new union management committee was elected.

Any negative thoughts about me in the past had seemingly evaporated, because I was asked to consider taking the chair. Without hesitation I agreed, but only on the basis that the Executive Committee would work with me in making the full reinstatement of the cost of living bonus our number one objective, and once it had been achieved, I would hand over the chair to another person.

I also requested, hum, thinking about that, perhaps I more like demanded, that during my term of office, the trade union would only resort to negotiating settlements of any disputes. Once all was agreed, I confirmed my acceptance.

I was very conscious of the fact that my demands at the AGM were bordering on the undemocratic, and they didn't have a chance in hell of standing up unless they were endorsed at a specially convened extraordinary general meeting.

But equally, I didn't need to be any kind of genius to work out that the COLB was both a highly topical and an emotional issue.

Therefore, any suggestion that we aimed to win it back was surely the right tune to be singing to the crowd at the time, no matter how difficult it might be to play in the future.

There was a much more direct reason for my stance. If I was going to be the union's chairman, with any future and usefulness, I had no option but to galvanise a defeated army pretty damned quickly. And I knew my proposals at the AGM would spread like wildfire through the membership in Stanley and camp by word of mouth, or whatever other means of communication were available.

Another reason for my action was to nip in the bud the distinct possibility of having the meeting boil over into an uncontrollable witch-hunt.

Well, at least that night, my tactics had worked a treat, on all counts. But I was well aware this was not the time or place for being smug about it. I, and the union Executive Committee, had to deliver, or we would be history. That was a very sobering fact.

From 2 April 1982, the Falkland Islands were to change like never before. The aftermath of invasion, occupation and liberation had taken its toll on morale, infrastructure and services.

The trade union and the employers quickly came to the very sensible decision, given that the circumstances in the Falklands were nothing short of chaotic, to put a freeze on negotiations on working and pay conditions for a period of time. On reflection, this decision might just have saved the union from total collapse and eventual extinction.

As you can imagine, just before the invasion, employers were on a winning streak, their self-esteem was at an all-time high, and they had momentum and were eagerly waiting for the winter SOA meetings to come around. Whilst in total contrast, the union had suffered consecutive, and humiliating defeats, the morale of the membership of the trade union was on the floor and their rank and file seriously divided.

(But I am sure the union would have settled for something far less dramatic than a war to deflect attention away from their very troubled doorstep.)

Thus, the decision to freeze the negotiations provided the union with the time and space, so desperately needed to regroup and plan the future way ahead. It was a very unstable and grateful trade union who grabbed with both hands the opportunity to freeze talks, I can assure you.

Having the luxury of time out, so to speak, the union set about putting its house in order. It was a wonderful chance to strip down and throw out the dead wood, then restructure the whole organisation, and to install regular and fluid communication between all those involved.

The many new formats introduced included delegates' meetings being held at least once a month, with the delegates filing records of those meetings to the General Secretary at head office. If a delegate was a member of the Executive Committee, he would make a verbal account of his monthly meeting to the committee.

It was also agreed that the Executive Committee would meet on the last Friday of each month to discuss the material input from the delegates' meetings, and any other issues. Previously the committee would meet very ad hoc.

Executive Committee meetings were also going to be much more formal than in the past; there would be set agendas, formulated by the General Secretary.

I, as Chairman, would conduct the meetings, sticking rigidly to the agenda, only allowing for other topics to be raised and debated under any other business.

I would also implement a 'golden rule'. I would not permit a meeting to continue beyond one and a half hours. Experience had told me that if you allowed a meeting to go beyond that time period, you could visibly detect people getting irritable and rapidly losing concentration.

I encouraged other changes too, such as no more voting by show of hands. Somehow, this practice had replaced the much more democratic method of voting by ballot paper, as laid down in the union's very own rulebook. I firmly believed that the show of hands method was very intimidating.

I also introduced a form of delegation, within the Executive Committee. In the past, if anything needed to be decided, or acted upon, it was usually left to the General Secretary or the Chairman – a certain way to undermine democracy.

Whilst I was happy that both continued to attend to many of the issues, delegation of responsibilities to others gave them a feeling of being a part of a team, and by having to report back to committee on their areas of responsibilities, got them used to being a type of messenger/communicator between members and committee.

Putting it all rather bluntly, I had felt in the last couple of years, certainly since Dick Goss's death, the leadership of the union had become far too dictatorial, which in turn had resulted in membership, and committee members, being disjointed and ineffectual.

We, the union, had a very serious mission ahead of us, and the only way to deal with it was to be very serious, committed and above all, organised, so that we had the best possible chance to achieve our objectives.

At the beginning of the negotiations in the winter of 1983, the Sheep Owners Association and the General Employees Union started off the first round of discussions in a pretty low-key fashion. Sort of 'skirting around the minefield', if you like.

As in previous years, there had been an exchange of agendas, so with this formality completed, it was very obvious to both sides that COLB was on the table for discussion, with the SOA seeking abolition, whilst the union wanted full reinstatement.

You could hardly get further apart on the subject than that. I also knew there was very little, if any, scope for flexibility to reach a negotiated settlement.

Despite all the improved and new in-house practices, I was still very concerned that once we got into heavy, hard and difficult debate on this business, I still might not be able to keep my team disciplined.

I was also mindful, and fearful, of the old habits of verbal abuse, lost tempers, and fists thumping table tops at the opposition, whenever people got the slightest bit frustrated or confused.

Consequently, I attempted to eliminate this risk, or at least as best as I could, by suggesting to my team that we should dispense with the old format of everyone chipping in and having their say on a subject. As of now, I should be spokesperson on all agenda items, and if a delegate felt at any time he was unhappy with the way things were panning out, he should attract my attention, as discreetly as possible, asking to speak, or calling an adjournment by way of a coffee break or suchlike.

In the past, total bloody chaos reigned, when six separate conversations would be going at the same time, and some of them nothing to do with the subject that should have been debated.

These new tactics might appear obvious and sensible to you, but they were revolutionary in the trade union movement of the Falkland Islands in 1983.

Despite some mumblings I got grudging agreement, but I knew I had no guarantee that my proposal for procedure would be adhered to.

To my surprise, it would be me who called the first coffee break. After an hour of running over the meeting schedule with SOA, a thought struck me: if the real issue was going to be COLB, then why not try and get them to discuss and agree all the other issues on the agenda first?

During the break, I explained my idea to the committee. I believed the only issue the SOA were focussed on was the cost of living bonus, therefore, I reckoned their guard would be down on other issues on the agenda. I also thought they might just be in an unusually generous mood, and willing to concede on increases in dirt money, shearing and table hand rates, painting and peat cutting rates, etc.

I realised that it would not be good timing to give my committee my honest opinion on getting any agreement on a wage increase, nor the possible outcome of the COLB. For the moment, I felt that was not important.

The committee agreed we should try my idea. Happy, I made a cup of tea and munched a handful of biscuits. After the break, I went straight in and put the proposal to the SOA, who readily agreed. I was very satisfied. No, I was positively excited. I was struggling to contain my composure. You see, in getting the SOA to agree, I had managed to defuse a potentially volatile situation, which had the possibility of the first session of talks being stalled from the outset.

Some of the early part of the negotiations touched on matters of extreme trivia – how much milk the cookhouse should get, store opening times etc., issues that surely should have been resolved between the delegate and manager on the farm. But it enabled us to start storming through the agenda and the mood lightened up by the minute.

By the end of day two, we were left with the principal subjects to discuss. As we entered into dialogue on a wage award, SOA moved very quickly, and immediately laid down an unconditional marker.

They were not prepared to discuss a wage increase without it being linked to the abolition of COLB. No more playtime. The cards had been laid firmly on the table and it was time to get down to the real business of the day.

There were some early skirmishes on the subjects, but I could see the immediate tension on everyone, therefore, I suggested we call it a day and sleep on it overnight. Everybody readily agreed.

Once the sheep owners had left the union building I dropped another bombshell. I asked the committee to stay on for an hour to discuss the play for the next day.

Why was it such a bombshell? In the past, it had been normal for everyone to bolt out of the office door as quickly as possible, and dash off down to the pub to meet old friends they had not seen for a while.

I did not push my luck too much. After the hour, I called a halt to any further debate for the day, certain that no one had the solution to the problem before us. It was looking increasingly likely that I was going to be left holding the baby, because none of my team had shown signs of a genuine desire to spend too much time debating the problem and seeking a solution.

From that meeting on, I had been left in no doubt, that the whole bloody COLB business had become an emotional issue for my members, and any rationale had long gone out the window.

However, this was the night that I, for the first time, realised that everything was not all negative. This would be the night I saw the light, brother.

If it proved we could not reach a negotiated settlement with the sheep owners, then the union *did* have another option, other than industrial action: independent mediation.

Why had this not dawned on everyone else before? Then hope faded as I stopped to think. After all, the union had rejected this out of hand last time it had been suggested.

But I went home with a bit of a spring in my step.

The Sheep Owners Association were due to arrive at our office at 9 a.m. the next morning. I had made arrangements to meet my group an hour earlier, yet another new concept, previously it was not unusual for members from both sides to amble into the venue at very similar times, and often more concerned about the antics of the night before, or the degree of pain in their heads or stomachs from consuming considerable amounts of alcohol and food at a social gathering.

For the SOA members, this would have been with wealthy and influential friends, for my boys it would have been down the pub with the lads.

I had asked my guys at the very beginning of the week's meeting to stay off the booze, and I promised them we would have a proper party when business was finished.

In the past the meetings had never been viewed as business, just an annual fixture which was a small part of a much larger social and vacation picture.

The first thing I did in the morning was to seek the opinion of my delegation once again as to what I should do in the case of an impasse.

The reply was again very disheartening: 'Stop the meetings', 'Call a fucking strike', 'We are not giving in'. The mandate was very narrow.

I did not put my new idea of arbitration forward; I felt it was not the time. I also felt I needed to keep some powder dry. I might just be wrong about SOA, but I didn't hold out much hope of that.

Without thinking about it at the time, when I called for the meeting to start, I did so with the most uncouth, or perhaps the most profound, words you could imagine: 'Let battle commence'.

The whole day was to develop into something more than a battle. It became a full-scale war of words. With zero give, and double zero tolerance, on either side.

I abandoned my position as the mouthpiece and, instead, I adopted a sort of umpire role, letting the teams get on with it, and whilst the game was unfolding all around me, I watched, listened and learnt. This was going to be the only way I would get inside the opposition's head, I couldn't do it fighting from the front.

The ploy worked. I got the message, they were simply pitching their lot on the basis that the union had conceded 50% already, therefore there was no just case to avoid the obvious step of abolition.

As the debate unfolded I saw a chink of light. I felt that the union was approaching the thing from entirely the wrong direction; there was a desperate need to change tactic, an excellent time to bring on the debutant fast bowler.

My foot soldiers were weary and badly needed a rest, so I

decided to finish the day by dropping a bomb, which I hoped would land right in the middle of the SOA camp.

Looking directly at the opposition's leader, I said, 'It appears to me that we are getting nowhere here, everyone is just going around in circles.'

'Bloody right,' he shouted back.

'Okay then,' I said, 'that's the first thing we've agreed in hours, so let me ask you a question. Are you basing your case on emotion, or fact?'

The chairman of the SOA gazed at me with a quizzical expression, and replied in a single word: 'Fact.'

'Fine,' I said. 'What are the facts?' (Bombs away.)

'What do you mean?' he snapped. (I detected evasive action, usual thing when a bomb is coming down towards you.)

I repeated the question, more firmly and crisply. I was sure my single bomb had landed right on target, because almost immediately, one of his team members, realising his leader was in difficulty, leapt to his feet and called out, 'It's been a long day, Terry. Don't you think we should call it a day now?'

I turned to him and said, 'I do believe you are absolutely right, but before we go home can I have an answer to my question?' (I thought when bombs went off there was a bloody great bang and all sorts of commotion ensued. Not with mine.)

There was a pregnant pause, followed by complete silence. Then out of the blue someone said, 'We can't afford it.'

Without hesitation I replied, 'Now that is something that has never been suggested before.'

Then as one, they all sang out, 'That's right, we can't afford it.' As I looked at each one of them sat around the table, I could see a sparkle in their eyes and expressions of relief on faces; some were even managing to smile again.

I took a deep breath and said, 'Very well. I find your comments quite a revelation, therefore I think now is a good time to adjourn the meeting, and perhaps we could commence proceedings in the morning by you proving it.'

Once again my comment visibly shook one or two. As they were getting out of their seats, I noticed their smiles had evaporated just as quickly as they had appeared. As they trooped out of the office, there was much muttering and mumbling under breaths.

Like the night before, I again asked my team to stay on, just long enough to explain my tactic, which was one of trying to create doubt and confusion among the members of SOA. Smoke 'em out, type of thing.

For the first time I could see one or two of the guys thinking there was some hope to this very tricky issue, aware that the guys were 'dead on their bums'. I called an end to the session.

First thing next morning, the SOA team entered the conference room with a very apparent air of confidence, even a bit of a swagger. What were they up to?

I did not need to wait long for my answer. As the meeting commenced their chairman focussed his gaze in my direction. 'You asked for proof, Terry. Well, here it is.'

One of the other farm managers stood up, and tossed a document on the table. I reached out for it, and as I picked it up, I could tell it was a statement of accounts. 'Look at that and you will see I made a loss. There is the proof that we cannot afford to continue with COLB,' he said.

'That's right,' the SOA spokesmen chipped in.

I hesitated, then said, 'I think I would appreciate a little time to go over this with my delegates,' as I flicked over the pages. 'What say we adjourn now and our General Secretary will give you a telephone call when we are ready to reconvene.' I was trying to show as little emotion as possible. Somehow I felt I was not being very convincing.

'Excellent,' said their spokesman. As they got up, many turned towards the exit with very satisfied expressions on their faces. I was sure they were thinking to themselves, 'That had stuffed you one, Betts.'

Once I was sure they had all departed, I suggested to my colleagues that we make some tea, and take a look over the document.

'I think that means we're fucked,' said one of the West Falklands delegates. 'They said they can't afford it and you have the proof in your hands.'

I told them to take a good look at it, and tell me what they saw and what they thought.

I watched them, first one, then the other, passing the document around after leafing a few of the pages, never pausing for a moment to look at balance sheets or profit and loss accounts or suchlike.

After they had finished, we all huddled around the table. I knew I needed to pay special attention to the West Falklands delegate. His comments had warned me that he had the potential to pull the bung out of the union dinghy.

He was not alone. Other delegates were just as discontented, and then they began to let off steam. Can't afford it, my ass. They can afford to buy new airplanes, and Land Rovers, travel, and take six months' vacations in the United Kingdom and other parts of the globe. Plus owning farms, homes and other assets in Stanley and other parts of the world, but yet they say they can't afford the cost of living, bullshit, was the general consensus of opinion. With some justification, it must be said.

'Look,' I said, 'they have tried to call our bluff. These accounts tell us nothing, and certainly do not give us the global picture of the farmers' economic position.'

Everyone in the room fell silent. I could tell they were on the back foot, and had not expected the SOA to respond in such a manner to my request to provide proof. Furthermore, no one understood the so-called evidence presented anyway. I went on, 'These accounts are two years old, they are the accounts of a small farming company which represents, at best, 5% of the woollen industry, and if you look closely at the administration costs you can see that salaries are a very low percentage. These accounts are worthless.' Then I stopped. 'Wait a minute, they might just be what we need. We all know who the big player is on their side, who controls the big farms and who calls the shots: FIC.'

In reality, they held the voting power, they led SOA in any direction, on any subject, if they so desired. If they voted for or against an issue, it was carried or tossed out accordingly. They were also the ones, after all, via the SOA mouthpiece, that were the leaders of the attack on the cost of living bonus in the first place.

I decided not to tell my boys my train of thought. I did not want them to get too excited, for two reasons. One, they might give the game away to SOA, and two, they might raise their expectations too highly.

Neville, the General Secretary, went into his office and telephoned SOA to advise them we were ready to reconvene.

Shortly after their arrival I told them that we had looked over the accounts and we thanked the manager for providing them, but that we felt they were inconclusive on their own, and we wondered if FIC could provide their accounts.

This request shook the heavyweights on their side to the core. No!!! was the short, sharp and rapid response. 'Why not?' I questioned, well aware that I had rattled the cage and started a little bit of fighting, and I was beginning to enjoy it. 'Come on, you guys. FIC are the major producers in this industry, if you are unable to provide financial evidence which shows that you cannot afford the cost of COLB, why should I, or the union members believe you?'

By now the members of SOA were showing obvious signs of anger and some began to lose control of their emotions.

Don't you believe us? Do you think we have something to hide? And anyway, our accounts will not be completed until next year etc., were the type of responses.

At this point, I felt there was a serious possibility of the meeting plummeting into chaos, so I said that if SOA would not, or could not, show us satisfactory proof of their argument, there was little point carrying on the negotiations for the time, and suggested that they might like to go back to their office and think things over.

'Yes we will go,' said their spokesman, 'but we have nothing to think about.'

'That's up to you, but I want you to understand that we are ready to continue the meetings as soon as you are ready.'

I was very concerned, but all we could do now was sit tight and play the dreadful waiting game.

For two days there was not a sound from the SOA. Then, just as I was beginning to give up hope, we got the call. SOA invited me to go down and meet their Chairman and General Secretary at Barton House. I put the telephone down and told Neville to get his hat and coat on. Neville and I sat down, as we had been invited to do. Once in my seat I instantly asked what it was they had to say. 'Nothing,' come the amazing and hugely disappointing reply. 'We have nothing more to give you,' said the Chairman.

I stood up and beckoned Neville to do the same. Staring straight into the eye of their Chairman, I said, 'In that case I think the meetings are closed and we have a stalemate situation. Thank you and good afternoon.'

The meeting had lasted barely a minute, but as we left, I had time to notice that they appeared to be just as disturbed as me about the position.

Neville and I went back to the union HQ very dejected. I asked him to get in touch with our delegates, who wasted no time getting to the office.

I told them of the latest events, and that it appeared to me that we had reached a very unsatisfactory situation, which had put everyone in a dilemma.

'Does that mean we go on strike, che?' someone questioned.

Very angrily, I snapped, 'No it fucking doesn't. Is that the only bloody thing you are able to think about? Don't you realise we're in this goddamn mess because of a bloody stupid strike action, all because we had not tried hard enough to work things out by dialogue.'

Quickly realising that tension was developing, the dear old General Secretary steadied the ship by politely saying, 'What next then, boss?'

I threw my hands in the air and honestly declared, 'I really do not know, I really do not know. But I do know one thing, we are not going on bloody strike, and that is it.'

Within a day or two of everyone drifting off back home, very unhappy with the state of affairs, the union received a telephone call from Rex Hunt, the Islands Governor (or was he Civil Commissioner then?) He had heard negotiations had reached deadlock, then after making it clear that it was not for him to interfere in such matters, he emphasised his concern about the wider implications, and offered his assistance. Finally, he invited me to go to his office immediately at Government House, to chat things over.

Rex Hunt greeted me warmly and invited me into his office. After a period of open discussion, he asked if I had ever considered arbitration. I told him I had, but I had only discussed the idea very briefly with one or two of the union members and they did not appear to like the idea at all.

It was at this very moment I jumped in feet first and said to him, if it was an available option, the union must seriously consider it.

Once the words were out of my mouth, I felt quite shocked. What the hell was I saying? I had no right to make any such comment on the union's behalf, without their prior approval.

I will admit that just about everything I said, and did, during that meeting, I probably did in the most undemocratic way. But in my defence, I felt completely isolated, and what I was saying and doing, I firmly believed was in the best interests of the trade union membership, and when it came to choice, there did not appear to be a hell of a lot of alternatives.

To his credit, I think Rex realised there was a chink of light. Making no promises, he offered to have a word with SOA, and subject to all parties being willing, he would make his best endeavours to find a suitable individual.

We agreed that it was highly unlikely that such a person could be found in the Islands to carry out such an onerous task, therefore it was almost certain someone from overseas would have to be sought and approved by each side, and this would take time.

I departed hurriedly for the union office, and told Neville the basic details and asked him not to call the delegates just yet, it could all be a false dawn.

An hour or two passed, then the telephone rang. It was the Governor again. He confirmed that SOA had agreed to the idea, in principle.

A couple of weeks later, Neville told me that a chap had been identified with the right credentials for the job of arbiter. His CV would be passed on to us, and subject to all sides agreeing his appointment, arrangements would be made for him to pack his bags and come down. But there was one vital condition: whatever the arbitrator decided, was final, and must be accepted by both sides, favourable or not.

I asked him to give me a call as soon as he received the letter from GH with the man's details. In the meantime, he should call all the members of the Executive Committee and ask them to attend a committee meeting at 5 p.m.

It was 4.30 p.m. before the Secretary confirmed the letter had been received. From the moment I saw Mr Derek Wilkinson's details, I felt he was the man.

At 5 p.m. it was time to lay the cards on the table with the executive committee, who had now all arrived and were sitting in the conference room, no doubt waiting for me to tell them what the urgency was all about.

As I walked into the conference room, more than a little nervous, someone said, 'This must be important, TSB.'

I made myself comfortable in my usual chair, and looked at each one of them and said, 'It is not only important, but it is also extremely sensitive.'

I explained the chain of events over the last month or so, and why it was that up to this point I had been acting pretty much alone. Once I had finished, I put the letter from GH referring to Mr Wilkinson on the table and invited them to read it, and to give me their opinion. I then braced myself for the backlash.

As the letter was being read and passed around to each committee member, no one said a word. Then someone broke the silence: 'Can you sell it to the members?'

The question gave me the opportunity to drive home the stark realities of the situation, perhaps for the last time. Seizing my chance, I replied, 'I don't think it is a question of selling it to the membership, I believe if the union declines this window of opportunity, there is a real possibility it could spell the beginning of the end for the trade union. You are all aware what happened to the union the last time we took industrial action on this matter. You should also understand, if we lose the argument under arbitration, you, and the membership, will at least know it was because the SOA has a case. That might be hard for all of us to take, but no one on this committee could be held responsible.'

Then I asked, 'Give me your support, and I will take whatever the union membership want to throw at me. You can stand back and let them abuse me, if they feel that way inclined. Furthermore, I will put in all the time necessary to prepare the union's presentation case, and finally, having just raked over the rule book myself, let me remind you that you do have the power within the union rules to make the decision to go to arbitration without the members' consent.'

The moment I mentioned this, everyone instantly agreed to support me. I was so relieved, I am sure that if I had lost the vote that night, I would have been forced to resign. I would not have been able to have led the union through a self-destructive strike.

The next day, the Governor said that both parties had agreed to the nomination, and it was agreed that a joint statement should be made to the general public.

That night, via local radio, the public statement was read out. The reaction in some quarters of the trade union was extremely hostile. Several members were incensed to learn of the union's decision to accept arbitration by way of the joint communiqué. I was soon feeling the full force of their displeasure and anger.

Between the time of making things public and the arbiter's arrival in the Islands, I was to receive a few letters and many telephone calls from members accusing me of betraying them, and saying how stupid and naïve I was to be trusting the Government, and that I had played right into the hands of the employers.

I thought I would be prepared for some disquiet, but I was quite taken aback by the level of anger expressed by some callers. The experience was unpleasant, insulting and in one or two isolated cases, threatening.

I must say, from my preliminary meeting with Mr Wilkinson, I felt whatever the outcome, here was a man that would listen to both sides even-handedly and would make a fair and just decision.

From the very outset, he gave the impression of having a grip on things, and that he had arrived in the Islands to do a job, not to socialise, or be befriended by anyone.

I was very happy with his refreshing approach, and his method of operation was simple enough. He informed us that he would meet first one side, then the other, in the conference room of Government House, which the Governor had made available. A venue that was all very agreeable and suitable as a neutral ground.

Sir Rex and I would not always see eye-to-eye on trade union matters, but on this very delicate topic he was exemplary.

As Mr Wilkinson sat at the end of the conference table, the whole procedure was very much like going to court to give evidence to the judge. He rarely adopted a questions and answers policy, he only wanted to listen, and appeared to write down everything that was said.

Only on the final day did he change tack slightly, when he asked if we had anything more to add to our case. Satisfied that we had not, he then asked me what appeared to be a fairly innocuous question.

He asked, 'You did say the union would need to think again if the SOA could demonstrate they were not in a position to finance the cost of living bonus, or words to that effect?' Correct, was my reply. Nodding his head, he politely said, 'Thank you.'

As I left Government House, I was sure the statement had made a profound impression on him. I became even more certain a day or two later, when he asked me the same question, ironically enough, in the accountant's office of the Falkland Islands Company, who were not only my employers but also part of the SOA team I was negotiating against.

Finally, the day arrived when it was time for him to deliver his final verdict, and as far as the union and SOA were concerned, it was an irrevocable decision.

We were all summoned to Government House. Upon arrival, we all went directly to the conference room and settled in our seats and waited.

I looked across the line of my team, and I noticed the boys were edgy. I then turned towards the SOA team. I thought they all appeared to be very calm.

Mr Wilkinson began by saying that he was very grateful to us all for our openness, honesty and patience. He then made it abundantly clear that he had listened to all the submissions carefully, and had deliberately taken all the time required to make a clear assessment of the arguments made from both sides.

He then went on that he was satisfied that the trade union had a grievance, and declared that the cost of living bonus should be reinstated to the workers at full capacity. In the light of the financial information he had been able to view, he also awarded two wage increases in favour of the employees represented by the General Employees Union.

I reacted to this remark by sitting bolt upright. As I did so, I looked directly across the table at my opposite number; his face showed an obvious sign of shock.

The arbitrator continued that the first award of 2.5% should be implemented with immediate effect, the second, also of 2.5% must be introduced six calendar months from today's date.

I thought to myself, my Christ, he certainly has been digging deep, and he has dropped several mighty bombshells.

He finished his very brief but earth-shattering statement by saying that if any of us would like clarification on his findings, to say so now, but he would not listen to any protests or pleas.

There were plenty of open mouths on the Sheep Owners Association side, but they were not producing words.

In a flash it was all over, the door had been firmly slammed on the matter.

Before getting up to leave, still slightly stunned by it all, I again looked across the table at their Chairman. He was now visibly shaken, and his face had paled. He was not alone, all his colleagues had been floored.

We went back to union headquarters and for a short while basked in the glory. I was delighted for the workers, this was their day of triumph. They didn't know it just yet, and they would not know until Falklands radio released the news later in the evening.

The workers had waited a very long time for success at this sort of level. That realisation did move me a little, and satisfied me a great deal.

Yes indeed, it was their victory, a victorious occasion for them and their immediate families. A day they could feel proud to be union members once again, a day their union had delivered.

Patrick, the man at the local radio station, who had been following the story all the way, called the union office within minutes of us getting back from Government House, and asked me to join the SOA Chairman in an interview on the radio that night.

About an hour later, I was somewhat surprised to get a call from the SOA Chairman, who asked if it would be okay to go along to the studio together. He then offered to give me a lift to the radio station from his office.

Upon my arrival at the SOA headquarters, he greeted me warmly, and we climbed into his car.

I remember the very short journey well. Barely a word was spoken between us. I could only think about how awful he must have been feeling, but I could not offer any sympathy; it was not necessary, nor would it have been ethical. But he was a very decent man, and in his moment of defeat, he was being extremely gracious towards me.

During the interview, I made every effort to deal with the facts, and would not be tempted into any vitriolic remarks. Patrick tried once or twice; that was his job and he was very good at it.

But as far as I was concerned, I was not going to play ball. I had to think ahead. This was the camp agreement; there was still the matter of the hourly paid workers agreement in Stanley to attend to, and the issue of COLB was bound to be a central issue. The union's work would not be complete until these workers had their full cost of living bonus reinstated as well. This was not the time to be shouting my mouth off.

But, for a brief moment, I did remember one or two of those people who had given me a very hard time over the matter. I did think they had had a sock firmly put in their mouths, and I was inwardly very satisfied about that.

With the interview done, I left the radio station at the same time as my injured opponent, who offered me a lift to wherever I wanted to go. I thanked him for his offer, but I didn't want to be in his sombre company any longer.

Now it was time to go and join my colleagues in the pub, and share a beer or two with them.

By the time I got to the Rose Hotel, it was 9 p.m. The antiquated law still required pubs to close at 10 p.m., so there was not time to get many beers down.

The delegates, however, had clearly lost no time, and they were in very fine form. One or two were even singing.

My father-in-law, Les Lee, was also in the bar. As I was waiting for my drink he came up to me and shook my hand and said, 'You did very well, Terry. You saved the union today. We are all very proud of you.'

I was a bit embarrassed by his very generous compliment, but I took it as sincere and genuine. He was one of the most honest and decent men I have ever had the pleasure to meet in my life. We had struck up a good relationship, and he became a good friend and advisor. I liked him a great deal.

A little while later he came back up to my side and touched me on the arm and said, 'Did you ever think about your job?' I looked at him quizzically. 'I reckon if you had lost today, they would have sacked you, or made your life so unbearable you would have left.'

'No, of course not,' I replied. It was a genuine answer. I had never thought about that aspect of things before, but from the moment he mentioned it, I wondered. Briefly, it had a sobering effect on what was intended to be a very non-sober night.

To be fair, my employers had always appeared to accept my dual role as employee and trade union activist. Sure, it was a tricky balancing act for me, and it must have been very difficult for them also, I suppose, but they never ever applied any pressure on me, and I think they can take considerable credit for that, because there must have been times during my union career when I tested their resolve to the maximum.

I walked out of the pub that night with a very happy group of union delegates. I was thrilled for them; they would be able to go back to their respective farms with their heads held high.

By the end of 1983, the union had partial success on the reinstatement of the full cost of living award for all its members in Stanley.

Despite the arbitrator's decision on the matter in the winter, the resistance from the Stanley employers to concede on the issue was surprisingly strong, particularly from my employers.

However, offering to take the matter to arbitration should the item not be resolved by negotiation had the desired effect. Thus it was agreed that full cost of living would be implemented in two stages by 1985.

During the whole time I was involved in union matters in the Falklands, the cost of living bonus dispute would be the most demanding, sensitive and rewarding piece of labour relations I would ever be tasked to resolve.

There were other issues that were innovative, revolutionary and challenging. Some succeeded, whilst others did not, for one reason or another.

Consolidation of membership, followed by a recruitment drive, were very successful in the traditional areas, but a new concept to form a sister union to represent the new landowners was a complete failure.

An idea to encourage women into the union movement had little success, but Eva Alazia would create trade union history in the Islands by becoming the first woman elected to the Executive Committee shortly after I gave up the chair. I would like to think that my idea to encourage women into the union fold had something to do with her historic achievements.

When I took the chair, membership level was barely 60% of its potential for the workers covered under the two traditional agreements, Stanley showing the worse figures of the two groups. But within a year, the percentage had increased to 98%.

There was no doubt that the very impressive growth had much to do with the union's success on the cost of living issue, but it was not this factor alone.

The union had become a much more organised, purposeful and professional outfit, as it went about its daily business. The organisation had undergone dramatic internal and external changes to underpin this, and to rid itself of a very poor public relations image, including the opening of the headquarters office from 60 hours a month, to 40 hours a week. This change alone had the effect of making the union more readily available to its membership, and the general public.

After the Falklands War, visitors to the Islands dramatically increased. People from the international media, British Parliament, members of the Royal Family, international business people and others, were now regularly dropping in on the Falklands.

In the past, the union had little contact, and even less exposure, to these influential individuals or groups.

By announcing we were open for business, the union began to get itself pencilled in on visitors' agendas, and thus reached out to a much wider audience.

I have mentioned that I did not always see eye-to-eye with Sir Rex on labour relations. The most notable issue was the construction of the International Airport at Mount Pleasant, often incorrectly referred to as RAF, Mount Pleasant.

The union had been lobbied by members about the total lack of employment opportunities at the airport complex site, some 35 kilometres from Stanley.

The facility was being constructed by a United Kingdom consortium, collectively known as LMA: John Laing Construction Limited, Mowlem International Limited and Amey Roadstone Construction Limited.

It was alleged that when Islanders approached the contractors for employment, they were told, 'If you are Falkland Islanders, we're not allowed to employ you.'

The union became very concerned about these reports, and I was instructed to approach Sir Rex.

The wonderful thing about Sir Rex was that he was a very approachable man. Once he knew what I wanted to discuss with him, he readily agreed to meet me.

We met in his office at Government House. Once tea had been poured and biscuits offered and taken, we got straight on with the issue at hand.

I asked if it was true that employers at the airport were not allowed to employ Falkland Islanders, and impressed upon him that if it were the case, the union considered it to be a grave act of discrimination against both union members and Falkland Islanders as a whole.

He denied that any such restrictive procedures were in place, but when asked why it was that no one from Stanley or camp had been employed, no suitable explanation seemed to be forthcoming. I also felt that the truth was being used rather sparingly.

There was plenty of talk about the problems to the major employers if too many workers went off to work on the airfield, and the many jobs that would not get done as a result of a grave shortage of labour.

I felt a very feeble attempt was being made to put up a smoke screen. Therefore, as politely as I could, I indicated the union would not accept that reasoning. In fact it was only likely to harden the view that undemocratic practices were being carried out against them. Furthermore, it was the union's opinion that the action of denying Falkland Islanders the opportunity to work on this project was simply because employers had effectively lobbied the Government, using a very flimsy excuse, to deny the worker the freedom to up and leave for better-paid employment.

Sure, the employers were worried, but their concern was that they knew they would be under considerable pressure to increase their salaries in a competitive marketplace – a situation I am sure the union would have noted. After all, it had been reported that employees on the airport contract were earning many times more than their counterparts in Stanley and the camp.

The meeting continued with agreement and disagreement on various side issues, such as the number of men likely to seek employment in a free labour market, taking into consideration the very long hours, extremely remote location, very basic accommodation, no easy form of transport from Stanley to the site, coupled with a worker culture which preferred to go home at night, or over the weekends, to be with their families. But none of these issues was the critical factor.

No, what troubled the trade union was the possibility that the basic fundamental right of man to be free to choose his place of employment might be being denied. Secondly, there was a great opportunity for workers to learn skills not normally available to them in their present employment.

I reminded the Governor of the building of the Stanley airport in the 1970s, when 15/16-year-old boys were learning to drive heavy plant and machinery.

Eventually, the conversation dried up. I got the impression the Governor felt he was in a bit of a tight corner and was no longer comfortable about continuing the debate. The meeting closed, with the Governor suggesting to me that he should make a statement on the local radio to clarify the overall position.

That night, he duly made his broadcast, which, in my opinion, was nothing more than a load of patronising labour relations claptrap.

What is interesting is that, after the Governor's radio address, the union received news that even Falkland Islanders residing in the UK who had sought to work on the project were declined by the contractor if they became aware of their birthplace. One or two did make it, by using deceptive measures.

If there was no system in place to stop Islanders being employed on the project, why was it that so few Islanders ever worked on the site, and nearly all of those that did get through the net, didn't even let their families know they were in the Islands, for fear of losing their highly paid jobs? All rather strange don't you agree?

In truth, our little trade union was not equipped to do much about it. What a pity it was that it would be a year later before we made contact with the TUC (Big Brother). They would surely have been better equipped to assist us to redress a highly political and extremely unjust act.

The whole episode made me pause for thought. I had believed that we Falkland Islanders were liberated in 1982, not castigated; too many lives had been lost for that, surely?

Sadly, Islanders had been denied, by someone in authority, the right to offer their labour freely, which would have improved their standard of living and given them the opportunity to learn new skills, which they could then have put to good use in the interest of the whole Islands community, after the project had been completed.

No one has ever admitted responsibility, but there are people out there who should sleep uneasily at nights. Whoever you are, and wherever you might be, God damn you.

Taking the chair of the trade union required me to take on some extra baggage, legacies of Dick's era, I suppose. These were honorary appointments to committees like immigration and housing, responsibilities that just took up valuable time. Committee members had no authority, they were just advisory groups to the Governor in Council.

But Sir Rex Hunt did invite me to join the board of the newly formed Falkland Islands Development Corporation. In accepting, I was to make a little piece of Islands history by being present at its inaugural meeting in Government House in July 1984. Sir Rex and I were now batting for the same team.

FIDC was just one more of the Shackleton concepts. The idea being that it would take responsibility for stimulating the Falkland Islands economy, by measures of land reform and other commercial diversification.

38

With the TUC in London
(But not elected in the General Election)

In 1985, the Falkland Islands Government had inquired if I would be prepared to take some training with the Trade Union Congress in London. The union Executive Committee felt this was not an offer to refuse, therefore it was accepted.

However, by the time everything had been set up, flights, programme, accommodation etc., another issue became the focus of the Executive Committee's attention, which involved me, and was scheduled to take place at the same time as the TUC visit.

I was due to take my training during October and November, over a six-week period, but there was the question of the Islands General Election. The union felt I should put myself forward as a candidate; they were very eager to have 'their man', as they put it, in Legislative Council again – a new generation of Dick Goss, if you like.

After much discussion, it was finally agreed that I should stand as the unofficial candidate of the GEU, but that I would still go to London for the tuition.

Due to the voting system within the Falkland Islands, camp members could not vote for me. I could only be elected by the constituents of Stanley as a Stanley candidate, therefore a huge section of the union voting block was not able to vote for their desired choice.

I should point out that campaigning in an election in the Falklands was a pretty low-key affair. It was not a very dramatic or tense occasion; there was no party politics then, nor today, thus, nearly all candidates followed their own beliefs.

Interestingly, the union did *not* give me a mandate either, they simply believed the organisation would be better placed if they had someone 'on the inside' and they entrusted me as their flag bearer.

Eventually it became apparent that eight other candidates would contest the four Stanley seats against me.

I arrived in London in early October 1985; this was a time when mainland Britain had just come out of a community-splitting, family-dividing miners' strike, which had raged on in the UK for most of the year.

By all accounts, it was probably the nearest thing to civil war you could get, and I was going to be hosted by those very close to the defeated. I was also coming from Islands whose community, almost to a man, regarded the British Prime Minister, Margaret Thatcher, as a heroine. An accolade which I was fairly sure was far removed from the views of the Trade Union Congress and the trade union movement of the United Kingdom, especially those who had been directly or indirectly involved in the miners' strike.

Strangely enough, I was to be accommodated in the Mount Pleasant Hotel in London. Strange, because that was also the name of the area in the Falklands where the International Airport had been built. It had been opened back in May of 1985 by HRH Prince Andrew, thus enabling me to make my journey in very comfortable conditions. I had been allocated a seat in the top deck of a 747 jumbo jet, so I arrived in England, rested and raring to go.

However, I had not been in the United Kingdom for 17 years and I had no clear memory of services and places, so I spent the free weekend adjusting to an enormous populace and familiarising myself with the underground network and taxis.

On the Monday morning, I made my way to Congress House in Great Russell Street, and was welcomed to the home of the Trade Union Congress by the organisation's General Secretary, Norman Willis. The meeting proceeded as if we were long lost friends and I was impressed by his warmth and hospitality. He enabled me to feel at home immediately, but I had nothing to be tense about anyway, I was in the company of the Falkland Islands General Employees Union's affiliated friends (I would get a rude awakening later on).

Mr Willis asked me to fill him in on the Falklands union, and after a coffee or two, he presented me with a very special present. This was a plate to commemorate the exploits of the Tolpuddle

Martyrs, who had been banished from England to Australia in chains, for their beliefs.

I was thrilled to pieces with the gift, which I assumed was only handed out on very rare occasions.

After swapping questions and stories, I got on to the subject of the miners' strike. As the conversation progressed, he asked me if I would like to meet Arthur Scargill, the miners' leader. If so, he would arrange it for me.

I think I surprised him with my response of 'No thank you,' and he asked why. Never one to be short of an opinion, I explained that I did not wish to meet him because, in my view, he had taken his eye off the ball during the miners' strike. It was a personal belief of mine, that he could have negotiated a successful outcome for the miners on a couple of occasions, but I thought he had got distracted by politics, and instead of reaching a deal, decided to switch tactics and made an attempt to bring down Margaret Thatcher and her Conservative Government.

I had to admit that I had made my assessment purely from listening to the BBC World Service and UK Forces Radio, 8,000 miles away in the Falkland Islands.

Then I went on, his failure had grave consequences for the trade union movement.

Norman looked at me rather curiously, but he was diplomatic and made no comment on my remarks. He just said, 'Well, if there is anyone you would expressly wish to meet, you just have to let me know.'

He was such a kind and generous man that I felt more than a bit rude for being so outspoken in my opinions on the miners' strike.

My programme was set in a way that would allow me to attend as many seminars and work and talk shops as possible, with the objective of gathering information about labour relations, health and safety at work, negotiating skills, work study and job evaluation and many other union related matters.

There was also time set aside for meetings with heads and deputy heads of several union organisations, such as the Municipal Boilermakers and Allied Trade Union, the National Union of Public Employees and the Transport and General Workers Union.

There were also other meetings arranged with individuals, organisations and the media, which included a television interview with an Argentine television crew headed by a Mr Ronnie Boyd, radio interviews with BBC World Service, and lunch with the staff from the Falkland Islands Government office.

So, although the whole course was centred around core union issues, the programme was much wider and more varied than that.

The Falklands were very topical in the United Kingdom in October 1985. Many people that I met in the trade union sphere firmly believed the Falklands War had had a profound effect on the result of the last general election in the UK, which had not resulted in a satisfactory outcome for the trade union movement as a whole. The events in my homeland, back in 1982, were thought responsible for the Conservatives' convincing victory, which many described to me as due to Margaret Thatcher milking the victory cow.

On many occasions, classroom sessions were delayed, or seriously interrupted, because of the barrage of questions thrown at me about the war, the weather, population, sheep and penguins.

Many thought we were simple-minded sheep shaggers. I would joke with them and say, we might be sheep shaggers, but we are certainly not simple-minded.

One or two would even come up to me and touch me, as if I were a music or film idol, or even off another planet. Many had never seen a real live Falkland Islander in the flesh before. It was also a fair bet that many of them had never heard of the Falklands, or didn't know where in the world they were, before the war started. That has all changed now, and how.

But there was the other side of the coin too. I would experience extreme abuse and insults regarding my birthplace, people finger-prodding me in the chest and shouting at me in a violent rage, how futile the whole Falklands War had been. What a waste of so many lives. 'Maggie's War' many called it.

Margaret Thatcher might have been a heroine in the Falkland Islands and in many parts of the UK in 1985, but she was certainly not in this neck of the woods.

One morning I had made my way from the hotel to an office where I was to meet a gentleman to discuss negotiation skills.

'Well then, tell me about the trade union in the Falkland

Islands,' he began, so I proceeded to give him a general overview of the General Employees Union, the membership, and the kind of areas and agreements it worked within.

He seemed to be keenly interested, then I went on to say, 'There is something you should know, however. It is quite an unusual thing really, especially for a trade union, that is. But Falkland Islanders as a whole, and the members of the GEU in particular, are all very big supporters of Margaret Thatcher and the Conservative Government. So much so, that affixed to a wall, behind the General Secretary's desk in the office of the trade union in Stanley, there is a framed photograph of the British Prime Minister.'

The man's face instantly went red, and he exploded into a violent rage. He jumped up from his seat and started thumping his desk top, then he proceeded to dash around his office, shouting 'NO, NO, NO.'

I sat in my chair, watching his antics in total disbelief. I had been winding him up slightly, but his response was bordering on the ridiculous.

Once we got on to the subject of negotiating skills, I found him impressive, but he had spoiled things just a little bit with a very dramatic and unimpressive display of lost control.

As the weeks went by, my hotel room became more and more cluttered with books, papers and research material. It was looking more like a library each passing day, and I was going to need a couple of very understanding military personnel at the check-in desk at Brize Norton to allow me to carry all my accumulated luggage on the flight back home.

I was probably overdoing it on collecting information material, but I was very aware that my trip to the United Kingdom was for the overall benefit of the GEU. It would be stored in the union's headquarters, not only for the use of the Executive Committee, but also the vast majority of the union membership, who I hoped would be encouraged to stroll into the office to browse through the material and broaden their knowledge.

As for the establishment of personal contacts on my visit, I regarded this exercise as a 'card-collecting mission' to pass on to the General Secretary, who would then have for the first time a comprehensive list of contact numbers for individuals and organisations at his immediate disposal. Including professional services, such as accountancy and law; the union had never had this type of support before.

Legal or accountancy firms did not exist in the Falklands, even in 1985. It might have been possible to seek advice on a legal issue from the local Judge, but if he thought his advice was likely to conflict with his employers (FIG), that avenue would be closed off immediately.

As I have hinted before, had the union had these contacts a year earlier, when all the nonsense was going on about employing Falkland Islanders on the International Airport project, I am sure the union would have been much better equipped to have been far more forceful on the issue.

I had a couple of unforgettable experiences whilst in the United Kingdom, events that had nothing to do with trade union matters.

One took place in late October 1985. Somehow, representatives of the Falkland Islands Company had acquired an invitation from the sponsors of Tottenham Hotspur Football Club (Holsten) for me to spend a day with them, as their guest at the club during match day.

Absolutely thrilled to bits, I travelled to the ground with another Spurs fan/friend, who was working in the FIC office in London.

Once we had consumed a rather large welcoming gin and tonic, we were given a conducted and detailed tour of the ground and the stadium, inside and outside. Then it was back to the bar to consume a few more drinks before sitting down to an excellent lunch.

After lunch, we were invited to go off to the sponsors' box to watch the game against Leicester City, in the maximum of comfort. A certain Mr Gary Lineker and Alan Smith were the two Leicester City strikers and they both scored to give Leicester a 3–1 victory. But for once, the result did not mean much to me that day, I was having such a wonderful time, and my mind was struggling to take everything in.

When the match had finished, I was taken back, with my friend Ray, to the Bill Nicholson suite, to present a Falkland Islands silver coin to commemorate 150 years of British Rule to the man of the match, who was to receive it on behalf of Tottenham

Hotspur FC. It just happened that the man of the match that day was a certain Glenn Hoddle.

After shaking hands and passing the coin over to Hoddle, I started to make my way off the podium, but before I had gone a couple of steps, Mike Rollo, the club's commercial manager, grabbed me lightly on the shoulder, and asked, 'Where do you think you're going?'

I remember thinking, what the hell is going on here? Well, to my complete surprise, Glenn Hoddle was then asked to present me with one of the club's crystal ship's decanters. I knew that there had only been 500 of these wonderful objects made to commemorate the club's centenary, so I was totally agog.

I still vividly recall Hoddle's words to me after we shook hands for a second time: 'You do appreciate what you have been given here, don't you?' Indeed I did.

It was one of those rare moments when this Falkland Islander was speechless. As a nine-year-old boy, when I first became a Spurs fan, 8,000 miles away, I would have dreams and fantasise about moments such as this. Now 27 years on, I was standing on a podium at White Hart Lane, being handed a Tottenham Hotspur centenary crystal decanter by Glenn Hoddle, as the guest of the club's sponsors.

What a day, what a moment. Mr Von Muller, the sponsor's representative, gave me a lift back to my hotel, and as I got out of his car he presented me with a Holsten Pils tie. I was one very happy Spurs fan.

The last I knew, the silver coin sits in the club's oak room. The beautiful decanter sits in my son's lounge. It is my wish that it will remain the property of my family for generations to come, standing centre stage somewhere, to demonstrate our loyalty to this great football club.

Also during my short visit, it had been organised for me to meet another idol of mine, Lord Shackleton, at the House of Lords to witness a working session, then to take tea and have a chat about his two Falkland Islands economic reports.

Lord Shackleton was a very fine gentleman, and a huge Falklands friend. I found him to be extremely intelligent, quick-witted and light-hearted, all of which made him very easy company.

I remember we both had a bit of a laugh when he asked me if I wanted tea.

'Sure,' I replied.

'Fine, but what will you have?' he inquired.

'Tea of course, what do you mean, what will I have?'

He smiled and said, 'Okay, but will it be Ceylon, Chinese, Indian, or whatever.'

Trying to make little of my obvious display of ignorance, I responded, 'Oh Christ, I didn't think having tea was such a technical and complicated affair. I'll have whatever is going.'

With a twinkle in his eye, he turned to a lady who was waiting very patiently by his side and duly requested the tea of his choice.

'Now, will you have toast and marmalade, Terry.'

'Okay,' I said, 'providing I don't have to choose between six different types of marmalades.'

He laughed out loud, and said, 'No, not at all. Chunky and orange. How's that?'

During tea, we chatted about topics in his economic reports on the Islands. In fact, we concentrated mainly on two subjects, land sub-division and fishing.

The Falkland Islands Government had already implemented an element of his recommendations on land sub-division. However, somewhat tragically, nothing had been done about the recommendation to exploit and develop the huge amount of fish stocks around the Islands. This fact, I knew, concerned and upset Lord Shackleton greatly.

(As it turned out, within a year of our meeting, the situation changed greatly, when Sir Geoffrey Howe, on behalf of the British Conservative Government, finally declared a Falkland Islands Fisheries Interim, Conservation and Management Zone.)

After tea, Lord Shackleton took me on a walkabout of the Lords, during which he invited me to sit down with him on a large wool-stuffed cushion, called the 'Woolsack', usually reserved for the Lord Chancellor, I believe. As we sat upon this historical and prestigious piece of furniture, he lightly patted the top of it and said, 'There's a piece of Falkland Islands wool in here, you know, Terry.' I didn't know, in fact, but from that day on, I have never forgotten.

I must also admit, that as I was sitting upon the Woolsack with one of the United Kingdom's finest peers, I briefly let my mind slip away.

I was thinking to myself how my life had changed. Twenty years ago I had been packed off to Lively Island as a no-hoper with the potential of becoming a troublemaker.

I pondered for a moment on that idea, then I began to wonder. Perhaps nothing had actually changed. I was still making trouble, the only difference was, I was making it in a totally different environment, for a completely different reason.

Whatever the reasoning, it didn't really matter a great deal. But I will tell you this, having the opportunity of meeting great people like Lord Shackleton, and absorbing just tiny fragments of their vast knowledge, was an education that one can never gain in a classroom.

I also found it a far more interesting way to learn – I was a naughty and impatient classroom student.

Like most things when you are enjoying yourself, the weeks slipped by all too quickly, and it was time to take my long 18-hour flight home.

Everyone at the TUC had been superb, I could not have wished for better treatment. The whole experience had been a privilege and something that will live on in my memory.

As soon as I got home, I would be going straight into the annual negotiations with the Stanley employers.

Talking of employers, it was also time I went back into the FIC office and did a day's work for mine. Once again they had been wonderfully understanding and supportive. They had assisted me in every way possible to ensure that I could make the trip to the UK, and even arranged some engagements for me whilst I was there.

I was keen as mustard to pass on my experiences with the TUC to the Executive Committee. Upon reflection, I might have been guilty of trying to introduce one or two things far too quickly. As a result, my good intentions would be suffocated by frequent overdoses of caution and doubt.

Oh, by the way, I did not return home as an elected member of the Legislative Council either; being absent from the Islands during election time proved to be a bridge too far, and I finished 30 votes short of being elected.

39

From Member to President
(My objective achieved, it's time to step aside)

Just over a year later, it had become apparent to me that the time had come to plan my withdrawal from the union.

The Executive Committee had been made aware that I was not going to be seeking re-election as their Chairman at the 1986 Annual General Meeting in November. Therefore, it was decided I should start to work closely with the Vice-Chairman, Gavin Short. Gavin was young, energetic and full of enthusiasm, and many in the Executive Committee saw him as my natural successor.

Part of the reason for my decision to move on was that I had become increasingly aware that many people were referring to the trade union organisation as 'Terry Betts's union'. It could, of course, never be that, it always was, and always had to be, the membership's union. But I felt this image was not healthy for the GEU.

I also remembered a promise I made to every one present the night I was elected to take the chair: 'I will recover the cost of living bonus for you, then I will give the chair to someone else.'

Looking back, the statement was very arrogant and presumptuous of me. Who the hell was I to assume I would automatically be re-elected to the chair, if I had failed in the first year to achieve the results we did? That aside, the election of Chairman was a democratic process of voting by secret ballot.

The union had started chipping away at employers, in particular the Falkland Islands Government, about the need for the introduction of health and safety legislation at work.

As a result of the war, things would change very rapidly in the Falkland Islands, and new and very demanding issues would challenge the trade union and the employers.

The Government realised that as the Islands were going to be catapulted into the 20th century, there was a need for a new administrative structure to handle the inevitable requirement for a vast amount of law reform and legal practice. They were also aware that they might well need expert legal advice and representation themselves.

Law reform was, of course, required to put such very important issues as health and safety into practice. FIG Attorney General Michael Gaiger, and his predecessor David Lang, were very understanding and cooperative on this matter.

From the union side, the project ended up being Gavin's baby as he got to grips with the subject from the outset.

Gavin continued to impress everyone by grasping things very quickly. I was extremely happy about that, because more and more of my time was being demanded by my employers who were continuously promoting me through the ranks. I was now in senior management, as the company's Works Manager.

The negotiations with the employers were a bit of a stroll in my final year, and the union membership was oozing confidence, but the organisation was no closer to financial stability. Come to think of it, very little was in the Falklands in those days, not even Government.

Therefore, I tried to put into place one last piece of restructuring before my departure, a system whereby the union could raise funds through the membership and the general public without either feeling the pain, or even noticing they were paying. Membership fees alone were insufficient to maintain and administer the trade union, as they always had been.

My idea was very basic. I thought of raising funds whilst the union membership and their guests were having fun. We had our own building, therefore all we needed to do was convert a section of it into a compact but suitable bar/lounge area, ideal for leisurely things such as reading, the usual games of darts and cards, general chitchat etc., and for getting the members together, especially at the end of the working week, to discuss topical work and union issues – a very important and logical way to promote trade union awareness.

It could also serve as a place for formal and informal forums, allowing members to express themselves on important matters whilst they were happily spending money over the union bar counter, thus enabling the organisation to build up capital reserves for the very first time in its history.

When I presented my humble plan to Committee and members, all agreed it was a good idea, but sadly, as it required a degree of self-motivation, it was never to get off the ground.

Sadly, it is a fact of life that the most difficult thing to change in a man is his habits, and our members were not going to change theirs. They just carried on drinking at the local pub, shovelling their money into the pockets of people who, in general, did not care if they had a job or not, or if they were well paid or not. What a great shame for the union and its membership alike.

At my final Annual General Meeting I outlined our achievements and progress over the years, under my chairmanship, whilst highlighting the tasks left undone that would still need to be attended to.

I had only been five years at the very top of the Falkland Islands trade union tree, but it had been a wonderful experience, and extremely satisfying.

I was sure I had become a much better, and wiser man, from the whole affair. I had learnt that to do your best for the benefit of others could be very uplifting and rewarding.

Having grown men coming up to you terribly stressed, and trusting you with their most intimate personal or family matters, then sending them off with some hope and gratitude, all because of a few comforting or well-chosen words, followed by the appropriate action to resolve their problems, sticks firmly in the memory.

During my time in the union, I would also discover that employers were not unreasonable people. If you took the time to sit down with them and talk things through in a calm manner, they would often listen, and you could change their minds.

As one might expect, I had taken my responsibilities as union leader very seriously, and now I could leave the organisation, satisfied with the knowledge that it was in a very good state of health.

But whatever good things I might have achieved, I would have been totally ineffectual without the support of wonderful characters like Neville Bennett, Mary Jennings and Wallace Hirtle. All were outstanding union General Secretaries during my term in office. There were many others, too numerous to mention, who gave so much of their free time to serve their fellow man, as members of the Union Executive and as delegates (shop stewards).

That night, I was to be in for quite a surprise. After closing the Annual General Meeting, the Vice-Chairman rose to his feet and informed me that the Executive Committee, on behalf of all the members of the trade union organisation, would be glad if I would accept the honour of being the union's first honorary President.

I was totally gobsmacked. I was very touched, and truly flattered by the invitation. To have refused would have been nothing short of an insult, so naturally I accepted.

As I did, I thought to myself, it is not every day you go down in Falklands history in such a way. I suppose I must have impressed someone.

Just before leaving the General Employees Union office as its honorary President, I fixed my eyes on that framed photograph of Margaret Thatcher in her blue attire, and I thought to myself, this sure is a unique organisation indeed.

Those farsighted forefathers of the movement: Barnes, Brechin, Howatt, Sedgewick, Evans and Harrison, along with some very notable, and honourable disciples, such as Goss, Rowlands and Summers, can all rest in peace.

Because no matter what the future holds, these men have carved their names in the history of the Falkland Islands. Each one of them is directly responsible, in their own way, for the further development and improvement of the workplace for future generations of workers in the Falkland Islands.

FROM THE BOTTOM OF MY HEART, THANK YOU VERY MUCH.

MAY GOD BLESS YOU ALL

40

Sir Rex Invites Me on Board
(The Falkland Islands Development Corporation)

Apart from my union responsibilities, I had others just as demanding and no less important. One of these was the Falkland Islands Development Corporation. As I have already mentioned, in 1984, Sir Rex Hunt invited me to become one of the original members of the board.

The concept was another egg out of the basket of Lord Shackleton's economic report, version number two, I do believe.

The organisation was set up to be responsible for the development, among other things, of the Falkland Islands economy, by advising on methods of diversification in the agricultural industry. It was also to identify new areas of commercial opportunity, especially for a private sector, which was quite a challenge, because there was no free and fluid private sector to collaborate with.

From its inauguration there was also another negative factor the board of FIDC had to endure in the early years. This was the crucial pivot to any kind of new economic development – funding.

The Corporation's finances, in the beginning, came from the Overseas Development Agency in the United Kingdom. From my personal experience and observation, this was an unfortunate way to begin business, because the main sponsors were often slow to react to proposals, and I felt they often did not, or perhaps could not, get a real grasp of the Islands' essential needs, and there always seemed to be too much paper required to cover one's ass.

The Corporation has had many critics, and it is probably pretty fair to say it has made mistakes during its time. That had to be expected. But there cannot be any doubt that the Corporation can claim some credit for being part of the development and expansion of a present-day vibrant and competitive private sector.

The Corporation was handicapped in the early years because it had to initiate commercial concepts completely cold, without any broad and varied historical commercial data or practice to develop from.

The Falkland Islands was a single-industry and single-product economy: sheep ranching and raw wool.

There were other difficult, and unique, scenarios for the Corporation to deal with. There was little to no infrastructure or facilities to acquire or transform into new commercial projects. This problem was compounded by the near-feudal system in which the woollen industry was operated, and the monopolisation of retail, freight, shipping and many other services in the Islands.

These wholly negative aspects, not surprisingly, produced a populace with little hope, or ambition, for running their own business.

Thus, sadly, there was hardly anyone knocking on FIDC's door with a business initiative, which probably forced FIDC into business the wrong way around. Instead of the people coming to FIDC, FIDC went out to the people. Which I am convinced resulted in too many people wearing the wrong clothes.

The Corporation also had to be mindful of the lack of competitiveness in the private sector. It did not wish simply to identify commercial opportunities, and then allow them to be operated and controlled by the existing monopoly.

All these problems meant that FIDC would be robbed of its ideal role, which should have been to provide administrative back-up and/or advice, plus providing the initial working capital to kick-start the commercial projects.

As it was, FIDC was not much more than a quasi-governmental body which was forced to take the lead, always a recipe for potential cock-ups, making the organisation an easy target for snipers sitting on their butt ends doing nothing more than willing failure.

Another factor which made life extremely difficult for anyone tasked with changing things commercially in the Islands was the chronic lack of capital. Fishing revenues were still three years away.

This was almost certainly due to the fact that those few who had been making any money over the previous 150 years in the Falklands had tucked it all away into overseas bank accounts. The revenue from their considerable profits had gone into the pockets of shareholders and directors overseas.

Furthermore, because the Falklands economy had been driven from a single source for 150 years, the community was vastly uneducated and inexperienced regarding commerce. This, in turn, naturally led to a lack of drive and an often apathetic attitude towards commercial development, bred from a previous lack of opportunity.

Not a conducive environment for the FIDC to begin to promote the need for a diverse economy, especially as the changes required would also force the transformation in the attitude of existing employers and employees.

Economic development would also contribute to a dramatic change in the way of life in the islands that so many had assumed was regulated for the whole of their lives.

The Falkland Islands economy has been transformed since 1987 by the sale of fishing licences, but it must be recognised that the FIDC has played its role in diversifying and expanding the Islands economy in many areas.

Tourism and the production of vegetables by a method called hydroponics are testimony to that. The vegetables have even found a place in the export market.

Since 1984, the FIDC has needed to change itself in structure and outlook. But it continues to be a crucial player as one of the guardians of the Islands economy. The Corporation offers planning, advisory and financial assistance, identifies additional sources of income, export opportunities and import substitution, assists with training and provides business information services, encourages rural development and diversification, in conjunction with the Department of Agriculture, promotes tourism, through direct assistance for companies and the Falkland Islands Tourist Board, optimises the opportunities for the development of the Falkland Islands economy and ensures that the social and environmental impact of development is positive, whilst creating an infrastructure beneficial to businesses.

I trust that as one of the longest serving members of the FIDC board, I made a useful and positive contribution to the development of the Falkland Islands economy. I can assure you, I always did my best, and I thank Sir Rex for the opportunity.

41

The Hospital is on Fire
(Nine civilians die)

If the morale of Islanders had been lifted by the visit of Thatcher and the celebrations of the 150th anniversary of British resettlement of the Islands in 1983, then it was to be brutally shattered by the horror of events in the early hours of one April morning in 1984.

Just two years and eight days after the invasion of the Falkland Islands, another traumatic event took place, a disaster that would take three times more civilian lives than the invasion, occupation and subsequent liberation.

I think many of the resident population of the Falklands who had lived through the war were still traumatised in one way or another by the experience, and its aftermath. But they had been bravely trying to carry on with a normal way of life. But life was hardly normal any more, and confidence would be badly shaken once again.

In the small hours of 10 April 1984, the capital's population were woken up by the wailing noise of fire sirens.

I first thought that it was an air raid warning, but soon it was clear it was a fire, and very close to our house. Looking out of the kitchen window I thought the Government Secretariat was ablaze, as it had been back in the 1950s. But I quickly concluded that the flames were too big and bright to be the Secretariat, which was constructed of concrete blocks.

Just as I realised where the fire was, the local radio station confirmed it was the King Edward Memorial Hospital which was ablaze.

The noise of the fire sirens had woken everyone up. Suddenly Severine, who was now ten years old, began screaming and sobbing, and when I picked him up he was trembling with fear.

If I had thought the experience of the war had not affected him, I was now left in no doubt about that. The sound of the fire warning had got him into a total state of panic. He thought war was breaking out again. After some time his mother and I got him calmed down.

We all got dressed, and I decided that we should go and take a drive around, mainly to show Severine that the Argies were not back in town.

When we got outside, I noticed heavy black smoke was blowing over the house and small lumps of what appeared to be plastic were flying ablaze in the air. For some reason I looked up into the back garden, and to my surprise, I discovered that a small section of one of our timber garden fences had been set alight by these tiny fireballs.

Moving quickly, I soon put the fire out. Once that was done, I decided I should remove a five-gallon can of fuel I had stored in the workshop, just in case the shed caught fire and it exploded into the night air.

Eventually we climbed into the FIC red Ford Escort van, which was now a perk of the job, and set off. As we did, I was still very concerned about Severine. His fit of hysteria had shocked me immensely.

As we drove along a street called Reservoir Road, past the east end of the top football field, I noticed a man running along a grass bank above us.

I vividly remember saying to Melody, 'Don't you think that's a bit odd? That bloke up there, he's running flat out away from the scene of the fire.'

The other thing that I remember about this person was that he was not someone we knew; by that I mean he was a stranger in town.

So what, you may be thinking. Well, some time later the Falkland Islands Government pressed charges against a serviceman for arson, a case they would lose in a court in England. Still to this day I wonder, had we seen a person running away from a crime scene?

I did not drive around for too long, and after dropping Melody and the children off home, I took a walk down to the hospital area for a better view of things.

When I got there, the building was a huge ball of fire, with firemen shouting instructions and busying about with various types of fire-fighting equipment, battling against monstrous flames and intense heat as they struggled to contain the fire, and then bring it under control, whilst they, and others, tried to ensure that everyone inside the building was taken out unharmed.

The scene was one of chaos, destruction and high drama, in an atmosphere of tension, some confusion and extreme bravery.

A nearby dwelling had also caught fire, and fire fighters were spraying other homes and buildings in the area which were now becoming threatened by the size of the blaze and a fairly strong westerly wind.

I was standing by a small garage, at the junction between St Mary's Walk and Reservoir Road, when I noticed a work colleague, John Leonard. He appeared very disturbed, as he watched people going in and out of the garage, which was owned by a chap called Sydney Lyse.

It was Sydney's house, which was some 30 metres to the east of the hospital, that was set ablaze and eventually gutted, as a result of the fire being carried along by the strong breeze.

I called out to John and asked what was going on in the garage. 'Garage,' he shouted, 'more like a bloody mortuary than a garage. Eight people have lost their lives, Terry, and they've put the bodies in there. There maybe more yet.'

It became even more numbing as John began to tell me the names of those who had perished, seven females and a male, which by some cruel twist of fate included the Chief Fire Officer's wife, along with a mother and her week-old baby daughter, and a nurse from England who died attempting to save the lives of others.

There were four or five people who did escape the hospital fire that night, due to their own courage and the outstanding bravery of others.

It was a catastrophe beyond comprehension; people had survived the bloody war, only to lose their lives in the hospital, in the most tragic of circumstances. How could such a terrible thing have happened?

I remember going into work in the middle of the morning. Everybody was very quiet; obviously the tragic events of the night had taken over everyone's mind.

Then Nick Hadden caught the mood of everyone present, when he broke the silence and said, 'I don't know about you lot, but after what I have witnessed this morning, I can't concentrate on work, I'm going home.'

It was as if a teacher had suddenly declared that class was finished for the day. Everyone got up, put their coats on and went home.

The mood of the people of the Falklands was one of disbelief, sorrow and shock, especially as it came so close after the war, and I know some of the mental wounds from that terrible experience were harshly reopened. The community appeared to close ranks as it united in grief, turning out in large crowds to attend the funeral services that followed.

Churches were full to overflowing, many people stood in the streets, in the cold as the driving rain lashed against them, to pay their last respects to those lost, their families and friends. The death of the young mother and her child probably had the most profound effect on the tiny community, but everyone lost was mourned by the Islands community.

The loss of life was not the only loss for the community. It had also lost the only hospital facility in the Islands. To their credit, the authorities moved quickly and effectively, by ordering the conversion of the capital's main Town Hall into a makeshift hospital for a short while.

Later, a new building to the west of Stanley was then made ready for temporary use, and the military, as usual totally adaptable, rapidly constructed a facility to the east of Stanley, in an area known as the Canache. The two facilities proved capable of dealing with the population's medical requirements until the new hospital became functional.

I recollect that Sir Rex called for an immediate inquiry into the possible cause of the fire. Of course, there had been the usual amount of speculation and theory as to how the whole thing might have been caused. One of these was an electrical fault, but the commission for the inquiry quickly dismissed that idea. Instead, it reached a far more damning conclusion, which was that the fire had been man-made.

Seven years later, a Mr Shorters was tried for arson. However, he was acquitted at the Old Bailey in London. What an ironic tragedy it would have been, if 255 servicemen had lost their lives to save and protect the lives of the Falkland Islanders, whilst the alleged actions of another might have been responsible for the deaths of so many.

42

From the Boy to the Boss
(and rehabilitation)

Rehabilitation after the war was slow, and not without pain, and the hospital fire was a crucial blow to this phase. Rehabilitation was not just about the need to rebuild infrastructure and vital utilities, but social life, and people's confidence, which had been shattered. The way of life had also been changed beyond all recognition, for ever.

Islanders were not getting together like they had before the war, people were staying at home, and it was almost impossible to go down to the local pubs and have a drink and a chat as before.

This was because they were packed to the rafters, people were jammed in shoulder to shoulder, due in the main to the huge number of military personnel in and around the tiny town. A situation that would not change until the airport at Mount Pleasant opened in May 1985.

Upwards of 4,000 or 5,000 British service personnel were living about the city, or on floating units called 'coastels', which were moored along the shore to the east of the capital, or in huge tents and other shelters in areas around Stanley Airport.

Whilst the presence of the military was very welcome and obviously necessary, it was putting an even greater strain and stress on the limited amount of social and recreational areas and services available.

Minefields had also restricted access to sandy beaches and other areas that had been popular for picnics, walks, or the traditional berry picking.

There were two plusses about the minefields, however. Many of the peat banks were now out of bounds, ringed off by minefield fencing, and those beaches mined were now acting as a form of defence against any Argentines who might have fancied running ashore for a spot of war games.

As for me, after fronting the Insurance Department and the Shipping Agency for the Falkland Islands Company, I was then promoted to Works Manager, a hugely responsible position.

Overnight, I had accepted the responsibility for the proper care and maintenance of all the company's fixed assets in Stanley, such as dwellings, warehousing, offices, retail outlets, port facilities, fuel supply and distribution, plant and machinery.

My responsibilities also extended to the camp. I would be required to carry out some maintenance work and new buildings in those areas.

I would also be tasked with the day-to-day distribution of labour, drawn from five separate departments, a labour force for which I was now both their union representative and immediate boss. A unique situation, don't you think? It could only happen in the Falklands.

I was also required to ensure we had stocks of materials to carry out the construction of new buildings, or to implement improvements and maintenance – a stock that would be mainly ordered and drawn from a supply line 8,000 miles away in the United Kingdom. Let's face it, you could not allow your work force to get halfway through rewiring someone's dwelling, then run out of cable.

As Works Manager, I also needed a good general knowledge of several trades. I must admit I was more than a bit concerned about my total lack of knowledge in one or two disciplines in the beginning.

I was also uncomfortable about my inheritance, inasmuch as I knew my predecessor had been regarded as a bit of a 'know it all', which had resulted in a lack of, or grudging team support. So I decided to appoint a small group of people as heads of departments, people I felt I could trust, who would be willing to be part of a team concept. A team that would guide and advise me, when and wherever necessary.

The idea was very simple. Each of the men I chose would run his department but be directly responsible to me. As it turned out, all these guys were wonderfully loyal and supportive to me. Never once did they let me down, therefore I am compelled to mention who they were: Colin Goodwin (Garage), Montana Short (Painting & Decorating), Orlando Almonacid (Carpentry & Shipwright works), Joe Booth (Electrical) and Billy Morrison (Stevedoring and general labour).

Billy, if you recall, had been my boss in the past, and had put great faith in me. It was now my turn to repay him.

To complete the changes, I also introduced an end-of-week meeting between the heads, so that we could get together to chat about the week's achievements, or failures, future projects and timescales, and of course any labour concerns and requests.

I was also responsible for hiring and firing of the labour force in this area, but I never employed anyone without consulting the head of department (and, of course, the General Manager).

My move to create these new and very simple ideas had three immediate and very positive results for me. Firstly, I was not going to be alone in carrying the load of responsibility. Secondly, I had brought the labour force onside. And finally, I could draw off the knowledge and skills from top-class staff, in their various trades.

There was one other thing that I was very conscious of. I knew from the very beginning of my new role in the company that I had no option but to be a firm and fair boss.

I made it clear that I would not tolerate the consumption of alcohol at work. This might sound bloody obvious to anyone, but believe me, when I became Works Manager it was rife and pretty much out of control in one area in particular.

The significant difference between me and all the other previous Works Managers was that I had been there, and done it. I knew what went on when it was raining, or when certain ships were being discharged. I had seen the pilfering first hand, I not only knew that it happened, but to whom it happened too.

I had come up through the ranks, I was aware of all the party tricks, hidey holes, the job dodgers, therefore I knew one or two of the guys would test my new authority. It was so bloody predictable.

When you move on in life, there is always someone who is standing still in theirs, who thinks you should spend more time thinking about where you have come from, rather than where you might be going to.

So, one day, sure enough, the inevitable happened. Two chaps decided to take no heed of my first circular, which stated if anyone were caught drinking, or found drunk at work, they would be fired instantly.

The first chap, unfortunately, was an old school mate. I had gone to one of the sheds where we stored bales of wool. The gang were loading wool on to a forklift truck and then on to trailers, and eventually on a ship.

I walked into the shed, and almost immediately the old school friend and former workmate walked up to me. He was reeking of booze and clearly unstable on his feet. A few words were said and I was left with no choice but to fire him. I say I had no choice; if I had not done anything, I would have been seen as weak and also not a man of my word, which would have resulted in losing their respect and my authority.

The second guy was that drunk, that when I opened the door of the Land Rover he was sitting in, he actually fell out of the vehicle. I had come across him trying to back it into a space half its width.

I was never fool enough to kid myself that I would stamp out the practice of drinking at work altogether, because the few left doing it went underground, and they were never going to be shopped by their mates. Which, to be honest, was fine by me. But I am sure that I greatly reduced the practice, and as a result, I made the workplace a much safer environment. Furthermore, the employees were also left in no doubt as to who was boss.

During one winter, a Managing Director of the company, David Britton, was down in Stanley, whilst the regular Stanley Manager, Terry Spruce, was back in the United Kingdom on several months' leave.

I got on with David very well; he had the qualities in a man that I appreciate, right up front, prepared to make a decision and stand by it, never one to blame someone else.

We had also been combatants in labour relations between the trade union and the company, but we had a respect for each other's position, and left it at that.

Anyway, one day I was walking down the office corridor with him, when out of the blue he said, 'I am very happy with your contribution to the company, Terry. You seem to be enjoying your responsibilities.' (In fact, I think I became a bit of a workaholic, I was always at work.)

The corridor was too narrow for two people to walk side-by-side, so I walked slightly behind him. 'Yes, I love it here,' I said. 'I enjoy my work and the company has always treated me well.' They had, and right up to the day I left, they continued to do so.

'Well,' he said, 'I think you are in pole position to be the next General Manager of this establishment.' Now what David was saying was quite something, a Falkland Islander had never been appointed the Manager of the Falkland Islands Company. Okay, one or two, perhaps, might have stood in for a very short period, but I was being told that I was in pole position to make company history.

I said, 'I am very grateful for your consideration, but I have no intention of waiting for Terry Spruce to be knocked over by a bus before I become the Manager of the FIC.' Then I went on, 'I also do not intend to draw my pension from the company. When the time is right, I will depart the firm and start my own business.'

He asked, 'What will you do?'

Again I replied honestly, 'I don't know yet, but I will when the time comes.'

Deciding not to press me any further, he said, 'Okay. Well, let's wait and see what happens. In the meantime, remember what I have just said to you.

I thanked him, not so much for his kind consideration, but more the way he took my reaction to it.

As we worked side-by-side that winter, David taught me many good management practices, and how to conduct oneself in business. He was a stickler for accuracy, punctuality and detail. I quickly learnt that behind that 'no nonsense' image was a generous, warm and caring man, who simply did not care for fools and vagabonds. The lads in the local trade union had nicknamed him 'Electric Whiskers' because of his very pronounced moustache. I think he took his nickname as a compliment, because it made him out to be a bit of an action man, which in fact was exactly what he was. I got to know him very well, and because of that, I think I saw him quite differently than the union boys.

Once, whilst I was head of the trade union and Works Manager of the company, he said to me, in private, of course, 'You make sure your union guys give me 6½ hours' work a day, and I'll make sure I give them 8 hours' pay.'

I knew exactly what he meant. I also knew he would. What troubled me was, I was not sure if I could deliver. I was confident enough about the FIC employees, but other working areas were not renowned for their energy, nor a vast amount of productivity – their working environments were not conducive to either. But I never told him that.

Things have changed in the workplace since I was involved in the trade union 17 years ago, as one might expect, but I would like to make one other point regarding matters relating to labour relations.

Many employers and authorities have allowed themselves to be fooled that to pay a minimum salary is cost-effective. Nothing could be further from the reality.

Falklands labour practice history clearly shows, where employers pay a negotiated salary, often many times above the minimum agreed hourly rate, geared entirely to productivity levels agreed over a specified period of time, it makes for a positive working environment, and both the employer and employee are happy.

Contract shearing in the camp, stevedoring with the FIC and production of crushed stone with FIG are excellent examples of my case.

Both sides are content because the employer gets the job done within a time frame he desires, and at a cost he can pretty accurately budget.

The employee is happy because of job satisfaction via the incentive scheme, which boosts his earning capability.

43

Controversy and Politics
(I publicly call my politicians 'dumb and stupid')

Just before leaving the UK in November 1985, I had been interviewed by an Argentine television crew headed by a chap called Ronnie Boyd. He had interviewed the likes of Alastair Cameron, who was the Falkland Islands Government Representative in London, and Lord Shackleton about the Falklands situation since the war, and what were the hopes and aspirations of Islanders for the future.

The interview was hardly earth-shattering, until I was asked by the interviewer what I thought about the Islands Legislative Council's refusal to approve a request from him, and his crew, to go and visit the Falklands. Their intentions were to shoot footage and interview elected councillors and other members of the Islands' community, primarily to put together a TV programme for Argentine consumption, about Islanders' reactions to current Argentine relations, and feelings about the future.

My reply was brutally honest. I said that I thought the decision was dumb and stupid.

When I returned home, I was interviewed by Patrick Watts on the local radio. He was only too eager to ask me to repeat what I had said in the interview with Boyd in London, and without hesitation, I duly obliged.

'Why do you say that?' he asked. I replied by saying, that in my opinion, I firmly believed that a golden opportunity had been missed by the councillors, and others, to express their real feelings about a highly sensitive situation. Furthermore, had they approved the visit, it would have been a wonderful chance to allow Boyd and his crew to see first hand, how British we all were.

I suppose I had pushed councillors into a corner a little bit and as a result they tried to rubbish my comments by lamely saying that Boyd would just have doctored a documentary to demonstrate something pro-Argentina.

Interestingly, a day or two later, I was at a cocktail party at Government House, when by chance, I overheard one very senior government official say to His Excellency the Governor, 'What did you think of Betts's comments?'

The Governor's reply was, 'It needed to be said, but perhaps in a different manner.'

I moved on with my gin and tonic, most satisfied.

What I hadn't reckoned on, was that I would be part of the Legislative Council 14 months later, despite missing out in the General Election of 1985.

However, a by-election was called on 20 January 1987, because Lewis Clifton had surrendered his Stanley seat to take up the very important post of the Falkland Islands Government representative in the London office.

This time, I decided to stand as my own man. I would be challenged by the local Judge and a female resident. When the votes were counted, I had polled more votes than the other two candidates put together, a most satisfying and resounding victory.

To be honest, I don't think I campaigned on any particular issues to win so handsomely, but I do recall making an original slogan: 'It is time to shed our colonial cloth and create our own identity.' I was deadly serious, but I think few realised what a radical statement I was making.

I was particularly pleased that I had beaten one of my opponents so resoundingly, because this person would often stop me in the street, then say that I had only achieved things in life because I was a Freemason. The individual never believed it had anything to do with natural ability or burning ambition.

I was a member of the Falkland Club, which many in the community, and this person in particular, wrongly assumed was a Freemasons' lodge.

My victory was sweet success at a time I needed a little uplifting. After thirteen and a half years of marriage (a great deal of it memorable), Melody and I went our separate ways. She had been a good mother and wife, and we all know that everyone makes mistakes from time to time.

Mine was that I should have made much more of an effort to save the marriage. It was a great shame, and life became especially difficult for Severine, who would spend too many hours at home alone, on a computer, whilst I wallowed away in self-pity and drenched my brain with Johnnie Walker whisky – a grave error of judgement.

Once elected to Government, I was pretty sure about two things. The first was that I knew there would not be any welcoming party from my new political colleagues because of my previous comments about them. The second was that it was almost certain I would be invited by them to clash with my brother at some political forum.

I thought their tiny mind game was very risky for them, and the inhabitants of the Falkland Islands. Politics is a no prisoners game, therefore if I put up a very poor show against my brother, not only would I return home a complete fool, but it would reflect very negatively on the Falklands, and worse still, quite possibly, very positively for the Argentines.

Their moment of sweet revenge came when councillors were invited by the senior FIG Administrator to select the Falkland Islands Government representatives for the all-important political forums at the United Nations General Assembly, who debated on the Falklands dispute, or the Committee of 24, who met to discuss decolonisation issues.

I was chosen, overwhelmingly, to represent the Islands at the UN General Assembly, not because of individual political aptitude. No, simply because my brother Alec had been ever present at the UN since his departure from the Falklands, immediately after the Falklands War during which, he vigorously supported the Argentine claim on the Islands.

One thing the councillors did not know, rather than being daunted by the prospect, I was actually willing it to happen.

44

*How Politics Worked in the Falklands
(with a few opinions thrown in)*

The small group of eight elected councillors was, I suppose, like any small elite club: there are some members you get on with, there are others you tolerate, just. That was to be the case for me during my time in the Legislative Council.

All sessions of the Legislative Council were held in public, in the Court and Council Chambers. In addition to the elected councillors, the other members present at a full session included the Governor as the President, and the Commander of British Forces with a non-voting seat, who naturally advised the house on defence matters, the Chief Executive, as head of administration, the Attorney General and the Financial Secretary, who presented the Annual Budget to the house, usually around May. The Clerk of Councils completed the number.

The structure, and procedure, has been much improved in the last year or so. The Governor no longer presides over the sessions of Legislative Council, he has been replaced by a 'Speaker of the House', who, significantly, is a native-born Islander.

In the writer's opinion, this very important change is a huge step in the right direction to eventual full autonomy for the Falkland Islanders (shedding that colony cloth I had been talking about 18 years earlier).

I recall my first Legislative Council session fairly well. I was not the slightest bit nervous about making my debut public appearance. Why should I have been? I had been jumping up and down in front of the public, singing songs in rock bands for years. I had done many interviews on television and radio, I had even given live sports commentaries on radio, in front of watching spectators, so standing up in the Court and Council Chambers to speak publicly was not going to have my knees knocking.

Besides, within this small team of power, I had two cousins, two ex-school mates, and a former drummer of the several rock groups.

Unfortunately, Falklands politicians were all too often involved in issues that should have been handled by a town council, which had somewhat controversially been abolished in the early 1970s. Therefore, one of the first issues I got my teeth into was the repositioning of the local refuse tip. This appalling eyesore had been a huge environmental blunder; it had inexplicably been sited to the west end of the town after the Falklands War.

The prevailing westerly winds resulted in thick smoke and debris from the many fires drifting towards the populated area, along with the stench from rotten meat and so on. The winds would also lift paper and plastic, flattening them against the galvanised wire fencing, creating an appalling sight.

The refuse dump itself had become a very popular hunting venue with some members of the public, who scavenged for fruit and vegetables, timber, vehicle spares and even porn magazines, all being dumped by the truckload when the military were massed to the east of Stanley.

I would eventually be successful in assisting to get the public nuisance closed, and a new site opened, which is still operational today on the south coast, in an area called Eliza Cove, far enough away from the city to be out of sight, and far less offensive to the public. But I doubt if it is that much more environmentally friendly.

Even when there were major political issues to be dealt with, elected representatives probably only played bit parts in the decision-making. The three elected Executive Councillors would certainly have been much more involved than the other five. But even then, all the papers for the Executive Council and the Legislature as a whole would have been drafted up, with a summary and a recommendation included, by a civil servant, usually on an extremely over-generous salary and possibly with only a short-term commitment to the Falklands.

One of the most significant political issues for the Legislative Council of 1987 was the need to set up a legal structure for the new fishing regime, which would need to include guidelines for management and control, whilst containing the vital economic components, such as levelling licence fees, that would be beneficial to the Islands economy and attractive to the international fishing vessel owners.

Before going any further, I should point out that the Falkland Islands have their own laws, and any amendments to those laws, or the introduction of any new laws, can only come into force in the following manner.

Firstly, any amendment or any new law/s proposed would be framed by the Islands Attorney General (a new kid on the block in terms of administrative and political influence), who would almost certainly seek the advice of the UK Foreign Office legal adviser.

Once he had received the appropriate nod and a wink from his learned friend, he would place his draft legislation before the Governor of the Islands, the Secretary of State and then the Falkland Islands Executive and Legislative Councils.

Upon the final drafts being approved at Executive Council level, they would then be presented before the Legislative Council. If passed in a full session of the House, they would finally be laid before the Secretary of State, for signature (hopefully).

Bloody long-winded process, don't you think? Oh, and just for good measure, if there was no Falklands law in place to cover a given need, UK law was often adopted.

I certainly cannot claim any personal involvement that swung anything one way or the other on the legal aspects of the Falklands Fishery, but I would be very much involved with licence allocations later in the year. Licence awards, for the first season of 1988, contributed handsomely to the Falkland Islands revenue, which leapt from about 4 million to nearly 40 million overnight. This was easily the biggest economic transformation in the Islands history. The accolades for all this newfound wealth must belong to Lord Shackleton. For it was he, and his team, who had recommended the exploitation of the Falklands fish stocks as a revenue earner for the Falkland Islands in his two economic reports.

It was a great pity that the Falklands War was not enough to prompt the British Conservative Government into action on this lucrative potential then. In fact, it took them another four years before they took any positive action, and even then, probably only because they had received a short sharp poke in the ribs.

It was the signing of a fishing agreement between Argentina,

Russia and Bulgaria in 1986, to fish in the southwest Atlantic, which had the effect of enforcing fishing restrictions within the Argentine 200-mile Exclusive Economic Zone (EEZ), that forced the British Government's hand. Subsequently, on 29 October 1986, they announced the introduction of a 150-mile Falkland Islands Interim Conservation and Management Zone (FICZ) around the Falklands. This basically covered the same area as the Falkland Islands Protection Zone (FIPZ) introduced in September 1982. The one significant difference was a pronounced, and specified, median line to the southwest of the zone.

At the same time the British Government also announced that they reserved the right to extend the FICZ to 200 miles, in accordance with the 1982 United Nations Law-of-the-Sea Convention, and just for good measure, they declared their right to exclusive jurisdiction over the Falklands Continental Shelf.

This action pissed the Argentines off immensely, and they encouraged their neighbours in Latin America to force Britain to hold bilateral talks with Argentina on fisheries and other issues.

The terms set out in the declaration of the new FICZ made it clear to all, that the new regulated fishery would be managed, controlled and financed by the Falkland Islands Government, under the laws of the Falkland Islands. In my opinion, this decision was politically very significant because it gave the Islands Government some international political standing.

Easily the most significant internal political change in the Falklands for 152 years took place in 1985. This was when the British Parliament announced the Falkland Islands' first constitution, its first political handbook, if you like.

Some of the new internal political rules were dramatic. For the first time, all members of the House would need to be elected; no longer could anyone be appointed as a member to Executive or Legislative Council because they were a buddy of the Governor.

Thus, when Clifton, Blake (A.T.), Blake (L.G.), Edwards, Cheek, Goss, Lee and Keenleyside were returned to office in the General Election of October 1985, they were the first members of a fully elected House in Falkland Islands political history. A landmark indeed.

Another issue of immense importance, written in the constitution, was the principle of the right to self-determination. The inclusion of this fundamental right was a major political coup for councillors of the Falkland Islands at the time.

I find it rather odd, and highly hypocritical of the United Nations, that whilst this principle is enshrined in their own charter, they cannot see fit to grant it to the inhabitants of the Falkland Islands.

The Argentines have a somewhat odd perception of the issue. They claim self-determination should not apply to Falkland Islanders, because they consider we are a transient, or impermanent, population, thus not a 'people'. Quite stupid sometimes, those Argentines. It is for this reason that I have gone on at some length in this book to detail my family roots in the Falklands. Once anyone understands this, they would have to agree that the Argentines stand on very thin ice indeed.

Nineteen years on, there has been some further fine-tuning to the constitution and fifteen years from now, I suspect still more changes will be required to the structure for political process, as one should expect with an ever-changing situation, economically, commercially, environmentally and politically, coupled with a growing self-belief and desire to run the day-to-day affairs of the Falkland Islands for ourselves, just as it should be.

But whatever might happen, it was the councillors of 1985 who provided us with the basic tools to build our house for the future. In time a Constitutional Day should be put into the Falklands calendar.

In several passages of this book, I deliberately insert my personal viewpoints on sensitive issues covering politics, economics, labour relations, the public sector and many other things relating to the well-being of my homeland and its many inhabitants.

I accept that some of my ideas might cause considerable controversy; but when you are attempting to shake a few apples out of the tree, this is inevitable.

With this in mind, I suggest that it cannot be sensible any longer for the Falklands to maintain the position of Governor as head of the governmental structure. The whole idea of a people being run under a kind of dictatorship (actual or not), which the position of Governor has got to imply (even if not practised), as defined in our own constitution and laws, must smell of colonialism.

It is surely a situation that will not be tolerated in international politics, even if others who decry colonialism operate control of its people under a very thin veil, which they disguise as democracy.

We Falkland Islanders must be looking towards a political structure that is tailor-made for our Islands and our inhabitants, which at the same time impresses upon the international political arenas that we are indeed serious about self-determination and, perhaps even more importantly, self-governance of our own territory.

The latter, I would agree, is a very debatable subject within itself, simply because there may well be many variations of a theme.

Perhaps now is the appropriate moment for the birth of innovative and ground-breaking political concepts.

By this I mean the power and influence to be entrusted to Islanders, natives or adopted Falkland Islanders, who hold the reins of authority and power, be it in the political structure, or the administration framework set up to support it, be they Premiers, Chief Executives, Ministers for Transport, or whatever grand titles we wish to bestow on them.

The idea being that we begin to dismantle the old rat-infested regime, brick by brick, and replace it, also brick by brick, with a comfortable and highly commendable new home, suited for all committed Islanders to live in.

Anyone wishing to do business, or discuss matters concerning the Falklands, has to do so with a short-term overseas contractor, barely able to remember where Fox Bay is, as head of our administration. This image is hardly conducive to impressing upon strangers around the world that we Islanders actually run our own day-to-day administrative affairs, let alone convincing them that we run the Government.

Therefore I am totally convinced that there is no sane reason on earth why the Chief Executive, the head of administration, should not be a Falkland Islander.

It is also nonsensical to believe, or expect, that a person on a three-year contract from overseas can have a true grasp of what the Falklands' needs are in the short term, let alone the medium to longer outlook, on many wide-ranging and ever changing issues.

No, it must make sense for a Falkland Islander to head the administration. The individual simply has to be far more acceptable to the populace, and one would assume, much more accountable also. But perhaps most important of all, as an Islander, they would surely be much more in touch with local affairs and the community, and certainly have nowhere to hide.

I must make it crystal clear that my comments are not an attack on those who have served in the post in the past, nor the person who fills the seat now, but the situation is unacceptable, and Islanders should demand change.

My word, I enjoyed that little outburst. Now back to how Government worked. From my experience, one of the most important tasks for councillors each year in office was the budget session of Legislative Council.

Once the draft budget had gone through a couple of preliminary stages, it would be presented to the Legislative Council in formal session by the Financial Secretary. At this stage elected representatives rarely raised any significant issue; this was always reserved for Select Committee.

Legislative Council would go into Select Committee (secret session, if you like) to debate the budget, following an adjournment of the Legislative Council.

At this stage of legislative proceedings, the Governor, Attorney General and Commander of British Forces would drop out of the action.

Select Committee would be chaired by the Chief Executive, but it is really the Financial Secretary's playhouse. It is also here that he finds out for the first time what elected representatives really think of his proposed budget and what they are desirous of deleting or inserting.

Before the influx of fishing licence revenue, the Financial Secretary invariably had a few favourite fiscal lollipops to suck on, as he tweaked away to ensure a balanced budget. Often it was annoying little things, such as a penny increase on postage, hiking up Government House rentals, personal taxation and import duty on alcohol and cigarettes.

To my knowledge, the Falklands has never had Value Added Tax, and I hope it may never be necessary.

One of the main problems with the Financial Secretary's prudent budget in these times was that it completely lacked imagination. There were never any ideas coming forward on how to stimulate or create growth in the economy. In reality, the budget was just a piece of administrative bookkeeping. A year later, the Financial Secretary always had the pleasure of standing up in Legislative Council with a smile on his face, to report to the House that an unexpected windfall from one source or another had been forthcoming, therefore he was delighted to announce that the previous year's budget had miraculously balanced out. He would never admit to a surplus; if there happened to be one, he would hold his breath, hoping no one would notice, and slip it into the national reserves.

This ad hoc accountancy practice made it bloody difficult to explain and justify to the electorate.

Anyway, for a couple of days elected councillors pored over the Draft Estimates, as the Government's fiscal document was drawn up into public sector departmental heads, and sub-heads, listing such items as approved and actual expenditure for the previous year, while forecasting and proposing expenditure for the coming year. This covered a whole range of expenditure items, which varied depending upon departments, such as Aviation or the Hospital, Secretarial or Customs.

I seem to recall that the Public Works Department was the most expensive department to operate, and generated the largest deficit.

The problem with the revenue generated by nearly all departments within the structure, up to 1986 at least, was that it was usually earned from one original source and they simply invoiced one another for services or procurements provided. Few ever generated 'new money'; a notable exception, perhaps, was the Customs & Harbour Department.

During Select Committee sessions, departmental heads were called in to present, and often defend, their department's performance of the year, and the expenditure requests for the forthcoming term in front of an eager, or rather irritated, group of councillors, depending on what time of the day you went in. It seemed to me that they always had the most convincing case for a new vehicle or a couple of additional staff.

They were, if nothing else, past masters at pulling the wool over councillors' eyes.

Then there was the unexpected: a major catastrophe, such as the hospital fire. A case would be put up for increased manpower and/or equipment, so as to avoid a similar incident. Councillors would be putting their heads on the block not to take these recommendations seriously and provide the funds. To accommodate this type of extraordinary expenditure, there would be a need to draw down from a special reserve fund.

Much time was spent haggling on small numbers, not enough on the larger ones – not that there were many big numbers in a £4 million budget.

The situation changed dramatically the following year, as we sat in Select Committee with something like £40 million forecast to be spurting into the revenue tank, a monumental leap to £20,000 per capita, and with everyone, from the trade union to departmental heads shouting, 'I want some of that.'

With hindsight, it is very debatable if we coped very well with that pressure, but I do know that councillors were not alone. Administration, even the electorate themselves, were 'cash shocked' as the economy exploded, changing everyone's way of life overnight. No one had prepared in any quarter for the vast sums and the knock-on effects, be they good or bad, and they were not all good.

From experience and observation up to the year I left the Falklands, I have drawn the following conclusion about the administrative part of FIG: it has been guilty in the past of acting as though it was the only business in town.

Which, as I am sure you will be aware, is the philosophy of socialist states. We also know what appalling track records they have.

I would not think the Falkland Islands Government, or its Administration, would wish to be considered as running a socialist state, but if it wishes to avoid any further misunderstanding, I believe the Government should simply play a role in setting out the ground rules which are sensible, reasonable and conducive for commerce, then let the commercial people get on with running the businesses.

This new, and much healthier, approach would be much more cost-effective, far less labour-intensive, and much more productive for the Falkland Islands Government, hence the people it represents.

Sure, I hear the screams from the public sector workforce, terrified of the word 'privatisation'. This labour group has now been allowed to become the largest and most influential in town, due entirely to Government's willingness to overload departments with staff. Several heads of department have been permitted to build little empires, whilst they swallow up just short of half the national income on salaries alone, not including pension or operational costs. Jesus Christ, you don't need to be a rocket scientist to understand that in economic terms this is unsustainable.

The FIG estimates scream out for cost-cutting. They also demonstrate huge areas of Government monopolistic control in the market place, which I think curtails private sector development and sits like a heavy weight on economic development and expansion.

I am not suggesting everything is simply thrown to the wolves. Important utilities should remain within Government control, but by releasing parts of the public sector to the private sector, it should reduce the cost to the state, who are running non-profit-making, inefficient public service departments.

It is also a way to encourage the private sector to take over the responsibilities of running and offering certain services to the community, which the Government could then slip out of gracefully.

Now I might be wrong, but it is a fair bet that the main reason the private sector has not been allowed to take up more control is due entirely to the powerful Civil Service. These employees hold the belief that they have a job for life, and privatisation would disrupt this.

Local politicians try, rather lamely, to deny this philosophy, but any moves by them, or other lobby groups, such as the Chamber of Commerce, to hand over parts of Government to the private sector, get a rapid rebuff from Civil Servants, who very quickly corner their senior administrators and councillors, who then slip into a total farce on privatisation and eventual submission to the Civil Servants' wishes.

Senior administrators, because they don't like the idea in the first place (I will cite examples shortly) elected councillors, because they need votes in the next election, and they were well aware that the biggest voting power block was the Civil Service workers.

I feel it is a great shame councillors do not have the balls to go down the privatisation road. If they did, they would soon feel a great deal of satisfaction, as dozens of surplus-to-requirement overseas contractors packed their bags and winged their way off in search of another golden goose.

Privatisation would also spell the end for what I call 'the calendar watchers'. You know, those Civil Servants who amble into work at 8 a.m., and rush out again at 4.30 p.m., having spent all day checking the calendar to work out the next break for local and overseas vacations, or fretting about how much money someone in the private sector might be making.

I do have a message for these type of people; protect and sit in your nest by all means, but I tell you this, should Government go into some form of contraction because it was unable to economically sustain your every demand, it might well be that someone will shit in your nest, and you will be forced to leave it.

I vividly recall a FIG representative trying to impress upon the Chamber of Commerce that they had heard the organisation's plea for privatising certain parts of the public sector, by offering funeral services as a test case. This was basically the making of coffins and providing very basic funeral arrangements. Who was ever going to make a viable business out of 20 deaths a year? That just about summed up Government's thinking about commercial practice. The whole thing was farcical, and Government knew it. However, they went through the motions, so they could then say to the private sector, 'No one wants privatisation. We offered it and no one responded.'

On another occasion, two or three years later, the Falkland Islands Government approached the matter once again, again as a result of pressure from the Chamber of Commerce.

I knew they were no more sincere now than before. It was obvious they had been rattled by the Civil Service workers, because FIG would only look at possible sectors being privatised if they were taken over by employees already within the departments – a kind of take-over, or buy-out, system from within. This concept closed out the existing private sector from any privatisation programme, and the Civil Servants had now been given power to veto any privatisation plans.

Therefore, I have failed to be convinced that the Government has done anything to break up some of its monopolies of assets and services, a very strange kind of behaviour considering they were always very anti the Falkland Islands Company, for the very same reasons, in the past.

It is for this reason that I feel FIG has given a lot of lip service to privatisation but to date they have shown no positive action. In fact, it might be argued quite the reverse, as over the years they have steadily got themselves more entrenched, by taking up share equity in companies or forming joint ventures of their own.

It might even be argued that in the latter exercise, they have simply permitted a licence to print money for the partner, or formed a mechanism in which FIG was simply throwing public funds away.

Overall, their actions could be argued to have resulted in the FIG becoming even more dominant and monopolistic in their fields, which might even suggest that FIG is in direct conflict with the private sector, because no competition exists.

This situation can only have the effect of further oppressing the private sector by depriving it of opportunity, as FIG continues to build an even stronger socialist-state type system. Very unhealthy in all aspects, and it cannot be conducive to encouraging new friends and investors to the Falkland Islands.

Shall we move on? It would be remiss of me to imply that the budget session was simply about departmental issues. There were, as you might expect, a multitude of things going on in the Islands, which required councillors' constant attention.

Electricity supply was badly disrupted during the war, but since then, we had renovated the old, and built a new section to the powerhouse, installed additional generation plant, erected new sub-stations, and laid many miles of new service lines.

Domestic water supply suffered a similar fate, which had required us to rebuild our treatment, storage and supply services; this project was expected to be complete by mid-1988.

The capital's road network was severely damaged; a small amount had been rebuilt, and major works would be carried out during 1988/89 financial years.

Housing was regarded as a number one priority by the Legislative Council. The housing stock in the Islands capital had been increased by 47% since 1982, but demand was heavy, residents, returning Islanders, immigrants and business personnel who were participating in our fishing industry, all required accommodation.

It was projected by the end of 1988 to the middle of 1989, that the number of houses in Stanley would have increased by a further 18% on the current figure.

Education had been supplemented by the construction of new boarding hostels in Stanley, and that year, the Islands Legislative Council approved funds of 5 million pounds to build a new secondary school complex.

It was envisaged that by the end of that year, a new office unit would have been completed for our teaching staff involved with the education of our children in the countryside.

I pointed out that education standards in the Falkland Islands were now on a par with those in the United Kingdom, with opportunity to proceed for further education and university studies.

As you can see elected Councillors had much on their plates.

45

Nominated for the United Nations
(It means I will clash with my brother, who will represent Argentina)

As I expected, after the end of the budget session, councillors nominated the Falklands Representatives to attend the United Nations debate on the Falkland Islands to be held in November of 1987. The two chosen were John Cheek, who had a lot of experience in such matters as he had attended several conferences in the past, and me.

I was delighted, although it was very hard not to show that I wasn't surprised by my colleagues' choice. To contain my inner feeling of excitement, I announced that I was flattered by their decision to trust me with such enormous responsibility and I was very grateful for the opportunity to represent my country at such a high level.

I will admit one thing: I was disappointed that my first foray into international politics would be with John. It was not a question of not liking the man; in fact, like his father Fred, he commanded a certain level of respect and trust. No, my problem with John was that I was sure I would find him to be intransigent on tactics with the Argentine representatives in New York.

I felt we needed to get amongst the Argentines, in the corridors, cafés, wherever and whenever facilities or opportunities presented themselves.

It seemed rather ludicrous to me to travel all the way to New York just to deliver a speech, as a petitioner in support of the British Government's position over the Falkland Islands. I firmly believed this notion was an awful waste of valuable time and public money and the loss of a great opportunity to do much more.

Therefore, it seemed to me it would be much better to do a little bit of ankle tapping, rattle one or two cages, whilst at the same time, showing a little bit of diplomacy and maturity, attempting to heal a few very obvious open wounds as a result of the Falklands War, as we delivered our message to them firmly, politely and clearly.

The Falkland Islanders' viewpoint on the position of the Falkland Islands extended, I believed, to much more than just sovereignty. Recognition as a native people, development of an independent economy, opening up of the Islands to international trade and communication, and the right to self-determination might do for starters.

Yes, I fancied a little bit of eyeball-to-eyeball poker playing, but I knew John would only consider such ideas as outlandish. Don't think for one moment I was not aware of the seriousness of our task; I was very conscious indeed of that.

I know you are itching to know, but I was not interested at all in what my brother's thoughts about the situation, nor was I the slightest bit perturbed by the fact that he would be representing Argentina and supporting their sovereignty claim over our Islands. To be honest, as far as I was concerned, it was quite irrelevant.

I think this was an area where some of my colleagues had created a little bit of tunnel vision for themselves, and as a consequence, became far too preoccupied and focussed on the prospect of brother versus brother at the United Nations. I can understand that there must have been some element of excitement about this quite unique event, but I think they got a bit carried away, and in so doing, lost the plot a little bit. Fortunately for them, but thankfully for the inhabitants of the Falklands, I did not.

Before I departed for New York, one or two councillors had tipped me off that John would not be interested in mixing it. They advised that he would adopt a pretty regimental approach, which would likely be, 'Get in, get on with it, and get out', whilst keeping a very low profile in the process.

I knew there was a fat chance of the latter. Too many of the world's media had become aware of the potential brotherly clash.

As far as I was concerned, Alec had made his political bed and he was going to have to lie in it. But I had made one decision: no matter how much we disagreed on politics, I would try my best to maintain a brotherly relationship outside of it.

It's simple really. Alec believes the Falkland Islands belong to Argentina, I have always strongly disagreed with him.

By now you know my personal opinion. I believe Falkland Islanders should support the British claim to our Islands at the United Nations on its justifiable merits. But I do not accept that the status quo is tenable as a long-term option. In fact, I think for all Falkland Islanders it is a very dangerous stance to even try and maintain.

When the time is right for all, it is only sensible that the Falkland Islands belong to the Falkland Islanders. It's a distant vision, but at the end of it I envisage peace for everyone who has been, or will be, involved in the political pain ahead.

Soon the waiting was over and I was winging my way to London. Just before departing the Falklands, however, one other matter of importance happened to me. I was elected to the Executive Council, by my fellow councillors.

Perhaps the simplest way to describe Executive Council is to liken it to the upper house. Three of the eight elected members of the Legislative Council (the lower house) are elected to the Executive Council for a one-year term. The elected members of Executive Council are the only members of this particular part of Falkland Islands political structure who have the right to vote on matters discussed in Executive Council session, with one notable exception. The elected members could be overruled by the Chairman, the Governor, in consultation with the Secretary of State. (See what I mean about potential dictatorship under a Governorship structure.)

Prior to the constitutional change in 1985, Executive Council consisted in the main of appointed members who could out-vote the people's elected representatives on any issue they fancied. So now I was one of three, elevated to higher order.

The flight from the Falklands to RAF Brize Norton in Oxfordshire took its usual 18 hours, with a 1½-hour pit stop in the middle of the Atlantic Ocean, at Ascension Island, to refuel the aircraft and change flight crews, all of whom were members of the Royal Air Force.

Sleep was not something I ever got much of on those very long-haul flights from the Falklands, so I arrived in England pretty tired, but there was little time for rest. Once through Customs, it was into an awaiting car and off to London, where we checked into a hotel, took a quick shower and changed clothes, before going to the Falkland Islands Government office at 29 Tufton Street.

Once there, we immediately began to discuss various topical issues with the London based representative, Mr Lewis Clifton.

Lewis was a workaholic and 110% committed to the cause. Thus he had not left a stone unturned to maximise the use of our time in the city – meetings with members of the Foreign and Commonwealth Office, across-the-board media exposure, social gatherings, etc. – whatever was deemed essential in promoting the Falkland Islands.

It was also not unusual for Lewis to be in his office between 6 a.m. and 6.30 a.m., having scoured the UK newspapers for anything about the Falklands which might be worthy of further promotion, or in rapid need of clarification or denial. Lewis would have the article/s photocopied and down the fax line for his superior's attention the moment he arrived in his office in Stanley, awaiting further instructions, if any.

Oddly enough, it was Lewis's switch to London which had created the by-election that I won. I did not know him terribly well then, but I have often recalled the image of him hosing out excrement which the Argentines had plastered all over the Post Office in Stanley immediately after the surrender.

I would get to like and respect him very much. Lewis epitomised one of the new age of Falkland Islanders, one who had become confident of the future, because of the Islands' anticipated wealth from fishing, an individual who had been given a little bit of power and influence and had a burning desire to represent first and foremost the interests of the Falkland Islands and their inhabitants. Many people have had responsibility for the Falkland Islands in an office in London over the last 150 years, before the Falklands opened its own office doors in 1983. But very few would have had the interests of the Falkland Islanders foremost in their minds.

There have been, and continue to be, many outstanding people who do not, or have not, had any official responsibility to the Falkland Islands and their people, but they have, nonetheless, been so solid in their support for us that without them, we would never be where we are today.

I must say, before flying off to the United States, I was well satisfied with the rearrangements that had been made to my passport. The document had been quite impressively redecorated on one of the inner pages, which now boldly displayed in bright red lettering at the top 'OFFICIAL'.

Suddenly my mind began to drift back in time, to when I was lying, so ill, in my bed in the Victory Bar 30 years ago, the time when I saw the image of a man's face poking itself around the corner of a fluffy white cloud, and heard a voice from the skies saying, 'Not yet, not yet. You have things to do.'

46

*New York, Brothers Clash
(and a tough time over Falkland fishing licences)*

The British Airways flight across the Atlantic from Heathrow to New York was fantastic, and all the little benefits of flying other than economy class were most appreciated.

But pleasure turned to despair whilst making our approach into J.F.K. airport. It was snowing, in fact, it was a bloody whiteout, and I began to shit myself. I was the world's worst airline passenger; any slight bump and I would be rigid in my seat, gripping the arms with white-knuckled hands.

Somehow the pilot made a perfect landing in what was most definitely zero visibility, and I started to relax once again.

Quite unexpectedly a bit of drama was about to unfold, as our transport pulled up outside a hotel entrance. Doors were opened, luggage gathered, and we made our way directly into the foyer of the Tudor Hotel, which was on Second Avenue and Forty-Second Street.

I naturally assumed it was our hotel. John was a seasoned traveller and I suppose I leaned on him a bit for travel awareness, especially in New York, where I had never been in my life before. But as soon as I went up to the reception desk, chaos and confusion began to break out.

As I handed my passport over to the chap at the desk, he looked at me and smiled, then he started to chat to me in Spanish. Then he handed back my passport in a rather jovial fashion, and said, 'Señor Betts, Señor Betts, *habitacion tres cero cuatro.*'

I shrugged my shoulders, and turned to John. 'I think he thinks I'm Alec, and if we are not in the wrong hotel then I'm a bloody Argie.'

By now, John was wide-eyed and standing rigid by the hotel lifts. Suddenly the doors opened, and out stepped my brother and a Colonel Balcarce, who was a representative of the Argentine Foreign Ministry.

John paled slightly, and needed no further convincing that we were indeed in the wrong hotel. Bags were rapidly gathered together, a car was called, and in no time at all we were being loaded into a vehicle and taken away to where we should have gone in the first place, which was a hotel in Lexington Avenue, on the corner of Fifty-Fourth Street.

Check-in was a far less exciting affair, but no sooner had I got to my bedroom and thrown my suitcase on to the bed than the telephone began to ring.

The caller turned out to be a Victoria Graham of the BBC, who wanted to interview me about my reasons for being in New York and my pending clash with Alec. Jokingly I said, 'You're too late, we've already clashed.'

Rather excitedly she said, 'What do you mean?' I went on to explain to her what had happened at the Tudor Hotel.

'I know,' she said.

Startled by her comment, I said, 'Jesus, news gets around faster in New York than it does in Stanley.' She laughed, and then told me she had been speaking to Alec, to ask him if he would agree to an interview. That was why she was calling me, to see if I would oblige.

'Sure,' I said, 'but I'm a bit tired. When and where have you got in mind?'

'What about thirty minutes?' she said.

Finally it was agreed that I would meet them two hours later, at the United Nations Building.

So much for low profile. The press had wasted no time in getting the brother battle saga into motion.

Unsure about how to get to the UN, I called John and told him what had been arranged. It was an error, in hindsight, because it got him unnecessarily concerned, and he insisted on joining me.

I had gathered that if his company was wanted, he would have been asked by the interviewer. As it turned out, when we got to the interview room, he got rather unceremoniously turned away and was invited to go and sip coffee somewhere else.

As John and I reached the main gates of the UN, and reported to a security guard, I looked across the street, and thought someone was waving at me. I began to feel, like Crocodile

Dundee, Jesus, these Americans are bloody friendly. As the figure got closer, I could still not make out who it was, but whoever it was, they still kept waving at me. Finally, as the man was halfway across the road, I could see for the first time that it was Alec. Even though I had seen him briefly at the Tudor Hotel, it was only now that I noticed his hair was completely grey.

It then flashed through my mind that the last time I had really seen him, he had dark brown hair, and that was when we parted at the top of Davis Street in June 1982, a week after the Falklands War, after I had asked him if he was an Argentine spy.

As soon as he reached me, we shook hands, but the atmosphere got rather chilly instantly. Alec offered his hand to John, but he refused to reciprocate and turned his back.

Fortunately, there was little time to dwell on the matter, because Victoria Graham appeared at the gate and we were led off to the UN building.

I was surprised by the size of the room in which we were going to carry out our historical interview. It was so tiny that we were virtually sitting in one another's laps.

Before the interview began Alec offered me a copy of his new book. I looked at it, leafed through some pages, then handed it back to him, replying rather coldly, 'It's not much use to me, I don't understand Spanish.'

I could tell I had offended him by my response. Pausing for a moment, he offered it to me again and asked me if I would take it back to the Islands and give it to some friends there. I readily agreed.

By the way, whenever Alec and I are discussing the Falklands, he always refers to them as the 'Islands', a kind of neutral and general title for what he now considers are 'Las Malvinas'. However, I am far less gracious to him, I always say the Falkland Islands.

Once Victoria had dispensed with a little bit of small talk and satisfied herself that we brothers were not going to trade blows with each other, we prepared for the interview.

The questions raised were pretty predictable: the war, what did we do during it? What was it like now to be in opposing camps, with totally different political views on the Falklands? Could we ever be like normal brothers again? etc., etc.

I also remember that there were moments of extreme tension between Alec and me, and often strong verbal confrontation. I was particularly aggressive to him in response to anything he might have said in favour of the Argentines' claim over the Falklands.

When Alec suggested that the Argentines had a strong legal and historical claim to the Falklands, I implied that if any whiz-kid lawyer representing Argentina had a strong legal case, they would have been off to the international courts years ago, so bollocks on that count. And if Argentina was making a case on some crazed notion of inheritance from a Spanish viceroyalty, then double bollocks on that count.

Granted, my behaviour was far removed from diplomacy, but it was mighty effective. It even made the interviewer blink once or twice.

Once Victoria Graham terminated the interview, and microphones were turned off, Alec began to get emotional. After a while we shook hands again and went our separate ways.

Whilst in New York, I would have to deal with another highly sensitive political issue. Now that I had been elected to Executive Council, one of the many responsibilities of this committee was to approve the allocation of fishing licences for the first season of 1988, the second commercial fishing year.

I remember receiving telephone calls at my hotel from the Chief Executive, who was communicating with me from London, and Tony Blake on his farm at Little Chartres in West Falklands.

I recall taking one of these calls whilst in the shower and I also remember two issues above all others. The first was the question of the number of licences to be awarded to two Spanish organisations, ASPE and ANAMER. I knew nothing about either – probably just as well. The number of licences involved was 16, so because I was totally unbiased, I naturally thought it reasonable that it should be 8 apiece.

This seemed to give some people, including the Foreign Office, apparently, a lot of problems. My suggestion therefore was considered inappropriate and unhelpful. The final recommendation to FIG by the influential powers was 15–1 in favour of ANAMER. I never knew why.

The second issue regarding licence allocation was not only very important, but also a highly sensitive and historical political matter for me. Sensitive, because it involved my colleague down the corridor, who was a 50% shareholder of one of the first ever locally owned registered Falkland Islands fishing companies, called Fortuna.

The local directors of Fortuna had turned more than a few heads in the local community, but especially in the FIG administration and the Foreign Office in London. For authorities in both hemispheres Fortuna was a bit of a fly in the ointment.

When the Falkland Fishery was opened, officials and authorities did not envisage that Falkland Islanders would form their own companies for the purpose of being involved in the fishery, dear me no, that was not the idea at all.

The Falkland Islands Government adopted a policy of forming joint ventures with whomever they fancied, with a considerable guiding and influential hand from the Foreign and Commonwealth Office, and one or two others outside the Falklands whose intentions might have been just a little bit questionable.

However, from the telephone conversations with the Chief Executive, it was clear authorities were greatly troubled by Fortuna's participation in the licensing round and that much debate had ebbed and flowed as to whether to grant licences or not to the local company.

As was usual in this situation, a little bit of covering one's ass was required, and the safest and surest way to ensure this was to test the opinions of a couple of Falkland Islands elected representatives, namely, Tony Blake and myself.

I can tell you this, if Tony and I had said no licences, that would have been the outcome, because that was exactly what they wanted to hear. But Tony and I were adamant; Islanders simply had to be permitted to participate in an industry that was going to exploit some of the Falklands' natural resources. Not to support Islanders would have been an act of treachery. It would also have sent out all the wrong signals to potential foreign partners, thus almost certainly driving home the death nail for any future hopes of Islanders wishing to carry out a commercial practice in the fishery.

Although stopping short of saying so, the senior administrator was unhappy with our stance, either because of his differing personal opinion, or because of great pressure being placed upon him from higher authority. To this day I can only speculate.

We were then encouraged to think that it was too soon for local companies to participate, they should wait and could have their chance after a year or two. But once again, Tony and I would have none of it. How could we? To accept that it was too soon for local people, who had taken the courage to give up secure employment, and face the risks that go along with commerce, to share in a resource that belonged to the Falkland Islands, thus Falkland Islanders, was absolutely ludicrous.

I rather suspected that in a last-ditch effort to stop Islanders' participation with a local company entering the fishery, certain people tried hard to create a certain kind of problem about John Cheek being an Executive Councillor who was gaining favour from his political position.

The only thing I could see that John Cheek and his business partner, Stuart Wallace, had been guilty of, was that they had been one step ahead of authorities and everyone else. They had seen a commercial opportunity and gone for it.

Once it became obvious to everyone that Tony and I would not budge, then came the vexed question of the number of licences to be awarded. I vividly remember four being bounded around by officials for a while. I don't know why but Tony and I doubled the figure, and we stuck with it.

Reluctantly, everybody eventually agreed on eight licences being awarded to Fortuna via foreign vessel owners. In the Falklands Fishery, the licence was awarded to a specific vessel, not a company or vessel owner.

It is possible that Tony and I had participated in a little bit of Falkland Islands history-making that day. I am convinced, had we not stuck to our guns on that day in November 1987, the number of Falkland Islanders involved in business in the Falklands Fishery today would surely be much less, if any at all.

I remember thinking to myself with a great deal of satisfaction that, on the day Fortuna were celebrating their tenth anniversary, sometime in 1997 in Stanley, and the directors of Fortuna were paying tributes to those who had enabled them to achieve their first decade in business, I was omitted.

I was not offended – quite the opposite, in fact. I was delighted on two counts. One, that they were able to celebrate ten years in business, and two, I had missed out on some of Stuart's awful cheap booze.

But above all I am delighted that I can live with the memory of how it all actually came about.

47

The Falklands Within the United Nations Machinery (with more of my own political opinions)

Before moving on to the presentation of speeches at the UN, it might be helpful if I gave you a kind of resumé of how this whole Falklands thing began to get debated at the United Nations in the first place, and the structure and procedure which enabled Falkland Islands elected representatives to speak on behalf of the people of the Falkland Islands, as petitioners for the Government of Great Britain and Northern Ireland.

Should you get slightly confused, worry not, you will not be alone. I also accept that what I write is open to debate, argument and even correction. That said, here goes.

Surprisingly, perhaps even unfortunately, the 'Falklands Issue' probably found its way on to the United Nations agenda as a result of the UK raising the issue of Article 73 of the UN Charter, signed in San Francisco in 1945, which established that all member states that had, or assumed, the responsibility of administering overseas colonial territories whose people had not yet gained, or developed, their own Government, were obliged to submit a list of the said territories to the UN, with the object of complying with its obligation of developing and assuring self-government in the territories concerned.

The Falkland Islands figured among the 43 colonial territories included in the original list submitted by the UK.

I am sure the United Kingdom's intentions were nothing but honourable, but she must have had no idea of how many headaches and diplomatic efforts and man-hours of research and debate this listing was going to cause the UK, the Falkland Islands and Argentina in future UN sessions.

Suddenly debate began, and gained dynamic following, which resulted in the adoption of Resolution 1514 (XV), 1960, and as the Falklands issue picked up impetus, further resolutions were passed,

1654 (XVI) and 2065 (XX) in 1961 and 1965 respectively. This provided the juridical basis for the UN to study and consider means of decolonising territories and the appropriate legal path towards this aim.

There is a long and slow bureaucratic procedure before an issue will be noted and listened to by the appropriate committee.

The Falklands question fell under the Non-Self-Governing Territories issues which were considered by the Decolonisation Committee. The Committee of 24 was designed with the task of analysing, informing, debating and then recommending measures, aimed at putting into effect the principle of decolonisation on the basis of the mandate of the UN Resolution 1514 (XV).

At the beginning the Decolonisation Committee was subdivided into sub-committees, and it was Sub-committee III that was given the responsibility of dealing with issues concerning small territories.

The special committee's recommendations are passed on to the Fourth Commission of the General Assembly, and this, in its turn, reports to the Plenary of the General Assembly.

Within the Fourth Commission, we find the Third Sub-committee (sometimes called the Group of Seven) and a step further down the scale, the Decolonisation Committee or C24.

The special committee authorised petitioners to appear before the committee when dealing with the Falklands Issue. However, petitioners had to be presented by, and included in, the official delegations that represented the United Kingdom (Argentina also). They could not participate as citizens with a particular interest in the issue, but had to be considered as representatives of the Island community.

I wondered, if Falkland Islanders are not considered a people, how is it that we were permitted to speak at the UN on the subject of the Falkland Islands?

48

Warming up for Centre Stage
(Then the day of deliverance at the UN)

Once in New York, naturally John and I called upon the British Embassy, where we were greeted by the UK Ambassador to the United Nations, Sir Crispin Tickell, who was an absolute gentleman. He impressed me immensely. He was ever so calm, and spoke with such eloquent ease. This guy was hot stuff.

I might be able to stand up and fight my corner, but I do it in a very brash kind of manner. Sir Crispin could cut a piece of metal in half with his educated mind and razor-sharp tongue, as he pleasantly smiled at you. I was greatly pleased that he was on our side.

We chatted away all rather informally, whilst taking a sort of general overview of the political position and tactics that might be employed in the UN. But it was nothing like battlefield planning.

As a matter of courtesy, John and I outlined our planned speeches, not in terms of content, but more in the way of the general theme, and who would cover what.

John and I did not even sit in the same room together, at any time, to write our speeches, but we did discuss and agree between us who would cover what. We did not want to be repetitive at the UN session, therefore I was to cover how the Islanders' way of life had improved in recent years, with the considerable investments made by the FIG in a whole array of areas, also to highlight the greater participation of Islanders in the day-to-day affairs and decision-making, in the areas of commercial and economic development.

That was fine. However, any hopes that I had been harbouring about getting amongst the Argentine representatives in the corridors, to perhaps curdle a coffee or two, were soon dashed.

My colleagues back home had been correct, John was not up for that kind of thing. I had to settle for just delivering my speech. Well, almost.

Officially John and I were delivering a joint statement before the Fourth Commission of the General Assembly, as petitioners, for the Government of Great Britain and the United Kingdom. But of course we were delivering speeches, on behalf of the Falkland Islands Government and its inhabitants, not a bloody joint statement.

Once in the assembly hall, I was to get quite a surprise. I thought we would be seated with the British delegation; instead, we were shown to seats much higher up in the auditorium and quite some distance away.

I made myself comfortable in my seat, which was on the aisle, with John sitting immediately beside me. I had just got settled into my chair when I got another almighty surprise.

This time, my attention was drawn to people making their way towards me; I looked up to find my brother and a colleague with Islands connections standing almost at my side. Alec smiled and said, 'Good morning.' I was so taken aback that I did not offer a reply.

As they began to place themselves in the seats on the opposite side of the aisle to me, I began to think to myself, how bloody bizarre, and in some ways surreal, the whole thing was.

However, I pretty quickly adjusted to the unexpected. Rather than feeling daunted by the prospects of big brother sitting opposite me, as I would be making a case for the Falkland Islanders, against his adopted country, on the stage of the most significant international peacemaking forum in the world, I found it extremely stimulating.

Also the idea that Alec and I were going to make Falklands, perhaps even international, political history, was so exhilarating that I began to feel the adrenaline pumping through my body. I was on a high and raring to go.

How could I be anything else? This was one of the biggest occasions in my life. Furthermore, a lot of people back home were putting their trust and faith in me, and quite frankly, having one's brother sat just a few feet away from you, as one stood up and delivered a maiden speech (sorry statement) in such an illustrious venue, could not have been any more satisfying.

Because of my defined role that day, my speech was not designed to bring the house down, or to get members of the UN (especially Argentine) jumping up on their feet requesting that I be thrown out. My statement was merely an account of the facts, information that was intended to get across to all at the United Nations that we were a native people who must have the right to self-determination and the freedom to choose our own government, and underlining that, given these fundamental rights, the Falkland Islanders were well capable of looking after themselves and keeping their own house in order. I highlighted progress and development in as many areas as possible to support this argument, whilst also taking every opportunity to swipe the rug from underneath the Argentines' feet.

I suppose, to sum up, I was to do the spadework, whilst John followed up with the heavyweight political punches.

49

My Speech to the UN
(with supplementary comments to broaden out some points)

The first point I made was that I was addressing the committee on behalf of the inhabitants of the Falkland Islands, as their elected representative. I was making this point because, just two years earlier, prior to the Falklands 1985 constitution, some members of the Legislative and Executive Council were not elected, they were appointed by the Governor. This was clearly political progress.

The next point was to impress upon the forum that the elected representatives of the Falkland Islands were speaking on behalf of the people of the Falkland Islands, not necessarily, or just simply, offering support to the Government of the United Kingdom.

I went on to say that it was also an opportunity to enable us to provide them with an update on statistical and other factual information on the Falkland Islands. Which, from time to time, was wrongly transmitted to the assembly by those who did not wish them, or anyone else, to hear evidence from a community which they believed did not have the right to self-determination, as enshrined in the charter of the United Nations. (This was a direct attack on the Argentines, and also begged the question of the right to self-determination of Falkland Islanders by the UN itself.)

Then, having gone through the formality of introducing myself, I highlighted the general substance of my speech, which was to furnish the assembly with evidence of growth in our business and industry, population and economy, whilst also box ticking improvements in our social system and infrastructure, since the unprovoked military attack by Argentina on our islands and their inhabitants' way of life.

The comments were a double slap in the face for the Argentines. I was also breaking new ground, uncharted territory, by referring to the Falkland Islands as 'our islands'.

I went on to poke the Argentines in the ribs once more, by stating that my involvement in the day-to-day affairs of our islands, both economically and politically, was now typical of a Falkland Islander today. But only possible because we had the protection of the British forces from any would-be aggressor, to uphold our wish to mould and shape our future under our own government.

Although I was fully focussed on my speech, I did find time to shoot a quick glance at Alec and I noticed he was watching intently and appeared a little anxious.

I then proceeded to explain how we in the Islands had been steadily progressing to achieve our aims since 1982. I began by throwing more sand into the eyes of the Argentines by saying that as a result of the Argentines invading our islands, and the need for British forces to evict them, so as to restore democracy and the wish of a people to remain under a government of their own choosing, we had to spend considerable time, effort and money on rebuilding and expanding infrastructure and social services. I then outlined the progress in electricity and water supply, roads, housing and education.

I was driving home these points on education and other issues to emphasise to the Argentines in particular the dramatic changes since they were around prior to 1982. Students were now continuing school until they were 16 years old (14 in my day) with the opportunity to gain further education at college and university in the United Kingdom, all sponsored by the Falkland Islands Government.

Digressing slightly, I can proudly boast that it was during the time that I was an elected councillor that we adopted a 'MUST EDUCATE our children, at ALL COSTS' policy. The concept being that a much better educated community, not just academically, but also vocationally, would surely equip Islanders better to become leaders in trades and other skills, head our administrative departments, become businessmen and women, and also be the political leaders of the future.

I was also given the honour, by the head of education, to officially open the new Camp Education office after it had been completed. I could just imagine what some of my old schoolteachers would have thought if they had been around that day, witnessing one of their most difficult students officially opening the education department's newest facilities, whilst nervously anticipating some prank unfolding.

Well, now back to the UN. Then I went on to explain that plans were in hand to build a better internal transport system, to improve travel on both East and West Falklands. The general idea was to open up the countryside and link the very isolated camp communities by building 'all weather tracks'.

Once again it was the council I served on which took the decision to get behind the project and provide the funding.

I then got on to another aspect of communication: the Falkland Islands Government were nearing an agreement with a commercial company for the installation of a new telecommunications system for the entire Islands and internationally, which was to be financed from our own resources.

It was very important to emphasise that we were funding things ourselves. Many still believed we were totally dependent on financial assistance from the UK Government.

For the reader's benefit, the contract for telecommunications was closed with Cable and Wireless PLC. The result of the deal opened up telecommunications for the first time with the whole of the Falklands and the world. Before, it was not possible for people living in the West Falklands to call friends and family in Stanley, let alone the world.

Turning my attention to agriculture, I said the Falkland Islands had seen great changes in the past seven years. I then highlighted the statistical facts in the overall shift in land ownership in the Falkland Islands. In 1980, the Falkland Islands Company held 44%, other absentee owners 46% and Falkland Islanders 10%. In 1987 the figures made much different and more suitable reading: Falkland Islands Company 27%, other absentee owners 14% and local ownership 59%.

Once again I had to take my opportunity to drive home to the UN that it was the Falklands Government, no one else, who was bringing about a distinct and important change of land ownership in the Falklands. I also had to press home this point because in the past I was aware that we were very exposed to Argentine criticism in the UN that not only did we not have any political power, but we also did not have any meaningful land ownership. I hoped my figures would plug that hole.

I then went on to explain that the agricultural sector had seen other changes besides the sale of land; many farmers now embraced tourism as an important supplement to their income from wool, by converting unoccupied accommodation into comfortable tourist lodges.

The subject of tourist lodges allowed me to neatly slip into tourism as yet another area which had considerable potential to be a major contributor to the Islands economy, and although it was early days, I was able to report that three tourist lodges now offered a high standard of accommodation, and coupled with the sub-division of land programme, large houses on other farms were being upgraded to accommodate tourists comfortably.

I informed the UN that a tourist board had been set up, and that the manager of this board was a Falkland Islander.

The point I was making was that we were actively looking at ways to develop and expand our economy, and that Islanders were getting the opportunity to lead the way in these projects. Furthermore, I wanted to drive home to Argentina and the members of the UN that we were standing on our own two feet, and that we were determined to support ourselves financially.

Just for the record, I would become a director of the tourist board in the early days, and my hopes that the industry would provide a meaningful contribution to the Islands economy have been realised. However, it is my opinion that tourism could become an even bigger revenue earner for the Falkland Islands than fishing, with a lot of potential for the private sector to participate in the industry, providing FIG stands back and lets it.

At the moment it centres on cruise-liners making day visits. This has been extremely sensible, because it allows large numbers of visitors to come, see and spend, without the need of accommodation and other facilities for tourists wishing to stay a few days or a week. But I believe, for the tourist industry to reach its full potential, it will need to embrace large investment – which should be sourced from the private sector in the Falklands and overseas – in efficient and easy travel by air, and comfortable and hospitable accommodation. That is, good hotels and airlines.

I am convinced that a business group would consider investing in a five-star hotel providing there is an air link to fill it. For that you need good reliable airlines and at least two flights in and out of the Islands a week. This would give the tourist the option of a three/four day stopover.

The only thing FIG needs to do is reinvest some of the money generated from the industry by way of improving facilities, services and information related to the industry, and, as I repeatedly say, to lay down the ground rules, to ensure the fullest safeguards against environmental and social destruction. Then leave the businessmen and women to do the rest. There you go, back on my opinionated high horse again.

Back to my address. I then moved on to the other areas in which Falkland Islanders had been actively involved: the operation of small, medium and large businesses, ranging from bakeries to woollen mills, restaurants to building construction companies.

I was well aware that the Argentines repeatedly claimed that the commercial activity in the Islands was dominated by the Falkland Islands Company, a UK-owned business. This was, of course, correct in the past, so I was trying to demonstrate another important change.

I was able to beat the drum a little when I turned to the introduction of the Falkland Islands Interim Conservation and Management Zone, and blow rather loudly on the trumpet that, since its inception, we had been able to multiply our incoming revenue many times over, and almost overnight.

I wished also to stress that we had managed the area to the satisfaction of conservationists and fishermen alike; furthermore, such was the interest from international commercial fishing operators that demand to access our resource was heavily oversubscribed. The Falkland Islands was also moving to expand its own involvement in the fisheries, the Falkland Islands Government was now in possession of a port facility which might lend itself to onshore facilities such as cold storage and bunkering.

The fun thing about what I was doing was that the membership of the UN had not heard this stuff about the Falklands before, they had only ever listened to 'It's British, it's Argentine, decolonisation'. This was a completely new slant on things: 'We are Falkland Islanders, we can support ourselves, we have the right to self-determination', etc. I was also pretty sure that the Argentines were not very comfortable about the unorthodox manner in which I kept poking them up the rectum.

By the way, I must admit that it was debatable if we were satisfying conservationists, it was not what I really meant. I should have said marine scientists, who believed, to sustain the squid species, there was a requirement for an escapement level of 40% of the previous biomass. It was believed at the time that these targets were being achieved.

Unfortunately there were to be some miserable failures, and mistakes, in the fast and sometimes furious transformations that were taking place in the Islands.

One example of this was the FIG's joint ventures via its development agency arm, Stanley Fisheries Limited, who entered into, as it had to really, vessel ownership and charter. But we were all too inexperienced (I was a member of the Stanley Fisheries Board, also I had some minuscule involvement in these ventures, but nothing whatsoever to do with the administration and operational aspects of them).

Because the Government element of the partnership completely lacked any knowledge about commercial fishing operations and the markets, they had to depend upon their joint venture partners, who in some cases had no experience of fishing the South Atlantic or trading the fish species, which probably resulted in the wrong type of vessels, crews and equipment being purchased and used for the operations.

The consequence of these factors was that FIG caught a very heavy commercial and financial cold and were forced to bale out, several millions of pounds down on one such joint venture investment alone.

It would be harsh to criticise anyone in particular in the administration of the FIDC, Stanley Fisheries or FIG. I am sure their intensions were honourable. Perhaps there was too much pressure on them to provide a quick-fix success story. But there was, as there always is in these matters, a silver lining to the dark cloud.

More local companies were formed, and they were able to strike up their own joint ventures with foreign partners who had a wealth of professional experience in the international fishing industry, and by investing serious amounts of money, the local companies were able to demonstrate to FIG just how it could be done.

When I eventually went into business a year after the UN experience, I was fortunate enough to be involved with three local companies, over a decade, who did just that.

Just another example to support my argument that Government should stay out of business.

The port facility (FIPASS) that I referred to is a six-barge unit, locked together and secured to piles which had been driven into the sea bed of Stanley harbour. The two outside units offered berthing facilities, whilst the remainder provided surface area for discharging and loading of vessels, warehousing offices and catering facilities. Additionally, there is a roll-on, roll-off point.

The whole unit was linked to the shore by a bridge which provided easy access for transport and personnel. The structure was built in Middlesbrough for the British forces in the Islands, and once transported to the Falklands, it was put into position by the military, apparently at an all-in cost of approximately £25 million.

Interestingly when the military moved to their new base at Mount Pleasant, it became surplus to their requirements, and it was offered to the FIG, who purchased it for approximately £2.5 million. You must agree, not a bad deal, and as a member of Executive Council at that time, I naturally gave my full support to the purchase of the unit. Seventeen years on, it is still the central port facility of the Falklands capital.

As for the facility being used for fisheries support services, the idea never really took off, all rather disappointingly. But one Islands fishing company, Polar Limited (of which I was a company director), did make a pioneering capital investment there in 1989, by building a 900 cubic metre cold storage.

I wound up my speech by informing the assembly chairman that the message from the inhabitants of the Falkland Islands was this:

'They are more than happy with their present situation. Which is one of enormous growth and prosperity, under a Government of THEIR choosing. If the ISLANDS PEOPLE changed that view at anytime, THEIR elected representatives will be happy to let this committee know.'

Strangely enough, in a fairly recent e-mail I received from my brother, referring to my UN speech, he remarked, 'I think you failed to get on to the central issue of the sovereignty dispute.'

Had my brother not understood what I was doing or saying, because I had not used the word 'sovereignty' in any portion of my speech? Rather worried, I then began to wonder how many other people had not understood. Please, there are many ways to skin a cat, you know.

50

A Stroll, a Chat and Back Home
(You did well, said John. Let's buy a building, said
Lewis)

I knew once the speeches were over at the UN, I would be collared by media, and sure enough, before I could leave the assembly hall, I was approached by a lady with microphone in hand. She began shaking her head, and muttering, 'How awful, how dreadful, you must feel terrible having done what you have just done against your brother.'

Looking straight at her, I said, 'Terrible? How is that? I have just had one of the most exhilarating times of my life, representing the people of the Falkland Islands. How can that be terrible?'

She began to put her microphone in her shoulder bag, then proceeded to run off in a flood of tears, too upset to do her interview.

Once out of the main hall and into the corridor, the media were there left, right and centre. I found myself getting jostled about a bit, so I made my way towards one of the café areas to find myself a bit of space. A persistent Canadian reporter was right on my tail and I knew I wasn't going to shake him off, so I stopped and asked what he wanted. 'Like to do an interview with you and your brother,' he said, with an assured smile. Then I noticed Alec standing nearby so I agreed to get it over with.

In those days the UN had a row of telephone booths in a hallway, if memory serves me well, six or eight of them, in a slight curve. In a flash this reporter had it set up that Alec and I would do a live telephone interview to Canada. He mentioned that some German station was also involved.

I was placed in a booth at one end of the block and Alec at the other end. Once hooked up, off we went, answering questions which were being fired at us by the radio interviewer.

I must admit I loved every minute of it. I think Alec was more than a bit upset at my frankness. But this was politics not brotherly love, and the gloves were certainly off.

Following this interview, I was the target of the press in New York pretty much until I left. At times it felt like I was someone famous – perhaps I was, but I was never daunted by the attention. In fact, I think I rather enjoyed it. But I never forgot my reason for being at the United Nations, which I took deadly seriously.

I would see Alec on one or two more occasions, but the atmosphere was always tense and conversation was limited at best. We were never left alone to discuss anything in a casual or informal manner, there was always an expectant audience.

One day, just before John and I left New York, we were taking a well-earned bit of free time, going to sights of personal interest. Once we had reached the Empire State Building, we decided to go up on to the observation deck, because the weather conditions were perfect for the maximum 80-mile view in any direction.

For those of you who don't know, the Empire State Building is 1,454 feet high, and your journey to the observation deck is an experience in itself, as you whiz up in the lift to your destination in less than 60 seconds, which feels like you have left your stomach behind on the ground floor. Once at the observation level, you can take the view from inside, or step outside on to the decking and walk around, which was what we chose to do.

As we were taking in the most spectacular of views, John began smiling. 'You did a very good job indeed at the UN, Terry.'

Those few words made me feel ten feet tall. John was not a man renowned for passing out compliments.

Once back in London, we had a further meeting with the Foreign Office, just a hello, how do you do, and how did it go, type of gathering.

But John and I did take part in a very rewarding exercise. The London Representative, Lewis Clifton, alerted us that he had identified a building which had the potential to become the permanent office complex for the Falkland Islands Government, and would we like to go with him and view it. Sure enough, was the response.

The first thing that struck me was its excellent location, alongside New Scotland Yard and St James's tube station, and close enough to the FCO.

The building was another matter. It was derelict. But when you looked beyond its very poor state of repair, you could see that with a fair amount of refurbishment, it could be a wonderful place to fly the Falklands Flag, and for use as a kind of Falkland Islands embassy, right in the heart of London. This was a place that would enable us to make a pronounced statement to the world. Which was: the Falkland Islands have arrived in town, and we are alive and very much kicking.

Perception was the keyword. If the Falkland Islands were going to have a representative in London, with support staff, then they should have the best possible building to work from as they worked to deliver our message, and positively advertise the Falklands.

Everyone was doing their very best at 29 Tufton Street, but conditions were cramped and the pressures for information, meetings and presentation were increasing by the day. It was clear the present office facilities could not cope.

Like Lewis, from the very beginning, I could see the potential for the property. I was more than happy to go back to the Falklands and lend my full support to the purchase and refurbishment of the building. And would you believe it, all for the amazing price of about £1.2 million.

Within nine months, the office, appropriately called 'Falkland House' and situated at 14 Broadway, was opened for business. Since August 1989 it has been the hub for all things Falklands in London, for most of this time under the patriotic, proud, extremely loyal and highly skilful leadership of the Falklands Representative, Sukey Cameron.

It must be said that the inhabitants of the Falkland Islands have always been extremely fortunate in that they have always had representatives in London of the highest calibre. There have only been four of them since the first office opened in 1983, and they are all worthy of mention.

The first was Adrian Monk, the same chap that paid me 5p an hour for filling sheep pens on Golding Island, the late Alastair Cameron (Sukey's brother), Lewis Clifton and, from 1990, Sukey Cameron.

Before departing the London office on one occasion to head off on my 8,000 mile journey back home, Sukey asked, if she could arrange with air movements at Brize Norton to grant me some excess baggage allowance, would I be prepared to carry back some urgent medical supplies for the hospital.

Well, how could I refuse? A few moments on the telephone, and she had forced some military person to submit to her unique way of gentle persuasion, and she duly handed me a few packages to put in my baggage.

I found out later that the urgent supplies were thousands upon thousands of condoms. When I became an elected councillor, I had no idea that protecting the interests of the electorate would have to go that far. However, I hope my small contribution was put to good use.

51

*I Quit My Employers and Start My Own Company
(But I needed to choose some business partners)*

I would be invited to represent the Falkland Islands at two more very important forums in 1988, one in Blackpool in October and the other in Bermuda the following month, but first, other major events were to take place in my life.

In the early part of 1988, I made a decision of a personal nature that has probably changed my life for ever. After ten and a half years with the Falkland Islands Company, I decided now was the time to leave them, to set off in pursuit of my own business, a world of mystery and fresh challenges.

The FIC were very amicable about my departure. The manager, Terry Spruce, arranged a farewell party, and I was presented with several fine gifts, which I have appreciated and enjoyed. But the finest gift of all this company had given me, during my time in their employ, was to teach me the basic skills of management and business. They had been very good employers, and I have nothing but the greatest respect for them.

Even on the day of my departure, they told me if my business venture did not work out, I would always be welcomed back. You have no idea how comforting those words were as I embarked on a high-risk venture in the infancy of the Falklands fishing industry. High-risk because I knew nothing about the fish species, the various types of vessels used in such an operation, or about markets.

FIC was a company which sometimes came under severe public and government criticism. Sure, they jealously guarded their commercial patch and tried to hang on to as much private sector dominance as possible. But let me tell you one thing: when the new boom fishing business opened up in town, the company could have blown me and anyone else trying to get into it clean out of the water. But they chose not to. Okay there was a deal struck between the company's UK-based owners Coalite and the FI Government over nine seven-year-licenses. I, and others, started in the fishing industry as nothing more than fish licence brokers. The FIC could have easily acted as a broker for these fishing companies and their fishing fleets, because they knew most of the fishing clients via their shipping agency. But the perceived 'big bully' commendably backed off, and settled for the agency business and support services, such as supplies and retail.

The decision to move from the FIC was not entirely my own. I had been under pressure by the representatives of a Japanese fishing fleet to set up my own shipping agency and I had also been tapped by the newly formed Sullivan Shipping Agency to become their manager, but I was not in the mood to cease being an employee for a company whom I liked a lot to become an employee for someone I knew nothing about, and who was in competition with the FIC.

I had made up my mind, when I left the Falkland Islands Company I wanted to leave to do my own thing. I wanted, no, rather I craved, the challenge of standing or falling by my own decisions.

I told the Japanese that I would set up a company, if they would agree to my company applying for some of their licence applications.

The one thing that I was able to take to any company which I might form was that I, like the FIC, knew many of the clients involved in the new industry.

Some people were of the opinion that I started business because I was an elected councillor and I had inside information. That is, of course, total crap. I had inside information all right, but it was gained by working for the FIC as a reliable, dependable and totally loyal employee.

Another thing I had decided was that I would need a local business partner. I did not want to go into the unknown alone. I had spoken with a few guys about the idea of starting up a business together, but I guess they all felt it too risky.

Then one morning, I was walking up Ross Road, and met Pete Gilding. We stopped, and chatted, then I put the idea to him. Unlike the rest, he was immediately positive. Pete and I would have several meetings at his home on Philomel Hill, over the next couple of weeks.

With Pete on board, I began to feel that we needed a third member for the group, but Pete was adamantly against this idea. However, after a day or two, I gave Gerry Johnson a telephone call. Gerry was an energetic and progressive-thinking Islander who was already operating, with his wife, a very successful retail outlet in nice new premises in the centre of town. Just the man, I thought, to complete our little team.

After telling Gerry a few very basic points, I asked him if he would have any interest in joining Pete and me in forming a company. I was surprised and delighted when he said he would be, so I invited him to meet me for lunch at Monty's restaurant and go over the idea in a little more detail.

The meeting with Gerry was a breeze. He was totally positive, and I left Monty's no longer in any doubt that the company should be a partnership of three, and that Gerry Johnson should be that third person. Now it was time to go and put it to Pete.

Pete was wholeheartedly supportive of me, as he always would be over the 13 years that we spent in a business relationship together. So that was it.

Strangely enough, the naming of the company had little to do with me. I had left Pete and Gerry together at Pete's house one day, rather exhausted, fed-up and undecided on the subject, should it be JBG, GJB, JGB or whatever.

The next day, we met and it was agreed that JBG rolled off the tongue better than any of the other combinations: J for Johnson, B for Betts and G for Gilding. So the company was officially registered in the office of David Lang, The Falkland Islands Government Attorney General under the name JBG Falklands Limited.

We issued three £1 shares to ourselves. Pete paid £1, Gerry 3p because that was all the money he had in his pocket at the time, and I paid £1.97. It was 8 April 1988, and we were up and running for business.

As the only business in the beginning was to broker fishing licences, and any income from this source was six months away, we knew the company would not have any income for half a year, at best. Therefore, we were well aware that we would either need to fund the operation from our own pockets for that period, or to be extremely creative. We readily agreed to the latter, which we did manage to achieve.

I must admit it took me a little time to settle in my new

surroundings. In the first week of setting up the new company and moving into our new office, I twice found myself standing on the doorstep of the FIC office at 8 a.m. before I realised I no longer worked there. It's true, old habits die hard.

52

The Workload, Plus Political Ideas for the Future
(Lord Shackleton receives his freedom of Stanley, I tie him up)

In 1988, my workload had reached astronomical levels; it had peaked to around 20 committees or advisory boards, ranging from important and high level to the downright unnecessary and boring.

The more important were the Executive and Legislative Councils, Standing Finance and Education Committees, Executive and Corporation boards of the Falkland Islands Development Corporation, Tourist Board, Stanley Fisheries Ltd, Housing and Immigration Committees, which ensured that a mountain of paper was finding its way home on a daily basis.

I will be honest and admit at times it was very difficult, no, impossible to stay on top of it all. It also got very exasperating. Just as you thought that you were about finished getting through everything, another pile of papers would arrive, always for your immediate attention.

It was also not unusual to get a very important paper the day before you were expected to meet and make a decision on the subject. Little wonder 'deferment' became a regular course of action at many meetings of the highest level, which frustrated politicians and general public alike.

Despite committing the enormous amounts of our own time and energy required to attend all the meetings, read documents, and/or carry out any research that had to be done, elected councillors had to go out and do a day job to earn a living. Therefore, I don't think any elected councillor could realistically claim to be on top of everything that was going on.

As a result, a situation developed that was far from ideal. FIG administration were drafting up papers galore, on a whole array of subjects and slinging them out like confetti.

I am reasonably certain this situation might have forced councillors into a position where we often just had time to flick through files and only focus on issues which the individual considered important, or simply noted the administration's conclusions and recommendations on a paper which they regarded as important, urgent or otherwise.

There was no doubt that the pressure was especially intense on the elected members of the Executive Council, who had the greater workload of all the elected representatives. But there was no easy or obvious solution.

That said, the elected members of the Executive Council introduced a system that would enable us to spread the burden, with the aim of trying to ensure that at least one of us knew something about every item on the Executive Council meeting agenda. Tony Blake, John Creek and I adopted a very simple and effective practice with confidential papers: we agreed to split the agenda items into equal parts and to hold meetings on the morning prior to the Executive Council sessions. We turned these sessions into semi-social events, working breakfasts and suchlike, and it all worked rather well. But late papers were always a problem and would often screw up our best-laid plans.

Thankfully, things have changed somewhat for the better these days; councillors have their own office, with a research assistant and they also draft papers (one or two, anyway). This is a tremendous step in the right direction.

But surely the time has come to elect full-time councillors. And I believe a strong argument exists to elect even more councillors, certainly 10, but perhaps 12. When I say 'full-time', I mean individuals elected to office for four years on a salary paid by the state. These extremely important people should not only be expected to take the lead and the responsibility for the development and expansion of our democracy, but also all the day-to-day affairs that go with it.

Using Falklands salaries of today as a benchmark, this should cost FIG a mere £1,000,000 a year (on the basis of 10 elected), £100,000 a year each, possibly even tax free, with itemised allowances on top.

This progressive step should ensure that candidates of the highest level put themselves forward, thus providing the electorate with the maximum range of choice.

The system should also be devised in a way that enables any

elected representative who might act in an improper manner, to lose their job, thus forcing a by-election. Not only would this protect the electorate's interests, it is a fair democratic process, and the penalty carried could have a severe financial effect on the councillor and should act as a suitable deterrent.

Other arguments that support the case for 10 (or 12) councillors, as opposed to 8, are that it should help to ease, and spread, the workload. Elected members should have official office status, Ministers for Transport, Agriculture and Fisheries, Education, Health and Social Welfare.

It is my opinion that the introduction of such an obvious and truly democratic system would go some considerable way to blowing Argentina's political argument against us clean out of the water.

But I also believe the actual cost to the Falklands taxpayer of these much improved services to them might be considerably less than the present system of paying councillors and several Civil Servants, who I am sure the new mechanism would very quickly identify as surplus to requirement. This fundamental change in the structure of the Civil Service's administration, I feel, would likely finance full-time councillors on its own.

It must also be obvious that elected members with defined responsibilities and a functional office would remove a considerable amount of the workload presently sitting on the desk of administrative staff or officials.

I rather suspect that under the new scheme it might also be prudent for the Government to physically move certain staff members from their present locations to the offices of elected members. Relax, I am only suggesting that the individuals' working environment would change, not their terms and conditions (yet).

I am totally convinced, that given the few changes I have suggested, it is a certainty that the electorate would be less confused about who is actually in authority, get a faster and more efficient service, and much better value for money. If not, they would know exactly who to hang out to dry.

Another potentially very important benefit to the electorate, and perhaps the Falklands in the wider political arena, in my opinion, is it is more likely to encourage the first steps to the important issue of party politics. If there were 10 or 12, it would naturally bring about a kind of bonding between small groups of elected members, uniting some, whilst dividing others, rather than the present system of 8 individuals perhaps being pushed or swayed by effective lobbying or, even worse, making decisions on important issues simply because the individual believes it to be right or wrong – or because they dislike or approve of someone or something.

But to have party politics in a meaningful way you need at least two parties. That might be more difficult in the small populace of the Falklands. Oh, well, food for thought, don't you think?

Without doubt, one of the biggest disappointments for me in my 30 months in politics was not to see Lord Shackleton whilst he was in the Islands in 1988.

He had been nominated by the Legislative Council to receive the Freedom of Stanley, an honour to be presented to him by the elected councillors on behalf of the people of the Falkland Islands for his outstanding contribution to the Islands' financial boom.

A public gathering had been arranged at the Town Hall, to enable as many of the public as possible to attend the presentation of the scroll to the great man. Unfortunately, I was in agony, stretched out in my bed in 6a Pioneer Row, with mumps. I must admit I had some very impressive additional lumps on my body, which were also very painful; however, there was a little bit of unexpected pleasure for me.

Lord Shackleton had arrived in the Islands, rather inexplicably, without a tie to wear for the occasion. As I was lying in my bed feeling rather sorry for myself, my mother announced that Pete King and the Chief Executive, Brian Cummings, had come to see me. As they both came running up the stairs, arriving rather breathless at my bedside, I thought to myself, what a wonderful gesture of compassion. Alas, it was soon evident that they had only arrived to seek a tie for the honourable peer.

Despite being a little the worse for wear physically, I had not lost my appetite for grasping a chance to put my little personal touch into Lord Shackleton's day of honour in the Falklands. Easing myself ever so gently into a sitting position in my bed, I pointed in the direction of a cupboard and said to the Chief Executive, 'Inside that cupboard there you will find about twenty or thirty ties. Pass them over to me and I will select one for you.'

THE COLONY OF THE FALKLAND ISLANDS

HONORARY FREEDOM OF STANLEY

In Recognition of his long association with the Falkland Islands and of the outstanding contribution which he has made to the economic development of these Islands and the well-being of their people;

We, the undersigned representatives of the people of the Falkland Islands, in acknowlegement of our sincere gratitude and appreciation;

Hereby Confer upon The Right Honourable the LORD EDWARD ARTHUR ALEXANDER SHACKLETON, K.G., P.C., O.B.E., Baron of Burley, the Honorary Freedom of Stanley.

In Witness whereof we have hereunto set our hands this tenth day of January 1988.

The Hon. B. R. Cummings,
Acting Chairman of Executive Council
and President of Legislative Council.

The Hon. H. T. Rowlands, O.B.E.,
Member of Executive and Legislative Councils.

The Hon. T. S. Betts,
Member of Executive and Legislative Councils.

The Hon. A. T. Blake,
Member of Executive and Legislative Councils.

The Hon. J. E. Cheek,
Member of Executive and Legislative Councils.

The Hon. L. G. Blake, O.B.E., J.P.,
Member of Legislative Council.

The Hon. C. D. Keenleyside,
Member of Legislative Council.

The Hon. R. M. Lee,
Member of Legislative Council.

The Hon. E. M. Goss, M.B.E.,
Member of Legislative Council.

The Hon. Mrs. C. W. Teggart,
Member of Legislative Council.

For the first time in days, I forgot about my discomfort and began to eagerly rummage through the bundle of ties. Finally, I found what I was looking for. I picked up a blue one and handed it to Brian. 'I think you can be sure that Lord Shackleton will find this most agreeable.'

Clutching the tie, the Chief Executive and Peter wished me a speedy recovery and then rushed off to their very important function.

I lay back down on my bed, feeling very much happier. To be honest, I felt a bit like that naughty schoolboy again. Why? Oh yes, well, the tie I had given them for Lord Shackleton bore the emblem of the Transport and General Workers Union (TGWU). It had been given to me by the organisation's national secretary, George Henderson, whilst I was in London in 1985.

The idea of Lord Shackleton receiving his 'Freedom of Stanley' scroll decked out in a trade union labour movement tie gave me immense pleasure. I was equally certain it would have pleased Lord Shackleton.

In the middle of 1988, I decided to take a short break from politics and spend some time with my two children on a holiday back in the UK, and to make a business trip in Japan.

The children had had a bad time following the separation of their mum and dad, and I really felt I owed them something, especially Severine. He did not get the same loving attention from me as a result of the marriage breakdown as I am sure Amelia did from her mum.

It was the children's first time in England and Severine found London all a bit too much to deal with, but once we moved out of the city and travelled to Cornwall, we all began to relax and have a wonderful time, just the three of us in the village of Looe for a week, where we stayed in a very well-run little family hotel.

It was so great to be dad again, but all too soon for the kids, and me, I had to get back on the road again.

After my business had been completed in Japan, I returned to the UK. With the time difference, my 1 August was 36 hours long. Once back in England, I rejoined my children and continued our holiday.

Unfortunately, the English summer was wet and miserable. It

seemed to rain every day, and frequently messed up the best laid plans for outdoor activities. It reminded me of the terrible weather stories the British press often wrote about the Falklands. When it was time to head back home, the children were more than ready.

53

*Labour Party Conference and CPA in Bermuda
(First Falklands elected representative to attend
a party conference)*

Within a month or so, I was travelling back to the UK once again, in transmit to Bermuda. I had been asked by my elected colleagues to represent the Government of the Falkland Islands, this time to attend the Regional Conference in Bermuda of the 18th West Indies, The Americas and South Atlantic Conference of the Commonwealth Parliamentary Association.

This time I was travelling alone, and I was not going to be in conflict with my brother at the other end, so I assumed I would be free from media attention – not that either prospect would have bothered me.

I arrived in England just as the UK political party conferences were about to get into full swing. The Falkland Islands Government had agreed to adopt an idea from a company called Profile, who suggested that the Government should present and promote itself at these conferences. FIG had decided for some time that it should 'hit the road', and wherever possible it would show its face in an attempt to maintain the support it already had, and to seek to gain new friends and allies.

Oddly enough, I rather suspected that the motivation to attend party conferences came about as a result of councillors' paranoia that the Labour Party was not to be trusted in any shape or form, and if the Conservatives were ever to lose power in Britain, then the Falklands could be up the creek without a paddle.

I always felt this fear factor was ill founded, but I was fully supportive of the need to get out and blow one's own trumpet.

So as a part of this campaign, the political party conferences were seen, correctly, as an excellent way to promote the good name of the Falklands, by manning a stand at these forums, to meet, greet and chat to as many Members, or former Members of

Parliament as possible, and anyone else who might be interested in the Falklands, whilst shoving a nice glossy brochure or video in their hands.

I just happened to be in London at the time the Government representative, Lewis Clifton, was packing boxes in the back of his car to head off for the Labour Party conference in Blackpool. When he rather casually said, 'You're a Labour boy Terry, do you fancy joining me?' Without hesitation I replied I did. I would not have missed the chance to meet Labour Party members whilst promoting the Falklands for anything.

When we reached Blackpool, the weather was bloody miserable. It rained and blew a gale all the time we were there, and the sand was even drifting in the streets like snow. But the conference was a success for the Falklands; we had a lot of visitors to the stand and we were able to educate more than one or two about the Islands and I believe we also gained some new supporters in the process.

One thing is certain: this inaugural venture into promoting the Islands' cause became a watershed for what has been a continuous programme of positively portraying the Falklands, not only in the UK, but the world. I consider myself very fortunate to have been involved at the very beginning.

I would also like to say, Labour Party support is now taken for granted by most Falkland Islanders, but it was quite a different story back in 1988. Falkland Islanders then were so pro the Tories and Thatcher that they almost despised the Labour Party.

On a personal note, I had been keen to meet the Labour Party leader, Neil Kinnock, but for some unexpected reason it was not possible. The same thing happened to me in 1985, when I was pencilled in by the TUC to meet him. I was starting to get a complex. However, I was introduced to his good lady wife, and I did meet, and had my photograph taken, with the deputy leader, Roy Hattersley, whilst he was at the Falklands stand.

So there you go, my attendance at the conference once again created a little bit of history; I was the first Falkland Islands councillor ever to attend a party conference.

With my duties at Blackpool done, it was time to start thinking about getting my bags packed for Bermuda, and the Commonwealth Parliamentary Association Conference there.

I arrived in Bermuda on Saturday, 12 November 1988, and after being welcomed at the airport I was taken off to join the rest of the delegation, who were staying at the Stonington Beach Hotel, and later in the afternoon I attended the welcoming reception held in the lobby of the hotel and hosted by the joint Presidents of the Bermuda Branch of the CPA, the Honourable F.J. Barritt, CBE, MP, who was the Speaker of the House of Assembly, and Senator, the Honourable A.S. Jackson, MBE, JP, President of the Senate.

The weeklong conference would include seven working sessions, which were held in the Lecture Hall of the Department of Academic Studies of the Bermuda College.

Once the Island's Governor, a chap called Langley, had officially opened the conference, we were all out on the lawn in front of the hotel for a photo-call and then back to Bermuda College to get on with business of the day.

Any hopes I had of not being noticed had been dashed during the weekend, when an enthusiastic radio presenter announced my arrival, where I was staying, and what I thought about one or two things. A local newspaper also released a picture of me and printed an interview, which was all very tame and mostly factual.

Once I had settled into my seat and the first session had got underway, I soon noticed that the topics were very much centred on one general area of the globe. The title was 'The Economic Development of the Caribbean'. Why the Falkland Islands had been lumped into the same region as the Caribbean by the CPA I do not know. Today the Falklands are more appropriately located in the CPA region of the British Islands and Mediterranean.

The speakers had been identified for all the working sessions prior to the conference, so for a few days, I listened and just got involved in the questions and answers break, but I had not come all this way just to listen, and later in the week I got my chance to speak.

However, if I had not got into the centre of things on the opening day of the conference, I was certainly centre of attraction and attention at the social event that evening, and I must say, it was not of my own doing.

All the delegates had been invited to a reception hosted by His Excellency the Governor and Lady Langley at Government House. Bermuda also had a deputy Governor, and the Premier and Vice-Premier were Islanders.

Well, the drinks were going down pretty well and the gathering was generally interesting.

The Governor and his wife, along with their entourage, were 'mingling' at their party, and soon enough I found myself face-to-face with His Excellency. I introduced myself and then I proceeded to shake hands with him and his wife. Then he said something to me which I just had to respond to.

After 16 years I am not absolutely certain about the accuracy of what was said, but I do believe it was something like this.

'Ah, so you're the chap the media are making all the fuss about.'

I replied rather casually, 'Oh is that right?'

He smiled and then said, 'The Falkland Islands, I wouldn't want to go to those far-flung islands,' and then he began to laugh.

Naturally, as the loyal people they were, the whole entourage started to laugh along with him. I am sure everything was meant to be a light-hearted joke and that the Governor didn't really mean what he said, but as I felt we were all having a bit of fun, and also because I was well aware that I needed to stand up for myself, or I would have been seen as the little wimp from the Falklands by the rest of the guests for the remainder of the evening, I looked him straight in the eye, and replied, with a clear and evenly balanced voice so all could hear, 'Oh you needn't worry, sir, because you will never be invited.' Then I took a step back and grinned at him.

Suddenly the laughing stopped and silence fell, but to the Governor's credit he picked up the pieces very quickly and got everyone lifted again before he moved on, and as he did he lightly touched my arm, and in much less dramatic fashion whispered, 'A fighter, I like that.'

The next morning it was back to business. Of course, it is always business – coffee breaks, meal times, bus rides, cocktail parties, always explaining who you are, where you come from, what it is you do etc. But that is all part of public life.

Delegates had come from 18 different islands, or island groups, from Belize to St Helena, Turks and Caicos Islands to Montserrat, Trinidad and Tobago to the Falkland Islands.

There were also observers present, including the CPA Secretary General, Dr The Honourable David Tonkin, from Australia – bloody fine man in my opinion. The United Kingdom had a delegation of three, which included Mr Norman Hogg, Labour

Member of Parliament for Cumbernauld and Kilsyth; Canada and the USA also had observer representation.

I was particularly pleased to meet Mrs Ruth Pridham, who was a member of the Executive and Legislative Council from the Island of St Helena; I took the opportunity to reassure her that the Falkland Islands Government would continue to offer employment opportunities to the people of St Helena, a message she was delighted to receive, because at that time the Island had a huge unemployment problem, and those in employment received very low incomes.

In the Falkland Islands, we had the reverse problem, we did not have enough human resources to carry out all the work that we needed, or wished to be done. In fact, many people were doing two jobs, so it seemed to make very good sense, both politically and humanely, to bring in a British cousin labour force to help ease their unemployment problems. In fact many from St Helena who have come to our Islands over the last 15 years or so have settled into the Falklands way of life and taken up permanent residence.

Well, after two working sessions on economic development, the debate moved on to educational development matters, then the subject switched to matters relating to migration, drugs and the social and economic implications.

Finally I was able to get a go on the rostrum; I just couldn't come all the way to Bermuda without having something to say to the gathering. I was surprised at the number that did, however.

My opportunity came when the debate had been flowing on natural resources. After much waving of my hand, I eventually got called up to speak. It was wonderful to hear the announcement over the public address system: 'The next speaker will be the Honourable Terry Betts from the Falkland Islands.'

I had no opportunity to prepare a speech, but that was no big deal. I knew the essence of the subject being debated, so that was enough.

Without being long-winded about it, the comments I made suggested that a country could have as many natural resources as it wished, but unless they were properly controlled and managed by its own government, which also needed to ensure that any commercialisation of these resources was developed by its own people, as much as possible, to maximise the revenue return to all sections of the community, or it would be greatly devalued.

Again, I highlighted the point that it was not up to governments to play businessmen, they should just be the umpires, making sure the players played by the rules; the local private sector, without or with outside foreign partners, should be encouraged to make investments and re-investment, to produce as much added value products from a single raw material as possible. That way, the maximum revenue fell into the country, and benefited the community across the board. If a government simply allowed foreigners to exploit its natural resources, it went without saying that the country of origin received the least financial return.

I concluded that management and control were crucial to the success of any exploitation of one's natural resources. 'Sell all your trees and you have nothing left to build your own house.'

As I stepped down off the podium to a generous round of applause, once again I felt I had represented the people of the Falklands in the proper manner, and not simply taken a free bus ride.

The conference was very neatly rounded off with a farewell dinner at the Southampton Princess Hotel, on that night 'Princess' was a very apt name, because the guest of honour was Her Royal Highness, the Princess Alexandra, accompanied by her husband Angus Ogilvy, who became Sir Angus a year later, I believe.

I would imagine there must have been about 300 guests sitting at several tables, all nibbling our way through a 14-course meal.

After dinner had been washed down with a nip of one's fancy, and we had toasted Her Majesty the Queen, we all stood up and turned outwards to face the Royal party. Even as they were coming down the stairs, I sensed the Princess was going to come my way; eye contact suggested so.

Sure enough, once on floor level, she immediately swung to her left and walked directly up to me. I bowed my head and gently shook a tender hand. I seem to recall that she was quite beautiful. She asked me several questions about the Falklands; in fact, we slipped into a little chat, which was only broken up when her husband encouraged her to move on.

As she moved away and disappeared, I felt quite honoured. Actually, I was bloody elated. After all, I was the only guest on the lower deck that spoke with a member of the royal family that night.

I will always remember that she was light and gentle in conversation. She also expressed a deep and genuine interest in the Falklands. She was indeed a 'Princess'. She would visit the Falklands 12 years later and I would miss her. What a bugger.

So all that was now left to do was get on home, via the United Kingdom. I suggest you take a quick look at your atlas sometime. Then you will see that from Bermuda to the United Kingdom, to the Falklands via Ascension Island is a long hike home.

But I must admit I was in good form as I started out on my travels, thanks entirely to Malcolm Smith, an officer in the Bermuda police. Malcolm's brother, Alex, was living in the Falklands and had arranged for us to meet. Well, Malcolm had become aware of my flying phobia, so he took me down to the police club, where we partook of some delightful Scottish malt, which fired up my engine room rather well. Then he drove me off to the airport and bid me farewell.

For the first time I sat in my allocated seat aboard the aircraft and fully relaxed as I began to reflect on Bermuda's charm and beauty.

Compared to the Falkland Islands landmass of 4,700 square miles, Bermuda is minuscule in size, just 22 square miles, but they had a population 31 times the size of the Falklands, 62,000 spread over 8 parishes, with some 2,000 in the tiny capital, Hamilton.

I was impressed with its political structure. But what really stirred the blood for me was the businesslike attitude, fresh, vibrant and so bloody purposeful. It made me a little bit jealous. It was something that I dreamed the Falklands could become. Envy regarding success appeared to be non-existent; it was a disease back home.

They also had something else: millionaires, lots of them. How I wished the Falklands had them. Not one or two, but 100 or 200. I was also told to remember, success breeds success. I am equally sure that wealth breeds further wealth.

54

Prayer Breakfast with the President of the USA (Thanks to the House of Representatives and the US Senate)

Before pulling the curtain down on 1988, let me tell you about another experience I had during what was a very eventful year. I had received an invitation from the House of Representatives and the US Senate to join them at the 36th annual national prayer breakfast meeting to be held at the Washington Hilton in Washington DC and also to meet with members from both the US Senate and Congress, at the Capitol.

The invitation was not a political one, it was personal, so I did not have any authority to speak on behalf of the people of the Falkland Islands, or the Falkland Islands Government. Whenever asked about the Islands, which I was, frequently, my reply would deal with fact alone, or I would express my own personal opinion.

I have found over many years of experience that no matter what level of company you are in, the most regular asked questions about the Falklands are: What is the size of the population? How big are the Islands? What's the weather like? Do you shag sheep?

Even after you have answered the questions accurately, the response is always the same: Just two thousand people, I had no idea they were that large, I thought you had snow all the time, I really thought you shagged sheep. People's response to statistical facts about the Falklands I often find quite entertaining.

What is the national prayer breakfast? Apparently, back in 1942 at the height of World War II, a handful of Senators and Representatives discussed how they might be of personal and spiritual support to one another. They decided that if they could gather now and then to pray together, they might discover an added resource, which would be sustaining value. And so, very informally, they began to meet, and it has grown and continued ever since.

On this occasion, the annual prayer breakfast was attended by 3,700 guests, which included Senators and Representatives from all over the USA, His Royal Highness Prince Bandar bin Sultan, Royal Embassy of Saudi Arabia, and Dr Billy Graham. But the most distinguished guests of all were the President of the United States Ronald Reagan and the First Lady.

Now I have no intention of attempting to overplay my breakfast with the United States President. I was not introduced to him. But I did spend the whole of a breakfast session just five metres or so away from where he and the First Lady sat, which gave me plenty of time to make observations.

I was slightly surprised by his lack of height. It was that old visual trick television plays on us that had given me the wrong impression. I also noticed that he had a crocked little finger, and Mrs Reagan was always smiling and very attentive to her husband. It was also very evident that even at this most tranquil and peace-loving occasion, security was heavy.

On the theme of prayer, I must tell you a little story so I don't forget. I once had the privilege of serving the former Archbishop of Canterbury, Archbishop Carey, a cheeseburger from a burger van my wife and I were operating at the Goose Green sports, on East Falklands. I recall watching him munching away at our wares as he waddled away. It was not the fact that he was eating a burger that interested me, it was the fact that he was wearing trainers.

Well, back to Washington DC. During my time there I met a man who I would like to mention. Although important in his own right, he was not Royalty, a President or a Prime Minister, nor a rock star. But a very nice English gentleman called Harvey Thomas.

Harvey had been a secretary of some importance to Margaret Thatcher, and had the misfortune to get himself blown up by the IRA when they attacked the Grand Hotel in Brighton, where those who mattered in the Conservative Party at the time were staying.

As he was handing me a signed copy of his book, Harvey said to me, 'Terry, I went up through three floors, and came back through four.' As he made light of what must have been a terrifying experience, I was impressed by his bravery and loyalty.

Of course my time in Washington was not all about prayer; in fact, it was a brief part of it. I had many meetings with small, and not so small, groups of Senators and Representatives, all were very welcoming, and many discussed the Falklands at some length and in a favourable light, they were much more interested and aware than I had expected.

I also have to say that I enjoyed my time in Washington DC much more than New York. I think it had much to do with the fact that in DC, I had more time on my hands, was free of the media and could visit places of interest at leisure, which made it much more relaxed than my New York experience.

But there were other important aspects, many more open spaces, none of those head-spinning high risers. I understand the reason for this is because no building is permitted to be built higher than the Washington Memorial. How very intelligent.

One of the most exciting visits I made was to the National Air and Space Museum. Whilst standing on a platform just feet away from the capsule of Apollo 11, I was amazed how small the module was that took man to the moon. It was awe-inspiring, as I stood there gazing at it. My mind began to slip back to the days when Robin Luxton and I were playing make-believe outer-space journeys in the tree at the Victory Bar.

But if the Air and Space Museum was thrilling, the sight of the Capitol building inside and out was unbelievably breathtaking. Like London, Washington is bristling with internationally famous landmarks, the Lincoln Memorial and the White House.

However, once you approach and start to feel the Vietnam Veterans Memorial, it tempers much of what else is around. I am not talking about Frederick Hart's fine sculpture of the 'Three Servicemen' but the soul-searching, polished black stone wall which bears the names of more than 58,000 Americans who died or are still missing in Vietnam.

As I entered one end of the site, and slowly disappeared beneath ground level, reading some of the names as I went along, then gradually climbing back up to ground level at the other end, I found the whole experience quite numbing, a tragedy of an unbelievable scale to mankind, created by man himself. I would go back to Washington DC in 1992, and I just had to go back to the memorial again, this time with fellow Falkland Islanders Tony Blake and Charles Keenleyside.

55

*A Tragic Death and the End of My Political Road
(My business partner dies and I resign
from Government)*

Once more it was a long journey back home, from the United States, but when I got there, I was delighted to learn that my company, JBG Falklands, had been highly successful in the licence applications for the 1989 fishing season, gaining 16 licences. Gerry had apparently caused quite a stir in the community by saying to the media that our new company was 'a force to be reckoned with'. It was probably true, but Falkland Islanders were not renowned, nor regarded, for speaking out so confidently about a private sector success.

If 1988 had been a busy and successful year for me, 1989 was to be a dramatic and traumatic year.

Pete, Gerry and I had every reason to be optimistic about the future. We were a good partnership and we got on very well with each other. We were all very different personalities, which I think complemented one another.

On one particular evening, I went home from the office very happy with life in general. I was looking forward to a dance that was taking place in the Town Hall in the evening. In the late afternoon, there had been reports that a Spanish fishing trawler was on fire and in trouble, but later it was confirmed that all the crew were off and safe, so I didn't think much more about the incident.

However, at some point, it was decided that the fire brigade should go on board the ship. The local fire brigade in the Falklands was made up by volunteers from the community; Gerry was one such volunteer, and I understand that his main role was to work off the breathing apparatuses.

I went out for the evening's entertainment, and after a long night of dance and drink I made my way home. I had only been in bed ten or fifteen minutes when I heard a voice calling out repeatedly from downstairs. My partner and I got up and went down to the kitchen to see who it was. A relative of my future wife was in the middle of the kitchen in an uncontrollable state.

She was the mother-in-law of one of the fire fighters, so it was obvious something had gone terribly wrong on the fishing trawler. When she finally broke the news that her son-in-law and Gerry had died, I was shocked, but I quickly realised this was not the time for me to lose control. I now had a responsibility and I would need to keep a cool head. It was not going to be very easy.

Gerry Johnson was not only my business partner, he was also my third cousin. If that were not enough, so was Robert Finlayson, the other man who died on board. Their bodies had been found inside the ship, somehow separated from their safety harnesses, with empty oxygen tanks. They had presumably died of smoke inhalation; Gerry was just 29 years old, Robert a little younger.

It was the small hours and I had probably had too much to drink, but I needed to try and keep a grip of my senses, get into my car and wake Peter Gilding up at his house and deliver the dreadful information to him.

But for some reason, I went to Bertie Ford's home first (Bertie was best mates with Pete and me) and told him, then I took the short journey to Pete's house on Philomel Street and broke the news to him. Naturally, Pete was every bit as stunned as me and I knew it was going to be a long hard night.

Pete and I agreed that we should go back to the office and communicate with everyone from there, because, in addition to the terrible situation we had, Gerry's wife and very young son Daniel were both back in Brighton, in the UK.

I am not clear any more about the exact chain of events, but liaison was established between the police in the Falklands and their counterparts in England, who agreed that when they arrived at Jenny's home to deliver the most awful news, the police in the Falklands would simultaneously let us know back at the office and then Pete would telephone to try and console her.

It was a sincere and brave attempt by Pete. He was quite wonderful in his manner and with the words, but in reality he had been given an impossible task that night. How could he comfort the poor woman who had just received the worst news of her life, from 8,000 miles away.

Pete and I did everything we possibly could to assist in a whole variety of aspects. Some were very sombre and sobering, others were just matters of comfort and assurance.

It had been the wish of the family that Gerry's body be transported back to the UK so he could be buried there. It had also been agreed that Pete would escort our partner's body back to his grieving relatives, staying on for the funeral and lending his support to the distraught family.

I recall going to the chapel in the King Edward Memorial hospital with Pete, to have my last private moment with Gerry – one of those terrible moments in life that you simply have to go through, but I am so glad I did. I have wonderful memories of Gerry; he was always a bundle of laughs, energetic and bright, but now his life had been snuffed out, just like a candle.

As I stood in the rather chilly room, I did not have a clue how to react. How was one supposed to behave, with your close friend and business partner lying lifeless before you?

I just stared at the body laid out on a bed, then I stepped forward and lightly stroked his cheek with the back of my right hand, then I bent down and kissed him on the forehead. He was so cold. Then I whispered, 'God bless, my friend.'

As I stepped back, I began to choke up and, fighting back the tears, I looked at Pete and in a trembling voice I said, 'I think it is time to leave.'

I do not wish to go on any more about this hellish tragedy, other than to say that for a while it tore close friends and the company apart. JBG Falklands Limited may not be commercially active these days, but it does live on, and on 20 May each year, I always remember the loss of a very good friend. It was indeed a traumatic event.

The dramatic event of 1989 was a political drama, unparalleled in the political history of the Falklands. It began and concluded during the budget session of the Legislative Council.

A bill had been tabled to approve the granting of agricultural subsidies to all the farm owners. The Bill was structured in such a way that if passed, much of the financial benefit would pass into the hands of the absentee landowners. By this I mean companies based in the United Kingdom, or elsewhere in the world. The largest of these was, of course, the Falkland Islands Company.

I was not interested in who the absentee landlords were. For me, that was not the issue, it was the very idea of paying x pence per kilo of wool produced which was the crux of the matter. The principle absolutely horrified me.

At 11 a.m. the House adjourned for the regular coffee break. I went up to John Cheek, who was standing alone munching a biscuit. 'I cannot accept this bill, John. It means endorsing public funds to be transferred to overseas bank accounts. There is no way I can support such a bill, I would be betraying the people who elected me.'

John immediately stopped sipping his coffee, and looked at me very seriously. 'What are you going to do then?' I told him I would have to think about resigning my seat. He said nothing else, but I could tell his mind had gone into overdrive.

I left him in his thoughts and I would spend the rest of the interval debating a different subject with Robin Lee. Robin and I got on pretty well with each other and our politics were not miles apart. He had come up to me, to ask why it was that I did not support the sale of Port Howard to Falkland Islanders.

I explained to Robin that I had no problem whatsoever with the most significant farm on the West Falklands going into Islander ownership; in fact, it was a tremendous idea to wrest the ownership of land out of absentee owners' hands, especially given the bill that was now on the table. But I had to admit to him that I was troubled with the sale proposal for Port Howard, principally because of the structure of the new ownership.

I went on to explain to Robin that I felt the deal, in essence, was nothing more than a commercial transaction between Waldron's and the brothers Lee, financed by the commercial wing of the Falkland Islands Government. On that basis, the purchase of the land did not invite any meaningful participation of the other Islanders, especially those presently employed on the farm, who had been loyal servants to the old regime.

I could accept a new company which owned Port Howard, with the brothers holding 51%, perhaps even 60%, of the share equity, but I could not accept that a good deal was being done in the interests of as many Falkland Islanders as possible with the brothers holding 90/95% of the company.

It would be totally naïve of anyone to believe that there would be any kind of democracy within the board of directors of the company with that kind of shareholding, which basically meant that the employees on the farm, who had given so much in the past, would simply be moving from one dominant employer to another. I think by the end of the coffee break Robin was getting my point, even though he tried lamely to convince me otherwise.

I am a little bit hazy in terms of how things unfolded in the House regarding the further debate on the Agricultural Subsidy Bill but I do recall that nothing had been concluded by lunchtime. As I was leaving the Town Hall, John grabbed me lightly by the arm and said, 'Were you serious about resigning?' Yes of course, I replied. 'Hum, let me think about it over lunch.'

I walked the 100 metres or so down to the Upland Goose, where I was meeting my future wife Arlette for lunch. I told her I was sure I would resign. I did not need her approval, but I did seek her opinion, which, as it happened, did not differ greatly from mine.

After lunch I walked back to the Town Hall and made my way into the Court and Council Chambers. I was immediately greeted by a rather excited Governor and Attorney General. Upon seeing me, one of them said, as they turned and pointed to the doorway of the Registrar's office, 'We have a problem in the back there, John Cheek and Wendy Teggart are threatening to resign. Will you go and try and talk some sense into them?'

Before I could respond, the other gentleman looked at me rather flushed, and excitedly said, 'They won't bring the Government down, you know, if they think that. They won't bring the Government down,' he repeated.

Putting my hands up in the air, I looked at the Governor and said, 'Hold it, hold it. You're talking to the wrong man, you're talking to the wrong person.' I paused, then said, 'I'm going to resign too.'

The Governor then pointed in the direction of the Registrar's office and said, 'You had better go in there and talk to the others, and when you are ready I will reconvene the House.' Then he and the Attorney General went in one direction, I the other.

Upon entering the office, I immediately noticed Wendy standing under a window on the far wall. She was clearly distressed, whilst John appeared to be fired up, in a state of mind that was like a mixture of anger and agitation.

As soon as he saw me, he said, 'You in or out? Are you with us or not?'

I looked at Wendy again and said, 'Sure, but what's been going on here?'

The question was not answered by either of them, then John went on to say, 'When the House is reconvened, I wish to speak first.'

Rightly or wrongly, I instantly began to feel that someone was trying to make capital out of this situation, so I delivered a clear message to both of them. 'Hey you guys, you do whatever you want to do. I just want to go to sleep with a clear conscience tonight.'

Once the Governor had been informed we had made a final decision, he duly called the House into formal session. I remember my old friend Patrick Watts standing in the gallery, doing recorded highlights of the session for local radio. As I passed in front of him he said, 'You're not going to resign, are you, TSB?' I nodded my head.

I can still vividly remember his reaction, as he stood at the controls of his radio equipment, shaking his head in disapproval. I knew right there and then, if Patrick did not approve, then the general public would most likely feel the same. Patrick's opinion was quite influential in the small community.

I knew also that it was election year. I had done nothing wrong during my 30 months as an elected councillor, therefore it was not unreasonable to assume that if I threw my hat in the ring again, I would have a more than even chance of getting re-elected in just four months' time.

But that did not concern me right there and then. I could only be honest with myself and ask, could I vote for a bill that would shovel out money from the public purse to the benefit of shareholders overseas? The answer just had to be NO.

There was one final act to be played before the largest political rebellion in the history of the Falkland Islands Legislative Council was carried out.

John tabled an amendment to the Agricultural Subsidy Bill, which, in essence, was the subsidies that would be made available by the Falkland Islands Government to farmers with the exception of any absentee landowners. I seconded the amendment.

But from the very beginning we knew we had a problem to reverse the tide. To be successful with the amendment we had to get a simple majority vote in favour, or the original bill would be carried forward.

Our obvious disadvantage was that one of the elected members for Stanley, Charles Keenleyside, was not in the Islands, so we were 4–3 down in the representative stakes and the 4 against were farmers/landowners or their representatives.

Thinking back, this situation was quite horrifying and totally undemocratic, because four of the elected councillors were going to vote on expenditure of public funds that either directly or indirectly advantaged themselves.

One was a farm owner, two were in the process of becoming owners, the other one was a farm manager for the Falkland Islands Company, which, as I have explained, would be the greatest beneficiary of the grant under the original bill. Surely a clear case of conflict of interests if ever there was one. It was 1989, and still Falklands democracy was showing itself to be nothing more than a bunch of bullshit.

Anyway, just before the voting process began, three of the elected representatives from the farming community, Eric Goss, Robin Lee and L.G. (Tim) Blake, drew their lines in the sand without hesitation or the slightest regard for scruples and made it clear they were going to vote against the amendment. Wendy, John and myself were going to vote for it. That meant it all fell down on the shoulders of the one remaining member of the House present, A.T. (Tony) Blake, who had not made his intentions known.

I had always viewed Tony as a genuine guy, with a very open mind; therefore, I began to feel there was some hope that we could snatch victory out of the jaws of defeat.

It must have been extremely difficult for him, as he knew all eyes were upon him as he was the last one to stand up to speak, and cast his vote. He had been thrown into a situation which was not his own doing, and now he was going to decide the outcome of this pulsating and controversial contest.

But within seconds of him getting to his feet, I knew we had lost it. His body movement immediately indicated discomfort at the responsibility that lay on his shoulders.

I sat in my seat watching his every move; he was in anguish. I was thinking to myself, what was it that was so troublesome for him? It was surely a clear-cut decision – this could not be a 'grey' problem, it was black or white. Then at the end of his address he voted. Unbelievably he abstained. Fucking hell, I immediately thought to myself, how could you abstain, Tony? Was this the ultimate in gutlessness?

His decision meant that huge sums of taxpayers' money would find their way to overseas bank accounts never to be seen again. At the time, I was very annoyed with him. However, I later found out he had little or no choice, he had been given a clear direction by his electorate, mostly FIC farm employees and/or his bosses, that he should not vote with the amendment, so the only thing he could do was to comply with their instruction.

He told me afterwards that the only action he could take to demonstrate his disagreement with his electorate was to abstain. He was absolutely correct, but how frustrating.

After all the tension, the vote had ended in a draw, the amendment had been lost, and my political career was over. All that was left now was for John, Wendy and me to stand up in turn and formally announce our resignations from the Legislative Council.

The term of the present Council still had four or five months to run before the next General Election, but it was able to stagger through until the House was dissolved six weeks or so prior to the election.

Ironically, within two years both the major absentee landlords sold out their sheep farming assets for exhorbitant prices, considering they were selling non-profit-making businesses which had no hope of making profit for the foreseeable future. Worse still for the poor old taxpayer, the deals struck were funded, directly or indirectly, in one form or another, from the public purse, which meant the Government had allowed itself to get stuffed, not once or twice, but on multiple occasions.

There were many financial costs to the public purse other than the purchase price of the land and assets from the Falkland Islands Company. I understand that prior to the time of FIG closing the deal with FIC on the purchase of Goose Green, Fitzroy, Walker Creek and North Arm, FIG had sought, and been given, expert advice by an independent evaluator as to the worth of the assets. This was given at £3.1 million.

If that is correct, it is quite amazing that FIG agreed a purchase price of 5 million. If that were not enough, it is alleged that FIC rather cleverly threw in Port Stephens, a large farm at the bottom of West Falklands, which was at the time being operated by local farm owners, with mortgages provided by the FIC. The allegations are that FIC offered to transfer the mortgages of these assets at an additional cost of £750,000 to FIG.

Allegedly, FIG agreed to the combined deal, but only on the basis that FIC re-invest £500,000 back into the Islands. If this is true, I could just imagine how difficult it must have been for the representatives of the Falkland Islands Company to contain their pleasure, as they readily agreed to close the deal.

All I can say to my dear Falkland Islanders by way of some sort of comfort, each time you go into the internationally famous Upland Goose (built by my great-great-grandfather) for a drink or dinner, for Christ's sake enjoy yourselves.

Firstly, it is alleged that we Gosses had it stolen from us, and now it is highly likely you provided the funds, via FIG, for FIC to buy it back again, and left them with a bit of spare change as well.

Apart from paying far too much, FIG have since written off £1 million worth of share capital investment, inserted umpteen variations of a theme on grants and subsidies and certainly up to the year 2000 prevented commercially-minded board members from raising funds to limit the overall financial burden. Any taxpayer should not be impressed.

I do not know a great deal of details regarding the purchase of Port Howard, but I am fairly confident that the price paid was £750,000, 50% of which was funded indirectly from the public purse. Then at some point, the overall price was written down by 50%. If you add in the annual grants and subsidies, all-in-all, it might have been a great deal for the Lee Brothers, but I think you must agree that it has been a pretty piss-poor one for the taxpayer.

As for politics, well, I did stand twice more, but on each occasion I failed to be elected. Each time, I polled 25.1% of the vote, and each time, I finished about 30 votes short.

I was always ready to grasp the political nettle and jump out in front of the trees, saying highly controversial things like, 'I would talk to the Argentines about long-term peace in the southwest Atlantic.' I believed we should let Argentines into the Islands, in the interest of long-term security in the former. And the latter, for the purpose of demonstrating to them, that their lifelong understanding of the Falklands, was not as they had been educated. I considered I did very well to get 25% of the vote.

With politics out the window, I was now able to fully concentrate on the business front, which had gone well, considering we spent most of the second half of the year reeling from Gerry's chilling death.

In an attempt to bolster the administration aspect of JBG, as a result of the vacuum left by Gerry, we employed a General Manager, Dik Swale, who had been the first Spanish teacher in Government schools since the '82 War. Dik (that is how he spells it) was a great asset to the administration of the company, but naturally, all policy and decision-making continued to be made by Pete and myself, and there was much going on.

We were soon buying up property to establish a home base; we did not think it appropriate, or professional, to be operating out of a Portakabin. We also saw the need to try and spread risk and get ourselves involved in more meaningful business than licence brokering.

To achieve this, JBG Falklands Limited forged a joint venture partnership with one of the largest fishing companies in Vigo, Spain, called Pescanova Limited.

JBG Falklands were one of the first companies to secure one, of only four, long-term licences. (That's if you can regard four years as long term.) Issued by the Falkland Islands Government, our licence was for the vessel *Sil*, to target a squid type called loligo (calamari to the Spanish), the preferred squid type for the Spanish and other European markets.

Two Spaniards, Jacobo Fontan and Manuel Fernandez, and I had a meeting with the Falklands Director of Fisheries in the refurbished Bayona Yacht Club, in Vigo, to present the joint venture business plan, which, without question, contributed greatly to clinching this unique licence for the *Sil* (which I believe it still enjoys today).

So the 1980s draw to a close. At the end of this decade my politics are over, my football-playing days are over, my first marriage is over. But before moving on to the 1990s, allow me to reminisce a little bit about my football days.

From 1969 to 1989, football had been very rewarding for me, not just as a way to keep reasonably fit, but I had been a fairly successful player, picking up six League Championship medals, and being selected as a member of the national team on 102 occasions.

This record enabled me to join a very elite club indeed, Bill Jones, Tom Perry, and good old Terry (Rubber Duck) Peck, as the only players at that time to reach the landmark of 100 or more appearances for his country.

I had also captained the team on 49 occasions and scored 19 goals. Considering I played most of my games as a defender, that was quite a good scoring rate. I had been a member of 14 shield-winning sides, also a Falklands sporting record. The shield was a competition between the Falklands and the Royal Navy, on odd occasions it was triangular, with the Royal Marines involved as well. Not premiership stuff, but it was the highest level you could play at in the Falklands.

There were also no lush green or level football pitches, potholes and stones were not uncommon, and the elements often dominated a game, with winds in excess of 30 knots, sometimes accompanied with hail squalls or horizontal rain, which meant the ball was more often than not high up in the air or out of play. Any team that kicked off against the wind needed to go in at half time not more than three down. If your luck was really out, the wind would change direction at half time and you would be forced to play against the odds for the entire game.

56

Marriage, Cold Stores, Office Blocks, Fishing Companies

Now it is time to lift the lid, and disclose a few things that came out of the 1990s basket of my life. The decade began, primarily, with me focussed on developing and pioneering business ventures within the Falklands Fishery for my companies, with foreign and Falkland Islands partners. As it progressed, I would take up the responsibility of caring for many other business interests, spread over the entire Islands, when I was elected the President of the Falkland Islands Chamber of Commerce in 1996.

On 21 April 1990, I got married for the second time. The date was deliberate, it was Her Royal Highness Queen Elizabeth's actual 62nd birthday; not her pretend one in June.

My bride was a Falkland Islander who had been living in the UK for nearly 20 years, so although we knew of each other, we did not know one another. I had met her at a Falkland Islands reunion party held in Ham Hall, in Richmond, Surrey, in August 1988.

It was the opening day of the English football season, Spurs had beaten Manchester City 3–1 and I was in a very good mood. Arlette was living in Plymouth, with her three daughters, and from our chance meeting we got along pretty well, and after a while she agreed to join me in the Falklands. The girls followed at intervals.

The wedding was to be a day out for the whole of Stanley. We had hired the Town Hall and a military band, which just happened to be in the Islands to celebrate the Queen's birthday, agreed to come along and play at the wedding ceremony, whilst some 800 guests attended a pretty lively wedding reception and dance.

Canon Gerry Murphy, the priest for the Anglican Church, agreed to perform the service. When we had asked him, I was a little doubtful that he would, seeing as it was not a church wedding, but he was very positive. 'I think I owe you one, Terry,' he said.

What he was referring to was a time when I was an elected member of the Legislative and Executive Councils, and one day I stopped to chat with him. Pretty soon the subject turned to the very poor state of repair of the church itself. After nearly 100 years of very little maintenance the structure was starting to show some alarming signs of fatigue.

Standing there together, Canon Murphy asked me a very straight, but honest question: 'Do you think the people really care about the church, Terry?'

I replied, 'Of course they do, Gerry. Look, I don't attend very many home matches, and I am certainly not a season ticket holder, but the church to me is a principal landmark, a symbol of the faith, in the heart of a democratic and civilised city. The fact that it is the tallest building in town gives it a sense of physical strength and its distinctive features so obviously represent the Church of England, it is perhaps the one thing more than any other that demonstrates to the community and visitors alike that we are British. After all, if we were indeed Argentine, the most symbolic building of a religious nature in the town would be undoubtedly Catholic.'

'My, my,' he said, 'I would never have looked at it like that.' Then with a smile and a slight sigh, he asked, 'It will take an awful lot of dedication, hard work and money to put it all right. Do you think the Government would or could help in any way?'

'Let me see what I can do, I'll have a chat with some of the other Councillors.'

I am not sure how it came about, but with my mind made up to raise the matter in the House, I was pleasantly surprised to be beaten to the punch. L.G. Blake (Tim) stood up and spoke ever so elegantly and appropriately about the structural problems of the church and suggested why FIG should consider helping out.

I was on my feet as soon as he finished his appeal, to lend support to the idea. Eventually, a scheme was agreed, whereby the Government would match 1 for 1 any monies raised by the Church.

With this news, the Church Council swung into action and were quite magnificent in organising fund-raising events. Soon enough, with the support of all sectors of the community and others outside, enough money (I am told £1 million) was raised to complete the works required, and to make some very agreeable additions. Now the church stands proud and shining, as the main centre for the congregation of the faithful, and those who are not so inclined, for religious and ceremonial occasions.

I am still not a season ticket holder, and I still do not attend many home games, but I can tell you this, it gave me a great deal of satisfaction to help out in the restoration of 'God's National Stadium'. I also hold a great deal of admiration for Canon Murphy. He was a quiet-spoken man, who had very sensitive ears and a good pair of eyes, which meant he was well aware of how best to serve and support the community.

I recall going to his house, (the deanery) one afternoon. His accommodation could be very difficult to live in at times, but he never complained. On this particular day, the house was cold and the smoke from the chimney was filling the kitchen more than it was letting out into the chilly winter air.

Gerry had noticed that I was aware of his lack of comfort. He winked an eye, and then said to me, 'Ah, Terry, when it gets really cold in here, I put on three or four jumpers. When it starts to get warmer I take them off, one at a time.'

'What about the smoke?' I asked.

'Oh, if the kitchen gets too blue, I open the door and let it out that way.' The remark summed up the man's character. Apparently he had also distinguished himself in the green shirt of Ireland playing international rugby union.

I don't know about his Rugby history, but I do know that after completing his work in the Falklands, he moved on to the Tower of London. If there are special places in heaven, then there must be a spot for Canon Gerry Murphy there. But then Gerry would have a better idea than me.

Unfortunately, my marriage was to be a fairly short one. Fast, and perhaps all too often a furious affair, with booze playing a central role in the never-ending dinners and parties, Arlette and I separated after just eight and a half extremely turbulent years. I think by the end, one was just as tired as the other from the whirlwind experience. That said, there are a few happy memories.

The licence brokerage business is an untold story about the history of the Falklands and its private sector. In the early 1990s it was pretty much the most important business, but each year since 1987, it had become much less lucrative (I stop short of saying worthless).

The reason for this makes a sorry tale. In the beginning, there were just a few local companies involved in the illex squid licence business in a meaningful way, thus the fees for the successful agents were very valuable. It was the only way, then, local companies could generate income, to re-invest and take a meaningful stake in the industry for the longer term. The reason for this was that there had been no indigenous fishing industry in the Falklands, therefore no expertise or infrastructure.

News of the financial rewards soon became street and public house hot gossip and soon enough, new companies appeared and within a few short years the business was ruined.

The main reason for this was that other companies wishing to get into the market were prepared to undervalue their services, which only played into the hands of the foreign vessel owner, who employed a tactic of playing one company off against the other. These almost pimp-type companies, in their short-sightedness, perhaps even worse, blindness, were unwittingly actively aiding and abetting the foreign vessel owner in the rapid contraction of the brokerage fees, until they were worth one tenth of what they had been.

The irresponsible and commercial incompetence of these few companies, believing they were being some sort of smart-arses, had drastically reduced vital revenue to a still very young and fragile local private sector (new money), from approximately £1.2 million to little more than £120,000. (The totals may not be 100% accurate, but certainly accurately reflect the trend.)

It must also be said that FIG can take no credit either, because they stood back and let it happen. Some would even say that one or two senior officials and elected representatives mischievously encouraged it, allegedly motivated by sheer jealousy that some local businessmen just might get rich, and that would never have done. I would not know if that was true or not, but from my worldly travels, the one thing I have found to be very common and annoying in all small communities is that terrible human condition called envy, which seems to cloud the mind and blur the vision.

As all the local companies gradually became slaves of the

brokerage trade to the Japanese, Korean and Taiwanese boat owners, it was very necessary to go and visit these countries and companies, making long, expensive and time-consuming journeys halfway around the world, fighting for some peanut returns, from a foreign boat owner, for your own country's natural resources – just the bloody point I tried to make at the CPA meeting in Bermuda.

On one such journey, Pete and I decided we ought to go, uninvited, to Seoul, Korea, because although we had secured half the Korean licence allocation in the Falklands the previous fishing season for an organisation of boat owners known simply as KOSAC, rumour around town was that others were trying to gatecrash the commercial arrangement between us and the boat owners' association, so rather than sit on our butts we thought we had better get into action and kick some.

Finally we made our destination. Once there, we soon made arrangements to meet with the President and other senior members of KOSAC, who found our initiative to travel all the way to their offices in Korea, to raise the issue of potential competition, surprisingly challenging.

Although we failed to get anything firm on the next season's allocation, they had been suitably impressed by our approach, which was certain to have some bearing on their final decision. See what I mean, their decision. Our bloody resource, yet they would decide if we could participate or not.

As it happened, we also had a meeting with a boat owner company outside of this organisation, whose representatives became very interested in setting up a joint venture with JBG Falklands, in the Falklands. The commercial plans were much more than just licence brokerage.

Pete and I were very aware that there was a need to climb out of the snake pit called licence brokerage; the future was to develop a meaningful long-term business, but each time we tried, we were either pulled back in by the boat owners, or pushed back in by the likes of the Falkland Islands Government.

Once we got back home, the joint-venture company JBG/SAJO was officially registered, and the foreign partner deposited a six-figure amount into the JV account in the Falkland Islands, as agreed in Korea. The capital was to be invested in the commercial projects we had each approved.

These plans were presented to FIG officials, and some elected representatives. The latter gave verbal support for the projects. In view of this support, we were confident that the allocation of a fishing licence for the Korean vessel would be successful. But alas, this was the Falklands. Elected representatives had little say in the matter, and other influential powers saw to it that it was not granted. Therefore, the opportunity for JBG/SAJO to lead the private sector down a new, and far more beneficial road, whilst devising a vital section of the Falklands fishery and the Islands economy, had been tragically lost. The JV was wound-up, and the 'new money' repatriated to Korea.

Despite this inexplicable betrayal by our own authorities, we would make other attempts to try and break the foreign boat owners' stranglehold on our fishery, which also failed. Not because the commercial intent was weak or unsustainable. No, because of the Falkland Island Government's inability to make what should have been clear-cut decisions in the project's favour. Oddly enough, even when its development arm was strongly recommending some of our plans, Government still found reason to permit the foreigner to monopolise the Falklands illex fishery.

However, there were moments of very satisfying success, as we beat off the pack of wolves in the brokerage business before it got buggered up.

One of these occasions was back in London, when I was again meeting the largest organisation representing the Korean boat owners.

The only person who could speak English on their side was the translator, therefore every single detail had to be channelled via him. It would prove to be a laborious task. Every time I answered or asked a question, 15 of the 18 wanted to put their spoke in. Long periods of time would pass, when they would just discuss things among themselves.

By the end of a very long day nothing had been resolved and I drifted off back to my hotel totally knackered and in need of a refreshing shower, a change of clothes and a very long whisky. Saturday and Sunday was the same bloody routine, 12 hours each day of endless Korean and very little English, about the details of an agreement between us to apply for Falklands fishing licences.

Interestingly, on this occasion, I was not just representing my company but also Fortuna Limited. We had formed a kind of pact, which was to hang on to what we had with the Koreans and keep every other bugger out.

Worryingly, after three days of inconclusive talks, it was now Monday. I was flying back to the Falklands at midnight and I had to check in at 9.30 p.m. at RAF Brize Norton to catch an 18-hour flight back home, so I had to get the deal done before I left.

By lunchtime, it appeared to me that I was no closer to getting an agreement signed than when I first met them. So, I decided that it was time to push things on. To achieve this, I needed to cut out the multiple conversations in Korean so I shouted at the translator, asking him to relay the concept of an agreement as I saw it.

My very direct approach caught the group's attention, and they all sat and listened without interruption until the translator had completed transmitting my message.

Then their senior representative spoke to each one of his delegation. When he finished, he looked coldly at his translator, and spoke very firmly to him. The interpreter turned and touched my arm, then said, 'The President says why don't you go and tell your boss that we think it should be done differently.'

I did not look at the translator, I stared straight at the President and said, 'I've got a better idea. Why don't you tell the President I am the boss.' For the first time in four days, I think the interpreter actually translated exactly what I had said.

Things then began to move quickly and suddenly pieces of paper started flying left, right and centre. Finally, the group's President and I were signing documents that were hastily prepared. As each document was finalised, I was pushing a copy into my briefcase.

By 6.30 p.m., it was done, and I was making my way, with a very supportive wife, to the lobby, with the ink still wet on the papers. I still had to get back to my hotel, to arrange some transport to get up to Oxfordshire to catch my flight.

As the lift reached the ground floor, the doors opened. I was about to step out, when suddenly, I came face-to-face with a representative of an arch rival company.

I bid him a very good day. He glared and grunted something back at me, so to cheer him up, I waved some papers over my head. 'Is this what you are looking for? If it is, you're five minutes too late.'

I left the hotel totally exhausted, but although I climbed into the waiting taxicab worn out, I was extremely satisfied with the knowledge that for one more year, JBG Falklands and Fortuna would hold on to the licences (20 each).

The early 90s also became a crossroads period for JBG Falklands. Apart from the frustrations with the fishing companies from Asia, we had also become disillusioned with our Spanish partners. Thus, JBG decided to opt out of the partnership with Pescanova SA in the Falklands joint venture company, Polar Limited. After Polar, we formed a new joint venture company with another Spanish partner, which we called JBG/Eurofishing.

But Pete and I had not limited JBG Falklands to the fishing business alone, we also decided to build an office block and conference centre in the middle of the town. This time, the partnership was not with a fishing company, but a legal firm from Aberdeen, who themselves had become pioneers in the Falklands by having the foresight to realise there would be a need for legal representation and advice in the rapidly changing environment of the Falkland Islands.

Thus, they had set up an office in Stanley in August 1988 as C. & P.H. Chalmers. Gavin Farquhar, who skilfully bedded the company down, and into society, superbly represented them in those early days. They would later amalgamate with another legal firm, which operates successfully as Ledingham Chalmers in the Falklands still today.

The business concept that we agreed upon was to provide office units for ourselves, whilst letting out the other units, which would also provide facilities for business meetings and conferences.

The investment, in Falklands terms, was not inconsiderable. We had to purchase land then a prefabricated kit unit from the United Kingdom, arrange transportation from the UK and employ a building contractor to carry out a 'turnkey' project.

The joint venture raised the investment capital in two ways. Firstly JBG Falklands and C. & P.H. Chalmers took up an equal amount of share equity. The remainder was borrowed from the only bank in the Falklands (still the case), Standard Chartered Bank.

It was not an ideal time to be borrowing money from a bank, at

2 or 3% above base rate, which meant our borrowing was being paid at 17% eventually. However, within nine months of planning the project, we moved into the new building, which we called Atlantic House. Yet another company was formed, this time, Stanley Business Centre Limited, and in no time, the office units were fully occupied.

We supplemented the earnings from lets by operating a stationery supplies business. The combination worked very well, which ensured we were able to service debt and, as the business grew, generate profit.

The ultimate aim was achieved some ten years later, which was to have a functional home base for the company, with modern assets, free of all debts and liabilities.

I would like to mention that before giving up our interests in the subsidiary company Polar Limited with the Spanish partners Pescanova SA, JBG Falklands had been fully involved in the first major piece of onshore fishing infrastructure to be built in the Falklands, on the floating port facility in Stanley. The idea being, we would provide a support service to assist in developing Falklands fishing industry.

It was a project that required not only logistical planning, from importing the prefabricated structure, power generation units, storage and cargo handling equipment, but also a major human resource factor: importing and accommodating a foreign labour force of nearly 30 men from Chile and Spain.

The plan itself was simple enough: build a cold store unit which could hold approximately 900 cubic metres of frozen fish in blocks. This project, and the building of Atlantic House, not only demonstrated serious capital investments by a local joint venture company in the Islands, but it also showed that a local fishing company could support, and provide, benefits in financial and employment terms to other sectors of the Islands community, and in so doing, we were an active player in the important role of stimulating the Islands economy. (A point missed, sadly, by the Government.)

I will highlight just a few benefits to the economy. The importation of a transient labour force during the 13-week contract to build the cold store provided the FIG with some unexpected revenue from letting to us a campsite which had been closed down for months and was going to be dismantled. Furthermore, local businesses who owned and operated retail and social services and facilities benefited from the arrival of the short-term workforce through their purchasing.

Both the office and cold store ventures provided employment opportunities and better than average salaries for Islanders during construction phases and beyond. Once completed, Islanders were given full-time employment at the cold store and in the office units. Oh yeah, we were pioneers all right, and we certainly played our part in developing and expanding the Islands economy.

57

Lunch and Dinner With Royalty
(A Cup Final with Tottenham Hotspur)

Before going on with other business stories, I would like to tell you about some other unusual and unique happenings in this Falkland Islander's life, thus far.

One of these events took place in September 1990. I had been invited by the Governor and Mrs Fullerton, along with a handful of other guests, to take dinner at Government House with HRH the Duke of Kent.

The last member of the Royal family whom I had been introduced to in the Falklands had been HRH Prince Andrew back in 1985, after he had laid the foundation stone for the new hospital which was to replace the building destroyed by fire in 1984. On that occasion, it was nothing more than a handshake, as Sir Rex stopped and introduced me to the Prince as they were walking by.

This time, it was a meal, and I was indeed honoured. I should mention that dinners, after Sir Rex Hunt's period as Governor, had become much more formal affairs, 7.30 p.m. for 8 p.m., and on your bike by 11 p.m.

As we were gathered in the main lounge, taking our aperitifs, Mrs Fullerton came up to me and said, 'When dinner is over, Terry, I will arrange for HRH to sit on that settee.' She pointed to a small piece of furniture. 'So make sure you are nearby, and I will arrange for you to sit by him.'

After dinner, I made my way towards the settee with a glass of brandy. Mrs Fullerton had skilfully guided the Duke of Kent there, and whilst his Royal Highness was making himself comfortable, she said, 'Why don't you sit here, Terry?' signalling politely with her left arm to the vacant space. With a cheeky little boy's grin, I replied, it would be my pleasure.

I did not know much about the interests of the Duke of Kent, other than the Freemasons, but I was aware that he was the President of the Football Association; I wasn't that well up on Freemasonry, so I thought that football would do as a good conversation opener. It worked a treat, and we chatted away with ease for about an hour. I remember saying to him that I believed Spurs would win the cup that season. Bugger me, they did.

Within six months of meeting the Duke of Kent, I would have my next Royal engagement. This time I had been invited to lunch with HRH Prince Philip.

Once again, there was a very small gathering, about 16 people I would have thought. Once more, we were in the main lounge at Government House, drinks had been served, and the Governor was taking His Royal Highness around the room to introduce him to the few guests individually. When they reached me, I said who I was, and what it was I had done.

His Royal Highness then looked at me, and said, 'Oh, so you're one of those industrial rapists, are you?' What he said could be heard all around the room; everyone stopped what they were doing and glanced towards us.

Just like the time with the Governor in Bermuda, I knew I needed to react, and bloody quickly. So I did. I said, 'I beg your pardon, sir, but I have the greatest respect for conservation and the environment. I am well aware that if we do not preserve our fish stocks, then I am out of business, so it makes no sense for me to be an industrial rapist.' HRH smiled, and moved on.

After lunch, and whilst the Royal guest was engrossed in conversation with a small group of people, the Governor slipped away from his side, came up to me and said, 'Well done, Terry. I think he quite enjoyed you standing up to him.'

As the Governor moved away again to join his distinguished guest, I thought to myself, to be honest, I couldn't care if he did or did not like what I said. Prince or no Prince, I was not having anyone suggesting to me that I might be an industrial rapist.

Well, moving on from Royal dining sessions, you will be aware that I am a passionate Tottenham Hotspur football fan. Something I will be for the whole of my life.

One day, I was sitting in the lobby of my hotel in Coventry Street, right in the heart of London, with my wife and business partner, and a long gin and tonic, contemplating getting myself ready for yet another journey back home.

Pete and Arlette were both sitting opposite me, with big grins on their faces. Then Arlette said, 'You are not going back to the Falklands tonight, Terry, because I've got two tickets for the Cup Final, Tottenham against Nottingham Forest.' After a brief pause she went on, 'Not just for the match itself, but also for pre-match drinks, lunch, and then for a post-match reception.' I was elated, I was filled with uncontrollable joy. I told you I had some happy moments in my marriage.

Cup Final day was to be one of the most memorable of my life; I have written about my wonderful experience, six years earlier, when I was the guest of the club at White Hart Lane. But this event was quite different, and absolutely special.

The 1991 Cup Final just happened to coincide with the 30th anniversary of Tottenham Hotspur becoming the first team of the 20th century to win the FA Cup and Football League double. Because of this, many of the double-winning team players were present at the pre-match and lunch gatherings.

The first person I would meet, however, as I approached the entrance hall was Martin Chivers. Martin was one of the great Spurs goalscorers of the 1970s. As I chatted away to him, I reminded him about his scorcher of a goal against Wolverhampton Wanderers in the final of the UEFA Cup. Shaking his leg and laughing, he said, 'I can still feel my foot tingling as I hit that one, and watched it screaming into the Wolves' net.'

As I began to move around the room, I met more great stars, and I found myself chatting away to many of my schoolboy heroes. Spurs legends like Cliff Jones, Bobby Smith, Dave Mackay, Maurice Norman, Terry Dyson, were just a few from the double winning team of 1961 and Frank Saul, who scored the winning goal against Chelsea in the first ever all-London Cup Final, in 1967, which Spurs won 2–1. We reminisced and took photographs like long-lost friends.

But there were other famous people around, other than football stars that morning. I also had a few laughs with Bruce Forsyth.

Lunch was served in a huge hall, for what must have been about 1,000 guests. The hall was decorated in a sea of navy blue and white: walls, ceiling, tablecloths, balloons etc.

As luck would have it, I was sat with a chap who printed the match programme for Tottenham. He asked me what I was doing in the evening, to which I replied that I didn't know. I did in fact know, I had made arrangements to meet Lewis Clifton for dinner, but I just had this feeling that something might be on offer by the tone of his question.

I was right, because he went on to say, 'It's too late now. If I had met you before, I could have arranged for you to come back to the hotel after the match, and join the team and other guests for dinner.' Fucking hell, I thought, that would be some deal.

Then I said to him, 'Yeah, bit of a shame.'

He looked at me with quizzical eyes. 'Let me have a think about it, and let's meet up here after the match. Is that okay?'

As kick-off time was approaching, I was getting a little nervous. Tottenham were favourites to win, but in these types of games you can never tell. It was time to leave the hall and walk across to Wembley. The adrenaline immediately begins to pump through your body, as the deafening noise of your fellow fans chanting Tottenham, Tottenham begins ringing in your ears and echoes out around the stadium. Just as I was adjusting to the atmosphere, something quite remarkable happened.

Here I am, entering Wembley Stadium with 80,000 fans packed inside this wonderful old arena, and as I am walking down the steps to the row where my seat is, I hear above all the noise and jubilation, 'TSB, TSB.' I thought I must have had too much champagne already, so I ignored it. As people stood up to let me get to my allotted seat, I heard a voice calling again, 'TSB, TSB.' Fuck it, I can't be going mad. So in one last-ditch attempt to convince myself I was normal, I looked up.

To my sheer delight and total amazement, I saw a long-time Falklands friend and mate, Steve Jennings. He was jumping up and down with his friends, not more than 12 rows away. Okay, there was nothing extraordinary about two Falkland Islanders, 8,000 miles away from home, who supported the same football club, being at the FA Cup Final. But it was quite remarkable that we were in such close proximity to each other, with another 79,998 people packed in the stadium.

I knew from that very moment, it was going to be my day, and Tottenham would win. The boys did not let me down, even if it did require extra time, and Gary Lineker missed a penalty.

After the game, I made my way back to the hall for after-match drinks, which I badly needed; my throat was dry and I had almost lost my voice from all the singing and shouting, but I was one very happy teddy indeed.

As planned, I met up with Mr Eastman. He was every bit as pleased as me. 'Look,' he said, 'I can't do anything about the dinner, it is too late, but if you come to the Park Hotel at 11 p.m., I'll be waiting in the foyer and I will let you in.'

Jesus Christ, my day was just getting better and better.

At 6.30 p.m., the drinks session was over and it was time to disperse. Also as planned, I met Lewis Clifton in the early evening for a meal. But I am sure I could not have been the greatest company, because my mind was elsewhere. After a while I told him what had happened and what had been planned. He fully understood why I wished to curtail the evening with him, and wished me a very happy hangover.

I was on the doorstep of the hotel at 11 p.m. prompt, and true to his word Mr Eastman was waiting in the foyer. As soon as he noticed me, words were said to a doorman, who then let me in. I was then shown into the banqueting hall, where it was clearly obvious that dinner had been finished, and it was now party time.

With the exception of Paul Gascoigne, who had been carried off the field after just 15 minutes of play with knee ligament damage, and Gary Lineker, who was with his wife and very ill son George, all the players who had helped Tottenham to victory that day, were now, not unexpectedly, letting their hair down.

There were other well-known sports personalities and heroes of yesteryear at the party, former British heavyweight boxing champion Henry Cooper was one. I remember Arlette just had to go up and touch the fist that had laid out Muhammad Ali.

We had been given a table to sit at, and glasses filled with champagne, which kept flowing all night, and pretty soon I was having a ball along with everyone else. I recall a bunch of the players getting up on a small stage, pretending to be a rock band. The goalkeeper, Norwegian Eric Thorstvedt, was beating shit out of the drums.

But, perhaps the highlight of all, on this most memorable of days for me personally, had to be when I was actually allowed to hold the FA Cup itself, aloft.

The commercial manager, Mike Rollo, held one handle and I the other. Oh yes, it will be a day that this Spurs fan will remember for as long as my mind allows me to.

It is also gratifying to know that no matter whatever happens in this world, I will always be the first Falkland Islander to ever hold the FA Cup. All thanks to Tottenham Hotspur Football Club, and of course Arlette, who arranged the tickets.

58

*Pleasure, Leisure and the Cruel Side of Business
(But the ultimate business challenge presents itself)*

Life was not all work and Tottenham Hotspur, as you could imagine. I travelled to many countries, for leisure and pleasure, in the 1990s. On one such occasion I took my wife to the birthplace of her ancestors, or at least we assumed so.

With her family names of Henricksen and Hansen, they had to come from some Scandinavian country, so we took a ferry from England to Gothenburg, Sweden.

The trip was a 24-hour party. Once safely in the Swedish port, we checked into the Radisson Hotel. We were actually there at the time of her 44th birthday, on 2 May, a day that gradually descended into one of arguments and tantrums.

Even dinner proved a disaster. We went out for a Chinese meal, and were served up something that was typical Mongolian, which did not excite my taste buds one little bit. I would not stop moaning about the quality of the food, and the price I paid for it, from the moment I settled the bill. We went back to the hotel, totally pissed off with the whole day.

I decided to order two brandies from the hotel bar, and for some reason, I asked to pay cash. This was 1990, and I just couldn't believe the £16 the barman was asking. But I shrugged my shoulders, took a deep breath, and said, 'Oh fuck it, give us two more, will you.'

I have to say I was mightily impressed with Sweden. The cleanliness, wherever you went, restaurants, the streets, public transport and toilets, made countries such as the UK look untidy, even filthy.

We travelled by train down the southwest coast of Sweden, from Gothenburg to Malmo, where we stayed for a couple of days, eating, drinking and sleeping – I must admit, I have no idea in which order – before taking the short hop by ferry to our next destination, which was Copenhagen, to begin my wife's family pilgrimage.

I found Denmark completely different to Sweden. Carlsberg or other lagers are central to a Dane's way of life, from when one opens one's eyes in the morning (it could even be accompanied by schnapps) until closing them in the small hours of the following morning. That said, the Danes are very friendly and hospitable people, whereas I found the Swedes to be a little more reserved.

Back in the Falkland Islands, many Falkland Islanders had made friends with seamen from Denmark over the years, when the small sea freighter which carried the Islands' supplies from the United Kingdom every three months arrived in Stanley.

Before leaving the Falklands for our trip to Copenhagen, we had been strongly recommended to go and visit the Tivoli Gardens, so we took the advice, and what a spectacle it is. I discovered that the gardens are one of the oldest amusement parks in the world, with a vast array of games and rides. There are dozens of restaurants covering every imaginable international culinary delight. Several large stages are often used as venues for live concerts, for the world's top artists in all types of music.

The gardens are riddled with wonderful walkways, from which you take in the splendour and the beauty of the flower gardens, trees, ponds, birds, insects and animals. Then finally, at the end of the evening, there is a magnificent fireworks display.

On one fairly quiet Sunday afternoon, my wife and I were casually walking around the streets of Copenhagen, when we noticed a group of people rushing off down a particular street. Neither of us had the slightest idea what the hell all the fuss was about, but none the less, we just had to go and take a look, so we decided to go down a small side street parallel to the main crowd.

As we were strolling along, we came upon a dark blue van with blackened windows. Quite by accident, we had happened to stumble upon the Rolling Stones, who were in the city doing a gig.

It soon dawned on us, that we were actually at the back of a hotel, and the mass of people had obviously been rushing to the front in the hope of getting a glimpse, kiss, touch or autograph of their rock idols. As we approached the van, the band members, with the exception of Mick Jagger, were just getting out of the vehicle and going into the hotel. So by pure chance, apart from us and two or three security guards, there was not another soul in the street.

Not being a Stones fan, I did not find it a big deal, but I did find myself feeling slightly guilty that I was standing where hundreds of genuine fans dearly would have loved to have been. The only thing that impressed me about the whole experience was the size of Keith Richard's gold wristwatch. It was the largest piece of gold jewellery I had ever seen in my life. Arlette was delighted, and got plenty of waves and kisses blown at her by the band members. Actually, I think Keith Richards was blowing the kisses at me.

For the last 18 years, travel has been a way of life for me. On one of my journeys, I would travel to Szczecin, the largest city in the northwestern part of Poland, which has a long maritime and shipyard heritage. Many of the ships I had seen and enjoyed a meal on, were now rusting away inactive at docksides.

On this particular trip, I was accompanied by JBG Falklands General Manager, David Hall. The purpose of the visit was purely business; we were keen to set up a joint venture with one of the old-established Polish fishing companies, called Gryf, who had been operating for many years in the Falklands fishery.

I am not sure why, but once in the UK we took a plane to Frankfurt in Germany, where we were met by a chauffeur, who then took us all the way by car from the German city, to the Polish port of Szczecin, which is just across the border with Germany.

It was a very long car journey from Frankfurt, and we did not see much along the way because it was pouring with rain, as we travelled along and brushed the outskirts of Leipzig and Berlin. The journey only really brightened up when we reached the Polish/German frontier. Once there, we were greeted by authorities, who checked and stamped our passports, and by the many smiling street traders, who were showing off their gold teeth as they began to try and sell us items such as cigarettes and alcohol.

Had I known what was in store for us when we would reach my hotel in Szczecin, I would have gladly bought a bottle or two of whatever it was they were selling as whisky, or some genuine vodka.

As it happened, the business aspects of our visit to Poland went very well, but the accommodation was shocking, quite unbelievable. Of all the hotels I have ever stayed in my entire life, this had to be the worst. Block walls had huge holes in them, which had been covered with bed sheets, rubble and debris lay everywhere in the foyer area. It just looked as though someone had got halfway through a refurbishment job, then walked out and left it.

Both the check-in desk area and the bar were covered in dust. A single bottle, labelled Johnnie Walker Red Label Whisky, stood on the middle shelf behind the bar counter. It was also covered in dust, and looking ever so lonely.

The lift appeared as though it had been manufactured a hundred years ago, and when the man pressed a few buttons, not surprisingly nothing worked. After a while, we gave up, and walked up several flights of stairs to the bedrooms.

Once inside my room, it appeared to me more like a prison cell. Having been a policeman, I knew what a prison cell looked like. The bedcover was designed like the top of a canoe, apparently so you could slide your body into your bed and seal yourself off from vampire-like mosquitoes. One of the travel brochures I had read explained that in this city, accommodation could range from luxury hotels to fleapits. I could not work out why we had selected a fleapit.

I had, of course, arrived very shortly after the revolution. Poland had gone from being a Russian satellite state, and was feeling the pain of growing out of its embryonic phase of democracy.

What I had always admired in the Poles was their honesty, hard work and amazing will to fight to achieve their dreams. They were going to need all three in abundance to climb up and out of their dark and traumatic past. But I believed and hoped they would. They are a people that have been pushed and shoved around for centuries, and now, because of their courage to go it alone, they deserve success and happiness.

Often, as I walked around and observed the scale of the challenge that lay ahead of them, I would think back to the many occasions when I had been very well entertained by ships' captains on several of the Polish fishing trawlers in Port William. They would often express their concerns for family and friends back home in Poland, during the misery days of communism. With tears in their eyes, they would say, 'The Polish people are Catholics, Terry. How can a Catholic be a communist?'

We left Poland full of hope for them, and for our business objectives with Gryf. All we now had to do was to go back home, and convince the authorities that our plans were worthy of support, by providing a fishing licence.

Leading up to the allocation of the 1992 fishing licences by the Falkland Islands Government, JBG were very active on the lobbying front for several international business interests from Japan, Poland, Spain, Korea and Taiwan. As a result, there were success stories, but also deep frustration.

JBG had settled in well with its new Spanish partners in the joint-venture partnership, JBG/Eurofishing. These Spanish partners were from a company called Rampesca, made up of eight Fontan brothers led by Jacobo.

Together, we had achieved an element of our business goals, but just as it appeared we had jumped the major hurdles, there came a huge and unexpected disappointment. We had done the hard bit, or so we thought. We had secured three loligo licences for a Spanish boat owner, who had agreed to place three of his vessels into JBG Eurofishing. But before we could start celebrating, Jacobo Fontan was on the telephone from Spain to inform us that the vessel owner had fallen seriously ill. So ill, in fact, that there was a real possibility he might not survive.

Eventually the boat owner decided that his health was more important than business, and he would not invest in the Falklands project. Thus, we had to decline the offer of the licences from FIG.

In one fateful swoop, JBG Falklands, via its joint venture company Eurofishing, had been robbed of a secure and prosperous future. The best-laid plans of Eurofishing, which was to own and operate three medium-size fishing trawlers, a very courageous and progressive plan at the time, were completely wrecked.

Worst still, salt was to be thrown in the gaping wound. The licences we had turned down were then offered to competitors, in what was a very competitive commercial field, making it almost impossible in the future to retrieve the position lost.

I did not think for one moment it could, but the situation actually got worse. I had felt the business trip to Poland had been a success. Well, it was, in terms of managing to get a signed agreement between ourselves and one of the most experienced and respected fishing companies. Bugger me, the Falkland Islands Government once again offered this new joint venture company, JBG/GRYF, a loligo licence, and they too turned it down, deciding at the eleventh hour not to enter into a long-term commercial venture with us.

I could not believe JBG Falklands' appalling bad luck. Two projects, which we had thoroughly thought out, and planned on the basis of sound commercial concepts, which only required the tools to build upon, and those tools had been gained, but an unforeseen illness, and a nervous foreign partner, left all the business plans in ruins.

The double whammy was, I think, catastrophic for JBG Falklands and I don't believe the company ever fully regained its confidence, even though it continued to trade for a couple more years.

The relationship with the company Gryf of Poland terminated within a month or two, and even though JBG and the Fontan brothers continued a working relationship by working with the vessel the *Ferralemas*, the partnership did not remain for very long and JBG pulled out of JBG-Eurofishing a little while later.

However, as always, as one door closes, another opens. In April 1992, with the dagger still quivering in JBG Falklands' heart, a new commercial relationship began with another local fishing company, the first ever registered in the Islands, as a matter of fact, Southern Cross Limited.

This company, which had been formed on 1 April 1986, and had obviously, somewhere along the line, lost the plot. Therefore, its majority shareholders, Christophersens of Uruguay, who held 80% of the shares at the time, instructed its Falklands partner to come and speak with me.

Because of the sale agreement with the Spanish company Pescanova SA, a system was devised for Pete Gilding and me to become directors and shareholders of Southern Cross Limited as individuals, rather than JBG Falklands, the company.

Finally, a working understanding was reached, once the Uruguayans agreed to one fundamental issue, which was that I would assume full responsibility for the restructuring of the company, in consultation with the Uruguayans and the Falklands partners, and I would be responsible for the initial commercial planning.

The Uruguayans also agreed to the new shareholding, only on the basis that a certain turnover figure was reached in the first year of trading. The agreed sum was, in fact, achieved in the first three months under the new company formation.

Having shifted the balance of power (51/49 in our favour), I began to plan my next task, which was a tactical and diplomatic removal of the Uruguayan shareholders altogether. Why? Because FIG fisheries policy was set in such a way that if we wished to become long-term players in the Falklands loligo fishery in particular, it was absolutely necessary that I finalised an agreement with the Uruguayans that effectively removed them from Southern Cross Limited, so that the company became 100% owned by Falkland Islanders. Step-by-step, and over a period of perhaps two years, the objective was achieved.

I have always rated that success as one of the highest achievements in my 13 years in the Falkland Islands fishery, simply because, if Southern Cross Limited had not been entirely owned and operated by resident Falkland Islanders, there was never going to be any hope of getting the company into the much larger commercial picture, in the joint ventures Southern Cross Limited would eventually form with its Spanish partners, Chymar SA, firstly Golden Chance and then Golden Touza Limited, followed by all the subsidiary companies that spun off from that in the future.

The introduction of Southern Cross Limited to Chymar SA came about by a piece of inspirational thinking.

I had received a telephone call from Antonio Cordero, a representative for the Spanish boat owners in the Falklands.

Antonio had called me to enquire if JBG Falklands were available to do business with some people he knew back in Spain. Naturally I had no intention of reneging on JBG's agreement with Pescanova, so I correctly replied that we could not. But instantly, an idea came to my head, and I said, 'But I think I do know someone who might be able to.' Then I told him of Southern Cross Limited.

The result of that telephone call from him was the moment which kicked things off between Southern Cross Limited and the Spanish company Chymar and the initial joint venture company was formed. Out of that came Golden Touza Limited, which now, quite rightly, stands as one of the most respected leading local fishing companies in the Falklands today.

I am extremely happy and proud that I took a leading role in the rescuing and rapid commercial expansion of Southern Cross Limited, and in every other commercial thing it would be involved in over the next nine years from 1992 to 2001. This included vessel ownership and operation, investments in marketing, cold storage companies, properties and factories, and the pioneering aquaculture programme through the local company Falklands Fresh Limited.

Southern Cross Limited has the potential for a bright future (for as long as there is a sustainable fishery) because the company has been built on solid commercial planning, which also ensures that people who live in the Falkland Islands are right in the heart of the commercial action, with a meaningful shareholding.

59

New York and Washington DC for a Drop of Politics

In 1992, I found myself on an unexpected trip to New York and Washington DC. It came about because elected representatives of the Falkland Islands had declined individual invitations to attend a seminar at Airlie House Conference Centre in Virginia, near Washington DC under the auspices of the Institute for Conflict Analysis and Resolution, at George Mason University, which had been organised to coincide with the 10th anniversary of the Falklands War.

The colloquium was to be attended by a wide range of scholars, researchers and political and economic leaders from the United States of America, Argentina, the United Kingdom and the Falklands. The subject was 'The Falklands/Malvinas Conflict, Ten Years On'.

I tell you this, I thought it quite remarkable and totally irresponsible of the councillors to turn down the invitations to attend such a topical issue regarding our Islands and to make a useful contribution. Here was a golden opportunity to stand up and be counted for what we are, Falkland Islanders, in the presence of influential figures who had been representatives of the UK Foreign Office or the United States Embassy in Buenos Aires, or very closely associated with the Argentine Foreign Ministry, along with academics who had written papers or published books on the subject.

As I was not a scholar, researcher, political or economic leader, how did I get invited? Simple, really. Once all the elected members had refused, invitations were sent out by the organisers to former elected councillors of the Islands, and eventually three of us, Charles Keenleyside, Tony Blake and I, agreed to attend.

It was now left up to four Islanders (we had been joined by Lewis Clifton) to express personal opinions, not the ideal situation for the people of the Falklands. However, this situation did not deter me in any way. I was going to make a full and active contribution.

Before going to Washington, we had been invited to attend a conference in New York organised by the Glad Foundation to debate the concept of global peace. By some quirk of fate, or otherwise, the Falklands had been identified as a potential base to launch this highly commendable idea.

Unfortunately, after a few days of discussion and some very enjoyable social events, it became pretty obvious that the ambitious plans needed a lot more thought, and it was extremely unlikely the Falkland Islands would be hosting such a project within the next few hundred years.

Please don't think I am scoffing at the idea. I would never want anyone to think that I was mocking anyone who was desirous of world peace. But I felt the sponsor of this attempt was still very short of an awful lot of nuts and bolts, which Tony, Charles and I were sure we could not supply.

With that decided, the three of us soon headed off to catch a train to Washington. Once we had purchased our tickets, we checked our luggage in and then we went off in search of a shoeshine boy to put some life back in our well-worn-looking shoes, then to relax with a cold beer and some good old American fast food. We did not stop shovelling the calories until we were called to our waiting train by a boisterous black gentleman, who was singing out the train stops en route, and finished with a wonderful crescendo of 'All—— a— bo——ar–d.'

During the journey, I was playing, over and over again, the cassette recording of my song 'Two Fifty-Five', which had been finished just before going to the States.

I had gone to a recording studio, at Eastcote, in London, to record my song. Unfortunately, I could not give the project my full time and attention, which resulted in a couple of friends putting it together in their own style, then passing me a copy just before my flight. But no matter how much I tried to convince myself that it was fine, I was hugely disappointed with the end product. The song had been changed beyond recognition, and it was nothing like I really wanted, or expected. I was gutted. It was not the guys' fault, they had done their best, and after all, I had only given them the lyrics and a basic melody to work with.

Finally, we arrived in Washington DC. Airlie House was set in several acres of colourful and peaceful grounds that provided spectacular views and a variety of wildlife, which included beavers who seemed to spend all day doing their best to fell trees.

Our accommodation was clean and adequate, but we were not allowed telephones or televisions in our rooms. The idea was that we should become totally immersed in the subject matter for the whole of the time we were there.

The representatives from the Falklands made a pronounced contribution to the forum. So much so, that a few very surprising and extremely positive results for the Islands came out of the conference.

It was great to be working with Tony on an international issue. I had got my wish to do this during our time as politicians at places such as the United Nations. Of course, I would be kidding myself if I thought for one moment that this forum was anywhere near that level of debate or importance. It was not. But it was a session in which the Falklands was the centre of attention. Therefore, it was an honour to be present, but much more importantly, to be identified as Falkland Islanders, with a clear view about the Island's long-term future, and how we, as individuals, saw relationships developing with our neighbour, who still did not understand, or accept, that we were a people in our own right, no longer behaving like a baby trying to hide behind the parental legs of Great Britain, metaphorically speaking.

Tony and I adopted a few tactics that maximised the transmission and reception of messages between ourselves, or the gathering, whilst also maximising our ability to spoil, or interrupt, the exchange of communication between those we chose to.

To achieve the former, NEVER sit alongside your colleague/s, always position yourself opposite, or preferably, diagonally from your team player. This way, you maintain maximum eye contact with each other. This allows you to transmit and receive body language between each other to the fullest effect. Just like good bridge players.

As for the latter, ALWAYS find a sitting position inside the enemy camp. Sit beside, or in between, two people who are not in your team. This allows you to greatly restrict or eliminate verbal and written message exchange between your opponents during working sessions. One other thing, for those who have not yet experienced it, when going into battle, be prepared and know your subject.

As part of our preparation, Tony and I would get up very early in the morning, well before breakfast, and take a walk in the beautiful gardens whilst planning strategy.

A classic mistake often made is when two people from the same side start talking over each other about the same topic, or even worse, delivering two different and conflicting messages at the same time. With careful tactical planning this sloppiness should never happen.

Well, I think that is quite enough about TSB negotiating theory, so let's get on and tell you about the conference itself.

In the chair was Dr Christopher Mitchell, who, it seemed, had more letters after his name than there are in the English alphabet. Barely 30 seconds into his opening address and I was up on my feet interrupting him.

He had begun by saying that we were all gathered together to discuss and look for possible solutions to the Falklands/Malvinas dispute between Great Britain and Argentina.

It was this remark that had me up on my feet and waving my arm, calling out, 'Excuse me, excuse me, Mr Chairman.' I got his, and everyone else's attention, rather quickly.

Looking my way, he said, 'Would you like to say something, Terry?'

'Yes I would, Mr Chairman. Yes indeed I would,' I replied. 'I would like to point out that there are three groups of people involved in this dispute, not two. They are Great Britain, the Falkland Islands and Argentina. I assume that is why we are all here today. Thank you, Mr Chairman.'

As I sat down again, I immediately thought, if I did nothing else for the rest of the conference, I had firmly laid down the Falkland Islanders' identity card for the rest of the meeting.

Unfortunately, I got the feeling the Chairman took my comments rather personally, and was slightly upset by my interjection and correction to his statement. But for the remainder of this forum, it was clearly understood that there were in fact three parties to the dispute. Had I, or some other Falkland Islanders, not been present at this meeting that morning, I have no doubt that this simplest of errors would not have been corrected.

In fact, at this particular session, it was two of the British delegation who got upset with my firmness on the issues, not the Argentines. One was so upset that he even felt compelled to approach me in a quiet part of the gardens, after a long day's session, and ask me why the hell I was being so abrasive, to which I replied, 'Perhaps you are overestimating your own intelligence.'

This remark pissed the academic gentleman off immensely, as he immediately fell off his educated perch and came crashing down to land at my level. He wheeled away saying, 'Fuck you.'

'Fuck you too,' I said, 'and I will see you in the bar for a drink later.' Rather disappointingly, he didn't show up.

Generally, it is now pretty much understood and accepted that Falkland Islanders are very much part of the Falklands/Malvinas dispute, and any debate about the subject must include Falkland Islanders; just as it should be.

Our presence at Airlie House would also score a major and very gratifying success. By the end of the three-day meeting, we had got two of the six Argentines to agree that we Falkland Islanders had to be recognised as a people. One went even further, much further than even we Falkland Islanders could have dared imagine. A trusted friend of the Argentine Foreign Ministry returned to Buenos Aires and immediately suggested to the Foreign Minister that the Falklands was without question British. Somewhat surprised, and very annoyed with their old amigo, the Argentine Foreign Ministry made a public statement disassociating them from the distinguished Señor forthwith.

The statement came as a complete surprise to me. But I tell you this, when I heard the news back home in the Falklands, I was very pleased indeed. And I thought to myself, for those in the Falkland Islands who felt our presence in Washington had been worthless, the words and actions of one Argentine might well have proved beyond all reasonable doubt that our visit was in fact vindicated.

Before leaving the United States, Tony and I decided to stay for the long weekend, because it was May Bank Holiday back in the United Kingdom. We hired a car, in which Tony drove the two of us over 1,100 kilometres in just three days. It took us the best part of one and a half hours to break free of Washington central, but once we did, it was on to the West-8 highway.

Tony had wanted to go to Titusville, which apparently had been the site of the first oil drilling, at a place called Oil Creek, so off we went. There were some remains of oil activity of yesteryear there, but the site was generally lush green grass. After a gentle stroll around, we concluded our brief visit by purchasing a bottle of Coca-Cola and a chunk of confectionery called a cow's tail from the tiny local general store. Then we walked out on to the veranda and flopped into two vacant cane chairs, and put our feet up on the railings and relaxed, before we headed on to the Blue Ridge Mountains. I kept singing the John Denver song, 'Country Roads'. Do you remember how the first line of the song goes? You don't? Well, here it is. 'Al-most hea-ven, West Vir-gin-ia, Blue Ridge Mountains, the She-nan-do-ah Ri-ver'.

I must tell you, a bloody strange thing happened to us. It was about 9/10 p.m., we were, hungry, thirsty and tired. As we were going up the motorway towards Pittsburgh, we could see the large sign with the distinctive green lettering signalling the Holiday Inn up ahead.

Fantastic, I thought, a quick bite to eat, a drink, shower and hit the sack. As we got to the end of the motorway the road forked off. Decision time. 'Left or right,' Tony called out.

'Christ knows,' I said.

We went left. As we did, the Holiday Inn sign disappeared. After driving around some of the local streets for a while, failing to find the hotel, we admitted defeat, and pulled up and asked a local for directions. We got two minutes of lefts and rights, and a loud and reassuring 'you can't miss it'.

So we drove off on our way again. I am not exactly sure what happened, but after taking several lefts and rights, we were back on the motorway. Once again we reached the now familiar fork-road. Naturally, this time we took a right, but just as before, the bloody Holiday Inn sign did its disappearing act again. Do you know something, we never saw it again. After driving around for about another hour, we stopped off at the next hotel we came across, more than a little fraught. If anyone knows where that bloody hotel is situated, will you please drop me an e-mail or something, and let me know. I must go and stay there one night, out of sheer spite.

By the time my head hit the pillow, I was fast asleep. The next morning I felt much better. It is surprising what a good night's sleep and a healthy breakfast can do for one's morale. We left Pittsburgh in good spirits, to make our way to Buffalo, to take a look at Niagara Falls.

Whilst at Buffalo, Tony and I sat down at a table and started reminiscing about Washington DC. Tony had been struck by the Vietnam Veterans Memorial in Constitution Gardens, just as I had been on my first visit there in 1988, and the magnificent surroundings of Airlie House.

After a while, we realised we had overstayed. It was getting dark, and Tony no longer felt like driving any more that day, so we found a hotel and stayed the night. The next morning, bright and early, we headed off for our journey's end, by car anyway, which was New York.

Once we had delivered the car to the car hire company, Tony looked at me and said, 'Well, TSB, we got culturally ventilated with ballet in New York and a piano concert in Washington DC, mesmerised with the Holiday Inn mirage in Pittsburgh, and finally pissed in Buffalo. I guess it's time to catch a plane and get back home.'

I gave him a slight pat on the back, and said, 'Damn right, mate. Let's get going. I've got a business to run.'

Actually, whilst in the UK waiting to get my flight back home, I went in to see my bank manager, Chris Morton, at NatWest in the High Street in Southampton. Chris came from one of the Channel Islands and had developed a great interest in the Falklands. He would always make an excuse to call me into his office, whenever I was in the bank, for a chat about my home and the way of life back there.

On this occasion, he called me into his office and said, in a rather excited tone, 'It's on.'

I was dumbfounded, as I had to admit. 'What's on?'

'The Rotary lunch, you're guest speaker.'

'Oh Christ, I am sorry Chris, I had forgotten about that.'

'Well, will you still do it?'

Slightly panicked, I said, 'When is it? I'm leaving next Monday.'

'Great,' Chris replied, 'because it's Friday. I'll pick you up from your house, and drive you there and fetch you back. Is that okay?'

Completely off my guard, I said, 'Yeah, okay.'

Sure enough, on the Friday, he arrived in his car at my front door and off we went to his Rotary Club. I remember him saying to me that the club had 45 members, and that 43 had confirmed they would be showing up for the lunch. He impressed upon me that considering it was high summer, holidays etc., this was a remarkable turnout. A Falkland Islander, as their guest speaker, had clearly stirred a lot of interest. 'Good,' I said, 'I always prefer to sing to a full house, rather than one where you can hear yourself fart.' He laughed loudly.

I had never been to such an event before, so as we were driving along, I asked him a few questions about protocol. Just as well I did, because I found out from his commentary that these things were very formal. One or two people needed to be addressed in a certain manner, and there was a precise routine. It was not just a question of roll up, down some food and beverage, jump up, do a speech, take a bow and bugger off. Actually, when I got the nod to step forward and deliver my speech, I did so using a theme about the positive aspect of having 'nothing'. It had often been said to me, especially in England, 'Why do you live in the Falklands? There is nothing there.' So I felt the Rotary luncheon was an ideal occasion to highlight the good things about 'nothings' in the Falklands.

After giving factual statistics about the usual old stuff on weather, population, the size of the Islands, cultural and social activities, what was driving the economy etc., I finished my speech by reading out my top ten list of nothings: no unemployment, no crime, no poverty, no pollution, no need to lock doors of cars and homes, no murders, no Aids, no drugs etc., until I got to the end of my list. Then I concluded, with a bold and breezy statement: 'Now you see why I live in the Falklands.' Bang, right on cue.

They were all out of their seats giving me the most generous applause. Then the members peppered me with a series of questions. Even amongst these intelligent people there was still much ignorance about the Falklands – very alarming really.

60

Political Forum in Salta, Argentina

The next time I was to be mixed up in an organised debate on the Falklands was in 1996. This time, it was the VI Argentine–British Conference (ABC) arranged by the Argentine Council for International Relations and the South Atlantic Council. These meetings had been established in 1990 for addressing bilateral Argentine–British relations and particularly the situation in the South Atlantic. Let me tell you, whenever the Argentines refer to the South Atlantic, they mean the Falkland Islands.

The main objects of the ABC were (a) to encourage further understanding and contact between Britain and Argentina, (b) to provide an unofficial but influential forum for exchange of views and ideas of mutual interest, and (c) to provide the flow of information between the two countries.

The previous meetings had been held in Streatley-on-Thames in 1990, followed by further meetings in Bariloche, Argentina 1991, St Catherine's College, Cambridge, England 1992, Mendoza, Argentina, 1994 and the last in Keble College, Oxford, England in 1995. This time we were all going to congregate in the beautiful province of northwestern Argentina called Salta. I was one of three Falkland Islanders invited to attend with the British delegation, Graham Bound (author of *Falkland Islanders at War*) and Lewis Clifton were the other two Islanders.

We were also joined by the Falkland Islands former Chief Executive, David Taylor, CBE, and former Chief of Staff, British Forces, Falkland Islands, General Sir Robert Corbett, KCVO, CB, along with four members from the House of Commons: Tam Dalyell (now Father of the House) MP, Martin O'Neill, MP both from the Labour Party, Kenneth Carlisle, MP, and Jacques Arnold, MP from the Conservative Party. Also in the British delegation line-up were political heavyweights such as the Deputy Speaker of the House of Lords, Baroness Hooper, and Viscount Montgomery of Alamein, CBE. The Chairman for the British delegation was also Vice-chairman of the South Atlantic Council in England, Mr Hugh Carless, CMG. The 27-strong British delegation was completed with members from the clergy, academics and journalists.

The Argentine delegation was headed by Carlos Muniz. He was also President of the Argentine Council for International Relations (CARI) and had been Ambassador to the United States and the United Nations, and was also a former Minister for Argentine Foreign Affairs and Worship. He was supported by members and ex-members of the Argentine Senate, such as Senators Eduardo Menem, the brother of the country's President, Carlos Menem, Emilio Cantarero and Jose Millan. The former Senators included Lanari and Lafferriere. In addition to the aforementioned, the Argentine team also included other politicians as well as having their mix and match of academics, Church leaders and journalists to make up their team of 27.

I remember on the flight down to Buenos Aires, talking away to Tam Dalyell, MP. He told me that the only other Betts he had ever known was Barbara Castle. Apparently, she was the daughter of Frank and Annie Betts, born in Bradford on 6 October 1910 (that made her a Libran like me). She had been a member of Harold Wilson's cabinet of the 1960s, and she had also been widely tipped, at one time, to be the first female Prime Minister. That would have been very palatable.

I was looking forward to arriving in Argentina. I had not been there since 1978, and I had never been to the capital before, so I was very eager to see the changes, if any, their new democracy had brought about for them.

In the airport terminal, I got my first taste of change. I instantly became aware of the total lack of military personnel in the area, compared to when I had last been in an airport in Argentina. Then, every other person appeared to be in military uniform and shoving a gun up someone's nostrils. It was a pleasant and very welcome surprise.

We had about 11 hours' free time before we had our first engagement, which was a cocktail reception given by Sir Peter Hall at the British Embassy, therefore I was able to get my head down for a few hours. I have to admit, I was half expecting the media to be around poking microphones in my face, or making notes following a comment that I might have made.

I was not sure if my brother knew I was coming to Argentina, but if he did, I thought it would be a fair chance he would be in the capital, and if he were in Buenos Aires looking for me, the press would know about my arrival, and if/when he and I met, the media would be there too. I was somewhat relieved not to find anyone waiting for me at the hotel when I arrived, but if I thought I was going to get in and out of Argentina without the attention of the press, I was wrong.

Before flying on to Salta, I attended a lunch hosted by the head of the Buenos Aires Stock Exchange, who I remember was being quite bullish at the time about economic growth in the country, and what an important role Argentina was going to play within Mercosur (South America's trading version of the European Union). God knows what he thinks now.

Friday 25 October 1996, the sixth meeting of the Argentine–British Conference (ABC) got under way, well eventually. We had to sit and be attentive to opening speeches from the Presidents of the two delegations, Hugh Carless and Carlos Muniz, and finally, from the Governor of Salta.

The morning session started with a 'How things are in Argentina and Britain' from a speaker's viewpoint. Other topics ranged from 'Bilateral relations' to 'The future of fishing', 'Communication between the Islands and the Continent' to 'Joint scientific research'. Under the spirit of the talks, I am not permitted to give details of the aforementioned, or any of the other subjects discussed, so I shall respect that stance.

After the morning's debate, the delegates split into two main groups, one under the banner of 'Economic and Political' the other 'Cultural, Social and Academic'. I chose the former, and Graham the latter. I think Lewis joined the same group as me. I should point out that during the whole period, interpreters were being used, which I think was just about the only similarity to the United Nations.

I remember one day getting very fed up with one of the former Senators on the Argentine side, who lost his composure at one point, and suggested that everything that was being discussed was pointless, because everything in the southwest Atlantic belong to Argentina, fish, oil whatever. I laid into him, via a translator, which resulted in him spending the remainder of the day avoiding me. Therefore, I was somewhat surprised when a photo-call had been arranged, that he insisted on standing alongside me.

I also crossed swords with one of the Labour MPs, when I thought he was not correctly relaying the Falklands perspective to the assembly. As before, there was no doubt that Falkland Islanders should be present at this forum. Looking Argentines straight in the eye, and some of the British, whilst standing our ground on some issues, and listening to others' points of view was extremely valuable.

As it happened, the ABC itself was now questioning its future role, and its further usefulness, and the discussions did not appear to reach any conclusion, at this meeting anyway. The forum closed with debate and reports from the rapporteurs.

On Sunday we were back in Buenos Aires. Then bang, it happened. As I walked into the hotel, to my surprise, and delight, I was greeted by my brother Alec and nephew Paul.

I had not seen Paul since March 1982, over 14 years. I began to remember our last time together. I had hired a tractor and trailer. Paul was just short of his 14th birthday, and he had been helping me to cart the peat home. He was a lovely boy, and he got on pretty well with his uncle Terry.

Paul loved the Falklands, but he had been about to leave for Argentina. Alec never had any faith in the Falklands educational system, and he was sending Paul off to Argentina for, as he saw it, a better education. As it turned out, it was just weeks before the Falklands invasion. All day Paul was saying to me, 'I wish I didn't have to leave the Falklands, Uncle Terry.' I didn't say it, but I wished he didn't have to leave either, but it was not for me to say or decide.

The only blessing about the whole thing was that he missed the fighting in the Falklands. Whatever he saw or heard would have been on Argentine television or fairytale propaganda. Now, 14 years on, he was standing in front of me, a slim, fine-looking 27-year-old man.

Suddenly, without the slightest warning, the media appeared, it seemed from everywhere. Photographers began clicking their cameras, interviewers jostled for position with microphones and cassette recorders shoved in my face, others with pens and note pads at the ready.

I was furious, and I glared at Alec and said, 'Did you tell these bastards I was arriving here today?'

He looked at me, a little startled, and then shrugged his shoulders and said, 'I didn't tell anyone, I only found out that you were in Argentina myself the other day.'

I snapped back, 'Oh, come on, Alec, that is utter bullshit. Someone told them I was coming here. I tell you what, I'm pleased to see you. I'm very happy to see the both of you, and I'll go and get changed. Then we will go and have a bite to eat together, because it's your birthday tomorrow, and it would be a rather nice thing to do. In the meantime, you can get rid of these arseholes.' I pointed to a group of men waiting to do the 'exclusive interview', then I pushed through them and made my way to the lift.

By the time I got to the room, I took a drink out of the mini bar and sat down on my bed and began to think.

It was not that I was bothered about the press, in as much as doing interviews. I could handle both of them okay, but I had left the UK wondering if I would have the chance to meet up with Alec. Then we could put our political differences to one side for the night, and enjoy a little bit of social time together. So seeing him and Paul, in the lobby, was a wonderful surprise. But why the hell had he called the press in? It had to be him who had told them. That's what pissed me off. I had only wished for a quiet family reunion, not a bloody media party.

When I got back down to the hotel lobby, it was noticeable that a few feathers had been ruffled, but the press had gone, and I smiled at my two family members, then said, 'Let's go out and catch up on one or two things over a beer.'

We found a nearby cafeteria, and went inside. I had not seen Alec since the UN meetings nine years ago, and then it was briefly and in difficult circumstances, so there was much to catch up on. We chatted away for several hours, almost entirely about family issues. Any subject that could get us into a political argument was avoided.

After a while I suggested that we go out and properly celebrate Alec's birthday. It was only then that I realised they had made plans to leave that night. Fortunately, it did not take long to persuade them to stay and enjoy themselves, but before moving on, I needed to go back to the hotel for something. When we got there, it was like walking into a film shoot as we entered the hotel. I noticed Falkland Islander Graham Bound, who had been at the ABC meeting with me, among the group in the lobby, obviously now with his press hat on. I believe he was working freelance for the BBC, and one of the programmes he had worked on was *BBC Calling the Falklands*.

My blood pressure started to rise again, and I said to Alec, 'Okay, if you didn't alert the press, then let's get it over with. But Graham, and *Calling the Falklands*, gets first shot.'

I called Graham towards us. He was delighted. The idea of getting the exclusive story almost made him orgasm.

So we pushed our way through the crowded room, and made our way into the small breakfast area, bolted the glass doors behind us and recorded the interview.

Oddly enough, although very much in opposite camps regarding the Falkland Islands and who they belonged to, we had much in common on other issues relating to the colonial past, and our time growing up in that environment.

The interview, which was for a 30-minute programme, took about two hours to complete. After it was in the can, Graham asked if Alec and I would agree to go down and have our pictures taken, the next morning, at the Argentine War Memorial, built to commemorate the Falklands War. Alec was all for it, but I would not have anything to do with that idea.

By midnight we were through with interviews. I felt the night had been well and truly fucked up, so I turned to Alec and Paul and said, 'Let's find the nearest Johnnie Walker bottle and give this birthday boy a night out to remember.' We all got smashed.

The next morning we said our farewells, and I was off on my journey back home. If it had been possible to fly direct from Buenos Aires to Stanley, my flight time would have been just over two hours. As it was, I had to fly to Santiago de Chile, which was about the same flight time, then in the early hours of the next morning, catch a LanChile flight which would take me to the Falklands via Puerto Montt and Punta Arenas. Therefore, with stopovers, another nine-hour journey. Kind of crazy, isn't it?

I should add that whilst in Buenos Aires, the Argentine Foreign Minister, Dr Guido Di Tella, invited me to take dinner with him. I was not alone, two other Islanders were there, and someone else well known to the Falklands.

It was a very low-key occasion, which was purely intended to be a gesture of goodwill. However, I had made it clear to my fellow Falkland Islanders that if I got the chance, preferably alone, I would raise the issue of fisheries with the Foreign Minister. We in the Falklands were getting increasingly worried about migratory fish stocks (the illex squid) and we believed Argentina was not doing everything it could to stop foreign fishing vessels from overfishing. Once again I must point out I was just being an opportunist, trying to take the chance to support the Falklands position, this time from a commercial man's point of view. It was clear I had no official role and, as usual, I would not pretend otherwise.

On arrival, we were given a short conducted tour of a small section of the house, which included his grandson's bedroom. The boy was in the room at the time, watching a video of *Pingu the Penguin*.

Dr Di Tella had amused some, and infuriated some other Falkland Islanders, when he sent about 500 copies of *Pingu the Penguin* as a Christmas present to Islanders, all part of his so-called 'Falklands charm offensive'. I got the impression he thought the whole thing was a light-hearted joke.

Later on in the evening, I had my chance, as both commercial man and ordinary citizen of the Falkland Islands, to raise the fishing issue with him. I am not a marine biologist in any shape or form, but just as I had indicated to HRH Prince Philip, I had a genuine interest in seeing that fish stocks were sustained, because I would be out of business and because I was well aware that many of my fellow countrymen would not be able to realise many of their dreams without the millions from fishing revenue gained by the sale of fishing licences for this species.

I was also aware that if the Falklands was going to develop and widen its political options, it could only achieve them if we could support ourselves financially. Therefore I felt it was my duty to take the chance to raise this very important issue with the Argentine Foreign Minister, regardless if he listened or not, or if he could, or would, do anything about it.

Whilst the Falkland Islands Government had been exemplary in its management control, by maintaining a limited commercial fishing period and trying to deter poaching, it has been argued that the Argentines have been far less responsible, and perhaps, even encouraged practices that would harm the buoyant Falklands economy, irrespective of the danger to the fish stocks, by not properly implementing appropriate preservation and conservation measures. A view I shared.

In real terms, the Falkland Islands fishery zone only offers a very short commercial window of interest for this squid, which is more or less a 10–12 week period, from March to the end of May.

Licences are sold by the Falkland Islands authorities to cover longer periods, but catch levels for the other times are always very much less than the fishing fleets can obtain by fishing in the licence-free, uncontrolled international waters outside the management of the Falklands and Argentina. Or in the more competitive waters in Argentina, who offered a cheaper licence, and a much longer fishing period.

Therefore, even though the Falkland Islands Government has been very responsible about management, and sustainability, regarding fish stocks, it has been pretty much powerless to do anything much about the danger of overfishing alone.

The Falklands has always needed a partner who was willing to share these responsibilities, and the obvious one to forge that partnership with was Argentina, the only other country with a commercial fishery for this species in the area at the time.

However, because it was Argentina, as far as the UK Government was concerned, the sticks and carrots had to be dished out by the UK Foreign Office, and from past experience, Falkland Islanders never regarded that as the best place to go to get the most positive of results regarding Falklands interests which involve the Argentines.

That said, the British Government has made efforts, through the establishment of the South Atlantic Fisheries Commission, and the scientific sub-committee, which has resulted in the pooling of resources from Britain, Argentina and the Falklands to collate, and provide, vital data in an effort to reach a conclusive and lasting policy.

But even with these very useful groups in place, the Argentines had been unhelpful. Often their information was slow in coming forward, and thus dated and on occasions even useless. What the Falkland Islands needed, was a partner who shared the same aims and objectives, which must be to sensibly regulate their own fisheries, and to unite, as one, on the issue of protecting the uncontrolled migratory fish stocks.

This would require all parties concerned to forge, and if necessary force, enough signatories to a treaty, which could be ratified and enforced by the United Nations, that would provide the framework to abolish uncontrolled fishing on high seas, to eliminate the extreme possibility, which existed then, and even more so today, of the annihilation of the *Illex argentinus* squid.

The Foreign Minister was gracious enough to hear me out on my very direct points of view that night, and was even hospitable enough to recharge my brandy glass.

Although I wanted to believe what Dr Di Tella said in response was sincere, I somehow felt he was not telling me the real reasons why Argentina was not playing ball. I surmised that it had more to do with the overall global view Argentina harboured regarding the Falklands, and South Georgia. You see, the Argentines insist that South Georgia, South Orkneys and the South Sandwich Islands belong to them also.

When we eventually got back to the Falklands, Graham, Lewis and I were interviewed by Patrick Watts, at the local radio station. In a response to a question from Patrick about what had been discussed at the meetings, we informed him we were not in a position to discuss anything said during the ABC meetings. However, as a result of the visit to Argentina, we all felt that the practice of a total ban on Argentine nationals visiting the Islands should now be lifted, because we felt it was not in the best interests of the Falkland Islands and fellow Falkland Islanders. I argued that isolating ourselves was counterproductive; we needed to open up, and demonstrate to all Argentines who would not feel intimidated by coming to the Islands that we were nothing like their indoctrination had taught them to believe. We spoke English, not Spanish, we had a British heritage and cultural way of life, we supported Spurs, not Boca Juniors, we were not downtrodden colonials, but a vibrant and prosperous community. There were many good reasons to allow the Argentines in, and as far as I could see, no good reasons to keep them out.

Our remarks caused fireworks. I remember my old mate Neil Watson getting on the telephone from Long Island, saying we were trying to reinvent the wheel. It was not a question of reinvention, it was like putting the spare wheel on the car so it could get going in the direction the driver chose. Neil, naturally, had support, but so did we, and this was very encouraging.

Unfortunately, it would not be until 1999 that the ban was eventually lifted, but when it was, I am certain it has been a very positive step forward in our democratic political development. It showed the Falkland Islands Government as taking the lead, not following along. At least I hope that's how it was done.

61

I Meet a Brother for the First Time in my Life (Also, HRH the Princess Royal, Norway and Taiwan)

I'll start with the brief encounter with the Princess Royal, then get to the more important tale. (Excuse me, Your Royal Highness.)

HRH arrived in January 1996, and once again, I would have the good fortune to be able to meet with another member of the Royal Family. My first had been her father, when he arrived in Stanley in 1957. I was a snotty-nosed, freckle-faced and frozen little schoolboy, standing in front of the Christ Church Cathedral steps, waving my tiny union flag, and cheering Prince Philip as loud as I could.

This time, I was a clean-shaven, well-behaved, well-dressed, law-abiding citizen who had been invited by the Church Canon, Steven Palmer, to attend a gathering at which the Princess Royal was to officially open the refurbished Parish Hall.

Having finished her duties, she was being led out of the main building by Canon Palmer, but just before departing, he was kind enough to gently direct the Princess in my direction. He made some complimentary comment about my contribution to the church restoration campaign, which encouraged Princess Anne to offer her hand, which I took, and released, in the appropriate manner. Not that I was counting, but that was the fifth member of the Royal Family I had had the good fortune, and pleasure, to meet. There would be one more.

Now I am going to turn the clock back to 1993. In the early part of that year, my half-brother (same father) Arnold and my sister-in-law Mary arrived in the Falklands. It was Mary's first visit to the Islands, and Arnold's first time back home since he sailed away on the SS *Lafonia* way back in 1949. Then, there was no international airport, no fishing industry, no Islands constitution, half the number of houses, few business people and a handful of policemen.

Arnold was struck by the change in attitude of many Islanders. People were much more outspoken than when he was growing up.

Arnold, who was now 60 and living in New Zealand, wanted to come back to see dad one more time. Our father was 79, and still pretty sharp and bright. They had not seen each other since 1970, when my dad made a visit to the United Kingdom, where Arnold and Mary were living at the time. As it turned out, Arnold's decision was a good one, because once dad reached his 80th birthday his physical condition rapidly declined.

I was also delighted that he had made a return home, because I had never seen him in my life before. We had never spoken on a telephone to each other either, nor had we even exchanged letters or Christmas cards. No contact whatsoever.

Going to collect him and Mary from the airport was a bit like enacting the Cilla Black television programme *Surprise, Surprise* – you know the one, that tear-jerker where she is interviewing someone about a long-lost relative, who then just happens to pop out from behind the curtain, reducing the interviewee/s to tears and near cardiac arrest.

Arnold and I did not go through any of those dramatics, but I was stunned by one thing when I first clapped eyes on him. I was amazed how much he looked like dad; of us all, he was the most like him. I was also impressed by his very obvious physical fitness. Unlike the guests on the Cilla Black show, we greeted each other as if he had just been away for a short holiday. We got on like a house on fire instantly. It really was as though we had known each other all our lives.

For once, the drive along the bloody nightmare 35 kilometres of stone-spitting road was hardly noticed as we chatted away virtually non-stop, only interrupted when Arnold would rather excitedly point out a landmark he knew to Mary.

Arnold and Mary had a wonderful time in the Islands, catching up on numerous things, and also reminiscing with dad, other members of the Betts family and friends about a whole array of matters. He spent time on our brother's farm at the Boundary and, of course, there was the pilgrimage to Pebble Island, where he trod over every blade of grass and explored every building and area that brought back memories of his living past on the Island.

Arnold never went anywhere without his video camera, shooting cassette after cassette of family gatherings or Falklands scenery. When in Stanley, we spent as much time together as possible. He would often pop into the office, or jump in the Discovery with me, to observe the various businesses I was operating.

Like everything, when you are having fun, the time arrives all too soon for you to stop what you are doing and get back to your routine life, so after several jam-packed weeks of fun and meeting people, they were on the way back to New Zealand. The trip out to the airport was a much more quiet affair than when they arrived, so once we had dropped them off at the air terminal, we wished them a safe onward journey, and a 'see you later'. I did see Arnold later, three years later in fact, but this time in much more sombre circumstances.

Also during 1993, I made a business trip to Kaoshiung, which is in the south-western part of Taiwan. About 1.5 million people live in Kaoshiung, which is very industrialised, and they pay a heavy price. The air is heavily polluted, noise levels and crime are also very high and traffic jams continuous.

I wondered in amazement as I watched scooters passing by with what seemed like the whole family on board, all wearing masks over their noses and mouths. But it is not just the air that's polluted, so is the sea. The main river is called Love River, but I was horrified to see the oil slicks and amount of debris that were floating about around the dockside. Love River was not a very appropriate name for this waterway.

I went down to the dockside to look at some fishing vessels, used for catching squid in the Falklands and other parts of the world, also to view one or two fish factories. It was the fishing vessels that were largely responsible for polluting Love River. The fish factories were a hive of activity, as man and machine laboured at top speed, shifting, lifting, filleting, sorting, packaging, stowing etc.

Although the trip had been very useful regarding expansion of knowledge about the industry, and getting an understanding of who the players were in the fishery, it was not entirely successful in terms of direct commercial benefit to my businesses at the time. That followed a little bit later, when we managed to entice the

Taiwanese to take up 70 illex fishing licence's at a time when FIG couldn't sell them to anyone. Thus we generated £7,000,000 to the FIG revenue for the year in one stroke. But socially, the people were very pleasant, and I did enjoy the all-night street market, but I was not sorry to leave when the time came. I would very much like to visit the capital Taipei one day, which I understand is quite beautiful and industry-free.

On the way to and from Taiwan, I stopped off at Hong Kong. The hotel we stayed in at Hong Kong was quite magnificent, it was said to be the second finest in the world. We chose a room, for an extra $30 a night, with an outside wall that was totally made of glass. This gave us the most spectacular views of Hong Kong harbour.

Outside the hotel were gold-painted Rolls-Royces, with chauffeurs standing by, all apparently complimentary for guests to do shopping trips or one-way journeys to the airport.

Another thing about Hong Kong, in those days, which tested one's nerve to the full, was the fact that your jet had to be expertly navigated between the high-rise buildings as it made its approach to the airport. I understand only specially trained pilots were allowed to fly into this airstrip.

Things had not changed much since my first visit in 1991. People were still trying to sell fake Rolex watches in Nathan Street, and once again, I was not tempted. But I do remember that I did buy a Game Boy game, well actually 31 of them, all for US $30. Back in the UK, that would have been the price for just one.

When I got back to England, I gave the game to a friend's son, who was just a little pleased with his gift, as he went off to school the next morning, grinning from ear-to-ear to show it off to his mates.

Another country I visited was Norway. This was in 1994. Ray Robson and I had been asked by fellow members of the board of directors of a newly formed Falkland Islands fishing company called Consolidated Fisheries Limited to attend a fish seminar and trading show in Trondheim.

Consolidated Fisheries Limited had been set up to target a species of fish called Patagonian toothfish; some people know it as mero and others call it South Atlantic seabass. Whichever name you prefer, it was assumed in the Falklands that this fish, which lay in the trenches of the seabed, 1,000 metres or more below sea level, might be an untapped resource of high commercial value.

The initial idea to commercially exploit this species was probably that of the Director of Fisheries, and the General Manager of the Falkland Islands Development Corporation, John Barton and Mike Summers, two Falkland Islanders who are very bright and forward thinking. (See what happens when Falkland Islanders run their own show.) As a result, a group of pioneering Falkland Islands commercial people, representing 18 local companies, got together and formed CFL, by taking equal share equity. At the time, nothing was really known about the fishery, by any of us, so three or four working groups were set up with various responsibilities, one of which I was chosen to lead.

In the very early days, information was the key, and our objective in Norway was to find out as much as possible about long-line fishing vessels, their equipment and techniques used, markets, etc. I had attended many shows in various parts of the world before, not just fishing, so I knew pretty much what to expect, or at least so I thought.

During the five days we were there, we spoke with, and listened to, shipbuilders, vessel owners, long-liner and long-line accessory makers, packaging material manufacturers, machinery makers and operators, and many experts on the best possible methods of fishing. Some grossly overestimated the ability of their own mechanical techniques to operate competitively and efficiently with the more labour-intensive 'Spanish system' in the South Atlantic waters. Ray also did a few press interviews etc.

By the end of each day, Ray and I would be overloaded with coloured brochures, fish news magazines and papers and what have you from the many stands that we visited, and when it was time to pack our suitcases and head home, we had very heavy luggage indeed, and once again, the patience and understanding of the load master of the RAF Tristar at RAF Brize Norton was going to be tested.

But I must tell you a story about one stand that we did not patronise. It was manned by Norway's most prominent, or infamous, depending how you looked at it, whale catcher vessel owner. The stand was situated in the best possible location for attracting attention, right at the entrance/exit door. The vessel owner had a variety of anti-Greenpeace tee-shirts for sale, in an assortment of colours, laid out on a table. The one he was wearing himself was probably the most outrageous and provocative of them all. It depicted a whale with a harpoon through it, and the caption, in very bold letters, read: 'Fuck Greenpeace'. I have to tell you, his was the busiest and best-supported stand at the show.

One other thing stuck in my mind from my visit to Norway. A guest speaker, referring to conservation measures, said, 'Big fish eat little fish'. He is right. Conservation is vital, but also be realistic.

62

When Father is Father, Son is Son, and Father Dies

Now I will change the subject altogether. I am going to tell you a true story about something which happened between a father and son. It is a tale that I hope will encourage any young person who has ambition or dreams. The story warns that you must be prepared to fight for what you want; you will be required to dig deep, and work hard, to achieve your objective. There will be times when you think it is all beyond you, you are alone, and no one cares or understands you, not even your parents, as it appears all is lost and you will never achieve your mission.

It's a story that I hope will enable you to understand that sometimes parents have to be very strong for your best interests, and also sometimes parents are right.

Severine took up a five-year apprenticeship, as an electrician, with the Falkland Islands Government in 1989. After a couple of years, he was granted a two-year practical electrical course, sponsored by FIG, with Eastleigh College, in Southampton. However, there was a problem: the course had to be completed in just one year.

In the beginning, things went pretty smoothly, then he began to get bogged down, and as it was becoming harder and harder for him, frustrations began to creep in. With a strange environment, no family or old friends nearby, and working with other students who had time on their hands (they had two years to do what Severine had to do in one), Severine became desperate. So much so, that one day, just before Christmas in 1994, I got a call in my office from him, pleading to come home.

Well, I am not your 'don't worry about things, son, come home and forget it, you can try some other time' sort of dad. Instead, after hearing him out, I said, 'I tell you what, I will arrange for you to come home and have Christmas in the Falklands, so you can be with family and friends. But then you go back to finish the course, and I will tell you why.' I paused for a moment, then in a very firm voice I said, 'Because you are a Betts, and the Betts's are not quitters, so you're not quitting on me. But far more importantly, you are not quitting on yourself. Deal or no deal?' He came home and stayed for ten days. He had a really enjoyable break, then he went back with renewed enthusiasm and vigour. Not only did he finish his training, but he actually finished with the top student award for his category of studies.

I am very proud of my son's achievements. I wish success to many other sons and daughters out there in that big bad wide world. And just remember one more thing, no time for bullshitters.

The next father and son story is very different. At the end of February 1996, my father became very ill and was confined to hospital. The doctors carried out extensive examinations and diagnosed him as having terminal cancer.

Before going into hospital, dad had been living in one of the sheltered accommodation units in the hospital compound, which had been built from the very generous cash donation of Sir Jack Hayward, and the people of Guernsey, I believe.

Digressing slightly, I should mention that the people of Jersey had also donated several millions to us after the Falklands War, which was put to very good use for much needed housing in Stanley, which is called the Jersey estate. I must say one other thing, Sir Jack really does need to get a proper football team, other than Wolverhampton Wanderers, but it is true that he responded quite manifestly to the tragedy of our hospital fire back in 1984. But perhaps I should get back to the story about dad.

I had gone up to see him one Sunday morning, and to my horror, I found him lying in a heap on the bathroom floor. Fortunately, I had a friend with me, and once we had alerted the hospital and got assistance, we managed to get dad into a wheelchair, then we pushed him around to the main hospital and eventually got him tucked up in bed.

Later in the afternoon they carried out the examinations, after which, the doctor had a personal and frank chat with me, which left me in no doubt about the seriousness of my father's health. The doctor also presented me with quite a dilemma: should we tell my father or not? After some considerable thought I decided dad should know his fate, but I asked the doctor not to mention it to him that day.

Once the doctor and I had finished our little heart-to-heart conversation, I went off to see dad, but he had dropped off to sleep, so I took the opportunity to go home and tell my wife the news. I had been fine right up to that point, but as soon as I told her I began to cry uncontrollably for a little while.

(Arlette and I have had our problems, but during the period of my father's short hospitalisation and immediately after his death, she was truly magnificent. She organised the logistics of pulling together a family which was spread around the world, to get to the Falklands for his funeral. I really could not have got better support than I did from her at that time.)

With dad now in hospital, at least I had the comfort of knowing he would have immediate and constant care, and there would be no more fears of finding him on a floor stranded.

The next day when I went up to see him, he appeared much fresher, even with a twinkle in his eye. But I instantly noticed he was behaving rather oddly. He was swearing every second word, which was very unusual for him. When he saw me he said, 'Hey what are you up to?'

A bit surprised, I said, 'I've come to see you, obviously.'

'You know, don't you?'

I had no idea how to react, or what to say. Then he repeated his words. Trying to act cool, I said, 'I know what?'

He sat on his bed, then looked at me with sad and shining eyes and said, 'I'm dying.' Just like that, he threw the words out at me.

I was now struggling desperately to keep my composure. I tried putting up some kind of pretence by saying, 'You, dying, look at you, you're like a spring chicken getting around.'

'No, no, I'm dying,' he insisted. 'The doctor has told me.'

I remember holding a glance with him briefly, then I walked up to him and put my arms around him. There were no tears, but the hug was firm from each of us; words were not required. Then when we parted, he swung himself on to his bed and sat up with pillows supporting his back, and said, 'I would like a favour, I would like a bottle of whisky.'

Dad had always enjoyed his Johnnie Walker Red Label whisky and, given the situation, I said, 'Just a minute, I'll go and ask the matron.

Dad snapped, 'Don't ask her, she will only say no.'

I ignored his remark, and I went straight off and asked her if it would be okay if I carried out my father's request. I could tell she wanted to say no, but when she looked at him on his bed, knowing his predicament, she turned towards me and said, 'I think on this occasion it is in order, Terry.'

I went straight back to dad and told him I would nip down the road to the West Store and get his whisky. He smiled, then made himself more comfortable. Then completely out of the blue, he said, 'I've got something to tell you, Terry. I have not included you in my will.' He looked at me a little nervously.

I touched him lightly on the cheek, and said, 'I don't think you need to worry about that, dad.' (As it happened, he only made his will in his dying breath.)

Then dad made a comment, which was just about the ultimate compliment a father could make to his son, 'I have left you out because you don't need my help. You have made a success of your life on your own.' It was difficult not to show him that his comment had hit the soft spot, and I was struggling desperately not to get emotional in his company. To avoid this happening, I disappeared out of the ward to get his whisky. As I went I could hear him saying, 'Don't be too long. I'm bloody thirsty.'

Now I had to wrestle with another problem. I had been scheduled to travel to Uruguay, to conduct a business meeting with Spanish business partners from Chymar SA on planning the further development of the joint venture company Golden Touza Limited. I kept thinking about what the doctor had said to me: 'Your father is dying, all we can do is make the rest of his life as comfortable as possible.' It was not a question of being weak, but I felt I should put the matter to my father, let him decide if I should go to Uruguay or not. I would only be away for a week.

When I got back to the hospital, and after pouring dad a very lengthy measure, then a much shorter dram for myself, I sat down by his bedside and asked him what I should do about the trip to South America. Without a split second's hesitation, he said to me, 'Go son, go. Don't worry about me, I'll be fine. You go and I will look forward to you coming back.' It was what I really wanted to hear, but if he had said stay, then I would have stayed, no question.

Three or four days later, I did depart for the Uruguayan capital; once again fellow director Ray Robson accompanied me.

I had been in bed little more than an hour on the first night when the telephone rang. I knew instantly that it would be my wife, and that it would be news about dad. Sure enough, it was Arlette, and in a very balanced and soft voice, she said, 'I'm sorry, Terry, but dad passed away just a short time ago.' It was 2 a.m. on 3 March.

At first, I didn't answer, I couldn't answer. The silence was only broken when Arlette informed me of a few intimate details.

Needless to say, I did not sleep for the remainder of the night. I kept tossing and turning in my bed, then getting out and walking around my room. Dad's words kept ringing in my ears: 'Go, son. Don't worry about me, go.' It was not a question of guilt that was troubling me, it was the fact that I was not there to share his last moments with him. What's more, I could not get back home until the next LanChile flight, still a few days away.

I was showered and dressed by 6.30 a.m. I had decided I would carry on with the meetings as planned. I knew, given my hopeless position, dad would have wanted me to get on with things.

I joined Ray for breakfast. I did not tell him anything at that stage, and we went off and met our Spanish partners, on cue. But I could not focus properly on the debate. I think it would have been better if I had told everyone right there and then, but I thought at first it would be easier to try and work on.

Somehow, I did manage to stagger through the morning session, even though there were several interruptions because Arlette made regular calls to keep me updated on the plans for getting various scattered family members to the Falklands.

At the lunch break, Ray and I went off to a small restaurant, and midway through the meal, I just had to break the news to him. Ray was wonderful, so understanding, and for the rest of the visit, and the journey back home, he became very much like a brother to me. Ray has been like that in my life, always popping in and out.

We agreed that when the meeting reconvened, I should tell the Spanish right away, but we also agreed that as I could not get home, it would be better to occupy my mind, rather than just leaving me in a hotel bedroom to suffer in silence.

When we got back to the meeting room and I made my

dramatic announcement, immediately the Spanish partners wanted to close files and folders and call a halt to proceedings. But I encouraged them to push on.

As it happened, nothing was positively achieved that day, nor the next. As much as I tried, I could not stop my mind drifting back to the last conversation that I had with my father. I repeat, I did not feel guilty for leaving him, but I just wondered if dad had neatly planned it this way, to get me out of the Islands, then go off on his journey to eternal life. I will never know, but I will not dwell on it for the rest of my life. Dad can let me know when I see him again.

When I got back to the Falklands, I had little to do in terms of final arrangements because Arlette had been so efficient. As one or two family members had not yet arrived from overseas, the funeral had been arranged for 13 March. Dad would be buried just 65 paces away from the front door of our house. I know, I have stepped it out many times, whilst walking to the office. The town's cemetery is that close to Lafone House, which was the home I had purchased just two months earlier.

Once the funeral service had been completed by the graveside, Canon Stephen Palmer, family and friends came back to our house to have a tea or something a little stronger. Then quite off the cuff, guitars and accordions started to come out of their cases, and the music began to flow. I am sure it must have got dad tapping his toes just one last time, as Billy Morrison and Owen McPhee rattled out Scottish reels on their accordions. Dad enjoyed music; he had been a reasonable accordionist himself.

There was one thing to be thankful for, dad had had a full life, and had managed to remain a very aware person who could hold conversation on a wide range of subjects, right up to his final days. Although he had kept himself very much to himself, especially in the latter part of his life, at 83, he bowed out pretty gracefully.

Strangely enough, when I walked slowly up to dad's graveside, and then looked down upon his coffin, my mind flashed back to the time when I nearly killed him and myself in a car accident.

We had both been down to the pub. I was driving us back home. This was a year or two after the war, the roads in Stanley were full of potholes and I was weaving in and out of them. I then turned the van sharply into Drury Street. As I swung the wheel hard to the right to avoid another hole, I am sure the steering locked in. I was certainly not driving too fast, given the appalling conditions of the road surface that was impossible. Whatever, I could not get the steering wheel to turn to straighten the vehicle to head along the middle of the street. Out of control, we went straight into the concrete foundation of Willie Bowles's peat shed. Upon impact, I lurched forward. The steering wheel immediately collapsed, and I hit my forehead very hard on the rim of the shattered windscreen frame, splitting my forehead open, which resulted in blood spurting out all over the place from a gaping wound. The force of the impact had also knocked the wind out of me.

In fact, for a minute or two, I was struggling with my breathing. The only thing I can vividly remember was Willie Bowles somewhere nearby saying, 'Are you all right, che? Just hold it there, and I'll get some help.' I have no idea where Willie thought I might be going, but his words were of great comfort and I remember remaining calm even though I was blinded with my own blood.

I was not aware of it at the time, but as a result of the sudden and violent impact, dad had been catapulted out of his seat and thrown straight through the windscreen and on to the road. Amazingly, his only injuries were a multitude of facial scratches, from the windscreen exploding in his face. Some members of the Falkland Club, who heard the noise of the crash, came running out into the street and immediately went to dad's aid.

After a little while, Willie managed to attract the attention of a driver going past the front of his house. Incredibly, I managed to climb out of my crumpled vehicle, which was a total write-off, and get into the Land Rover, and then Charles Clifton transported me to hospital, which was only a short distance away. But by the time I got to the hospital, my woollen jumper was wringing with blood.

It was a little while before the doctor arrived but when he did he needed to put 20 stitches in my head wound, and one or two in other cuts above my eyelid and on the bridge of my nose.

The whole thing took the doctor some time, mainly because he was heavily under the influence. I remember him frequently swearing as he struggled and stumbled, desperately trying to coordinate his hands and mind so that he could put the stitches in. I became more concerned about him than myself. Once he finished his handiwork, I walked home (amazing, isn't it?) and made my way directly to bed.

It was the next day I really felt the aches and pains all over my body. My chest was particularly sore. The doctor came around to the house to examine dad and me. He was not concerned about my cuts, scratches and bruises, but he carried out a thorough check on my chest. Once satisfied, he explained that had the steering wheel of the van not been designed to collapse upon sudden impact, there was a real possibility it would have stoved my chest in and killed me.

Shortly after the doctor left the house, my dad came shuffling into my bedroom to see me. When I got my first glimpse of him, I wanted to burst out into raucous laughter. My painful body deterred me from that, but he did look so funny, with his face and bald head smothered in hundreds of tiny scratches.

It must have been the brush with death at that time which made me think of it now I put my hand in my pocket, pulled out a pound coin and threw it down into his grave and said, 'Have one on me.' Then I turned away and stood back some distance to await other family members to join me, after they had filed past his resting place with their own thoughts. Once everyone had finished his or her individual rituals, we took the short walk back to the house, and dad's life was celebrated in a way that none of us had planned.

It would be hypocritical of me to say that dad and I were the best of mates. It was only in the last ten years or so of his life that we did get along pretty well. For most part of my life, he had not liked me very much, and he had often told me so. I do not know why. Perhaps it had to do with the fact that I had always been an individualist with a wild sense of imagination, a fascination for doing things out of the ordinary, and was not prepared to accept the way of life that others had dictated for him and many other generations of Falkland Islanders. Which I am sure often meant I was misunderstood by many people, so I suppose it was hardly surprising that should include my father.

A son might be your flesh and blood, but you can never be his mind.

Fathers who try shall carry the pain till the very day they die.

A son might carry the family flag, if he is blessed to live long enough.

A father might guide, teach and defend. But other forces decide how it will end.

TSB 2002

63

This and That

Two months before my father's death, the long search for my own home ended when I purchased a five-bedroom Scandinavian kit home situated on an acre of land next the Islands cemetery. The house had been built by the Falklands Islands Company for its first, and I believe only, Chief Executive, at an extortionate cost – apparently double what I actually paid for it.

There had also been clear evidence of improper labour control, and a high level of helping oneself to some of the building materials, and unfortunately, despite the enormous capital outlay, the project was never properly finished.

I will also be very honest about one other thing; I never liked the place, it was my wife who was the enthusiastic one about the property, and it took several viewings of the interior before I appreciated the value of the purchase. But that was the crux to what would become a problem: I saw the purchase of the house as nothing more than an investment, not a home. The place was littered with top-quality fixtures and fittings, so I agreed to buy it at FIC's asking price. But I never had a good feel about it, irrespective of the marriage breakdown. For me, it would never be a place where I would be happy.

There always seemed to be too much attention paid by others to the material values for my liking. My subsequent divorce would see to it that I would not have to worry about that any more, which was the biggest bonus of the whole fiasco.

But I had learnt a lesson from that bloody awful experience, which was: never buy something when you are swayed by other forces, just because it appears grand; only purchase something that makes you feel good, regardless of whether it is cheap or expensive. Only then you will enjoy it.

Let's move on to a much more cheerful subject. One of the most out-of-the-way places I have ever visited was Reykjavik, the capital of Iceland; actually I would make four trips there between 1995 and 1997. On my first visit, I had gone, once again, to look into the possibility of yet another joint venture, which again got off to a promising start, but would come to an inglorious end.

One of my fondest memories of Iceland was when I went with my new business partners to a tiny island called Flatey for the weekend, to discuss the business plan and agree and sign a letter of intent. Flatey is halfway between the coastal port of Stykkisholmur, and another coastal place called Brjanslaekur, which is serviced by a ferry twice a day in the high season, once a day for the rest of the year. It pissed with rain all weekend we were there, but the people (about 20) and the corrugated-clad homes reminded me of a tiny sheep farm settlement back home.

I also vividly remember a couple of visits to Stykkisholmur, and a husband-and-wife team who appeared to have tourism pretty much stitched between themselves in the small village. The wife operated a retail outlet, and the husband had a high-speed and very luxurious boat, which he used to take tourists out on, weaving his way between tiny islands and through the roaring white waterways, against tidal currents that were apparently as much as 20 knots.

Whilst at sea, he would get his assistant to do a small trawl for shellfish, which would then be opened and eaten straight from the shell (that's what you call fresh) and washed down with the most delicious white wine. I was well impressed with the vessel owner's very simple and effective initiative in overcoming the local law, which prohibited him from selling wine on his craft. He would give his clients the wine free of charge, and sell them the glass. Now that's what I call smart. I liked his style.

Regrettably, after four visits to Iceland, and the Icelanders making several visits to the Falklands, I was to be deeply disappointed about the outcome of the commercial plans of chartering a trawler and purchasing a very modern long-line vessel.

Although the project failed, I have peace of mind with the knowledge that it certainly was not the fault of the Falklands partners, who not only met all their obligations to the joint venture, but much, much more.

No, it was simply this, the trawler experts failed to operate the vessel expertly, and long-liner owners failed to manage the long-liner properly, nothing more, nothing less. It meant, however, that we were required to engage Charles Morrison, a top-class London lawyer to defend our case.

I will tell you something else. I have never dwelt on what might have been, with this very good commercial idea. I would advise anyone in business, or contemplating it, if a business concept doesn't work out as planned, forget it, instantly. Never think of it as failure either. It is only the lazy or jealous observer who measures failure; everyone else is too busy, or positive, to think about it at all.

As I tell you some of my tales about my commercial ventures, it is clear that at least one department of the FIG administrative machinery, the Fisheries Department, has given me a chance. But then, for the most part, my colleagues and I were dealing with a native Falkland Islander. Strange it frequently turned out differently when we were not.

Remember, it is not the introduction of a constitution in itself that will ensure a native people the end of colonialism. It is only when the native people write the constitution themselves that they will have the power to bury it. Then freedom begins.

64

President of the Chamber of Commerce

Outside my own business responsibilities, from 1996 to 1999 I would be given further trust and faith by the commercial sector of the Falkland Islands as a whole by being elected as President of the Falkland Islands Chamber of Commerce.

This, as you can imagine, was a hugely important position in the Falklands private sector. I knew from the moment I took the chair, I would have to be a good listener and observer, whilst employing a tactic which carefully and correctly steered the Chamber Council in the right direction in its deliberations and decision-making on behalf of the membership.

Of course, whenever there is a change at the top, that person will always have a slightly different way of viewing things, and how they might be done, and I was not going to be an exception to this.

I had been slightly concerned in the past that there was potential for self-interest, rather than take a natural and global position and view as the chair. Therefore I made myself a promise, a simple little rule: I would first and foremost care for the well-being of the Chamber of Commerce as a whole. To do that, I would be required to absorb and distribute information in an even-handed manner. It sounds all so logical and simple, but let me tell you, in a small community, it can actually be very difficult to practise.

Another issue which I wished to get to grips with was the function of the office. I felt it was just an untidy shoe box being used as little more than a base for the Secretary for administration purposes only. I decided the Chamber's image needed a good shake-up. It needed to be much more upbeat, and the most obvious place to begin was with its headquarters, the hub from where it all stemmed.

The Chamber Council needed to ensure that the office filled a multitude of vital roles, from an information-gathering and distribution centre, to a place where strategy could be planned and launched, and an awareness centre for the general public. In addition, the Chamber base needed to act as a conduit for the dissemination of information. In business there is always a demand for easy, regular and reliable access of information.

The main elements of commercial education the office needed to provide, for the use of all its membership, were a library, access to computer facilities, administrative assistance and to act as a post box. The Chamber of Commerce also produced a *Business Directory*, whilst also publishing and distributing a weekly news bulletin.

To achieve all these aims, I considered several changes were required, and damn quickly. We began with new office opening times, five days a week, Monday to Friday, from 9 a.m. to 5 p.m. This, at a stroke, immediately improved accessibility and effectiveness not only for the membership, but also the Chamber itself.

Whilst one or two improvements were achieved by basic good housekeeping, others would take a little longer to put in place. But I should just briefly state that the Chamber Council was elected democratically, as you would expect: nine members, serving a one-year term. In my time as President, the Council would meet once a month.

One of the most useful forums for direct communication with elected representatives, and the heads of Government departments was through a regular informal question-and-answer forum. I always found it rather interesting that senior administrators and elected representatives regarded themselves as separate, not one working for the other.

Although this was an 'off the record' meeting, all manner of things could be raised and discussed.

I was very fortunate to be President at the time of a visit to the Islands from a delegation of some 20 business people, predominately from the Grampian area of Scotland. Many of the group had a special interest in the oil industry, but representatives from related services, which included solicitors and auditors, also made the journey.

The Chamber Council was fully involved in arranging the visitors' programme, which was littered with the usual cross-section of meetings and social occasions, both formal and informal, and, of course, their accommodation.

It was the first visit of its kind to the Islands by such a large and varied group of business people from the United Kingdom. It had almost certainly been prompted by the huge UK media coverage the Falklands had been getting, headline stories that were often extremely exaggerated, about the potential oil and gas reserves in the licensed blocks to the north of the Falkland Islands. Therefore, this group of entrepreneurial wise men were coming to look, listen and seek any commercial opportunity. If, in fact, opportunity existed at all. Unfortunately, the delegation arrived in high spirits and great expectations, but they appeared to leave much less hopeful of developing commercial activity. Some even spoke out, quite strongly against FIG.

Hosting this group from Scotland did highlight, once again, the very poor office facilities available to the Chamber: cramped, tatty decor, untidy, very poorly furnished and often cold. It was simply ridiculous to try and continue to work for the good name and positive promotion of the Chamber of Commerce in such conditions. The whole atmosphere gave off a very negative image. So I was determined that during my presidency (which actually lasted three years) I was going to get this organisation a proper home.

Apart from the image issues, I knew that if the Chamber had its own purpose-built unit, regular meetings would not only be held in pleasant surroundings, but acting as host for social events, and some formal sessions, when guest speakers could be invited to address members on matters of interest, could be a very good way of raising funds. Therefore, I was sure that the building should be multipurpose, not just an office. It needed to include a bar to provide refreshments and a room designated for functions.

As it was, we had to rely on the goodwill of the owners and management of the Upland Goose or Malvina Hotel. It was not an ideal situation for all, it was not a money-spinner for the hotel proprietors and it was often disruptive for the hotel guests.

Having our own building would enable the Chamber of Commerce to raise much-needed funds from the operation of a bar, funds that would help finance the administration and other costs. A home base could serve as a facility for a cross-section of the community together, not just the private sector, as they discussed topical issues, be it formally, or informally.

You recognise the plan? That's right, it was the same idea that I had tried to get off the ground with the trade union ten years earlier. The Chamber's only income was from membership fees, and acting as agents for DHL. The Falkland Islands Development Corporation had always been very supportive to the Chamber, probably because of the good relationship which had been built up, resulting from the regular meetings held between the two organisations. The FIDC support was often financial.

Once again, just like the trade union, the reaction from members to the idea of a multipurpose office unit was extremely apathetic. I was very disappointed that many of the members had not grasped what it was I was trying to achieve for them.

Despite getting a pretty frosty response to my idea from the membership, my non-stop encouragement to the Chamber Council kept them positive. We also received the understanding and exceptional support of the Falkland Islands Development Corporation, especially from their General Manager, Hugh Norman, with whom the Chamber of Commerce had built up a very good working relationship. This enabled the two sides to work out, over time, a suitable arrangement which would allow the Chamber to have its home base, even though it was not as owner-occupiers, as I had really wished.

I was a very proud President of the Falkland Islands Chamber of Commerce the night the new complex was officially opened, by the Falkland Islands Government's Chief Executive, Andrew Gurr, even though some members childishly snubbed the ceremony because he was invited to open the building.

In my reply to the Chief Executive's speech, I once again outlined the basic idea behind the project, and highlighted the facilities that were now readily available to members of the Chamber of Commerce.

I will always regard the opening of this multipurpose unit as one of my major contributions to the Falkland Islands Chamber of Commerce, which I truly hope will be for the benefit of all in commerce in the Falkland Islands. The fact that the building stands at all is testimony to the close working relationship the FIDC and the Chamber of Commerce had at the time.

I have mentioned the *Business Directory*; this very important document was first printed and released during my Presidency. In my introduction to the 1998/99 edition, I wrote:

> As President of the Falkland Islands Chamber of Commerce it gives me great pleasure to provide the introduction to this very important document.
>
> The main thrust of this booklet is to highlight those in commercial practice and to demonstrate the wide range of services members of the Private Sector can offer. The content within is not solely for domestic consumption but also to act as an information tool to potential business interests worldwide. Such is the importance of marketing and receiving business information quickly, efficiently and accurately, the Directory can also be found on two web sites on the Internet. These are: Falkland Island News Network http//www./Sartma.com and FIGO www.fidc.orrg.fk
>
> My comment will naturally focus on the interests of the Private Sector, but it will become obvious to the reader that there is a considerable amount of information about the Falkland Islands Government as well as numerous social and recreational facilities contained inside the Directory.
>
> The business community in any civilised country is a very important organisation, which contributes greatly to a country's economy, quality of life and development opportunities. The Falkland Islands commercial sector is no exception to the rule.
>
> The Inhabitants of the Falkland Islands are very proud, loyal and honest people and therefore they are highly commendable to the international business world as a partner, agent, associate or any other formulation of business arrangement one might wish to develop.
>
> There is a tendency worldwide for bureaucracy to deter or obstruct business investment and growth. Although the Falkland Islands is not perfect in this regard, it does provide a reasonable atmosphere to register and operate whilst operating some very attractive aspects which include favourable company and personal taxation, Zero Value Added Tax, limited import duties and no Capital gains Tax (except in specific areas of Oil exploration and exploitation).
>
> The objective of the Chamber of Commerce is to assist in the consolidation and development of the private sector.

Therefore I trust that the contents of the Directory will enlighten and guide everyone in forging new businesses in the Islands and worldwide.

Terence Severine Betts
President.
1996–1999

I am not sure if the comments made about taxation in 1999 are applicable today, therefore anyone contemplating a business venture in the Falklands should make a close check on these matters beforehand.

During 1999, I was beginning to spend more time out of the Islands than I was in them, to attend to the pressing commercial needs of business interests. Therefore, I considered it only sensible that I did not offer myself for re-election at the 1999 AGM. It was time for me and the Chamber to move on.

But no matter what I do, or don't do, where I live, or don't live, I am a Falkland Islander who only cares for the future generations of Islanders. So I will warn, despite the Falkland Islands Government's very responsible attitude in maintaining a minimum level of funds in capital reserves (I am told around £100 million) and the prudent management of some sectors of the fishing industry, I continue to worry just as much now as I did when I was the Chamber of Commerce President back in the 1990s about the wealth of the Islands, hyped up by the world media in particular. I am no more convinced now than I was then about the ability of the Islands to achieve a sustainable and viable economic growth pattern that will allow the development and expansion for a vibrant and prosperous commercial sector which could play a leading role in the structuring of a solid economic base. I liken the Falklands economic situation to a huge bright colourful balloon, hovering rather precariously over the point of a very sharp needle. I sincerely hope it doesn't land on it. My worries now are the same as they were then:

First, an overstaffed and inefficient Government Civil Service, which takes too large a chunk out of annual revenue to support it, coupled with a serious deficiency in the Falklands fishery in the area of the migratory squid species. I accept, that in terms of fighting the cause for proper management and control of overfishing in this area, the Falkland Islands Government has been exemplary. But, on the question of ensuring that the maximum revenue is received into the Islands from Government charges, and supporting the private sector in substantial commercial agreements with Asian boat owners and others, then the Government has been nothing short of pathetic.

I would like to point out that my remarks about the Civil Service have to do with the system, not any individuals in particular, although one or two of them might well hang their heads in shame, if they are still in the Islands, that is. Therefore, I would suggest that there should be a sound shake-up of the Civil Service, aimed at improving efficiency and cost-cutting.

The Chamber of Commerce should insist upon the proper management and development of our natural resources – such as domestic fish stocks, tourism, mineral water, the production of wool and other farm products, oil and gas, precious stones and whatever else there might be – which allows for the minimum of Government intervention and ensures the maximum encouragement and involvement of the private sector.

Both Government and businessmen should understand that it is not enough to extract raw material and export it. With this policy, the Falklands will only ever gain the minimum income from its natural resources. Authorities and businessmen should work together to produce added value. There is much more money for businesses and the Government to be earned by participating in the production of fish products than there is by owning or chartering a vessel and dumping the raw material at the dockside in Vigo, Spain. Or simply allowing boat owners from Asia to pay a licence fee, and that's it.

Equally, it is simply not enough to bottle fresh spring water, then put it in the West Store and hope it retails. Thought needs to be put into presentation, and attractive packaging is a good start. Wider markets than the Falklands themselves should be explored.

If the woollen industry generates income that sustains their businesses, the Falkland Islands Government should cut subsidies immediately, unless it is providing funds for the production of other agricultural goods which have a better than even chance of washing its own face commercially.

I am sure that if these examples are implemented, along with many others, the Falkland Islands, and my fellow Falkland Islanders, can indeed look forward optimistically to a future that offers opportunity for those that desire it, and security for those that do not. When this has been achieved, the politicians, and the Civil Servants who are supposed to support the politicians, can all lie easy in their beds at night.

65

I Take Mother to Argentina to See Her Son

Switching back to family issues, my mother was going to celebrate her 70th birthday on 22 January 1998, so I decided that I should take her to Argentina to see Alec. She had not seen him since the War of '82 and I figured that the chances of the two of them seeing each other again in the Falklands were becoming extremely remote.

From a very personal point of view, I think it might be highly risky for Alec to make a return to the place of his birth, even now. I really do believe that one or two people would make an effort to complicate his life if he suddenly showed up in Stanley.

My mother had never been off the Falklands in her entire life, so going on a jet was quite a unique experience for her, and the prospect of going to Argentina, even if it was to stay with her eldest son for a week, was a pretty daunting one.

Unfortunately, our journey was delayed by 24 hours, because the plane that came into the Falklands from Chile sustained damage to some hydraulic landing gear, which had meant that the gruelling journey along the 35-kilometre MPA road to the International Airport had been a complete waste of time. The pre-flight check-in, and the waiting around in the airport lounge, had all been in vain, and the whole exercise would have to be repeated the following day.

Now aware that the plane we were due to travel on had a fault, my mother's imagination about the plane's future airworthiness had begun to run a little wild, and I was cursing our luck, as I had to spend some considerable energy and time on dispelling her fears, which were eventually eliminated, by several bottles of Carlsberg with friends in the Rose Hotel.

The next day, we were on our way, and after a night's stopover in a hotel in the Chilean capital, Santiago, we began what turned out to be a long and tiring journey to Alec's home, which is in a small village called Agua de Oro, some 40 kilometres from the airport in Cordoba, which has a population half the size of Stanley's.

The problem, which we had not anticipated, was that we had to fly from Santiago to Mendoza in Argentina, before going on to Cordoba, and the stopover time in Mendoza was eight hours. I must say, despite the journey and stopover times, mother was superb, and held up really well, never once complaining.

There was one awkward moment, when we arrived in the airport at Mendoza, with an unhelpful and at times uncertain Argentine immigration officer. After a couple of rounds of him saying, Las Malvinas, and me replying, Falkland Islands, then both of us standing looking at each other, shrugging our shoulders, he passed the passports back to me and then said, 'welcome home' in Spanish. I pretended not to understand what he was on about, and replied in English, with a comment that bore no relation to his welcoming greeting.

As we touched down in Cordoba, I could tell that my mother was getting more and more excited about seeing members of her family that she had not seen in 16 years, and others she had never seen in her life before, such as the three grandchildren from Alec's third marriage, who had all been born in Argentina and did not speak a word of English. It was going to be quite amusing listening and watching her communicating with them. All mother's words in Spanish ended in 'O' and I could also envisage plenty of hand signals and what have you also being used.

Although slightly concerned about mother's reaction to actually being in Argentina and meeting Argentinians on their home patch, outside of family that is, I was much more concerned about the heat in Cordoba. It was high summer and the weather was very hot, almost three times what mother had been accustomed to. But once again she surprised me and acclimatised very well.

Heat, however, was not to be the problem on the first night we arrived, because the heavens opened up, and in no time at all, flood conditions prevailed, accompanied by the most spectacular electrical storm, which gave off loud crackles and bangs. The lightning felled trees, and during the course of the night, two people lost their lives. Mother had been terrified of lightning storms all her life, and unknown to me, she spent the whole night pacing her bedroom floor in tears. But after a good breakfast, in the company of her boisterous family, the trials and tribulations of a very long journey, and the dramatic performance of uncontrolled natural energy, were soon forgotten.

I never considered for one moment that my idea to fetch my mother into the heart of what many, perhaps even she herself, viewed as the enemy's territory was foolhardy. I perceived the whole thing as a family pilgrimage, and I was reasonably confident everyone else would see it that way.

But during the whole time (five days) we were there, I was very aware that at any time media attention could spoil the visit for my mother. Therefore, when Alec received a telephone call, shortly after breakfast, from someone well known in the Argentine Foreign Ministry who was enquiring about mother and me, I began to fear the worst. But after a short while on the telephone, Alec invited me to talk with the caller, and following my conversation with him, I was happy that nothing out of the ordinary was going to take place, for the moment anyway.

The climax of the visit for me came on the third evening. The children had gone to see friends, and it was about 10.30 p.m. Mother and Alec were sitting opposite each other around the open kitchen fire, and Alec was playing country songs on his old acoustic guitar. Between each tune, he and mother would slip into conversations about times gone by in the camp, and other parts of the Falklands.

After an hour or so, they were so engrossed that they were totally oblivious to the fact that I was even in the same room as them. I was feeling a bit tired, so I got up as quietly as possible and snuck off to my bed. When I put my head on my pillow, I had a sense of great satisfaction, as I could hear Alec singing 'Country Roads' and mother talking over the top of him.

I knew then I had achieved my objective. I believe she went back home to the Falklands with her mind a little more settled. Five years on, the memories of the trip live on with her, and memories are all she is likely to have.

66

*Another Royal, and a Few Other Things
I've Seen and Done
(South Africa, Namibia, landholdings)*

Moving back to business, by the end of 1998, my business interests had become pretty much consolidated within the activities of Southern Cross Limited and its joint venture company Golden Touza Limited, and the satellite companies which developed from that joint venture. There was still the stationery business, and my interests in Consolidated Fisheries Limited. But by now, all the other ventures that were full of promise, from countries such as Iceland, Denmark, South Africa, Namibia, Japan, Taiwan, Korea, the People's Republic of China, Uruguay and Chile had not taken root as the thriving businesses they should have become. But I am satisfied that none of that was any fault of mine, or my local partners.

I have never been afraid of hard work, nor to commit time and effort entering into pastures new to seek a commercial opportunity that might be of benefit to my Falklands partners, the Islands economy as a whole, and, of course, myself. And despite having walked down several blind alleys, I am a much wiser and happier man for those experiences, delighted with the knowledge that for many years, I was right up at the sharp end, instigating ideas and working my bollocks off to try and make them a commercial success.

Even though the businesses had become very centralised, I still didn't need to worry about spare time. The Atlantic House group of businesses kept me very busy, and I still had my responsibilities to the Chamber of Commerce, as their President, and also as the Chairman of the board of directors for a company called Falkland Landholdings Limited, who owned and operated the farmland purchased by the Falkland Islands Government from the Falkland Islands Company back in the early 1990s. But now let me tell you something about Landholdings.

Rather interestingly, I had been invited by the FIG to take the position of Chairman because of my commercial background. I was up for the challenge, but as always, I am not a 'yes man' and unfortunately, even with the introduction of a full-time Managing Director I soon realised that many good commercial and common-sense projects would be interfered with by meddling and unhelpful politicians.

The politicians (one or two, probably) vigorously argued that, as elected councillors, they were the representatives of the FIG share-holding. It was a strange position for them to take, because I was aware that in other commercial companies in which they had significant or meaningful shareholding, they left the board to get on with the day-to-day business of those companies pretty much. It was, in my opinion, a farcical situation, and especially as I knew, in the strictest of commercial terms, they were not the share-holders' representatives. The Government shareholding was entrusted in the signatories of the company share certificates, who were namely the Financial Secretary, Derek Howatt, and the Chief Executive, Andre Gurr, at that time.

But in fairness to the politicians, I thought I understood their dilemma, which rolled back to the very moment FIG purchased the assets from the Falkland Islands Company, because then, not only did the Government acquire a loss-making business, it also took on, in the main, dilapidated machinery, equipment and settlement infrastructure, coupled with a labour force that would become demanding to ensure their jobs and accommodation were protected at all cost – without the slightest interest, or understanding, that a business really should try and 'wash its own face'.

Furthermore, other elements of the sale locked the FIG into terms and conditions with the farm managers which demanded that their personal terms and conditions of employment would at least equal those of their previous employers.

These contracts were loaded with benefits in kind, and completely devoid of any need for the individuals to be imaginative and commercial thinking. Which became a real barrier when trying to introduce a sensible private company mentality and structure.

I am not attacking the individuals involved (they were very smart cookies), no, I am critical of the FIG stupidity, when agreeing with the antiquated arrangement.

The elected councillors were constantly pressurised by the

employers, the management and certain members of the public who were related to both, all of which were also the electorate, to basically maintain the status quo. If they didn't, they could kiss their vote goodbye at the next General Election. Therefore, straightforward and commonsense business practice was not what the elected councillors wanted to hear. I suspect that what they really wanted from the board of Falkland Landholdings was a partner in the social welfare matters of the employees, as the company spluttered along in the pretence of being commercial.

I only wish the politicians had been upfront with me at the very beginning. Then I would not have taken the responsibility on, because I would have been aware that commerce was just a front. I would have preferred honesty, rather than constantly having to endure the bullshit of being told 'only representing the shareholders' best interest' when I asked why a piece of land or other assets so obviously surplus to company requirements could not be sold in a proper commercial manner as a means to raise much needed capital.

I have to say, it was a bloody strange interpretation of the shareholders' interests, when each commercial project was denied, then the funds required by the company were derived from the public purse, in one form or another. I thought, as Chairman, I had been given a task to turn the company around, and to try and make it profitable. That was my foolish mistake.

Eventually, as in most things, I was not attending enough board meetings because I was more often in Spain than the Falklands, and I resigned. Regrettably, without being able to make any positive contribution to Falkland Landholdings and its shareholders. But believe me, I did try my best, and for a while, I was genuinely committed and gave it all my best efforts, but once again, it would be another one of those adventures called 'useful experience' to throw into one's life kit bag.

I would like to slip back a little, to 1997 and tell a tale about a trip I made to South Africa and Namibia. This time I was accompanied by the office manager, Ian Doherty. The trip was fishing-related business, with a plan to bring new people into the Falklands fishery.

Getting to Cape Town was a pretty complicated affair from the

Falklands. We took the regular flight from Stanley to Chile. After spending the night in the Chilean capital we then travelled to Argentina, and on to Brazil. Then we had to take a Varig flight to Johannesburg, before we moved on to Cape Town, where we stayed for a day and held our preliminary meetings with our hosts, who were full of enthusiasm.

Following these meetings, we moved on to Namibia, firstly to Windhoek, and then on to the principal fishing port of Walvis Bay. Unfortunately, when Ian and I arrived, we were put into a hotel which was some 500 metres downwind of a huge fishmeal plant. It did not matter where you were situated in the hotel, it was impossible to escape the obnoxious smell.

The two stories I want to tell you about this trip are about life itself, and the shocking surprises it sometimes has in store for us. One morning, Ian and I had been taken by car by the owner of a fishmeal factory in Walvis Bay. As we approached the factory gates, I was amazed to see a long line of people, for as far as the eye could see, from two directions, queuing at the factory gates. They were all black.

I first thought that they were just waiting to be let in to go to work, but as we got closer, the crowd started to mill around our car, then began banging on the vehicle as we drove slowly along, and started shouting at our driver, the factory owner.

I asked him what it was all about. 'Oh,' he said, 'they are wanting work. It is always like this every bloody morning. I'll give one or two a job today.'

'They'll be happy about that,' I said.

'Until tomorrow,' he replied. 'I only give them work for a couple of hours, or a day, at best.' I flopped back in my seat rather flabbergasted.

The sight of the poor souls, desperately begging for work which would earn them a few dollars, if it was their lucky day, only to have to repeat the exercise the following day, sickened me. I felt very uncomfortable, watching them going through their emotional pleading, and I was mighty relieved when I left. But as you can tell, the fact that I felt compelled to tell you about this experience, means I have not, and will not, forget it.

Then we went back to Cape Town for a couple of days to continue our business meetings. Well, as for the end of apartheid, you really have to be kidding. On one Saturday morning, I was walking in a small area of Cape Town, with a white guide, and we passed three or four black children, between eight and twelve years old, I would say, huddled in a small group on the corner of the street. As we walked by, they immediately began begging us for food and money. They were absolutely filthy and stank to the high heavens as they stood in front of us, with bare feet and ragged clothes, trembling with fear. I had seen many beggars in my life, including children, but I had never seen any who were so filthy and frightened.

I turned to my companion and asked why they were in such a physical and mental state. He looked at me and said, 'These kids will have been buggered and urinated on by many people. That's the way it is here.' I wanted to throw up on the spot. I asked him to take me out of the place immediately. There was nothing I could do for their poor miserable souls, and I walked away totally disgusted with my fellow man, who had been carrying out such unspeakable atrocities. I thought to myself, little wonder some of these children fought back and became trained killers at such a young age.

Finally, the more observant of you will have noted that I mentioned I have had the honour to meet six members of the Royal Family, and thus far, I have only given you details about meeting five of them. The last was HRH the Prince of Wales, who came to the Falkland Islands in March 1999. I was introduced to His Royal Highness in the Community Hall at Goose Green, that's right, the very building where 110 civilians had been imprisoned during the Falklands War in 1982. For once, being Chairman of the board of Falkland Landholdings, who are the owners of Goose Green, actually gave me some kind of privilege, for a brief moment anyway.

I was introduced to the Prince as he was circulating and meeting the gathering in the hall. I don't believe there were any significant exchanges of conversation between us, even though we did talk for a couple of minutes. I do recall trying to outline some of our commercial plans for the future, whatever they might have been. It mattered not anyway, because I expect shareholders eventually savaged them.

However, the Prince did seem to have a genuine interest in rural development and its environment. I am sure it would not have escaped such a quick and keen mind that Goose Green lacked much, and was in desperate need of a good old shot in the arm from someone, from somewhere, and pretty damned quickly.

67

The End of the Marriage, Then the Business

By the middle of 1998, it was abundantly clear that my second marriage was in trouble, and I had it confirmed when I arrived at the home of friends in Tasmania, which was the first stop of a business trip I was making to Australia.

I must admit that when the news had been broken to me, it was simply a statement of the obvious; rather than any surprise or shock. The news was, however, a hammer blow to my wife's supposed best friend, whose husband it was that she had got herself involved with.

I will have to be honest, I had not been happy in the marriage for some time, and although I ambled on with it, I could see that it had no future. My only regret was not having had the courage to call it a day myself, much earlier. But like all bad business, you sling it on the scrap heap of history, and forget about it.

Well, in an ideal world maybe, but I was not granted that luxury living in the Falklands. In fact, I was even expected to humiliate myself by living in the same house as my estranged wife and her mother, who my wife had brought back to the Islands, even after the news of the relationship with the other man was public knowledge, and inserted her into my own home, without my permission.

I was told by people who should have known better, just to put up with it and pretend nothing was out of the ordinary, whilst lover boy even had the effrontery to drive up my long driveway to the back door of the house, to take his new lover out for the evening. She would be dressed in the finest attire, eagerly awaiting her chauffeur, and drive off on a night of pleasure right under my very nose, whilst all I was supposed to do was remain cool, and not react in any provocative manner. Was I mad, or were my legal representatives, and everyone else, living in cloud-cuckoo-land?

Even if I went out for a drink, or to some social occasion at one of the few hotels, it would not be unusual to have to endure the presence of these two people in the same room. Just what any sane man did not need. At times, I would even go into the pub and have to tolerate my legal representative leaning over a bar laughing, joking and drinking with my wife.

By the way, I am only telling you these stories to give you a feel for another aspect of life in the Falklands; I am not attempting to rewrite the pages from *Heartbreak Hotel*, God forbid, nor am I making any attempt to be insulting to my ex-wife.

However, I would not want you to think that I could accept, or in fact cope, with this crazy situation. It was totally unrealistic to pretend that all was fine. The ridiculous position I had been put in pretty quickly began to affect my daily life, coupled with the now routine commercial projects which had restricted my activities to projects in hand only. Rather than allowing my creative mind to bring any new ideas to the table, the combination of these and other factors made me feel a little suffocated, and I am sure I became a little stale. I badly needed a break from the environment I was living in, in the Falklands. As it happened, my business partners realised this too.

After a little while, everyone in the business felt I could serve the business interests much better in Spain, working more closely with our partners, and other experts, on various aspects of the commercial consolidation plan. For a time, it seemed to work very well. I was enjoying my new environment, free of any mental torment, and learning things of great interest in relation to the global fishing industry. I was fortunate that I had always enjoyed the respect of my Spanish partners; the only difference now was that we had also become very good friends.

But things were not allowed to run smoothly for too long, due, unfortunately, to the fact that a clean break from my wife was becoming very protracted, and the whole thing ended up in one bloody great mess. Which probably meant I was away from the Falklands longer than first planned, which naturally resulted in me seeing less and less of my Falklands business partners, and eventually, over a period of time, I detected a gradual breakdown in communication in our commercial relationship. In truth, it probably started some time before I went to Spain.

I think it really began when we stopped being a trio on a daily basis in the office. It was little things at first, a difference of interpretation on a commercial point, and sure enough, like pop stars, the cracks in the band began to appear, and then widen, as we all developed our individual interests outside the commercial partnership. As this trend developed, we gradually seemed to have less and less in common regarding projections of our commercial world.

It was no one's fault in particular, I am sure, but like brothers and sisters, you grow up, and then you part. Socially, things with the chaps and their families were fine; perhaps they were even too good when we all got together. But sadly, even these occasions began to be spoilt by individual preference for the company we kept. We were becoming increasingly like three individuals (which of course we were) rather than a team.

If I could make one other observation, it was that too much trust and confidence was being placed on office staff. Perhaps I was as much to blame as anyone else for that.

At some point, in the early part of 2000, I was reasonably sure in my own mind that the local partnership, in its original structure, was doomed. After a while I began to openly discuss the matter with my partners whilst in the Islands. But I was probably too frank and abrupt about the whole very sensitive subject. Therefore I decided, if necessary I would leave.

The trouble was, no one really wanted me to go, but I had started the ball rolling and the split was now inevitable. However, I did manage to make one more major commercial contribution for the partners of Southern Cross and Golden Touza Limited before my working days in the Falklands under the partnership finished on 31 May 2001.

My 'swansong' was this. I had become aware of a new business venture, which was in its embryonic stages, whilst in Spain, and I was sure it was just the sort of project for the joint venture to participate in. So once back in Stanley for a board meeting, I had no hesitation in putting the idea to the Spanish and Falklands partners in Golden Touza Limited.

The project was aquaculture, and in particular the introduction of oyster spat into the Falklands. Although I was immediately sold on the idea, I found that I had more sceptics than supporters among the seven board members of GTL. But with the chairman of the board's support, and after a little bit of poking and prodding, I eventually managed to get a meeting together in Atlantic House between the two parties already working on the project, who were the Falkland Islands Development Corporation and Simon Hardcastle, and representatives of GTL.

A series of meetings followed in the Falklands, Chile, Spain and London, and eventually, the joint venture company Falklands Fresh Limited was formed. Then the company began to expand its plans to include the exploitation and commercial development of other local Falklands inshore seafood products, such as crabs, mussels and two species of fish.

My involvement in this new challenge gave me renewed interest and vigour, but the aftermath of my divorce would not go away, and the settlement arrangements were hanging over me like a big black cloud and tempered the 'good mood' atmosphere.

Before things really nose-dived, in terms of a business relationship, in March 1999, one of my business partners and a close friend for many years, Pete Gilding, invited me to join him on a trip on a small cruise ship. The voyage would take us to sea for 25 days on and off; and our first port of call would be South Georgia, my first visit there in the 30 years since I departed on the RRS *Shackleton* in March 1969. This time, I would circumnavigate South Georgia.

As we did so, we also made several landings at places of interest. I remember we had a dram at the graveside of Ernest Shackleton before setting a course for Tristan da Cunha.

On our way to Tristan da Cunha, Peter had mentioned to the ship's captain that I had been on ships before, and I knew how to drive. One morning, when I was on the bridge, the captain invited me to steer the vessel. I readily agreed and got my hand in for an hour, which I enjoyed immensely. I'm not sure if the rest of the crew and passengers did, however.

Before reaching Tristan da Cunha, we lay off Gough Island whilst the ship and a small team on the island chatted to each other by radio, and others clapped binoculars upon one another.

We also spent a day on Nightingale Island, which is all part of the Tristan da Cunha group. From Tristan da Cunha we sailed for St Helena and finally disembarked at Ascension Island.

It was a wonderful adventure. Pete and I became really close again – it was like old times.

I suppose the highlight of the whole trip for me would be the visits to St Helena and Tristan da Cunha. Both are only serviced from the sea, and on many occasions, when a ship arrives at

Tristan, it is not possible to land there because of the constant trade winds, which create a permanent sea swell.

So it was to be for us on the first day we arrived, but unlike many other visiting ships, we had three days, so we waited for our chance to get on the island. The second day was perfect for a landing.

We all eagerly stepped ashore with broad grins on our faces and armed with cameras, well aware that we were very privileged people indeed to ever set foot on this volcanic island.

One of the most prominent features of the island is the distinctive scars of the 1961 volcanic eruption, which has left the river of molten lava as a mound of black volcanic rock which runs into the sea. Given the close proximity of the volcanic site to the small village, it is quite remarkable that only one house was lost. However, the inhabitants were forced to evacuate, mainly to the UK, but the islanders could not settle, and nearly all returned two years later.

We spent a whole day wandering around the island, chatting with many of the 300 or so inhabitants. In its tiny village, called Edinburgh, I actually met a man who knew my father, whilst he was working on Pebble Island in the early 1960s. It was a chance encounter. We had pulled up to a gateway, in a Land Rover driven by the Chief Islander, Jimmy Glass, who was taking Pete and me off to the potato patches. The people of Tristan da Cunha claim to grow the finest potatoes in the world.

Anyway, a tall and lean man was standing at the gate, holding it open for us to go through. Once we had, Jimmy stopped the vehicle, and we all climbed out to chat with the man, who, I assumed, was in his late sixties. After a bit of small talk about the weather and suchlike, he asked where I came from. I told him the Falklands. Then he said, 'Oh, I worked on Pebble Island. I knew a man called Cyril Betts. Do you know him?'

With a grin on my face, I replied, 'I do actually. He's my father.' The man, whose name was Mr Andersen, just could not believe it.

I would leave Tristan da Cunha thinking to myself, if we in the Falklands thought we were pretty isolated before 1982, our isolation then was nothing in comparison to the inhabitants who live on this very remote 25-square-mile island today.

St Helena, like Tristan, is also unique, but not quite as cut off.

It is also twice the size. The total population is 5,650 approximately, but there is very limited employment and incomes are very low.

Pete and I got off the ship for the two days we were there, and stayed at the Consulate hotel, in the island's main street.

We knew many people on the island, because of the link with the Falklands, which provided employment opportunities for many St Helenians. We would always come across someone who had either been to the Falklands, or knew a family member or friend who had worked there.

One of the biggest challenges awaiting any visitor to St Helena is to walk up a very steep cliff face, which consists of 699 steps, called Jacobs Ladder. I managed to decline the offer to accompany a friend up the breathtaking open-air stairway, on the basis that if you want to return somewhere, you should leave something undone.

The Island of St Helena, was, of course, the prison island of Napoleon Bonaparte for five and a half years, and as one of my great-great-great-grandfathers, Richard Victor Goss, had been the boatswain on the ship that took him there, I had to visit his Longwood House, where he was confined until his death in May 1821.

Once inside, you are treated to a wonderful array of artefacts from that period: paintings, furniture, clothing, coins, letters, books etc., in every room of the house.

We also walked around the trenches in the garden, which Napoleon had dug so he couldn't be seen whilst out in the grounds. The gardens themselves are a multitude of colours, with beautiful flowers and plants all bathed in St Helena's ever-present daily sunshine.

Wherever you go in St Helena you will always hear country music being played. This reminded me of my visit to Bermuda.

Pete and I couldn't resist a ride around the island in a 1940s charabanc. I took videos of the splendid views, and other places of interest, such as the Governor's residence, called Plantation House, where we stopped to stroke and take photographs of the 200-year-old tortoise, who I think was called Jonathan. I would also like to record my thanks to the people of St Helena for their support to Falkland Islanders during and after our war.

After departing St Helena, it was off to Ascension Island, 700 miles to the northwest. It was only a two-day voyage, and once Pete and I had packed our bags, it was straight ashore, and a 12-hour wait in the capital, Georgetown, for my RAF connecting flight that was due in that night from the Falklands to take me off to the UK and then on to Spain. Pete was actually staying on in Ascension, to be joined by his wife and children for a short break in the island's sunshine.

It was the end of a wonderful 25-day journey, and I am delighted that I can think back on the whole experience with a bagful of very fond memories. I am also very grateful to Pete for the invitation to join him, and also for all his support and encouragement during the trip, which in hindsight I now realise was a genuine attempt, on his behalf, to try and pull the relationship together one last time.

Once I returned to Spain, I immediately began to contribute to the planning for lengthening one of the fishing trawlers, the *Hermanos Touza*, and also matters pertaining to the new venture in the Falkland Islands, Falklands Fresh Limited. This company's activities were very much at the pioneering stage, but it was clear that Golden Touza Limited had become a partner because we felt it could lend to the joint venture our wider commercial experience in fisheries, whilst also providing venture capital if reasonable and sensible.

With that decided, there was a need for a great deal of planning and logistical work to be carried out to enable the project to have a real chance of moving forward and succeeding. It was concluded that a unique and purpose-built factory unit was required. This entailed identifying manufacturers, getting the unit assembled and making it ready for shipment to the Falklands. Once there, it was then a question of getting it set up and running. This was going to require a lot of cooperation from authorities in the Islands, and from past experiences, this was something that worried me because I knew it would not be guaranteed.

We were also tasked with sourcing buyers, and markets, for species which would be new to the market place. We did have some early success by establishing a buyer in Estonia for one of the local fish.

It was a very interesting time and I was happy with my role and responsibilities. However, the relationship with my Falklands partners took a serious nose-dive when I put my weight behind the idea of Golden Touza Limited responding positively to a request from FIG to offer sponsorship for a high-level forum they had planned to stage in London in July 2000.

A misunderstanding developed into something that became a major issue with certain members of the board. It could have been so easily resolved, if those who were troubled by the matter had bothered to communicate with me directly.

I was certain GTL had been given a great opportunity to promote itself on a very large stage, an opportunity just too great to miss. Not only was the forum going to be attended by senior officials of the Falkland Islands Government, and elected councillors, but also by representatives from the United Kingdom Foreign Office, along with international businessmen and some serious heavyweights from the UK media. As an example, the forum was being chaired by Nicholas Owen from ITN.

As it happened, Golden Touza Limited did sponsor the formal occasion of the forum dinner, and did itself no harm whatsoever by putting up the sponsorship funds. But the partnership and trust between fellow directors in the Islands never recovered.

The problem might have been created because I had got the funding for the sponsorship without the full backing of some of my Falklands colleagues – a majority, not a unanimous vote. That might have been unprofessional of me, even though my actions were only meant to be in the very best interests of the company, which they later proved to be (and how).

Another problem developed after the forum. I had attracted media attention with some comments I made about the Falklands Government, regarding the new processing plant bound for the Falklands.

Some of my statements about unhelpful local authorities were recorded in the UK press and touched a very sensitive nerve with a certain senior member of FIG administration, which resulted in that individual dribbling down a telephone, or writing some schoolboy-type letters to fellow directors in Falklands Fresh Limited (or GTL).

Probably because they had not supported GTL involvement in the forum from the beginning, or they were too nervous to stand up to the childish behaviour of this official, at least one Falklands director chose to dissociate themselves from me, and my comments. It was just another signal that all was not well in the partnership.

However, within months of the Falklands forum issue, the board of Golden Touza Limited held its regular November meeting in the Falklands. The meeting was held in a very good atmosphere in Stanley, and we worked away as a cohesive and enthusiastic group, and it seemed all the previous problems had been forgotten. But in reality it was paper over cracks. It was at this meeting that the first idea of me selling my shareholding was raised. But once I indicated my opinion of their value, the matter was quickly dropped.

Things went downhill very quickly in the beginning of 2001, not entirely due to a breakdown of communications regarding commercial matters. My divorce, and the protracted settlement, fuelled an already out of control fire.

The combination contributed to a worsening of relationships, and by the time I arrived back in Stanley for the company board meeting in April, my business relationship with my Falklands partners was very fraught indeed. So bad was the atmosphere at times that I was deliberately, and blatantly, ignored by one of my partners who didn't even want me to come back to the Islands to attend the meetings.

Strangely enough, as my relationship was in freefall with partners in the Islands, my working relationship with the Spanish partners had grown from strength to strength; we became very close, as we worked together on the upfront issues.

But when I departed the Falklands on 7 April 2001, without as much as a goodbye from one partner, I flew back to Spain with mixed and confused emotions. On the one hand my Spanish colleagues were discussing the future plans with great optimism with me, whilst on the other hand, fellow directors were not talking to me, even though I remained a keen and active participant of the company on day-to-day affairs right up to the very end. On that flight back to Spain, I knew it was all over for me. It was just a matter of when.

Seven weeks after departing the Falklands, at 6.22 p.m. (Spanish time) on 31 May 2001, I walked out of the Chymar office in Vigo, Spain, having signed documents which confirmed, among other things, my resignation as a director of Southern Cross Limited, and subsequently, all its other commercial connections – a resignation which was all rather farcical, more like Hobson's choice. The real reasons, and the events leading up to my resignation, are still only known by a handful of people. I might tell all another time, in another book perhaps. I promise you, it will make fascinating reading.

68

I Have Been a Fortunate Man

As time slips by, I can only reflect upon my life and the many things I have participated in regarding Falkland Islands affairs. For someone who medical experts had predicted would not survive beyond my 10th birthday, I have managed to cram an awful lot into my life. Which, I hope, will be long enough to permit me to contribute still further, as I pursue fresh and new challenges which now stand on the horizon.

As I work towards some of these goals, I will be able to reflect on past achievements with a great deal of satisfaction and pride. I am satisfied that I have made a useful and meaningful contribution to Falkland Islands commerce, and to the economy of the Falkland Islands as a whole. I can also tell you that I did so with the clear aim of improving the standard of living and quality of life for my fellow Falkland Islanders, and of course myself.

My contributions to the private sector, and the Falkland Islands economy, have come via several channels, personally, through private company activities, as a President of the Chamber of Commerce, as a politician, as an honorary board member or company director of organisations such as the Falkland Islands Development Corporation or the Tourist Board. I have played a leading role in the improvement of working and pay conditions for the ordinary workingman in the Falklands, as the leader of the trade union.

Oh yes, that mystery voice of many years ago which encouraged me to fight on, as I was about to quit on life, was absolutely right. I had things to do.

I am viewing this period in my life (2003) simply as an interval, an intermission, time to take stock, and when the curtain rises again, I will, hopefully, be once more actively contributing in some meaningful way to the Falkland Islands and its inhabitants.

I cannot close this book without expressing more political viewpoints regarding the Falkland Islands, my country. It is a personal and frank opinion, and everyone will take it, or leave it, as they fancy, just as citizens of any true democracy should be able to. Ah, but sadly, the Falkland Islands are not a true democracy yet. That's why I was stripped of a vote as fast as possible. Even though I still pay my taxes to the Falkland Islands Government on my world-wide income.

Some of my opinions are these: whether we like it or not, the burning question of the sovereignty issue is no more resolved now than it was when we in the Falkland Islands were taking cover from the Argentine invading forces on the night of 2 April 1982. This fact should trouble all Falkland Islanders; it certainly bothers me. Be in no doubt, problems need solutions, just as questions need answers.

Before going any further, let's get one thing straight. I am only interested in a stable long-term future for Falkland Islanders. My loyalty, above all else, is to the Falkland Islander. Yes, of course I am British, and yes, I am proud of that fact. But that is not enough in this long-standing dispute.

All of us should contribute to looking for the long-term answer. I do not suggest for one moment that I have the solution, I am not that self-righteous, but I am putting you on notice that I am prepared to try and help to look for one.

The status quo is not a long-term option for Falkland Islanders. To try and maintain it, is, in my opinion, extremely dangerous. There is one thing that is as plain as the nose on your face, no government of Argentina will agree to give up its claim to the Falkland Islands, as the present arguments stand. That would be totally unacceptable to the people of Argentina, as I understand it.

The British Government, for the moment, say they will not cede sovereignty of the Islands to Argentina against the wishes of the people of the Falkland Islands. Now the status quo believers say, 'That's great, so let's leave it at that.' Well that is just the problem. It is not great at all, guys.

The status quo could be negative and dangerous, because there could be elements of potential high risk to Falkland Islanders. One is possible negative action from Argentina against us. This could be civil, in the form of stopping other national airlines flying in their airspace en route to the Falklands, or military, or a combination of both.

Another situation which could dramatically alter the status quo is that a future British Government might change its mind and heart towards the Falkland Islands and its native population, by striking a deal with the Argentines. Stranger things have happened in politics. A dramatic downturn in the UK or Islands economy, or both; unforeseen pressures on the UK, which would demand a much more home-based strategy; international terrorism; World War III; or ever closer ties within Europe, could force a serious change of attitude towards us.

I would agree that the Falklands have achieved one major political success over the last 18 years. This has been to get the Argentines and the British to recognise, and accept, that there are three, not just two, parties to this long-standing dispute (or have we?).

If this has come about it is only because Falkland Islanders have stood up on their own, and spoken out for themselves. Please never underestimate this fact.

Now that this has been accomplished, there is a need to build long-term security, prosperity, and peace, for many, many generations of Falkland Islanders to come, upon this vital foundation stone.

Being recognised and heard at last also means we have to be seen to be a responsible people, not a bunch of whingeing layabouts, or those same organisations or groups will get fed up and begin to ignore us again. I believe we have been given some time, and an opportunity, to put forward ideas that will complete the final picture of this particularly complex puzzle.

In the past and, more worryingly, now, I hear some Islanders saying, 'As long as nothing changes over the next twenty-five or thirty years, I don't care, che, because I'll be dead, and it won't bother me.'

I would suggest to those who think this way, that your view is a totally selfish and extremely irresponsible one. What about the Islanders aged between 1 and 40? Do you honestly not give a shit about them?

I firmly believe we should be fully utilising our window of opportunity, and I am pretty sure that the only constructive way to do that is to try and become problem solvers. We should not be in fear of getting one or two things wrong in our attempt to secure a lasting peace, because I am sure, as long as we can be seen to be making a genuine effort, we will be understood and tolerated.

Why do I desire a change at all? Because I still see Falkland Islanders feeling insecure, and ever so susceptible to actions that could have a hugely negative effect on our economy or the potential to develop it. The effect of any immediate cutting of commercial air links with the South America mainland, as we already know, can cause considerable damage to the Islands economy and, of course, freedom of movement. Worse still, at the other end of the non-resolved dispute scale, is the horrifying possibility of further bloody conflict.

Anyone in the islands from 2 April to 14 June 1982 will know that we were very lucky that Stanley, at least, and its civilian population, were not wiped out. It would be extremely foolhardy to try our luck a second time.

I think we can hold our heads up high, and say the events of 1982 were not our fault. In fact, we were perhaps the innocent victims. But if there were to be anything like a repeat of those events, I could well imagine we might be in the dock. The judge and jury just might find us guilty this time.

What I am writing is not an attempt to scaremonger, nor to identify areas of blame if things go wrong, I am just trying to get your attention, and on the basis that I now have that, what do I think might be done?

I would suggest that all three parties should work with organisations such as the United Nations, the European Community and perhaps even Mercosur (South American Trading & Political body), as hard as possible on a win, win, win situation, a solution that removes once and for all the sovereignty dispute. The motivation for all concerned should be the concept of lasting peace. With this in mind, I offer a contribution.

The first step is for everyone to recognise that the Falkland Islands' political problem is unique; whilst all minds need to be very open, no one should begin to compare the Falklands with a Gibraltar, Northern Ireland or any other situation. Once that is accepted, perhaps, the Falkland Islanders should suggest to Great Britain and Argentina that they both give up their sovereignty claim over the Falkland Islands. This might have the positive effect of neutralising the issue.

The ownership of the Islands should then be transferred to the Falkland Islanders, who would, naturally, have total autonomy. That way, there is no loser in the first crucial step of attempting to resolve the dispute, and thus, much face-saving, especially for the Argentines.

On the basis that this is acceptable to all, it would mean that everyone could really get down to serious business, because then a long-term peace plan has a real chance. Having reached this stage in the negotiations, it should then be possible for Argentina to confirm its end to making any further attempts to what they call 'recover' of the Islands. The positive benefits to all, when we have reached this stage, are obvious.

Of course, we Falkland Islanders would need to be sure that the home we are just about to acquire is not going to be attacked by a foreign neighbour who has a sudden change of heart. We must also be sure that we have the tools and resources to maintain and develop our property. The primary basis for this is, of course, a sound economy. The nuts and bolts of this will need to be worked out, and will involve a lot of very intelligent people who only have the long-term and future security of the Falkland Islander in the forefront of their mind.

Once the Argentine threat has been removed, many other things can happen, for example, the Argentines accepting that the Falklands does not belong to them. The new government of the Falkland Islands would be free, at last, to develop all kinds of commercial, social, cultural, environmental and political relationships with its South American neighbours, including Argentina.

Equally, if the Argentine Government recognised the Falkland Islands Government, in its own right, as the legitimate government of the Islands, and therefore no longer harboured any claims over our homeland, it might not be unreasonable for the Falkland Islands Government to invite the Argentine Government to establish an embassy or consulate in the Islands capital. As a natural process, from this place of officialdom, the Argentine flag would be permitted to fly.

But I would not try and kid my compatriots that this is the only reason for such a move. Just think of the unique way in which it could evolve. Not a single word of anger, not a single drop of blood.

I repeat, there would be a need for everyone involved in seeking a solution to clearly understand and accept the uniqueness of the Falklands issue. Once this principle has been accepted, it is then required to structure a unique settlement.

To this end, I suggest that when it is agreed to transfer the property to the Falkland Islanders, who must accept and conduct democratic self-governance as part of the deal, additional special circumstances should be attached to the transfer. This should include a structure which allows the Falkland Islands, and its inhabitants, to become integrated in some kind of way into the European Community, for the purpose of trade at least, and perhaps some form of domicile.

The Falkland Islands must ensure it can trade within Europe. In my opinion, this trading area will be one of the most important in this century, and that Falkland Islands should not be restricted from introducing the euro as its official legal tender, if it is felt economically and politically desirable. The Falklands would need to utilise a currency that has international standing.

The Falkland Islands should also have the flexibility and option to become a member of Mercosur in its own right. Again, I suggest this because it would allow the Falklands access to a geographically convenient market place. The idea is consistent with the concept of trying to maximise our trading options for the future development of our economy.

Even with the threat of conflict removed, there would still be the question of the Islands' defence, and what the defence needs of the Falkland Islands might be in a very different atmosphere to today. I suppose the obvious question, from Falkland Islanders' point of view at least is: 'What if Argentina reneged on the whole agreement and reverted to force?' A very reasonable question, but one that needs to be tackled, not simply put up as an excuse to obstruct a lasting settlement.

Whenever an agreement is reached, there is a considerable amount of trust. I would also imagine the peacemakers would not wish to appear stupid by agreeing a naïve plan.

As you know, I am not a militarily minded person, but if it was felt there was a need for a continued military presence, at least to cover the transactional and settling down period, then I suppose it is not unreasonable to think that the British forces remain, or to assume some sort of neutral force be stationed at Mount Pleasant International Airport. One thing is certain, it could not be argued that the Falkland Islands has the human resources to defend itself.

I admit, I have no bright ideas on this subject, other than very basic logic. But any solution that is acceptable to all concerned is surely likely to have a very welcome release of pressure on British military resources of today.

It also needs to be understood by everyone that we Falkland Islanders are British, and I make no apologies for highlighting this matter of fact again. We are many generations of British blood, and our natural tongue is English, our culture and social structure is naturally, not factitiously, one of British democratic principles. Therefore it needs to be noted that it is totally illogical to expect Falkland Islanders to sever their ties with Great Britain like the flick of a switch.

This is one part of the reasoning behind my suggestion of the European trading and domicile concept. I perceive this as a compromise to the status quo. I do not think there is any requirement for Falkland Islanders to embark on an act of diluting the continuance of our British heritage as we develop our own identity; our genealogical background would, in fact, be a fundamental fibre to our new self-confidence and future image.

As long as that is understood and accepted, I think it rather desirable in terms of national identity to have our own Falkland Islands passport, flag and other national symbols and systems, to give us the same rights, privileges and protection as any other European citizen. Remember, unless you keep an open mind on the need for uniqueness in resolving the Falklands problem, you will lose the train of my thinking.

So, if the Betts plan was that simple and easy to implement, why hasn't anyone thought about it, and done it before? Firstly, I do not think for one moment my ideas are that easy to implement, nor do I believe that all sides directly involved would readily agree to even consider my thoughts.

All I am attempting to do is to be a responsible and caring Falkland Islander, not an interfering one. I am just someone who is throwing some fresh ideas into the melting pot. If some people do take time out to consider my thoughts, that will mean there has at least been a process of debate, analysis and finally judgement on some, or all of them.

Some might even ask, 'Why stick your head above the parapet, Terry?' Well, it comes naturally. I have never had any fear of expressing myself, even if there has been a real possibility of being ridiculed.

I have been laughed at, by my fellow man, many times before in life, and most often when all I have been trying to do is look after their best interests. I also have a conscience, and I do not want something terrible to happen to the Falklands and Falkland Islanders which might make me question myself.

I am obliged, therefore, to try and contribute to a possible long-term peaceful settlement in the southwest Atlantic. So I am committed to trying to seek security, peace, prosperity and happiness, for the Falkland Islander in particular, but not exclusively.

Make no mistake, I have no grand ideas about myself. I am well aware that I am no scholar; I am not making any attempt to be a contender for the Nobel Peace Prize. I am simply doing what makes me feel better within myself, whilst trying hard to care for others who do not deserve to have to endure the same strife in their lives that generations of Falkland Islanders, people in Great Britain and Argentina have had to, and who continue to, because of this unresolved dispute.

By the way, it is not the first time I have tried to lend a hand in this problem. The last was probably in the early part of 1999, when I happened to be in Buenos Aires. Once again, I received an invitation from the Argentine Foreign Minister to take a meal with him. Naturally I accepted. Not wanting my friend from the Falklands to miss out, I took him along with me. Well that was one of the reasons, the other was that I wanted someone to witness what I said and did.

After a brief informal meeting, four of us sat down and had lunch at the Foreign Minister's office. First, we chatted openly about current events. He was very conscious of the fact that he would be out of office come the October elections in 1999. He went on to tell me that he had been trying to pull a meeting together with the British Foreign Minister, who was Robin Cook at the time, and elected councillors from the Islands.

Before the lunch finished, he asked me if I would be good enough to pass a message on to a councillor when I returned home. I was happy to agree.

As a result of what was discussed at that lunch, I was not surprised at all to learn a short while later that meetings had been arranged, and on 14 July that year, a meeting took place in London between the Argentine Foreign Minister, Dr Guido de

Tella, the British Foreign Secretary, Mr Robin Cook, with two Islands councillors in attendance, at which a document, simply called, 'Joint Statement', was signed. Councillors Mike Summers and Sharon Halford also signed as 'witnesses'.

One of the ground-breaking features of this agreement was the lifting of the ban on Argentine nationals entering the Falklands. Of course all I had done was to pass a message on back in the early part of the year. A message that the Argentine Foreign Minister wished to meet councillors, wherever, with his British counterpart.

Another subject I did talk to the Foreign Minister about was a business idea I had. I told him that I would really love to have a go at developing the Falklands natural spring water, put it into attractive packaging for local and tourist consumption, and a special pack for the Argentine market. He smiled and questioned, the Argentine market? 'Yes,' I said, 'you buggers would buy anything that comes from the Falklands, and I reckon a fortune could be made by selling Falklands water into Argentina.'

'Interesting,' he said, 'but how would you market it here, given the complicated politics.'

'Oh, dead easy,' I said, 'on the label of the bottle I would have an outline map of the Islands, with little black dots indicating strategic places, and I would market the product, as Agua de las Islas (Water of the Islands). That gets over the politics rather neatly.'

He gave a big smile, shook my hand, and then said, 'I think you might be a clever and dangerous businessman.'

I'M A FALKLAND ISLANDER TILL I DIE

We've been neighbour's for such a long time, this is a matter of fact
Separated by the Atlantic, nothing we can do about that
You say my country's not mine, it belongs to you
Friend, I must differ from this point of view

But there's one thing I know for certain, I'm a Falkland Islander till I die.
But there's one thing I know for certain, I'm a Falkland Islander till I die.

We've been brothers for such a long time, this is a matter of fact
We have the same mother and father, nothing we can do about that
You support the Agentine sovereignty claim
This hurts me and it caused our parents great pain

But there's one thing I know for certain, I'm a Falkland Islander till I die.
But there's one thing I know for certain, I'm a Falkland Islander till I die.

Can't you see whatever has happened, I hold no malice t'wards you
We all make errors of judgement, just as you did in eighty two
I just hope your democracy will prosper
And that might change your way of thinking

But there's one thing I know for certain, I'm a Falkland Islander till I die.
But there's one thing I know for certain, I'm a Falkland Islander till I die.

Music and Lyrics by Terry Betts
Arranged by Trevor Holman

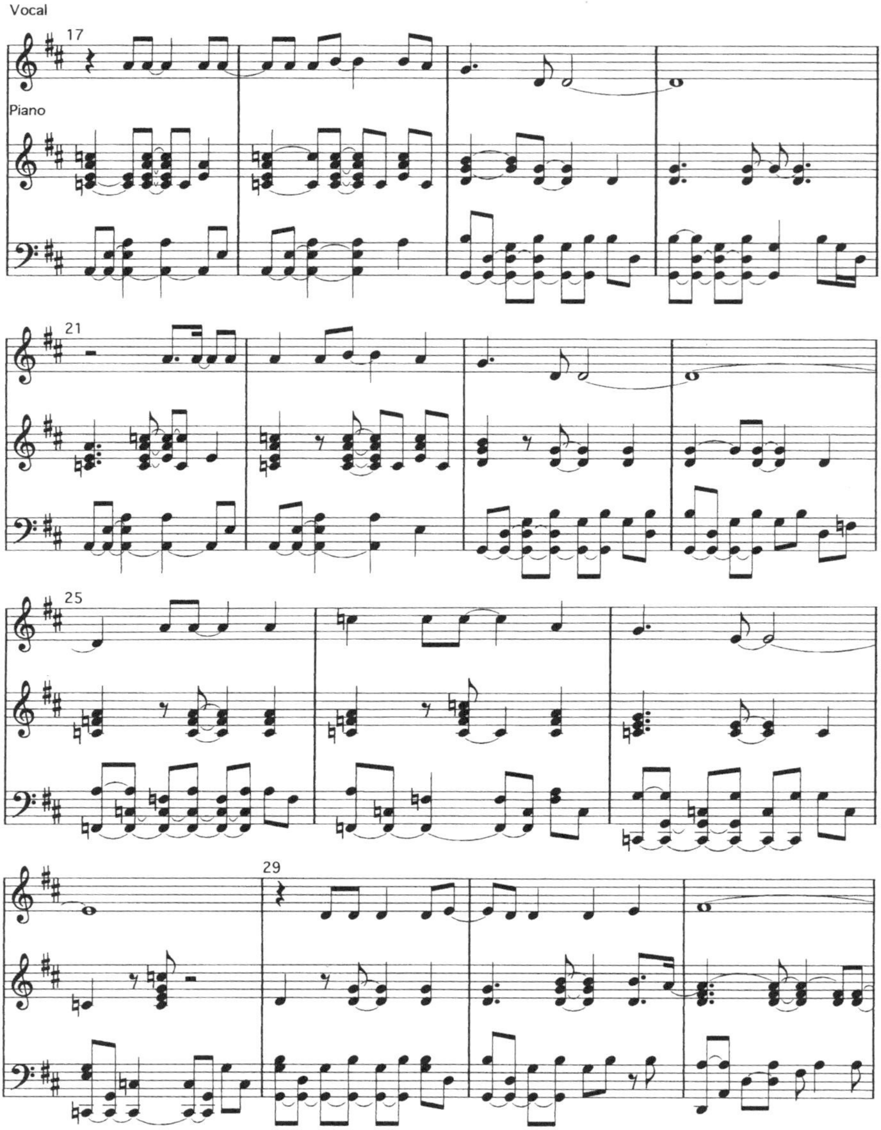
Vocal
17
Piano
21
25
29

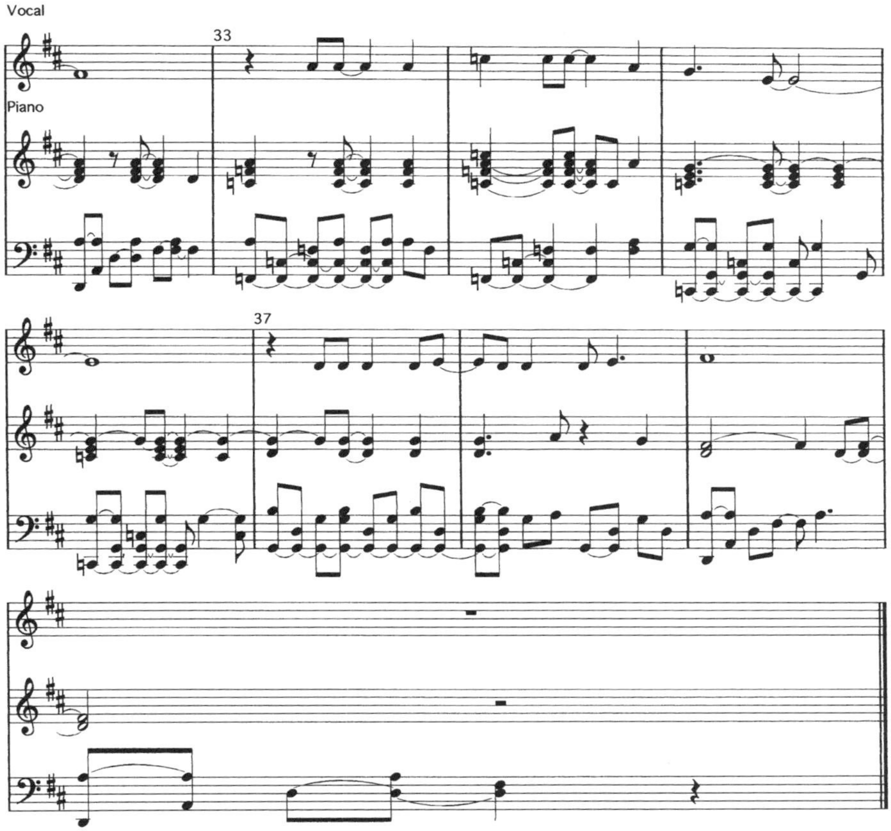
Vocal
Piano
33
37